A COMPANION TO 20th-CENTURY AMERICA

Edited

Stephen J. Whitfield

Blackwell
Publishing

© 2004, 2007 by Blackwell Publishing Ltd
except for editorial material and organization © 2004, 2007 by Stephen J. Whitfield

BLACKWELL PUBLISHING
350 Main Street, Malden, MA 02148-5020, USA
9600 Garsington Road, Oxford OX4 2DQ, UK
550 Swanston Street, Carlton, Victoria 3053, Australia

The right of Stephen J. Whitfield to be identified as the Author of the Editorial Material in this Work
has been asserted in accordance with the UK Copyright, Designs, and Patents Act 1988.

First published 2004
First published in paperback 2007 by Blackwell Publishing Ltd

1   2007

Library of Congress Cataloging-in-Publication Data

A companion to 20th-century America / edited by Stephen J. Whitfield.
p. cm. – (Blackwell companions to American history)
ISBN 0-631-21100-4 (hardcover: alk. paper)
1. United States–History–20th century. 2. United States–Historiography. I. Title: Companion to
20th-century America. II. Whitfield, Stephen J., 1942– III. Series.

E178.6.C65 2004
973.91–dc21

2003010121

ISBN-13: 978-0-631-21100-6 (hardcover: alk. paper)
ISBN-13: 978-1-4051-5652-3 (alk. paper : pbk)
ISBN-10: 1-4051-5652-X (alk. paper : pbk)

A catalogue record for this title is available from the British Library.

Set in 10 on 12 pt Galliard
by Kolam Information Services Pvt. Ltd, Pondicherry, India
Printed and bound in the United Kingdom
by TJ International, Padstow, Cornwall

For further information on
Blackwell Publishing, visit our website:
www.blackwellpublishing.com

Contents

Notes on the Contributors

Raymond Arsenault is the John Hope Franklin Professor of Southern History and Director of the University Honors College at the University of South Florida. A specialist in the social, political, and environmental history of the American South, he is the author of *The Wild Ass of the Ozarks* (1984), *St. Petersburg and the Florida Dream, 1888–1950* (1988), and the editor of *Crucible of Liberty: 200 Years of the Bill of Rights* (1991), and (with co-editor Roy Peter Clark) *The Changing South of Gene Patterson: Journalism and Civil Rights, 1960–1968* (2002). His *Freedom Riders* is forthcoming.

James L. Baughman is Professor of Journalism and Mass Communication at the University of Wisconsin-Madison. He is the author of *Television's Guardians: The Federal Communications Commission and the Politics of Programming, 1958–1967* (1985), *Republic of Mass Culture: Journalism, Filmmaking, and Broadcasting in America since 1941* (2nd edn., 1997) and *Henry R. Luce and the Rise of the American News Media* (rev. edn., 2001).

Anne M. Butler is Emeritus Trustee Professor of History from Utah State University and the former senior editor of the *Western Historical Quarterly*. The recipient of numerous research awards, she has published extensively on the history of the American West, especially concerning women.

Jerry Cooper is Professor Emeritus of History at the University of Missouri St. Louis. He is the author of *The Army and Civil Disorder: Federal Military Intervention in Labor Disputes, 1877–1900* (1980), and *The Rise of the National Guard: The Evolution of the American Militia, 1865–1920* (1997). He has served as Visiting Professor of Military History at the US Army Command and General Staff College (1989–90) and the US Army Military History Institute, Army War College (1990–1).

Roger Daniels is Charles Phelps Taft Professor Emeritus of History at the University of Cincinnati. He has written widely about immigrants from Asia and about immigration generally. The second edition of his *Coming to America: A History of Immigration and Ethnicity in American Life* appeared in 2002 and his *Guarding the Golden Door: A History of Immigration Policy and Immigrants since 1882* is forthcoming.

Hasia R. Diner is Paul and Sylvia Steinberg Professor of American Jewish History at New York University. She is the author of *In the Almost Promised Land: American Jews and Blacks, 1915–1935* (1977; reissued 1995), *Erin's Daughters in American: Irish Immigrant Women in the Nineteenth Century* (1984), *A Time for Gathering: The Second Migration, 1820–1880* (1992), *Lower East Side Memories: The Jewish Place in America*

(2000), and *Hungering for America: Italian, Irish, and Jewish Foodways in the Age of Migration* (2001).

Justus D. Doenecke is Professor of History at New College of Florida. He has been awarded the Arthur S. Link Prize by the Society for Historians of American Foreign Relations for *In Danger Undaunted: The Anti-Interventionist Movement of 1940–1941 as Revealed in the Papers of the America First Committee* (1990) and the annual book award of the Herbert Hoover Presidential Library Association for *Storm on the Horizon: The Challenge to American Intervention, 1939–1941* (2000).

Richard M. Fried teaches recent US history at the University of Illinois at Chicago. He is the author of *Men Against McCarthy* (1976), *Nightmare in Red* (1990), and *The Russians Are Coming! The Russians Are Coming! Pageantry and Patriotism in Cold-War America* (1998).

Glen Gendzel is Assistant Professor of History at Indiana University-Purdue University at Fort Wayne. He has written articles and reviews for *Western Historical Quarterly, Business History Review*, the *Journal of Interdisciplinary History, California History*, and *The Public Historian*. He has also contributed to *The Encyclopedia of American Studies* (2001), *The Encyclopedia of the Vietnam War* (1996), and *The New York Times Almanac* (from 1998). His research focuses on the progressive movement in California.

Steven M. Gillon is Professor of History and Dean of the Honors College at the University of Oklahoma. He is the author of *The Democrats' Dilemma* (1992), *Politics and Vision: The ADA and American Liberalism, 1947–1985* (1997), and *That's Not What We Meant to Do: Reform and its Unintended Consequences in the Twentieth Century* (2000), and co-editor (with Diane B. Kunz) of *America During the Cold War* (1997).

Jama Lazerow is Professor of History at Wheelock College. He is the author of *Religion and the Working Class in Antebellum America* (1995), which won the E. Harold Hugo Memorial Book Prize. He is currently working on a book about the Black Panther Party, entitled *The Awakening of a Sleeping Giant: New Bedford, the Black Panthers, and the 1960s*.

Eugene E. Leach has since 1975 taught at Trinity College (Hartford), where he has directed the American Studies Program and chaired the History Department. He has edited and written for several encyclopedia projects and lectured on topics in US history in Poland, Nicaragua, and Venezuela. His book *Interpreting the American Dream* is forthcoming.

Charles H. Lippy is the LeRoy A. Martin Distinguished Professor of Religious Studies at the University of Tennessee at Chattanooga. He is the author of *Pluralism Comes of Age: American Religious Culture in the Twentieth Century* (2000), and *Do Real Men Pray? Images of the Christian Man and Male Spirituality in American Protestantism* (forthcoming). He is co-editor of the *Encyclopedia of the American Religious Experience* (1988) and of the forthcoming second edition of the *Encyclopedia of Religion in the South*.

Joseph A. McCartin is Associate Professor of History at Georgetown University. He is the author of *Labor's Great War: The Struggle for Industrial Democracy and the Origins of Modern American Labor Relations, 1912–21* (1997). In 2003–4 he is also a Fellow at the Charles Warren Center for Studies in American History at Harvard University, and is writing a book on the 1981 strike of the air traffic controllers and the decline of the American labor movement.

Wilfred M. McClay is SunTrust Bank Chair of Excellence in Humanities at the University of Tennessee at Chattanooga, where he is also Professor of History. He is currently an Adjunct Public Policy Fellow at the Woodrow Wilson International Center for Scholars, a member of the advisory board of the National Endowment for the Humanities, and a member of the Society of Scholars at the James Madison Program of Princeton University. He is the author of *The Masterless:*

Self and Society in Modern America (1994), which won the Merle Curti Award of the Organization of American Historians. Among his other books is *Religion Returns to the Public Square: Faith and Policy in Modern America* (2003).

Charles McGovern teaches American Studies and History at the College of William and Mary, and is Curator at the National Museum of American History, Smithsonian Institution, Washington, DC. He has written *Sold American: Inventing the Consumer, 1890–1945* (forthcoming) and co-edited, with Susan Strasser and Mattias Judt, *Getting and Spending: Twentieth-Century European and American Consumer Societies* (1998). He has curated numerous Smithsonian exhibitions on American popular culture and is at work on a social history of American popular music.

Michael E. Parrish is Professor of History at the University of California, San Diego. He is the author of *Felix Frankfurter and his Times* (1982) and *Anxious Decades: America in Prosperity and Depression* (1992). He specializes in legal and constitutional history and in movements for political reform since the Progressive Era.

Carroll Pursell is Adeline Barry Davee Distinguished Professor at Case Western Reserve University. He has been President of the Society for the History of Technology, and has won its Leonardo da Vinci Medal. He is also a Fellow of the American Association for the Advancement of Science and has served as President of the International Committee for the History of Technology.

Leo P. Ribuffo is Society of the Cincinnati George Washington Distinguished Professor of History at George Washington University. His publications include *Right Center Left: Essays in American History* (1992) and *The Old Christian Right: The Protestant Far Right from the Great Depression to the Cold War* (1984), which won the OAH Merle Curti Prize. He has served as book review editor of the *American Quarterly* and *American Studies International*, and has contributed reviews and essays to many newspapers and magazines, including *Dissent*,

Christian Century, New York Newsday, and the *Philadelphia Inquirer.*

Norman L. Rosenberg, the DeWitt Wallace Professor of History at Macalester College, is the author of *Protecting the "Best Men": An Interpretive History of the Law of Libel* (1990) and co-author of a number of books including *In Our Times: America Since 1945* (7th edn., 2003). Primarily writing in legal and cultural history, he is also the author of several dozen articles. His classroom work has earned him the Burlington Northern Award for Outstanding Teaching.

Edward S. Shapiro is Professor Emeritus at Seton Hall University. He is the author of *Clio from the Right: Essays of a Conservative Historian* (1983) and *A Time for Healing: American Jewry since World War II* (1992). He is also the editor of *Democracy, Communism, and the Cold War: Letters of Sidney Hook* (1995).

David B. Sicilia is Associate Professor of History at the University of Maryland, College Park. A specialist in American business, economic, and technology history, he is co-author or co-editor of six books, including *The Greenspan Effect* (2000) and *Constructing Corporate America: History, Politics, Culture* (2003). In the spring of 2003 he served as Fulbright Professor in the Department of Intercultural Management and Communication and in the Department of English at the Copenhagen Business School.

June Sochen is Professor of History and Women's Studies at Northeastern Illinois University in Chicago. She is the author and editor of fourteen books, including *From Mae to Madonna: Women Entertainers in 20th Century America* (1999). Her recent research has been on Hadassah in 1920s Palestine and on a study of children's experiences in twentieth-century America.

Paul S. Sutter is an Assistant Professor of History at the University of Georgia, where he teaches US and environmental history. He is the author of *Driven Wild: How the Fight Against Automobiles Launched the Modern Wilderness Movement* (2002).

Douglas Tallack is Professor of American Studies and Pro-Vice Chancellor at the University of Nottingham. He is the author of *The Nineteenth-Century American Short Story: Language, Form and Ideology* (1993) and *Twentieth-Century America: The Intellectual and Cultural Context* (1991). He is also the editor of *Literary Theory at Work: Three Texts* (1987) and *Critical Theory: A Reader* (1995).

Jon C. Teaford is Professor of History at Purdue University. He is an authority on American urban history and has written eight books, including *The Twentieth-Century American City: Problem, Promise and Reality* (1986). His most recent work is *The Rise of the States: Evolution of American State Government* (2002).

Reed Ueda is Professor of History at Tufts University and has been a visiting professor at Brandeis and Harvard. Pursuing research in social and immigration history, he has written *West End House* (1981), *Avenues to Adulthood* (1987), and *Postwar Immigrant America* (1994). He has been Research Editor of *The Harvard Encyclopedia of American Ethnic Groups* (1980) and edited, with Conrad E. Wright, *Faces of Community* (2003). He has received fellowships from the National Endowment for the Humanities, the American Council for Learned Societies, the Woodrow Wilson International Center, and the Charles Warren Center of Harvard University.

Hans Vorländer is President of the German Association of Political Science and Chairman of the Academic Council of the Federal Agency for Civic Education, Germany. Among his books are: *Nationale Identität und Staatsbürgerschaft in den USA* (2001), *Integration durch Verfassung* (2002), and *Demokratie. Geschichte, Formen, Theorien* (2003).

Stephen J. Whitfield holds the Max Richter Chair in American Civilization at Brandeis University. His eight books include *Into the Dark: Hannah Arendt and Totalitarianism* (1980), *A Death in the Delta: The Story of Emmett Till* (1988), *The Culture of the Cold War* (2nd, expanded edn. 1996), and *In Search of American Jewish Culture* (1999). He was a Fulbright Visiting Professor at the Hebrew University of Jerusalem in 1983–4 and at the Catholic University of Leuven and Louvain-la-Neuve, Belgium, in 1993, and was visiting professor at the Sorbonne in 1994 and 1998.

Allan M. Winkler is Distinguished Professor of History at Miami University in Ohio. He is author of eight books, including *The Politics of Propaganda: The Office of War Information, 1942–1945* (1978), *Home Front U.S.A.: America during World War II* (2nd edn., 2000), and *Life Under a Cloud: American Anxiety about the Atom* (1999), and co-author of the college textbook *The American People: Creating a Nation and a Society* (5th edn., 2000) and the high school textbook *America: Pathways to the Present* (3rd edn., 1998).

Introduction

Stephen J. Whitfield

"The American Century" is the title that the magazine publisher Henry R. Luce bestowed on the past century, even before it had run half its course. In an editorial appearing in the February 17, 1941 issue of *Life*, the weekly that Luce invented, he expressed a vision that – perhaps even more than the reverberant term he devised – merits consideration as a way of understanding what the United States has meant in the framework of world history.

When his editorial appeared, Nazi Germany had already conquered much of Europe; and its oppressed peoples might well have wondered how and when an unprecedented tyranny might ever be defeated. Allied with the Third Reich was another totalitarian power, the Soviet Union, leaving only Great Britain to resist the Nazi juggernaut. In Asia the most populous nations on the planet were also beleaguered – whether in the convulsions of civil war (China) or under imperialist rule (India). At such a moment, the United States was not merely isolationist; it also looked isolated. Officially neutral, this republic of slightly under 134 million people was still recovering from the most severe crisis that its capitalist economy had ever suffered. What was about to happen in 1941 were turning points that neither Luce nor anyone else could have been expected to foresee: the German invasion of the Soviet Union, which would turn the largest nation on earth into a tenacious enemy, and the Japanese attack upon Pearl Harbor, which would turn the greatest industrial power on the planet into a champion of collective security against the Axis. Only four years after Luce's editorial, a full-scale war of catastrophic destructiveness would leave his country the dominant power on earth. That position of hegemony the US would hold until the end of the American century.

In 1941 Luce might have seemed guilty of exaggeration, if not of delusion. By 1945 he could have been credited with eerie foresight. From the perspective of the twenty-first century, what he intended in urging both a repudiation of isolation and a promotion of national values has taken on special resonance. For he advocated an acceptance of global responsibility to advance the two benefits that he claimed had made the United States so appealing a society: its abundance and its freedom. (Full employment would not be reached until after American entry in the Second World War, and white supremacy would still be legally enforceable for another generation.)

Only a month before Luce's editorial was published, President Franklin D. Roosevelt had proclaimed something similar, tabulating the Four Freedoms that needed to be vindicated in battle: Freedom of Speech, Freedom of Worship, Freedom from Want, Freedom from Fear. Unlike FDR, Luce was neither a Democrat nor much of a liberal. But the magazine magnate captured something about the national mood too, and managed to articulate the American dream (itself a phrase that had been coined, by historian James Truslow Adams, only a decade earlier). If the United States was to pay a high price in blood and treasure during the war, and was to project unrivaled military and economic might thereafter, the ideals that Luce identified had to be of universal value and not merely the special but parochial aspirations of his fellow citizens.

The twenty-nine chapters that constitute this *Blackwell Companion* can be read as sites for testing what the Time, Inc. tycoon proposed. How, over the course of the twentieth century, has the nation approximated the democratic prospect? To what extent have the ideals of prosperity and liberty been realized? How has the promise of opportunity been rendered, squandered, fulfilled? Start at the beginning. The year 1897 marked the end of the bleak depression that had begun four years earlier, and – a year before the acquisition of an empire in the wake of the Spanish-American War – inaugurated a spectacular period of economic growth. Until the shocking collapse of the stock market in 1929, the gross national product (GNP) more than tripled (when dollars are held constant). Per capita GNP more than doubled, which meant that, by 1910, increasingly comfortable Americans were living in the greatest industrial power in the world. That was still true nine decades later, when globalization was often understood to be a synonym for Americanization. How such productivity was managed, how such resources were allocated and deployed – these are themes that inevitably emerge in a book about the American century. This book is about freedom too. How was the value that was so alluring to millions of immigrants pursued, defined, redefined, betrayed, or achieved? How was it compelled to compete with other ideals? The proportion of the foreign-born at the end of the century was comparable to its dawn, and was drawn even more from Latin America, Asia, and Africa than from Europe. How so variegated and diverse a populace achieved stability and order, while exalting an ideal of freedom, is integral to the story of twentieth-century America too.

This volume is intended to challenge readers to imagine the past anew, to consider it from a multiplicity of perspectives and approaches, and to appreciate how recent scholarship has required a re-conceptualization of the last century. The authors have tried to do justice to the elusive, intriguing, and complex fate of experiencing the American century. All of these scholars have taken into account the ways by which recent research and reinterpretation inevitably destabilize the past, and have sought to make such revisions as accessible and intelligible to readers as possible. Some contributors have approached their topics chronologically, in terms of decades (which do not necessarily occur in conventional ten-year intervals). But most chapters are designed to trace a phenomenon over the course of time. These historians are all experts in their particular fields, and have engaged in analysis as well as synthesis. Whether they have succeeded is ultimately the judgment of the readers of this *Companion*. But all of the contributors have earned the gratitude and admiration of the editor of this volume.

PART I

Time-frames

CHAPTER ONE

1900–1914

EUGENE E. LEACH

At the dawn of the twentieth century, few Americans were confident that they understood their country. In 1865 the Union victory in the Civil War marked the climax of a national narrative to which most Americans subscribed, whether they approved the narrative or not. By 1900 the nation's story had grown congested with subplots and hidden texts. There was no longer a widely shared consensus about what it meant or where it was heading, in part because the story had grown so complex, in part because such diverse groups now claimed a right to read it. Old-stock Americans believed their ancestors had possessed a sense of purpose and command which now eluded them. Immigrant newcomers knew little of the nation apart from the promise of decent livelihoods provided by its giant economy. African Americans had, perhaps, the steadiest perspective on their society, because they knew all too well where they belonged in it: at the bottom. All other groups – including that biggest of "minorities," women – felt they were moving. The whole country was growing bigger and more crowded. But the motion seemed random, the growth undirected. It was not that the center did not hold, but rather that those who looked for a center couldn't find one.

Historians of this period have been searching for a national center and striving to frame its narrative ever since. Almost all of them have concurred that the political record of 1900–14 was dominated by a loose phenomenon they have called – often with distaste, always with qualifications – "the progressive movement." If this essay concentrates on the historiography of progressivism, that is not because nothing else happened in these years, but instead because progressives influenced or attempted to influence almost everything that did happen. Progressivism can be viewed as "the way in which a whole generation of Americans defined themselves and responded to problems at the turn of the century" (Link and McCormick 1983: 3). The most powerful engines of change in this period may have been technological and economic innovations. The automobile, air travel, the movies, large-scale electrification, national marketing of retail goods, and a host of other developments were fueling prosperity and transforming the material conditions of American life. Yet the nation's inventors, engineers, entrepreneurs, financiers, and managers did not set out to redirect American history or leave a legacy for later generations. The progressives did. They were the most determined shapers of the nation's narrative in this period, the most deliberate history-makers. This too makes their work integral to the era of 1900–14.

To a great many Americans in the waning years of the nineteenth century, the country felt as if it was falling apart. After staving off political dissolution in the 1860s, the United States had rapidly built an economy that led the world in both agricultural and industrial production. But the epic changes wrought by industrial capitalism had come at the price of constant conflict and volatility. In the tempestuous 1890s the deepest depression so far experienced left 20 percent of the work force unemployed. Angry strikers in Pennsylvania, Illinois, and the Rocky Mountain states brought to a peak the years of clashes between capital and labor; and angry farmers aggressively challenged the power of established parties and rising corporations. The lynching terror drew the color line in blood across the South, and anxieties about rising immigration generated the first calls to restrict it.

Preserving union and keeping order had always been a struggle in a society so vast and loose-knit that centrifugal forces seemed perpetually on the verge of overcoming the forces of cohesion. By 1896, when all the elements of discord were gathered up in a climactic presidential election, many citizens believed the integrity of the country was once again in jeopardy. And to a degree they were right. The preindustrial, mostly rural, relatively homogeneous social order was disintegrating. A stable new order was yet to be established.

Worse than rampant disorder, in the eyes of many, was the menace of a coercive order purchased at the price of liberty and opportunity. Individuals could scarcely grasp, much less stand up against, the scale and speed of the nation's demographic and economic growth. Counting 63 million inhabitants in the census of 1900 (more than any European nation save Russia), the United States had grown demographically to 76 million a decade later. More than 13 million immigrants entered the country between 1901 and 1915, a number greater than the immigration total for 1868–1900. In 1860 there were sixteen cities with as many as 50,000 people; a half-century later there were 109 of them. The capitalization of the new United States Steel Corporation ($1.4 billion) boggled minds in 1901. By 1913 a congressional investigating committee discovered that a single investment banking firm, the House of Morgan, held director-ships in 112 corporations with aggregate assets of more than $22 billion. In 1914 Henry Ford opened an automobile plant that employed under one roof nearly as many people as had lived in America's largest city, Philadelphia, in 1790. Giant corporations, political machines, and unions had more weight to throw around than state and city governments. Such concentrated masses of money, power, and people might easily turn into a society of herds commanded by tyrants.

Never before had there been such substantial grounds for feeling, as Woodrow Wilson said in the 1912 presidential campaign, that "the individual has been sub-merged" and "individuality is swallowed up. All over the Union, people are coming to feel they have no control over the course of affairs" (quoted in Diner 1998: 200). What was new in the new century was a widespread feeling of bewilderment and helplessness. Americans not only knew they no longer controlled "the course of affairs." They were not sure they knew who did.

Into this predicament marched battalions of reformers who around 1910 began to call themselves progressives. In 1912 Theodore Roosevelt formed a new party that used this name, but the progressive movement was a much bigger, messier, more plural, and more durable phenomenon than the Progressive Party. Even to call it "a movement" may suggest more unity than it really had. Nearer the truth would be to characterize it as a collection of loosely related reform movements. Among the many progressivisms was a drive to root out corruption in city governments that began in the mid-1890s; a Populist-tinged midwestern progressivism led by Senator Robert LaFollette of Wisconsin that tenaciously represented the interests of farmers and workers; a relatively elitist and conservative eastern progressivism led by the Republican Theodore Roosevelt and the Democrat Woodrow Wilson that specialized in building the regulatory powers of the federal government; and a "social justice progressivism" that specialized in safeguarding the welfare of women, children, and other vulnerable groups. The name "progressive" denoted one of the few qualities all these shared: a common determination to restore to their communities, their lives, and their country a direction they could call "progress."

The movement's objectives were as diverse as its parts. Many progressives wanted to remove corruption from government, so they supported the secret ballot, the direct election of US Senators, women's suffrage, home-rule charters for cities, the replacement of patronage with civil service jobs, and professional-manager forms of city government. Progressives campaigned for laws and government agencies to regulate business, to the end that private enterprise respect "the public interest." "Gas and water socialism" – municipally owned utilities – represented an extreme of progressive intervention in the economy; more typical were efforts to increase the powers of existing regulatory agencies (the Interstate Commerce Commission), to create new agencies (the Federal Trade Commission, the Pure Food and Drug Administration, the Women's Bureau, the Federal Reserve Board), and to file anti-trust lawsuits. Progressives backed a huge array of private and public initiatives to relieve the distress of society's weaker members: settlement houses serving immigrant families; workmen's compensation laws, to make employers liable for accidents on the job; minimum wage and maximum hours laws for women; restrictions on child labor; compulsory school attendance laws; modest protections for unions; widows' pensions; and a mildly redistributive income tax (the Sixteenth Amendment). Finally progressives advocated measures to impose their morality and ensure their dominion over immigrants and the poor: prohibition; Jim Crow segregation; anti-vice (mostly prostitution) campaigns; and restrictions on immigration.

The historiography of progressivism has been almost as disjointed and argumentative as progressivism itself. Before the shifting course of that historiography can be traced, three large patterns of interpretations of the past must be identified.

First, since scholars inaugurated the history of progressivism – and indeed of the whole period 1900–14 – they have constantly widened their perspective, discovering new dimensions of the subject. Progressivism has come to be recognized as an immense, diverse, even protean phenomenon. This has made for a pattern of historiographic dispersal, to the point that some scholars have wondered whether a coherent "progressivism" ever really existed.

This pattern of diverging interpretations has been rebutted by a second pattern, of rough consensus on the overall nature of progressivism. Almost all historians have agreed that progressivism was a movement to fix flaws in the nation's polity, economy, and society that had built up during the preceding period. The Gilded Age had been marked by depressions, industrial violence, corruption of public officials, growing disparities between rich and poor, growing insecurity, the erosion of democratic institutions, and in response to all these, movements for wholesale change. Progressivism sought to reverse these trends. Its reform thrust was toward control, including control over other, competing models of social change. Far from being revolutionary, progressivism may be understood as a counter-revolutionary movement, not just unradical but concertedly anti-radical. It sought alternatives to the status quo left over from the Gilded Age as well as antidotes to the revolutionary forces let loose during the Gilded Age.

In sum, rather than seek to transform the existing political economy or the existing social structure, progressivism tried to make the best of them. In *The Age of Reform*, the enduring historical masterpiece on this period, Richard Hofstadter astutely called eastern progressivism "a mild and judicious movement, whose goal was not a sharp change in the social structure, but rather the formation of a responsible elite, which was to take charge of the popular impulse toward change and direct it into moderate and, as they would have said, 'constructive' channels" (1955: 163–4). Some historians have suggested that the real project of the progressive period was to put America more firmly on the Gold Standard by re-gilding the Gilded Age, applying a shinier and more durable coating to mask the baser metals beneath. In one form or another, progressives addressed all the principal divisions in the American society of 1900–14, including those of race, ethnicity, and gender.

A third pattern in the interpretation of progressivism has been rough agreement that progressives also wrestled with issues of class. They did this more self-consciously than any previous generation of reformers, though with no greater enthusiasm. For the progressives universally deplored class division as un-American and class conflict as a social malignancy. They were decidedly anti-Marxist and anti-socialist as well, despite efforts by moderates in the Socialist Party of America to link up with left-wing progressivism. In their interpretations of this period, historians have chosen variously to emphasize class conflict, hold it at arm's length, or deny its centrality. But all have acknowledged the specter of class haunting America in 1900–14 and, like the progressives themselves, all have kept a wary eye on it.

The first historians of progressivism were members or admirers of the movement. In their view the progressives were champions of "the people" in their perennial struggle to defend their freedom against "the interests." On one side stood the majority of Americans: holders of small property, eager for opportunity, jealous of their rights. On the other stood the forces of predatory privilege: the railroads, manufacturing corporations, banks, and the entrenched parties that served them. The progressives defied the overlords of the new industrial economy. In the first scholarly study, *The Progressive Movement* (1915), political scientist Benjamin Parke De Witt wrote that "men became economic slaves . . . Slowly, Americans realized that they were not free" (1968: 14). As a principled movement of the whole "people," progressivism transcended political and social divisions. De Witt called it the "expression of fundamental measures and principles of reform that have been advocated for many years by all political parties" (p. vii). In their landmark text, *The Rise of American Civilization* (1927), Charles and Mary Beard painted in heroic colors the progressives' drive "towards social democracy." After the reformers had finished with the political economy bequeathed from the Gilded Age, "it was so battered and undermined at the base that the men of the age which had constructed it imagined, perhaps with undue fright, that the solid earth was crumbling beneath their feet" (1930: 543).

A substantially different interpretation was advanced four years later. John D. Hicks also identified progressivism as a movement of democratic protest against overweening economic power and corrupt political authority (1931). But he held that a particular segment of "the people" – poor farmers – made up the backbone of the movement. This agrarian movement was more defined by class interests than the miscellaneous paladins of reform who figured in the accounts by De Witt and the Beards. According to Hicks, progressivism was essentially an expansion of the reform efforts set in motion by the Farmers Alliances and the Populist Party of the 1880s and 1890s. Elizabeth Sanders recently reasserted important elements of Hicks's interpretation, arguing that the "roots of reform" throughout the period 1877–1917 lay in "politically mobilized farmers . . . driven to establish public control over a rampaging capitalism. The periphery [of poor agrarians] generated the bulk of the reform agenda and furnished the foot soldiers that saw reform through the legislature" (Sanders 1999: 1, 3).

After World War II a group of gifted historians developed a reading of progressivism that in some respects remains the most persuasive account. Though they acknowledged the Populist "seedbed" of many progressive proposals, they characterized progressivism as a middle-class reaction against Populism. According to George Mowry, Richard Hofstadter, and Arthur Link, progressivism represented a protest by the safe and sane middle against alien and dangerous extremes. The core progressives were predominantly urban, unlike the agrarians; they were predominantly white collar, unlike the wage-earners; they were comfortable, in distinction to the sybaritic rich; and they were better educated than any other segment of the population. What most clearly distinguished them, however, was their location between classes that they associated with disorder (the workers or proletarians) and with despotism (the business moguls or plutocrats). "Nearly all the problems which vex society have their sources above or below the middle-class man," wrote a California progressive cited by George Mowry. "From above come the problems of predatory wealth . . . From below come the problems of poverty and of pigheaded and brutish criminality" (quoted in Mann 1963: 35). Mowry profiled the typical progressive as an individualist who "became militant when he felt himself hemmed in between the battening corporation and the rising labor unions" (1946: 37). Or as the progressive attorney Louis D. Brandeis announced, the movement's aim was to take up "a position of independence between the wealthy and the people, prepared to curb the excesses of either" (quoted in Hofstadter 1955: 164).

But though the progressives readily identified themselves as "middle class," they resisted defining themselves by their class position; nor did they admit that they had class-specific interests. Instead they thought of themselves as people of the "middling sort," virtuous and respectable citizens representing the solid center of society. Industrialization, by creating barbarian classes "above" and "below" them, had made this status a position of peculiar vulnerability. They felt exposed and surrounded. They aspired to rise above sordid class conflict, hoping to restore America to its original classlessness.

Representative progressives, according to this reading of the movement, were figures like Jane Addams, who regarded class conflict as the root of all the country's evils. For her the Pullman strike of 1894 epitomized "the danger and futility involved in the open warfare of opposing social forces," which made "the search for justice and righteousness in industrial relations . . . infinitely more difficult" (Addams 1961: 158–64). Impartial referees, she thought, should separate the combatants and then resolve their private differences in light of the public interest. By deploying the objective and neutral middle against the selfish and irrational extremes, mediation could turn the progressives' "betweenness" into a position of strength.

With *The Triumph of Conservatism* (1963), historian Gabriel Kolko challenged the Mowry–Hofstadter thesis of progressive moderation and middleness, and located the progressives squarely on the side of "the interests" and the governing class. Kolko argued that progressives' campaigns for federal regulation of corporations were "invariably controlled by leaders of the regulated industry, and directed toward ends they deemed . . . desirable." Thus, for example, the 1906 Hepburn Act (giving the Interstate Commerce Commission increased authority to control railroad rates) and agencies like the Bureau of Corporations (1903) aided the corporations by quieting their critics and stabilizing markets in their industries. Kolko concluded: "It is business control over politics rather than political regulation of the economy that is the significant phenomenon of the Progressive Era" (1963: 2–3). James Weinstein joined Kolko in contending that "few reforms were enacted without the tacit approval, if not the guidance, of the large corporate interests." But instead of considering progressivism "conservative," Weinstein maintained that it represented "corporate liberalism," a sophisticated strategy for defending business interests by disarming critics and co–opting opponents (1968: ix–x).

This perspective on progressivism effectively exposed the defects of the old interpretation of the "people vs. interests." Not all proponents of progressive reform were democrats or idealists. But the revisionist interpretations of Kolko, Weinstein, and others simply ignored segments of the progressive movement that did not fit their theses, such as the thousands of women and men who worked in settlement houses. *The Triumph of Conservatism* never mentions progressives like Jane Addams or, for that matter, historians like Richard Hofstadter.

A subtler and ultimately stronger challenge to the Mowry–Hofstadter interpretation of reform politics in 1900–14 was first sketched by Samuel P. Hays and then elaborated by Robert Wiebe. Their accounts melted progressivism into what Hays called *The Response to Industrialism* (the title of his 1957 book) and that Wiebe called *The Search for Order* (the title of his 1967 book). For Mowry and Hofstadter proactive reformers assembled in purposive "movements" made the history of this period. Hays and Wiebe portrayed progressivism in terms of Americans' "response" to external forces and their "search" for a stability that largely eluded them. At the turn of the century, industrial capitalism was creating a modernity that made all things new: methods and mechanisms of production and distribution and communication, forms of social relatedness, values, ways of interpreting experience. Progressive reform campaigns were interpreted by Hays and Wiebe as strategies of adaptation to these immense, bewildering changes. The key to Americans' "adjustment to industrialism," Hays held, was organization. Manufacturers, distributors, workers, and farmers learned how to act collectively in trusts, unions, and other kinds of associations. Thus they gained a measure of control over the marketplace and a measure of security in their economic lives. Gradually a loose society of independent producers, self-sufficient families, and autonomous communities was transformed into a far more integrated and interdependent society dominated by large organizations. Reformers changed with the times.

Wiebe refined the "organizational thesis" that has left an enduring mark on the historiography of progressivism. Like Hofstadter, Wiebe proposed that most progressive leaders came from the urban middle class. But he placed stronger emphasis on the reform activism of a new middle class composed of professional people and "specialists in business, in labor, and in agriculture." Common to these two groups was their "consciousness of unique skills and functions." In a word they were experts, whose productive property lay in their knowledge and brains. This new middle class had made its peace with the economy and society created by industrial capitalism. Indeed many progressives – lawyers, accountants, engineers, executives – were employed by the corporations. "Most of them lived and worked in the midst of modern society and accepting its major thrust drew both their inspiration and their programs from its peculiar traits," Wiebe claimed. Like a great many inhabitants of industrializing America, progressives were adepts of organization, eager "to join others like themselves in a craft union, professional organization, trade association, or agricultural cooperative" (1967: 112). Wiebe called their style of reform "bureaucratic": "suited to the fluidity and impersonality of an urban-industrial world. They pictured a society of ceaselessly interacting members and concentrated upon adjustments within it" (p. 145).

By the 1960s there was less consensus about the nature and composition of progressivism than ever. Who were the core progressives? Historians had variously nominated creative politicians, ex-Populist farmers, corporate fixers, humanitarian idealists, immigrant workers, the old middle class and the new middle class. What was their purpose? Historians had variously argued that the chief mission of progressivism was to clean up political corruption, stabilize the political economy, save industrial capitalism, care for its victims, head off socialist revolution, achieve efficiency, restore order, restore competition, restore civility, restore democracy. Little wonder that some scholars began to doubt that a phenomenon described so differently by so many investigators had ever really happened. Perhaps, Peter Filene suggested in 1970 and Daniel Rodgers in 1982, "progressivism" was, historically speaking, a mirage. Perhaps there had never been a coherent "progressive movement," but only a passel of disparate movements, sharing nothing but the same dates. The suspicion lingers. For example, one historian has recently contended that "progressivism" has become so elastic and applied to so many different things that "its utility as a historical category is threatened." The "essential common denominator" of progressivism lies in nothing but the "rhetorical formula" of advocating "united public action against corrupt forces" (Connolly 1998: 8). Yet most historians of the early twentieth century have continued to find unity and utility in the concept of progressivism, for a number of reasons.

First, however flimsy and scattered the movement has sometimes seemed to later observers, to the historical actors themselves progressivism was real and important. One purpose of De Witt's pioneering study of progressivism in 1915 was "to give form and definiteness to a movement which is, in the minds of many, confused and chaotic" (1968: viii). Its champions certainly thought of themselves as belonging to a recognizable collectivity. Even if progressivism amounted to little more than "a style of political behavior," at least the style was uniform and widely shared, as James J. Connolly has noted: "Each set of Progressives – whether settlement house feminists, elite male municipal reformers, antitrust crusaders, or ethnic politicians – presented themselves as the leaders of a communal response to the actions of illicit interests and the problems of urban-industrial life" (1998: 8).

Second, since the 1980s most students of progressivism have chalked up its awkward pluralism to its protean character and to the confusing nature of the transformations to which progressives were responding. The movement was disparate because it was very broad, they have decided; and this very breadth suggests its significance. The parable of the blind men and the elephant seems apropos here. That different groups of Americans in 1900–14 grasped different parts of the progressive "elephant," that no one saw the whole animal, does not mean no elephant existed. Nor does it mean that the different parts of progressivism were not related to one another.

Third, recent historians have regained a sense of the coherence of progressivism by recovering an awareness of the movement's international context. Seconding Roosevelt's nomination for the presidency in 1912, Jane Addams called the new Progressive Party "the American exponent of a worldwide movement toward juster social conditions, a movement which the United States, lagging behind other great nations, has been unaccountably slow to embody in political action" (quoted in Rodgers 1998: 74). Historians have established that the American progressives were participating in a process of adaptation to industrial capitalism that had analogues in the industrialized nations of Western Europe. James Kloppenberg and Daniel Rodgers have written superb studies of transatlantic convergence and cooperation. Kloppenberg analyzed the sometimes parallel, sometimes intersecting intellectual histories of American progressivism and European social democracy (1986); Rodgers masterfully mapped a whole North Atlantic community of "social politics," in which American progressives were more often borrowers than lenders of reform ideas (1998).

The historiography of progressivism remains rambunctiously heterogeneous. There is no "standard account." A sensible book that comes closest to being such an account, however, is the careful synthesis published by Arthur S. Link and Richard L. McCormick in 1983. The authors represent two generations of historians: Link began writing about progressivism in the 1940s, McCormick in the 1970s. These scholars relied principally on the Hays–Wiebe "organizational thesis," but combined with it the Mowry–Hofstadter perspective on progressives' attitudes and added anticipatory glances toward the broader context explored by Rodgers: "The progressives made the first comprehensive efforts to grapple with the ills of a modern urban-industrial society." Striving not to dismantle industrial capitalism but "rather to ameliorate and improve the conditions of industrial life," the progressives initiated processes of ambivalent accommodation with "industrialism" that would go on long past the period 1900–14 (Link and McCormick 1983: 3, 21).

From the perspective gained from a century's distance and stacks of previous studies, historians today see aspects of progressivism that were not clearly visible in the 1950s or even the 1980s. Wider-angle lenses enable them to discern patterns and connections in the jostling welter of particular movements, leaders, communities, and groups. One result is the possibility of achieving a more inclusive, panoramic image of the period, without necessarily losing the high resolution that close-ups provide. In any case the task of mapping the landscape of progressivism is, of course, a work in progress. I conclude with a sketch that indicates where the work is now and where it appears to be leading.

The most significant contemporary trend in study of this period may be that of putting American developments in a larger framework. Eager to shed the entrenched parochialism of their trade, American historians are exploring the implications for the United States of taking part in an industrial capitalist revolution which, though centered in the North Atlantic region, had consequences all over the world. Though no one then spoke of "globalization," more and more goods, people, and ideas were flowing across national boundaries. Improved means of trans-oceanic communication (by cable) and transportation (by steamship) led to increasing international trade in globally organized markets. Immigrants retained more of their old-country characteristics than did previous immigrants, partly by choice, partly in defense against the prejudices of native-born Americans, partly because – isolated in ghettos – they had no choice. In major cities and industrial towns, immigrants and their children made up most of the population, a highly visible "foreign" presence.

To many of the native-born, all this came as a shock. "Americans had grown up with the placid assumption that the development of their country was so much unlike what happened elsewhere," Hofstadter observed, "that the social conflicts troubling other countries could never become a major problem here" (1955: 166). At the turn of the twentieth century, titanic economic and demographic shifts were eroding distinctions between "here" and "there." In matters of material production, Europeans learned more from Americans than the other way around; but as Rodgers and Kloppenberg have demonstrated, American reformers often took inspiration from Europeans, as did a great many American intellectuals and artists. In this period the Armory Show introduced Americans to modernist art, and Sigmund Freud introduced them to depth psychology.

The United States was far from being a passive participant in these epic changes. Massive immigration depended on government policy, which in turn responded to booming industries' appetite for cheap labor. Policy also drove the republic out into the world beyond its borders. The US decisively emerged from its former isolation by acquiring a modest Caribbean and Pacific empire in 1898, then, under Roosevelt, Taft, and Wilson, behaved diplomatically like the great power it had become.

One of the touchstones of progressivism, in fact, was its readiness to embrace the nation's entry into the mainstream of world history. Americans had earlier identified their exceptionalism with their strengths and virtues. Signs of reversion to the benighted ways of the Old World were to be deplored. In contrast, progressives were inclined to view the shrinking of differences between the New World and the Old dispassionately, or to call it maturity. Convergence with Europe was not, in their eyes, retrogression, but joining with other advanced nations in a modernization that held high promise for them and perhaps for all of humankind.

To be sure, American exceptionalism persisted. Convergence with Europe was to be selective. Most progressives were fervent nationalists. The most celebrated of them all, Theodore Roosevelt, was an unapologetic imperialist who called his domestic program "the New Nationalism." Progressives of all stripes were determined to defend distinctive elements of the national culture. In relative terms the United States was less rigidly class-divided, more capitalist and Protestant and moralist, more resistant to state power and socialism, than were any of its industrialized peers; and progressives were happy to keep it that way. Other aspects of American peculiarity, however, progressives were eager to discard. Most, for example, were uncomfortable with the ethnic heterogeneity that set the United States apart from its rivals; cultural pluralism (the precursor of today's "multiculturalism") was a minority position among progressives. Many were also happy to cut back on what they viewed as the excesses of democracy. Thus literacy tests enjoyed wide support among progressives in the South (for denying the franchise to undesirable voters) as well as in the North (for barring undesirable immigrants).

This readiness to compromise democracy points to the progressives' heavenly city: a managed democracy, that is, a democracy that worked to their satisfaction because it was managed by people like themselves. Many progressives were sincere proponents of the secret ballot and of plebiscitary instruments like initiative, recall, and referendum. But considered as a whole, the movement's commitment to purifying democracy has been exaggerated. More basic to the progressive enterprise was a commitment to gaining control of democratic institutions that had, they believed, been corrupted by venality or grown inadequate to the needs of a modern society.

The agrarian and labor radicals of the Gilded Age had wanted to purify a society corrupted by sin. For progressives the problem was not just sin but also the inefficiency of institutions that allowed sin to flourish. The economy and society were corruptible because they were sloppily organized and haphazardly led. The solution to both sin and inefficiency was intelligent, diligent management. That meant using the scientific method to direct economic and social change; it meant constant gathering and analysis of data, constant measuring and monitoring of results, constant evaluation and adjustment of policies. Progressives believed that managerial methods gave them the capacity to overcome drift and to master history over the long haul. For static laws enforced in courts, they substituted frequently amended regulations applied by administrative agencies; for converted hearts, they substituted scientific reason and expertise; for millennialist visions, they substituted perpetual problem-solving. "The rules" they lived by were not fixed principles or laws but orientations based on probabilities; their techniques stressed "constant watchfulness and mechanisms of continuous management" (Wiebe 1967: 167). Most successful reform campaigns of the period exhibited the new emphasis on painstaking data-gathering, organization, and management. Employed by Carrie Chapman Catt, president of the National American Women's Suffrage Association, these methods were crucial to building support for the Suffrage Amendment; employed by the American Saloon League, they helped build a winning coalition behind the Prohibition Amendment; thanks to social workers like Florence Kelley and Josephine Goldmark, these methods brought countless gains in protections and services for workers and their families.

Not all progressives were equally infatuated with managerial methods. Republican progressives in the big urban centers of the Northeast and Midwest were the most prone to believe that honest, efficient management cleansed all sins. Rooseveltians even distinguished between "good trusts" that owed their size to superior efficiency and the "bad trusts" that had grown big by corrupt practices. These were the progressives who exhibited the "conservative" or "corporate liberal" orientations described by Kolko and Weinstein. Westerners and Southerners who came to progressivism by way of Populism and the Democratic Party tended to distrust big concentrations of private economic power, whether well managed or not. To the proponents of Woodrow Wilson's "New Freedom," trusts were bad just for being trusts.

But all progressives believed in good *public* management. All believed in cleaning up government and making it an effective instrument for policing "the interests." Business, labor, and even the champions of reform causes had grown mighty by mastering organizational and managerial skills. Now government, representing the welfare of the public, had to catch up. Thus progressivism reacted decisively against the ethos of laissez-faire. Any society needs to be governed, progressives believed, and none more than a modern industrialized society. Competing interest groups arise from a multitude of differences, whether of economic situation, section, race, ethnicity, or religion. As groups proliferate and organize, their interests collide. Members of each group become less cognizant of the values and needs of other groups, more intent on getting their own needs satisfied and their own values respected. A public interest grows hard to define, even harder to assert. Under these conditions, progressives believed, the state has the obligation to adjudicate fairly among interest groups and to furnish services left unprovided by the market economy. In practice this meant a larger and more active government. "Regulating a new society – using government and law to control the behavior of institutions, individuals, and groups – was a conspicuous feature of that outburst of state activism that we call the Progressive movement," according to Morton Keller (1994: 1).

Though progressives accepted the legitimacy of both interest groups and government, they were less sure about the legitimacy of parties. Parties had begun as mechanisms for brokering and bargaining among private interests in a relatively homogeneous preindustrial society. But the immense complexity of a modern industrialized country had overloaded party circuits, making them less efficient and more corruptible. Progressives were prone to rely on the state to undertake balancing functions previously performed by parties, and to replace the crass give-and-take dealings of politics with the theoretically just and transparent calculations of management.

The trusts and disorders of the Gilded Age demonstrated the incapacity of laissez-faire liberalism to keep capitalism sound and stable. Progressives were liberals who saw the necessity to revise the old formula for achieving order and security. They recognized the need for government to perform functions which – in a complex capitalist society – the market and human nature would not automatically fulfill. Progressives remained liberals, determined to preserve as much space for personal choice as social needs would allow. But they were liberals in search of a viable balance between government and liberty. Order was a precondition of liberty, and in 1900 order demanded the expansion of the state.

This understanding of progressivism, as liberalism in the process of reinventing itself, helps explain the faith in management, which was a way of exercising power that was free of all the things that tainted power in liberals' eyes. Being essentially scientific, management was animated by impartial reason. In theory, at least, its books were open; it operated in public hearings, courtrooms, and government documents rather than in smoke-filled rooms or locked boardrooms. Thus it was intellectually neutral. More importantly, it was politically neutral; the power of a regulatory commission or a bureau of labor statistics stood above privilege and partisanship. Managerial power was supposed to be disinterested. Regulators mediated or arbitrated between private interests, taking neither bribes nor sides. At an extreme progressives could pretend that management had nothing do with power, but was a purely mechanical process. Progressives venerated markets kept honest and efficient by neutral regulation.

Like many reformers, progressives were clearer about what they were against than what they were for. They were against dishonesty, secrecy, and greed. They were against class privilege and class solidarity. They were against predatory interest groups. They were against irresponsible power, whether wielded by bullying corporations, venal bosses, or conspiratorial unions. They were against dogmatic ideologies, especially those of the left. They were against overt, swords-drawn conflict. Perhaps more than anything else, they were against the partisanship of politics-as-usual. They loved the ideal of a public. They said that they wished to lead the whole country, not a class or party; and they wished to lead it neither to the right nor to the left, but forward. To move the country forward required rising "above" politics. When they tried to describe their political principles, progressives avoided crass words like "power," "self-interest," and "bargain." They preferred to use august words like "democracy" and "public interest" or austere words like "interdependence," "efficiency," and "administration."

A particular favorite was the word "control," a managerial word that connoted order purged of interest, conflict, and the open exercise of power. Yet try as they often did to deny it, the control that progressives desired entailed political deal-making and the exercise of power. The progressives were more like their wayward countrymen than they liked to acknowledge. Like all political actors, they had distinct class interests, cultural biases, and partisan instincts. As Hofstadter and Mowry noted decades ago, progressive leaders belonged to a middle class that was acutely anxious about its status in a class-divided industrialized society. Progressive leaders and the bulk of their followers were white Protestants of British heritage, a shrinking segment of the population. And Roosevelt, Wilson, LaFollette, and other progressive giants were reform-oriented politicians, superbly skilled in the arts of steering the interests they represented through conflicts and compromises.

George Mowry called "paradoxical in the extreme" the typical progressive's ability to combine "his own intense group loyalties with his strong antipathy to the class consciousness of organized capital and organized labor" (quoted in Mann 1963: 38). Naïveté accounted for some of the dissonance between the chaste neutrality that they professed and the interest-driven politics that they pursued. Probably the swift pace of events accounted for more of it; progressives' perceptions and ideas lagged behind their motives and actions. If they identified their peculiar values with "the public interest," confusion was as much to blame as deceit. But the gap between progressives' rhetoric and their practice also reflected blindness, hypocrisy, and arrogance. While proclaiming their reverence for science, democracy, and the public interest, not infrequently the progressives were infected by racism, ethnocentrism, class snobbery, and patriarchy. Progressives could be found in the ranks of the most illiberal causes of the day: prohibition, immigration restriction, gunboat diplomacy, movie censorship, rigidly moralistic approaches to vice, assaults on the First Amendment rights of unionists and leftists, and opposition to the social and economic equality of women.

Their record in race relations was particularly lamentable. 1900–1914 was a period of stagnation or deterioration in the conditions of life for black Americans. "Scientific racism" was riding high; and the incidence of lynching, having peaked in the 1890s, barely abated. A few prominent white reformers joined with blacks led by W. E. B. DuBois to found the National Association for the Advancement of Colored People (NAACP) in 1909. To be sure, President Roosevelt entertained Booker T. Washington in the White House and appointed African Americans to some federal posts. But President Wilson resegregated the federal civil service and trumpeted his delight with D. W. Giffith's racist cinematic masterpiece, *Birth of a Nation*, despite anguished NAACP protests. Progressives mostly supported the disenfranchisement and segregation of blacks in the South and exhibited indifference to their predicament everywhere else.

Ultimately progressives were themselves an aggressive interest group. They could justly profess to be more broad-minded and far-sighted than other groups. Their claims to virtuous high-mindedness are less persuasive. They were as determined as other groups to defend their own interests, as ready to use coercive means to achieve their ends, as avid to gain power. Management, their preferred remedy for social ills was more than the objective tool progressives liked to think it; it was also a subtle weapon that they deployed in the low-intensity interest-group wars of their time. Moreover, whenever progressives were forced out of their stance as apolitical middlemen and apostles of reason, whenever they were forced to choose sides in class and culture conflicts, they knew which side they were on. They stood with the established institutions that kept order, guarded property, and fueled prosperity: the law, the churches, the schools, the government, and the corporations. Industrial capitalism had transformed their country, and they accepted its work. Their purpose was to reform the complicated America that they had inherited, not to transform it again.

But if progressives were often disingenuous, and sometimes illiberal, they were seldom duplicitous. Though a century's hindsight enables us to see the limitations of this "progressive period," progress there surely was; and progressives were responsible for most of it. Especially in gender relations progressivism sponsored enormous advances. The movement was itself a vehicle for women's emergence from domesticity and subservience. Women led the social justice wing of the movement and took part in all branches of it. The most unequivocal gains in rights and welfare were made by and for women: increasing participation in higher education and the work force, protections for working women, services for mothers and their children, and decisive progress toward the Suffrage Amendment of 1920. The progressive ethos facilitated all these developments. Its emphasis on rationality, gentility, and service helped usher women into realms of power and work from which they had always been excluded.

On the score of inclusiveness and tolerance, in fact, the progressives have a better record than their contemporaries, or their predecessors in the Gilded Age, and certainly than their successors during the Great War period and in the 1920s. Though the hectic pluralism of American society disturbed them, the progressives dealt with immigrants, workers, and African Americans with a measure of sympathy and a sense of duty. They proposed to solve the "problems" of pluralism with management, education, and voluntary Americanization. The generation of political actors that followed them attacked these problems with repression and exclusion: 100 percent

Americanism, the Red Scare, immigration restriction, and nativist organizations such as the Ku Klux Klan.

This essay has addressed a segment of American society that aspired to control the rest of it, and for the most part succeeded. The progressive formula for a managed democracy that took hold in 1900–14 eventually became the prevailing approach to governing the political economy. What began in protest and reform ended in established institutions and orthodoxy. After the reactionary 1920s, progressivism swept back into power with the New Deal, and has remained a force to be reckoned with ever since. If the United States grew up under a regime of laissez-faire capitalism and classical liberalism, in its industrial maturity it has relied on the welfare-state capitalism and corporate liberalism that the progressives pioneered. The world they made – of a managerial state adjudicating among organized interest groups and supporting a market economy dominated by big corporations – is the world we still inhabit.

Where is the historiography of 1900–14 heading a century later? It seems likely that historians will have less to say about progressivism and more about the rest of American society: the myriad groups and sectors that the progressives sought to control. Under the aegis of the "new social history" and "history from the bottom up," they will sustain a focus that most younger historians have already adopted, on the divisions of race, ethnicity, gender, and class. The many "others" who lived far from the centers of American power – people of color, the immigrant working class, farmers, women – all made their own contributions to the national narrative in 1900–14, including contributions to the development of progressivism.

Though most recent scholarship has explored divisions of race, ethnicity, and gender, historians must also continue to probe divisions of class in the early twentieth century. Class division seems highly pertinent to the history of progressivism, as a number of historians have already established. J. Joseph Huthmacher (1962) and John Buenker (1973) argued some time ago that progressivism cannot be understood without appreciating the role played in progressive political coalitions by urban working-class voters. The Socialist Party of America attracted nearly one million votes in 1912 for its presidential candidate, Eugene Victor Debs, largely because – according to Nick Salvatore (1982) and Irving Howe (1985) – its socialism was an undoctrinaire, native-born ideology that had wider appeal than most progressives cared to admit. Progressivism may have been a defensive movement, designed to undercut the appeal of the left by ministering to workers' interests. David Montgomery also showed that the obstreperous radical labor federation called the Wobblies (Industrial Workers of the World), founded in 1905, was not the only manifestation of working-class militancy in the Progressive Era (1987). He described the whole period from 1909 till 1922 as one of resurgent working-class solidarity and activism. In light of this pattern, progressive initiatives to improve the lot of workers, plus later campaigns to suppress left parties and unions (1917–22), may have had the same basic motive: to keep the working class from making too much history.

Finally, historians will surely expand their explorations of the international contexts of American history in the early twentieth century. The United States became a potent actor not just in the North Atlantic region but across the planet during this period, which partly anticipated the "globalization" of our own time. The topic of American exceptionalism will continue to compel investigation, to assess the balance between factors that distinguished American development and factors that were drawing the country into transnational networks and patterns. Surely it is significant that in an age of explosive revolutions (in Mexico in 1910, in China in 1911, in Russia in 1917), the most dynamic actors on the American scene were middle-class reformers. Surely it is significant, too, that reform movements akin to progressivism (though more statist) occurred in Great Britain, France, and Germany. Those who know only progressivism – and only America – cannot deeply know either.

REFERENCES AND FURTHER READING

Addams, Jane (1961) [1910] *Twenty Years at Hull-House*. New York: New American Library.

Beard, Charles A. and Beard, Mary R. (1927) *The Rise of American Civilization*. New York: Macmillan.

Blum, John Morton (1965) *The Republican Roosevelt*. New York: Atheneum.

Buenker, John D. (1973) *Urban Liberalism and Progressive Reform*. New York: Scribner.

Connolly, James J. (1998) *The Triumph of Ethnic Progressivism: Urban Political Culture in Boston, 1900–1925*. Cambridge, Mass.: Harvard University Press.

Croly, Herbert (1964) [1909] *The Promise of American Life*. New York: Capricorn Books.

De Witt, Benjamin Parke (1968) [1915] *The Progressive Movement*. Seattle: University of Washington Press.

Diner, Steven J. (1998) *A Very Different Age: Americans of the Progressive Era*. New York: Hill and Wang.

Filene, Peter G. (1970) "An obituary for 'the Progressive Movement,' " *American Quarterly* 22, pp. 20–34.

Fink, Leon (1997) *Progressive Intellectuals and the Dilemmas of Democratic Commitment*. Cambridge, Mass.: Harvard University Press.

Hays, Samuel P. (1957) *The Response to Industrialism, 1885–1914*. Chicago: University of Chicago Press.

Hicks, John D. (1931) *The Populist Revolt: A History of the Farmers' Alliance and the People's Party*. Minneapolis: University of Minnesota Press.

Hofstadter, Richard (1955) *The Age of Reform: From Bryan to FDR*. New York: Alfred A. Knopf.

Howe, Irving (1985) *Socialism and America*. New York: Harcourt Brace Jovanovich.

Huthmacher, J. Joseph (1962) "Urban liberalism and the age of reform," *Mississippi Valley Historical Review* 49, pp. 231–41.

Keller, Morton (1994) *Regulating a New Society: Public Policy and Social Change in America, 1900–1933*. Cambridge, Mass.: Harvard University Press.

Kloppenberg, James T. (1986) *Uncertain Victory: Social Democracy and Progressivism in European and American Social Thought, 1870–1920*. New York: Oxford University Press.

Kolko, Gabriel (1963) *The Triumph of Conservatism: A Reinterpretation of American History, 1900–1916*. Chicago: Quadrangle Books.

Link, Arthur S. (1954) *Woodrow Wilson and the Progressive Era, 1910–1917*. New York: Harper and Row.

Link, Arthur S. and McCormick, Richard L. (1983) *Progressivism*. Arlington Heights, Ill.: Harlan Davidson.

Mann, Arthur (ed.) (1963) *Progressive Era: Liberal Renaissance or Liberal Failure?* New York: Holt, Rinehart, and Winston.

McCormick, Richard L. (1986) *The Party Period and Public Policy: American Politics from the Age of Jackson to the Progressive Era*. New York: Oxford University Press.

Milkis, Sidney and Mileur, Jerome M. (eds.) (1999) *Progressivism and the New Democracy.* Amherst: University of Massachusetts Press.

Montgomery, David (1987) *The Fall of the House of Labor: The Workplace, the State, and American Labor Activism, 1865–1925.* Cambridge: Cambridge University Press.

Mowry, George E. (1946) *Theodore Roosevelt and the Progressive Movement, 1900–1912.* New York: Hill and Wang.

Rodgers, Daniel T. (1982) "In search of progressivism," *Reviews in American History* 10, pp. 113–32.

—— (1998) *Atlantic Crossings: Social Politics in a Progressive Age.* Cambridge, Mass.: Harvard University Press.

Salvatore, Nick (1982) *Eugene V. Debs: Citizen and Socialist.* Urbana: University of Illinois Press.

Sanders, Elizabeth (1999) *Roots of Reform: Farmers, Workers, and the American State, 1877–1917.* Chicago: University of Chicago Press.

Weinstein, James (1968) *The Corporate Ideal in the Liberal State, 1900–1918.* Boston: Beacon Press.

Wiebe, Robert H. (1967) *The Search for Order, 1877–1920.* New York: Hill and Wang.

CHAPTER TWO

1914–1929

GLEN GENDZEL

For Americans, the years from 1914 to 1929 raised questions without easy answers. Could the United States remain neutral in a world at war? Could Americans make a difference in that war and in the peace that followed? What was the proper role of the United States in world affairs? Would the democracy that Americans fought to defend abroad prevail at home? Was it possible to build lasting prosperity with minimal regulation and almost no welfare state? What was the proper relationship between business and government? The era of World War I and the 1920s touched on all of these vital issues but gave them only incomplete and unsatisfactory resolution prior to the onset of the Great Depression.

Challenges to Neutrality

When Woodrow Wilson became president in 1913, he sensed prophetically that "it would be an irony of fate if my administration had to deal chiefly with foreign affairs" (quoted in Baker, IV: 55). A renowned scholar of American government, Wilson brought the progressive reform movement to a climax by signing the landmark New Freedom legislation. Yet for all his mastery of domestic politics, Wilson, like most Americans, had little foreign policy experience. The United States had recently acquired the Philippines, built the Panama Canal, intervened in Central America, and increased its foreign trade and investment substantially. Yet none of these international involvements seemed to break through the traditional attitude of secure detachment from world politics that historians have dubbed "isolationism" (Adler 1957).

In 1914, Americans were shocked out of insular complacency when the great powers of Europe suddenly declared war on each other. Britain, France, Russia, and (in 1915) Italy were the Allies; Germany, Austria-Hungary, Bulgaria, and (in 1915) the Ottoman empire were the Central Powers. The Great War, as it was called, only underscored the need for separating the United States from Europe. President Wilson proclaimed official US neutrality and urged Americans to "be impartial in thought as well as in action" (Link, XXX: 394). Four months later, he dismissed the European conflagration as "a war with which we have nothing to do, whose causes cannot touch us" (Link, xxxi: 423). Nonetheless, three challenges to American neutrality would arise between August, 1914, when the war began, and April, 1917, when the United States intervened on the Allied side.

The first challenge to neutrality arose in the court of public opinion. As the Great War bogged down into a bloody stalemate, few Americans could remain impartial for long. Though German immigrants rooted for the fatherland, and Irish immigrants hoped England would lose, the preponderance of American sentiment favored the Allies for three reasons. First, Germany waged war with extraordinary cruelty and ruthlessness; second, upper-class Americans had close ties with England; third, most of the Allies were parliamentary democracies whereas the Central Powers were military autocracies. A war between democracies and despots left Americans inclined to root for the democracies, although pro-Allied sentiment did not translate into support for US intervention. Public opinion remained strongly opposed to American participation in the war under any circumstances.

The second challenge to neutrality arose for reasons of profit. US corporations sold immense quantities of munitions, the "sinews of war," to the Allies and not to the Central Powers (Burk 1985). This lopsided trade developed for reasons beyond American control. Britain clamped a highly effective naval blockade around Germany, so the only customers for American exports were on the Allied side. Yet it was only the Allies who *needed* large quantities of American exports. Britain and France had nothing comparable to the massive German arms industry. The Germans would have imported American foodstuffs if possible, but apart from severe civilian hardship, their war effort was not substantially affected by the British blockade. If the Allies, on the other hand, could not import American munitions, they would lose the war (Coogan 1981; Vincent 1985).

Trade drew the United States out of strict neutrality. The value of US exports to Britain and France more than tripled between 1914 and 1916, while at the same time the value of US exports to Germany fell by over 90 percent (Birdsall 1939; Burk 1985). To cut off munitions exports in order to protect American neutrality would have damaged the US economy and assured victory for the Central Powers – hardly a "neutral" outcome, nor one necessarily in the best interests of the United States. For this reason, when the Allies ran out of ready cash to purchase munitions, President Wilson authorized private loans from US banks to the British and French governments. Loans kept the munitions trade going, but they placed the United States in a position one historian characterizes as "non-belligerent non-neutrality" (Coogan 1994: 81).

The third challenge to neutrality was a new weapon of war: the submarine. Germany's small fleet of *Unterseebooten*, or U-boats, could slip past the British blockade and sink cargo ships or passenger liners heading into Allied ports. Under international law, countries at war could stop and search civilian vessels and confiscate munitions headed for enemy ports. Warring countries were not allowed to attack civilians or to confiscate cargo other than munitions. Great Britain was the first to violate international law by confiscating virtually all cargoes headed for the Central Powers, including food and medicine. Wilson lodged only minor protests because the British refrained from attacking civilians (Devlin 1974). U-boats, on the other hand, were ineffective if they surfaced to stop and search civilian vessels. This procedure forfeited the element of surprise and left U-boats vulnerable. Instead, the Germans freely attacked Allied cargo ships and passenger liners, endangering civilian lives in order to maximize the submarine's effectiveness as a weapon.

Despite the U-boat threat, Americans continued traveling on British and French passenger liners as they had before the war. Germany issued public warnings that such travelers faced possible attack, but under international law, neutral citizens had every right to free passage through a war zone, and the Germans had no right to attack passenger liners. The inevitable disaster came on May 7, 1915, when a German U-boat torpedoed Britain's *Lusitania*, which carried over 2,000 civilians. Of the 1,200 passengers and crew who died in the attack, 128 were Americans. The *Lusitania* was carrying munitions at the time, but from the standpoint of international law and American public opinion, nothing excused the wanton murder of civilians on the high seas. Many Americans called for war over the *Lusitania* outrage, but President Wilson clung to neutrality: "There is such a thing as being too proud to fight" (Link, xxxiii: 149). He faced pressure from interventionists such as ex-President Theodore Roosevelt, who charged that anything less than war would be cowardly and dishonorable. On the other side, however, isolationists, pacifists, and pro-Germans sided with Secretary of State William Jennings Bryan, who urged Wilson to preserve neutrality by embargoing trade with countries at war and forbidding Americans to travel in the war zone.

Wilson chose a middle course by insisting on "neutral rights," meaning the right of Americans to trade with countries at war and to travel freely in war zones. Even though the British blockade also violated those rights, Wilson pointed out that the British, unlike the Germans, had not harmed any US citizens. After the *Lusitania* incident, Wilson demanded that the Germans cease attacks on unarmed civilian ships. Surprisingly, in August, 1915, the Germans agreed to spare passenger liners; and a year later this pledge was extended to all civilian ships. The Germans secretly began stockpiling U-boats to strike a decisive blow against Allied shipping in the near future, and they wished to avoid US intervention in the meantime. But to the public it seemed that Wilson had won a great diplomatic victory by forcing the Germans to curtail submarine warfare (Clements 1987, 1992).

This apparent triumph came just in time to aid Wilson's re-election. With the campaign slogan "He Kept Us Out of War," he eked out a narrow victory in 1916. Claiming a new mandate from the American people, Wilson tried to mediate a settlement to the war still raging in Europe. On January 22, 1917, he delivered a dramatic speech calling for "Peace Without Victory." Wilson offered to help negotiate an armistice based on a return to prewar borders with no punishments for either side. Only a peace among equals could prevent a war for revenge in the future, he warned. Wilson also offered his vision of a new world order based on democracy, disarmament, and free trade that he hoped would emerge from the ashes of war. But Wilson's words came too late; just nine days later, Germany announced that it would begin unrestricted submarine warfare on February 1, 1917. The Germans assumed that the United States would enter the war on the Allied side at that point, but they believed their U-boats could sink so much Allied shipping that Britain and France would have to surrender before US intervention could make any difference (Smith 1965; Cooper 1980).

As Americans began dying on the high seas again, victims of German U-boat attacks, Wilson published the Zimmermann Telegram on March 1, 1917. This document, which had been intercepted and decoded by British intelligence agents, was a secret dispatch from the German foreign minister to the German ambassador in Mexico City. It offered a military alliance between Germany and Mexico (plus Japan). The scenario was not far-fetched, given that Wilson had recently ordered two separate US invasions of Mexico and that relations between the two countries were severely strained (Tuchman 1958). The Germans hoped that the prospect of war with Mexico and Japan would deter the United States from entering the war, but their plan backfired. The Zimmermann Telegram only raised American indignation and convinced Wilson that the Germans would never accept peace until they had been beaten in war.

America in the Great War

Historians still debate why the United States entered World War I. At one time, it was accepted that the US needed to defend neutral rights and national interests against German aggression (Smith 1965). Then the "revisionist" interpretation suggested that American bankers and munitions-makers had pushed the country into war because they had heavily invested in the Allies and could not afford to let the Germans win (Tansill 1938; Cohen 1967). Some self-proclaimed "realists" later criticized Wilson for insisting on the abstract principles of neutral rights and freedom of the seas, rather than explaining to the American people that vital national interests were at stake in preventing a German victory (Kennan 1951; Osgood 1953; Gregory 1971; Ambrosius 1991). Other historians maintained that the United States went to war to gain access to world markets for US corporations. American participation, in this view, was aimed at Soviet Communism and European imperialism as much as at Germany (Mayer 1959; Levin 1968; Williams 1972; Gardner 1984).

Interpretations aside, the United States would not have gone to war unless President Wilson desired it. His speeches suggest that he wanted American participation in the war in order to create a new world order. At first, by offering to mediate, Wilson tried to achieve that goal peacefully. But when the Germans showed their determination to win at any cost, he reluctantly joined the coalition against them. Only by helping to win the war could Wilson shape the peace. This was the argument Wilson presented to Congress on April 2, 1917, when he asked for a declaration of war: "The world must be made safe for democracy" (Link, xli: 519–27). Isolationists in Congress protested; but they were outvoted, and the United States went to war four days later.

US intervention in the Great War came just in time to save the Allies from defeat. In 1917 Russia dissolved in revolution, and the new Bolshevik regime made a separate peace with Germany. Wilson cooperated with the Allies in sending forces to intervene, but they failed to restore Russia to the war. Russia's withdrawal from Allied ranks closed the eastern front and relieved over a million German troops for transfer to the western front. With this infusion of manpower, Germany planned a knock-out blow against the Allies in France before enough Americans could arrive to make a difference. The gamble almost worked: the United States could not raise a modern army overnight. Drafting, training, and equipping 4 million "doughboys" to fight in France took a full year after the US declaration of war, which gave the Germans their window of opportunity.

In the spring of 1918, Germany launched its last-ditch offensive in France. Exhausted British and French troops held off the German onslaught largely on their own. Six months later, the American Expeditionary Forces under General John Pershing played a major role in the Allied counter-offensive, but by then the Germans were already militarily beaten (Trask 1993; Woodward 1993). European historians tend to downplay the US contribution to victory, but American historians emphasize the psychological boost to British and French soldiers who knew that the Yanks were coming. Though rather small and late, intervention was decisive because it tipped the balance. True, the United States lost "only" 115,000 dead, compared to over 4 million Allied losses. But the principal American contribution to victory was non-military: the US government spent a phenomenal $35 billion on the Great War, much of it for supplies to keep the Allies fed and fighting. Dollars as well as doughboys turned the tide in Europe; the Allies could not have won without men, money, and *matériel* from the United States (Trask 1993; Woodward 1993; Mosier 2001).

War is always a catalyst for social and economic change, and the Great War was no exception. Progressive reformers like Wilson had been struggling for years to expand the regulatory state, and the war helped them to advance their "social engineering" agenda. The Wilson administration substantially increased federal power over business. In particular, the War Industries Board (WIB) allocated resources, shut down non-essential industries, standardized products, and set prices. Though still haphazard and inefficient, the WIB was the closest that the United States had yet come to centralized economic management; and historians cite it as a forerunner of the New Deal. Businessmen protested at first, but federal control of the economy proved necessary when critical industries such as railroads and shipbuilding failed to mobilize adequately on their own (Cuff 1973; Leuchtenburg 1995).

Other key wartime agencies included the War Labor Board, which arbitrated between employers and workers, and the Food Administration, which encouraged farmers to produce more and consumers to consume less. More controversial was the Committee on Public Information (CPI), which disseminated official government propaganda in support of the war effort. Fearing dissent, Wilson authorized a campaign to "sell" the war to the American people; but the CPI distorted his message about a war against militarism and autocracy. Instead, the CPI's advertising executives and public relations consultants portrayed the war as a crusade against inhuman, evil "Huns" who had to be exterminated. In the days before radio and television, the CPI produced millions of pamphlets, posters, and newsreels. The committee also recruited 75,000 public speakers known as "four minute men," who gave brief pro-war speeches at public gatherings. All these voices screaming for death to the Huns drowned out Wilson's high-minded war aims, while creating a home-front atmosphere conducive to political repression and abuse of civil liberties. Private vigilantes took the CPI's message to heart by burning German books and harassing German Americans. Popular hatred and sporadic acts of violence spread to socialists, pacifists, intellectuals, immigrants, and anyone else who failed to meet the test of so-called "100 percent Americanism" (Schaffer 1991; Zieger 2000).

Congress fueled wartime intolerance by passing two laws that practically repealed the First Amendment. The Espionage Act of 1917 barred any criticism of the military in wartime; even worse, the Sedition Act of 1918 outlawed any "disloyal, profane, scurrilous, or abusive language" against the US government in general. Although both laws went far beyond the requirements of national security, they were rigorously enforced. Over 2,000 Americans were tried and punished for exercising their right of free speech. These repressive laws were upheld by the Supreme Court essentially on the grounds of military necessity in wartime, which set an unfortunate precedent that would help to justify the internment of Japanese Americans in World War II.

The Lost Peace

President Wilson neglected civil liberties during the war because he was preoccupied with shaping the peace. His vision of a new world order received further expression in the "Fourteen Points" speech of January 8, 1918. Wilson listed features of the fair, democratic peace for which Americans were fighting, and he called for "a general association of nations" to prevent future wars (Link, XLV: 534–9). The League of Nations, as it became known, was supposed to replace the old balance-of-power alliances with a general alliance against war itself. Potential aggressors would be deterred by the international community's united stance against them. Some historians dismiss Wilson's "collective security" plan as hopelessly idealistic, but others applaud his devotion to building a lasting peace through international cooperation (Kennan 1951; Osgood 1953; Link 1979; Clements 1987; Knock 1992).

Trouble began for Wilson's peace when the war ended on November 11, 1918. Germany requested a conditional armistice based on the Fourteen Points, and the Allies accepted it under pressure from Wilson. Weeks later, Wilson joined other Allied leaders at the Paris Peace Conference to hammer out the final peace treaty. For months, Wilson negotiated himself into exhaustion by arguing for gentle peace terms that would avoid another war with Germany. His bargaining position, however, was difficult because the other Allied leaders knew that the League of Nations was Wilson's utmost desideratum. They threatened to stay out of the League if Wilson blocked their demands for vengeance against Germany. In this way, the Allies forced Wilson to compromise most of the Fourteen Points.

The Treaty of Versailles that emerged from the Paris Peace Conference was harshly punitive. The victorious Allies tore off huge chunks of territory from the Central Powers, confiscated overseas colonies, and imposed $33 billion in "reparations" on Germany. Some aspects of Wilson's Fourteen Points did appear in the treaty, however. In Central and Eastern Europe, imperial monarchies gave way to parliamentary democracies. Wilson's advocacy of national self-determination led to the creation of new states such as Poland, Yugoslavia, and Czechoslovakia. Wilson also persuaded the Allies to accept colonial possessions taken from the Central Powers only as temporary "mandates" that would be set free some day. This was the first time that European imperialist powers had promised independence to colonial subjects. But the treaty's saving grace, from Wilson's point of view, was the League of Nations: the collective security apparatus that would keep the peace in the future. All the great powers agreed to join, and Wilson probably consoled himself by thinking that whatever the treaty's flaws, the League would resolve them in the future.

Sadly, however, Wilson's dream fell apart when he returned to the United States. Under the Constitution, the Senate must approve all international treaties by a two-thirds majority. Despite months of debate and numerous roll-call votes, the Senate never ratified the Treaty of Versailles; and the United States never joined the League of Nations. It is tempting to blame this failure on the "Irreconcilables," a small bloc of isolationist senators steadfastly opposed to any US involvement in world politics that might lead to war (Fleming 1932; Guinsburg 1982). Yet four out of five senators voted for the Treaty of Versailles in some form in 1919 and 1920. With artful compromises, Wilson could have secured Senate approval for US membership in the League of Nations; but he refused to accept any amendments to the treaty he brought back from Paris. Wilson instructed Democratic senators to vote against the treaty with amendments, and Republican senators refused to vote for the treaty without amendments. This partisan stalemate, compounded by Wilson's intransigence, prevented the treaty's ratification (Ambrosius 1987; Cooper 2001).

Wilson's opponents deserve some of the blame for the Lost Peace. Henry Cabot Lodge, chairman of the Senate Foreign Relations Committee, displayed a deeply partisan and personal animus. But Lodge and other treaty opponents also voiced genuine concerns about the loss of US sovereignty and congressional prerogative if membership in the League of Nations should obligate the United States to wage war in the future. By refusing to address these legitimate concerns about collective security, Wilson prevented the United States from joining the world organization that he had created. Senate objections could have been worked out later if the United States had joined the League at the outset, but Wilson himself obviated this possibility by spurning any amendments to his treaty. Hence the question for historians is why he refused to compromise. The likely answer is that after months of hard bargaining with Allied leaders in Paris, Wilson was in no mood for dickering with opponents in Washington (Ferrell 1985; Clements 1987; Heckscher 1991).

As the Senate debated, Wilson embarked on a national speaking tour aimed at persuading the American people to support his treaty. It nearly killed him. The ailing President traveled 10,000 miles in three weeks; he delivered forty speeches to huge audiences before he finally collapsed from exhaustion. Rushed back to Washington, Wilson suffered a severe stroke on October 2, 1919. The left side of his body was paralyzed and his judgment was affected. For the next six months, while the First Lady and the White House physician kept the President isolated, the Treaty of Versailles languished in the Senate, then went down to final defeat. Americans heard about the treaty's shortcomings from its critics while Wilson was unable to respond. Disillusionment was inevitable once Americans realized that their crusade to make the world safe for democracy had ended up expanding the British and French empires instead. Millions of veterans and their families concluded that their sacrifices had been wasted because the peace did not turn out as Wilson had promised.

The Aftermath

Much went wrong for Americans in 1919. The booming war economy screeched to a halt when the Wilson administration cancelled billions of dollars in war orders. Four million workers went on strike as inflation and unemployment soared. The nation's first general strike shut down the city of Seattle, and the city of Boston dissolved into anarchy when the police force walked out. Even worse, 1919 also marked the beginning of the Spanish flu epidemic, the world's deadliest in over five centuries. At least 20 million people died of influenza worldwide, including half a million Americans – more than four times the number killed in the Great War. Thousands of doughboys survived the horrors of trench warfare only to sicken and die on their way home (Crosby 1989).

There were also twenty-five major race riots across the United States in the "Red Summer" of 1919, so called because the blood of blacks and whites flowed freely together in the streets of American cities. Racial tension was high, owing to competition for housing and jobs; but most riots began when newspapers published exaggerated or false stories about alleged black crimes, which sent white marauders into black neighborhoods. Dozens of victims, mostly African Americans, perished in Red Summer riots across the South and the Middle West, but worst of all was the Chicago riot of July 27–31, 1919. White mobs beat African Americans to death in the streets, while black mobs set fire to white neighborhoods. This horrifying ordeal lasted for five days and left 38 dead, 537 injured, and over 1,500 homeless. An even worse race riot occurred two years later in Tulsa, Oklahoma, where the death toll is still under investigation (Tuttle 1970; Shapiro 1988; Madigan 2001).

African Americans had faced mob violence before, but in Chicago and elsewhere, white rioters were surprised to encounter mass resistance. The "New Negro" spirit of militant defiance was a product of the Great War. Almost 400,000 African Americans had joined the Army, urged on by W. E. B. DuBois and other black leaders. Eager to prove their equality and patriotism, African-American troops found themselves in segregated units with white officers and relegated to menial chores like unloading ships or burying the dead. Yet they also had a taste of racial equality in France, courtesy of hospitable civilians who did not share white American attitudes toward race (Barbeau and Henri 1974). For these reasons, black veterans came home from the Great War determined to defend their communities and to make their own country safe for democracy. As DuBois wrote in 1919, "We return. We return from fighting. We return fighting" (quoted in Goldberg 1999: 91).

The year 1919 also marked the beginning of the Red Scare, a shameful blot on the record of American civil liberties. When the Great War ended, many Americans were in a patriotic fervor with no one left to attack. Trading their anti-German hysteria for anti-radical hysteria, some acted as though the war were still going on, but against a new enemy: "Reds," the generic term for socialists, communists, radicals, anarchists, and union organizers. The Russian Revolution had already raised fears of Communism when Attorney General A. Mitchell Palmer warned that the United States was next in line. The Red Scare began with vigilante attacks by returning war veterans against union members belonging to the Industrial Workers of the World. The climax came on January 2, 1920, when federal agents staged simultaneous mass arrests in 33 cities across the country. About 5,000 suspected radicals were eventually imprisoned for months without trial, and hundreds of immigrants were summarily deported. Prominent judges and legal scholars protested the Wilson administration's abuse of constitutional rights.

The Constitution suffered a further insult in 1919, when the Eighteenth Amendment prohibited the sale, possession, and consumption of "intoxicating liquors." The movement for prohibition of alcohol dated back to the temperance crusade of the nineteenth century, but it gained popularity after 1900 as a reform panacea. Businessmen expected that prohibition would increase labor productivity; social workers hoped it would reduce poverty and family violence; progressives believed it would hasten the assimilation of immigrants. Prohibition got a boost from the Great War, which triggered patriotic calls for conserving grain and manpower. The war also stirred up hatred of German Americans, who happened to own most of the big national breweries. Congress banned the sale and manufacture of alcohol as a temporary wartime measure on August 10, 1917. Four months later, Congress approved the Eighteenth Amendment. Most of the states that ratified the amendment did so as a patriotic wartime gesture, but the Eighteenth Amendment did not receive final ratification until six weeks after the armistice. The war was over, but prohibition had just begun.

Like prohibition, woman suffrage was an old idea that gained new popularity during the Great War. Despite decades of suffrage campaigning, only eleven states had granted voting rights to women by 1914. Most men, and a lot of women, too, believed that suffrage would undermine family values by inviting the filthy world of politics into the home. Women progressives such as Jane Addams built support for woman suffrage by turning this argument on its head. They suggested that a little motherly housecleaning was exactly what American politics needed. This rhetoric helped win new converts to woman suffrage. During the Great War, women took men's jobs in farms, factories, and offices or volunteered for service as nurses, recreation workers, and military recruiters. Previously opposed to suffrage, President Wilson endorsed it during the war to recognize women's contribution (Lunardini and Knock 1981). Congress passed the Nineteenth Amendment on June 4, 1919, and it was ratified on August 26, 1920. White women finally attained the right to vote in every state. But African Americans of both sexes were still unable to vote in the South because of disfranchisement laws unaffected by the Nineteenth Amendment (Keyssar 2000; Perman 2001).

Back to Normalcy

President Wilson called on the American people to treat the 1920 election as "a great and solemn referendum" on US membership in the League of Nations (quoted in Clements 1987: 220). He hoped that the two parties would take clear stands on the issue so that Americans would have a chance to vote on it directly. The Democratic nominee, Governor James Cox of Ohio, endorsed the League and joined Wilson in urging Americans to accept international obligations. All the Republican front-runners for the presidential nomination in 1920 were outspoken isolationists opposed to the League. But rather than give the American people a clear choice, the Republicans straddled the issue in their platform and nominated an obscure Ohio senator, Warren Harding, whose principal qualification for the presidency was that his views on the League were unknown. The 1920 election became a referendum, not on the League of Nations, but on the past two decades of progressive leadership. Harding offered "not nostrums but normalcy . . . not surgery but serenity," which appealed to Americans grown weary of reform crusades at home and abroad (quoted in Ferrell 1985: 227). Harding implied that he would leave things alone for a change, and voters approved by electing him in a record landslide. But what did "normalcy" mean in practice? In foreign affairs, it meant withdrawal from world politics and a return to isolationism. Private business continued expanding American trade and investment abroad, but US diplomats focused on quixotic issues like recovering war debts from former allies and negotiating a treaty to outlaw war. Although the United States took the lead in international arms control efforts, it avoided even the appearance of cooperation with the League of Nations (Cohen 1987).

Domestically, the progressive spirit lingered in the 1920s in the form of third-party insurgencies, public power projects, and federally subsidized health care for poor mothers and children. It was clear, however, that progressives no longer set the nation's political agenda. Riven between rural native-born and urban ethnic factions, the Democratic Party was in disarray throughout the decade (Burner 1968; Craig 1992). Republican conservatives used their control of Congress and the White House to abandon the progressive commitment to social justice and the regulatory state. Anti-trust laws went unenforced as merger waves swept through the ranks of business and income taxes were reduced so that wealthy Americans benefited most (Keller 1990; Hawley 1992). These policies reflected intimate ties between big business and the Republican Party that came to light in the Teapot Dome scandal of 1924. Several Harding administration officials went to prison for taking bribes from oil companies. Despite the scandal, however, Republican pro-business policies continued under President Calvin Coolidge, who had been Harding's Vice President. Coolidge assumed the presidency when Harding died in 1923, and was easily elected in 1924.

GOP dominance throughout the 1920s rested on a combination of low voter turnout and high economic growth. Republican office-holders and their business allies proclaimed that the United States had entered a "New Era" of permanent prosperity (Hicks 1960; Buenker 1976). The economic boom was concentrated, however, in a few industries: construction and real estate thrived as every major US city added a skirt of middle-class suburbs and a crown of skyscrapers. Sales of consumer appliances like refrigerators, washing machines, and radios also soared. But the biggest booming business of the 1920s was the automobile industry. The personal car, previously a luxury item, became affordable for every middle-class family and many working-class families. Automobile registrations in the United States soared from under 8 million in 1920 to over 23 million in 1930, by which time Americans owned two out of three automobiles in the world.

Henry Ford, icon of the automobile age, had introduced the first mass-produced affordable car, the Model T, in 1908. In 1914 he cut the price in half and doubled the wages of his employees to stimulate sales. Less well known is that Ford investigated and punished workers for smoking, drinking, swearing, or joining a union. He was also a confirmed anti-Semite who published attacks on the international Jewish conspiracy. None of these activities detracted from Ford's folk-hero status, however. The muckrakers of the Progressive Era had criticized "robber barons" in the popular press; but in the 1920s, Ford and other businessmen basked in the glow of public esteem. A best-selling book of the decade was Bruce Barton's *The Man Nobody Knows* (1925), which portrayed Jesus Christ as a "forceful executive." In a decade when businessmen attained godlike status, Americans were ready to accept the Son of God as the consummate businessman (Barton 1925; Ribuffo 1981).

Cultural Ferment

The 1920s brought dramatic changes in American morals and standards of behavior inherited from the Victorian era. Historians often cite this decade as a cultural turning point, when the nineteenth-century work ethic gave way to a new ethic of leisure and consumption (Horowitz 1985; Cohen 1990; Dumenil 1995;). For women, the 1920s offered hope of escape from restrictive gender roles, starting with the everyday prison of Victorian attire. The "New Woman" of the 1920s shed her steel corset, wore shorter skirts, and bobbed her hair as acts of self-liberation. Social commentators heralded the appearance of "flappers," which *Webster's Dictionary* defined at the time as young women "somewhat daring in conduct," suggesting that more than fashion was at stake (quoted in Critoph 1975: 145). The New Woman was more independent than her mother's generation, less reliant on men, and less willing to follow social rules. She rejected domesticity and demanded the same right as men to combine career with family. To be sure, women still faced discrimination in education and employment, but new professional opportunities beckoned, women's labor force participation increased, and the Equal Rights Amendment was introduced. For these reasons, historians find many antecedents of modern feminism in the 1920s (Becker 1981; Brown 1987; Cott 1987; Dumenil 1995).

African Americans, like women, were also on the cutting edge of cultural change in this decade. Half a million black sharecroppers left the rural South for the urban North during the Great War, and another million followed in the 1920s. Locked in a cycle of debt and poverty, terrorized by lynch mobs, many southern blacks were eager to start new lives in the North. The migrants still encountered racist hostility in northern cities, where they were forced to live in crowded ghettos and work for low wages in menial jobs. But at least they escaped the indignities of Jim Crow segregation, and black men even gained the right to vote by moving north. Freed from the repressive legacy of slavery, black communities in northern cities enjoyed a cultural efflorescence. A literary movement called the "Harlem Renaissance" protested racial injustice and celebrated the black experience and culture, while jazz emerged as America's greatest indigenous art form. The new music began in New Orleans early in the century and joined the black migration north to Chicago and New York, where it drew patrons of both races. Black pride, cultural autonomy, and self-expression reached new heights. Harlem in the 1920s was also the headquarters of Marcus Garvey, founder of the United Negro Improvement Association (UNIA). A flamboyant showman, Garvey struck other black leaders as undignified and impractical. Still, his "back to Africa" message encouraged racial pride and separatism. Garvey scorned integration and urged black people not to rely on white people for anything. He founded a string of black-owned businesses, including the Black Star Shipping Line, before he was convicted of fraud and deported to Jamaica in 1927. It was a sad end for the most popular black leader of the decade. About 2 million African Americans joined the UNIA to share Garvey's back-to-Africa fantasy. It was a way for them to express doubt that racial equality would ever occur at home in America.

Among white Americans, multiple social and ethnic conflicts marred "the tribal twenties" (Higham 1988). Behind much of this strife lay the ongoing feud between country and city. By 1920 a majority of the population lived in towns and cities, but rural Americans defended their provincial way of life against cosmopolitan modernity. Three different controversies of the decade expressed this underlying urban–rural conflict. The first was over prohibition, which was openly flouted in northern cities. Overall levels of drinking declined when working-class saloons closed down, but many city-dwellers persisted in drinking anyway. They flocked to underground cocktail bars called "speakeasies," and organized crime flourished as mobsters like Al Capone capitalized on the urban demand for alcohol. By the end of the 1920s, prohibition had reached a stalemate as rural politicians clamored for law enforcement and urban politicians blocked them at every turn (Clark 1976; Pegram 1998). This standoff affected the 1928 presidential race: Al Smith, an urban "wet" candidate opposed to prohibition, lost the election, but won a majority of the big-city vote.

The second urban–rural conflict of the 1920s was over immigration. Nativism was strongest in rural areas because it was mostly in cities that immigrants and their children were a majority. As with prohibition and suffrage, the Great War marked the turning point for the nativist movement. In this case, it accentuated hostility against foreigners, or "hyphenated Americans," for their alleged lack of patriotism. After the war, the Red Scare further fanned the flames of xenophobia: many radicals were foreign-born, so immigration restriction took on national-security overtones. As immigration surged upward again, nativists warned that foreigners were about to inundate the United States and cause "race suicide." In 1924 Congress bowed to nativist pressure by setting strict immigration quotas in the National Origins Act. The law favored north-west Europe over southeast Europe and barred all immigration from Asia. Quotas were quite effective: the United States averaged a million immigrants a year before 1914, but only 400,000 a year in the 1920s and 50,000 a year in the 1930s. Without fresh infusions from the old country, immigrant neighborhoods of American cities went into decline – much to the satisfaction of rural nativists (Higham 1988; Dumenil 1995).

The third urban–rural conflict of the 1920s was over religion and morality. Protestant fundamentalism experienced a great revival in rural areas, especially in the South and among rural migrants to Los Angeles and other cities. Fundamentalist preachers attacked the theory of evolution and insisted on the literal truth of the Bible. Tennessee's law against the teaching of evolution was upheld in the Scopes Trial of 1925. Ostensibly a battle between science and religion, the Scopes Trial juxtaposed secular modernism based in cities with rural America's religious tradition-alism (Ginger 1958; Larson 1997). Similarly, the Ku Klux Klan, a dormant relic of the nineteenth century, reappeared in the 1920s as a social club for native-born white men and women opposed to modernist culture. The reborn Klan was popular in small towns, rural areas, and cities of the West and Middle West; most Klan members lived outside the South. Like the old Klan, the new Klan attacked blacks; but immigrants, Jews, Catholics, homosexuals, radicals, and intellectuals joined the list of Klan victims in the 1920s. Some historians portray the new Klan as "hooded populism" opposed to local elites, but anyone (including non-elites) who violated old-fashioned morals could face Klan terrorism (Blee 1991; Moore 1991; Lay 1992, 1994).

In the long run, the city would prevail in its decade-long *Kulturkampf* with the country. Agriculture was mostly exempt from New Era prosperity, so children of the farm kept swarming to the bright lights of the big cities. Despite immigration restrictions, the nation's urban population grew by 15 million in the 1920s as urban migration reached record levels. Country folks voted with their feet for a share of the prosperity, excitement, and cultural dynamism centered in cities. But the dream they were chasing abruptly disappeared at the end of the decade.

The Great Crash

In recent years, some historians have attempted to rehabilitate the reputations of Republican presidential administrations in the 1920s (Murray 1969, 1973; Trani and Wilson 1977; Hawley 1992; Ferrell 1996, 1998). Nonetheless, it is hard to resist a teleological skepticism toward policies that ended in disaster. The New Era reached a feverish peak in the late 1920s under President Coolidge and his successor, Herbert Hoover, who was elected in 1928. As Secretary of Commerce under both Harding and Coolidge, Hoover had supervised the pro-business regime, so he seemed like the perfect caretaker for New Era prosperity. Hoover took office amid a wild stock market boom. Prices had doubled between 1925 and 1928; they doubled again in 1929, making Wall Street the wonder of the world. Prosperity and inflation accounted for some of the boom, but the "great bull market" occurred mainly because of increased demand for stocks and rampant speculation.

Millions of new investors entered the stock market in the 1920s. At the start of the decade, just a few hundred thousand individuals owned all the publicly traded shares of corporations, but by 1929 the number of stockholders had reached 9 million. This still represented less than 8 percent of the population, but the stock market became a mass phenomenon. Even those who did not own stocks followed the market's relentless advance. Across the country, Wall Street brokerage houses opened branch offices with waiting rooms and ticker-tape machines connected to New York. Average folks, hearing stories of shoeshine boys and taxi drivers enriched by the market, eagerly plunked down their life savings to get a piece of the action. Business leaders and Republican politicians hailed the diffusion of stock ownership as a sign that New Era prosperity had reached the masses, but it only ensured that falling prices would hurt more people than ever before (Sobel 1968; Galbraith 1972; Parrish 1992).

Speculation also helped trigger the Wall Street stampede. Investors bought trendy stocks, like Radio Corporation of America, in hopes of turning a quick profit regardless of the company's performance. They also bought shares in investment trusts whose sole assets were shares in other investment trusts, building speculative pyramids vulnerable to collapse. Many investors bought stocks "on margin," borrowing money to purchase stock, with the stock itself serving as collateral for the loan. This practice was extremely dangerous because if stock values declined, banks issued margin calls, requiring borrowers to supply more collateral or repay their loans immediately. If prices fell widely across the market, many investors would be forced to liquidate their portfolios in order to meet margin calls, creating an avalanche effect. Americans took out $21 billion in margin loans between 1926 and 1929, which fueled the stock-buying binge. It also increased market volatility and susceptibility to panic.

In March 1929, President Hoover took office proclaiming that "the future is bright with hope" (quoted in Warren 1959: 53). Seven months later, however, the Great Crash struck Wall Street. Between October 24 and October 29, 1929, the stock market lost about 40 percent of its value. Prices had been stagnant for weeks, spreading fear among speculators who were gambling on continued increases. As some sold out, prices drifted downward, and more speculators were forced to sell in order to meet margin calls. As wave after wave of selling hit the market, stock prices plummeted rapidly, though there were occasional rallies led by New York bankers hoping to stem the panic. Prices continued to fall for the next three years, until $75 billion in stock values had simply disappeared. Despite Hoover's assurances of prosperity's imminent return, the Great Crash plunged the nation into the Great Depression.

New Era prosperity was vulnerable to collapse all along. Its greatest weakness was income inequality: Republican policies boosted corporate profits and made wealthy Americans wealthier than ever, but the windfall did not trickle down to workers and farmers. In a decade of declining union membership, workers were powerless to fight for their share of prosperity (Bernstein 1966; Montgomery 1987; Goldberg 1999). As wealth concentrated in fewer hands, there were not enough customers left to purchase the mass-produced goods pouring off assembly lines. By 1929, the top 5 percent of Americans received one-third of all national income, and rich people did not buy enough consumer goods to sustain the new mass-consumption economy. Manufacturers tried to stimulate consumer demand with installment-plan credit and heavy advertising. But burdened with income inequality, the New Era was doomed, especially after the Great Crash, when wage cuts and mass layoffs forced consumers to halt new purchases (Schlesinger 1957; Parrish 1992; Leuchtenburg 1993).

The end of the 1920s brought the end of illusions about permanent prosperity. It also tumbled businessmen from their lofty perch. Yet Americans were still not ready to expand federal power to meet the economic emergency. Before 1914, progressives had increased the power of government to regulate big business, but not until after 1929 would another generation of reformers resume the process during the New Deal. Likewise, it would take another world war to disabuse Americans of their isolationism and to accept global responsibilities commensurate with great power status – for good or ill.

REFERENCES

Adler, Selig (1957) *The Isolationist Impulse: Its Twentieth Century Reaction.* New York: Abelard-Schuman.

Ambrosius, Lloyd E. (1987) *Woodrow Wilson and the American Diplomatic Tradition: The Treaty Fight in Perspective.* New York: Cambridge University Press.

—— (1991) *Wilsonian Statecraft: Theory and Practice of Liberal Internationalism during World War I.* Wilmington, Del.: SR Books.

Baker, Ray Stannard (ed.) (1927–39) *Woodrow Wilson: Life and Letters*, 8 vols. Garden City, NY: Doubleday, Page.

Barbeau, Arthur E. and Henri, Florette (1974) *The Unknown Soldiers: Black American Troops in World War I.* Philadelphia: Temple University Press.

Barton, Bruce (1925) *The Man Nobody Knows: A Discovery of Jesus.* Indianapolis: Bobbs-Merrill.

Becker, Susan D. (1981) *The Origins of the Equal Rights Amendment: American Feminism between the Wars.* Westport, Conn.: Greenwood Press.

Bernstein, Irving (1966) *The Lean Years: A History of the American Worker, 1920–1933.* Baltimore, Md.: Johns Hopkins University Press.

Birdsall, Paul (1939) "Neutrality and economic pressures, 1914–1917," *Science and Society* 3, pp. 217–28.

Blee, Kathleen M. (1991) *Women of the Klan: Racism and Gender in the 1920s.* Berkeley: University of California Press.

Brown, Dorothy M. (1987) *Setting a Course: American Women in the 1920s.* Boston: Twayne.

Buenker, John D. (1976) "The New Era business philosophy of the 1920s," *Illinois Quarterly* 38, pp. 20–49.

Burk, Kathleen (1985) *Britain, America, and the Sinews of War, 1914–1918.* Boston: Allen and Unwin.

Burner, David M. (1968) *The Politics of Provincialism: The Democratic Party in Transition, 1918–1932.* New York: Alfred A. Knopf.

Clark, Norman H. (1976) *Deliver Us From Evil: An Interpretation of American Prohibition*. New York: W. W. Norton.

Clements, Kendrick (1987) *Woodrow Wilson: World Statesman*. Boston: Twayne.

—— (1992) *The Presidency of Woodrow Wilson*. Lawrence: University Press of Kansas.

Cohen, Lizabeth (1990) *Making a New Deal: Industrial Workers in Chicago, 1919–1939*. New York: Cambridge University Press.

Cohen, Warren I. (1967) *The American Revisionists: The Lessons of Intervention in World War I*. Chicago: University of Chicago Press.

—— (1987) *Empire Without Tears: America's Foreign Relations, 1921–1933*. Philadelphia: Temple University Press.

Coogan, John W. (1981) *The End of Neutrality: The United States, Britain, and Maritime Rights, 1899–1915*. Ithaca, NY: Cornell University Press.

—— (1994) "Wilsonian diplomacy in war and peace," in Gordon Martel (ed.) *American Foreign Relations Reconsidered, 1890–1993*. London: Routledge.

Cooper, John Milton, Jr. (1980) "World War I: European origins and American intervention," *Virginia Quarterly Review* 56, pp. 1–18.

—— (2001) *Breaking the Heart of the World: Woodrow Wilson and the Fight for the League of Nations*. New York: Cambridge University Press.

Cott, Nancy F. (1987) *The Grounding of Modern Feminism*. New Haven, Conn.: Yale University Press.

Craig, Douglas B. (1992) *After Wilson: The Struggle for the Democratic Party, 1920–1934*. Chapel Hill: University of North Carolina Press.

Critoph, Gerald E. (1975) "The flapper and her critics," in Carol V. R. George (ed.) *"Remember the Ladies": New Perspectives on Women in American History*. Syracuse, NY: Syracuse University Press.

Crosby, Alfred W. (1989) *America's Forgotten Pandemic: The Influenza of 1918*. New York: Cambridge University Press.

Cuff, Robert D. (1973) *The War Industries Board: Business–Government Relations During World War I*. Baltimore, Md.: Johns Hopkins University Press.

Devlin, Patrick (1974) *Too Proud to Fight: Woodrow Wilson's Neutrality*. New York: Oxford University Press.

Dumenil, Lynn (1995) *The Modern Temper: American Culture and Society in the 1920s*. New York: Hill and Wang.

Ferrell, Robert H. (1985) *Woodrow Wilson and World War I, 1917–1921*. New York: Harper and Row.

—— (1996) *The Strange Deaths of President Harding*. Columbia: University of Missouri Press.

—— (1998) *The Presidency of Calvin Coolidge*. Lawrence: University Press of Kansas.

Fleming, Denna F. (1932) *The United States and the League of Nations, 1918–1920*. New York: G. P. Putnam's Sons.

Galbraith, John Kenneth (1972) *The Great Crash of 1929*, 3rd edn. Boston: Houghton Mifflin.

Gardner, Lloyd C. (1984) *Safe for Democracy: The Anglo-American Response to Revolution, 1913–1923*. New York: Oxford University Press.

Ginger, Ray (1958) *Six Days or Forever? Tennessee v. John Thomas Scopes*. Boston: Beacon.

Goldberg, David J. (1999) *Discontented America: The United States in the 1920s*. Baltimore, Md.: Johns Hopkins University Press.

Gregory, Ross (1971) *The Origins of American Intervention in the First World War*. New York: W. W. Norton.

Guinsburg, Thomas N. (1982) *The Pursuit of Isolationism in the United States Senate from Versailles to Pearl Harbor*. New York: Garland.

Hawley, Ellis W. (1992) *The Great War and the Search for a Modern Order: A History of the American People and their Institutions, 1917–1933*, 2nd edn. New York: St. Martin's Press.

Heckscher, August (1991) *Woodrow Wilson: A Biography.* New York: Scribner's.

Hicks, John D. (1960) *The Republican Ascendancy, 1921–1933.* New York: Harper and Row.

Higham, John (1988) *Strangers in the Land: Patterns of American Nativism, 1860–1925,* 2nd edn. New Brunswick, NJ: Rutgers University Press.

Horowitz, Daniel (1985) *The Morality of Spending: Attitudes Toward the Consumer Society in America, 1875–1940.* Baltimore, Md.: Johns Hopkins University Press.

Keller, Morton (1990) *Regulating a New Economy: Public Policy and Economic Change in America, 1900–1933.* Cambridge, Mass.: Harvard University Press.

Kennan, George F. (1951) *American Diplomacy, 1900–1950.* Chicago: University of Chicago Press.

Keyssar, Alexander (2000) *The Right to Vote: The Contested History of Democracy in the United States.* New York: Basic Books.

Knock, Thomas J. (1992) *To End All Wars: Woodrow Wilson and the Quest for a New World Order.* Princeton, NJ: Princeton University Press.

Larson, Edward J. (1997) *Summer for the Gods: The Scopes Trial and America's Continuing Debate over Science and Religion.* New York: Basic Books.

Lay, Shawn (ed.) (1992) *The Invisible Empire in the West: Toward a New Historical Appraisal of the Ku Klux Klan of the 1920s.* Champaign: University of Illinois Press.

—— (1994) "Hooded populism: new assessments of the Ku Klux Klan of the 1920s," *Reviews in American History* 22, pp. 668–73.

Leuchtenburg, William E. (1993) *The Perils of Prosperity, 1914–1932,* 2nd edn. Chicago: University of Chicago Press.

—— (1995) *The FDR Years: On Roosevelt and his Legacy.* New York: Columbia University Press.

Levin, N. Gordon (1968) *Woodrow Wilson and World Politics: America's Response to War and Revolution.* New York: Oxford University Press.

Link, Arthur S. (ed.) (1966–94) *The Papers of Woodrow Wilson,* 69 vols. Princeton, NJ: Princeton University Press.

—— (1979) *Woodrow Wilson: Revolution, War, and Peace.* Arlington Heights, Ill.: AHM.

Lunardini, Christine and Knock, Thomas J. (1981) "Woodrow Wilson and woman suffrage: a new look," *Political Science Quarterly* 95, pp. 655–71.

Madigan, Tim (2001) *The Burning: Massacre, Destruction, and the Tulsa Race Riot of 1921.* New York: St. Martin's Press.

Mayer, Arno (1959) *Political Origins of the New Diplomacy, 1917–1918.* New Haven, Conn.: Yale University Press.

Montgomery, David (1987) "Thinking about American workers in the 1920s," *International Labor and Working-Class History* 32, pp. 4–38.

Moore, Leonard J. (1991) *Citizen Klansman: The Ku Klux Klan in Indiana, 1921–1928.* Chapel Hill: University of North Carolina Press.

Mosier, John (2001) *The Myth of the Great War: A New Military History of World War I.* New York: HarperCollins.

Murray, Robert (1969) *The Harding Era: Warren G. Harding and his Administration.* Minneapolis: University of Minnesota Press.

—— (1973) *The Politics of Normalcy: Governmental Theory and Practice in the Harding–Coolidge Era.* New York: W. W. Norton.

Osgood, Robert E. (1953) *Ideals and Self-Interest in America's Foreign Relations: The Great Transformation of the Twentieth Century.* Chicago: University of Chicago Press.

Parrish, Michael E. (1992) *Anxious Decades: America in Prosperity and Depression, 1920–1941.* New York: W. W. Norton.

Pegram, Thomas R. (1998) *Battling Demon Rum: The Struggle for a Dry America, 1800–1933.* Chicago: Ivan R. Dee.

Perman, Michael (2001) *Struggle for Mastery: Disfranchisement in the South, 1888–1908.* Chapel Hill: University of North Carolina Press.

Ribuffo, Leo P. (1981) "Jesus Christ as business statesman: Bruce Barton and the selling of corporate capitalism," *American Quarterly* 33, pp. 206–31.

Schaffer, Ronald (1991) *America in the Great War: The Rise of the War Welfare State.* New York: Oxford University Press.

Schlesinger, Arthur M., Jr. (1957) *The Age of Roosevelt: The Crisis of the Old Order.* Boston: Houghton Mifflin.

Shapiro, Herbert (1988) *White Violence and Black Response: From Reconstruction to Montgomery.* Amherst: University of Massachusetts Press.

Smith, Daniel M. (1965) *The Great Departure: The United States and World War I, 1914–1920.* New York: Wiley.

Sobel, Robert (1968) *The Great Bull Market: Wall Street in the 1920s.* New York: W. W. Norton.

Tansill, Charles C. (1938) *America Goes to War.* Boston: Little, Brown.

Trani, Eugene P. and Wilson, David L. (1977) *The Presidency of Warren G. Harding.* Lawrence: Regents Press of Kansas.

Trask, David F. (1993) *The AEF and Coalition Warmaking, 1917–1918.* Lawrence: University Press of Kansas.

Tuchman, Barbara (1958) *The Zimmermann Telegram.* New York: Viking.

Tuttle, William M., Jr. (1970) *Race Riot: Chicago in the Red Summer of 1919.* New York: Atheneum.

Vincent, C. Paul (1985) *The Politics of Hunger: The Allied Blockade of Germany, 1915–1919.* Athens: Ohio University Press.

Warren, Harris Gaylord (1959) *Herbert Hoover and the Great Depression.* New York: Oxford University Press.

Williams, William Appleman (1972) *The Tragedy of American Diplomacy,* rev. edn. New York: Dell.

Woodward, David R. (1993) *Trial by Friendship: Anglo-American Relations, 1917–1918.* Lexington: University Press of Kentucky.

Zieger, Robert H. (2000) *America's Great War: World War I and the American Experience.* Lanham, Md.: Rowman and Littlefield.

CHAPTER THREE

1929–1941

MICHAEL E. PARRISH

Between the collapse of the stock market in 1929 and the Japanese attack on Pearl Harbor in December, 1941, most Americans endured harsh material conditions. In this decade the longest economic depression in the nation's history was recorded, which is why the first generation of American historians who attempted grand narratives of the period tended to stress the myriad forms of social struggle within the United States. Political, economic, social, legal, and ideological conflict in the 1930s gave shape and dramatic momentum to the interpretations first offered in the 1950s and early 1960s by Basil Rauch, Dexter Perkins, Arthur M. Schlesinger, Jr., James MacGregor Burns, William Leuchtenburg, and Frank Freidel.

On the eve of the 1932 election, which pitted Republican incumbent Herbert Hoover against Franklin D. Roosevelt, the unemployment rate was approaching one quarter of the labor force. Social struggle was virtually everywhere. In the nation's capital, army troops commanded by General Douglas MacArthur drove protesting World War I veterans from their tented bivouac with tear gas and rifle butts. In the Midwest, attempts by landlords and courts to evict tenants from their urban apartments or to foreclose on bankrupt farmers encountered violent popular resistance. Industrial workers across the country, seeking recognition for their unions, shut down cities such as San Francisco and Minneapolis in 1934 and occupied automobile factories in 1937. The labor movement itself erupted in conflict and split apart in 1935–6, as insurgents led by John L. Lewis bolted from the American Federation of Labor and created the Congress of Industrial Organizations (CIO) to organize the mass-production industries such as steel, automobiles, and textiles.

The American Communist Party and the Socialist Party gained new followers. So did other vocal protest movements, whether led by Louisiana's Senator Huey Long, who espoused Share Our Wealth, or by Upton Sinclair, the old muckraker who championed End Poverty in California (EPIC), or by a charismatic radio priest, Father Charles Coughlin. The presidential election of 1936 that returned Roosevelt and his New Deal program to the White House exposed the rawest class divisions of any such contest in the twentieth century. The forces of what he called "organized money" had become "unanimous in their hate for me," FDR told his supporters, "and I welcome their hatred" (quoted in Parrish 1992: 360).

When the United States Supreme Court declared unconstitutional the core reforms of the New Deal in 1935–6, as well as numerous state laws aimed at specific economic problems generated by the depression, Roosevelt and his supporters in Congress proposed to restructure the Court by adding additional justices. This "court-packing" plan produced the most serious constitutional crisis since the Civil War and Reconstruction, polarized even Roosevelt's newly-formed political coalition, gave fresh momentum to the administration's opponents, and stalled the New Deal. Finally, the rise of aggressive totalitarian regimes in Nazi Germany, Italy, and Japan, which were willing to achieve their geopolitical objectives through military force, precipitated a bitter struggle between so-called isolationists – who feared American involvement in another world war – and those seeking greater American military preparedness and an enlarged role for the nation in international affairs. That debate ended at Pearl Harbor.

Continuity or Caesura?

This first, founding generation of scholars who framed interpretations of the American experience during the Great Depression and the New Deal often placed events within a longer framework of political-economic struggle, one that pitted the welfare of ordinary men and women against the ruthless power of businessmen and financiers. The "people" were embattled against "the interests." As Justice Oliver Wendell Holmes, Jr. elegantly described it, "one of the eternal conflicts out of which life is made up is that between the effort of every man to get the most he can for his services, and that of society, disguised under the name of capital, to get his services for the least possible return" (quoted in Posner 1992: 124). In this 1930s version of that continuing American drama, therefore, Roosevelt played Thomas Jefferson, the defender of the yeomen farmers and sturdy artisans, against Alexander Hamilton, the patron of the bondholders and merchants. FDR was Andrew Jackson slaying Nicholas Biddle's "monster" Second Bank of the United States. The policy and ideological links between FDR, the New Deal, and the turn-of-the-century progressivism of Theodore Roosevelt and Woodrow Wilson seemed clear enough. Leading New Dealers like Harold Ickes, who served as Secretary of the Interior, had been avid supporters of Theodore Roosevelt's Bull Moose insurgency. FDR himself had modeled his political career after cousin Teddy's and had served as assistant secretary of the navy under Wilson. Like Wilson, FDR espoused (even if he did not always honor) America's international responsibilities for peace and order.

Schlesinger, for example, equated Jacksonian democracy with New Deal democracy and later placed the 1930s in one of the many repeated "cycles" of liberal reform stretching from the Revolution to President Lyndon Johnson, who once proudly declared that Roosevelt had been "just like a daddy to me" (quoted in Asbell 1961: 256). Carl Degler, a younger member of the founding generation, offered a similar framework when he called the New Deal "the third American revolution" (1956). Leuchtenburg, in a much admired essay entitled "The New Deal and the analogue of war," noted both the programmatic and rhetorical reliance of FDR and his advisers upon the experience of World War I when they were devising programs to combat the economic crisis (1964). In his famous first Inaugural Address, Roosevelt asked Congress for "broad executive power to wage war . . . as great as the power that would be given to me if we were in fact invaded by a foreign foe" (quoted in Leuchtenburg 1963: 41). Only one prominent member of the founding scholarly generation entered a dissent against this generally Whiggish view of the seamless American political tradition and the New Deal. In his 1955 classic *The Age of Reform*, Richard Hofstadter, although an ardent liberal, questioned the intellectual trajectory from progressives to New Dealers. The former, he argued, remained pre-eminently Victorians who were devoted to the task of spiritual regeneration. They hoped to save both the souls and the economic autonomy of the American people. The New Dealers were hard-boiled pragmatists instead, and cared less for saving souls than for simply saving bank accounts. Progressivism resembled a convention of ministers; the New Deal became a gathering of lawyers. Wilson, the moral absolutist, embodied progressivism. Thurman Arnold, who enforced the anti-trust laws while ridiculing them as an empty ritual in his celebrated 1937 critique, *The Folklore of Capitalism*, remained for Hofstadter the prototypical New Dealer.

Among the founders, of course, the decade of the 1920s – the interlude between progressivism and the New Deal – served usually to highlight the differences between those political leaders devoted to the general welfare of the American people (progressives and New Dealers) and Republicans like Warren Harding, Calvin Coolidge, and even Herbert Hoover. These presidents have been portrayed as supine servants of the property-owning classes, the corporate magnates, and the grandees of Wall Street. When it came to interpreting the causes and the duration of the depression, the founders rested their analysis upon the claims put forward by many New Dealers at the time, with later assistance from the disciples of the English economist John Maynard Keynes. The fault was generally ascribed to the maldistribution of income, produced not by the inscrutable laws of economics, but by the short-sighted fiscal and monetary policies of the Republican administrations from Harding to Hoover.

The founders were absorbed with the formidable task of explaining the origins of the Great Depression, the roots of the New Deal in the past and the impact of its innumerable programs. These historians seldom attempted to compare in depth the American experience during the decade with what befell other industrial societies. An exception was John Garraty (1974, 1986). Nor did issues of gender often intrude into these narratives, besides an obligatory discussion of the roles played by very prominent New Deal women, like Eleanor Roosevelt, Frances Perkins, Molly Dewson, and Lorena Hickock. Nor did the founding historians venture to explore – despite critical discussions of New Deal failures, or its problematic legacy for the future in World War II and beyond – the decline and fall of the New Deal order. The disintegration of American liberalism more generally since the 1960s has been much examined.

A half-century of scholarship since the path-breaking work of Schlesinger, Leuchtenburg, Freidel, Hofstadter, and Degler has been heavily influenced by the racial and gender struggles of the 1960s and 1970s. New perspectives into the Great Depression-New Deal era have been introduced. Yet its central interpretative issues have been left unshaken, as recently demonstrated in David Kennedy's monumental volume (1999) in the Oxford History of the United States series. Why did the Great Depression endure far longer than any other economic downturn in American history? Were the Keynesians correct in their analysis and proposed solutions? Did the fault lie with Roosevelt and the New Dealers, either because they were too orthodox in their economic thinking to implement a full-scale Keynesian fiscal policy, or because they were too radical in their rhetoric and other initiatives, which frightened timid capitalists? If the New Deal owed a substantial intellectual and programmatic debt to the old progressives, do we include Herbert Hoover among the creditors? Was he the last of the old presidents or the first of the new? What legacies from the Progressive Era and the 1920s did the New Deal draw upon? Did the New Deal ever have a coherent theory and method for combating the depression? Who were the true beneficiaries of the major New Deal reforms in business, labor, and social welfare? Who bears responsibility for the impasse between the Supreme Court, the administration, and Congress? Was there a real "constitutional revolution" in the 1930s, inaugurated by Roosevelt's war on the Court? Why, in the face of palpable threats to its economic and geopolitical interests in Europe and the Asia, did the United States remain isolationist for so long? Did the war years from 1941 to 1945 finally achieve what the New Deal could not: a new American consensus, built on the promise of economic growth and membership in a community of consumers? Or did longer-term developments, rooted in the popular culture and consumer culture of the 1930s, forge a new sense of shared values, yet predicated ultimately upon the material fulfillment of individual desires and hostile to the more collective aspirations of many New Dealers? Did the New Deal, in short, promote the institutional and ideological relationship that ultimately doomed liberalism?

In the Beginning

Two shattering events – the stock market crash in the fall of 1929 and the Japanese attack on Pearl Harbor in early December, 1941 – framed this period, firmly etched in the memories of those who lived through them. About the first, no historical scholarship has yet altered or surpassed the general conclusions reached by John Kenneth Galbraith (1954) and by Robert Sobel (1968). Galbraith's droll witticisms alone repay frequent rereadings of the volume. By slashing personal income, corporate, and especially capital gains taxes in the 1920s, Secretary of the Treasury Andrew W. Mellon, aided and abetted even by Democrats in Congress, encouraged a massive shift of private funds into the stock market. That shift was further hastened by the dearth of public debt opportunities that arose from the Republican plutocrat's passion for balanced federal budgets. In an effort to shore up European monetary systems by discouraging the flight of foreign funds to the United States, Mellon and his allies at the New York Federal Reserve Bank also kept interest rates low in America, which made it easier for those drawn to the market to finance their purchases through brokers' loans, sometimes with as little as 10 percent down. With good reason, one vexed Democrat called Mellon, whose own economic interests included Gulf Oil, Alcoa Aluminium, and the Pittsburgh National Bank, the "fairy godfather of the bull market" that roared on until the fall of 1929 (quoted in Sobel 1968: 54). The value of some common stocks soared 100 percent without having paid a single dividend.

As long as more buyers than sellers remained active, the capital gains reached astonishing levels. But given the distribution of income and the thinness of the market, the bubble was bound to burst. When it did, the commercial banks and other lenders (including major corporations such as Standard Oil and General

Motors), which had sunk billions into brokers' loans, found themselves holding depreciated paper assets. They could not be turned readily into cash, thanks to both panic and the discounting rules that governed the Federal Reserve System. The result became the worst liquidity crisis in American history, with banks unable to meet the demands of depositors or to extend further credit. By the end of 1930, a thousand commercial banks had failed. With America's financial machinery frozen stiff, those who had been dependent upon such credit in Europe and Asia also felt the chill. Despite President Hoover's lament that America's economic woes had been imported from abroad, the reverse appears to have been the case.

The stock market bust and the ensuing liquidity crisis exposed myriad structural flaws in the nation's economic institutions. Foremost were its decentralized, under-capitalized banking network, its jerry-built structure of corporate holding companies, its primitive accounting standards, and the near-total lack of aggregate, reliable information concerning employment and production. But neither the collapse of equities in 1929–30 nor the massive liquidity crisis that followed "caused" the Great Depression, or explains why it lasted so long in terms of high unemployment, lagging investment, and stagnant production. By 1934, the New Deal had restored the American banking industry to health through a combination of liquidations, revamped federal reserve rules, federal deposit insurance, and the infusion of new capital courtesy of the federal government. After 1934, interest rates remained about the same or lower than during the boom years of the 1920s. Yet private borrowing and investment languished and even the mounting expenditures of the New Deal failed to make up the difference.

At the time conservative opponents of the New Deal placed the blame for this continuing condition upon the administration, especially its programs raising taxes and assisting labor, which, the critics complained, frightened capital and retarded new private investment. Echoes of these complaints can be found in historical critiques of the New Deal by Edgar Robinson (1955) and by the less vitriolic Gary Best (1991) and Robert Eden (1989). On the other side of the ideological spectrum, Keynesians – both then and recently – point to FDR's fiscal conservatism, as evidenced in his unwillingness to engage in substantial federal employment programs beyond the Public Works Administration (PWA), the Civil Works Administration (CWA), and the Works Progress Administration (WPA). More public investment, so this argu-ment goes, would have generated economic recovery prior to the defense buildup of 1940–1.

These perspectives, however, failed to take account of the profound structural impasse that plagued the economy during the decade, which Michael Bernstein illuminated in his path-breaking study, *The Great Depression* (1987). Between 1920 and 1940, he pointed out, the American economy began its historic transition from a core in highly labor-intensive industries that centered on producers' goods to a structure that was far more capital-intensive and oriented toward the provisioning of services and consumer goods. The former was an economy of sweat and muscle, smoke stacks, mines, and raw materials, and remained dominated by agriculture, construction, extractive industries such as coal and iron, manufacturing processes like textiles (which had changed little since before the Civil War) and railroads (which had once driven economic growth). The emerging economy, built largely on electri-city and discoveries in the physical sciences, was characterized by research laboratories, the distribution of finished goods to individual consumers, the collection and processing of information of all sorts, and the production of entertainment and leisure activities. The cotton farmer, the coal miner, the carpenter, and the locomotive engineer symbolized the old; the refinery technician, the chemist, the car salesman, the bank teller, the government bureaucrat, and the motion picture producer symbolized the new economy.

Unfortunately, when the market crashed and the depression began, this epic structural transformation – so familiar to the economic world of the twenty-first century – had barely commenced in the United States. In terms of sheer numbers, the great bulk of the labor force remained rooted in the old economy, especially in agriculture and in extractive industries. These sectors were plagued by excessive competition (some of it global in nature), surplus labor, low profitability, and limited potential for new investment. Because of malapportionment and other factors, however, these same sectors of the economy dominated the nation's political structure from the level of state government to the US Congress. Small wonder that both the states and the federal government spent considerable time and money attempting to rescue agricultural sectors (including the dairy industry), mining, and railroads. On the other hand, the economic sectors of high growth potential in consumer goods, services, entertainment, and research and development lacked the critical size and political influence to drive both the economy and the polity on a different course until after World War II.

Although the structural problems of recovery efforts were not among his central objectives, Bernstein's fresh perspective on them reinforced scholarship that had previously sought to rehabilitate the reputation of President Herbert Hoover, so often the fall guy in depression narratives constructed through the 1960s. Beginning with the work of diplomatic historian William Appleman Williams, who contrasted Hoover's pacifism with Roosevelt's more imperial designs, and proceeding through the more detailed studies of Hoover's attempts to cope with the economic crisis by Carl Degler, Albert Romasco, and Joan Hoff Wilson, the Great Engineer emerged less as a failed leader than as "the last progressive." As Secretary of Commerce in the 1920s, Hoover had been the chief promoter of the radio and aviation industries in the 1920s, thus playing midwife to two important sectors of the new economy. He was also the first presidential candidate to utilize motion pictures systematically as a medium for advancing his career. And, unlike FDR, the country squire who lacked much business sense, Hoover never doubted the potential of capitalism to generate new growth through innovations rooted in science and technology.

As Hoover's defenders asserted, his initiatives in the face of the economic crisis should be contrasted with those of previous presidents, not with those taken by Roosevelt, who had the benefit of his predecessor's failed efforts. Judged on this scale, Hoover took unprecedented steps to mobilize other government sectors as well as private industry, finance, and philanthropy. He created the Reconstruction Finance Corporation (RFC), which by the end of his term was making loans not only to faltering industry, but also to states and local governments, for self-liquidating public works. FDR and the New Dealers built upon this foundation by broadening the RFC's mandate to the point where it became the single largest source of new capital to underwrite a host of government projects, ranging from crop storage to the distribution of electric power by municipalities. Hoover's Federal Farm Board lacked the authority to regulate agricultural production (he opposed such coercion), but nevertheless set a precedent for federal price supports. And soon forgotten were his three Supreme Court appointees, even though Chief Justice Charles Evans Hughes, Owen Roberts, and Benjamin N. Cardozo decisively reoriented that tribunal in a more progressive direction on economic issues as well as civil liberties and civil rights.

Hoover's reputation was so tarnished that he did not address another Republican National Convention until the 1950s, yet the efforts of Hoff and other historians to refurbish his place in history risked becoming so orthodox by the late 1970s that keepers of the Roosevelt flame like Schlesinger rose up in revolt and reminded readers of the Great Engineer's not inconsiderable failings. Willing to seek a reduction in railroad rates for drought-stricken farmers, he had resisted giving them direct federal relief, because it would dry up private charity and sap their self-reliance – a theory he maintained as the unemployment lines grew longer. He relied too long on "voluntary cooperation" to promote recovery, especially in banking and unemployment, and blindly insisted on the efficacy of moral suasion despite overwhelming evidence to the contrary. Unaccustomed to elective office and addicted to giving commands as a corporate executive, Hoover lacked the most rudimentary political skills required of his office, in a complex constitutional structure dependant upon compromise, negotiation and persuasion. Despite vocal protest from leading economists, he signed a whopping increase in tariff rates that helped to choke off international trade. And, obsessed with the rising federal budget deficit by 1932, he advocated and won a substantial tax increase in the midst of double-digit unemployment and plummeting demand. It bears noting, however, that both the tariff increase and the tax hike enjoyed broad support from the Democratic leadership in Congress.

The Fate of Liberalism

While Hoover's historical stock rose faster in the 1960s and 1970s than the Radio Corporation of America's dividend in the 1920s, Roosevelt's took a nose dive. FDR became the victim of the era's social and political turmoil, especially the civil rights movement, the rediscovery of poverty, and the war in Vietnam. In addition to attacking the current standard bearers of the Democratic Party and the liberal project, especially John F. Kennedy, Lyndon B. Johnson, and Hubert H. Humphrey, civil rights activists and antiwar leaders inside and outside of the academy turned a critical eye on FDR's failings. While conceding that the New Deal curbed the worst abuses on the stock exchanges, gave industrial workers the right to organize unions, and legislated both Social Security and the first public housing program, these scholars stressed the faults rather than the virtues of the Roosevelt administration. With few exceptions, they noted, New Deal programs like the Civilian Conservation Corps practiced rigid racial segregation. Eleanor Roosevelt and Harold Ickes arranged for Marian Anderson to sing at the Lincoln Memorial, but the President refused to support legislation to make lynching a federal crime. New Deal social welfare programs such as Social Security and the Fair Labor Standards Act excluded the poorest and most exploited workers – farm laborers and domestics – while perpetuating the low-wage advantage enjoyed by many southern industries. Finally, Roosevelt often denounced French colonialism, but did little to prevent the restoration of that nation's empire in Southeast Asia, with all of the Cold War consequences that followed for the United States.

The founding generation of New Deal scholars had not neglected Roosevelt's conservatism and the limitations of his programs. Yet many of the revisionists of the 1960s – often labeled New Left historians – saw such policies as part of a longer, more sinister process. Corporate liberals, beginning in the Progressive Era, were portrayed as having attempted to solve the contradictions of capitalism by utilizing the power of the state to secure their own domination while providing the palliative of a few social welfare programs for the rest of society. Although they emphasized different aspects of the New Deal's failures, Howard Zinn (1966), Paul Conkin (1967), and Barton Bernstein (1968) reached similar conclusions on key points. The New Deal was presented as usually opting for conservative solutions to specific problems, notably with regard to commercial banking; FDR's programs proved incapable of generating economic recovery, which came only with war-induced spending beginning in 1940; any effort to redistribute wealth and income failed miserably; the Democratic administration did not realign the political system along true liberal-conservative lines; and the status quo on matters of race was upheld. "The story of the New Deal," wrote Conkin, "is a sad story, the ever recurring story of what might have been" (1967: 73).

His pithy volume offered the most balanced, yet devastating, critique of FDR and the New Deal. While conceding that the aristocratic Roosevelt's bout with polio became an equivalent to a log cabin that allowed him to identify with various beleaguered minorities, Conkin rooted the New Deal's shortcomings in the President's own lack of mental rigor. Justice Holmes once described FDR as possessing only a "second-rate intellect, but . . . a first-rate temperament" (quoted in Kennedy 1999: 100). While some earlier historians, especially Schlesinger, had favorably contrasted FDR's pragmatism and his willingness to experiment with the dogmatic ideological posture of other depression-era leaders such as Britain's Stanley Baldwin, Conkin reminded readers that true pragmatism stressed disciplined inquiry and empirical verification. Such intellectual habits were sadly lacking in a White House preoccupied with short-term political solutions and the nation's electoral cycle.

For Conkin and others, the New Deal's chaotic approach to the problems of agriculture illustrated the perils of such shallow pragmatism. The first Agricultural Adjustment Act paid commercial farmers a subsidy for not planting basic crops, with the cost passed on to urban consumers through a tax levied on food processors. The growers with the largest acreage, of course, reaped the most benefits; and the program took purchasing power from the pockets of poor and displaced thousands of sharecroppers and tenants who did not own their own land. When this strategy stirred opposition even inside the administration and through a grass-roots organization, the Southern Tenant Farmers' Union, the New Deal responded with additional programs such as the Resettlement Administration, the Farm Security Administration, and Subsistence Homesteads. These were intended to pacify rural discontent by keeping a handful of marginal producers on the land. Although among the most class-conscious of all New Deal efforts, these step-children of the New Deal's agricultural program did nothing to redress the basic inequities within agriculture, nor to mitigate the ordeal of the transition from country to city for most of the rural dispossessed, nor to cure the long-term problems of surplus production.

Although rarely classified as a New Left history, Ellis Hawley's monumental *The New Deal and the Problem of Monopoly: A Study in Economic Ambivalence* (1966) confirmed both the conservative influences shaping administration policy toward business and a general incoherence over the decade. The National Recovery Act (NRA), regarded at the time as the centerpiece of the New Deal's initial recovery efforts, emerged out of frantic efforts to head off Senator Hugo Black's bill, which would have mandated a thirty-hour work week for companies and employees engaged in interstate commerce. Whatever the constitutional and economic difficulties with Black's bill, they paled in comparison with the problems that soon plagued the NRA, given the conflicting goals of those who wrote the enabling statute. Administration spokesmen, notably Rexford Tugwell and the starry-eyed national planners around him, saw the NRA as a mandate for broad-gauged federal regulation of the economy. The President would be given the ultimate authority to impose "codes of fair competition" that would scientifically control supply and demand and rationally allocate resources, while also insuring the welfare of labor and consumers. Through suspension of the anti-trust laws the NRA, under the skillful direction of enlightened government managers, would promote business cooperation rather than cut-throat competition. Many hard-nosed business-men, on the other hand, regarded the law's suspension of the anti-trust laws as simply an opportunity to gain government endorsement for private cartels and the policies of trade associations that lacked legal enforcement. Invited to the drafting table, partisans of organized labor won provisions intended to guarantee the right of workers to join unions, free of employer coercion or discrimination.

Given these incompatible objectives, the National Recovery Act soon generated more strife than cooperation, even before the Supreme Court unanimously declared the NRA unconstitutional in 1935. As business representatives descended like locusts upon Washington to shape their particular "code of fair competition," the Tugwellian national planners found themselves consistently understaffed and outmaneuvered. This was a consequence of the federal government's stunted administrative capacity, later stressed by Theda Skocpol and Kenneth Finegold (1982). While corporations in highly concentrated industries dominated their code writing, in more competitive sectors the race usually went to those who caught the first train to Washington. And with consumer groups pushed to the margins of influence, cries of monopoly soon reached Congress. Prices rose before wages under the NRA, precipitating – along with employer resistance to unions – a wave of strikes, many of them violent, in 1934–5.

Even after the Supreme Court gave the faltering program a decent burial in 1935, Roosevelt and some of his congressional allies continued to seek NRA-like panaceas for recovery. For example, the Guffey–Synder and Guffey–Vinson Acts were passed to limit competition in the coal industry, the Connally Act outlawed the shipment across state lines of so-called "hot oil" produced in violation of state quotas, the Robinson–Patman Act prohibited discounts or rebates to large-volume buyers, and the Miller–Tydings Act exempted so-called "fair trade" laws from anti-trust prosecutions. But when the economy took another nose dive in 1937–8, largely as a result of both significant budget cuts approved by Roosevelt and the first payroll deductions for Social Security, the President did an abrupt about-face and reverted to venerable progressive policy. He denounced monopoly, initiated a new anti-trust crusade in the Department of Justice and welcomed a broad congressional inquiry into the anti-competitive practices of business. From the National Recovery Act to the Temporary National Economic Committee, the New Deal had come full circle on economic policy in four years, without solving the central problem of unemployment.

The New Left's revisionist conclusions about the New Deal did not go unchallenged, however, even in the late 1960s. The assumption that Roosevelt and his administration bore responsibility for the domestic and foreign policy failures of later Democratic Party-liberal regimes struck many historians as an untenable, perverse argument. Jerold Auerbach thoughtfully examined the perspective and the conclusions of many revisionist works and found them wanting with respect to their understanding of the basic historical context of the 1930s. Roosevelt and his advisers, Auerbach insisted, did not function in a political or constitutional vacuum. They could not impose their policy preferences by fiat upon a supine society. The US Congress continued to sit and legislate throughout the decade; and although it delegated broad authority to the executive and the burgeoning federal bureaucracy, the basic responsibility for shaping the nation's laws was never abdicated (Auerbach 1969).

By virtue of seniority, Southern Democrats controlled Congress until 1938, when Republicans made significant gains and tilted the national legislature even further to the right. Although southern congressional leaders welcomed certain New Deal initiatives, such as cheap electric power and aid to agriculture, labor and social welfare reforms that threatened the region's economic and racial status quo were resisted. The Senate Finance Committee, chaired by Pat Harrison of Mississippi, for example, impeded the administration's efforts to implement a more progressive federal tax system between 1935 and 1937, although the label of "soak the rich" somehow still clings to the New Deal. Thanks to Congress, it was nothing of the kind, as Mark H. Leff demonstrated (1984).

The Rule of Law

Revisionist historians, who discounted the restraints imposed on Roosevelt and the New Deal by Congress, also tended to ignore an even greater obstacle to reform: the federal courts. Virtually all federal judges had been appointed by Republican presidents, from Harding to Hoover, and by 1935 had issued scores of injunctions against major programs of the New Deal. And in 1935–6, the Supreme Court declared unconstitutional the core of the government's initial recovery efforts for agriculture, industry, debtor relief, and coal mining, in addition to a state law that had attempted to fix minimum wages. Those judicial vetoes brought down the wrath of Congress and the administration because they appeared to place in jeopardy other laws winding their way through the courts, notably the National Labor Relations Act and the Social Security Act. Even former President Hoover denounced the Court's five against four minimum wage decision and urged the Republican Party to support a constitutional amendment to overturn it.

Roosevelt and a small coterie of his advisers chose a different, radical course. Given a powerful mandate by the voters in November, 1936, the President sent his Judicial Procedures Reform bill to Congress the following February. The centerpiece of this measure would have allowed the President, with the consent of the Senate, to appoint one additional Supreme Court justice, up to a limit of six, for each sitting justice who had reached the age of 70 and did not retire. This "court-packing" plan drew immediate opposition from both Democrats and Republicans in Congress. Former critics of the Supreme Court defended it as the pillar of legality and constitutional government, while Roosevelt was portrayed as a power-hungry tyrant who differed little from the dictators of Europe. Soon after the President's assault, however, the Supreme Court narrowly upheld a new minimum wage law and approved both the National Labor Relations Act and the Social Security Act. Congress almost simultaneously killed the President's "court-packing" plan.

While FDR's epic confrontation with the Supreme Court counted for little in general revisionist interpretations of the New Deal, this constitutional drama had always played a significant role in the more traditional narratives by both political and legal-constitutional scholars. The orthodox account can be found in Edward Corwin's classic *Constitutional Revolution, Ltd.* (1941) and more recently in William Leuchtenburg's *The Supreme Court Reborn: The Constitutional Revolution in the Age of Roosevelt* (1995). They portray the Hughes Court as dominated by ideological conservatives (Pierce Butler, Willis Van Devanter, James McReynolds, and George Sutherland), who were sometimes joined by the Chief Justice himself and Owen Roberts. They blocked even the moderate reforms of the New Deal until forced to capitulate in 1937 by Roosevelt's re-election and the threat of his "court-packing" legislation. The Supreme Court, in short, bent before the winds of the New Deal. Politics, not law, produced a constitutional revolution; or, as one New Dealer expressed it, "the President's castor oil seemed to work" (quoted in Parrish 1992: 271).

This interpretation of the "constitutional revolution" of the 1930s has been forcefully challenged by a group of constitutional scholars. Peter Irons, Richard Friedman, Barry Cushman, and G. Edward White have attempted to demonstrate the following propositions: poor lawyering had much to do with the New Deal's initial downfall before the Supreme Court; law, not raw politics, shaped much of the Supreme Court's behavior towards the legislation of the New Deal; and the real constitutional revolution came before 1937 and after that date with the appointment of new Roosevelt justices. Irons (1982) placed much of the blame for the constitutional impasse of 1935–6 not upon the justices, but upon the hasty, shoddy drafting of early New Deal statutes and their inept defense by mediocre lawyers in the Department of Justice. That situation did not change until graduates from more elite law schools took command of the drafting and later litigation.

Cushman's provocative *Rethinking the New Deal Court* (1998) argued convincingly that a strict liberal versus conservative division among the justices does not adequately explain why the New Deal suffered its series of judicial defeats in 1935–6. Justice Cardozo, for example, was highly sympathetic to the administration, yet voted to strike down the National Recovery Act, as did reactionaries like McReynolds and Butler. Justices Brandeis and Stone, both considered liberals, joined the majority opinion to overturn the initial congressional attempt at debtor relief and to block Roosevelt's removal of a member of the Federal Trade Commission without legislative approval. On the other hand, a minimum wage law was sustained before Roosevelt announced his plan to pack the Court (a fact well known since the 1950s). Nor did the justices have much to fear from the proposal, given the outpouring of immediate opposition in Congress; and yet the Court majority continued to constitutionalize New Deal programs even after 1938, when FDR lost support in Congress.

The meticulous efforts by Cushman and others to put legal process and legal categories back into the constitutional story of the 1930s have not persuaded those scholars who continue to believe – as did many contemporaries – that external events such as the sit-down strikes and Roosevelt's re-election strongly influenced judicial decision-making in 1936–7. On the other hand, there is a general consensus about another important, but often neglected, constitutional tale of the decade: how the Hughes Court expanded the constitutional protection of civil liberties and civil rights when these issues were not high on the agenda of Roosevelt and the New Deal.

Between 1930 and 1941, with the Chief Justice taking the lead, the Supreme Court required the states to observe specific protections of the Bill of Rights, including freedom of speech, press, assembly, and religious expression. The Court struck down racially discriminatory voting procedures, ordered the admission of an African-American student to the all-white law school in Missouri, and mandated the appointment of legal counsel to all persons charged with a federal crime and of state-appointed counsel to indigent defendants facing capital charges. This other "constitutional revolution" expanded the role of the federal courts into new areas of American social life, even as the justices were empowering Congress and the President to orchestrate the economy without strong judicial oversight.

Coming Home

Even while ignoring salient constitutional issues, New Left critics also assumed that the desperate economic situation of the decade provoked the American people to consider and endorse programs far more radical than any that Roosevelt offered. The New Deal has therefore been depicted as frustrating the possibilities of more fundamental changes in the social-economic order. The administration certainly gave little help to Upton Sinclair's gubernatorial campaign in California with his proposals for turning idle factories and farms over to the unemployed in order to End Poverty in California (EPIC). And the President's supporters did everything possible to destroy the credibility of Huey Long, who appeared likely, under the banner of Share Our Wealth, to challenge Roosevelt – until the Senator from Louisiana was assassinated in 1935.

But the historical evidence for a broad-based revolutionary movement, dedicated to the overthrow of American corporate capitalism in the 1930s, has remained exceedingly thin, despite scholarly attempts to prove otherwise. The conclusions reached by our keenest cultural and intellectual historians, including Richard Pells (1973), Warren Susman (1984), and Lawrence Levine (1993), provide compelling testimony against such a thesis. A citizenry that continued to purchase and play the board game *Monopoly* and that packed motion picture theaters to enjoy *It Happened One Night, Top Hat, Gold Diggers of 1935*, and *The Great Ziegfeld* was not poised for revolution. In the 1939 Frank Capra film *Mr Smith Goes to Washington*, Jefferson Smith (Jimmy Stewart) fought old-fashioned corruption in Washington. He did not overthrow the United States government.

Farmers who blocked the marketing of crops or threatened violence against judges at foreclosure time hoped to save their individual farms, not to advance the collectivization of agriculture. In 1936–7 the sit-down strikers at General Motors wanted recognition of their union, not responsibility for running the automobile factories. Communists made important contributions to labor militancy, but party leaders endorsed Roosevelt and the New Deal until the Soviet–Nazi Pact in 1939. The party's greatest achievements, aside from espionage, came through its representation – within the established legal system – of victims of southern racism, like the

Scottsboro defendants. Alan Brinkley's portraits of Senator Long and of Father Coughlin (1982) effectively disposed of the myth that either the Kingfish or the radio priest constituted a viable, radical alternative to the New Deal. Coughlin's monetary panaceas had no relevance to either labor markets or income distribution. Long skewered FDR's aid to bankers and big business and advocated heavier taxation on the rich, but intended the proceeds from Share Our Wealth reforms to finance the defense of petit-bourgeois capitalism at gas stations, barber shops, grocery stores, and bowling alleys. Such investments were unlikely to bring socialism to America.

Amid the hard times of the 1930s, a new national consensus was beginning to take shape. It was hardly free of conflict, but it could be discerned as organized ultimately around a consumer culture that survived and expanded even during the Great Depression. In 1930, for example, the year Hughes became Chief Justice, more than a thousand banks closed their doors, unable to pay their depositors. The first federal census of unemployment reported that 3 million Americans could not find a job. The homeless who slept on park benches covered themselves with used newspapers that were called "Hoover blankets." The nation's economy, social relations, and political system all seemed to be coming apart. But in that same year, a small Detroit radio station launched a new program that soon spread across the country. Called *The Lone Ranger*, it began with the *William Tell Overture* and the voice of an announcer who introduced the hero astride "a fiery horse with the speed of light, a cloud of dust, and a hearty 'Hi-yo, Silver.' " In that same year, too, stores introduced consumers to Twinkies, Snickers, Wonder sliced bread, and Worcestershire sauce; and four airlines were founded. Braniff, TWA, United, and American were all under-capitalized; but they would soon knit America together in new ways.

Hughes retired as Chief Justice in 1941, six months before the Japanese bombed Pearl Harbor. In that year the Supreme Court upheld the New Deal's Fair Labor Standards Act, which mandated uniform national standards (with exceptions) for minimum wages and maximum hours, and also abolished child labor. In that fateful year American families first consumed Spam, began to use shopping carts at A & P supermarkets, and were able to stay in hotels that were franchised and dine in restaurants by Howard Johnson. America, so the Pledge of Allegiance went, was increasingly becoming "one nation, indivisible, with liberty and justice for all." Of course, it was an ideal, not a fact, either in 1930 or in 1941 – or even in 1945, when the Second World War ended. But the New Deal, the Hughes Court and the manufacturers of Twinkies, Spam, and Wonder Bread, plus the operators of the major radio networks and the Hollywood studios, collaborated to forge an America knit together as never before in history by a common array of consumer products, popular culture, political entitlements, and legal standards.

While capitalists gave consumers Birds Eye frozen vegetables, vitamin pills, Walgreen drugstores, and nylon stockings, the New Deal was providing federal deposit insurance for bank accounts, standardizing real estate appraisals through the Home Owners' Loan Corporation, demanding uniform corporate accounting methods (courtesy of the Securities Act), guaranteeing nation-wide unemployment insurance and old age pensions for retirees and also creating a national framework for resolving disputes between labor and management. The Supreme Court validated these new national standards and imposed new rules upon the individual states with respect to the Bill of Rights and the Fourteenth Amendment. In short, the years from 1929 to1941 were a historical moment when America seemed to be on the precipice of social disintegration, but also when political, economic, and legal institutions came together to forge a stronger, more perfect domestic union.

A few scholars, notably Lizbeth Cohen (1990), have imaginatively explored this terrain. Industrial workers in Chicago, she argues, overcame racial, ethnic, and religious divisions to form new industrial unions during the 1930s, thanks to the collapse of corporate welfare programs as well as oppressive conditions on the shop floor. But their solidarity also arose from the spread and adoption of more standardized forms of consumer products, leisure activities, and popular culture. The casualties of this process were often local ethnic markets, newspapers, and theaters, as well as venerable corporate policies that sought to divide and conquer the work force. The winners were the CIO organizers in the industrial heartland who could pitch their appeals not only to Poles, Czechs, Hungarians, and Appalachian hillbillies, but also to these same groups as common consumers who needed the security and purchasing power provided by unions.

Labor organizers who gave their support to reform were not alone in sensing by the 1930s that the rise of a consumer-oriented economy had changed fundamentally the relationship between employers and employees as well as that between government and business. Opposition to unionization and government-induced social welfare programs inspired much hostility to the New Deal, especially after 1935 and especially among southern employers. Yet significant sectors of the business community gave their support to reforms that promised to level the economic playing field across regions and within particular industries. Unionization and government-mandated welfare programs, such as Social Security, unemployment insurance, and minimum wage laws, were among the strategies that liberal capitalists pursued with determination before and during the New Deal. Building upon the initial research of Thomas Ferguson (1991), who demonstrated the powerful corporate support for the New Deal among capital-intensive, service-oriented firms with small blue-collar labor forces, Colin Gordon deepened and extended this analysis across a wide range of New Deal initiatives (1994).

With the collapse of private welfare programs after 1929, a number of corporate leaders looked to government to spread these costs across industry. And faced with the failure of both trade associations and the National Recovery Act to curb cut-throat price competition, many of these same business leaders also looked to strong national unions as another way to rationalize the economy further and to reduce the advantage enjoyed by their low-wage competitors in regions of the South and West. The most sophisticated of these corporate liberals were Gerald Swope of General Electric, Walter Teagle of Standard Oil, Henry Harriman of the Chamber of Commerce, Louis Kirstein of Filene's Department Stores, and Marion Folsom of Eastman-Kodak. They readily perceived the nexus between the purchasing power to be generated by such reforms and the profitability of their own companies. In short, the most symbolic and significant reforms of the New Deal – the National Labor Relations Act, the Social Security Act, and the Fair Labor Standards Act – garnered crucial support from some big businessmen and would not have survived without their support.

On the eve of Pearl Harbor, the Roosevelt administration was getting major assistance from key corporate leaders and the heads of the CIO in forging a new social contract for a consumer society between capital and labor. Emblematic was the collective bargaining agreement negotiated between United States Steel and the United Steelworkers of America. That social contract, challenged only briefly after the war by Walter Reuther and the United Automobile Workers, provided unionized workers with steady income, including some fringe benefits, in exchange for maintaining labor discipline. Union wages were extended across the industry, and management's basic control over investment and the pace of technological innovation was accepted. As Gordon points out, however, this social contract – the crown jewel of the New Deal – functioned on the premise of a self-contained, expanding national marketplace, which would be largely insulated from the opportunities and turbulence of a world economy. And that premise was about to be invalidated, owing to the hot war that began in 1941 and then the cold one that soon followed.

It is now several decades since William Appleman Williams, the *enfant terrible* of diplomatic historians, undertook to demolish "the myth of American isolationism" in *The Tragedy of American Diplomacy* (1959). After World War I, he brilliantly argued, the United States spurned membership in the League of Nations and the World Court; but the absence of these formal institutional ties did not mean that the country lacked a presence or failed to influence the course of economic change around the world. American bankers extended loans and credits of considerable magnitude to governments and private investors in Europe, Asia, and Latin America. American businessmen developed mines, plantations, utility systems, oil wells, and railroads across the globe. Williams nevertheless tended to overdraw his case. Most of this direct overseas investment was centered in the western hemisphere (principally Mexico, Canada, and Central America); and apart from agricultural exports, income from foreign trade constituted a relatively small fraction of total wealth in the US. Both in prosperity and depression, American firms concentrated on the domestic market which, because of the high tariffs of the 1920s, remained largely immune from foreign competition.

Until the military regimes in Europe and Asia began their march in the mid-1930s, Roosevelt proved to be the equal of Hoover as an economic nationalist. Nor was he willing to challenge the framework of neutrality laws that limited American trade and finance with countries at war. He not only endorsed congressional efforts to tighten these rules, but also enforced them during the Chaco War between Bolivia and Paraguay by barring arms shipments from the Curtiss–Wright Corporation. Roosevelt extended this ban as well even to the civil war in Spain, a decision that denied aid to the republican government then under assault from its own military as well as from volunteers from Germany and Italy. He also torpedoed efforts at international monetary stabilization in the vain hope that devaluation would boost the domestic price level and expand exports, but neither measure had much impact on recovery. He opened trade with the Soviet Union, which proved a limited boon to farm equipment and electrical manufacturers, and allowed Secretary of State Cordell Hull, who was a fanatic for free trade, to negotiate a series of so-called reciprocal trade agreements. But none of the agreements significantly lowered general American tariffs or expanded international trade. At the same time, these brief efforts at projecting economic interests abroad drew fervent support from major oil companies, firms eager to share in the bounty of the Middle East, and from high technology firms anxious to expand their exports.

The Nazi–Soviet Pact, the outbreak of war in Europe in 1939, and further Japanese advances in China rekindled Roosevelt's dormant Wilsonianism and reinforced emerging political and economic interests that defined the nation's future in a global rather than simply a national context. In tracing this transformation, no scholar has yet surpassed the sweep and cogency of Robert Dallek's *Franklin D. Roosevelt and American Foreign Policy, 1932–1945* (1979) or chapters 13–16 in David Kennedy's *Freedom from Fear* (1999). By 1941, FDR clearly hoped for a decisive event that might trigger war with the Third Reich. At the same time, he hoped that economic sanctions would dissuade Japanese leaders from their expansion in the Pacific, buy time for further military preparations, and avoid a war on two fronts. He misjudged imperial Japan, and only Hitler's unfathomable decision to declare war on the United States after December 7 brought FDR the conflict that he saw as unavoidable in Europe.

Roosevelt and the New Dealers could not have foreseen the military and economic globalization in which the United States was engaged on an unprecedented scale after 1945. In order to secure American influence, it would be necessary to promote foreign investment and trade in such a way as to stabilize the economies of Europe and Asia, but in so doing the social contract forged in the 1930s between labor and capital was undermined. The consequences of those decisions for the New Deal coalition and American liberalism have been cogently analyzed by Judith Stein in *Running Steel, Running America: Race, Economic Policy, and the Decline of Liberalism* (1998). But that is a historiography best left to others.

REFERENCES AND FURTHER READING

Asbell, Bernard (1961) *The Day FDR Died*. New York: Holt, Rinehart, and Winston.
Auerbach, Jerold (1969) "New Deal, old deal, or raw deal: some thoughts on New Left historiography," *Journal of Southern History* 35, pp. 18–30.
Bernstein, Barton J. (1968) "The New Deal: the conservative achievements of liberal reform," in B. Bernstein (ed.) *Towards a New Past: Dissenting Essays in American History*. New York: Random House.
Bernstein, Michael (1987) *The Great Depression: Delayed Recovery and Economic Change in America, 1929–1939*. New York: Cambridge University Press.
Best, Gary (1991) *Pride, Prejudice, and Politics: Roosevelt versus Recovery, 1933–1938*. New York: Praeger.
Brinkley, Alan (1982) *Voices of Protest: Huey Long, Father Coughlin, and the Great Depression*. New York: Alfred A. Knopf.
Burns, James MacGregor (1956) *Roosevelt: The Lion and the Fox*. New York: Harcourt Brace.
Cohen, Lizbeth (1990) *Making a New Deal: Industrial Workers in Chicago, 1919–1939*. Chicago: University of Chicago Press.
Conkin, Paul (1967) *The New Deal*. Arlington Heights, Ill.: Harlan Davidson.
Corwin, Edward (1941) *Constitutional Revolution, Ltd*. Claremont, Calif.: The Pomona Colleges.
Cushman, Barry (1998) *Rethinking the New Deal Court: The Structure of a Constitutional Revolution*. New York: Oxford University Press.
Dallek, Robert (1979) *Franklin D. Roosevelt and American Foreign Policy, 1932–1945*. New York: Oxford University Press.

Degler, Carl (1956) *Out of Our Past.* New York: Harper and Row.

Eden, Robert (ed.) (1989) *The New Deal and its Legacy: Critique and Appraisal.* Westport, Conn: Greenwood Press.

Ferguson, Thomas (1991) "Industrial structure and party competition in the New Deal," *Sociological Perspectives* 34, pp. 498–523.

Freidel, Frank (1952–78) *Franklin D. Roosevelt,* 4 vols. Boston: Little, Brown.

—— (1964) *The New Deal and the American People.* Englewood Cliffs, NJ: Prentice-Hall.

Friedman, Richard (1994) "Switching time and other thought experiments: the Hughes Court and constitutional transformation," *University of Pennsylvania Law Review* 142, pp. 1891–943.

Galbraith, John Kenneth (1954) *The Great Crash: 1929.* Boston: Houghton Mifflin.

Garraty, John (1974) "The New Deal, National Socialism, and the Great Depression," *American Historical Review* 78, pp. 907–44.

—— (1986) *The Great Depression.* New York: Harcourt Brace.

Gordon, Colin (1994) *New Deals: Business, Labor, and Politics in America, 1920–1935.* New York: Cambridge University Press.

Hawley, Ellis (1966) *The New Deal and the Problem of Monopoly: A Study in Economic Ambivalence.* Princeton, NJ: Princeton University Press.

Hofstadter, Richard (1955) *The Age of Reform: From Bryan to FDR.* New York: Alfred A. Knopf.

Irons, Peter (1982) *New Deal Lawyers.* Princeton, NJ: Princeton University Press.

Kennedy, David (1999) *Freedom from Fear: The American People in Depression and War, 1929–1945.* New York: Oxford University Press.

Leff, Mark H. (1984) *The Limits of Symbolic Reform: The New Deal and Taxation, 1933–1939.* New York: Cambridge University Press.

Leuchtenburg, William (1963) *Franklin D. Roosevelt and the New Deal, 1932–1940.* New York: Harper and Row.

—— (1964) "The New Deal and the analogue of war," in John Braeman, Robert H. Bremner, and Everett Walters (eds.) *Change and Continuity in Twentieth Century America.* Columbus: Ohio State University Press.

—— (1995) *The Supreme Court Reborn: The Constitutional Revolution in the Age of Roosevelt.* New York: Oxford University Press.

Levine, Lawrence (1993) *The Unpredictable Past: Explorations in American Cultural History.* New York: Oxford University Press.

Parrish, Michael E. (1992) *Anxious Decades: America in Prosperity and Depression, 1920–1941.* New York: W. W. Norton.

Pells, Richard H. (1973) *Radical Vision and American Dreams: Culture and Social Thought in the Depression Years.* New York: Harper and Row.

Perkins, Dexter (1957) *The New Age of Franklin Roosevelt, 1932–1945.* Chicago: University of Chicago Press.

Posner, Richard A. (ed.) (1992) *The Essential Holmes: Selections from the Letters, Speeches, Judicial Opinions, and Other Writings of Oliver Wendell Holmes, Jr.* Chicago: University of Chicago Press.

Rauch, Basil (1944) *The History of the New Deal.* New York: Creative Age Press.

Robinson, Edgar (1955) *The Roosevelt Leadership, 1933–1945.* Philadelphia: Lippincott.

Romasco, Albert (1965) *The Poverty of Abundance: Hoover, the Nation, the Depression.* New York: Oxford University Press.

Schlesinger, Arthur M., Jr. (1957–60) *The Age of Roosevelt,* 3 vols. Boston: Houghton Mifflin.

Skocpol, Theda and Finegold, Kenneth (1982) "State capacity and economic intervention in the early New Deal," *Political Science Quarterly* 97, pp. 255–78.

Sobel, Robert (1968) *The Great Bull Market: Wall Street in the 1920s.* New York: W. W. Norton.

Stein, Judith (1998) *Running Steel, Running America: Race, Economic Policy, and the Decline of Liberalism.* Chapel Hill: University of North Carolina Press.

Susman, Warren I. (1984) *Culture as History: The Transformation of American Society in the Twentieth Century.* New York: Pantheon.

White, G. Edward (2000) *The Constitution and the New Deal.* Cambridge, Mass.: Harvard University Press.

Williams, William Appleman (1959) *The Tragedy of American Diplomacy.* Cleveland, Oh.: World.

Wilson, Joan Hoff (1975) *Herbert Hoover: Forgotten Progressive.* Boston: Little, Brown.

Zinn, Howard (ed.) (1966) *New Deal Thought.* Indianapolis: Bobbs-Merrill.

CHAPTER FOUR

1941–1950

ALLAN M. WINKLER

The United States underwent a tremendous transformation in the 1940s. The experience of fighting the most extensive war in world history brought profound changes in all parts of American life. In both foreign policy and domestic affairs, the nation found itself vastly different at the end of the decade than it had been before.

The United States developed into the strongest nation in the world in the 1940s. It had become an imperial power in the Spanish–American War of 1898, but was less dominant than many of the European nations, which had been collecting colonies for years. Its entrance into World War I in 1917 had enhanced its stature by tipping the military balance and bringing about Germany's defeat. It resisted further large-scale involvement after that war, however, and paid more attention in the 1930s to its own depression-era concerns. All that changed with the onset of World War II. Even before it began to fight, the United States was an integral player in the struggle. After officially entering the war, the nation harnessed its industrial might and entrepreneurial ability into the greatest military machine ever known, and that effort resulted in victory in all theaters of battle. The war established the nation as a superpower whose actions would help determine the fate of the rest of the world and laid the foundation for the Cold War conflict that followed.

At the same time, World War II raised new issues and resulted in new configurations of political and social authority at home. The struggle led to the further growth of presidential power in a process that had begun during the New Deal of Franklin D. Roosevelt. It resulted in the development of more centralized economic planning, which affected the lives of all Americans. And it encouraged efforts to end discrimination on the part of a number of groups, African Americans and women in particular, who had found themselves treated as second-class citizens in the past. In all areas, the war provided the framework for the postwar years.

The World of Foreign Affairs

World War II was well underway before the United States joined the conflict. Fighting in Europe broke out in 1939, even as Japan waged an undeclared war in Asia on the other side of the globe. Though not a formal protagonist in the European conflict, the United States played a huge role in sustaining Great Britain and the Soviet Union as it proceeded at the same time along a collision course with Japan. The surprise attack on Pearl Harbor in Hawaii on December 7, 1941 brought America into the war against Japan. While some critics argued in subsequent years that Roosevelt manipulated the attack to join a war the American people did not want, more recent historians have countered that claim. Roberta Wohlstetter, in *Pearl Harbor: Warning and Decision* (1962), demonstrated that while it was possible to find references to Hawaii in the cable traffic, there were so many other messages coming and going that it would have been impossible to track the Japanese plans. Still, Roosevelt was relieved that the United States was now officially involved in a war he recognized the nation could not avoid, and he was even more so when the German dictator Adolf Hitler declared war on the United States after the attack. Now the nation could buckle down to defeat the Tripartite Pact powers of Germany, Italy, and Japan.

As the United States prepared to fight, Roosevelt had a vision of what the postwar world should be like. In a speech to Congress early in 1941, the President spoke of the "four essential human freedoms": freedom of speech, freedom of worship, freedom from want, and freedom from fear. That summer, he met the British Prime Minister Winston Churchill off the coast of Newfoundland, and the two leaders issued the Atlantic Charter, underscoring their commitment to a democratic world with self-determination and equal trading rights for all. As a counterpoint to those idealistic war aims, most Americans fought for a conception of the kind of life they remembered back home. War correspondent John Hersey once asked a young marine in Guadalcanal what he was fighting for. After reflecting for a moment, the soldier sighed and said, "Jesus, what I'd give for a piece of blueberry pie" (1970: 74).

The Allies were in serious trouble by the time the United States entered the war. France had fallen, while Great Britain struggled to withstand a relentless German bombing barrage. The Soviet Union likewise found itself facing the prospect of defeat. In the Pacific, the Japanese drove American General Douglas MacArthur from the Philippines and consolidated their power there.

The military situation began to improve toward the end of 1942. The Soviets resisted the Germans in a brutal campaign at Stalingrad. Operation Torch landed forces in North Africa and over the course of the next year the Allies proceeded into Italy and what Churchill called the "soft underbelly" of the Axis. On June 6, 1944, on D-Day, the Allies crossed the English Channel and landed on the Normandy coast in northern France. Persistently, the Allies pushed on to Paris, and then into Germany. Horrified at the German concentration camps they liberated, and overwhelmed by the inhuman loss of life they discovered, they finally brought the European war to an end on May 8, 1945.

In the Pacific, the American victory at Midway in mid-1942 paved the way for an island-hopping campaign that took one piece of land after another on the way to a final attack planned for the Japanese homeland. That invasion proved unnecessary when the United States decided to use its newly-developed weapon – the atomic bomb – instead.

The United States had embarked on what became known as the Manhattan Project even before it had entered the war. In a letter to President Roosevelt in 1939, the internationally-known physicist Albert Einstein speculated that enormous energy might be released if atoms could be split apart in a self-sustaining chain reaction and wrote, "It is conceivable . . . that extremely powerful bombs of a new type . . . may be constructed" (quoted in Winkler 1993: 13). Hinting that Germany was already trying to build such a weapon, Einstein encouraged the United States to begin what became the greatest engineering enterprise of all time. In the last three years of the war, this top-secret project built 37 installations in the United States and Canada, employed 120,000 people, and cost the astronomical sum of $2 billion. After testing one atomic device in New Mexico in July 1945, the American military had two bombs ready in early August to use on Japan.

The first bomb, a uranium weapon named "Little Boy," fell on Hiroshima on August 6, 1945. It killed 70,000 people immediately and injured 70,000 more. Three days later, the second bomb, a plutonium device called "Fat Man," fell on Nagasaki, killing 40,000 and injuring 60,000 more. Both bombs demolished buildings as well, and left the two Japanese cities as piles of rubble. Other bombs, in cities such as Tokyo, had brought about similar destruction, but in Hiroshima and Nagasaki the devastation had been caused in each case by just one bomb. Traumatized by the attacks, the Japanese accepted American terms, and on September 2, 1945, the long and bloody war came to an end.

Why had the United States decided to use the new bomb? Policy makers in the immediate aftermath of the war justified their decision with the argument that it forestalled an invasion and saved American lives. Yet subsequent scholars have argued that there were other alternatives, such as a blockade, or a diplomatic concession that would have permitted the Japanese to keep their emperor after surrender, that could have been tried. In *A World Destroyed: The Atomic Bomb and the Grand Alliance* (1975), Martin J. Sherwin maintained that the bombs were used because Roosevelt and his top officials had always assumed the bombs would be used whenever they were ready. Barton J. Bernstein made a similar argument in "Roosevelt, Truman, and the atomic bomb: 1941–1945: a reinterpretation" in 1975. And J. Samuel Walker has pointed out perceptively in *Prompt and Utter Destruction: Truman and the Use of Atomic Bombs against Japan* that it was "an easy and obvious military decision" (1997: 75). The bomb had always been intended for military use and planners operated on that assumption.

The Second World War contained the seeds of the Cold War that followed. Winston Churchill once remarked that the only thing worse than fighting with allies was fighting without them, and tensions on the part of the major powers had often threatened to tear the Grand Alliance apart.

The United States had long been suspicious of the Soviet Union. After the Russian Revolution of 1917, the administration of Woodrow Wilson had refused to extend formal diplomatic recognition to the new Communist regime, and such recognition only came in 1933, when Roosevelt assumed power. During the war itself, the United States, Great Britain, and the Soviet Union met in a series of top-level conferences – at Teheran, Yalta, and Potsdam – where they papered over differences and made the decisions necessary to push on to a successful military conclusion. But the friction remained, and surfaced even more visibly after the war.

The United States and the Soviet Union had fundamentally different visions for the postwar world. Americans hoped to spread the values of liberty, equality, and democracy, and to create an environment where economic enterprise could thrive. The

Soviets needed to rebuild after the devastation of the war, and wanted internal security, particularly along their western flank. They also were committed to Communist ideology, downplayed during the war, and confident of the inevitable triumph of the proletarian state.

Tensions surfaced as the war drew to an end. East and West came into conflict over the shape of the future government of Poland. The Yalta Conference of February 1945 sought to resolve the issue but produced only a vague and imprecise agreement that could be interpreted in different ways. When Harry S. Truman became President after FDR died in April of that year, he lectured Soviet Foreign Minister Vyacheslav Molotov about the need for the Russians to follow his interpretation of the Yalta accord. Molotov, taken aback by the abrupt conversation that failed to observe the niceties of diplomatic protocol, protested, "I have never been talked to like that in my life." Bluntly, Truman retorted, "Carry out your agreements and you won't get talked to like that" (Truman 1955: 82). Relations went downhill from there.

Economic issues likewise split the Russians and Americans apart. Six days after the end of the war in Europe, the United States cut off economic and military aid to the Allies. Though the policy affected all nations receiving such assistance, it hurt the Soviet Union most of all. At about the same time, the United States hedged in response to a Soviet request for a large loan. By imposing severe restrictions requiring Russia to pledge "nondiscrimination in world commerce," American policy makers effectively guaranteed that the Soviets would go their own way.

Containment became the basis of American policy toward the Communist threat. George Kennan, a prominent State Department official, summed up the situation best of all in an article in the influential journal *Foreign Affairs*. "The whole Soviet governmental machine, including the mechanism of diplomacy," he wrote, "moves inexorably along the prescribed path, like a persistent toy automobile wound up and headed in a given direction, stopping only when it meets with some unanswerable force" (1947: 574). Soviet efforts to expand had to be contained wherever necessary around the globe.

The Truman Doctrine was the first step in America's containment policy. As the Soviet Union pressured Turkey for joint control of the Dardanelles, the passage between the Black Sea and the Mediterranean, a civil war in Greece set Communists against the British-aided right-wing monarchy. When Great Britain informed the United States that it could no longer provide economic and military aid to Greece and Turkey, America moved into the void. In 1947, at Truman's request, Congress appropriated $400 million in assistance to the two countries.

The next year, Congress acceded to the plan proposed by Secretary of State George C. Marshall to provide even more aid to nations still reeling from the impact of the war. Speaking at the Harvard University commencement of 1947, Marshall pointed to the impact of economic chaos in the growth of Communist strength and said, "The patient is sinking while the doctors deliberate" (quoted in Winkler 2000b: 29). It was time to take immediate action. After Western European governments made a series of massive requests, the United States agreed to provide $13 billion over a four-year period to sixteen cooperating nations.

Next came the creation of the North Atlantic Treaty Organization (NATO) in 1949. This peacetime military alliance, the first since the United States had fought in the American Revolution, marked a major transformation in America's approach to

foreign affairs. It declared that for the 12 nations forming the alliance, an attack
against one would be considered an attack against all.

In the aftermath of the Communist victory in the Chinese civil war and the Russian
detonation of an atomic device, the United States clarified its containment policy
further. NSC-68 was a document presented to the National Security Council in 1950
describing the challenges facing America. "The issues that face us are momentous,"
the document said, "involving the fulfillment or destruction not only of this Republic
but of civilization itself." Conflict between East and West was unavoidable. Negotiation was useless, for the Soviets refused to bargain in good faith. If the United States
hoped to meet the Russian challenge it had to quadruple defense spending. "A more
rapid build-up of political, economic, and military strength and thereby of confidence
in the free world than is now contemplated," NSC-68 stated, "is the only course
which is consistent with progress toward achieving our fundamental purpose."
(quoted in Winkler 2000b: 26). With the advent of the Korean War in 1950, the
United States embarked on the recommended course.

Scholars have debated the origins of the Cold War for decades. In the early years after
the end of World War II, many policy makers and commentators justified the stance of
the United States as a bold and courageous attempt to counter the Communist threat.
Arthur M. Schlesinger, Jr. summed up the argument of "orthodox" scholars in a
widely-reprinted essay, "Origins of the Cold War" (1967). In the 1960s and 1970s,
as the war in Vietnam eroded confidence in American foreign policy, "revisionist"
historians argued that the United States engaged in actions that were misguided and
insensitive and contributed to the increasing tension. Barton J. Bernstein, articulated
that approach in 1970. In the 1980s, still other historians, including John Lewis
Gaddis, in *Strategies of Containment: A Critical Appraisal of Postwar American
National Security Policy* (1982), called themselves "postrevisionists" and sought to
balance the arguments of both sides. With the end of the Cold War, the debate flared
up again, as scholars such as Melvyn P. Leffler (1992) used their greater access to
Russian records to assess just how serious a threat the Soviet Union was.

The Growth of Governmental Power

Both the economy and the governmental bureaucracy expanded enormously during
the 1940s. World War II made huge demands on American enterprise as the economy
operated at full tilt. Building on the pattern established in the New Deal, the
government became even more focused and centralized than before.

Franklin Roosevelt presided over the process. During the 1930s, a host of new
agencies had proliferated to deal with the ravages of the Great Depression. In an
effort to promote recovery and provide necessary relief, FDR pushed the nation to
craft its own version of the welfare state, and the New Deal, with its many alphabet
agencies, was the result. The Democratic Party, now firmly committed to a liberal
course, dominated public life. With the onset of war, however, there were new
demands to be met, and so, as Roosevelt observed in 1943, the United States shifted
direction. The New Deal, he declared, had come about when the patient – the United
States – was suffering from a grave internal disorder. But then, at Pearl Harbor, the
patient had been in a terrible crash. "Old Dr. New Deal," the President said, "didn't
know 'nothing' about legs and arms. He knew a great deal about internal medicine,

but nothing about surgery. So he got his partner, who was an orthopedic surgeon, Dr. Win-the-War, to take care of this fellow who had been in this bad accident" (see Winkler 2000a: 96). Roosevelt's light-hearted quip reflected a fundamental change in direction, as Alan Brinkley has shown in *The End of Reform: New Deal Liberalism in Recession and War* (1995). Liberalism was now harder to sustain, even as the government continued to grow.

Winning the war entailed working closely with the business community, which had been badly discredited by the crash of 1929. During the New Deal, Roosevelt had called businessmen "economic royalists" and had taken actions that infuriated them. Now he invited their assistance, for he knew he needed their help in producing the necessary weapons of war. Dollar-a-year men, who remained on corporate payrolls and drew but a nominal salary from the government, came to Washington and organized a productive effort unparalleled in the past. The administration provided incentives and tax breaks that basically underwrote the entire cost of plant expansion. It developed the "cost-plus" system whereby the government guaranteed all development and production costs and paid a percentage profit in addition on all goods produced for the war. With that support, business boomed and business and government together became partners in what came to be known in later decades as the "military-industrial complex."

Coordination was an important part of the production process. The administration insisted on the organization necessary to ensure that necessary materials, often in short supply, arrived where they were needed most. To that end, Roosevelt appointed a series of agencies to oversee the entire economic effort. If one agency failed to do what it was expected, in characteristic fashion, the President simply created another with overlapping responsibilities to try to get the job done. A War Resources Board, established in 1939, was the first step, but FDR was unwilling to support a policy of extensive regulation at this time. After the German blitzkrieg of the Low Countries and France in 1940, he resurrected the National Defense Advisory Commission, which had been created in the last war. When it proved ineffective, he created the Office of Production Management in early 1941. A year later, after Pearl Harbor, the President established the War Production Board, led by Donald Nelson, a top executive from Sears, Roebuck, and Co., but its failure to gain control of military procurement doomed its efforts. Finally, in 1943, the President created the Office of War Mobilization, superimposed on all the rest, to be led by James F. Byrnes, a former Supreme Court justice, who came to be known informally as "assistant president" and who got the job done.

This huge effort to create what Roosevelt called "the great arsenal of democracy" came at a cost. The number of Americans working at government jobs rose from 1 million to 3.8 million between 1940 and 1945. Big government was now an unavoidable part of modern life. Federal expenditures rose from $9 billion to $98.4 billion in these same years. The total American bill for World War II was more than $330 billion, a sum ten times larger than the direct expense of World War I.

Whatever the cost, the results were impressive. By the middle of 1945, the United States had produced 80,000 landing craft, 100,000 tanks and armored cars, 300,000 airplanes, a million guns, and 41 billion rounds of ammunition. Those materials made the difference between victory and defeat. And the huge organizational effort underscored the role of the federal government in public affairs.

World War II was an overwhelming success for the Allies on the battlefield and in the productive sphere. Americans enjoyed the return of prosperity, and later looked back fondly on the experience of the wartime years. For many of them, the conflict was, in the phrase journalist Studs Terkel helped popularize in his Pulitzer Prize-winning book, a "good war" (1984). They had defeated the Axis powers, and both veterans and homefront workers could take pride in a job well done. In subsequent years, however, scholars began to describe the struggle in much greater complexity than before. There were outsiders whose experience was not always positive as the nation struggled with the exigencies of war. And then there were the 110,000 Japanese Americans, described most recently by Roger Daniels in *Prisoners Without Trial: Japanese Americans in World War II* (1993), who were evacuated from their homes and interned in ten detention camps in seven western states, whether they were citizens or not, in the greatest violation of civil liberties in the history of the United States. In "The good war? A reappraisal of how World War II affected American society," Richard Polenberg reflected on the way the war worked "to narrow the scope of individual freedom and to reinforce illiberal tendencies in virtually all areas of life, but especially in class, gender, and race relations" (1992: 297).

As World War II drew to an end, Harry Truman hoped to revive a liberal approach. Like Roosevelt, Truman believed that the federal government had the responsibility for ensuring the social welfare of all Americans. He too was committed to assisting the less fortunate citizens of the United States who were unable to help themselves in a rational and systematic way.

Less than a week after the end of the war, Truman asked Congress to pass a 21-point program to ensure stability in the postwar years. He demanded full employment legislation, a higher minimum wage, greater unemployment compensation, and federal housing assistance. In the next ten weeks, he added demands for health insurance and legislation to control atomic energy to his list. Several years later, after winning re-election, he declared to Congress and the country, "Every segment of our population and every individual has a right to expect from our Government a fair deal" (Hamby 1992: 488). The phrase "Fair Deal" became the name for his domestic program, which included the measures he had proposed repeatedly since taking office.

While big government was now a permanent fixture of American life, not all Americans accepted it willingly. The Republican Party, in particular, resisted the relentless expansion of the federal bureaucracy. It wanted to see Congress re-establish its own authority and cut the executive branch back to size, and to limit government intervention in the business world and private life. Led by Senator Robert A. Taft, known to supporters as "Mr. Republican," the party fought the President at every turn.

The first battle came over the Employment Act of 1946. This measure was an effort to apply the theory of British economist John Maynard Keynes to preserve economic equilibrium and prevent another depression in the future. His assertion that massive spending could help end the Great Depression had been vindicated by the experience of World War II. Now liberals wanted to institutionalize that approach. The original full employment bill committed the government to maintain full employment by monitoring the economy and taking remedial action, including both tax cuts and spending programs, in case of decline. Conservatives countered that this approach undermined free enterprise and moved the country one step closer to socialism. Responding to pressure from the business community, Congress shredded the bill.

As finally passed, the act created a Council of Economic Advisers to make recommendations to the President for an annual report, but it stopped short of mandating the government to use fiscal tools to maintain full employment when difficulties loomed ahead. Big government may have become a fixture in the postwar years, but there was resistance to giving it additional power.

Another battle took place over the position of labor in American society. The New Deal had provided working men and women with the right to choose their own unions and to bargain collectively with management. The union movement had grown stronger and union membership had soared. Now Republicans wanted to check union growth and circumscribe unions' right to engage in the kind of disruptive strikes that occurred as the Second World War came to an end. In 1947, with majorities in both houses of Congress, they passed the Taft–Hartley Act, which restricted the tools unions could employ. It spelled out unfair labor practices (such as preventing non-union workers from working if they wished) and outlawed the closed shop, whereby an employee had to join a union before getting a job. The law gave the President the right to demand an 80-day cooling off period in strikes affecting national security and required union officials to sign a non-Communist oath if the government was to protect their rights. Union members and leaders were furious at the measure. Truman vetoed it, giving an angry explanation for his action on nation-wide radio, but the Republicans overrode the veto and the bill became law.

Some parts of Truman's Fair Deal program worked, while others did not. Legislators expanded social security programs, raised the minimum wage, and achieved modest gains on the housing front. But the administration failed to establish a national health insurance program or to provide federal aid to education. Because of the national commitment to spend whatever was necessary to support American efforts in the Cold War abroad, there was often correspondingly less money to spend for liberal reform projects at home.

Still, Truman kept the liberal vision alive in the late 1940s. There was now a general acceptance of the role the federal government could and should play in American life. The Fair Deal ratified many of the initiatives of the New Deal, and led Americans to take programs like social security for granted and to look to Washington for leadership in national affairs. According to both William E. Leuchtenburg in *In the Shadow of FDR: From Harry Truman to Bill Clinton* (1993) and Alonzo L. Hamby in *Liberalism and its Challengers: From F.D.R. to Bush* (1992), the liberal approach was now a firmly entrenched part of public policy.

Efforts to Promote Social Reform

During the 1940s, groups discriminated against in the past began to assert themselves more vocally and to demand more equitable treatment. As they played their part in the war effort, African Americans insisted on an end to the discrimination they faced in both civilian and military life. Their efforts at helping themselves led to further attacks on segregation in the postwar years and in time provided an example for Latinos and Native Americans who were similarly disfranchised in the United States. Meanwhile, women responded eagerly to new opportunities available to them in the work force, and looked back fondly on their experience in wartime industry as the women's movement unfolded in the decades that followed.

At the start of World War II, blacks faced discrimination on many fronts. Unemployment remained high, as one out of every five workers lacked a job. The United States Employment Service honored employers' requests for "whites only" when filling jobs and perpetuated existing hiring patterns. In the military services, African Americans could not join the Air Corps or the Marine Corps, could work only in the all-black messmen's branch of the navy, and found themselves segregated from whites in the army and confined to the few regular black units created after the Civil War. They bristled when the army, like the Red Cross, separated blood plasma according to the donor's race.

The administration hardly seemed sympathetic to the prospect of change. Secretary of War Henry L. Stimson believed that blacks were inferior and declared, "Leadership is not embedded in the negro race yet and to try to make commissioned officers to lead men into battle – colored men – is only to work disaster to both" (quoted in Blum 1976: 185). President Roosevelt was likewise more concerned with military issues than minority rights, and midway through the war said, "I don't think, quite frankly, that we can bring about the millennium at this time."

Yet African Americans were impatient. Some simply moved away from the South, where segregation was most entrenched, and headed toward industrial centers in the North. Others became more assertive and subscribed to the "Double V" campaign proclaimed by the *Pittsburgh Courier*, a widely circulated black newspaper. Troubled by their experience in World War I, where they had fought valiantly only to return home to repeated slights, they were determined to fight this time for freedom on two fronts – both at home and abroad. It was necessary, the *Courier* observed, to push for "victory over our enemies at home and victory over our enemies on the battlefields abroad" (Blum 1976: 208).

The demand for equality was spearheaded by A. Philip Randolph, head of the Brotherhood of Sleeping Car Porters. In January 1941, he proposed a massive march on Washington with the slogan "We loyal Negro American citizens demand the right to work and fight for our country." Concerned about the prospect of tens of thousands of blacks in the streets of the nation's capital, Roosevelt met with Randolph in mid-June 1941 and tried to talk the union leader out of holding the demonstration. When the President's powers of persuasion failed to get Randolph to back down, Roosevelt signed Executive Order 8802 declaring that "there shall be no discrimination in the employment of workers in defense industries because of race, creed, color, or national origin," and creating a Fair Employment Practices Committee (FEPC) to investigate complaints and take appropriate action. With that victory behind him, Randolph called off the march.

Meanwhile, African Americans pressed for change on other fronts as well. The National Association for the Advancement of Colored People (NAACP) and the Urban League, both established earlier in the century, continued to publicize grievances, exert political pressure, and use the courts to try to end discrimination. The Congress of Racial Equality (CORE), a new organization, counseled blacks to take nonviolent direct action to promote racial equality and conducted sit-ins in a number of cities. In Washington, DC, for example, black students picketed with signs reading "We die together. Let's eat together" in demanding the desegregation of a local restaurant. Similar protests took place in Baltimore, Chicago, Denver, and Detroit.

Sometimes racial tensions resulted in violence. In Detroit, a city overcrowded with war workers, the hot summer of 1943 sparked a bloody race riot. Scuffles between blacks and whites in a recreation area near the black ghetto of Paradise Valley escalated into more serious trouble. Rumors, including one story that whites had thrown a black woman and her baby off a bridge, caused the situation to get out of hand. Blacks looted and destroyed white-owned stores, while whites pulled blacks off of streetcars and out of theaters and beat them. By the time the riot ended several days later, 25 blacks and 9 whites were dead, and 675 people were injured. Another uprising occurred in Harlem, in New York City, the same year.

World War II broke down some of the barriers that had existed in the past and brought about some significant change. Neil A. Wynn pointed to the economic and social advances in *The Afro-American and the Second World War* (1976). Even more important according to Richard M. Dalfiume in "The forgotten years of the Negro revolution" (1968), agitation during the war laid the groundwork for the civil rights activity of the years ahead. Now, further change was necessary, for an explosive force was building that could not be contained. As Walter White, head of the NAACP, observed, "A wind *is* rising – a wind of determination by the havenots of the world to share the benefits of freedom and prosperity which the haves of the world have tried to keep exclusively for themselves . . . Whether that wind develops into a hurricane is a decision we must make" (quoted in Blum 1976: 219).

Pressure for racial change continued in the postwar years. Blacks in baseball, long confined to the Negro leagues, hoped for a chance to play in the all-white major leagues. That opportunity beckoned in 1947, when Jackie Robinson broke the color line as a player for the Brooklyn Dodgers. General manager Branch Rickey was well aware of the possibility of violence on and off the field, but he recognized that abundant African American talent could help the game. Signing Robinson to a major league contract was not a haphazard decision, but rather a carefully orchestrated action, as Jules Tygiel showed in *Baseball's Great Experiment: Jackie Robinson and his Legacy* (1983). Robinson lived up to all expectations, despite taunts and slights on and off the field. He was Rookie of the Year in 1947 and kept improving with time, opening the way for other African Americans in baseball and other professional sports.

Blacks protesting against lynching and other abuses pushed President Truman to take a stand in these same years. In 1946, he appointed a Committee on Civil Rights to investigate such problems, and listened carefully when it reported in 1947 that African Americans remained second-class citizens in all areas of American life. In February 1948, he went even further, sending a 10-point civil rights program to Congress. After the southern wing of the Democratic Party bolted that year, he issued an executive order barring discrimination in the federal establishment. He also ordered equality of treatment in the military services. Despite the fears of some white officers that integration would compromise morale, the administration stood by the change. Manpower needs in the Korean War led to the elimination of the last racial barriers, and the new policy became permanent when the army found that integrated units performed well.

Meanwhile, the NAACP slowly but surely pursued a legal path to end segregation. It argued cases, followed them through appeal, and took them all the way to the Supreme Court. In 1948, the Supreme Court outlawed the enforcement of restrictive covenants, barring African American from certain neighborhoods, and that decision opened up housing markets. A number of other decisions in these same years provided the underpinning for the landmark *Brown* v. *Board of Education* decision outlawing school segregation, which was finally handed down in 1954. While most of the extensive literature about the civil rights movement deals with the 1950s and 1960s and focuses on personalities and episodes which have become well known, Richard Kluger's *Simple Justice: The History of* Brown *v.* Board of Education *and Black America's Struggle for Equality* (1976) tracks the background in the late 1940s that made the movement possible.

Latinos faced the same kind of discrimination as blacks in the early 1940s. They often found themselves segregated, separated by skin color, with the added disadvantage of speaking another language as well. "For coloreds and Mexicans," a sign outside a Texas church read. Good jobs were hard to come by, and many Latinos lived in run-down areas. Without political influence, they found it hard to break the poverty cycle.

Wartime labor shortages made a difference in their lives. The draft drew some Latinos into the armed forces. Others gravitated to the cities in search of better jobs. In 1941, no Chicanos (Mexican Americans) worked in the Los Angeles shipyards; by 1944, 17,000 worked there. Latinos also worked in shipyards and aircraft factories in Seattle, Long Beach, Corpus Christi, and Albuquerque. Some headed for the nation's major war production centers: Detroit, Chicago, Kansas City, and New York.

Urban crowding caused tensions for Latinos similar to those felt by blacks. Some young Chicanos roamed the streets in groups or gangs, often wearing a distinctive costume – the zoot suit – consisting of trousers flared at the knees but tighter at the ankles, a loosely-cut coat reaching to mid-thigh, a long key chain, and a felt hat. It set the wearers apart and frightened white, middle-class Americans who associated it with gang violence. In June 1943, tensions erupted in Los Angeles when sailors sought revenge on Chicanos who had allegedly attacked them as they searched for women. Storming into bars and movie theaters, the sailors seized any Chicanos they could find, tearing the zoot suits off. Military and civilian law enforcement authorities either stood aside or arrested Chicanos without cause. If Latinos had felt vulnerable before, they felt even more insecure now.

The war affected life in the agricultural sector as well. Acute farm labor shortages led American growers to import Mexicans to work in the fields. Initially, owners wanted simply to open the border and hire workers at the lowest possible rate, but they were forced to accede to Mexican demands for contracts guaranteeing basic rights. An agreement in 1942 provided for transportation, food, shelter, and medical care, and led to the entrance of several hundred thousand *braceros* (helping hands) over the next few years.

The program continued after the war. Although labor shortages no longer existed, American growers wanted continued help in picking their crops. They also hoped to use the Mexican laborers to flood the labor market and depress wages. Negotiations between Mexico and the United States culminated in a migratory labor agreement which allowed growers to recruit their own undocumented workers without government involvement and provided few of the guarantees to the *braceros* that had existed during the war.

Conditions were tough for the *braceros*. In times of economic difficulty, troubles worsened. While *braceros* were expected to return to Mexico at the end of their labor contract, many stayed in the United States. Deportations drove them back during downturns, and the periodic search for illegal workers by immigration officials made all Chicanos feel vulnerable. As Rodolfo Acuña has observed in *Occupied America: A History of Chicanos* (2000), the 1940s were not easy years for Latinos.

Native Americans likewise saw the possibility of improving their lives during the war. Though they had long faced discrimination in the United States, and were still denied the right to vote in three states, they willingly served in the armed forces. Indians from tribes with a warrior tradition were especially willing to enlist. A number of them received public acclaim for their performance. Ira Hayes, a Pima from Arizona, was one of three survivors at Mount Suribachi on Iwo Jima, where marines managed to raise the American flag. Some Navajos worked as code talkers, since their language was so rare it could serve as a secret means of transmitting Marine Corps messages by radio and phone.

Indians participated in home front activity as well. Nearly 50,000 worked in war industries around the country. Two thousand Navajos helped construct a large ordnance depot in New Mexico. Others worked in airplane factories on the west coast and in plants in other wartime centers.

In the postwar years, Indians faced the consequences of the same technological developments as most Americans, but often had greater difficulties coping with the changes. As power lines reached reservations, Indians purchased televisions, refrigerators, washing machines, and cars, and the consumer culture inevitably affected traditional patterns. Reservation life lost its cohesiveness. Indians who had gravitated to cities often had trouble adjusting to urban life and encountered hostility from white Americans, much like that experienced by Latinos and blacks.

Meanwhile, they faced changes in the way the American government perceived them as well. Under John Collier of the Bureau of Indian Affairs, there had been a focus on preserving community values and tribal sovereignty. With the end of World War II, attention shifted to promoting assimilation to the larger American culture. As the nation worried about the Cold War and the impact of Communism, there was unprecedented pressure for conformity and consensus, and Indian policy was caught up in this national paranoia. Liberals involved in the civil rights movement and dedicated to the cause of integration came to see Indian reservations as relics of a racist past and promoted assimilation instead. Intertribal conflict and competition increased pressure for such integration. A commission in 1947 recommended the "discontinuance of all specialized Indian activity on the part of the federal government" and supported a policy known as termination, which continued into the next decade.

At about the same time, there was pressure for compensation for violations of treaty provisions in the past. The Indian Claims Commission Act of 1946 reviewed all grievances against the federal government and provided a ten-year period to process all claims. Compensatory payments would be made in money, not land, regardless of the priorities of Native American culture. Today, there is an increasing literature about the efforts of American Indians. In *"We Are Still Here": American Indians in the Twentieth Century* (1998), one of a number of accounts of Indians, Peter Iverson has pointed to the efforts Indians made themselves in their attempt to gain equal treatment.

Women's lives also changed dramatically during World War II. They had long been second-class citizens in the United States, denied access to many jobs and paid less than men in the positions they could find. During the Great Depression, conditions had worsened for them, as they competed with men who were having a hard time supporting their families.

The huge industrial effort opened new jobs to women, but the process took time. Initially, employers questioned whether women had the physical strength to do heavy work, and hoped that shortages of male laborers might not be so severe after all. Then, from late 1942 on, both government and industry waged a courtship campaign to persuade women to work in the factories. The Office of War Information issued messages designed to lure women into plants. One advertisement in Baltimore told women that war work was "a lot more exciting than polishing the family furniture." An advertisement in Seattle declared that "an American homemaker with the strength and ability to run a house and raise a family . . . has the strength and ability to take her place in a vital War industry" (Anderson 1981: 28).

Between 1941 and 1944, the number of working women rose from 14,600,000 to 19,370,000. At the peak of the industrial effort, women made up 36 percent of the civilian work force. At the same time, the demographic composition changed. While most working women in the past had been single and young, now married women began to work and outnumbered single women, and by the war's end, half of all female workers were over 35.

Even more important were the kinds of jobs women now held. Increasingly, they moved out of domestic service and into manufacturing, particularly in war industries. Women worked in airplane plants and shipyards as steelworkers, riveters, and welders. Rosie the Riveter, dramatized in a well-known poster by artist Norman Rockwell, showed a woman dressed in overalls with a riveting gun in her lap. She was strong, determined, and capable – and attractive at the same time.

Men were not always comfortable with the changes they saw. Columnist Max Lerner was concerned that the war was developing a "new Amazon" who would "outdrink, outswear, and outswagger the men." As women joined the military services as WACs (Women's Army Corps) and WAVES (Women Accepted for Volunteer Emergency Service), some soldiers were irate. One Marine Corps officer was said to have exploded, "First they send us dogs. Now it's women."

Women, on the other hand, were delighted with their new jobs. Money made a large difference. Wives of servicemen lost income when their husbands went overseas and jobs both helped make up the difference and eased the loneliness of separation. Evelyn Cook, who left her job as a cook to work in a navy yard, commented, "After all, I've got to keep body and soul together, and I'd rather earn a living this way than to cook over a hot stove." There was also an excitement as Jennifer Bucklin, a bus driver in Seattle noted, in doing "something women have never been allowed to do before" (Anderson 1981: 28).

Working women still faced problems. General Motors fired male supervisors and female employees found "fraternizing" or simply socializing with one another. Many women worried about what to do with their children while they were at work. Even when the government provided some day care facilities, most women preferred to rely on family members or friends. Women also earned substantially less than men doing the same jobs. At the Willow Run plant in Michigan in 1945, for example, women averaged $2,928 per year, compared to $3,363 for men.

With the end of the war, the government propaganda campaign shifted direction. Wartime work for women was temporary, messages proclaimed. *Women of Steel*, an

Office of War information film, quoted Edith Stone, a driver, as saying, "When my husband comes back, I'm going to be busy at home." Jane Stokes, an aircraft industry worker and union official, declared on the radio, "When this war is over – I'll get a manicure, put on the frilliest dress I can find, pour a whole bottle of cologne over my head, and *then*, I'll be *glad* to give up my Union chair in the Eagle Airie Room to some boy who comes marching home deserving it" (Anderson 1981: 59).

The changes in women's lives were immense, as Karen Anderson, in *Wartime Women: Sex Roles, Family Relations, and the Status of Women during World War II* (1981) and Sherna Berger Gluck, in *Rosie the Riveter Revisited: Women, The War, and Social Change* (1987), have observed. Yet for all the shifts, women remained committed to the traditional values of marriage and family as they had before, according to Susan M. Hartman in *The Home Front and Beyond: American Women in the 1940s* (1982).

When the war ended, many working women wanted to continue in their jobs, and some did. In 1940, only 15 percent of American wives were employed. A decade later in 1950, the figure had risen to 21 percent, and married women accounted for half of all working women. Yet the prevailing ideology still highlighted those who stayed at home.

In the first postwar years, there was some debate about the different roles women could play. A 1946 *Fortune* magazine poll captured the discontent some women felt. When asked whether they would prefer to be born again as men or women, 25 percent of the women interviewed said they would prefer to be men. A year later, in 1947, *Life* magazine ran a long photo essay entitled "The American woman's dilemma" that highlighted the problem. Women were caught between the traditional expectation, now reaffirmed at the end of the war, that women stay home and take care of their families, and a desire, based on their past experience, to have a paid job.

Pediatrician Benjamin Spock came down squarely on the side of staying at home. In *Baby and Child Care*, first published in 1946, he advised mothers to remain at home if they wanted to raise stable and secure children. Working outside the home, he suggested, might jeopardize their children's mental and emotional health. Enormously popular, the book helped define the child-rearing patterns of the postwar generation.

By the end of the decade, most doubts had passed. The baby boom, which began when servicemen came home from the war, increased average family size, and made the decision to stay home easier. The flight to the suburbs that changed the shape of American cities gave women more to do. In new homes in housing developments that sprouted up all over the country, they settled into the routines of gardening, redecorating, and transporting children to and from activities and schools. Still, as William H. Chafe observed in *The American Woman: Her Changing Social, Economic, and Political Roles, 1920–1970* (1972), the wartime experience provided a model for the future.

The 1940s in Perspective

The 1940s were turbulent years. Reluctantly, the United States accepted the responsibilities of leadership that accompanied its military and economic might. Once the nation decided to join the struggle to stop Germany, Italy, and Japan, it threw itself wholeheartedly into the effort. Americans came together in the greatest productive enterprise of all time, and in the process put the Great Depression behind them. The national mood improved overnight. Soldiers slogging through tropical terrain in Guadalcanal and thousands of similar spots sang "White Christmas," from the 1942 film *Holiday Inn*, and dreamed of all the things they associated with home. They were ready to shoulder responsibility for stopping aggression and to spread American values around the world.

The experience of war provided the framework for the postwar years. Other nations suffered far more casualties than the United States, but American might was clearly the cause of victory. With a second chance to play a major role in the international order, policy makers were determined to remain involved this time, and they accepted the task of serving as world policeman, particularly when they perceived a different kind of aggression surfacing on the part of the Soviet Union.

The Cold War that dominated the postwar years was rooted in the tensions that sometimes threatened to disrupt the Grand Alliance during the war. The major allied nations – the United States, Great Britain, and the Soviet Union – all had their own needs and priorities and their disagreements sometimes threatened to tear the alliance apart. They managed to stay together as long as was necessary to defeat their Axis foes, but then the friction could no longer be contained. Almost as soon as the war was over, an American commitment to worldwide democracy and free enterprise came into conflict with a Soviet desire for stability and security on its western flank, and the Cold War was the result. That conflict had a powerful impact on everything else that occurred in the 1940s and in the decades that followed. It fostered a nuclear arms race that sometimes threatened to incinerate the world. Funds spent for military defense left correspondingly less money for programs of social reform. Anti-Communist hysteria permeated the fabric of domestic life and created an atmosphere of fear and distrust.

At the same time, the World War II experience affected other parts of American life. Historians have debated the issue of continuity versus change in the years since the war. While acknowledging the enormous changes that took place, John W. Jeffries, in *Wartime America: The World War II Home Front*, has argued that in a variety of different areas "the war largely accelerated or confirmed developments long under way" (1996: 76). Allan M. Winkler, in *Home Front U.S.A.: America during World War II* (2000a), has suggested, on the other hand, that for all the continuities, change was ultimately more important. The war continued the pattern of governmental growth and executive expansion that had begun in the 1930s, and put the nation on a course from which there was no turning back. Political opponents might excise certain programs, but the basic commitment to a welfare state remained. Harry Truman followed in his predecessor's footsteps, as his Fair Deal built upon FDR's New Deal, and by the time Dwight D. Eisenhower assumed the presidency in 1953, these new patterns were a fixture of American life.

So too did wartime actions affect the configurations of social reform. The roots of the civil rights movement that made major gains in the 1950s and 1960s lay in the World War II years. The willingness to take direct action to resist discrimination during the war encouraged similar actions after the war that finally changed deeply-entrenched patterns in the United States. The experience of women working in industrial plants when men went off to fight overseas likewise influenced subsequent social arrangements. Though many women left their jobs and returned home after the war, the role they played in the 1940s served as a model for the women's movement in the decades ahead.

The United States began the 1940s still suffering from the ravages of the depression and reluctant to become overly involved in world affairs. As the decade ended, the nation was strong and secure, more prosperous than ever before, willing to play whatever role was necessary on the world stage.

REFERENCES AND FURTHER READING

Acuña, Rodolfo (2000) *Occupied America: A History of Chicanos*, 4th edn. New York: Harper and Row.

Anderson, Karen (1981) *Wartime Women: Sex Roles, Family Relations, and the Status of Women during World War II*. Westport, Conn.: Greenwood Press.

Bernstein, Barton J. (1970) "American foreign policy and the origins of the Cold War," in Barton J. Bernstein (ed.) *Politics and Policies of the Truman Administration*. Chicago: Quadrangle Books.

—— (1975) "Roosevelt, Truman, and the atomic bomb: 1941–1945: a reinterpretation," *Political Science Quarterly* 90 (Spring), pp. 23–69.

Blum, John Morton (1976) *V Was for Victory: Politics and American Culture During World War II*. New York: Harcourt Brace Jovanovich.

Brinkley, Alan (1995) *The End of Reform: New Deal Liberalism in Recession and War*. New York: Alfred A. Knopf.

Chafe, William H. (1972) *The American Woman: Her Changing Social, Economic, and Political Roles, 1920–1970*. New York: Oxford University Press.

Dalfiume, Richard M. (1968) "The forgotten years of the Negro revolution," *Journal of American History* 55 (June), pp. 90–106.

Daniels, Roger (1993) *Prisoners Without Trial: Japanese Americans in World War II*. New York: Hill and Wang.

Evans, Sara M. (1989) *Born for Liberty: A History of Women in America*. New York: Free Press.

Franklin, John Hope and Moss, Alfred A., Jr. (1994) *From Slavery to Freedom: A History of African Americans*, 7th edn. New York: Alfred A. Knopf.

Gaddis, John Lewis (1982) *Strategies of Containment: A Critical Appraisal of Postwar American National Security Policy*. New York: Oxford University Press.

Gluck, Sherna Berger (1987) *Rosie the Riveter Revisited: Women, The War, and Social Change*. Boston: Twayne Publishers.

Hamby, Alonzo L. (1992) *Liberalism and its Challengers: From F.D.R. to Bush*, 2nd edn. New York: Oxford University Press.

—— (1995) *Man of the People: A Life of Harry S. Truman*. New York: Oxford University Press.

Hartman, Susan M. (1982) *The Home Front and Beyond: American Women in the 1940s*. Boston: Twayne Publishers.

Hersey, John (1970) *Into the Valley: A Skirmish of the Marines*. New York: Alfred A. Knopf.

Hogan, Michael J. (1998) *A Cross of Iron: Harry S. Truman and the Origins of the National Security State, 1945–1954*. New York: Cambridge University Press.

Iverson, Peter (1998) *"We Are Still Here": American Indians in the Twentieth Century*. Wheeling, Ill.: Harlan Davidson.

Jeffries, John W. (1996) *Wartime America: The World War II Home Front*. Chicago: Ivan R. Dee.

Kennan, George (1947) X, "The sources of Soviet conduct," *Foreign Affairs* 25 (July), pp. 566–82.

Kluger, Richard (1976) *Simple Justice: The History of* Brown *v.* Board of Education *and Black America's Struggle for Equality.* New York: Alfred A. Knopf.

LaFeber, Walter (1997) *America, Russia, and the Cold War, 1945–1996,* 8th edn. New York: McGraw Hill.

Leffler, Melvin P. (1992) *A Preponderance of Power: National Security, the Truman Administration, and the Cold War.* Stanford, Calif.: Stanford University Press.

Leuchtenburg, William E. (1993) *In the Shadow of FDR: From Harry Truman to Bill Clinton.* Ithaca, NY: Cornell University Press.

McCullough, David (1992) *Truman.* New York: Simon and Schuster.

Olson, James S. and Wilson, Raymond (1984) *Native Americans in the Twentieth Century.* Urbana and Chicago: University of Illinois Press.

Polenberg, Richard (1992) "The good war? A reappraisal of how World War II affected American society," *The Virginia Magazine of History and Biography* 100 (July), pp. 295–322.

Schlesinger, Arthur M., Jr. (1967) "Origins of the Cold War," *Foreign Affairs* 46 (October), pp. 22–52.

Sherwin, Martin J. (1975) *A World Destroyed: The Atomic Bomb and the Grand Alliance.* New York: Alfred A. Knopf.

Terkel, Studs (1984) *"The Good War": An Oral History of World War Two.* New York: Pantheon Books.

Truman, Harry S. (1955) *Memoirs: Year of Decisions.* Garden City, NY: Doubleday.

Tygiel, Jules (1983) *Baseball's Great Experiment: Jackie Robinson and his Legacy.* New York: Oxford University Press.

Walker, J. Samuel (1997) *Prompt and Utter Destruction: Truman and the Use of Atomic Bombs against Japan.* Chapel Hill: University of North Carolina Press.

Weinberg, Gerhard L. (1994) *A World at Arms: A Global History of World War II.* New York: Cambridge University Press.

Winkler, Allan M. (1993) *Life Under a Cloud: American Anxiety about the Atom.* New York: Oxford University Press.

—— (2000a) *Home Front, U.S.A.: America during World War II,* 2nd edn. Arlington Heights, Ill.: Harlan Davidson.

—— (2000b) *The Cold War: A History in Documents.* New York: Oxford University Press.

Wohlstetter, Roberta (1962) *Pearl Harbor: Warning and Decision.* Stanford, Calif.: Stanford University Press.

Wynn, Neil A. (1976) *The Afro-American and the Second World War.* New York: Holmes and Meier.

CHAPTER FIVE

1950–1960

Richard M. Fried

Two certainties about the 1950s were detected at the time and persist today: the United States had become a nation both powerful and rich. Late in the decade, social critics questioned whether the wealth was either as widely distributed or as beneficent as its champions insisted; and later, with Vietnam, global power came to seem less of a godsend than was once imagined. We sense "the fifties" as a unique era that we think we know and often recall fondly. In fact the decade was more complex than the era we may wish to remember or imagine, a fidgety mix of anxiety and relaxation, sloth and achievement, complacency and self-criticism. Nostalgists recall an age of domestic tranquility – a 1970s television sitcom about the fifties was entitled *Happy Days* – but the label overreaches for a decade that opened with the ominous shadow of Senator Joe McCarthy and closed on such scenes as bus boycotts and sit-ins. Still, there was more than a grain of truth to the sentimental perspective.

Even dating the period presents a puzzle. Decades are simple enough, but perhaps we need to think in terms of a "long 1950s," starting with war's end in 1945, or soon after, when Cold War patterns congealed at home and abroad. It is also sometimes argued that President John F. Kennedy's "thousand days" resembled more the fifties than the sixties, so the decade could be extended to 1963, or perhaps even to 1965, when the "good" morphed into the "bad" sixties. Since the Korean War exacted an austerity that blends badly with our sense of the gaudy indulgence of the 1950s, and since 1950s styles extended into the following decade, some historians have even designated the "real" fifties as lasting from 1954 until 1964. Hence the term "the fifties" needs loose tailoring.

Chroniclers at the time were quick to notice that the nation had entered a new stage. They described the mid-century as marking a "big change" or a "great leap." The best contemporaneous work remains Eric F. Goldman's *The Crucial Decade*, published in 1956 and revised in 1961 as *The Crucial Decade – and After: America, 1945–1960*. Writing barely after the events, Goldman relied on contemporary journalism, plus interviews and feedback from the key participants (some even corrected his drafts). He weaves a narrative embracing both domestic and foreign policy, social as well as political history. His focus was shared by other early surveys of the postwar era in fixing on the nation's rise to maturity as a world power in the Cold War context.

Social history was subordinate to political history; Goldman depicts the vagaries of a public mood which underlay – sometimes resisting but generally supporting – the global initiatives of the administrations of Harry S. Truman and Dwight D. Eisenhower. *The Crucial Decade* portrays a citizenry that was often anxious about its vexing new responsibilities, but which generally rose to the challenge that the Cold War represented. So did American statesmen, whose policies depended on the support of "the faceless millions who proceeded to show a thousand faces ranging from utter inanity to utter good sense" (Goldman 1961: vii). Limning themes which endure in the literature to this day, Goldman's book remains immensely readable.

Historian William L. O'Neill's *American High* (1986) exemplifies the persistence of these early interpretive patterns. Here too the reader finds high achievement and low life. Citizens and leaders worked through a number of postwar tests: a housing shortage, the Soviet menace, the need to sustain prosperity, and the national shame of racial discrimination. O'Neill gives kudos to President Truman for meeting his chief challenge – from Moscow – with the measured policies of "containment." But *American High* rues Truman's election in his own right in 1948, since that unexpected victory blocked the more compelling political dynamic of the era. It was time for a change. A Republican victory in 1948 might have forestalled the worst of McCarthyism by obviating the partisan bitterness generated by defeat, which prompted so much support for McCarthy. O'Neill also finds the record of Eisenhower in office more than satisfactory, however laggard he was in improving civil rights for African Americans. The warmest praise in the book is saved for the "average" American, defined as a World War II veteran eager to shuck his uniform, to get educated via the GI Bill, to take a job, to occupy the mushrooming suburbs, to create the "baby boom," and then to get on with the business of life with few illusions, serious grievances, or utopian desires.

This postwar generation did get on with it and seemed, in the language of the day, rather "well-adjusted." In the recent remembrances of the generation that fought World War II, both in the trenches and on the home front, others have struck similar chords. A best-selling example is Tom Brokaw's *The Greatest Generation* (1998), portraying the cohort that came to maturity during the Great Depression and the global struggle against fascism. Perhaps that generation's appeal to us lies in our sense that they did their job, got on with life without much of what critics have variously described as a "culture of complaint" or emphasis on "rights-based" expectations, baggage with which their offspring were more often weighted down.

Even affectionate treatments of the period did not exempt it from criticism of such shortcomings as a casual tolerance of McCarthyism and of racial inequality. Neither O'Neill nor Goldman depicted the journey as untroubled, but both historians generally traced a march of progress. Other authors have found far less to praise in the era. Many of the more disparaging accounts reflect the radical judgments that entered the historical debate during the 1960s.

For example, Marty Jezer adopts an unambiguously critical leftist stance in *The Dark Ages* (1982). With the advent of World War II and the exhaustion of the New Deal, "corporate liberal" business interests became dominant, excluding and injuring virtually all others. This corporate elite's imperial reach bears responsibility for the Cold War, a costly, hazardous arms race, and a politics of repression. (Several of the targets of the congressional anti-Communists were treated as martyrs in this and similar works. But their haloes were knocked askew in more recent works dealing with "Venona," the top-secret project that de-crypted Soviet cable traffic to Moscow. Some of those named before congressional committees proved to be enmeshed in Soviet enterprises after all.) In the political economy of the Cold War, the undeserving fattened, while the deserving received thin gruel. Racism and discrimination abounded. But within the confining cloak of repression, a marginalized culture of dissent found hidden space from which it blossomed forth in the 1960s. The 1950s did indeed produce much bleakness for Jezer to present. While he offers an antidote to overly celebratory accounts, his version is more one-sided than most of those interpretations that he sought to refute.

A more nuanced but still dyspeptic view of the period emerges in George Lipsitz's *A Rainbow at Midnight* (1994), whose chief virtue is a detailed portrait of the lives of workers as they entered the 1950s. He enthusiastically depicts a working-class militancy born in the struggles of the 1930s and still vibrant, despite exertions by management, government, and labor union bureaucrats to tame it. Workers came out of the war schooled in shop-floor militancy and bent on shaping a postwar world to their liking. This militancy is tracked through a series of now-forgotten but dramatic general strikes in 1946–7 in various localities. The pugnacity of labor crested and receded, checked by the efforts of the corporate establishment and its allies in government. While not every industrial sector felt threatened by the post-New Deal labor settlement, early in the postwar era a powerful segment of corporate America was determined to reverse labor's gains and to reassert control over both shop floor and bottom line. These businessmen mobilized politically to ensure passage of the 1947 Taft–Hartley Act and to promote anti-Communist policies at home and abroad.

As the fifties dawned, in Lipsitz's telling, the radical ethos of the 1930s ebbed; and shop-floor militancy dwindled. Laboring men and women faced a more disciplined workplace, a hostile political environment, and a diminished field for oppositional politics or culture. Those left unfulfilled by the cultural and social status quo managed to create alternative spaces for self-expression. *A Rainbow at Midnight* treats insightfully such phenomena as roller derby, car customizing, and the eclectic origins of rock 'n' roll. This postwar genre emerged from a rich stew of interacting musical sources: rhythm and blues, country and western, zydeco, even Mexican and Caribbean music. Members of the working class thus compensated in their leisure pursuits for the autonomy lost on the job, for the absence of the "rainbow at midnight" that they had once anticipated.

Douglas Miller and Marion Nowak provide another jaundiced view of the age, by unmasking many of the sanctities and pomposities of the 1950s. One piety they debunk is piety: the authors take aim at the heavy religiosity of the decade. A "float to God," for instance, was entered in Eisenhower's 1953 inaugural parade. The float was said to resemble "an oversized model of a deformed molar left over from the dental exhibit" (quoted in Miller and Nowak 1977: 89). *The Fifties: The Way We Really Were* punctures the vaunted prosperity of the decade by emphasizing its uneven distribution and the growing concentration of wealth and income. Celebrants of the economic system boasted of how widely stock ownership had spread under "people's capitalism." But the authors point out that less than 1 percent of all families owned over four-fifths of all stocks. Society was not as classless as champions of affluence claimed.

But prosperity cannot be dismissed as merely a figment of propagandists, which is why it is useful to consult Harold G. Vatter's fact-laden *The US Economy in the 1950s* (1963). To be sure, three recessions occurred during the Eisenhower administration, of which Vatter discusses two in detail. Growth showed signs of deceleration. But if the economy was hardly comet-like, neither was it comatose. By 1960 per capita consumption had risen almost 50 percent since 1945. With government spending running about 20 percent of Gross National Product, the mixed economy was here to stay. Toward the end of the decade, the public made one of its periodic rediscoveries of the persistence of poverty. The Harvard economist John Kenneth Galbraith located pockets of poverty; but his popular 1958 book, *The Affluent Society*, affixed a more widely accepted label upon the era. While Vatter presents a sense of the sheer volume of the economy of the 1950s, Herman Miller, a scholar at the US Bureau of the Census, conveys a clearer sense of its shape. Compared to other nations, the distribution of wealth in America was relatively even. Not all reports from the economic front were cheering, but after World War II poverty was declining (Miller 1971).

The economy of the 1950s battened on altered demographics. The celebrated "baby boom" was inaugurated by the end of World War II and lasted through 1964. After the thin population harvest of the Depression, kids became the national bumper crop. Families were nuclear but large. The proportion of couples having a third or fourth child soared; the dramatic growth was registered among the well-to-do, not the poor. The impact of the new birth pattern rippled across the economy. Products came in "family size," and children became a vast market unto themselves. When Walt Disney telecast the heroics of Davy Crockett, the explosion of coonskin caps and similar regalia became the first of several marketing phenomena for junior consumers; and the price of raccoon pelts increased 3200 percent. Teenagers came to enjoy unparalleled purchasing power, and the popular culture soon reflected their disposable income. The baby-boomer age cohort, 76-million strong, caused a bulge in the nation's schools in the 1950s, and made education a more pressing issue than in earlier periods. They flooded college campuses in the 1960s and became an oversized participant in every subsequent life stage to the present. This generation learned to anticipate no less than the best, buoyed by its numbers to dictate to fellow citizens what Landon Y. Jones in his book of that title (1980) termed "great expectations."

The suburbs absorbed most of this population surge, becoming the zone of a dramatic cultural transformation and the scene of much of the prosperity of the 1950s. The construction drought during the Great Depression led to a postwar housing crisis. Married veterans often shoe-horned in with parents, or started families in relocated war-surplus Quonset huts. A solution would come – at the expense of open lands on the urban peripheries, where vast housing tracts replaced farms. The first Levittown was a swarm of look-alike single-family houses, which were made affordable by adopting assembly-line construction methods in an industry previously reliant on archaic techniques. This particular suburb took shape on a part of Long Island where potatoes had sprouted a year before. With the swelling of suburbia, the population and political clout of the central cities shrank; and that shift had dire consequences for the urban-anchored New Deal political coalition.

The federal government accelerated the suburban boom. The lending policies of the Federal Housing Administration and later the Veterans Administration favored single-family and suburban homes and encouraged, as did suburban governments and realtors, a policy of white-only development. An urban/suburban split between black and white populations developed. The effect was to keep the races segregated, even as other federal policies ostensibly shifted in the opposite direction. Federal transportation policy, notably the 1956 Federal Highway Act, quickened suburbanization, and favored auto over rail transit, the internal combustion engine over alternatives, and individual over mass commuting modes. An insightful, wide-ranging treatment of suburbanization and related processes, hardly confined to the postwar era, is provided by Kenneth T. Jackson's *Crabgrass Frontier* (1985).

Many of these trends received coruscating appraisals at the time. John Keats wrote such mocking critiques as *The Crack in the Picture Window* (1957) and *The Insolent Chariots* (1958); and Galbraith found fault with how social and economic choices slighted the public in favor of the private weal, to the long-term disadvantage of both. Among the indices were increasing pollution and traffic congestion. Suburbs, with their "little boxes on the hillside," endured much criticism. They were the sites of conformity and conventionality against which insurgents of the 1960s would revolt. However, there is evidence that those who trekked to the suburbs viewed their decision as rational and satisfying. In *The Levittowners* (1967), sociologist Herbert J. Gans finds the denunciations excessive. Homeowners living in the New Jersey Levittown that he studies lacked the sense of alienation, boredom, and stifling conformity from which they were supposed to be suffering.

Cities fared badly during the 1950s. Thomas J. Sugrue's *The Origins of the Urban Crisis* (1996) is an excellent case study which traces the dramatic impact of various trends of that decade upon an archetypal urban center and its black residents in particular. Sugrue limns Detroit's transition from the Arsenal of Democracy during World War II to a paradigm of all the problems of what came to be called the Rustbelt. During the period of African-American migration to Detroit, housing stock remained segregated; and white neighborhoods, aided by their political patrons, defended their turf, sometimes with violence. The hiring process adopted by the region's vast factories (some of which were already relocating to the Sunbelt) was also racially differentiated. Even in the seemingly prosperous 1950s, as deindustrialization gained momentum and derelict factory buildings and stores began to clot the landscape, one in five blacks in Detroit was jobless; and a subculture devoid of hope began to take over.

The 1950s gave voice to many critiques of American society, dissecting its mental as well as physical disposition. Americans were frequently chided as timid conformists, non-rockers of the boat, privatists, and members of a "silent generation." Yet for an age allegedly so complacent and cowed, the volume and profundity of such criticism are surprising.

Americans claimed to be an unideological folk. Sociologist Daniel Bell, a leading social analyst of the day, heralded "the end of ideology." Other observers suggested – some admiringly, others critically – that Americans had made an ideology out of not having one. A major tendency among historians was to identify "consensus" rather than "conflict" as the quintessential element of the national experience. In fact postwar liberals did grow more accepting of business than they had been in the 1930s, and conservatives became somewhat reconciled to the New Deal welfare state. Both segments of the spectrum proposed to solve social problems through economic growth. Or, alternatively, it was argued that historically most Americans shared a very loose and commodious set of doctrines, generally "liberal" (in the nineteenth-century British sense), entailing a commitment to individual liberty, property, and popular sovereignty. A topnotch analysis of both the ruling ideological tendencies of the period and the extensive and pointed social criticisms launched in the 1950s is Richard H. Pells's *The Liberal Mind in a Conservative Age* (1985).

Not everyone applauded the consensus, whether it was deemed liberal or conservative. A valuable study of the various conservative objections to the status quo is George H. Nash's *The Conservative Intellectual Movement in America: Since 1945* (1976). Those on the right were an assorted group whose members emphasized libertarianism, traditionalism, and anti-Communism in varying degrees. So conservatives sometimes found it hard to establish a consensus even among themselves. By contrast Maurice Isserman's *If I Had a Hammer* (1987) concedes that the age was marked by conservative consolidation, but highlights the activities of leftists who resisted the dominant political tendencies. As the Old Left of the 1930s withered, survivors and newcomers sought to forge a new one, piecing together strategies of Gandhi, remnants of Marxist thought, and pacifism, all of which might be enlisted to rectify social injustice. Isserman examines the frequently intersecting operations of obscure leftist journals, anti-Stalinist radical organizations, radical pacifist grouplets struggling against the Cold War doctrines of nuclear warfare, civil rights activists, and young campus-based seekers after progressive change. In such nooks and crannies survived the intellectual yeast that would grow into the uprisings of the 1960s.

In the practice of politics, the fifties often get low marks. Beginning with the feverish "McCarthy era" and then veering into a phase of stolid self-satisfaction, the decade exhibited a political tone that is hard to admire. McCarthy and the politics of anti-Communism have certainly not lacked for critics. Social scientists concerned with the sociological and psychological roots of the Senator's support were the first to make a comprehensive effort to locate him and his followers in a social context. These explorative essays were collected in 1955 in *The New American Right*, which Daniel Bell edited. Political scientists soon shifted the debate, identifying McCarthy's power as anchored less in widespread public anxieties than in institutions, notably the victory-starved, oft-defeated Republican Party and the US Senate. Berkeley's Michael Rogin, among others, makes the case that McCarthy's strength was rooted in traditional Republican conservatism (1967). In *The Politics of Fear* (1970), historian Robert K. Griffith, Jr. also stresses the extent to which privileges, immunities, and folkways peculiar to the Senate fixed McCarthy at the center of public life for the first five years of the decade.

New Left historians took a third focus, holding the Truman administration, the Democrats and liberals culpable for extremism, because they had established so many of the premises on which McCarthy and his allies would operate. The most noteworthy exponent of this view is Athan Theoharis, who cites Truman's messianic Cold War rhetoric and the promulgation of the loyalty program in 1947 (1971). Such initiatives sanctioned the notion of guilt by association which McCarthy would merely take to greater extremes. Theoharis later shifted his focus from Truman to J. Edgar Hoover, whose Federal Bureau of Investigation (FBI), relicensed in the mid-1930s to guard against subversion, began devoting much of its energy to harassing the Communists (and others on the left). Hoover's FBI became the institutional linchpin of a campaign that simultaneously operated on both covert and highly public levels to demonize and marginalize domestic Communists. Hoover is the subject of many biographical portrayals. Richard Gid Powers ably and enthusiastically fixes the FBI director's position in the popular culture, as well as in the political firmament, in *Secrecy and Power: The Life of J. Edgar Hoover* (1987).

Understanding "McCarthyism" has required a definition of the phenomenon that could transcend the Wisconsin Senator's antics to include other forms of what could be termed excessive anti-Communism. In *Nightmare in Red* (1990) Richard M. Fried offers a concise treatment of US anti-Communism in its broadest dimensions, tracing mid-century anti-Communism from its emergence in the late 1930s in the context of the menace of various international "isms" through its gradual demise in the 1950s. Ellen Schrecker offers greater detail in *Many Are the Crimes* (1998), while David Caute presents a vast inventory of McCarthyism's casualties in *The Great Fear* (1978). Two fine biographies of McCarthy, by Thomas C. Reeves (1982) and David M. Oshinsky (1983), are also available. Both are painstakingly researched. The chief interpretive difference lies in Reeves's view that McCarthy, early in his anti-Communist career, left behind his opportunism for the mindset of a true believer, a transformation of which Oshinsky is less certain.

Although Harry S. Truman and Dwight D. Eisenhower both bore responsibility for the buildup of McCarthy and the broader "ism" to which he lent his name, each President has had his defenders, who found other grounds for praise. At the end of Truman's administration, the Korean War dragged on, scandals nagged, and the political sourness that McCarthy epitomized worsened. The result was to put Truman's popularity at a low ebb. However, he eventually rebounded. He has been ranked among the "near great" in polls of students of the presidency, propelled chiefly by acceptance of such scholars and the general public of the premises of the Cold War consensus that Truman did so much to build. (When later that consensus dissipated, so did Truman's reputation among historians, but never among the general public.) Truman entered the popular culture as "Give 'em Hell, Harry," a straight-talking, unvarnished everyman, "the square root of America," in one pundit's phrase. The 1970s rock group "Chicago" even immortalized him in song. It is as a homespun folk hero that his memory endures.

David McCullough's eloquent biography takes a less smitten view, yet his *Truman* (1992) still resembles the plain-speaking politician of legend. Historian Alonzo Hamby provides a more nuanced, more detailed and subtler portrait (1995). It more than gives Truman his due, while elucidating the conflicts and anxieties that underlay his breezy, sometimes brusque exterior. Hamby effectively places Truman in his time and place as both heir to and executor of Franklin D. Roosevelt's political coalition and as director of postwar interventionist foreign policies. More critical is William E. Pemberton's brief biography (1989), which encapsulates much anti-Truman revisionist scholarship. While more measured than the treatments of Truman produced amid the rancor of the Vietnam War era, Pemberton's book blames Truman for the rise of the "national security state," which entailed globalist foreign commitments, a burdensome defense establishment, and the repressive domestic politics accompanying these choices.

Through the 1950s President Eisenhower maintained a sturdy personal popularity. But the end-of-decade political discourse that put a premium on vigor, motion, and catching-up-with-the-Soviets ascribed a certain tired complacency to his administration. John F. Kennedy promised an antidote for such fatigue. After New Frontier elan impelled the US into the war in Vietnam, and as social concord unraveled on the streets at home, the Eisenhower years suddenly began to glow more alluringly to one-time critics. Ike's fine sense of the balance between means and ends of global power, in the context of the nation's overreach in the 1960s, impressed many observers. If he promised less than his successors, neither did he disappoint the public so much. Soon "Eisenhower revisionism" was refurbishing his political reputation.

Political scientist Fred I. Greenstein offered one of the more striking revisions of Eisenhower's record; imagined vices became political talents. If he seemed not to be in command, this was deceptive; he was letting others tiptoe through political minefields ahead of him. If he seemed to lack ready answers for questions, perhaps this reflected a tactical sense that avoiding or delaying commitment was shrewder politics. Far from being a bumbling, grandfatherly type, Eisenhower was a Machiavellian manager who exercised "hidden-hand leadership," which enabled him to outmaneuver such foes as McCarthy, while minimizing the risks to the President himself (1982). Though placing less stress on his deviousness, historian Stephen E. Ambrose finds much to praise in Eisenhower's stewardship (1984). The record was not without flaws: McCarthy was left to run amok for too long; Ike failed to reshape the Republican Party after his design; the Cold War festered despite his desire for détente; he dragged his feet on civil rights. Ambrose nevertheless gives Ike high marks.

Such judgments of Eisenhower's leadership as these leave no mystery about his two smashing electoral triumphs. What is somewhat puzzling is the extent to which the Ike age had come, by its end, to be seen as something of an embarrassment. The Democrats could derive mileage from charges that the US had become a "second-class power," lagging behind the Soviet Union and needing a spurt of energy. A sense of the political dynamic existing during the campaign in 1960 – when, after all, Kennedy beat Ike's heir, Vice President Richard M. Nixon, by only the narrowest of margins – can be glimpsed in Theodore H. White's *The Making of the President 1960* (1961), the first of a series of election-year studies by White and the classic of that genre.

Regardless of who was president, the nation maintained a Cold War footing. A shrewd, nuanced assessment of the militarization of society and what it meant to the polity, the economy, and the culture is Michael S. Sherry's *In the Shadow of War* (1995). Its analysis begins in the 1930s and ends in the 1990s. "A 'cold war' mentality, constructed out of the experience of depression and world war, preceded the Cold War itself," the author argues (p. 88). Militarization colored every facet of American life, although Sherry is careful to note the limits of such influence. General Eisenhower was, paradoxically, more aware of the dire impact of militarization upon the quality of life and the strength of the economy than any other Cold War leader, and spoke eloquently of the harm that the arms race and the garrison state caused. His "farewell address" warned against the "unwarranted influence" of the "military-industrial complex" (quoted in Sherry 1995: 234). Despite Eisenhower's vigilance, militarization proved to be relentless – even during his own administration.

The largest unmet 1950s agenda item was civil rights. Though Eisenhower's own appointee, Chief Justice Earl Warren, wrote the unanimous *Brown* v. *Board of Educa-*

tion decision ruling segregated schools unconstitutional, the President was no fan of the decision; nor was he a civil rights enthusiast. Often Cold War anti-Communism gave foes of racial egalitarianism a potent weapon against seekers of change, but the need to win friends in the Third World also handed some leverage to proponents of civil rights. In the contest for public opinion around the world, the global exposure of such glaring disfigurements as lynchings, the daily operation of discrimination, and the indignities suffered by foreign diplomats of color in the South put pressure on the national government for amelioration. This dynamic had limits: the conservatism of which the nation's intense anti-Communism was an indication precluded a national discussion of the race issue that would bring in questions of class (Dudziak 2000).

Recent studies of the civil rights movement suggest the oversimplicity of assuming that the 1950s were no more than a High Middle Ages awaiting a 1960s Renaissance. Nor was the white South as homogeneous and uniformly resistant to change as convention supposes. Thus a dappled picture emerges in Pete Daniel's *Lost Revolutions* (2000), an analysis of the region during this decade. Technology took a heavy toll in altering southern agriculture, which had proven more resistant to change there than elsewhere. Postwar economic changes drove southern agricultural workers, largely black, off the land to cities in the region and elsewhere. Daniel cautions against acceptance of a static picture of separate black and white realms in the South. Despite the elaborate structure of segregation in law and custom, there were spaces in between, where the lines were blurred. Rock 'n' roll music was one instance; pioneers such as Elvis Presley melded elements of white and black musical traditions. The first volume of Peter Guralnick's biography (1994) delineates Elvis's debts – which he himself acknowledged – to aspects of black music, and specified the ways in which Presley and his sponsors managed to elide racial boundaries.

Yet to exaggerate the fading of racial lines would be to ignore the explosive resistance that the coming of the civil rights movement met. In 1955 Emmett Till, a 14-year-old black Chicagoan visiting his grandparents in Mississippi, was tortured and murdered for transgressing racial protocol in his approach to a white woman at a country crossroads store. This was a horrifying sample of the barbarism of Deep South race relations. *A Death in the Delta* (1988), Stephen J. Whitfield's review of the case, is most revealing. A further exploration of the ambience of rural Mississippi is John Dittmer's fine study of the development of the civil rights movement (1994). It is hard to know which is more remarkable: the benighted state of race relations in the Magnolia State in the 1950s, or the presence of what Dittmer calls "local people." These heroic African Americans, with deep roots in the state, fought the status quo well before the "outside agitators" spearheading the national struggle entered the scene.

Still, that movement did not simply burst upon the stage with the next decade. Much of the institutional infrastructure of the modern civil rights movement, from the NAACP to the profusion of highly organized black churches, was in place (Morris 1984). Moreover, studies of the civil rights movement in various localities illustrate how groundwork had been laid before the official discovery of the national civil rights movement and the media anointment of national leaders. William H. Chafe, for Greensboro, North Carolina (1980), and Robert J. Norrell for Tuskegee, Alabama (1985), have written two of a growing shelf of studies of the emergence of civil rights activism at the community level. A magisterial study of the early stages of the modern civil rights movement is Taylor Branch's *Parting the Waters* (1988).

With an eye to the upsurge of feminism in the 1960s, historians have taken a growing interest in the impact of the Cold War, prosperity, and suburbanization upon the status and consciousness of women. Betty Friedan's classic, *The Feminine Mystique* (1963), was a milestone in the rebirth of feminism and set the early interpretive pattern. She diagnoses the suburban housewife as suffering from "the problem that has no name," replicating day after day the same mindless tasks, steadily losing her sense of personhood. Friedan describes a sort of inchoate postwar crusade by magazine editors, academics, and the therapeutic professions to exalt domesticity and to devalue autonomous achievement by women in any other sphere.

Historians of the experience of women have taken up Friedan's interpretation. Elaine Tyler May's *Homeward Bound* (1988) ingeniously traces linkages between the broader outlines of Cold War policy and its domestic lineaments and the system of gender relations imposed on marital expectations and home life. She suggests that a domestic sexual "containment" – a growing valorization of sex, but confined to the traditional home – was a counterpart to containment in foreign policy. May found evidence that women who were traditional homemakers did manifest something of the unhappiness that Friedan attributed to them.

But such views may be bleaker than was reality. It is true that the political culture put a premium on feminine domesticity. One women's college president boasted ardently that his school had the largest ballroom in the state; another urged that women were better served if taught paella recipes rather than philosophical disputation. Yet many women did not float with this current, according to essays in Joanne Meyerowitz's *Not June Cleaver* (1994), which is named after the highly domestic materfamilias of the 1950s sitcom, *Leave it to Beaver*. Women operated as trade union militants, participated in early stirrings of the modern civil rights movement, and were activists in the peace movement (notably in protesting against the annual national civil defense drills of the Eisenhower years). Moreover, despite the image of women immured in the ranch house, many of them lived at least parts of their lives outside that cloister. The number of female workers climbed steadily in these years. That was especially true of married women, 30 percent of whom worked outside the home by 1960. Such rates may not be equated with an upsurge of feminism, but neither do they suggest placid domesticity.

The Cold War consensus was indeed a "guy thing"; after all, the diplomatist George Kennan formulated "containment" as a way to fend off Soviet "penetration." Yet men's roles, too, were fraught with tension in this decade. Such oft-remarked trends as the shift from "inner-directed" to "other-directed" behavior, the entombment of the "organization man" in "conformity," and an ever-more bureaucratic way of life levied a spiritual and physical cost. The role of the dutifully married, uncomplaining breadwinner imposed many contradictions, constraints, and even hardships. Men succumbed to growing and much-decried health hazards, including frequent heart attacks. Hugh Hefner's *Playboy* and the "Playboy ethic" that he preached suggested that, in a de-masculinizing world, men had a need to compensate. The revolt of the Beats also raised questions about the male niche. The more plastic gender roles evident by the 1970s got a bit of a head start in the 1950s (Ehrenreich 1983).

Other historians have found in these years seeds of trends which flowered in the next decade. Tie-dyed T-shirts and long hair would have to wait; this was the decade of the button-down collar and the crew-cut. But chroniclers of fashion trends in the 1950s noted that sport shirts began to outsell business wear; and males began to desert plain white for colored shirts, growing gaudier and less formal. Jackie Kennedy is remembered for bringing high fashion and elegance to the White House; but her predecessor, Ike's Mamie, was also highly fashion-conscious. She wore Paris styles, was tracked by fashion reporters, and even had a shade of lipstick – "Mamie pink" – named for her. Historian Karal Ann Marling has described these and other marks of the vivid, consumer-directed visuality of the 1950s in her entertaining *As Seen on TV* (1994), which frolics past such phenomena as the opening of Disneyland and the fads of painting by numbers and TV dinners. Marling stresses, as do so many commentators on consumerism, the emblematic moment of Richard Nixon's finger-jabbing "kitchen debate" with Nikita Khrushchev in Moscow's Sokolniki Park in 1959.

One can dismiss consumerism as a device to promote "false consciousness," to lull toilers who ought to be more restive. But in conjunction with other liberating forces running loose in the culture, it worked against the grain of the more disciplined civic approach called for by many of the nation's leaders during the Cold War. In *Deliberate Speed*, W. T. Lhamon, Jr., seeks a partial explanation of the subsequent cultural acceleration by linking music (bebop, rhythm and blues, the emergence of rock with such artists as Little Richard and Chuck Berry), fiction (Ralph Ellison, Flannery O'Connor, Vladimir Nabokov), and painting with consumer technology (television, the transistor radio, the long-playing record) and with the changing tempo in civil rights. ("Deliberate speed" was the pace of desegregation ordered in the second Supreme Court decision of *Brown* v. *Board of Education*.) Lhamon concludes that "the goals of the fifties are the givens of the present" (1990: 251).

Thomas Hine's *Populuxe* (1986) offers a more accessible tour of many of the same marvels, with emphasis on the material culture. Its manifestations – the consumer products, their design and the pervasive culture of plenty – were often gaudy. Barbie (b. 1959) and Ken and their wardrobes and other accessories were kid-sized symbols of the consumerism of the decade. Cars were sculpted to resemble rockets, beginning with the 1955 Chevrolet. Bermuda Pink refrigerators, TV dinners, the aerodynamic potato chip and its mushy consort chip dip (with the appropriate dishware), Tupperware, the ranch house, the sheath dress – these new things were flashily designed and not exorbitantly priced. Hine's book does not ignore harsher appraisals. If the decade had its repressive features, the *Populuxe* era is conveniently begun in 1954: the year of McCarthy's fall, the *Brown* decision, and the coming of rock 'n' roll. Suburban arrangements did result in waste, overly dispersed and segmented living, and some failed architectural ideas. (The abandoned "living garage" would have mingled furniture for daily living – tables and chairs – with the automobile, which was to become an *objet d'art*, as its focal point.) But Hine rejects some of the standard objections, claiming that suburbia was more tolerant and less conformist and that its houses were more admirable than critics had asserted.

Not all students of the decade have agreed that accelerating cultural flux and widening choice were unmixed blessings, or were even an option. Alan Ehrenhalt's *The Lost City* (1995) portrays the fifties as an age of limited choice. Your cereal was cornflakes; television was black-and-white; ballplayers generally stayed with one baseball team; life was structured and constraining. Freedom and choice would have to await the 1960s. But Ehrenhalt's account of the texture of life in three Chicago communities

– the white ethnic parish of St. Nicholas of Tolentine, the South Side Black Belt, and suburban Elmhurst – shows that with progress toward choice and change came losses too, especially the sense of community and rootedness that residents once took for granted. Thus such depictions, which have examined the social nexus of the decade, have replicated the splits in interpretation noted in more political studies.

Vince Lombardi, the great coach of the Green Bay Packers, grew up in the socially constricted setting that was to unravel after the 1950s. He wonderfully epitomized an older America, which took pride in duty, discipline, hard work, and loyalty. Lombardi was not reactionary (not that Packer fans would have minded); the team dismantled racial barriers, for example, more readily than did the host society. Although the Packers' glory days were in the 1960s, when professional sports became an all-consuming national addiction, Lombardi arrived in Green Bay in 1959; and to most worshipers his Packers stood for the 1950s. That Green Bay, Wisconsin, could become "Titletown" in an urban/suburban age hinted at a successful rear-guard action. By the late 1960s Lombardi had become very much a public figure. He inveighed against the altered culture – the decline of discipline, patriotism, and other vintage virtues – and became an icon of the political as well as sporting world. In 1968 both parties toyed with putting him on their tickets (Maraniss 1999).

That smallish Green Bay could become so celebrated a site owed much to the role of the media, especially television, in producing a national culture. The youth, adolescence, and maturity of television all occurred in the 1950s. Sets flew off the shelves then; so intense and vast was the consumer demand early in the decade that televisions were sold at gas stations and dry cleaners. By the late 1930s, radio had clamored so insistently for a place in the household that pollsters learned that the apparatus had become more important than indoor plumbing. In the 1950s television had similarly muscled its way into the home, 90 percent of which had at least one by the end of the decade.

An excellent overall treatment of the arrival of television within the larger constellation of mass media is James L. Baughman's *The Republic of Mass Culture* (1997). Television posed a sharp challenge to other means of communication: radio, movies, newspapers, and magazines, which tried to counter the threat but with varying degrees of success. Radio watched its stars migrate to the video screen, but managed to re-market itself to new niche audiences. "The tube" slurped up time which was once allocated to reading, so that some magazines and dailies did not survive. Baughman's balanced interpretation cautions against overstating the impact of television, however. It was not alone to blame for the failure of some newspapers and magazines, or the declining audience for Hollywood movies. The influence of television on politics should also not be exaggerated; television honchos boasted too much about the role of their medium in McCarthy's downfall, which they ascribed chiefly to the relentless exposure that his destructive behavior received during the televised army–McCarthy hearings. (Yet only two of the four networks offered full coverage, and much of the nation could not receive their signals.) Viewers were more skeptical than the critics of the medium feared; and while young Americans are always dismissed as "the TV generation," it was actually their grandparents, with more leisure to enjoy, who stared longest at the tube.

Another insightful treatment of the advent of television is Lynn Spigel's *Make Room for TV* (1992). The entry of that appliance into the parlor, long the haven of family privacy, had to be negotiated; this which was also true for such predecessors as the piano and radio. (Like television, radio had also been a potentially threatening new technology.) One virtue claimed for television was that it would bring the family together yet preserve traditional gender and social roles. Once the rougher edges of a young form of entertainment were smoothed (as when raunchier variety shows gave way to family sitcoms), television did generally fulfill that soothing function.

Since the 1980s the academic sub-field of cultural studies has taken serious interest in the 1950s. At its worst this curiosity has produced a temptation to read too much into cultural phenomena which may be isolated, incidental, or not very significant. Thus *film noir* is sometimes presented as a major statement of alienation and dissent from the dominant corporate hegemony. (A *film noir* hero typically confronts a situation in which he is a helpless suspect or victim facing an unjust system, a malign society, a world without hope.) Yet this genre or style was not a major draw at the box office. Was that limited popular impact therefore a sign of the oppressive power of the dominant forces of the status quo, or a tribute to the brave status of its practitioners or of its rebellious following? Or were there simply better alternatives on the marquee, or could bad lighting and low budgets at the studios be to blame? And were all the *It Came from Outer Space* and *The Thing* movies and their variations – or even the *oeuvre* of Alfred Hitchcock – as meaningful to audiences of the 1950s as they have been to later scholars? There is a tendency in cultural studies to fix upon the odd tree and to miss the forest. One 1997 book of essays, most of which do not make this mistake but usefully illuminate aspects of the culture, is *The Other Fifties*, edited by Joel Foreman. Essays in this volume touch on such revealing topics as the failure of the Edsel (the oddly styled new car introduced by Ford that proved a marketing fiasco), Nikita Khrushchev's unprecedented 1959 visit to the US, and themes discernible in early television programming.

It is tempting to differentiate between a soporific politics and a venturous culture marking the decade. But that disjunction produces a false dichotomy, since there was cross-pollination between these fields. A well-rounded, astute integration of the cultural activities of the 1950s with the wider world around is Stephen J. Whitfield's *The Culture of the Cold War* (1996), which manages to depict the repressive impact of Cold War political concerns upon the nation's culture, without missing those areas either of daring innovation or contradiction. The volume gives balanced treatment, for example, both to the timidity that afflicted Hollywood when it imposed the blacklist and to those streaks of daring visible in some of its offerings, such as Fred Zinnemann's *High Noon* (1952) and Elia Kazan's *A Face in the Crowd* (1957).

Perhaps the most complete introduction to the decade within one set of covers is the journalist David Halberstam's *The Fifties* (1993). Halberstam has flicked his line into most of the eddies and pools that constituted the stream of American life, so that *The Fifties* is striking for its length, its detail, and its even-handedness. Though he found plenty to criticize, his tone was temperate. Mini-biographies abound: of Kemmons Wilson, who bore responsibility for that key feature of the American landscape, Holiday Inn; of Ray Kroc, who made McDonald's a global cultural symbol; of the Beat writers such as William Burroughs, Jack Kerouac, and Allen Ginsberg; of Grace Metallious, whose heavy-breathing novel of 1956, *Peyton Place*, caused a sensation and hinted at coming changes in the role of American women and the American attitude to sex. *The Fifties* treats the stirrings of civil rights protest and lavishly describes a broad array of political, social, intellectual, and economic phenomena. Its author generally leaves interpretation to the reader, which will please some and madden others. The book can be strongly recommended as a Baedeker guide around the highs and lows, the variety and paradox that characterized the United States in the 1950s.

The decade mixed tension and relaxation, repression and emancipation, tradition and rebellion. It is tempting to infer that the dominant force was that of stability, and that the dissenters constituted a lonely group on the defensive. But that conclusion may miss the extent to which opposing trends were symbiotically connected. Mobilization for the Cold War, for example, encouraged conformity and an impatience with dissident views, but also summoned forth a trumpeting of definitions of what was being defended. Such ideological needs enabled excluded groups to create leverage, to get incorporated into the polity and society. As leaders rallied the nation to defend freedom, tendencies in art and in life-style that traditionalists found distasteful were paraded before the world as icons of that liberty: Louis Armstrong and other jazz musicians who could exemplify the diversity of the populace, abstract expressionism and other forms of modern art that were also sent on tours abroad, the unprecedented variety and bounty that the liberated average consumer could enjoy. The historian must therefore note the irony that the two major currents of the era – the mobilization of the Cold War and the emergence of an economy of abundance – had divergent and paradoxical effects on those who sought change and on those who wanted to halt it. Those two historical currents sometimes encouraged one side, sometimes the other – which is why this decade is in retrospect so perplexing, so difficult to categorize.

REFERENCES

Ambrose, Stephen E. (1984) *Eisenhower.* New York: Simon and Schuster.

Baughman, James L. (1997) *The Republic of Mass Culture: Journalism, Filmmaking, and Broadcasting in America since 1941*, 2nd edn. Baltimore, Md.: Johns Hopkins University Press.

Bell, Daniel (ed.) (1955) *The New American Right.* New York: Criterion Books.

Branch, Taylor (1988) *Parting the Waters: America in the King Years, 1954–63.* New York: Simon and Schuster.

Brokaw, Tom (1998) *The Greatest Generation.* New York: Random House.

Caute, David (1978) *The Great Fear: The Anti-Communist Purge under Truman and Eisenhower.* New York: Simon and Schuster.

Chafe, William H. (1980) *Civilities and Civil Rights: Greensboro, North Carolina, and the Black Struggle for Freedom.* New York: Oxford University Press.

Daniel, Pete (2000) *Lost Revolutions: The South in the 1950s.* Chapel Hill: University of North Carolina Press.

Dittmer, John (1994) *Local People: The Struggle for Civil Rights in Mississippi.* Urbana: University of Illinois Press.

Dudziak, Mary L. (2000) *Cold War Civil Rights: Race and the Image of American Democracy.* Princeton, NJ: Princeton University Press.

Ehrenhalt, Alan (1995) *The Lost City: The Forgotten Virtues of Community in America.* New York: Basic Books.

Ehrenreich, Barbara (1983) *The Hearts of Men: American Dreams and the Flight from Commitment*. Garden City, NY: Doubleday.

Foreman, Joel (ed.) (1997) *The Other Fifties: Interrogating Midcentury American Icons*. Urbana: University of Illinois Press.

Fried, Richard M. (1990) *Nightmare in Red: The McCarthy Era in Perspective*. New York: Oxford University Press.

Friedan, Betty (1963) *The Feminine Mystique*. New York: W. W. Norton.

Galbraith, John Kenneth (1958) *The Affluent Society*. Boston: Houghton Mifflin.

Gans, Herbert J. (1967) *The Levittowners: Ways of Life and Politics in a New Suburban Community*. New York: Pantheon.

Goldman, Eric F. (1961) *The Crucial Decade – and After: America, 1945–1960*. New York: Vintage.

Greenstein, Fred I. (1982) *The Hidden-Hand Presidency: Eisenhower as Leader*. New York: Basic Books.

Griffith, Robert K., Jr. (1970) *The Politics of Fear: Joseph R. McCarthy and the Senate*. Lexington: University Press of Kentucky.

Guralnick, Peter (1994) *Last Train to Memphis: The Rise of Elvis Presley*. Boston: Little, Brown.

Halberstam, David (1993) *The Fifties*. New York: Villard.

Hamby, Alonzo L. (1995) *Man of the People: A Life of Harry S. Truman*. New York: Oxford University Press.

Hine, Thomas (1986) *Populuxe*. New York: Alfred A. Knopf.

Isserman, Maurice (1987) *If I Had a Hammer . . . : The Death of the Old Left and the Birth of the New Left*. New York: Basic Books.

Jackson, Kenneth T. (1985) *Crabgrass Frontier: The Suburbanization of the United States*. New York: Oxford University Press.

Jezer, Marty (1982) *The Dark Ages: Life in the United States, 1945–1960*. Boston: South End.

Jones, Landon Y. (1980) *Great Expectations: America and the Baby Boom Generation*. New York: Coward, McCann, and Geoghegan.

Keats, John (1957) *The Crack in the Picture Window*. Boston: Houghton Mifflin.

—— (1958) *The Insolent Chariots*. Philadelphia: Lippincott.

Lhamon, W. T., Jr. (1990) *Deliberate Speed: The Origins of a Cultural Style in the American 1950s*. Washington, DC: Smithsonian Institution.

Lipsitz, George (1994) *A Rainbow at Midnight: Labor and Culture in the 1940s*. Champaign: University of Illinois Press.

McCullough, David (1992) *Truman*. New York: Simon and Schuster.

Maraniss, David (1999) *When Pride Still Mattered: A Life of Vince Lombardi*. New York: Simon and Schuster.

Marling, Karal Ann (1994) *As Seen on TV: The Visual Culture of Everyday Life in the 1950s*. Cambridge, Mass.: Harvard University Press.

May, Elaine Tyler (1988) *Homeward Bound: American Families in the Cold War Era*. New York: Basic Books.

Meyerowitz, Joanne (ed.) (1994) *Not June Cleaver: Women and Gender in Postwar America, 1945–1960*. Philadelphia: Temple University Press.

Miller, Douglas T. and Nowak, Marion (1977) *The Fifties: The Way We Really Were*. Garden City, NY: Doubleday.

Miller, Herman (1971) *Rich Man, Poor Man*. New York: Thomas Y. Crowell.

Morris, Aldon (1984) *The Origins of the Civil Rights Movement: Black Communities Organizing for Change*. New York: Free Press.

Nash, George H. (1976) *The Conservative Intellectual Movement in America: Since 1945*. New York: Basic Books.

Norrell, Robert J. (1985) *Reaping the Whirlwind: The Civil Rights Movement in Tuskegee*. New York: Alfred A. Knopf.

O'Neill, William L. (1986) *American High: The Years of Confidence, 1945–1960*. New York: Free Press.

Oshinsky, David M. (1983) *A Conspiracy So Immense: The World of Joe McCarthy*. New York: Free Press.

Pells, Richard H. (1985) *The Liberal Mind in a Conservative Age: American Intellectuals in the 1940s and 1950s*. New York: Harper and Row.

Pemberton, William E. (1989) *Harry S. Truman: Fair Dealer and Cold Warrior*. Boston: Twayne.

Powers, Richard Gid (1987) *Secrecy and Power: The Life of J. Edgar Hoover*. New York: Free Press.

Reeves, Thomas C. (1982) *The Life and Times of Joe McCarthy: A Biography*. New York: Stein and Day.

Rogin, Michael Paul (1967) *The Intellectuals and McCarthy: The Radical Specter*. Cambridge, Mass.: MIT Press.

Schrecker, Ellen (1998) *Many Are the Crimes: McCarthyism in America*. Boston: Little, Brown.

Sherry, Michael S. (1995) *In the Shadow of War: The United States since the 1930s*. New Haven, Conn.: Yale University Press.

Spigel, Lynn (1992) *Make Room for TV: Television and the Family Idea in Postwar America*. Chicago: University of Chicago Press.

Sugrue, Thomas J. (1996) *The Origins of the Urban Crisis: Race and Inequality in Postwar Detroit*. Princeton, NJ: Princeton University Press.

Theoharis, Athan (1971) *Seeds of Repression: Harry S. Truman and the Origins of McCarthyism*. Chicago: Quadrangle.

Vatter, Harold G. (1963) *The US Economy in the 1950s: An Economic History*. New York: W. W. Norton.

White, Theodore H. (1961) *The Making of the President 1960*. New York: Atheneum.

Whitfield, Stephen J. (1988) *A Death in the Delta: The Story of Emmett Till*. New York: Free Press.

—— (1996) *The Culture of the Cold War*, 2nd edn. Baltimore, Md.: Johns Hopkins University Press.

CHAPTER SIX

1960–1974

Jama Lazerow

We were young, we were reckless, arrogant, silly, headstrong – and we were right. I regret nothing!
(Abbie Hoffman)

For all their noisy rhetoric and noisy music, the sixties contributed nothing to America's national heritage, at least nothing that anyone in his right mind would care to treasure.
(Jonathan Yardley)

In a century of putatively distinctive decades, the sixties stand out as perhaps the most distinctive decade of all. At the dawn of a new century, a full generation later, the visual imagery of that time is, if anything, sharper in the American mind than at any time before. Thanks to television and movies the 1960s are back: civil rights marches and urban riots; soldiers fighting in Vietnam and citizens protesting at home; college students taking over campuses and hirsute hippies wearing unconventional clothing and flowers in their hair, taking drugs, dancing to rock music, celebrating the joys of "free love." What is most remembered – sometimes with a wistful longing for what might have been, sometimes with shame, even horror – is the upsurge of left-wing social and political activism known as "the Movement." In the collective memory, the contrast with the preceding and following decades could not be sharper.

To be sure there is much myth in these images, derived in part from the nostalgia of the so-called baby boomers (born between 1946 and 1964). 1969, for example, was a year of campus takeovers, shoot-outs between police and black militants, massive antiwar demonstrations, and the rock festival at Woodstock, New York. Yet the most popular song of that year was The Archies' "Sugar, sugar." Indeed, despite the Beatles-led British invasion and the popularity of "acid rock," the best-seller of the entire decade was Percy Faith's instrumental "Theme from *A Summer Place*." In fact misconceptions about the decade abound. In the early 1960s the leading right-wing student organization, the Young Americans for Freedom (YAF), outnumbered the leading left-wing student organization, the Students for a Democratic Society (SDS). Moreover, popular support for America's war in Vietnam remained strong until the end of the decade. Black Americans continued to support mainstream civil rights organizations, such as the National Association for the Advancement of Colored People (NAACP), in far greater numbers that those who identified with radical black organizations such as the Black Panther Party. Huge media events, such as the beating of demonstrators outside the Democratic Party's 1968 convention in Chicago, or the killing of four students at Kent State University during protests against the invasion of Cambodia in 1970, generated more hostility toward the victims than toward the perpetrators of the violence.

Indeed, viewed from the dawn of the twenty-first century, the New Left appears to be an exception to the conservative half-century after 1938. The descent of liberalism can be traced to the 1940s, despite what appeared to be its heyday in the mid-1960s; and by 1968 the grass-roots, anti-establishment New Right was in the ascendant. Adopting this perspective, younger scholars without direct experience of the decade – the "post-sixties sixties interpreters" – advocate a new, broader perspective, a move "from memory to history." They offer a version of what some call the "continuity thesis," which stresses longer, secular trends that the brief flirtation with 1960s radicalism barely interrupted. The decade thus did not represent a break in twentieth-century American history. One historian, Thomas Sugrue, has even suggested that in half a century "there won't be courses on the history of America in the sixties" (quoted in Perlstein 1996: 30–1, 37).

Very different is the view that "there has been nothing quite like it; nothing would ever be quite the same again," as Arthur Marwick has expressed it (1998: 806). For there is much truth to the decade's tumultuous image, and to the emphasis on left-wing dissent. In the late 1960s, SDS became the largest radical student organization in American history. The Panthers garnered significant support among young blacks precisely when the party advocated world socialist revolution. The Chicago demonstrations helped destroy the postwar liberal consensus on the welfare-warfare state. The national student strike following the Kent State killings was unprecedented in size and scope. Undeniably, those engaged in protest were a minority, even among the young, even during the most convulsive moments of the decade. But the social reform ferment of the early sixties, escalating into political apocalypticism by the end of the decade, had no parallel in American history, save perhaps the 1830s and 1840s.

The reach of radicalism certainly extended well beyond the meliorism of the Progressive Era. From the idealism of the young civil rights workers in the Student Nonviolent Coordinating Committee (SNCC), who envisioned their movement as a "beloved community," and the student activists of the New Left, who spoke of a nation renewed by "participatory democracy," to the urban revolutionary collectives of the Weatherman faction of SDS and the Black Liberation Army, and the rural communes in California and northern New England, everything was subject to question: political parties and private property, power and authority, sex roles and family arrangement, work and play, music and dress, language and thought. The release of energy, the expansiveness, the quest for something fresh and new, the sense of an "open-ended beginning," that everything was possible – all this characterized the sixties. As one early SDS activist remembered, the group's founding meeting in 1962 felt like the "dawn of a new age" (Miller 1987: 125). When acted upon, these utopian dreams drew a reaction – eventually, a "backlash" – and, as a consequence, the nation was more divided than in perhaps any other period since the Civil War.

Most historians rightly stress this turbulent aspect of the period. Unfortunately, the social, political, and especially cultural polarization of those years has kept the sixties part of the "immediate past" three decades later. Our understanding of a past era is thus more part of the contemporary political agenda than usual, certainly in contrast to our historical understanding of the 1930s, for example. That urgency has in turn retarded the development of 1960s historiography. For in the public arena much of the terrain is controlled by memoirists and politicians and, in the academy, by sociologists and political scientists instead of professional historians. The decade has refused to fade into oblivion, which is appropriate perhaps for a generation that sought to make history rather than read it, as one activist proudly proclaimed in 1964.

No decade has been more written about; a recent book on only some aspects of the period contains a bibliography of over sixty pages. Yet no decade has produced less dispassionate historical analysis. Until very recently historical debate has usually been dominated by those who lived through the decade and who engage in elaborate exercises of celebration (*The Sixties without Apology*) or condemnation (*The Unraveling of America*). Or, in one popular and remarkably resilient variation on the theme, expiation for the sins of the late sixties, exaltation of the idealism of the early sixties (*The Sixties: Years of Hope, Days of Rage*). This latter notion of a "good" (early) and "bad" (late) sixties – the "declension model" – dominates the writing of both liberal and left historians, including the post-1960s generation.

In sum, what one historian has said about the Panthers – that they are "symbolically central and yet historiographically underdeveloped" (Singh 1998: 61) – is a fitting epigram for the decade as a whole, perhaps because no sharply defined historical period has since appeared. Clearly, if we are ever to gain historical perspective on the 1960s, historians need to place the decade in the larger context of post-World War II history, while recognizing what made it distinctive, and moving beyond the self-serving politics of the moment. One way to do that is by approaching the sixties as a historical problem rather than as something to be defended or attacked, or even as a single narrative of events.

The Problem of Origins

The roots of the sixties tumult are obviously complex, and ultimately somewhat of a mystery. How did an apparently placid 1950s give way to a turbulent 1960s? How did the concerns voiced by particular groups become general, producing "a global unbinding of energies" (Jameson 1984: 207)? For many of the era's young radicals, who perceived the past as irrelevant and their present as unique, those questions did not need to be asked. For historians, though, the immediate sources of the upheavals can be glimpsed in the dramatic emergence of three activist strands that together presaged the birth of a New Left in 1960: civil rights, peace, and anti-imperialism.

On February 1, 1960 four black freshmen from North Carolina Agricultural and Technical College in Greensboro purchased some items at the local Woolworths, sat down at the lunch counter in the "whites only" section, and ordered cups of coffee. Refused service by a black waitress, they sat politely until the store closed, promising to return the next day to continue their "sit-down protest." The action sparked what became known as the "sit-in" movement, almost on cue as the 1960s began. The bold action becoming instantly famous on campus, four turned into a score the next day, and, by the end of the week, into a hundred. The following week, in High Point, North Carolina, the activist minister Fred Shuttlesworth witnessed a sit-in and immediately called Ella Baker, the executive director of the Southern Christian Leadership Conference (SCLC) in Atlanta, telling her: "This is the thing. You must tell Martin [Luther King, Jr.] that we must get with this, and really this can shake up the world" (Aldon Morris 1984: 201).

By the end of February sit-ins were reported in over thirty communities in eight states; by April over 50,000 had participated in some seventy cities in fourteen states. That month Baker organized a "Southwide State Leadership Conference on Non-violent Resistance to Segregation," which led to the founding of SNCC the following fall. The small action of the four freshmen had turned into a contagion. It was "like a fever," one participant said later (quoted in Carson 1981: 12). Indeed, it would help define a decade, as the sit-ins gave birth to something new. It was a sudden rush, a moment when, according to one activist, "everything broke loose" (quoted in Farrell 1997: 97).

How had it happened? The Congress of Racial Equality (CORE) had organized sit-ins during World War II; and CORE activists, along with the NAACP Youth Council and the SCLC, had organized over a dozen in the late 1950s. Moreover, the freshmen knew of CORE's efforts, of the Montgomery bus boycott of 1955–6, of recent sit-ins by NAACP youth in the bus station waiting rooms, parks, and hotels of nearby Durham. But the students who sat down at Woolworths were not part of a mass movement; there was none. For good reason, historians often trace the beginning of the modern civil rights movement to Rosa Parks's historic refusal to give up her seat, when "somewhere in the universe a gear in the machinery . . . shifted," as Black Panther leader Eldridge Cleaver said later (1968: 194). But 1960 inaugurated something novel. Like the dramatic strike upsurge of the mid-1930s after years of frustrated organizing efforts by union activists, something fundamental had changed.

But what? The shift cannot be attributed to media coverage; the action spread before any such exposure. Historians have speculated that these students were inspired in complex ways by what others like them had done. One of the Greensboro four recalled feeling "ashamed at how those young kids in Little Rock were braving it out" during the school desegregation crisis there. In turn a student from Alabama State University remembered: "When we discovered that the kids in Greensboro had made a move, we felt we were obligated to show our hand" (Bloom 1987: 157, 159). The decolonization movement then sweeping Africa, especially the revolution in Ghana in 1957, inspired many young black college students as well. Some observers have suggested that the sit-ins flowed naturally from 1950s civil rights activism, which by late 1959 had produced local "movement centers" that could spread the news and organize the action. In one of those centers, Nashville, Tennessee, the Reverend James Lawson recalled that upon hearing of Greensboro, he called people and said: "This is it, let's go" (Aldon Morris 1984: 202). Still others point to the young activists' optimistic assessment of northern public opinion and the federal government. Spontaneous or planned, inspired by domestic forces or international events, naïve or realistic, civil rights finally became a sustained movement, inspiring other sustained movements.

Concurrently something similar happened among peace activists. Every spring during the 1950s, as part of America's Cold War "readiness," New Yorkers were required to take shelter during a mock nuclear attack. Failure to comply carried criminal penalties. In 1955 twenty-eight pacifists, mostly longtime activists, publicly protested the drill; it was the first act of collective civil disobedience during the decade. Promptly arrested, they were denounced by the arraignment judge as "murderers," responsible for the deaths of millions; he even dispatched one of the rebels to Bellevue Hospital for psychiatric observation. Protests continued every spring, always mounted by a handful of dedicated activists, whose prison terms steadily lengthened. Then, on May 3, 1960, the "Ad Hoc Civil Defense Protest Committee" attracted some six hundred protesters, many of them first-time activists. Only twenty-six were taken into custody; there were simply too many to arrest. Meanwhile hundreds of college students in the area refused to participate in the exercise. Somehow the positions of those participating and those refusing had reversed; now those enforcing the drill seemed insane. By 1962 the exercises were canceled.

A third indication of the sea change was the reaction of young Americans to increasingly strained relations with Fidel Castro's Cuba. No one expected the national movement that materialized by the end of 1960 in the form of the Fair Play for Cuba Committee, which was especially popular on college campuses among middle-class males in their teens and twenties. More dramatically, the attempted overthrow of Castro the following year produced a significant crack in the Cold War consensus; the "Bay of Pigs" invasion sparked the first substantial postwar public protest against a military action abroad. Rallies attracted thousands in some two dozen cities and college towns. In New York the Old Left was involved in the demonstrations, as were some African-American leaders. On college campuses, though, the movement was new, despite rising interest in student politics at some elite schools as early as 1957. Again, something had happened, and kept happening, involving greater numbers and more issues. The result is what we have come to call "the sixties."

The *underlying* causes of this turbulence are more easily discerned than its immediate causes. To be sure, the genesis of the New Left (which spawned "second wave" feminism; gay liberation; and organized agitation by Latinos, Asians, Native Americans, consumers, the elderly, the disabled, and environmentalists) can be traced to modern civil rights activism, itself of complex origins dating from at least the late 1930s. But more broadly, at least a half-dozen factors help explain the decade's tumult, which ironically first buttressed the postwar American consensus, then exploded into social activism. The confluence of these factors helps explain the explosion, especially the paradox of apparent economic security alongside persistent injustice. Moreover, as in the Progressive Era, the mixture of confidence and anxiety, promise and danger, created a volatile combination for reform ferment.

The first three factors can be subsumed under the rubric of a postwar "victory culture," when publisher Henry Luce's 1941 prediction of an "American century" seemed a reality. Foremost was the general prosperity of 1946–73, the most sustained period of economic buoyancy in US history, with high rates of growth accompanied by low unemployment and inflation. Historian David M. Potter's *People of Plenty* (1954) typified the resultant mood among many intellectuals during what some dubbed the "fabulous fifties." Again as in the Progressive Era, such bright economic prospects generated a sense of possibility, perhaps especially among the more affluent young. For some, there was a sense that all problems could be solved, producing eventually a kind of post-scarcity radicalism. On the other hand, this prosperity was uneven, with stubborn pockets of poverty in rural areas and in the inner cities. There was also a reaction to the deleterious effects of a society that seemed increasingly materialistic, bureaucratic, and conformist, in which the individual was apparently eclipsed. The beginnings of such discontent could be seen among critics of mass society like David Riesman (*The Lonely Crowd*) and William H. Whyte (*The Organization Man*) and the tiny group of "Beats" like Jack Kerouac and Allen Ginsberg, who celebrated spontaneity, spirituality, and sensuality. In the 1960s such discontent would blossom into a new generation's quest for authenticity.

Rooted in economic pre-eminence was America's military strength, greater in the postwar period than any other nation had ever projected. In 1948 diplomat George Kennan captured the resultant sense of power – and its perceived requirements – when he told his staff at the State Department that the US controlled half of the world's wealth while making up only 6.3 percent of the world's population. He reminded his colleagues that their task was "to devise a pattern of relationships which will permit us to maintain this position of disparity" (quoted in Chomsky 1987: 15). Such dominance sometimes generated a sense that great changes were possible. Yet there was also the concomitant insecurity and anxiety of living in a nuclear world, both because of the "fallout" from the testing of nuclear weaponry and because – by the summer of 1949 – America's principal international rival, the Soviet Union, also had nuclear weapons.

The Cold War itself was a third underlying factor. Here, too, the contradictions between rhetoric (the moral imperative to defend "freedom") and reality (oppression at home and abroad) would generate social activism, especially among young people. The internationalization of the civil rights movement illuminated the problem: if the US sought freedom abroad, why not at home? Thus to remake the world on the assumption of America's preponderant power and moral example carried the seeds of its own destruction, for in the process national hypocrisy was exposed. Indeed the postwar consensus rested on the idea of the US capacity to dominate the world and to make inequality a residual fact in American life. The civil rights movement proved both notions wrong.

Demographic, cultural, and technological factors must be considered as well. The postwar reassertion of a "cult of domesticity" produced a "gender crisis," remarkably like an earlier one in pre-Civil War America. Among young women, the result was sometimes rebelliousness, as they watched their mothers labor (at home and often at the workplace) while official doctrine exalted women's domestic roles. Less often considered is the effect that fifties domesticity had on young men who identified with men of the world, like Fidel Castro (with his beard, fatigues, pistol, and cigar). Indeed, the "bad boys" of popular mid-1950s films like *Rebel Without a Cause*, *The Wild One*, and *Blackboard Jungle* stood in opposition to the kindly, indulgent television fathers of *The Donna Reed Show* or *Father Knows Best*. The young of both sexes, then, needed heroism – or a heroic struggle.

Meanwhile the dramatic increase in the numbers of young people produced the rudiments of a youth culture, complete with its own jargon, clothes, and music. In response came complaints from conservatives about the dangers of comic books, rock 'n' roll, and juvenile delinquency, with frequent warnings about the "devil's music,"

"Communist plots," and "race-mixing." The postwar expansion of universities produced a relatively insulated world that harbored many of these youths, whose political presence would be felt once their numbers grew to critical mass. Thus, in 1964, the year the first of the baby boomers entered college, hundreds of students trekked south to participate in Mississippi's Freedom Summer; that fall the Berkeley Free Speech Movement inaugurated an era of student protest on campus.

Finally, this was the first television generation. By 1960 nine out of ten homes had the technology. These young people watched and were watched, were subjected to promises of instant success and "revolutionary" products, and became targets of the advertising industry. Most crucially the Montgomery bus boycott and the violent battle to desegregate Central High School in Little Rock, Arkansas, were televised events. By 1963 the struggle for civil rights produced powerful images beamed around the globe: dogs attacking demonstrators attempting to desegregate Birmingham, Alabama, President John F. Kennedy's "A time to act" speech in response to the Birmingham events, King's "I have a dream" speech in Washington later that summer.

By the late 1950s, then, there were cracks in the postwar consensus. Social critics rebelled against the conformity and impersonality of the age. Rock 'n' roll music, combining elements of country-and-western, gospel, blues, and rhythm-and-blues, raised uncomfortable issues of race and class. The Beats rejected materialism and conformity, and embraced jazz, oriental philosophy, drugs, mysticism, and sex. A change of mood even animated middle-aged women: the housewives of the Women's Strike for Peace protested nuclear fallout, and opposed highway and bridge construction in cities as disparate as San Francisco and Memphis.

And still, Cold War anti-Communism, conservatism, and consensus remained powerful; the center held, "more or less" (Patterson 1996: 407). The late 1950s, it now appears, was neither a placid nor a turbulent era, but one of crosscurrents. Emblematic of the age, perhaps, was his first crossover hit, "You send me" (1957) by gospel-turned-soul-singer Sam Cooke: superficially placid yet seductive, even rebellious. With Cold War temperatures rising, then, with the emergence of the teenagers, Beats, peace activists, civil rights demonstrators, supporters of the Cuban revolution, and environmentalists, Americans of the late fifties lived with a sense of growing crisis but also of growing confidence that, with things to be done, problems could be solved.

In this dramatic story, finally, with its many immediate and underlying sources, the force of individual personality cannot be discounted, for 1960 was not only a year of protests against Cold War civil defense exercises, of student sit-ins, of rising support for the Cuban revolution, and of environmental protest. It was also an election year. In November Senator John F. Kennedy won a narrow victory over Vice President Richard M. Nixon in a presidential election, one that had not in half a century attracted so many voters. Kennedy was a complex character; and his term in office, foreshortened by assassination in November 1963, defies easy characterization. Historians recognize that he accomplished little in domestic affairs. As for foreign affairs, they are divided on his prudence regarding the Third World and the Soviets: his increasing involvement in Vietnam amounted to an invasion; and Cold War tensions also heightened, at least until 1963. At the same time there is much speculation about what he might have done had he not been murdered.

In any case, what seems to have distinguished him was his style: his sophistication, grace, eloquence, charm, vigor, all of which attracted those yearning for change. Kennedy's inaugural – or at least its imagery – demonstrated the contrast with what he was replacing. There was the outgoing President, Dwight D. Eisenhower, slightly stooped, bald, and wearing a heavy winter coat and muffler; the young President was, by contrast, the picture of apparent health, without overcoat or hat in the cold of a bitter January morning. On the other hand, Kennedy was deliberately cool, detached, in control, pragmatic, non-ideological – qualities that would later clash with youthful idealists. Indeed there was little in Kennedy's congressional record that suggested he represented a departure from the Cold War consensus. Nor did the campaign itself expose any significant issues that divided him from his opponent. And yet Kennedy seems to have won in great measure because he communicated that he intended to run the country ("to get the country moving again"), which in turn may have stimulated an incipient rebelliousness. That Nixon, only four years older than Kennedy, sought to offer the same prescription for leadership suggests that it was more the age than the man that made the difference. Still, there was something about Kennedy, and historians generally recognize it as a factor in explaining the sixties. On the eve of the election, the novelist Norman Mailer captured the moment when he wrote that the nation faced an "existential turn." Americans could choose the 1950s, he said, which represented "benevolence without leadership, regularity without vision, security without safety, rhetoric without life," under a leader whose followers "were most proud of their lack of imagination." Or the nation could "walk into the nightmare," behind a hero who could capture "the secret imagination of a people" (Mailer 1969: 15, 17).

Most crucially, Kennedy spoke eloquently of conquering "new frontiers" and pledged to "bear any burden, pay any price, meet any hardship, support any friend, oppose any foe to assure the survival and the success of liberty." Indeed, like his successor's "Great Society," Kennedy's program seemed to offer limitless possibilities. He generated "grand expectations" he did not fulfill. Meanwhile his reliance on technical expertise for liberal change clashed with a new generation's demands for moral renewal. But it would take the better part of the sixties to expose the discrepancy; and that, too, would stoke the fires of rebellion.

The Problem of Periodization

Almost as difficult as explaining why the sixties happened is making sense of what happened during the decade. Part of the problem, no doubt, is the enormity of events in such a compressed period of time. As one participant would later remark, it seemed that "history came off its leash" (Gitlin 1987: 3). But perhaps more pivotal is the difficulty of fitting key aspects of the era into the decade itself, whether the civil rights movement's roots in the 1950s or the Vietnam War's spillover into the 1970s. Indeed some historians write of a "long sixties" (from 1958 to 1974). Several college textbooks divide the era at 1963, putting Kennedy and the early sixties in one chapter and using the Vietnam War as the focus for the decade 1963–73. Others isolate the civil rights movement and "minority" movements, others foreign affairs, still others national politics. Some scholars have thrown up their hands and abandoned periodization entirely, adopting a thematic approach. In general civil rights dominates the writing of the early sixties, and Vietnam the later part. Yet just how much race and war interpenetrated by 1967 can be seen by the resonance of boxer Muhammad Ali's separate peace: "I ain't got no quarrel with them Vietcong" (Remnick 1998: 287).

History is not neat; that truism seems especially applicable to the 1960s. No single narrative or course of development can make sense of a decade of such complexity, and there are many ways to tell the story. Politically, for example, one might trace the course of the era from Kennedy to Nixon; in the realm of foreign affairs, from the Bay of Pigs to My Lai. And the changes within the decade do not always follow a linear pattern, while contradictions abound. Nevertheless, the continued emphasis on social activism as emblematic of the age suggests a four-stage "long sixties," or perhaps three stages and an epilogue. Historians usually tell the story this way, at least in some fashion. "Early" (1960–late 1963) is typically seen as an era of idealistic and optimistic protest. "Middle" (1963–late 1966) constitutes a transitional period of soaring confidence and rising anxiety. President Lyndon B. Johnson's Great Society programs, civil rights legislation, and favorable court decisions reflected and fed the former. But in this phase there was also frustration, disillusionment, and anger against the widening war in Vietnam, against the persistence of urban inequality, and against the recalcitrance of institutional authorities to yield to protesters' demands, all of which generated increasing popular resistance. "Late" (1966–late 1969), sometimes seen as lasting into the early 1970s, is the era of radical and even revolutionary fervor, marked by violence abroad and at home. The "Epilogue" (1969–74), a kind of American Thermidor, is the period of the Movement's demise (though new movements flowered), economic troubles, and conservative victory (stalled temporarily by the political scandals known collectively as "Watergate").

In forever returning to this periodization scheme, historians have rarely transcended the declension model. Take the saga of the black freedom movement, the most familiar of all the sixties story lines, told in numerous popular movies, documentaries, and memoirs, as well as in a huge scholarly literature. Much of this narrative has a "Whiggish" character; an air of inevitability hovers over the march to progress embodied in the movement's principles of freedom and justice for all, as does its descent into nihilistic violence when those principles are abandoned. The focus is on the opening years of the decade, a period marked by nonviolent direct action – sit-ins, freedom rides, marches, picketing, voter registration drives – aimed at dismantling the Jim Crow system in the South. By mid-1963 hundreds of thousands of citizens had participated in nearly a thousand such campaigns. Many of these demonstrators suffered extreme violence. More than two dozen died in the first half of the decade; and many hundreds more were beaten, shot, or injured in arson and bomb attacks. The idealistic young civil rights workers and those whom they enlisted in their cause nevertheless persevered, despite much frustration and many setbacks. Typically highlighted in this story are the March on Washington of August 1963 and the subsequent civil rights acts of 1964 and 1965.

In this telling, frustration with both the federal government and the mainstream civil rights leadership led to revolt, exemplified by the cries for "Black Power" in 1966, thus marking a turning point in the black liberation struggle. Emblematic of the change, it is claimed, were the urban riots outside the South. Harlem erupted for a week in the summer of 1964; Watts followed in 1965, Newark and Detroit in 1967. After King's assassination in 1968, there was a virtual national uprising. Meanwhile

Malcolm X's black nationalism became more popular, and the pressure rose on whites in bi-racial civil rights organizations like SNCC to leave and organize "their own." With black separatism flourishing and black militancy a new watchword, protest turned violent, most notably in the armed posture of the Black Panther Party for Self-Defense, founded in the fall of 1966. Two years later the Black Panthers formed a short-lived alliance with SNCC, a group founded on the principles of Christian nonviolence and love, soon to be ridiculed as the Non-Student Violent Non-Coordinating Committee. By 1971 the string had been played out. The Panthers experienced a violent schism, one element joining with members of SNCC and other militants in a loose confederation called the Black Liberation Army to carry out guerrilla warfare in the cities. This is declension history with a vengeance.

Late twentieth-century scholarship somewhat decenters this narrative, though the theme of decline remains. In keeping with the post-1960s historiographical trend to write history "from the bottom up," the new scholarship has privileged the local perspective. Ordinary folk, often older local activists on whom young civil rights activists depended, are at the center of the story, instead of national figures such as King. This shift in focus has produced a more radical reading of the civil rights struggle. Scholars increasingly appreciate not only that the sit-in demonstrators expressed a liberal demand for inclusion and initially complained about the pace – not the direction – of change, but also that their tactics represented a departure. At the same time King himself is seen as becoming increasingly radical in response. Other historians have stressed the tradition of self-determination and armed self-defense among local people that pre-dated the 1960s, and thus see Black Power as more than a product of the disillusionment of young civil rights workers. This story line fits the "continuity" interpretation, and thus supports the newer emphasis in sixties writing that rejects the decade as a significant historical break. Unfortunately this trend has done little to elucidate the nature of the crucial Black Panther Party, born at the same time as Black Power, amid the rising tide of urban disorders, but with roots in the anti-imperialist upsurge of the early 1960s. Nevertheless, historians invariably treat the Panthers as a prime example of the Movement's descent into violence.

Similar historiographical trends characterize the treatment of the New Left. This group – mostly white, mostly students – has received the most attention from scholars, most of whom agree that groups such as SDS were inspired by the civil rights movement, the era's "borning struggle." Again the emphasis has been on an idealistic, liberal early 1960s, what SDS president Carl Oglesby called the "bronze age." The liberal character of this phase is evident, for example, in the principal demand of the Berkeley Free Speech Movement for the right of full political expression. Moreover, many of these early activists were genuinely shocked when authorities did not yield to their righteous protests. So, like African Americans, these young whites sought personal empowerment through public, communal action. They had their expectations dramatically raised by JFK's soaring appeal to "new frontiers" and by LBJ's declaration that "we can do it all": to fulfill the promise of the New Deal by prosecuting a "war on poverty." Again the mixture of hope and despair proved combustible, as inequity (at home) and iniquity (abroad) became increasingly visible in the mid-1960s.

Here too, then, increasing frustration characterizes the mid-1960s, particularly with the escalation of the war and the failure of public demonstrations to stop it.

Meanwhile the influx into SDS of anarchistic elements ("prairie power") from 1965 on has been discerned as accelerating the descent into revolutionary adventurism in the late 1960s, and finally the fragmentation, chaos, and collapse during the Nixon years (1969–74). "By the end of the decade," social commentator Charles R. Morris wrote fifteen years later, "only the ugliness was left" (1984: 128). Typically, the sources of this descent are traced to the influence of the black freedom struggle. The Education Research Action Projects of SDS, which sought to build "interracial movements of the poor" beginning in the summer of 1963, stemmed from SNCC's style of organizing. The dissociative character of the post-1965 counter-culture, too, paralleled Black Power. The adoption of violent, revolutionary rhetoric, finally, echoed the Black Panthers: "equal parts Maoist jargon and black street rap" (Isserman and Kazin 2000: 226).

Thus, for most such historians, the early sixties represents a continuation of some of the best traditions of the 1930s progressives, if in new and somewhat untraditional ways. By contrast, the late 1960s represents an abandonment of class for race (and, increasingly, "identity politics" generally), political compromise for dogmatic purism, analysis for action. Ironically, what has been seen as the early New Left's strength (its moral vision, its belief in "participatory democracy," its willingness to engage in direct action) became its weakness: they were unwilling to compromise. Of particular concern to historians in this regard is the "backlash" that gathered strength in the mid-1960s, eventually destroying the liberal center, as the self-immolation of an increasingly nihilistic left made way for a resurgent right. Thus the debacle at the 1964 Democratic Convention over the seating of the Mississippi Freedom Demo-cratic Party is seen as having alienated both the left and the right from Johnson's liberalism, seriously eroding the labor-liberal-black coalition of the New Deal Dem-ocracy. Here historians sometimes charge the liberals with indecisiveness, in pursuing domestic and foreign goals on the one hand, and in confronting protests on the other hand. But the blame for the disappearance of the liberal center and for the rise of the right is typically placed at the feet of uncompromising radicals.

Outside this standard view, newer scholarship has begun to emphasize the spiritual elements of the New Left. One study, in trying to locate a common thread in what have come to appear as many movements rather than one Movement, identifies the "personalism" of the Catholic Workers as a key influence on the student New Left. Another, signalling a trend toward local studies, highlights the importance of Christian existentialism and the heritage of the Social Gospel for student radicalism in Austin, Texas, home to the largest campus chapter of SDS in the late sixties. But the use of these studies by other historians has actually reinforced the general direction of the scholarship. Consistent with the "continuity" thesis, radical Protestantism among the student left is seen by historians as rendering SDS "just another" in a long line of religiously-informed reform movements, while "personalism" is seen as an explan-ation for the failure of the late sixties New Left to compromise.

The emergence of the so-called counterculture has also been interpreted as a sign of decline. Generally recognized as having first appeared with the cross-country trip of Ken Kesey and his Merry Pranksters in 1964 and having reached flood-tide by the "summer of love" in 1967, the counterculture permeated much of the Movement as well as the lives of youth generally (partly by the design of political leftists). Here the emphasis on the personal has been viewed by historians as too easily leading to a mere politics of style and too easily absorbed by the larger culture. Even the "political" Yippies are seen as too media-reliant, in contrast to the more serious San Francisco Diggers. Meanwhile the "instrumentalist" political orientation of the New Left has been depicted as increasingly replaced by the quest for personal satisfaction (a corruption of the Movement's "prefigurative" or "expressive" politics). That development has been condemned by both liberal and conservative observers, though for different reasons. (To liberals it signals abandonment of structural change; to conservatives it represents a corruption of American values.) Moreover, the long hair, odd dress, music, and drugs alienated broad masses of Americans (Nixon's "silent majority"), it is noted, even some who supported racial equality and opposed the war. At the same time, as the Yippies' Abbie Hoffman remarked, a new way of life was eventually turned into a fad, marketed and sold, tapped by Hollywood, Madison Avenue, and the record industry. Like the philosophically vague "Black Power," then, the counterculture is seen as having been easily co-opted. Finally the communitarian movement of the late 1960s and early 1970s, which produced some two hundred times the number of communities that were established during the nation's last great communitarian phase in the antebellum period, is pictured as activists (literally) heading for the hills.

Even the antiwar movement, the largest peace movement in American history and still growing in the early 1970s, is made to fit into this narrative of decline, with the black movement again held responsible. In one version, the problem stemmed from SDS's refusal to lead the antiwar movement, despite early successes in getting demonstrators into the streets. According to this historiography, the SDS national office sought more fundamental issues on which to focus, first through SNCC-style community organizing, and then by organizing students as a "new working class." Then, by the end of the decade, virtually all historians agree, SDS leaders became slavish in their support for other (colored) people's revolutionary struggles, ironically a position derived in part from the war's exposure of systemic problems in America. Significantly, while late sixties radicals viewed the war as a logical result of US imperialism, many historians continue to see the conflict as a tragic error, rendering the radical position a decline from an earlier idealistic hope for peace. SDS has also been depicted as having been saddled with the war, almost against its will, again because of pressure from local campuses. But, because it was not an issue that could produce tangible, piecemeal results, the consequence was a tendency to swing from millennial expectation to apocalyptic despair. At the end of the story, then, the antiwar movement goes out with a whimper rather than a bang, even though its largest demonstrations were conducted in 1971. The Paris Peace Accords, signed in January 1973, came after the most intensive bombing in history, with hundreds of thousands dead in Nixon's first term. By then, historians agree, the Movement of the sixties was over. In this telling of the story, all that stood in the way of a triumphant right was Watergate, which would result in Nixon's resignation in August 1974.

In all this, the focus has been on explaining, sometimes bemoaning, what did not happen; and the blame has almost always been attributed to late sixties radicals and their "fatal entanglement with doctrines of violent revolution" (Isserman 1992: 34). Yet the two favorite whipping boys of that period, the Weatherman faction of SDS and the Black Panther Party, have received virtually no scholarly attention from historians. Why the Panthers, for example, should have been so successful so quickly

– beyond the facile focus on the media – is an issue unaddressed by historians. The striking absence of historical scholarship on this important group may have something to do with the fact that it had no idealistic, liberal, "bronze age," having begun as an armed revolutionary organization. And yet historians will have to come to grips with the dramatic increase during the 1966–71 period in the number of African Americans who believed violence would be necessary to bring about social change. They will also have to pay more attention to the role of state violence in the destruction of the Movement, most notably of the Panthers.

The new gender history of the sixties may offer some hope for a more sober analysis that places the era in context while still recognizing that the "long" decade (from 1958 to 1974) marked a distinct period of twentieth-century history. The first national women's liberation demonstration was the protest at the Miss America pageant in Atlantic City in September 1968 – which partly explains why a recent overview states flatly that the feminist movement was "barely a phenomenon of the 1960s" (Burner 1996: 261). But in a broader sense we now know that women, and women's liberation, were factors in 1960s struggles from the beginning. Moreover their story was paradigmatic of the sixties as a whole, in three revealing ways. First, the crisis in gender noted earlier was a product of postwar rising expectations. Increasingly women participated in the work force, attended college, and gained control over reproduction, all in the context of what Betty Friedan called the "feminine mystique." Secondly, like the early civil rights movement, the student New Left, and the counterculture, the consciousness-raising groups at the heart of women's liberation in the late 1960s exemplified the prefigurative politics that characterized the decade. Finally, and perhaps most important, like other movements of the 1960s, women's liberation quickly became a totalistic movement, seeking to remake the world. The women's movement had its excessive tendencies, yet survived the sixties in ways other movements did not. How and why, and its significance for a broader understanding of the "global unbinding of energies" that characterized the decade, is a project for twenty-first-century historians.

Those historians, like others seeking to place the 1960s in perspective, will write in the shadow of a fierce debate over its consequences – the source of much of the vitriol among late twentieth-century 1960s analysts. In the last decades of the past century, that debate has been dubbed "the culture wars." For, most agree, the changes in the wake of the sixties – though the causal relationship is disputed – were more personal and ideological than political and structural. And if, as one recent survey has suggested, the decade was twentieth-century America's Civil War, the nature and meaning of those changes will continue to divide Americans. The historian's job, however, is not to take sides and re-fight old wars, but to transcend the debate and to try to explain the origins, nature, and consequences of those wars. Therein lies the hope of understanding the 1960s as a historical era.

NOTE

For their help the author wishes to thank John Dittmer, Michael Downing, Maurice Isserman, Ted Morgan, Doug Rossinow, and Irene Scharf.

REFERENCES AND FURTHER READING

Andrew, John A., III (1997) *The Other Side of the Sixties: Young Americans for Freedom and the Rise of Conservative Politics*. New Brunswick, NJ: Rutgers University Press.

Bloom, Jack (1987) *Class, Race, and the Civil Rights Movement*. Bloomington: Indiana University Press.

Branch, Taylor (1988) *Parting the Waters: America in the King Years, 1954–63*. New York: Simon and Schuster.

Breines, Winifred (1988) "Whose New Left?," *Journal of American History* 75, pp. 528–45.

Brennan, Mary C. (1995) *Turning Right in the Sixties: The Conservative Capture of the GOP*. Chapel Hill: University of North Carolina Press.

Burner, David M. (1996) *Making Peace with the 60s*. Princeton, NJ: Princeton University Press.

Carson, Clayborne (1981) *In Struggle: SNCC and the Black Awakening of the 1960s*. Cambridge, Mass.: Harvard University Press.

Chomsky, Noam (1987) *On Power and Ideology: The Managua Lectures*. Boston: South End Press.

Cleaver, Eldridge (1968) *Soul on Ice*. New York: McGraw Hill.

Echols, Alice (1989) *Daring to Be Bad: Radical Feminism in America, 1967–1975*. Minneapolis: University of Minnesota Press.

Evans, Sara M. (1979) *Personal Politics: The Roots of Women's Liberation in the Civil Rights Movement and the New Left*. New York: Vintage.

Farrell, James J. (1997) *The Spirit of the Sixties: The Making of Postwar Radicalism*. New York: Routledge.

Frank, Thomas (1997) *The Conquest of Cool: Business Culture, Counterculture, and the Rise of Hip Consumerism*. Chicago: University of Chicago Press.

Gitlin, Todd (1987) *The Sixties: Years of Hope, Days of Rage*. New York: Bantam.

Gosse, Van (1993) *Where the Boys Are: Cuba, Cold War America, and the Making of a New Left*. New York: Verso.

Isserman, Maurice (1987) *If I Had a Hammer . . . : The Death of the Old Left and the Birth of the New Left*. New York: Basic Books.

—— (1992) "You don't need a weatherman but a postman can be helpful: thoughts on the history of SDS and the antiwar movement," in Melvin Small and William D. Hoover (eds.) *Give Peace a Chance: Exploring the Vietnam Antiwar Movement*. Syracuse, NY: Syracuse University Press.

Isserman, Maurice and Kazin, Michael (1989) "The failure and success of the new radicalism," in Steve Fraser and Gary Gerstle (eds.) *The Rise and Fall of the New Deal Order, 1930–1980*. Princeton, NJ: Princeton University Press.

—— (2000) *America Divided: The Civil War of the Sixties*. New York: Oxford University Press.

Jameson, Fredric (1984) "Periodizing the 60s," in Sohnya Sayres et al. (eds.), *The 60s Without Apology*. Minneapolis: University of Minnesota Press.

Mailer, Norman (1969) "Superman comes to the supermarket," in Harold Hayes (ed.) *Smiling Through the Apocalypse: Esquire's History of the Sixties*. New York: McCall.

Marwick, Arthur (1998) *The Sixties: Cultural Revolution in Britain, France, Italy, and the United States, c.1958–c.1974*. New York: Oxford University Press.

Matusow, Allen J. (1984) *The Unraveling of America: A History of Liberalism in the 1960s*. New York: Harper and Row.

Miller, James (1987) *"Democracy is in the Streets": From Port Huron to the Siege of Chicago*. New York: Simon and Schuster.

Morgan, Edward P. (1991) *The Sixties Experience: Hard Lessons about Modern America.* Philadelphia: Temple University Press.

Morris, Aldon (1984) *The Origins of the Civil Rights Movement: Black Communities Organizing for Change.* New York: Free Press.

Morris, Charles R. (1984) *A Time of Passion: America, 1960–1980.* New York: Penguin.

Patterson, James T. (1996) *Grand Expectations: The United States, 1945–1974.* New York: Oxford University Press.

Perlstein, Rick (1996) "Who owns the sixties? The opening of a scholarly generation gap," *Linguafranca* 6, pp. 30–7.

Potter, David M. (1954) *People of Plenty: Economic Abundance and the American Culture.* Chicago: University of Chicago Press.

Remnick, David (1998) *King of the World: Muhammad Ali and the Rise of an American Hero.* New York: Random House.

Rossinow, Doug (1998) *The Politics of Authenticity: Liberalism, Christianity, and the New Left in America.* New York: Columbia University Press.

Singh, Nikhil Pal (1998) "The Black Panthers and the 'undeveloped country of the left,' " in Charles E. Jones (ed.) *The Black Panther Party Reconsidered.* Baltimore, Md.: Black Classic Press.

White, Theodore H. (1961) *The Making of the President 1960.* New York: Atheneum.

CHAPTER SEVEN

1974–1988

LEO P. RIBUFFO

By 1974 the era of political, social, and cultural polarization that Americans had come to call the sixties was fitfully drawing to a close. An accord signed in January 1973 brought an uneasy truce to the Vietnam War, which had been the chief catalyst of the polarization. At the same time détente with the Soviet Union, which had persisted alongside the war, faced increasing criticism. Despite widespread polarization the sixties had been a prosperous time, and a sense that high economic growth could be sustained indefinitely had energized liberal efforts to build a Great Society. Conservatives had yielded to that effort, even as radicals envisioned more fundamental economic, social, and cultural change. In 1973, however, for the first time since the late 1940s, the median real income failed to rise. And in August, 1974, when the Watergate scandal ended in Richard Nixon's resignation, he was succeeded by Gerald R. Ford, a president as calming as his predecessor had been polarizing.

Sixties Legacies

These events mark a rough end of an unusually volatile "decade" (which, as a social-cultural period, distinct from the decimal system, started around 1965–6). But many of the social and cultural trends begun or enhanced in the sixties continued for years thereafter. That era had opened, or reopened, questions even more basic than the nature of legitimate government (or other) authority. When did life begin? How should it end? How should men and women live their lives in the interval? Conflicting hopes, fears, and expectations were re-orchestrated in the less prosperous and (at least temporarily) less confident "seventies."

Groups that had recently advanced through grass-roots mobilization both wanted to build on their victories and feared that their gains might slip away. African Americans now enjoyed legal equality and growing political power, but civil rights issues that affected the North as well as the South – notably affirmative action and compulsory busing of school children – left race relations volatile. The revival of feminism increased the number of women in the professions, blue collar work force, and public office. Yet this movement's most visible victories, congressional approval of an Equal Rights Amendment (ERA) in 1972 and legalization of almost all abortions by the US Supreme Court in *Roe* v. *Wade* (1973), precipitated immediate opposition. By 1973 there were 800 gay and lesbian organizations, many working to strike down sodomy laws and ban discrimination against homosexuals.

These social movements overshadowed – and for many Americans looking backward, continue to overshadow – domestic operations of the federal government. Nonetheless, government actions left at least equally important legacies. The federal courts expanded freedom of speech and assembly, while restricting religious ceremonies in public places, where explicit sexual acts were tolerated too. Even after the heyday of the Great Society, liberals in Congress managed to expand the welfare state during the Nixon era, and looked forward to further growth when the Democrats recaptured the White House. Actions regarded as secondary at the time sometimes had far-reaching effects. The Immigration Act of 1965 facilitated the country's fourth great wave of immigration, this time primarily from Asia and Latin America. These "new immigrants," like their predecessors, quickly began to modify what it meant to be an American.

By 1973–4 even men and women aloof from social movements could not avoid encountering significant changes in "the American way of life," a phrase on the verge of replacement by the looser "life-styles." While a small band of intellectuals promoted white ethnic identities, Catholics and Jews descended from the old "new immigration" of the early twentieth century married outside their faiths in numbers unimaginable in earlier generations. The rising rates of divorce, premarital sex, and cohabitation before marriage showed no sign of reversal. Neither did the rising rate of illegal drug use and violent crime. Harder to measure but nonetheless real was the decreasing formality in dress and modes of address. The sixties legitimated militant protest to a degree unprecedented since the thirties. Although usually appalled by the results, conservatives by 1973–4 had begun to learn lessons from their opponents' successes and their own defeats. Effective conservative mobilization required grassroots organization, dilution of fervor with amiability, and lobbies in Washington to influence "big government" while denouncing it.

Distrust of the federal government – a perennial aspect of the American sensibility – was exacerbated by the Vietnam War, the Watergate scandal, and well-publicized investigations of Central Intelligence Agency (CIA) covert actions during the Cold War. Although mass media had routinized the exposure of Washington corruption since the Progressive Era, this enterprise now acquired extraordinary prestige. In *All the President's Men* (1976), Hollywood presented as national heroes two journalists who helped to uncover the Watergate scandal. Under the circumstances, publishers and reporters were strongly motivated to discover or magnify subsequent scandals. As the sixties slid into the seventies, however, censure of lying presidents, congressional libertines, and intrusive bureaucrats rarely entailed a basic critique of American institutions. On the contrary, the popular post-mortem on Watergate held with journalist Jimmy Breslin that "the good guys finally won." If doubts arose, elite opinion leaders proclaimed that "the system had worked." Moreover, the venerable belief that luck, pluck, and hard work opened the way to success and personal fulfillment remained at least as strong, and perhaps stronger, than ever. Here, too, Hollywood adapted to the mix of moods. Along with the fictional news anchor in *Network* (1976), many Americans felt they were "mad as hell and . . . not going to take it anymore." Perhaps, as in *Three Days of the Condor* (1975), assassins lurked in the secret world of the CIA. Even so, in *Rocky* (1976) and *Saturday Night Fever* (1977), young men from working-class backgrounds still overcame adversity. And in the television mini-series *Roots*, the chronicle of a black family that endured slavery over many generations, freedom triumphed in the end.

Through it all the United States remained one of the most religious countries in the industrial world. Indeed, the number of Americans who told pollsters that religion was becoming increasingly important in their lives rose from 14 percent in 1970 to 44 percent in 1978. Anti-Semitism continued to decline except among African Americans. No reputable figure now questioned the legitimacy of a Catholic running for president. At the same time, theological liberals and conservatives within all major denominations were now increasingly at odds. Furthermore, countless Americans pursued a personal religious syncretism which, without any sense of contradiction, might include affiliation with a conventional denomination, respect for their neighbors' very different churches, perusal of a daily horoscope, curiosity about apocalyptic Bible prophecy, and interest in "new age" self-help.

In 1973–4 no aspect of American life seemed more permanent than some version of the Cold War. "Détente" with the Soviet Union had been accepted since the Eisenhower administration as a means to avoid apocalyptic confrontation and simultaneously weaken the Soviet Union. The term itself entered the standard diplomatic vocabulary during the Nixon years, when both sides formally promised to eschew pursuit of "unilateral advantage" and then pursued unilateral advantages. By 1973, avid cold warriors insisted that the Soviets were using détente to consolidate totalitarian rule at home and gain international ground on the United States. Specifically, they suppressed dissidents, restricted emigration, enlarged their nuclear arsenal, and supported Third World revolutionaries. In Vietnam there was none of the "reconciliation" promised in the peace accords (Garthoff 1994a; Schulzinger 1997).

From Ford to Carter

All of these developments ultimately affected Gerald Ford's presidency, but two problems required his immediate attention. Moved by friendship and a desire to move the country beyond its "long national nightmare," Ford on September 8, 1974 pardoned Nixon of all crimes related to Watergate. The economic problems Ford faced were not so easily addressed – or even explained. The annual rate of inflation in the fourth quarter of 1974 was 12 percent, the worst since 1919. But unemployment still reached 9.8 percent in mid-1975, the highest since the late 1940s. The causes of this "stagflation" were varied and deep-seated: slipping American economic power relative to other industrial nations, declining productivity, the capacity of large corporations to resist market pressures to lower prices, poor financing of the Vietnam War, zig-zagging fiscal and monetary policies by the Nixon administration and Federal Reserve Board, entry into the job market by large numbers of women and baby boomers, rising prices of primary products (especially petroleum), and public expectations that an inflationary spiral, once begun, would continue indefinitely. The cure was unknown and, at least at the time, probably nonexistent. In this economic environment, Ford was less willing than Nixon to acquiesce in liberal legislation passed by a Democratic Congress. While agreeing to extend unemployment benefits when the economy slipped into a recession during 1975, he vetoed bills intended to expand the welfare state. He sought a smaller federal deficit on the grounds that government borrowing "crowded out" more productive private investment. Ford also proposed to de-regulate major industries in order to foster competition and lower prices. Although the economy was recovering from the recession by late 1976, unemployment remained above 7 percent.

Ford both pursued détente and abandoned the controversial term itself in favor of "peace through strength." The United States and the Soviet Union almost came to terms on a second Strategic Arms Limitation Treaty (SALT II). In 1975, Ford did sign the Helsinki accords, which legitimated the post-World War II European boundaries, including those established by Red Army victories. In exchange, the Soviets joined other signatories in agreeing to respect basic human rights. To avid cold warriors, including Ronald Reagan, what Ford considered a promising deal represented "appeasement." Such complaints found a ready audience. More than any other event, the disorderly US withdrawal and fall of South Vietnam in the spring of 1975 convinced many Americans that their country was losing the Cold War. For some of them, this concern merged with deeper fears about the nation's future (Garthoff 1994a; Greene 1995; Schulzinger 1997).

Ford's was the first post-sixties presidency in ways beyond mere chronology. Not only were problems previously confined to the private sphere now volatile public issues, but political leaders, and their families, were expected to answer questions that would have been considered scandalous a decade and a half earlier. Ford's wife Betty welcomed the change and became a national heroine when she talked openly about her mastectomy for breast cancer. On the other hand, cultural conservatives denounced her realistic statement that her young adult sons might have used marijuana (which they had) and that her teenage daughter might have had a love affair (which she had not). Ford himself was asked whether he was smart enough to be President (Witcover 1977; Greene 1995).

After narrowly defeating Ronald Reagan for the Republican nomination, Ford faced Democrat Jimmy Carter, the former Governor of Georgia, in the 1976 election. The candidates' formulaic partisan attacks on each other obscured their commonalities. Ford was less critical of the welfare state than he sounded; and Carter, the most conservative Democratic nominee since the 1920s, was less supportive than he pretended. Both candidates favored a version of détente as a Cold War tactic. Both wanted to restore an optimistic national consensus, and Ford claimed already to have done so. Although both men felt uncomfortable with the country's most visible cultural issue – abortion – both also tried to adapt to the evolving "life-styles" of the electorate. More flexible than Ford, Carter underscored various aspects of his career and personality before different constituencies: naval officer, farmer, nuclear engineer, "populist" political outsider, and "born-again" Southern Baptist. In the end, however, the Democrat's 1.7 million-vote victory owed most to the sagging economy, the Nixon pardon, and doubts about the incumbent's ability (Witcover 1977).

The new administration opened with symbolic affirmations that recent national nightmares were over. In keeping with the new informality, and in a visible contrast to Nixon's "imperial presidency," Carter took the oath of office as "Jimmy" and walked part of the way in his inaugural parade. In his inaugural address, he acknowledged Ford as one of the good guys for helping to heal the country. The accompanying prayer services and parties highlighted racial, ethnic, regional, and religious diversity under an umbrella of national unity. Carter's first executive order established an amnesty program for draft evaders from the Vietnam War. He also supported legislation – ultimately passed in 1978 as the Ethics in Government Act – that set procedures for appointing special counsel to investigate possible crimes by high officials (Kutler 1990; Kaufman 1993).

Nonetheless, heightened expectations and the persistence of adverse trends combined to disable the Carter administration. Although the economy turned upward in 1977, the forces that had produced stagflation were only in remission. Détente with the Soviets remained inherently unstable. At the same time, Americans were less willing than fifteen years earlier "to bear any burden" (to recall President John Kennedy's words from 1961) on behalf of any national cause. If the "seventies" was the "me decade," as journalist Tom Wolfe claimed in 1976, it was not simply because the sixties had released unprecedented visions of individual fulfillment, but also because Americans felt that they had recently borne too many burdens (Carroll 1982).

Carter and Latter-day Progressivism

In this context Carter was out of step with the country when he stressed the limits of American power and prosperity. He was also out of step with the Democratic majority in Congress. After two Republican administrations, congressional Democrats expected to be courted and consulted by a president from their own party. More important, most wanted at least a modest expansion of the welfare state that had been created in the 1930s and expanded in the 1960s. Carter found his ideological inspiration in an earlier reform tradition. Offering an updated version of pre-World War I progressivism, he promoted spiritual uplift and efficiency, – the latter to be achieved, in this instance, by economic de-regulation (Hargrove 1988; Kaufman 1993). Insofar as there was a coherent political strategy, the administration hoped to hold on to working-class Democrats with modest concessions, while actively courting affluent voters by emphasizing such issues as conservation, consumer protection, fiscal restraint, and curbs on bureaucratic regulation. Unfortunately, because the politics of race, ethnicity, and gender had achieved fresh legitimacy, there were more "special interests" than ever to accommodate. This problem particularly afflicted the Democrats, always the more diverse of the two major parties. The administration itself necessarily included avid ecologists and fervent advocates of rural development, feminists who considered abortion a right and Catholics and evangelicals who thought it a sin, African-American proponents of affirmative action and whites only recently acquiescent in desegregation. Many white southern Democrats still joined Republicans in a congressional conservative coalition that had criticized the regulatory and welfare state since the 1930s (Fink and Graham 1998).

These forces, rather than Carter's idiosyncrasies as an "outsider," produced a series of embarrassments and legislative failures during 1977–8. As early as April 1977, Carter infuriated powerful Democratic senators by trying to cancel water projects that he considered ecologically unsound. The congressional conservative coalition defeated efforts to liberalize labor law, establish a consumer protection office in the White House, and reform Aid to Families with Dependent Children (AFDC), the

New Deal program often stigmatized as "welfare." Expecting to succeed where Nixon and Ford had failed, Carter offered a complicated plan to make the United States less dependent on imported petroleum. He too proposed the de-control of oil and natural gas prices but, unlike his Republican predecessors, also stressed conservation and proposed a "windfall" profits tax on energy companies. Carter hoped to rally the country around the energy crisis as the "moral equivalent of war."

Racial and sexual politics were probably more divisive than energy issues and certainly more visceral for most Americans. The election of a Georgian, a former segregationist turned advocate of racial equality, symbolized acceptance of African-American legal equality. The President himself actively recruited blacks to serve in his administration and in the federal judiciary. Yet blacks, who probably came out of the sixties with greater expectations than any other group of Americans, were disappointed by his economic conservatism. More importantly, controversies over affirmative action and compulsory school busing wracked communities, colleges, and work places. In *Regents of the University of California* v. *W. Allan Bakke* (1978), a fragmented Supreme Court approved affirmative action but rejected specific racial quotas. Instead of resolving a national controversy, this confused mélange of opinion, concurrences, and dissents served as a catalyst for further legal, social, and political acrimony. Carter lobbied for passage of the ERA and recruited women into his administration. He lacked the affinity for feminists and their issues that he felt with blacks and the cause of civil rights. Rather, they seemed much like labor leaders, a constituency that had to be appeased without alienating conservative voters or his own conscience. In 1977 he signed legislation that barred use of federal funds for Medicaid abortions. When some of his own female appointees openly protested that this action discriminated against the poor, Carter not only reiterated his personal opposition to abortion, but also observed that "many things in life . . . are not fair." (quoted in Fink and Graham 1998: 227).

Carter brought a distinctive approach to foreign relations. Frequently making analogies with the civil rights movement in the United States, he quickly adopted the cause of international human rights as his own. No president showed greater respect for small and non-white nations; none since Herbert Hoover was less inclined to use military force. At the same time, Carter's diplomacy fitted into the broader American diplomatic tradition. For instance, he believed that free trade and peace went hand-in-hand, and hoped to channel incipient revolutions into a democratic middle way between dictatorships of the right or left. Moreover, Carter's distinctive inclinations had to be adapted to international and domestic political realities, especially the inherent instability and growing unpopularity of détente. Carter institutionalized national (and Democratic) divisions over foreign policy with the appointment of Cyrus Vance, a chastened cold warrior, as Secretary of State, and Zbigniew Brzezinski, a strong cold warrior, as national security adviser. In May, 1977 the President declared his intention to move beyond the "inordinate fear of Communism" that had led the United States "to support any dictator who joined us in that fear" (quoted in Smith 1986: 66). Although this speech was misunderstood – and sometimes deliberately misconstrued – by many avid cold warriors, the President joined his recent predecessors in viewing détente as a means both to provide basic international stability and to change what he still called "totalitarian" regimes. Indeed, he openly chided the Soviet Union for violating the human rights of its citizens. At the same time, he proposed "deep cuts" in nuclear arsenals that the Soviets, who thought they were close to an agreement with Ford, rejected out of hand (Garthoff 1994a; Strong 2000).

Other foreign policy initiatives were more successful. Although the commitment to international human rights was less "absolute" than Carter claimed in one of his many hyperbolic moments, during 1977–8 the administration used rhetoric and withdrawal of aid to pressure several authoritarian governments. These actions saved lives, especially in Argentina, Brazil, and Chile. Highlighting his respect for Third World countries, Carter in 1978 became the first sitting president to visit sub-Saharan Africa. In 1977, after thirteen years of negotiations during four presidencies, Carter signed treaties that would turn over full control of the Canal Zone to Panama at the end of 1999. No early foreign policy decision was more consequential. Carter expected ratification of these agreements to provide a quick political victory and underscore American respect for small Third World nations. Yet in early 1978 the administration barely managed to win Senate ratification; it was by only one vote. Moreover the campaign against the treaties, framed in the context of widespread worries about the decline of American power, energized the grass-roots conservative movement (LaFeber 1979; Smith 1986).

Nor were conservatives alone in adapting to win followers in the seventies. Indeed, some movements that had only begun to congeal when pundits declared the sixties dead grew into strong interest groups during the seventies. Native Americans went to court to protect their sacred lands or claim compensation for broken treaties. Diverse immigrants from Latin America (whom the census began to group as "Hispanics" in 1973) derailed Carter's plan to crack down on illegal immigration. Responding to the increasing political clout of older Americans, Congress in 1978 raised the mandatory retirement age from 65 to 70 (Carroll 1982). If life was unfair, according to rival definitions of fairness, political mobilization could still render it less so. Nonetheless, pundits such as Tom Wolfe who saw a shift in the aggregate from the political to the personal were not entirely wrong. Looking back a generation later, a conservative commentator noted that forms of behavior that had recently been seen as cultural experiments or rebellious acts were incorporated into the "life-styles" of the upper middle class (Frum 2000). For instance, while marijuana and cocaine remained illegal, white recreational users were unlikely to be prosecuted, let alone convicted. Illegal drugs were celebrated virtually every week on the satirical television show *Saturday Night Live* and almost fetishized in popular movies such as *Up in Smoke* (1978).

Changing Life-styles and Ebbing Confidence

The "life-style" quest created a boom market in varied versions of mental healing and surrogate religions. During the Carter years, 19 million Americans were affiliated with the "human potential" movement. Some parts of this amorphous persuasion – notably psychotherapy, existential psychology, and the "new age" derivatives of theologically liberal Protestantism – were grounded in serious intellectual traditions. Others, like Scientology and EST, were insubstantial and occasionally dangerous. Most of them published their own guides to right living, variously defined. Some provoked exposés by former adherents. All were satirized in plays, movies, novels, and television shows. Most of them probably helped some people some of the time. Their popularity certainly should not have surprised anyone in an era of national nightmares and economic uncertainty. Indeed, this latest quest for health, wealth, and metaphysical meaning was as American as Sylvester Graham's cracker and Ralph Waldo Emerson's essays.

No change in personal "life-styles" was more consequential than the revolution in sexual morality that finally occurred a half century after it was first heralded and denounced. As usual, news media focused on the young and flamboyant, and especially on "singles" (a term just coming into general use). There were news stories on actors who appeared on stage naked and on citizens who made love *en masse* at the New York nightclub called Plato's Retreat. Yet attitudes were in flux among Americans unlikely to flaunt, or even admit to, a change. From the comfort of their living rooms, they made hits of *Charlie's Angels* and *Three's Company*, television series that featured, respectively, scantily dressed female detectives and sexual banter that would not have reached the networks a decade earlier. Shifting attitudes about sex, dreams of personal fulfillment, economic stress, and "no-fault" divorce laws in most states took a toll on what was called the traditional family, a term that usually evoked idealized memories of the unusually stable nuclear families of the 1950s. In 1979 one million heterosexual couples lived together outside of marriage; according to polls, only one American in four still stigmatized unmarried mothers. Once again, the trend was hardly confined to the over-publicized baby boomers. As divorce lost its stigma, the percentage of Americans in their forties who were married dropped from 84 percent in 1972 to 67 percent a decade later. According to the dominant cultural stereotype, exemplified in the film *Kramer vs. Kramer* (1979), middle-aged women left their husbands and children in search of liberation. Yet, as one social critic argued in retrospect, men were more likely to leave their wives (Ehrenreich 1983). The social costs of changing sexual mores included the "feminization of poverty." The number of female-headed houses grew from 2.2 million in 1971 to 5.9 million in 1979 (Stage 1983; O'Brien 1990; Frum 2000).

By the end of the Carter years, both the social changes begun during the sixties and the more recent economic slump no longer looked like ephemeral intrusions on "traditional" ways of life. As corporate profits dropped, big business grew less likely to accept federal regulation and acquiesce in unionization or wage increases. Except on Capitol Hill the counterattack by cultural conservatives was much more visible than its corporate counterpart. Grass-roots affirmations of "traditional values" proliferated. In 1977, singer Anita Bryant mobilized voters in Dade County, Florida, to overturn a civil rights ordinance protecting gays. The next year, a culturally conservative former member of the San Francisco board of supervisors assassinated Mayor George Moscone and Harvey Milk, the first openly homosexual member of the board. Also in 1978, California voters – many of them convinced that the state squandered money on the disorderly, undeserving poor – passed Proposition 13, drastically cutting property taxes (Carroll 1982; Peele 1984; Allyn 2000).

Economic stagnation and the erosion of "traditional values" also affected serious social thought. Conservative thinkers had not been silent during the sixties, but their ideas were submerged beneath a "captivating rhetoric of community, liberation, participation, and transformation." By contrast, the dominant social criticism that began to emerge during the Carter years affirmed scientific objectivity, hierarchical authority, and human fallibility (Purcell 1983: 83). Increasingly attentive to the failures rather than the successes of the welfare state, liberal social theorists Daniel Bell, Nathan Glazer, and Seymour Martin Lipset drifted toward what came to be called neo-conservatism (Fleming and Gottfried 1988). In *The Zero-Sum Society* (1980), economist Lester Thurow criticized American sloth and urged emulation of the disciplined Japanese. Christopher Lasch assailed therapy, self-improvement, and self-indulgence in *The Culture of Narcissism* (1979), a volume ironically displayed alongside Alex Comfort's *The Joy of Sex* (1972) and Jim Fixx's *The Complete Book of Running* (1977) in the self-help section of many book stores.

Despite signs of a conservative trend, the Carter administration approached 1979 with cautious optimism. In late 1978, Congress passed airline deregulation and lifted price controls on natural gas. Recognition of the People's Republic of China at the end of the year elicited few very vociferous complaints. Carter's mediation of the Camp David accords – a step toward peace between Israel and Egypt – was widely praised. Prospects were good for a SALT II treaty with the Soviets in 1979. Despite the risk of alienating liberal Democrats, the administration made curbing inflation the foremost domestic goal. The public had grudgingly tolerated a 9 percent rise in the consumer price index during 1978, and Carter expected government economies and wage-price guidelines to hold inflation to roughly that level in 1979. According to an administration public relations campaign launched in early 1979, the country faced new dilemmas in an era of limits, but Carter had gained control of these problems.

Within six months, everything seemed out of control. The central event was a revolution that drove the Shah of Iran into exile in January, 1979. Carter rejected military intervention, sought a centrist democratic government and, after that standard hope proved vain, tried to establish decent relations with the new Islamic regime. When Iranian oil production was disrupted, the Organization of Petroleum Exporting Countries (OPEC) took advantage of the situation by raising prices. Not only did the oil supply from abroad look increasingly precarious, but also one controversial domestic alternative looked increasingly dangerous. In March 1979, an accident at the nuclear reactor at Three Mile Island in Harrisburg, Pennsylvania, almost resulted in a meltdown (Carroll 1982; Sick 1986).

After further mediation by Carter, Israel and Egypt agreed to a formal peace treaty in March 1979. Three months later he signed the SALT II agreement with Soviet leader Leonid Brezhnev. But many Jews felt that Carter had pushed Israel too hard in the former instance, and avid cold warriors thought that the Soviets had won another victory in the latter case. After another futile search for a moderate alternative, Carter cut off military aid to Anastasio Somoza, the dictatorial President of Nicaragua, who then fled and allowed the Marxist-led Sandinistas to come to power in July. By that point, angry motorists lining up to pay high prices for scarce gasoline were as symbolic of Carter's administration as soup kitchens had been of Herbert Hoover's. The deterioration of Carter's coalition was almost as visible. In addition to Jews and staunch Cold-War Democrats, feminists criticized Carter, and their disaffection grew when he fired Bella Abzug as head of the National Advisory Committee on Women in January; from working-class Catholics, whose living standards were eroded by stagflation; and from Protestant fundamentalists and evangelicals, who saw that Carter was politically and culturally more liberal than he had sounded in 1976. Many union leaders and welfare-state liberals urged Senator Edward Kennedy of Massachusetts to challenge Carter's renomination.

The President spent the first two weeks of July secluded at Camp David seeking to shore up his coalition and unite the country. News media reported (inaccurately) that he was poring over analyses of the national "malaise" by Daniel Bell and Christopher Lasch. Then, on July 15, Carter addressed the country on the energy crisis and the "crisis of confidence." He linked a brief for the unpassed portion of his energy program with an appeal to Americans to transcend their selfishness and to sacrifice (modestly, and in the short term) to restore prosperity. This updated appeal to bear burdens for the country briefly enhanced Carter's popularity. Within the week, however, the President undermined his standing as an inspirational leader by abruptly reorganizing his government. Not only was the cabinet now less liberal and the White House staff more insular, but the President himself appeared erratic and petty (Ribuffo 1997).

Both the economy and the President's popularity continued to deteriorate. In July he reluctantly requested the resignation of United Nations Ambassador Andrew Young, the administration's foremost African American. Young had talked with representatives of the Palestinian Liberation Organization in violation of State Department instructions, and had lied about having violated that rule. Young's departure under these circumstances exacerbated already tense relations between blacks and Jews. In August, in accordance with the Ethics in Government Act, a special counsel was appointed to investigate allegations that White House Chief of Staff Hamilton Jordan had used cocaine at the New York disco Studio 54. Jordan was absolved but the political damage was done. In September, Carter's selection of Republican Paul Volcker, a fiscal conservative, as chairman of the Federal Reserve Board underscored his determination to curb inflation even at the cost of rising unemployment. The federal budget deficit fell from $48.8 billion in fiscal year 1978 to $29.6 billion the next year. Nonetheless, the consumer price index rose 9 percent between January and December, 1979. In early November Senator Edward Kennedy announced his presidential candidacy.

These developments were dwarfed by the seizure of the American embassy in Iran on November 4. The embassy had been invaded by Muslim militants in February but the occupation had been ended after two hours, on orders from Ayatollah Khomeini, the leader of the Islamic revolution. Relations between the United States and Iran seemed stable until Carter reluctantly allowed the exiled Shah to enter the United States from Mexico for cancer treatment on October 24. Although aware of the risks, Carter convinced himself of the dubious proposition that the Shah could not receive adequate care elsewhere. Certainly he was also moved by the advice of both Secretary of State Vance and National Security Adviser Brzezinski, as well as influential members of the bipartisan foreign policy elite, that the United States could not abandon a former ally. This time the Iranians held the embassy in Tehran as well as 66 Americans until Carter left office on January 20, 1981 (Sick 1986; Shawcross 1988).

The early phase of this hostage crisis coincided with a dramatic turn for the worse in Soviet–American relations. Notwithstanding SALT II, Carter had been growing increasingly wary of the Soviets since early 1978. In particular, he concurred in Brzezinski's judgment that Soviet sponsorship of a Marxist regime in Ethiopia and acquiescence in the deployment of Cuban troops in the Angolan civil war violated the rules of détente. In these circumstances, he favored a 3 percent real increase in military spending. Nor was this position devoid of political considerations. Prodded by such organizations as the Committee on the Present Danger, the premier lobby of the cold warrior interest group, Americans increasingly believed that the United States was falling behind militarily. Then, at the end of December, 1979, the Soviet Union invaded Afghanistan to replace one tottering Communist government with another. After an angry and futile confrontation with Brezhnev over the hot line, Carter pursued various tactics to force a Soviet retreat. He withdrew the SALT II treaty from Senate consideration, secured congressional approval for standby draft registration and an embargo on grain sales to the Soviets, led a boycott of the summer Olympics in Moscow, proposed a 5 percent real increase in defense spending, and stepped up the covert aid already in progress to anti-Communist guerrillas in Afghanistan. In January, 1980, he enunciated the Carter Doctrine. Any attempt by outside forces to gain control of the Persian Gulf would be "repelled by any means necessary, including military force" (quoted in Smith 1986: 230).

Benefiting from the tendency of voters to rally around a president during international crises, Carter easily defeated Senator Kennedy for the Democratic nomination. Yet as Kennedy's prospects of winning the nomination declined, his support in the primaries grew, a sign of Democratic doubts about Carter's abilities or economic priorities. Indeed, except for passage of legislation de-controlling the price of petroleum products, Carter faced failures and problems on every front while he campaigned against Republican nominee Ronald Reagan. In April 1980, an ill-conceived military mission to rescue the hostages ended when US helicopters broke down and collided far from Tehran. While the inflationary spiral proved impervious to interest rates as high as 15 percent, unemployment rose to 7.8 percent (Berman 1998; Kaufman 1993).

Carter's pledge of a presidency more ethical than others backfired in a scandal involving his alcoholic brother. In 1976–7, fraternity with Billy, a self-styled southern "good ol' boy," had helped Carter to soften his technocratic image. Subsequently, however, Billy lobbied on behalf of Libya, blurted out anti Semitic remarks, and in 1980 was investigated by Congress for allegedly profiting from his White House connections. Even Carter's promise in 1976 to celebrate and strengthen family values had come back to haunt him. When a White House Conference on Families finally convened in 1980, feminists and gay rights advocates clashed with cultural conservatives, who accused the administration of undermining the divinely-ordained nuclear family. Mobilizing around such issues, Republican political professionals joined with fundamentalist and evangelical clergy to create a "new Christian right." At the same time, culturally liberal Democrats and independents defected from Carter's coalition to support independent presidential candidate John Anderson. Reagan turned issues that Carter had used four years earlier back against him, especially the need to restore American greatness, protect traditional values, re-establish prosperity, and shrink an ostensibly wasteful federal government. In their televised debate, Reagan used informal geniality to ease fears that he was a dangerous extremist. What pundits mislabeled Reagan's "populist conservatism" is better understood as a conservatism belatedly adapted under his guidance to the growing informality of American life.

On election day, Reagan won 50.7 percent of the vote in a three-way race. Not only did the bulk of Protestant theological conservatives return to the Republican fold, but Carter received the smallest percentage of the Catholic and Jewish vote of any Democratic nominee since the 1920s. The Republicans won the Senate for the first time since 1952.

The Reagan Evolution

Although racially less diverse, Reagan's coalition was in its own way as complicated as Carter's had been. Whereas most citizens wanted the United States to sound tougher in foreign policy, there was no agreement on the degree of risk that the country should or would tolerate. Whereas Republican business leaders emphasized balancing the budget, proponents of "supply side" economics wanted large tax cuts. The small but prominent band of neo-conservative intellectuals – many of them Jewish – coexisted warily with new Christian right activists. "Reagan Democrats" were liable to leave the coalition if the new administration failed to deliver prosperity or chose to cut those parts of the welfare state from which working-class Catholics benefited. Participants in inaugural festivities ranged from Frank Sinatra, an erstwhile liberal Democrat and self-described "saloon singer," to the Reverend Jerry Falwell, leader of the Moral Majority, the foremost new Christian right organization. Reagan held his coalition together with the glue of his genial public personality. He cared most deeply about expanding American power and limiting some parts of the federal government; his inattention to the day-to-day governance fostered considerable flexibility in practice. Most importantly, Reagan began his presidency with gallantry. In April 1981, he was shot by John Hinckley, whose special delusion – unprecedented among would-be assassins – was that this murder would impress a young movie star, Jodie Foster. Reagan reacted with bravery and dark humor. Ford and Carter were brave too, as their naval careers demonstrated, but neither had brought to the White House a public image of heroism (Blumenthal and Edsall 1988; Cannon 1991).

In addition to Reagan's aura, the support of the "Boll Weevils," the latest Democrats in a congressional conservative coalition that dated from the 1930s, was crucial for the passage of the Republican economic program in 1981–2. The central feature cut federal income taxes by 25 percent over three years. But there was no comparable cut in federal spending. The administration blamed congressional Democrats. Yet this de facto compromise also reflected Reagan's belief that he should not and politically could not attack many welfare state legacies from the New Deal and Great Society. Moreover, Reagan sponsored the largest military buildup in American history (though, as the administration pointed out, the percentage of the budget spent on defense was lower than during the Kennedy administration). The budget deficit for fiscal year 1982 reached $110.6 billion. According to supply side theory, the cut in tax *rates* would produce a boom in investment and thus an increase in tax *revenues*. Rather, investment declined as the Federal Reserve Board with administration acquiescence tightened the money supply and the country sank into a recession starting in August, 1981. With a smaller working-class constituency than Carter, Reagan could accept the resulting unemployment rate approaching 10 percent.

Aspects of the welfare and regulatory state weathered the Reagan presidency with varying degrees of continuity. After claiming for years that Social Security faced "bankruptcy," he appointed a bipartisan commission to study the system's actual, and relatively small, financial problems. Following commission recommendations, Congress in 1983 raised the retirement age in stages and postponed cost of living adjustments. Another legatee of the New Deal, the labor movement, fared less well. In 1981, Reagan ordered the firing of striking air traffic controllers. Beyond the immediate issues at hand, including working conditions and the right of federal employees to strike, the President signaled his affinity with businesses that had begun to fight unionization more vigorously as their profits declined. Union membership fell from 23.6 percent of the work force in 1980 to 19.4 percent in 1984. Reagan accepted the gospel of deregulation with greater zeal than Carter and operated in a more favorable *Zeitgeist* than Ford. One tactic was to cut the staff charged with enforcement, for example, at the Federal Trade Commission and the Consumer Product Safety Commission. Another was to appoint foes of regulation. Preservationists had a place in the world, Secretary of the Interior James Watt remarked, but not in his department. In 1986 savings and loan associations (S & Ls) were permitted to move beyond the relatively stable mortgage market to more speculative investments. They promptly did so. To sustain the "Reagan revolution" in the long term, the President appointed federal judges favorable to the free market and skeptical of government regulation (Schwartz 1988; Schulman 2001).

While the President claimed to preserve the "social safety net," the heaviest burdens of his economic policies fell upon the poor, including the working poor. Means-tested anti-poverty programs were the least popular parts of the welfare state and thus the easiest to cut. For instance, the federal housing budget fell from $30 billion to $10 billion in 1987. Equally important were actions not taken. A Democratic administration would have promoted unionization as well as increases in the minimum wage and AFDC benefits to keep pace with inflation. The chief beneficiaries of Reagan's policies were the upper middle class and above all the very rich. By 1989, the upper two-fifths of the population received 67.8 percent of income and the lowest two-fifths received 15.4 percent, the highest and lowest percentages respectively in forty years. Liberal fears to the contrary, however, moralistic neo-conservatives and adherents of the Christian right were very junior partners in the Reagan coalition. With the exception of Secretary of Education William Bennett, a Catholic and a Democrat, none received a senior appointment dealing with domestic policy. New Christian right clergy were invited to attend prayer breakfasts and deliver invocations, and legislation eliminated the last vestiges of federal funding for abortions. Nonetheless, the White House gave only pro forma endorsements to the Right-to-Life Amendment and the restoration of prayer in public schools.

Probably no Cold War president entered office as convinced as Reagan that the Soviet Union was evil and that international Communism and its Third World clients were indivisible. Nonetheless, he was sufficiently practical to treat some Communist regimes with flexibility. A few members of the administration believed from the outset that the United States could roll back Communism and perhaps force a Soviet collapse. This old goal could be achieved through stern rhetoric, military buildup, and aid to anti-Communist groups. Reagan himself led the rhetorical offensive. In 1983, he called the Soviet Union the "focus of evil" in the modern world (quoted in Garthoff 1994b: 9). Two years later, he enunciated what came to be known as the Reagan doctrine. The United States, he said, would aid anti-Communist insurgents "from Afghanistan to Nicaragua to defy Soviet-supported aggression and secure rights that have been ours since birth" (quoted in Cannon 1991: 369). The American military buildup was intended partly to put a strain on the Soviet economy as Moscow tried to keep pace. Similarly, Reagan in 1983 endorsed the Strategic Defense Initiative (SDI), an expensive anti-missile shield that could be built, if at all, only at enormous cost.

Nonetheless, the administration resumed disarmament talks with the Soviets and largely abided by the unratified SALT II treaty. And acknowledging divisions within international Communism, Reagan visited the People's Republic of China in 1984.

From the outset Reagan differed sharply from Carter in his willingness to use military and paramilitary force against Third World countries and indigenous radical movements. Efforts to police the confusing Lebanese civil war led to the bombing of the US embassy and a US marines barracks in Beirut. The day after the latter disaster, on October 24, 1983, Reagan ordered troops to overthrow the Marxist government of Grenada, a small Caribbean island, on the dubious grounds that American lives were threatened. To his credit, after promising not to "cut and run" from Lebanon, he withdrew US forces. In the western hemisphere, however, Reagan was determined to make the Sandinista government of Nicaragua "say uncle." The main tactic was to support a rebel army generally called the Contras. In 1982 and 1984, a wary Congress passed legislation known as the Boland Amendment, banning aid to these anti-Sandinista rebels. Seeking to circumvent these restrictions, the National Security Council (NSC) continued to assist the Contras with contributions secretly solicited from private citizens and foreign governments (Draper 1991; Pemberton 1998).

As the recession lingered into 1983, only the most devout ideologists purported to know where the economy was heading in the long run. Even in retrospect, the conflicting tendencies are difficult to disentangle. Some of the medium-range problems were the result of bad business decisions: investments in outdated technology, creation of conglomerates whose managers lacked expertise in the constituent parts, corporate "raids" that maximized short-term financial gain rather than long-term productivity. While international competition, management choices, and improved technology combined to shrink the industrial work force, recent innovations offered the prospect of growth elsewhere. Companies founded between 1975 and 1983 included Apple Computer, Microsoft, and Cable News Network (CNN). In the short run, the economy emerged from the recession a year before the 1984 election.

Reagan administration actions provoked significant grass-roots responses from middle-class liberals and the residual community of radicals. The Sierra Club collected a million signatures to protest off-shore oil drilling. The military buildup and rhetorical offensive against the Soviet "evil empire" prompted a countervailing campaign to hold strategic arsenals at current levels. In 1983 a demonstration organized by this "nuclear freeze" movement drew a million demonstrators. Aside from African Americans and trade unionists, there were few comparable protests against scaling down the welfare state (Berman 1998; Pemberton 1998).

Except for black activist Jesse Jackson, all of the candidates for the Democratic presidential nomination tacked rightward in 1984. Jackson elicited enormous enthusiasm among African Americans and won support from some white liberals but never stood a chance of being nominated. His reputation eroded when, in a demonstration of the rising black anti-Semitism, he referred to Jews as "Hymies." A more likely nominee, "neo-liberal" Senator Gary Hart of Colorado, advocated a pro-business "industrial policy" to solve long-term economic problems. Hart sought especially to woo "yuppies" (young urban professionals), a constituency suddenly conceptualized, manufactured, and prized by politicians and marketers alike. Former Vice President Walter Mondale, the eventual nominee, recanted earlier enthusiasm for deficit spending and international restraint. His most imaginative tactic was choosing a woman,

Representative Geraldine Ferraro of New York, as his running mate. In the end, Mondale enjoyed even less success than Carter in portraying Reagan as an extremist. Reagan won 59 percent of the vote, solidified conservative Protestant support for his party, and even received 31 percent of ballots cast by the unemployed (Pomper 1985; Gillon 1992).

Conflicting "Life-styles" and the End of the Cold War

Liberals worried that the popular President was leading the whole culture in a conservative direction and, as film critic Tom O'Connor noted, they often cited *Rambo* and other patriotic films to prove the point. Insofar as there was a conservative trend in Hollywood, it was usually undermined by the conventions of popular entertainment and was sometimes explicitly opposed by liberal filmmakers. In the television series *Dynasty*, for example, not only did business leaders spend more time in the bedroom than in the boardroom, but their ethics in both venues fell short of exemplary. Most television families looked more complicated than their counterparts before the sixties. Viewers of *All in the Family* could laugh at Archie Bunker, the lovable bigot, and/or agree with him without saying so. In *Family Ties*, which President Reagan called his favorite television program, erstwhile counterculture parents coexisted affectionately with their prim, aspiring capitalist son. As was the case with government policy, the overtly political films of the Reagan years revealed polarization rather than an unambiguous conservative turn. Although no pointedly liberal film approached the *Rambo* series in popularity, at least four showed that aesthetic creativity survived: *Reds* (1982), a sympathetic docudrama about John Reed and the Bolshevik Revolution; *Matewan* (1987), perhaps the best film ever made about an American labor strike; and Oliver Stone's wrenching war movies, *Platoon* (1986) and *Salvador* (1986). Sex, nudity, profanity, and violence became more conspicuous. In this trend the three television networks lagged behind cable channels, and middle-aged parents lagged behind their teenage children – as the popularity of rock video channel MTV, founded in 1982, quickly demonstrated (Gitlin 1985; O'Brien 1990; Johnson 1991).

The attention that liberals as well as the media gave to the most vocal conservative Protestants obscured the complexity of the religious scene. By 1986–7, not only was the Moral Majority in decline, but televangelists Jim Bakker and Jimmy Swaggart were embroiled in sexual and financial scandals. Not for the first time, secular liberals wrote obituaries for theological conservatism as a cultural and political force. Not for the first time, they were wrong. Also in 1986–7, Operation Rescue was founded to disrupt abortion clinics; and televangelist Pat Robertson edged toward a presidential candidacy. Numerous grass-roots groups still mobilized effectively against Darwinism, sex education, and the ordination of women or gays in the clergy. Conservative Protestants thwarted the mass distribution of Martin Scorsese's film, *The Last Temptation of Christ* (1988). And "guppies", God-fearing urban professionals, spent millions of dollars on Christian rock music and romance novels, as well as on books interpreting current events in terms of Bible prophecy. Whether such adaptations of popular cultural forms served primarily to energize an alternative evangelical way of life, or subtly secularized it, remained an open question. Unquestionably the Catholic and Jewish communities continued to grow less insular, a development that brought greater acceptance in the wider society. As early as 1977, 82 percent of Americans polled said that they would vote for a qualified Catholic presidential candidate. In 1988 hardly anyone noticed that presidential contenders Bruce Babbitt and Alexander Haig were Catholic. Assimilation and acceptance also exacerbated within Catholicism and Judaism problems that had afflicted Protestants for decades: most notably declining fervor in general and proliferating doubts among the remaining faithful (Deedy 1987; Jorstad 1990; Martin 1996).

Denominational developments aside, the propensity of Americans to combine varied versions of "spirituality" remained at least as strong in 1988 as in 1974. For example, a sizable minority of Catholics adopted pentecostal practices and some evangelicals flirted with "new age" beliefs. Here as elsewhere, President Reagan personified incongruities that most Americans did not consider incongruous. The son of a Catholic father and a Protestant mother, he opened diplomatic relations with the Vatican in 1984, ruminated on fundamentalist Bible prophecy, and joined two-thirds of his fellow citizens in checking his horoscope. Indeed, his wife Nancy consulted with an astrologer in planning the presidential schedule.

Amid a more conservative political environment, the women's movement focused on securing ratification of the ERA and defending abortion rights. Although Congress extended the ratification period, the necessary two-thirds majority of the states was not achieved when time ran out for the ERA in 1982. The Supreme Court both reaffirmed *Roe v. Wade* and upheld legislation that barred government funding of abortion. Similarly, while President Reagan never made passage of a Right-to-Life Amendment a priority, his administration supported many such cut-offs. By 1980 the women's movement had established itself as a fully legitimate interest group. Yet in contrast to preservationists and proponents of nuclear disarmament, feminism as a coherent national movement did not prosper as the political axis moved rightward. One major problem was the "graying" of the movement as the post-sixties generation took earlier feminist victories for granted. Women enjoyed increasing success in winning elections, comprised one-third of union members, and no longer faced restricted admission to professional schools. Moreover, despite their opposition to abortion and the ERA, many conservatives adapted to feminist victories without formally embracing them. Forty percent of the delegates to the 1980 Republican national convention were women. Two years later Reagan appointed the first female justice to the Supreme Court, Sandra Day O'Connor. And the "gender gap" barely existed in the 1984 election, when he won 57 percent of the women's vote (Stage 1983; Davis 1999).

Conversely the gay and lesbian rights movement increased in dynamism partly in response to escalating attacks by cultural conservatives. In 1979, for example, the first national gay rights demonstration in Washington, DC, drew tens of thousands of participants. At most, a bare majority of Americans polled during the Reagan years opposed discrimination against gays; prominent politicians could still win votes by stigmatizing them. In *Bowers v. Hardwick* (1986), the Supreme Court upheld a Georgia law outlawing sodomy between consenting adults. The spread of Acquired Immune Deficiency Syndrome (AIDS) not only destroyed lives, but also had political consequences because at least two-thirds of the victims were homosexual men. For many Americans this "gay plague" legitimated their hostility to homosexuals; some leaders of the Christian right interpreted the disease as God's judgment on sexual sinners. Gays and lesbians disagreed among themselves about the proper collective response. Some pursued an effort to highlight the numbers of heterosexual AIDS victims in order to win wider support for medical treatment and research. Others, such as the militant gay activists in ACT UP (AIDS Coalition to Unleash Power), used civil disobedience to promote the same ends.

Amid the continuing cultural turmoil, Reagan in some respects shared the fate of many presidents re-elected overwhelmingly. That is, his second term was more politically difficult and legislatively less consequential than his first. There were only two significant legislative landmarks. In 1986 Congress slightly raised taxes, in a symbolic bow toward controlling the deficit, and revised immigration law, in a symbolic bow toward restricting the entry of illegal aliens. Also in 1986, the US bombed Libya in retaliation for a terrorist attack that killed American soldiers in Germany. The next year, however, the US surprisingly acquiesced in the fall of President Ferdinand Marcos of the Philippines. With the Cold War subsiding and human rights an unavoidable consideration since Carter's administration, Reagan was able to look beyond an inordinate fear of disorder in those Asian islands.

Nonetheless, the pattern of a less notable second term was broken by a significant scandal – the Iran-Contra affair – and an epochal event, the end of the Cold War. The Iran-Contra scandal was rooted in the persisting, inordinate fear of radicalism in the western hemisphere and an attempt to deal flexibly with the consequences of military intervention in Lebanon. As a result of that intervention, guerrilla groups allied with Iran kidnapped several Americans. Seeking to free these hostages and to arrange a modus vivendi with the Islamic government in Tehran, the NSC with Reagan's permission sold American arms to Iran. Then profits from these sales were transferred to the Contras. When these events were reported in the American news media starting in November 1986, the President offered a series of inaccurate and conflict-ing explanations. Whether Reagan formally approved the financial diversion to the Contras in violation of the Boland Amendment will probably never be known. Within six months, however, a special investigating commission, most of Congress, and the public professed to believe that the President had been merely inattentive while a rogue NSC operated on its own (Cannon 1991; Draper 1991).

Certainly Reagan's role in ending the Cold War helped to preserve his popularity during the Iran-Contra scandal. Yet it is by no means clear even in retrospect exactly what that role was. The major turning point came in March 1985, when Mikhail Gorbachev became leader of the Soviet Union. During the next three years, Gorbachev's government freed political prisoners, promoted religious liberty, cut the military budget, told his East European Communist colleagues that the Red Army would no longer protect their rule, arranged a truce in Afghanistan, and set free elections for 1989. The military quagmire in Afghanistan, partly a product of expanded US aid to the guerrillas, and the economic pressure brought by Reagan's military buildup contributed to the Soviet decisions to embark on *perestroika* (restructuring). So, too, did earlier advocacy of international human rights by Ford and Carter. Insofar as developments within the Soviet Union were affected by US policies, the Reagan administration operated with considerable skill. Despite qualms by avid cold warriors in his ranks, the President held his first summit conference with Gorbachev in November 1985. Three others followed, and Reagan and the Soviet leader both bickered and nurtured a personal rapport. The administration tried, on the one hand, to press for changes in the Soviet bloc without prompting a defensive reaction, and, on the other hand, to restrain its enthusiasm for Gorbachev lest he appear an American tool. Speaking in Berlin in June 1987, Reagan called upon Gorbachev to "tear down this wall" (quoted in Cannon 1991: 774). Negotiations were already under way, however, for an arms control treaty to eliminate medium-range ballistic missiles. By late 1988 the Cold War was essentially over in international diplomacy, though not in presidential politics.

Republican nominee George H. W. Bush, Reagan's Vice President, enjoyed several advantages over the Democratic candidate, Governor Michael Dukakis of Massachusetts. Bush had served two terms with the still extraordinarily popular Reagan. In 1988, 56 percent of Americans polled were "satisfied with the way things are going," compared to 19 percent in 1979. The economy suffered no permanent damage from a stock market crash in 1987; unemployment stood at 5.1 percent. Dukakis's self-presentation as an efficient manager recalled the cold, technocratic side of Jimmy Carter. Nonetheless Dukakis seemed capable of capitalizing on doubts about Bush's competence. Bush in turn assailed "that liberal governor of Massachusetts" for proposing inadequate military spending, opposing capital punishment, rejecting flag salutes in public schools, and sponsoring a prison furlough program that allowed an African-American murderer to escape and rape a white woman. Bush won with slightly less than 54 percent of the vote.

Despite its success, a campaign centered on fears of big government, black criminals, and the Soviet Union already looked atavistic, as Bush himself privately understood. To be sure, those fears were intrinsic to the "seventies." But that era, considered as a political, cultural, social, and diplomatic unit, had been fitfully drawing to a close since 1985. By that point, Reagan had reshaped the Republican coalition as well as national political discourse, his conservative economic program was in place, and intense cultural conflict at the national level had begun (temporarily) to ebb. With the close of the Cold War in 1988–9, the "seventies" came to a definitive end.

"Seventies" Legacies

It remains an open question, however, to what degree American ways of life had become more conservative – let alone more traditional – during the previous decade and a half. Despite repeated attacks on big government by three presidents, federal spending was 21.8 percent of the gross national product (GNP) during Reagan's second term. Social welfare spending, which had been 19 percent of the GNP in 1975, barely declined – to 18.8 percent – in 1987. Undeterred by repeated accusations of sloth, Americans devoted 7.6 percent of their personal consumption to recreation in 1988 compared to 6.9 percent in 1975. Rates of violent crime appear to have declined slightly but not the propensity to commit them; at least part of the decline was due to increased rates of incarceration. Neither proliferating celebrations of family values nor the threat of AIDS restored "traditional" sexual morality. Polls showed that only slightly more than a third of Americans thought premarital sex was always wrong. According to the Statistical Abstract of the United Sates, by 1987, out-of-wedlock births had risen to 17 percent among whites and 62 percent among blacks. Nonetheless, the abortion rate was roughly the same in 1988 as in 1975.

Fifty-one percent of women polled in 1988 preferred to "stay at home" rather than enter the job market. Yet chronic economic problems, high divorce rates, and increased opportunities combined to draw women into the work force. In 1988, the number of employed married mothers reached 64 percent. Ironically, traditional family values were probably more prevalent among the millions of immigrants trying to preserve non-American traditions (Jorstad 1990; Wattenberg 1991; Pemberton 1998).

Decades – perhaps especially those that are thought to last longer than ten years – leave legacies and burdens to their successors. So it was with the "seventies." Some cities, neighborhoods, and people never recovered from the recession used to bring down inflation. Structural economic shifts, attacks on the welfare state during three presidencies, and anti-union actions by businesses and the Reagan administration resulted in stagnant wages for most Americans long after the "seventies" ended. The dramatic expansion of national debt, though less damaging to the economy than conventional wisdom supposed, became a bipartisan political obsession. Bankrupt S & Ls, a product of the rush to deregulate, had to be rescued and their depositors compensated at the taxpayers' expense during George H. W. Bush's presidency. The post-Watergate special counsel law and the news media's post-Watergate propensity to magnify small scandals immobilized the Clinton administration for more than a year. Support of anti-Communist rebels in Afghanistan left an arsenal to anti-American Islamists whom the United States had helped to mobilize. And the confidence regained at the end of the "seventies" slid easily into the arrogance of the "world's only remaining superpower."

NOTE

An earlier version of this article was presented at the Fifth Conference of the Americas at the University of the Americas, Puebla, Mexico in October 2001. I would like to thank Edward D. Berkowitz for his helpful advice on content and style.

REFERENCES AND FURTHER READING

Allyn, David (2000) *Make Love Not War: The Sexual Revolution, an Unfettered History.* Boston: Little, Brown.

Becker, William H. (1999) *"Lean and Mean": Corporate Restructuring and the Resurgence of the American Economy in the 1990s.* Singapore: National University of Singapore.

Berman, William C. (1998) *America's Right Turn: From Nixon to Clinton.* Baltimore, Md.: Johns Hopkins University Press.

Biven, W. Carl (2002) *Jimmy Carter's Economy: Policy in an Age of Limits.* Chapel Hill: Univerisity of North Carolina Press.

Blumenthal, Sidney and Edsall, Thomas Byrne (eds.) (1988) *The Reagan Legacy.* New York: Pantheon.

Breslin, Jimmy (1975) *How the Good Guys Finally Won: Notes from an Impeachment Summer.* New York: Viking.

Cannon, Lou (1991) *President Reagan: The Role of a Lifetime.* New York: Simon and Schuster.

Carroll, Peter (1982) *It Seemed Like Nothing Happened: The Tragedy and Promise of America in the 1970s*. New York: Holt, Rinehart, and Winston.

Clecak, Peter (1983) *America's Quest for the Ideal Self: Dissent and Fulfillment in the '60s and '70s*. New York: Oxford University Press.

Davis, Flora (1999) *Moving the Mountain: The Women's Movement in the United States Since 1960*. Urbana: University of Illinois Press.

Deedy, John (1987) *American Catholicism: And Now Where?* New York: Plenum Press.

Draper, Theodore (1991) *A Very Thin Line: The Iran-Contra Affairs*. New York: Hill and Wang.

Ehrenreich, Barbara (1983) *The Hearts of Men: American Dreams and the Flight from Commitment*. Garden City, NY: Anchor Press.

Fink, Gary M. and Graham, Hugh Davis (eds.) (1998) *The Carter Presidency: Policy Choices in the Post-New Deal Era*. Lawrence: University Press of Kansas

Fleming, Thomas and Gottfried, Paul (1988) *The Conservative Movement*. Boston: Twayne.

Frum, David (2000) *How We Got Here: The '70s: The Decade that Brought You Modern Life (for Better or Worse)*. New York: Basic Books.

Garthoff, Raymond L. (1994a) *Détente and Confrontation: American–Soviet Relations from Nixon to Reagan*. Washington, DC: Brookings.

—— (1994b) *The Great Transition: American–Soviet Relations and the End of the Cold War*. Washington, DC: Brookings.

Germond, Jack W. and Witcover, Jules (1989) *Whose Broad Stripes and Bright Stars: The Trivial Pursuit of the Presidency, 1988*. New York: Warner Books.

Gillon, Steven M. (1992) *The Democrats' Dilemma: Walter F. Mondale and the Liberal Legacy*. New York: Columbia University Press.

Gitlin, Todd (1985) *Inside Prime Time*. New York: Pantheon.

Greene, John Robert (1995) *The Presidency of Gerald R. Ford*. Lawrence: University Press of Kansas.

Hargrove, Erwin (1988) *Jimmy Carter as President: Leadership and the Politics of the Public Good*. Baton Rouge: Louisiana State University Press.

Johnson, Haynes (1991) *Sleepwalking Through History: America in the Reagan Years*. New York: Doubleday Anchor.

Jorstad, Erling (1990) *Holding Fast/Pressing On: Religion in America in the 1980s*. New York: Praeger.

Kaufman, Burton I. (1993) *The Presidency of James Earl Carter, Jr.* Lawrence: University Press of Kansas.

Kutler, Stanley I. (1990) *The Wars of Watergate: The Last Crisis of Richard Nixon*. New York: Alfred A. Knopf.

LaFeber, Walter (1979) *The Panama Canal: The Crisis in Historical Perspective*. New York: Oxford University Press.

Lasch, Christopher (1979) *The Culture of Narcissism: American Life in an Age of Diminishing Expectations*. New York: W. W. Norton.

Martin, William C. (1996) *With God on Our Side: The Rise of the Religious Right in America*. New York: Broadway Books.

Mayer, Jane and McManus, Doyle (1988) *Landslide: The Unmaking of the President 1984–1988*. Boston: Houghton Mifflin.

Moen, Matthew C. (1989) *The Christian Right and Congress*. Tuscaloosa: University of Alabama Press.

O'Brien, Tom (1990) *The Screening of America: Movies and Values from* Rocky *to* Rain Man. New York: Continuum.

Olmsted, Kathryn S. (1996) *Challenging the Secret Government: The Post-Watergate Investigations of the CIA and the FBI*. Chapel Hill: University of North Carolina Press.

Peele, Gillian (1984) *Revival and Reaction: The Right in Contemporary America*. New York: Oxford University Press.

Pemberton, William E. (1998) *Exit with Honor: The Life and Presidency of Ronald Reagan*. Armonk, NY: M. E. Sharpe.

Phillips, Kevin P. (1990) *The Politics of Rich and Poor: Wealth and the American Electorate in the Reagan Aftermath*. New York: Harper Perennial.

Pomper, Marlene Michels (ed.) (1981) *The Election of 1980: Reports and Interpretations*. Chatham, NJ: Chatham House.

—— (ed.) (1985) *The Election of 1984: Reports and Interpretations*. Chatham, NJ: Chatham House.

Purcell, Edward A., Jr. (1983) "Social thought," *American Quarterly* 35, pp. 80–100.

Reichley, A. James (1981) *Conservatives in an Age of Change: The Nixon and Ford Administrations*. Washington, DC: Brookings.

Reimers, David M. (1992) *Still the Golden Door: The Third World Comes to America*. New York: Columbia University Press.

Ribuffo, Leo P. (1997) "Malaise revisited: Jimmy Carter and the crisis of confidence," in John P. Diggins (ed.) *The Liberal Persuasion: Arthur Schlesinger, Jr. and the Challenge of the American Past*. Princeton, NJ: Princeton University Press.

Rosen, Ruth (2000) *The World Split Open: How the Modern Women's Movement Changed America*. New York: Penguin.

Schulman, Bruce J. (2001) *The Seventies: The Great Shift in American Culture, Society, and Politics*. New York: Free Press.

Schulzinger, Robert D. (1997) *A Time for War: The United States and Vietnam, 1941–1975*. New York: Oxford University Press.

Schwartz, Herman (ed.) (1988) *The Burger Years: Rights and Wrongs in the Supreme Court*. New York: Penguin.

Shawcross, William (1988) *The Shah's Last Ride: The Fate of an Ally*. New York: Simon and Schuster.

Sherrill, Robert (1983) *The Oil Follies of 1970–1980: How the Petroleum Industry Stole the Show (and Much More Besides)*. Garden City, NY: Anchor.

Sick, Gary (1986) *All Fall Down: America's Tragic Encounter with Iran*. New York: Penguin.

Skidmore, David (1996) *Reversing Course: Carter's Foreign Policy, Domestic Politics, and the Failure of Reform*. Baton Rouge: Louisiana State University Press.

Smith, Gaddis (1986) *Reality, Reason and Power: America Diplomacy in the Carter Years*. New York: Hill and Wang.

Stage, Sarah J. (1983) "Women," *American Quarterly* 35, pp. 169–90.

Stein, Herbert (1985) *Presidential Economics: The Making of Economic Policy from Roosevelt to Reagan and Beyond*. New York: Simon and Schuster.

Strong, Robert A. (2000) *Working in the World: Jimmy Carter and the Making of American Foreign Policy*. Baton Rouge: Louisiana State University Press.

Thurow, Lester C. (1980) *The Zero-Sum Society: Distribution and the Possibilities for Economic Change*. New York: Penguin.

Wattenberg, Ben B. (1991) *The First Universal Nation: Leading Indicators and Ideas about the Surge in America in the 1990s*. New York: Free Press.

Witcover, Jules (1977) *Marathon: The Pursuit of the Presidency 1972–1976*. New York: Viking.

Wuthnow, Robert (1988) *The Restructuring of American Religion: Society and Faith Since World War II*. Princeton, NJ: Princeton University Press.

CHAPTER EIGHT

1988–2000

STEVEN M. GILLON

It was called "The Year of Miracles." In 1989, ship worker Lech Walesa and the Solidarity trade union movement had organized a series of strikes that crippled the Polish government. When Soviet Premier Mikhail Gorbachev refused to use the military to quell the uprising and instructed Poland's puppet regime to negotiate with the reformers, the Communist government collapsed, to be replaced the following year in the first free elections in sixty-eight years. In Hungary, the Communist government announced that it would no longer restrict travel to Western Europe. On November 9, 1989, the East German government stunned the world by announcing that residents of East Berlin would not be prevented from traveling to West Berlin. The Berlin Wall, the ultimate symbol of Cold War division, had suddenly been rendered irrelevant. Americans watched on television as jubilant Germans – East and West – tore down the Wall. Reunited families and total strangers danced atop the Wall, where only hours earlier armed guards had patrolled. One group of revelers hung a banner on the Wall reading "Stalin is Dead – Europe Lives."

The end of the Cold War also meant the end of the vaunted "Cold War consensus," the period after World War II during which Americans stood largely in agreement over foreign policy goals and often muted domestic concerns to further those aims. No longer consumed by the global struggle against Communism, Americans felt they had the luxury to focus on domestic concerns. Partisan divisions, often kept in check by fear of a common enemy, intensified during the 1990s as Republicans gained a firm foothold in the Congress and the Democrats controlled the presidency.

This essay will examine the impact of these changes on four areas of American life. First, in politics and diplomacy the demise of the Soviet threat allowed social and cultural issues to rise to the forefront of public attention, at the same time that it frustrated efforts to develop a coherent new view of the world. These epochal transformations bewildered the Republican President, George Bush, and swung the first election of the new decade to Democrat Bill Clinton, who promised to give more attention to domestic issues. His policies were stymied, though, by a resurgent Republican Congress and a sordid sex scandal that further eroded the public faith in government. Second, the end of the Cold War coincided with a technological revolution that transformed the way Americans communicated with one another and fueled the longest peacetime economic expansion in American history. Third, much of the technology, especially the growth of cable television, contributed to the growing fragmentation of public culture in the 1990s. Finally, despite all the changes, Americans continued to struggle with the enduring problems of race relations, and threats to the American way of life persisted, though they assumed different forms.

The Iran-Contra affair had removed some of the luster from Ronald Reagan's star toward the end of the 1980s, but as the 1988 election approached his conservative views remained popular with most Republicans. The logical choice for his successor was George Bush, who had served as Reagan's loyal Vice President for the previous eight years. In July, Bush decided to use his acceptance speech at the Republican convention to articulate his plans for the presidency. To energize the party's conservative faithful, Bush promised to continue the fight against terrorism abroad and big government at home. The centerpiece of the speech was a dramatic and carefully scripted promise not to raise taxes. "Read my lips," he said. "No new taxes." The Vice President also appealed to moderates by emphasizing his support for education and the environment. In a move that puzzled observers, and many of his closest advisors, Bush picked the untested Dan Quayle, a conservative senator from Indiana, as his running mate.

The Democrats had a difficult time finding a nominee to challenge Bush. The party's frontrunner, Colorado senator Gary Hart, quit the race after reporters disclosed that he was having an affair with a woman other than his wife. Michael Dukakis, a successful Greek-American governor of Massachusetts, moved to fill the void created by Hart's absence, and faced down a spirited challenge from African-American civil rights leader Jesse Jackson to secure the party's nomination. Dukakis believed that the Democratic Party had moved too far to the left since the 1960s. At the Democratic convention in August, Dukakis tried to skirt the sensitive social issues that had divided the party since the 1960s by declaring the campaign was about "competence, not ideology." To underscore his new centrist message, he chose stately Texas senator Lloyd Bentsen as his running mate.

The fall contest between Dukakis and Bush degenerated into one of the most negative in modern times. With polls showing the Republican ticket trailing Dukakis by more than 20 points, Bush's campaign manager Lee Atwater convinced the Vice President that the only way he could win was to tar the Democrats with the stigma of social liberalism. Following his cue, Bush campaigned as a cultural populist who told crowds about the "wide chasm" on "the question of values between me and the liberal Governor" (quoted in Dionne 1998: A1). The Republicans also exploited racial tensions. Bush's most effective advertisement featured Willie Horton, an African American who had raped a white woman while on leave from a Massachusetts prison. "If I can make Willie Horton a household name," said Bush's campaign manager Lee Atwater, "we'll win the election" (quoted in Greene 2000: 39).

Atwater was right: By late October, Gallup reported a "stunning turnaround" in the polls. On election day, Bush became the first sitting vice president since Martin Van Buren in 1836 to be elected directly to the presidency. The Democrats, however, managed to increase their margins in Congress, where they held an 89 vote margin in the House and 56 of 100 seats in the Senate.

President Bush declared that the end of the Cold War heralded a "new world order" in which the United States was the only superpower, the rule of law must govern relations between nations, and the powerful must protect the week. Initially, much of the optimism seemed justified. In a world no longer dominated by the Cold War confrontations, the prospects for resolving local disputes brightened. South Africans began to dismantle apartheid; military dictators in Latin America left or were removed from power, and Israeli and Palestinian leaders began a series of negotiations toward Palestinian statehood. Feeling secure now that great power tensions had disappeared, Bush focused on international drug trafficking. In 1989 he ordered American troops into Panama to extradite dictator and drug smuggler Manuel Noriega. In "Operation Just Cause," the largest American military action since the Vietnam War, 22,000 American troops invaded Panama and brought Noriega to the United States to stand trial.

The seed of revolution, planted in Eastern Europe, spread quickly to the rest of the Soviet Union. After a series of dramatic crises, culminating in an attempted coup by Communist hardliners in August 1991, a weary Gorbachev resigned as President of the USSR on Christmas Day, 1991. He recognized the new Commonwealth of Independent States and turned power over to Boris Yeltsin, the newly-elected President of the Russian Federation. The Soviet Union had dissolved. Bush seized the opportunity to continue the progress in arms control that began in the final years of the Reagan administration. In 1989, he announced that it was time to "move beyond containment" by integrating the Soviet Union into "the community of nations." The following year, NATO and the Warsaw Pact signed the biggest weapons cut in history. Bush and Gorbachev then signed the START I treaty, which cut their strategic nuclear forces in half. Two years later, Bush and Yeltsin came to terms on a START II agreement that called for further cuts and for the elimination of deadly multiple warhead (MIRV) intercontinental missiles by the year 2003.

Only China seemed to buck the trend toward greater openness in the post-Cold War era. Bush hoped to promote closer economic ties while also encouraging the ailing Chinese leadership to embrace democracy. His plan suffered a stunning setback in the spring of 1989 when the Chinese army brutally crushed a pro-democracy demonstration in Beijing's Tiananmen Square. A bloodbath ensued in which an estimated 400–800 young men and women were killed. The assault, covered extensively by American television, outraged the public and exposed an underlying tension in America's attitude toward the world: should the US emphasize its moral leadership by punishing nations which fail to live up to American standards of human rights, or should the US restrict itself to more practical questions of national security?

The New World Order also contained old-fashioned dangers. On August 2, 1990 Iraqi army troops smashed across the border of Kuwait. Residents of Kuwait City were awakened by the blast of rockets and gunfire. Iraqi leader Saddam Hussein had nearly bankrupted his country in an eight-year war with Iran and now needed Kuwait's huge oil reserves to pay his debts.

President Bush saw the invasion as a direct challenge to US leadership in the post-Cold War world. Over the next few months, in an impressive display of international diplomacy, Bush rallied world opinion against Hussein. The United Nations Security Council passed resolutions to enforce economic sanctions against Iraq in an effort to force it out of Kuwait. In November, it authorized use of force for the first time since the Korean War, giving Hussein a deadline of January 15, 1991, to pull out of Kuwait or face military action.

Public opinion was decidedly mixed about the wisdom of sending American forces into Kuwait, but Bush was determined to punish Hussein for his aggression. The President started the war on January 16 with a massive and sustained air assault. For nearly six weeks, US B-52 bombers and F-16 fighter bombers, flying up to 3,000 sorties daily, pounded Iraq. On February 23, the Allies launched a ground offensive that forced Saddam out of Kuwait in under 100 hours. Iraqi troops surrendered in droves. US forces lost only 184, compared with nearly 100,000 Iraqi deaths, mostly from bombing. On February 27, coalition forces liberated Kuwait and the President called off the attack, leaving a vanquished but defiant Saddam Hussein in power.

Despite their reservations about the war, Americans instinctively rallied around the troops once the war began. Millions placed yellow ribbons outside their doors as a show of support for American forces. Unlike the coverage of Vietnam, what Americans saw on their television screens included virtually no blood or death. The Pentagon imposed tough new restrictions on the press, forcing reporters to travel with escorts and exercising control over all reports from the Gulf. The victory produced an outpouring of patriotism and renewed faith in the military that had been tarnished since Vietnam. "By God, we've licked the Vietnam syndrome once and for all," Bush told a national television audience. The President reaped much of the credit for the operation. His approval rating shot to 89 percent, the highest ever recorded for a president.

While the President scored high marks for his adroit handling of the international scene, he never articulated a clear agenda at home. After only a few weeks in office, Bush angered voters and enraged conservatives by breaking his "no new taxes" pledge. "I've started going into the numbers, finally," Bush said, referring to the federal deficit, "and they're enormous." In 1990, Bush agreed to a compromise with congressional Democrats that included $133 billion in new taxes. The *New York Post*'s front page screamed the reaction: READ MY LIPS: I LIED.

The deficit package failed to stem the fiscal hemorrhaging. After seven booming years the economy began to sputter. While the GNP increased at an anemic 2.2 percent, unemployment crept upwards, housing starts dropped, and consumer confidence hit new lows. By 1992, Bush's approval rating sagged to 34 percent, with fewer than 20 percent of the public approving his handling of the economy. The public clamored for the President to take decisive action to revive the ailing economy, but Bush and his advisors decided on a hands-off approach.

Polls showed that Americans wanted more government involvement in issues ranging from education to health care, but the President's hands were tied by the huge budget deficit left over from the Reagan years. Bush signed only one meaningful piece of legislation: The Americans with Disabilities Act (1990), which prohibited discrimination against the 40 million Americans who suffered from mental or physical disabilities. Bush also paid a political price for his party's strong anti-abortion views. In the 1989 case of *Webster* v. *Reproductive Health Services*, a divided Supreme Court upheld a Missouri law that banned public facilities from performing abortions that were not necessary to save the mother's life. The decision enraged many moderate Republicans. Polls showed a widening gender gap, as many women, including many Republicans, feared that more Republican appointments could tip the court's balance away from abortion rights.

Bush unintentionally widened the gender gap when he replaced liberal Thurgood Marshall, the only African American on the court, with Clarence Thomas, an undistinguished black conservative who had served as head of Reagan's Equal Employment Opportunity Commission (EEOC). A former EEOC colleague, Anita Hill, stepped forward to charge that Thomas had sexually harassed her. The public debate over Hill's charges raised awareness about sexual harassment in the workplace. It also alienated many moderate women who were angered by the administration's unwavering support for Thomas.

The serious social problems that plagued the nation, and the President's lack of leadership, came into sharp focus when riots tore through Los Angeles in April 1992. After a mostly white jury in a Los Angeles suburb acquitted four white police officers accused of savagely beating African-American motorist Rodney King, African Americans in South Central Los Angeles erupted into the most deadly urban riot in over a century. By the time it ended three days later, 58 people lay dead, over 800 buildings were destroyed, and thousands more were damaged or looted. Bush traveled to the riot area and promised more federal aid. For many people, the response was too little, too late.

By 1992, Bush had compiled an impressive record of foreign policy successes, but the political ground had shifted beneath his feet, and he faced a formidable Democratic challenger in Arkansas governor Bill Clinton. A party moderate, Clinton appealed to fellow baby boomers by casting himself as a "new Democrat" who understood the concerns of the struggling middle class. Campaigning for president as a cultural conservative, he professed his support for capital punishment, promised to "end welfare as we know it," to make the streets safer and the schools better, and to provide "basic health care to all Americans." For traditional Democrats he offered a message of economic populism, promising to soak the rich and fight to preserve popular social programs. Despite lingering questions about infidelity and draft dodging, Clinton won the nomination earlier than any Democrat in more than two decades.

The campaign was complicated by the presence of an unpredictable third-party candidate, Texas billionaire Ross Perot. Perot tapped into public discontent with government and Washington by promising to balance the budget and cut the deficit. His position on most other issues remained a mystery. By July he was leading both Clinton and Bush in the polls, when he abruptly decided to leave the race. He returned just as unexpectedly in October, with only one month left, but largely in the role of spoiler.

While Perot was on hiatus from the campaign, Clinton moved to secure his followers by focusing attention on the economy. He promised to "focus like a laser beam" on economic issues. A sign hanging in his campaign office summed up the Democratic strategy: "It's the economy, stupid." Clinton also proved an effective and unconventional campaigner, chatting with young voters on MTV, taking calls on *The Larry King Show*, and playing the saxophone and discussing public policy with Arsenio Hall.

Voters rewarded Clinton on election night, giving him 43 percent of the vote, compared to 38 percent for Bush. Clinton's margin in the Electoral College was far more decisive. He won 31 states and 357 electoral votes. Perot received a bigger share of the vote – 19 percent – than any third-party candidate since Teddy Roosevelt scored 27.4 percent in 1912. The Democrats retained control of both Houses of Congress. Voters sent six women to the Senate and 48 to the House of Representatives. California became the first state to elect two women senators – Barbara Boxer and Dianne Feinstein – and Illinois elected the first African-American woman to the upper chamber, Carol Moseley Braun. Observers triumphantly called 1992 "the year of the woman."

The first president born after World War II, Clinton came to office promising to jump-start the economy and to use government power to develop solutions to pressing social problems. Congress passed the President's ambitious economic plan that used a combination of spending cuts and tax increases to reduce the deficit. In an ominous warning of partisan confrontations to come, not a single House Republican voted for the Clinton program. Some of the partisan rancor over Clinton's economic package stemmed from his earlier proposal to lift the long-standing ban on homosexuals serving openly in the military. After months of public debate, Clinton had been forced to retreat, agreeing to an unworkable "don't ask, don't tell" policy that pleased no one.

After passage of his economic program, Clinton focused his energies on passing a complex health-care proposal. The President asked the First Lady, Hillary Rodham Clinton, an accomplished lawyer with liberal leanings, to set up a health-care task force. In October 1993 the administration unveiled its plan, which would guarantee Americans medical and dental coverage and an array of preventive services. Business leaders and Republicans launched a successful campaign to convince the public that the plan was too costly, and the President too liberal. The proposal was dead on arrival on Capitol Hill. Scandal hampered Clinton's attempts to respond to the public's concern with domestic problems. An investigation into a failed real estate investment called Whitewater, reports that Arkansas state troopers had procured women for Clinton when he was governor, and a sexual harassment lawsuit file by Paula Jones, a former Arkansas state employee, all raised doubts about the President's character and distracted attention from his legislative program. After two years in office Clinton had the lowest poll ratings of any president since Watergate. Energized Republicans, led by Georgia firebrand Newt Gingrich, pounced on the helpless Democrats in the 1994 midterm elections. All 300 Republican congressional candidates signed a ten-point "Contract with America," pledging to trim government waste, cap welfare payments, raise military spending, and lower taxes. On election day, Republicans made major gains, seizing control of both houses for the first time in four decades and defeating thirty-five incumbent Democrats.

Clinton responded to the Republican triumph by what advisor Dick Morris called "triangulation": he moved to the center and co-opted Republican themes. His first move was to accept the Republican goal of balancing the budget in ten years or less. Clinton also supported a crime bill that would put 100,000 new police on the streets, and endorsed a strategy of "three strikes and you're out," giving life sentences to criminals convicted three times of felonies. Welfare reform was at the center of Clinton's new strategy. True to the terms of their "Contract with America," congressional Republicans collapsed nearly forty federal programs, including AFDC, into five block grants to the states. Clinton objected to the original legislation, but later signed a bill that maintained its central features.

By 1996, the president's effort to rebuild public support by co-opting Republican issues of welfare reform and crime and balancing the budget had become remarkably successful. Aided by an expanding economy and declining unemployment, Clinton watched his job approval soar to over 60 percent, the highest rating of his presidency. Polls showed that many voters were willing to set aside concerns about Clinton's character in favor of their satisfaction with the humming economy, and their general perception that the country was headed in the right direction. In the 1996 election, Clinton easily trounced Republican challenger Robert Dole, a 73-year old veteran of World War II and the oldest man ever to seek the presidency. Victories in 32 states and the District of Columbia gave him 375 electoral votes, compared to Dole's 18 states and 129 electoral votes. Though he became the first Democrat since Franklin Roosevelt to win a second term as president, Clinton's election did not represent a clear mandate, as the Republicans retained control of the House and gained two seats in the Senate.

As the first president elected after the end of the Cold War, Clinton faced a host of new foreign policy challenges. For all its perils, the Cold War had provided policy-makers with a framework, though often a narrow one, for interpreting world events and for calculating the national interest. Without a grand strategy to guide it, the administration appeared to lurch from one international crisis to another. The first occurred in the Horn of Africa, the northeast region of the continent, where many nations – Ethiopia, Sudan, and Somalia – had been suffering from drought, famine, and intermittent civil war. The situation grew grave in 1992 as fighting among rival factions threatened to cut off relief supplies to Somalia, leaving millions to starve. Pushed to respond by public reaction to television pictures of emaciated children, Bush had ordered nearly 30,000 troops to Somalia on a humanitarian mission to restore order and secure relief efforts. Initially, "Operation Restore Hope" suc-ceeded, but before long the rival clans tired of the US presence and began putting up resistance.

Clinton inherited a complex problem. The US troops could not guarantee the flow of supplies without fighting the clans, but engaging the rival factions risked getting bogged down in a quagmire. Without seeking approval from Congress, Clinton left nearly 9,000 troops in Somalia and expanded their mission to include taking on the local clans. In October 1993, eighteen US Army Rangers died in a bloody firefight with a gang of Somalis. Clinton quickly retreated, withdrawing the remaining America forces. "Gosh, I miss the Cold War," Clinton remarked after learning that American soldiers had been killed (quoted in Devroy and Smith 1993: A1).

The administration used the threat of military force more successfully closer to home in Haiti. In 1991, a band of military leaders overthrew the elected leader, Jean-Bertrand Aristide. The Clinton administration organized an international effort to restore Aristide, applying diplomatic pressure and convincing the United Nations to impose economic sanctions. The military regime showed no interest in giving up power voluntarily until Clinton decided to flex his military muscle, threatening to use the marines to expel the junta. With American warships looming off the coast, Haiti's military leaders backed down and allowed Aristide to return to power.

While uncertain about the use of military force in the post-Cold war era, the Clinton administration made economic policy the center of its approach to the world. In 1994, Clinton fought a tough legislative battle to win congressional approval of the North American Free Trade Agreement (NAFTA), and the Global Agreement on Tariffs and Trade (GATT). Both agreements lowered trade barriers between the United States and the rest of the world, increasing the pace of globalization.

Like his predecessor, Clinton stumbled over relations with China. During the 1992 campaign Clinton had criticized Bush for not punishing China for its human rights violations, but he changed his tune once in office. Emphasizing the importance of China as a trading partner, Clinton approved China's most favored nation status, despite that nation's continued crackdown on dissent. Russia also remained a major worry for the administration. If its domestic market collapsed it would send shock waves around the world. To help prop up the Russian economy, the administration developed a $4.5 billion aid package. At the same time, the administration worked closely with their Russian counterparts to reduce stockpiles of nuclear weapons. In 1994, the US signed the US-Russian-Ukraine Trilateral Statement and Annex, which led to the destruction of all nuclear weapons in Ukraine. Yeltsin and Clinton agreed to "detarget" US and Russian strategic missiles: instead of being programed to strike cities in their respective countries all nuclear weapons were aimed into the ocean. Of course, they could be reprogrammed in minutes, but the agreement represented an important psychological milestone.

Recurring crises in Iraq and the former Yugoslavia also plagued Clinton's administration. In Iraq, Saddam Hussein's refusal to cooperate with UN arms inspectors provoked several bombings by the United States. In 1994 and 1996, and again in 1998 under Madeleine Albright, America's first female Secretary of State, US forces bombed Iraq in attempts to force Hussein's compliance. Yet Hussein emerged defiant from each attack, and continued to frustrate US policy-makers.

The situation in Yugoslavia was more complex. The formerly Communist state plunged into civil war, as the Serbian-dominated federal government in Belgrade launched a brutal policy of "ethnic cleansing," first in the newly independent state of Bosnia, and later in Kosovo. The Yugoslav conflicts presented a challenge to foreign policy-makers: it was a case where no national interests seemed to be at stake, but where compelling humanitarian concerns seemed to demand some sort of response. After several years of waffling on the issue, the Clinton administration ultimately responded with force in 1995 to stop the fighting in Bosnia, and again in 1999 to counter Serbian aggression in Kosovo.

At the same time that he was flexing his muscle as commander-in-chief, Clinton was fighting a battle at home to keep his job as president. In December of 1998, he became only the second president in US history to be impeached by the House and, in January, tried in the Senate. The year-long drama that led up to the trial and consumed much of the nation's attention centered on an affair between Clinton and former White House intern Monica Lewinsky. When charges surfaced, a defiant president denied having had sexual relations with "that woman." After he made the same denials in a civil case, and to a grand jury, Kenneth Starr, the special prosecutor in the case, recommended that the President be impeached and removed from office for "high crimes and misdemeanors." To support his conclusion, he delivered a steamy report to the House detailing the affair and offering eleven potential grounds for impeachment.

After weeks of public hearings, the Judiciary Committee voted to send formal changes to the House which in turn approved two charges – perjury and obstruction of justice – and sent them on to the Senate for trial. The Senate rang in the new year by placing the president on trial. Over the next few weeks the Senators listened to often repetitive charges and countercharges by the House prosecutors and the White House defenders. When the final votes were counted the Senate failed to muster a majority on either count and fell far short of the constitutionally mandated two-thirds needed to convict the president.

Everyone came out of the affair with their reputations tarnished. The President enjoyed high job approval ratings, but the public gave him low marks for honesty and integrity. The GOP's pugnacious pursuit of impeachment backfired. Republicans appeared hypocritical, especially when some who condemned Clinton's behavior had checkered pasts of their own. The media's obsession with the affair, and all its sordid details, also came in for its share of criticism.

The public supported Clinton throughout the impeachment process because it gave him credit for the remarkable prosperity that characterized the decade. By the mid-1990s, the widespread use of personal computers, and the rise of the World Wide Web, formed the foundation of a communications revolution that promised to transform American business and leisure. The *Economist* magazine asserted in 1997 that the Web represents "a change even more far-reaching than the harnessing of electrical power a century ago." The information society propelled the economy to new heights as high-tech firms produced a surge on Wall Street.

By the beginning of the 1990s the impact of the computer on American life and the economy had become obvious to everyone. More than 90 percent of all businesses in the United States relied on the personal computer. More than one-third of families had a PC at home. In 1995, for the first time, the amount of money spent on PCs exceeded that spent on televisions. With the birth of the Internet and especially the creation of the World Wide Web in the early 1990s, the PC became the centerpiece of a technological revolution: the explosion of digital communications technology.

The key to the Internet was information: it empowered individuals by making available vast amounts of unfiltered information. In medicine, patients used the Internet to find out about new treatments, breaking the monopoly that physicians once had on medical information. In business the sharing of electronic documents flattened hierarchies and gave lower-level employees access to huge amounts of information previously the purview of managers. Investors could bypass stockbrokers and plan retirement benefits on-line. Politicians used the Internet to bypass the traditional media and communicate their message directly to voters.

For millions of Americans the Web helped break down cultural and geographic borders by creating virtual communities of shared interests. The technology promised to reconfigure the consumer society, providing buyers with new options and in-creased power. E-mail emerged as the most visible and commonly used feature of the new information society. By 1999, Americans sent 2.2 billion messages a day, compared with 293 million pieces of first class mail. Nearly every college and univer-sity in the country provided some form of e-mail access for its faculty, staff, and students. E-mail changed the workplace, allowing employees to conduct business from the road and from home.

The information revolution raised new questions and forced Americans to confront old problems. How should government balance the right to free speech on the Web with parents' interest in limiting their children's exposure to indecent material? The

Web also created new headaches for people trying to protect sensitive information. Hackers, ranging from curious teenagers to malicious governments, used the Internet to gain access to privileged information. Meanwhile, many people worried that the nation's reliance on computers would produce "technological segregation," aggravating the gap between the educational haves and have nots.

The surge in computer-related industry helped revive the US economy during the 1990s. By the end of the decade, the GDP, discounted for inflation was growing at an annual rate of 4 percent and unemployment had fallen to a quarter-century low of 4.7 percent. Productivity had risen to 2 percent, well above its historically slow annual growth trend of 1 percent since the early 1970s. All the while, consumer inflation had fallen to less than 2 percent.

The information revolution was the cornerstone of the new prosperity, accounting for 45 percent of industrial growth. From 1987 to 1994, the US software industry grew 117 percent in real terms, while the rest of the economy grew only 17 percent. The US software industry accounted for three-quarters of the world market, and nine of the world's ten biggest software companies were located in the United States. The industrial decline of the 1970s had led to stagnation; the growth of information technology in the 1990s produced staggering growth.

The nation watched as a new generation of computer moguls made millions from new inventions and rising stock prices. Wall Street was the most visible sign of the new prosperity. Between 1992 and 1998, the Dow Jones industrial average increased fourfold. The New York and NASDAQ stock exchanges added over $4 trillion in value, the largest single accumulation of wealth in history. With the tide rising rapidly for more than a decade, stock assets accounted for a larger share of household wealth than ever before. In 1980, only 6 percent of US households had such accounts for stocks or bonds. By 1997 the share had leaped to 37 percent, with a colossal pool of capital approaching $5 trillion.

Many people benefited from the booming economy. The poor did not get poorer in the 1990s. Their family incomes rose slightly, the poverty rate fell slightly, and the average pay for low-wage jobs increased. Minorities, especially African Americans, showed real economic gains. Yet while the poor were advancing by inches, the well-to-do were bounding ahead. In 1990, a corporate CEO earned 85 times as much as the average factory worker; in 1997, he made 324 times more. The information society's demand for educated, high-tech workers contributed to the income gap. The new technology placed greater demand on people who worked with their heads, not their hands.

By 1998, the combination of a healthy, growing economy, fiscal restraint, and the end of the Cold War had solved the budget crisis that plagued Washington since the early Reagan years. For the first time in decades, politicians had the opportunity to debate how to spend new revenue. The Clinton administration called for devoting the extra revenue to needed social spending. Congressional conservatives, on the other hand, called for limited spending on defense and social security, and advocated giving most of the money back through large tax cuts. Most of the states, which had been financially strapped for the previous two decades, also benefited from the healthy economy.

Economists pointed out, however, that while the deficit monster had been slain, the US still faced a mountain of debt, which was the cumulative amount of money the treasury owed its creditors. In 1999, the debt stood at $5.4 trillion, a third of it owed to foreign investors. According to the Congressional Budget Office (CBO), 15.2 percent of all federal outlays were to pay interest on the debt, a total of $245 billion annually.

"Our culture is in warp speed," observed a media critic. "We live on novelty, with new forms, new subversions generated daily" (Gabler 1995: M1). Television led the way in promoting the cultural subversion. The three major networks, which accounted for 90 percent of prime-time viewing in the 1970s, watched their audience share dip to 47 percent in 1998. By 1998, more than 75 percent of US households received dozens of channels via cable or satellite dishes. The technology allowed new networks – FOX, CNN, Warner Brothers – to siphon viewers, forcing greater competition for prime-time ratings.

The scramble for viewers encouraged the networks to experiment with different themes and ideas. Ellen DeGeneres's show had an episode where its central character, a lesbian, "came out" of the closet. By the end of the decade more than a half-dozen prime-time shows featured gay characters, though in less prominent roles. Television also attempted to tackle controversial social issues, from spouse abuse to teen pregnancy. Issues featured on the evening news one week turned up as plots in drama series such as *NYPD Blue* and *The Practice*.

The most common approach, however, was to lure people with more sex and violence. One study found that a sexual act or reference occurred every four minutes on average during prime time. Daytime television was dominated by racy talk shows where guests talked openly about their sex lives and their family feuds. Parental groups were especially concerned about violence. A 1996 poll showed two-thirds of the public believed television shows contributed to social problems like violence, divorce, teen pregnancy, and the decline of family values.

Conservatives also protested the often boastful promotion of violence and misogyny in rap and hip-hop music. The 1990s witnessed a remarkable ferment among musical artists as rap and hip-hop emerged as the new anthem of the youth culture. Created by black artists on the streets of New York and Los Angeles, hip-hop used repetitive samples of other musical tracks as background for the rhythmic vocals of rap singers. Many early rap artists used street poetry to deal with problems of the urban underclass, especially violence, sex, and racism. In 1998 rap surpassed country music as the nation's top-selling format.

Rap became less rebellious as it moved into the mainstream. By the end of the decade, suburban whites purchased more than 70 percent of hip-hop albums. Advertising firms used a muted version of rap to sell their products. In order to reach a broader market, many artists toned down their acts. Newer artists avoided controversy by writing songs that examined the pathologies of the black community, but avoided encouraging social activism. "The stuff today is not revolutionary," observed the host of a black talk-radio station in New York City. "It's just, 'Give me a piece of the action' " (quoted in Farley 1999: 2).

The debate over sex and violence missed the larger significance of an aspect of the evolution of popular culture: its continued fragmentation. Until the explosion in cable television and the proliferation of new networks, most of the viewing public watched the same television shows. As recently as the 1970s, more than a third of US homes tuned in weekly to watch *All in the Family*. With so many shows to choose from, the audience splintered into smaller subsets of viewers. Studies showed, for example, that blacks and whites watched completely different shows. Even the most popular shows, *Seinfeld* and NBC's medical drama *ER*, attracted less than 12 percent of the US population.

American culture may have been controversial but it sold, both at home and around the world. During the 1990s popular culture emerged as America's biggest export. The explosion in sales was spurred by the collapse of the Iron Curtain, rising prosperity, and the proliferation of television sets, video recorders, stereos, personal computers, and satellite dishes. American corporations moved aggressively to tap into the new markets. Foreigners were not only watching US television, they were eating American food, reading US magazines, and wearing designer clothes produced in America. American fashion – baggy jeans and baseball caps – became the global teenage uniform.

Despite the extraordinary influences that were transforming American politics and social life, one aspect of the American condition appeared remarkably resistant to change: race relations. The arrest of African-American football star O. J. Simpson for the murder of his estranged wife and her boyfriend – who were white – and his subsequent trial exposed the stunning racial divide that still existed in America. The Simpson trial became a singular media event, watched live by millions of Americans and discussed around the clock on cable television. Many of the trial participants became celebrities.

Both the verdict of the Simpson trial and its reception were viewed through race-tinted glasses. In his first trial, a mostly black jury acquitted Simpson; in his subsequent civil trial, a mostly white jury found him guilty. Polls reflected these opinions on a national scale: by large majorities, African Americans believed in Simpson's innocence, convinced that the American justice system intentionally discriminated against minorities and that rogue cops, such as Mark Furman, often tilted the hand of justice. Nearly 75 percent of whites found the DNA evidence convincing, rejected the suggestion that race played a role in the investigation and prosecution, and assumed Simpson's guilt. Perhaps the American system of justice was the final victim of the trial. Blacks and whites seemed to agree on one thing: there was a different justice for those who have money and those who do not.

The racial divide exposed by the Simpson case revealed itself in the continuing controversy over affirmative action. In November 1996, California voters passed Proposition 209, a ballot initiative that banned the use of race and sex in college admissions, contracting, and public employment. Men overwhelmingly supported the initiative (61 to 39 percent) while women disapproved (52 to 48 percent). Blacks and Latinos opposed it in large numbers. The ban on affirmative action had a dramatically negative impact on minority admissions to colleges and universities in the state.

As other states mimicked California, the nation engaged in an angry debate over race. Critics of affirmative action contended that quotas undermined black morale, contributing to "an enlargement of self-doubt," by creating the perception that successful blacks could not earn their positions. Proponents argued that affirmative action helped open the doors of opportunity for minorities and women, increasing their representation in the work force. In 1997 President Clinton established a national commission on race and spoke out in favor of affirmative action.

The end of the Soviet threat may have lessened America's fear of nuclear war, which was so palpable in the early 1980s, but it did not lower public anxiety about threats to the American way of life. Underneath the prosperity of the 1990s ran a current of fear: the nation preoccupied itself with worries about terrorism, both foreign and domestic. On the Internet, conspiracy theories flourished as a means to explain an increasingly complex world.

In February 1993 five people died and more than one thousand were injured when a bomb exploded in New York's World Trade Center. Federal agents traced the bombing to a group of radical Muslims in New York. American targets outside the US also found themselves vulnerable to attack. In 1996 a truck bomb exploded next to a military barracks in Saudi Arabia, killing nineteen US servicemen. Two years later, simultaneous bombs exploded in a crowded street in Nairobi and 450 miles away in front of the US embassy in Tanzania. The chief suspect in these bombings was Saudi millionaire Osama bin Laden, who called on Muslims to declare war against Americans.

The most violent and determined enemies, however, were not foreign terrorists, but alienated Americans. In 1996, the government captured the nation's most elusive terrorist, Theodore J. Kaczynski, a Harvard-trained mathematician who railed against modern technology. The FBI called him the "Unabomber" because his early targets were universities and airlines. His bombs killed three and maimed dozens over a seventeen-year period.

Kaczynski's actions paled in comparison to those of former Gulf War veteran Timothy McVeigh. On April 19, 1995 McVeigh parked a rented Ryder truck packed with a mixture of ammonium nitrate and fuel oil in front of the Alfred P. Murrah Federal Building in Oklahoma City. At 9:02 a.m. the bomb exploded. The blast killed 168 people, including 19 children. The first reaction of many Americans was to blame terrorists overseas, but the worst act of domestic terrorism in American history was home grown. McVeigh, who viewed himself as a freedom fighter, hoped the bomb would ignite a right-wing revolt against the federal government.

After the devastation in Oklahoma City federal and local law enforcement agencies cracked down on armed militias and "patriot" groups. They had limited success: according to some sources the number of militia and patriot organizations increased by 6 percent during the decade to 858 identifiable groups. While not all the groups practiced violence, they shared a similar view of the world, in which a sinister cabal of Jews and environmentalists sought world domination, usually under the auspices of the UN.

A larger culture of conspiracy fed the appetite of militia groups. Surveys showed more than three-quarters of Americans believed President Kennedy was the victim of a massive conspiracy, not a crazed and lone gunman. Filmmaker Oliver Stone popularized the conspiracy theme in his blockbuster movie *JFK*, which speculated that Lyndon Johnson and the military backed the assassination. One of the most popular television shows of the decade, the *X-Files*, tapped into the popular fascination. The show featured two FBI agents who struggle to disentangle a giant government conspiracy involving alien/human hybridization. "The truth is out there," the announcer intones.

Why the proliferation of conspiracy theories? Intense public mistrust of government and the media played a role. Real conspiracies in Vietnam, Watergate, and the Iran-Contra affair did little to boost public confidence and provided cynics with ample evidence that Washington was capable of deceit. The explosion of the Internet, coupled with the fragmenting of mass culture, produced a world in which facts could be manipulated. The Internet lacked the capacity to distinguish between reasoned fact and outrageous opinion. It also provided virtual communities where people could have running discussions about the death of Vincent Foster, the planned UN takeovers of America, and the always-popular cover-up of the Kennedy assassination. In the end, conspiracy theories abound because they impose a simplistic and coherent framework on a complex and often incoherent world.

Public fear reached a fever pitch in the months leading up to the new millennium. Government officials fretted openly about the possibility of a major terrorist attack, and many Americans worried that a Y2K computer glitch would paralyze business and government and produce social chaos. The nation breathed a collective sigh of relief when midnight passed without major disruptions. "Apocalypse Not," *Time* magazine labeled the occasion. At the dawn of the new century most Americans seemed to agree with the assessment President Clinton delivered in his final State of the Union address. "We are fortunate to be alive at this moment in history," he said. "Never before has our nation enjoyed, at once, so much prosperity and social progress with so little internal crisis or so few external threats" (quoted in Page 2000: 4A).

REFERENCES AND FURTHER READING

Atkinson, Rich (1993) *Crusade: The Untold Story of the Persian Gulf War.* Boston: Houghton Mifflin.

Beschloss, Michael and Talbott, Strobe (1993) *At the Highest Levels: The Inside Story of the End of the Cold War.* Boston: Little, Brown.

Blumenthal, Sidney (1990) *Pledging Allegiance: The Last Campaign of the Cold War.* New York: HarperCollins.

Brune, Lester H. (1998) *The United States and Post-Cold War Interventions: Bush and Clinton in Somalia, Haiti, and Bosnia, 1992–1998.* Claremont, Calif.: Regina Books.

Ceruzzi, Paul E. (1998) *A History of Modern Computing.* Cambridge, Mass.: MIT Press.

Devroy, Ann and Smith, R. Jeffrey (1993) "Clinton re-examines a foreign policy under siege," *Washington Post*, October 17.

Dionne, E. J., Jr. (1988) "Dukakis and Bush trade fire in heavy barrages," *New York Times*, August 31.

Drew, Elizabeth (1995) *On the Edge: The Clinton Presidency.* New York: Touchstone.

Farley, Christopher John (1999) "Hip-hop special," *Guardian* (London), March 19.

Fiske, John (1994) *Media Matters: Race and Gender in US Politics.* Minneapolis: University of Minnesota Press.

FitzGerald, Frances (2000) *Way Out There in the Blue: Reagan, Star Wars, and the End of the Cold War.* New York: Simon and Schuster.

Friedman, Lawrence Meir (1999) *The Horizontal Society.* New Haven, Conn.: Yale University Press.

Friedman, Thomas L. (1999) *The Lexus and the Olive Tree: Understanding Globalization.* New York: Farrar, Straus, Giroux.

Gabler, Neal (1995) "The culture wars," *Los Angeles Times*, September 17.

—— (1998) *Life the Movie: How Entertainment Conquered Reality.* New York: Alfred A. Knopf.

Gabriel, John (1998) *Whitewash: Racialized Politics and the Media.* New York: Routledge.

Goldman, Peter and Mathews, Tom (1989) *The Quest for the Presidency: The 1988 Campaign.* New York: Touchstone.

Graubard, Stephen R. (1992) *Mr. Bush's War: Adventures in the Politics of Illusion.* New York: Hill and Wang.

Greene, John Robert (2000) *The Presidency of George Bush.* Lawrence: University Press of Kansas.

Johnson, Haynes (1994) *Divided We Fall: Gambling with History in the Nineties.* New York: W. W. Norton.

—— (2001) *The Best of Times: America in the Age of Clinton.* New York: Harcourt.

Kolb, Charles (1994) *White House Daze: The Unmaking of Domestic Policy in the Bush Years.* New York: Free Press.

Maraniss, David (1996) *First in His Class: The Biography of Bill Clinton.* New York: Touchstone.

Marvin, David (1996) *George Bush and the Guardianship Presidency.* New York: St. Martin's Press.

Mayer, Jane and Abramson, Jill (1994) *Strange Justice: The Selling of Clarence Thomas.* Boston: Houghton Mifflin.

Morris, Dick (1997) *Behind the Oval Office: Winning the Presidency in the Nineties.* New York: Random House.

Oberdorfer, Don (1998) *From the Cold War to a New Era: The United States and the Soviet Union, 1983–1991.* Baltimore, Md.: Johns Hopkins University Press.

Page, Susan (2000) "President touts nation's prosperity, progress," *USA Today,* January 28.

Podhoretz, John (1993) *Hell of a Ride: Backstage at the White House Follies, 1989–1993.* New York: Simon and Schuster.

Posner, Richard A. (2000) *An Affair of State: The Investigation, Impeachment, and Trial of President Clinton.* Cambridge, Mass.: Harvard University Press.

Schlesinger, Arthur M., Jr. (1991) *The Disuniting of America: Reflections on a Multicultural Society.* New York: W. W. Norton.

Shilts, Randy (1993) *Conduct Unbecoming: Gays and Lesbians in the US Military.* New York: St. Martin's Press.

Starr, Kenneth (1998) *The Starr Report: The Findings of Independent Counsel Kenneth W. Starr on President Clinton and the Lewinsky Affair.* Washington, DC: Public Affairs Press.

Stern, Kenneth S. (1997) *A Force Upon the Plain: The American Militia Movement and the Politics of Hate.* Norman: University of Oklahoma Press.

Stewart, James (1997) *Blood Sport: The President and His Adversaries.* New York: Touchstone.

Vankin, Jonathan (1992) *Conspiracies, Cover-ups, and Crimes: Political Manipulation and Mind Control in America.* New York: Paragon House.

Woodward, Bob (1994) *The Agenda: Inside the Clinton White House.* New York: Simon and Schuster.

PART II

Places

CHAPTER NINE

The South

RAYMOND ARSENAULT

The first historian to survey the historiography of the twentieth-century South began with a caveat. Writing in 1965, Dewey Grantham complained: "No period offers more abundant materials for the writing of the region's history than the recent past, yet historians have scarcely begun to confront the southern experience in the twentieth century" (Link and Patrick 1965: 410). Commissioned to write the final essay in a volume entitled *Writing Southern History*, Grantham somehow managed to fill 35 pages adorned with 115 footnotes. But he did so only by liberally expanding the definition of history to include the works of journalists, sociologists, folklorists, economists, and political scientists. While this ecumenical approach produced an interesting and thought-provoking essay, it underscored the collective failure of southern historians to confront six decades of regional history. The South had passed through the crises of racial disfranchisement, World War I, the Great Depression, World War II, and the modern civil rights movement, not to mention massive urbanization, industrialization, and demographic change. Yet the sub-field of southern history had continued to focus almost exclusively, even obsessively, on the events of the eighteenth and nineteenth centuries, revisiting and reinterpreting lives and events that had been studied many times before. The lack of temporal balance among the region's historians was troubling to those trying to comprehend the continuities and discontinuities of the southern experience, or the place of the modern South in the wider world.

Fortunately, no such complaint can be lodged today. As anyone who has kept abreast of the book review section of the *Journal of Southern History* in recent decades can confirm, books and articles dealing with the twentieth-century South now number in the thousands, reflecting nearly four decades of intense and wide-ranging scholarship. The topics studied include everything from the boll weevil invasions of the early twentieth century to recent trends in southern politics, from the history of lynching to the evolution of rock 'n' roll, from the experiences of sharecroppers to the mores of Sunbelt retirees. Wherever one looks there are microstudies, state studies, biographies, meta-narratives, and even works of grand synthesis – some written by traditional political historians but many others authored by social and cultural historians, or by those who defy easy categorization.

All of this reflects broader trends in American historiography, suggesting that even if the South itself has resisted full integration into the nation, southern historiography has lost most if not all of its atavistic and parochial distinctiveness. The neo-Confederate and white supremacist historiography that once comprised the respectable main-stream of regional history now resides on the fringe of the scholarly world. Separating myth from reality in the southern context remains a difficult prospect for even the most talented and conscientious scholars, but the enterprise of regional history no longer operates in an arena of stifling political and racial orthodoxy. Why this is so is no mystery. The same forces that liberated the modern South also liberated the study of southern history: the civil rights movement, the restoration of black voting rights, the demographic shifts after World War II, and the technological innovations that disrupted regional homogeneity and isolation. The professional inclusion of women, non-whites, non-southerners, and historians educated outside the South opened up the field to new perspectives and initiatives. And even among the ranks of southern-born white males, the new context generated an expanding interest in the issues of race, class, gender, and social justice raised by the reality and possibility of historical change. In a region that was finally rediscovering and redefining its democratic heritage, regional history required new approaches, including greater and more searching attention to the recent past.

Predictably, this relative freedom has produced a diversity of interests and inter-pretations – and a nightmare for anyone attempting to make historiographical sense of it all. No essay can do justice to the full range and complexity of modern southern historiography. The best to be hoped for in this brief format is a sampling of some of the most influential or interesting works on the twentieth-century South, and perhaps a bit of speculation on why these particular works deserve our attention and how they fit together. Readers in search of a more comprehensive historiographical survey may want to spend a few weeks or months making their way through the pages of the *Journal of Southern History* (1934–   ), *The Encyclopedia of Southern History* (1979), *Encyclopedia of Southern Culture* (1989), or the appropriate essays in *Writing South-ern History* (1965), *Interpreting Southern History* (1987), and *A Companion to the American South* (2002), edited by John Boles. Part of the Blackwell Companion series, the Boles volume includes eleven essays that deal with specific aspects of twentieth-century southern history.

In the second half of the twentieth century the study of the modern South has attracted more than its share of talented historians. But, unlike most other sub-fields of American history, modern southern history is often associated with one person: C. Vann Woodward (1908–99), an Arkansas-born historian who produced an extra-ordinary body of research and writing. His work represented a rare combination of ground-breaking research, rigorous analysis, and graceful prose. Woodward ap-proached the study of his native region with unblinking honesty and a keen sense of irony, challenging the shibboleths of racial prejudice and class privilege. He was an iconoclast and regional expatriate who found a way to write as both an insider and an outsider, and as both a dispassionate scholar and an engaged public intellectual. Despite his intimate knowledge of the dark side of the past – of the foibles and immiseration of his fellow southerners – he retained an empathetic sensibility that helped him to understand the elemental realities of both the powerful and the powerless. As Sheldon Hackney, a former student, wrote, Woodward was above all else "a humanizing historian, one who recognizes both the likelihood of failure and the necessity of struggle" (Hackney 1972: 216).

Woodward also had great timing, emerging in the late 1930s when the South had reached a cultural and political crossroads and was in desperate need of intellectual guidance and historically informed criticism. Drawing upon the intellectual awakening of a crisis-ridden era and seizing the initiative from a largely moribund cohort of southern historians, he was able to set the agenda for coming generations of regional scholars. After a wartime hiatus, he accepted a teaching position at Johns Hopkins in 1947 and soon attracted some of the nation's most promising graduate students; after moving to Yale in 1961, he directed a total of forty doctoral dissertations before his retirement in 1977. Many of his protégés became leading regional historians in their own right. Woodward never sought to impose any undue order or limitations on his students, however; and several of them challenged their teacher on important points of interpretation and methodology.

Woodward pushed his readers and his students into a deep intellectual engagement with the major issues of regional life. He revolutionized the study of southern history primarily by insisting on tackling the big questions. He was not afraid to cut against the grain of conventional understanding, exposing the misdeeds and mythic distortions of even the most hallowed of regional heroes (Kousser and McPherson 1982: xvi). How did the white southern elite maintain economic and political power in the early twentieth century without significantly improving the miserable conditions under which most southerners, black and white, lived? Why did the South continue to lag behind the rest of the nation in virtually every category of measurement, from income and education to racial justice and political freedom? Why did a region blessed with impressive human and natural resources remain mired in political demagoguery, economic exploitation, and cultural complacency? How and why had the mid-nineteenth century dream of emancipation and racial equality been twisted into the twentieth-century nightmare of racial scapegoating, disfranchisement, and a Jim Crow caste system? Woodward – and the legion of historians who followed his lead – would not rest until these questions were addressed, not only by the academy but also in some measure by political leaders. While this activist edge has sometimes complicated and even obstructed the study of the modern South, it has also given the field a social relevance and intellectual vitality.

Among Woodward's publications, four are classics: *Tom Watson, Agrarian Rebel* (1938); *Origins of the New South, 1877–1913* (1951); *The Strange Career of Jim Crow* (1955); and *The Burden of Southern History* (1960). Each addresses a major theme of southern history. *Tom Watson* confronts the tragic aspects of southern political leadership and the perversion of populist reform in the twentieth century. *Origins of the New South*, generally considered to be Woodward's masterwork, explains, among other things, the perpetuation of economic exploitation, poverty, and colonialism in the decades following Reconstruction. *The Strange Career of Jim Crow*, his most widely read book, traces the rise and fall of segregation from its nineteenth-century origins to its ultimate demise during the 1960s. *The Burden of Southern History*, a provocative series of essays written on the eve of the civil rights and Sunbelt revolutions, explores the meaning of southern identity and the ironic and complex nature of southern distinctiveness. These four areas of inquiry – roughly defined as politics and reform, economic and social change, race and civil rights, and regional identity – do more than encompass Woodward's most important achievements. They also help us gauge the contributions of other scholars who have expanded our understanding of the twentieth-century South. In each of the sections below, a brief recounting of Woodward's interpretations precedes a discussion of important works that either address, reformulate, extend, or in some cases transcend the questions and issues that he first posed. Within each section, the discussion will proceed chronologically according to the era studied.

Politics and Reform

Woodward's PhD thesis, published in 1938, was a captivating and disturbing biography of a charismatic and radical Georgia politician. *Tom Watson, Agrarian Rebel* explored the grass-roots realities and lost alternatives of southern politics. As William Jennings Bryan's "fusionist" vice-presidential running mate in 1896, Watson forged an uneasy and fateful alliance between Democrats and third-party Populists, and – even more importantly – between economically distressed black and white farmers. Both experimental alliances ended in failure, as William McKinley's victory ushered in an era of Republican dominance in national politics and the Populist appeal to black voters brought a decade-long campaign of political terror and white supremacist repression to fruition. For Watson, defeat brought disillusionment and eventual metamorphosis into a demagogic and cynical political boss. After 1896, he not only abandoned the strategy of interracial cooperation but also turned on his former allies, advocating black disfranchisement and indulging in virulent racial (and religious) scapegoating until his death in 1922. Significantly, according to Woodward, the two halves of Watson's career reflected the general flow of southern politics at the turn of the century, from multi-party competition and agrarian reform to one-party rule and political demagoguery. In effect, the demise of Populism was a tragedy, as race trumped class, ending the likelihood of fundamental economic, political, and social reform. The first two decades of the twentieth century witnessed the flowering of a regional progressive moment, but what passed for reform after Populism represented either its demagogic perversion or a middle-class and largely urban alternative to agrarian radicalism.

From the outset many historians questioned the depth and nature of the Populist commitment to interracial cooperation and radical reform, but Woodward's dramatic telling of the Watson saga triggered an explosion of scholarly interest in the political peculiarities of the early-twentieth-century South. Reporting on the excesses of so-called "Dixie demagogues" had long been a staple of American journalism, but in the wake of Woodward's book a number of young historians joined in, authoring conscientious biographical portraits of colorful southern politicians. The best of these were Francis Butler Simkins's *Pitchfork Ben Tillman* (1944), Dewey W. Grantham's *Hoke Smith and the Politics of the New South* (1958), and Albert W. Kirwan's *Revolt of the Rednecks* (1951). By treating their subjects in a serious and unpatronizing manner, Simkins and other biographers fostered a greater awareness of the richness and complexity of early-twentieth-century southern politics. What they did not do, however, was to address adequately the most difficult questions raised by the popularity and persistence of southern demagogues. Indeed, a biographical synthesis invariably avoided the social analysis of mass politics in favor of a preoccupation with the moral and personal behavior of politicians. Despite years of diligent scholarship, why the post-Populist South produced a strain of agrarian radicalism that was as ineffectual as it was strident remained pretty much a mystery. Why, after disfranchisement, didn't a two-party system emerge? After all, one historian asserted, "fierce conflict did occur between personal followings or through intrastate sectionalism" (Hackney 1972: 205). To pose the riddle in more specific terms, as one scholar later did, "if factional strife between agrarian rabble-rousers and their more respectable opponents was so rampant and so bitter, why didn't the 'Solid South' come apart at the seams?" (Arsenault 1984b: 8).

Woodward himself recognized the limitations of biography early on, adopting in *Origins of the New South, 1877–1913* (1951) a much more analytical approach to the issue of continuity and discontinuity between Populism and progressivism, and to the social and political implications of disfranchisement and demagoguery. He generally emphasized the moderate and white supremacist nature of the region's reformers, who ranged from rustic neo-Populists to efficiency-minded urban progressives. They have continued to attract considerable scholarly attention, as political biographers (Holmes 1970) and state and local historians rediscovered the "liberal" and even "radical" aspects of southern politics. This collective and ongoing re-evaluation underscored the complexity of the reform impulse and for many years produced no clear synthesis of southern progressivism. Much of the confusion stemmed from a chronic inattention to the social analysis of politics. Only in the late 1960s did the faint outlines of a regional synthesis become visible. As historians began to pay more attention to voting behavior and to the social and cultural context of politics, at least some of the apparent contradictions and paradoxes of southern progressivism became comprehensible. Significantly, two Woodward students were at the forefront of this new approach. For Alabama Hackney used sophisticated quantitative methodology to explore patterns of political continuity and discontinuity and to measure the impact of turn-of-the-century disfranchisement on the character of reform. He found little evidence of continuity between Populism and progressivism, ideologically or electorally (Hackney 1969).

Five years later the representativeness of Hackney's findings in Alabama was soon tested and for the most part confirmed by a monumental quantitative analysis of disfranchisement. J. Morgan Kousser demonstrated the enormous magnitude and abruptness of legally-mandated disfranchisement all across the South, and showed conclusively that blacks were not alone in losing the right (or in some cases the will) to vote. Many impoverished whites, including thousands of ex-Populists and other political dissenters, were jettisoned from a political system that fostered a narrowed range of ideology and public policy: from corporate conservatism to an elitist form of progressivism that promoted social order at the expense of social or economic justice. The progressive South had exiled radical reformers to the fringes of regional life. Revising Woodward's estimation of the class limits of southern politics, Kousser argued that southern progressivism was for "middle class whites only" (1974: 229).

This conclusion prompted a general re-evaluation of early-twentieth-century southern politics. The first effort at synthesis was Jack Temple Kirby's *Darkness at the Dawning* (1972), which stressed the paradox suggested in his title. The southern reform impulse was real; indeed, Kirby argued that progressivism actually "ran deeper and broader in the South than in other regions . . . simply because there was so much more to do in the impoverished South." At the same time, he offered the startling conclusion that, from the southern progressives' perspective, the firm imposition and extension of disfranchisement and racial segregation represented "the seminal 'progressive' reform of the era" (pp. 2, 4). Searching for order, southern politicians and voters saw no contradiction between progressivism and vigilant white supremacy; in fact, with rare exceptions, they could not envision one without the other.

A second and more comprehensive attempt at synthesis came a decade later with the publication of *Southern Progressivism: The Reconciliation of Progress and Tradition* (1983). Dewey Grantham offered a more positive assessment of southern progressivism than did Kirby or Kousser. Without ignoring the racism and other unsavory elements of the progressive South, Grantham stressed the accomplishments of the reformers, who were, he concluded,

> the first southerners to make a concerted attempt to cope with the social problems growing out of the modern industrialized and urbanized system. Convinced of the benefits to be derived from economic progress and modern institutions but still self-conscious defenders of southern values, they sought to reconcile progress and tradition. . . . Their achievements, under the circumstances, were impressive. (p. 422)

One could say the same of Grantham's synthesis, which made a valiant effort to bring order and clarity to a complicated subject. Nevertheless, since the early 1980s the study of southern progressivism has taken an interdisciplinary turn that has raised new questions and reopened others. In a case study of Arkansas politics, Raymond Arsenault took Grantham and other southern political historians to task for ignoring "the social and cultural landscape of the early twentieth-century South" and for falling short of "a creative synthesis of political and social history – a synthesis that recognizes that politician-constituent interaction flows both ways." By downplaying "the social determinants of mass politics," the understanding of "mass leadership" is distorted (1984b: 9–10). Although few scholars heeded this call for quantitative grass-roots analysis of southern politics, a different sort of social history was realized. Mary Martha Thomas (1992) and Marjorie Spruill Wheeler (1993) published pioneering studies of the role of women as suffragists in the South. And in 1996 Glenda Gilmore's monograph on North Carolina, *Gender and Jim Crow*, integrated the study of progressivism with the emerging field of gender studies, demonstrating that in at least one southern state women played a critical role in reform politics. Gilmore's study employed a broad definition of politics and focused on African-American women. But Elna Green's regional study of the struggle over women's suffrage (1997), and Steve Kantrowitz's imaginative reinterpretation of the role of manhood and gendered conceptions of honor in Pitchfork Ben Tillman's South Carolina (2000) confirmed the value and necessity of reassessing the contributions of women and sexuality to southern politics prior to implementation of the Nineteenth Amendment. This reassessment is ongoing and will undoubtedly invigorate southern political historiography for years to come.

Throughout the 1940s and 1950s studies of the Progressive Era constituted the bulk of historical work on modern southern politics. Indeed, as late as 1965 Grantham complained that southern historians had "scarcely ventured at all into the period after 1920" (Link and Patrick 1965: 424). But by the end of the 1960s scholarly attention had begun to shift to the politics of the 1920s and 1930s, owing partly to the appearance of two remarkable books, George Brown Tindall's *The Emergence of the New South, 1913–1945* (1967) and T. Harry Williams's *Huey Long* (1969). Published as volume 10 of the widely acclaimed History of the South series by Louisiana State University Press, Tindall's comprehensive 731-page narrative was a worthy sequel to Woodward's *Origins of the New South* (volume 9 of the series). Tindall covered all aspects of regional life, but his analysis of politics – especially chapters that dealt with World War I, business progressivism in the 1920s, and the impact of the New Deal on the depression-era South – were among the most illuminating in the book. His overall interpretation of politics largely complemented Woodward's, placing stress on debilitating political, cultural, and economic cross-currents such as the Ku Klux Klan, religious fundamentalism, persistent sectionalism, and self-serving boosterism. Tindall's careful analysis of the New Deal era superseded all previous studies, but he might have done even better had he been able to draw upon Williams's portrait of Louisiana's Huey Long, whose challenge to President Franklin Roosevelt was cut short by assassination in 1935. *Huey Long* rivaled *Tom Watson* as a merger of magisterial biography and deft analysis. Williams's artful and largely sympathetic depiction of this reformer and demagogue activated other historians to study the politics of the 1930s (Hair 1991).

The ensuing proliferation of monographs filled gaps that even Tindall's compendium had failed to address. But, aside from differing assessments of Long, the growing literature on the New Deal era did not produce anything akin to the ongoing historiographical debate on southern progressivism. Indeed, despite decades of scholarship, the same could be said for the remainder of the century. Each era, from the 1940s to the recent past, has posed difficult questions and inspired extended inquiry. But no distinct schools of thought have so far emerged. What we do have is a few essential works and a much larger number of supporting monographs that collectively tell the story of southern politics since the beginning of World War II.

On the waning years of the New Deal, the most importance source is still V. O. Key's survey, *Southern Politics in State and Nation* (1949), which stresses the diversity of mid-century southern politics. Tindall's detailed account of wartime politics and the conservative coalition that challenged FDR's influence in the region and elsewhere is a worthy supplement to Key. On the confusing political crosscurrents of the late 1940s and early 1950s, when both reform and reaction seemed on the rise, Numan V. Bartley's *The Rise of Massive Resistance* (1969) and *The New South, 1945–1980* (1995), provide a good starting point. His work – including his collaboration with Hugh Davis Graham, *Southern Politics and the Second Reconstruction* (1975) – is also a good place to begin a consideration of southern politics in the post-Brown civil rights era. A 1972 anthology edited by political scientist William C. Havard is also essential. Designed as a sequel to Key's classic, Havard's *Changing Politics of the South* offers a state-by-state evaluation of political change since 1945, as does *The Transformation of Southern Politics* (1976), a more readable joint effort by a journalist and a political scientist, Jack Bass and Walter De Vries. Written on the eve of Jimmy Carter's election to the presidency, *The Transformation of Southern Politics* takes the story of political change into the mid-1970s and deftly analyzes the influence of race and class. *Politics and Society in the South* (1987), a less hopeful work written a decade later by two political scientists, Earl and Merle Black, covers similar ground but extends the analysis into the conservative Reagan era.

As these references suggest, much of the most significant work on post-1960 southern political history has been done by non-historians. One major exception is Dan T. Carter's 1995 biography of Governor George Wallace of Alabama. This careful rendering of Wallace's volatile career, appropriately entitled *The Politics of Rage*, focuses on the 1960s and what Carter calls "the origins of the new conservatism." But in a provocative companion volume, *From George Wallace to Newt Gingrich* (1996), the analysis is extended to the increasingly pro-Republican South of the 1980s and 1990s. Placing Wallace's racial politics at the center of conservative Republican ascendancy, Carter probes the origins and evolution of Richard Nixon's "southern strategy" during the national campaigns of 1968 and 1972 and traces the institutionalization of racialist, neo-Wallace Republicanism in the 1980s. Citing the racial impact of Reagan's ultra-conservative judicial appointments, the growing insensitivity to the plight of the urban poor, the gutting of the Justice Department's Civil Rights division, and the deliberate blurring of race, crime, and tax issues by George Bush and other Republicans during the 1988 and 1992 campaigns, Carter makes a strong argument that "the issue of race remained the driving wedge of American conservative politics" (1996: 80). This slim volume documents what John Egerton called "the Americanization of Dixie [and] the southernization of America" (1974). And it does so by combining scholarship and socio-political commentary in a style that harkens back to another turbulent era, to the passionate political engagement that informed and inspired *Tom Watson*, which gave rise to modern southern political historiography.

Economic and Social Change: From New South to Sunbelt

Woodward's work also exerted a powerful influence on the study of economic and social change in the twentieth century. In 1951 he created a new historiographical paradigm with the publication of *Origins of the New South, 1877–1913*, which highlighted false promises, racial and economic exploitation, economic colonialism, and social pathology. This "is not a happy story," Hackney observed.

> The Redeemers are revealed to be as venal as the carpetbaggers. The declining aristocracy are ineffectual and money hungry, and in the last analysis they subordinated the values of their political and social heritage in order to maintain control over the black population. The poor whites suffered from strange malignancies of racism and conspiracy-mindedness, and the rising middle class was timid and self-interested even in its reform movement.

Which characters, if any, are sympathetic? "Simply those who are too powerless to be blamed for their actions" (1972: 191).

Emphasizing the discontinuity between the planter-dominated culture of the Old South and the modernizing middle-class ethos of the New South, Woodward challenged the ruling mythology, as well as the views of leading interpreters of southern culture like W. J. Cash (1941). But this iconoclasm did not prevent his arguments from becoming the dominant school of thought among regional historians during the 1950s and 1960s. Against the backdrop of an emerging civil rights movement and accelerating demographic and social change, historians embraced Woodward's critique of the New South as a corrective to the earlier excesses of chauvinistic southern apologists. Thus a new orthodoxy evolved by the 1970s. The first serious challenge to his interpretation of the New South came in the late 1970s with the publication of a series of books on the political economy of modernization in the late nineteenth century. Emphasizing the persistence of planter hegemony and disputing Woodward's emphasis on the rise of a new middle class, social historian Jonathan Wiener (1978), economist Jay R. Mandle (1978), and sociologist Dwight B. Billings, Jr. (1979) argued that the South had followed the "Prussian" model of moderniza-tion. Landed aristocracies managed to maintain economic and political power by adapting to the dictates of modern capitalism and urban commercial culture. In this view, the planter elite did not yield to a new class of entrepreneurs and managers, but instead sustained itself well into the twentieth century, preserving and even extending conservative social values.

By the 1980s Woodward was facing a challenge of a different sort. As the new social history, women's history, cliometrics, and historical demography gained acceptance, the limitations of *Origins of the New South* became increasingly apparent. It had either overlooked or minimized a number of important topics, including the history of women, gender, family life, religion, ethnicity and immigration, African-American communities (as opposed to race relations), and various aspects of material and popular culture (Foster 1987; Ownby 1990). Here was an imposing research agenda that Woodward willingly acknowledged. Indeed, not only did he look favorably on the younger scholars trying to fill in the many gaps of historical knowledge left unaddressed by his generation, he also strongly encouraged one of his former students, Edward Ayers, to attempt a new synthesis. Indeed *The Promise of the New South* transcended his mentor's classic account by offering a wealth of fascinating detail on the public and private lives of southerners from 1877 to 1906. Yet so eclectic, inclusive and largely impressionistic an approach did not result in a funda-mental revision of the Woodward model.

Two syntheses of a different kind, Roger L. Ransom and Richard Sutch's *One Kind of Freedom: The Economic Consequences of Emancipation* and Gavin Wright's *Old South, New South: Revolutions in the Southern Economy since the Civil War*, offered little solace to those looking for such a new order. *One Kind of Freedom* presented the first systematic quantitative exploration of the origins and persistence of rural poverty in the postbellum South. For Ransom and Sutch, as for Woodward, the key element behind the immiseration of black southerners, and of the rural South generally, was sharecropping. This institution of racial control shackled the entire southern econ-omy to an outmoded and ultimately self-defeating agrarian order (1977). Other economic historians, like Robert Higgs, disputed these conclusions, however, argu-ing that poverty and economic underdevelopment in the early twentieth century had much more to do with the long-term impact of the Civil War and the collapse of the Confederate economy than with systemic problems in the region's market economy (1977). But the later work of Gavin Wright, which raised southern economic history to a new level of theoretical sophistication, provided strong support for Ransom and Sutch's sharecropper thesis, and for Woodward's notion of a highly exploitative colonial economy. Most importantly, by introducing the simple but elegant distinction between

Old South "laborlords" and New South "landlords," Wright altered the debate over the long-term implications of emancipation and Reconstruction (1986).

While relatively few regional historians have resorted to econometrics or economic theory, qualitative studies of the economic and social history of agriculture have flourished. Most works, like Pete Daniel's *The Shadow of Slavery* (1972), emphasize the persistence of poverty and racial exploitation; and many focus on the pressure of the Great Depression. The economic impact of the New Deal on southern farmers has also been studied. The exploitation of black farmers and other southerners by penal institutions and the convict lease system has received less attention from historians. But David M. Oshinsky's *"Worse than Slavery": Parchman Farm and the Ordeal of Jim Crow Justice* (1996) and Alex Lichtenstein's study of convict labor, *Twice the Work of Free Labor* (1996), have generated new interest in the sinister history of prison farms.

Until the final decades of the twentieth century the historical literature on the non-farm economy in the twentieth-century South was also relatively sparse. But in the 1980s and 1990s, an explosion of interest in southern labor history produced three major anthologies (Zieger 1991, 1997; Fink and Reed 1994) on organized labor and a series of path-breaking monographs that collectively investigate a broad spectrum of working-class life (see also Honey 1993). One important addition to the literature, Bryant Simon's *A Fabric of Defeat* (1998), explored the political implications of the mill workers' social isolation and racial and class insecurities in South Carolina. Other elements of the working-class South have attracted scholarly attention, from timber workers (Green 1978) to cigar workers (Mormino and Pozzetta 1987). These and other studies have tended to confirm the continuing weakness of organized labor in the region and the negative impact of racial divisions on political mobilization and social reform. Dominated by extractive industries and a patina of self-serving pater-nalism, the South remained mired in poverty, racial and class exploitation, and economic colonialism – the same deadly trio that Woodward had identified in 1951 – for the better part of the twentieth century.

Fortunately, during the second half of the century, as the South morphed into the Sunbelt, the region slowly but inexorably shed at least some of its burdensome New South baggage. The unburdening had begun in the 1930s, with the intrusions of the Great Depression and the New Deal, and accelerated during and immediately after World War II. The transition from New South to Sunbelt did not gain full force until the 1970s, but a region-wide pattern of urbanization and industrializa-tion was already in evidence by 1945. The public policies that helped bring about the new urban-industrial order are described in great detail in James C. Cobb's *The Selling of the South* (1982) and Bruce J. Schulman's *From Cotton Belt to Sunbelt* (1991). Several important aspects of the modern urban South, including the history of women, ethnicity and immigration, and the environment, have received inad-equate attention from regional historians. But since the mid-1980s a small but significant number of studies have tried to remedy these historiographical over-sights: most notably Margaret Ripley Wolfe (1995) in women's history; George Brown Tindall (1995) and Gary Mormino and George Pozzetta (1987) in ethnic-immigration history; and Albert Cowdrey (1983), Raymond Arsenault (1984a), and Robert Bullard (1990) in environmental history. While much basic work in these sub-fields remains to be done, the recent shift toward a more inclusive definition of social and economic history promises to liberate historiography from the confining paradigm of the New South.

Race, Segregation, and Civil Rights

Race has always been a critically important frame of reference for southern historians; indeed, in 1928 the region's most prominent historian, Ulrich Bonnell Phillips, insisted that the determination to maintain white supremacy constituted "the central theme" of southern history. Yet the first historian to make a major contribution to the field was the black scholar John Hope Franklin, the author of a seminal text, *From Slavery to Freedom* (1947). His final eight chapters chronicled a half century of African-American life, from the interracial turmoil of the Progressive Era to the Harlem renaissance of the 1920s to the racial crosscurrents of World War II and its immediate aftermath. Unfortunately, historians of the modern South were slow to grasp the significance of Franklin's work – except for Woodward, who not only cultivated Franklin's friendship but also followed his scholarly lead.

Initially presented as a series of lectures at the University of Virginia in 1954, *The Strange Career of Jim Crow* appeared in book form a year later. 1955 was a pivotal year: the Brown school desegregation decision was implemented with the encouragement of "all deliberate speed," Chicago teenager Emmett Till was lynched in Mississippi, and the Montgomery bus boycott was launched. Against a backdrop of quickening civil rights activity and rising massive resistance among white segregationists, Woodward's slim volume represented, as LaWanda Cox later put it, "a tract for the times that was also a history of such high quality as to remain for three decades the point of departure for scholarly discourse, controversy, and research on the origins and history of segregation" (Boles and Nolen 1987: 250). His thesis was disarmingly simple: racial segregation was not an immutable part of regional culture; instead it was an artificial and relatively recent construct that had accompanied a "capitulation to racism" in the 1890s. Only at the end of the nineteenth century, following the collapse of Populism, did a rigid system of *de jure* segregation emerge. Modern white southerners might therefore undo what their great-grandparents had done without sacrificing important parts of their heritage.

The extent to which *The Strange Career of Jim Crow* shaped the public debate on segregation and civil rights is difficult to gauge. But there can be no doubt about the book's impact on southern historiography. During the 1960s and 1970s, a series of monographs tested Woodward's thesis, with mixed results. For some areas, the argument that *de jure* segregation was essentially a twentieth-century institution seemed to hold; but for others, the imposition of codified Jim Crow clearly came much earlier than Woodward had thought (Williamson 1968). Woodward acknowledged that his work on the origins of segregation needed some correction (1971, 1986). Yet he refused to abandon his basic argument, even after many leading historians – including some former students – began to question the validity of his generalizations. One telling critique came from Howard N. Rabinowitz, who demonstrated quite conclusively that throughout the late nineteenth century the primary alternative to segregation was not integration but rather outright exclusion (1978). This approach ultimately gained wide acceptance, and most subsequent studies sustained the trend of pushing the origins of *de jure* segregation back in time.

Other historians turned to social psychology and the history of gender and sexuality as avenues of investigation into the dynamics and meaning of Jim Crow. For example, Joel Williamson produced the first true synthesis of "black–white relations" in the late-nineteenth and early-twentieth-century South since the publication of *The Strange Career of Jim Crow*. *The Crucible of Race* (1984) took advantage of three decades of monographic research and innovative theorizing on the interplay of race, personality, and culture. The result was a somewhat eccentric but highly imaginative analysis of how and why southern racism became increasingly aggressive and controlling between 1895 and 1915. Like Woodward, Williamson stressed the discontinuity between the racial regimes of Old and New South and identified a turn-of-the-century crisis that led to a new equilibrium of white supremacist oppression. But he did so in a way that demonstrated just how much the field had changed since the 1950s, when the dictates of a straightforward structure and a restrained academic tone were still in force.

A decade later, Williamson took this new free-wheeling approach a step further by criticizing the entire profession for focusing obsessively on the history of segregation when weightier and more troubling regional traditions such as lynching and racially-motivated capital punishment remained unstudied (1997). By that time several important studies of lynching, including W. Fitzhugh Brundage's ground-breaking analysis (1993) of Georgia and Virginia lynchings during the years 1880–1930, had already appeared in print. But Williamson's attempt to reset the profession's research agenda was only part of a deeper and long-standing suspicion that earlier generations of scholars had overlooked important aspects of early-twentieth-century black life. Even Woodward had underestimated the historical agency of black southerners and had rarely ventured beyond the boundaries of white oppression and black victimization. What was missing, many scholars now insisted, was a regional history that analyzed the internal dynamics of African-American life and that recognized not only the limitations but also the accomplishments of African-American institutions. For historians who had entered the profession in the wake of the civil rights and Black Power movements of the 1960s, the need to transcend the field of race relations was all but self-evident; and even among older scholars, the new interest in black history was palpable.

In 1989 the study of black life a century ago reached a new level of subtlety with the publication of the Bancroft Prize-winning *Dark Journey: Black Mississippians in the Age of Jim Crow*. Tracing the often brutal but sometimes ennobling saga of black Mississippians from 1890 to 1940, Neil McMillen painted a bittersweet picture of perseverance and survival that belied stereotypes of powerlessness and despair. Like the music of down-home blues, for which Mississippi had long been famous (and which fostered a growing body of scholarship in its own right), *Dark Journey* helped to establish a new tone in black social history, which did justice to the multiplicity of voices in the black community. A broader work published a decade later, *Trouble in Mind: Black Southerners in the Age of Jim Crow* (1998), evinced similar qualities. Whenever possible, Leon Litwack allowed the historical actors to speak for themselves. He reinforced the notion, which Howard Rabinowitz and others had advanced, that the tightening of Jim Crow restrictions was a response to signs of progress and protest among black southerners during the 1880s and 1890s. In this way, the historiography of Jim Crow was infused with a heightened sense of black historical agency and contingency.

In recent decades the racial adjustments of the 1930s have received considerable attention from historians, several of whom have detected and investigated early manifestations of civil rights activism. Beginning with Dan T. Carter's seminal study (1969) of the celebrated Scottsboro case, Richard Kluger's exhaustive account (1976) of the NAACP's campaign to dismantle the legal foundation of Jim Crow, and Harvard Sitkoff's analysis (1978) of the racial policies of the New Deal, the reach of civil rights historiography – once limited to the post-1954 era – has been extended back in time. Studies by John Egerton (1994) and by Patricia Sullivan (1996), for example, have confirmed traces of "the movement" before World War II, even though broad agreement remains that the war itself was an important turning point in the history of black America, North and South. The impact of wartime migration and the Double V campaign – the determination among black Americans to secure victory and advance democracy at home and abroad – has been amply documented. Egerton's *Speak Now Against the Day* offers the most comprehensive treatment of civil rights activity during the decade preceding the 1954 Brown decision, but August Meier and Elliott Rudwick's *CORE* (1973) and Kluger's *Simple Justice* remain essential works.

The literature on the classic phase (1954–68) of the civil rights movement is voluminous, though much of it has been written by journalists or movement veterans. For several years, when the movement was a recent memory, this largely narrative literature lacked an analytical edge. But since the late 1970s civil rights historiography has become increasingly sophisticated (Eagles 2000). Early classics that built upon the foundation established in *The Strange Career of Jim Crow* include two preliminary attempts at synthesis: Harvard Sitkoff's *The Struggle for Black Equality, 1954–1980* (1981) and the sociologist Manning Marable's *Race, Reform, and Rebellion: The Second Reconstruction in Black America, 1945–1982* (1984). Both scholars were nevertheless hampered by the scarcity of analytical monographs on modern black history and civil rights. The subsequent outpouring of research and writing on the recent South filled in many of the gaps. In particular, the freedom struggles in Mississippi and Alabama have inspired a rich literature (see especially Dittmer 1994; Payne 1995; Davis 2001; McWhorter 2001; and Thornton 2002). Biographers have also produced an extensive literature on civil rights leadership, especially on Martin Luther King, Jr.'s role as a national and international symbol of nonviolent direct action. Two Pulitzer Prize-winning studies of King, David J. Garrow's *Bearing the Cross* (1986) and Taylor Branch's *Parting the Waters* (1988), highlighted the activities and influence of the Southern Christian Leadership Conference, inadvertently reinforcing the popular misconception that King was the movement and prompting some historians to call for countervailing studies of other leaders and organizations. During the 1990s biographies of Fred Shuttlesworth (Manis 1999), Ella Baker (Grant 1998), Ruby Doris Smith Robinson (Fleming 1998), and Fannie Lou Hamer (Lee 1999) have mitigated this problem.

Civil rights historiography is still new, and the various debates among civil rights historians have not produced clear or consistent schools of thought. But in recent years the scholarly community has identified a series of polarities that provide some structure and direction to those hoping to make a contribution to the field. Energizing and enlivening it have been disagreements over the relative importance of politics vs. protest, legal redress vs. direct action, nonviolence vs. violence, local movements vs. national organizations, and black nationalism vs. racial integration, plus a methodological debate over the uses and abuses of oral history. There has also been a lively terminological discussion over whether it is more accurate to characterize the civil rights movement as a "freedom struggle," as well as considerable controversy about the proper historiographical balance between studying the movement and its opponents. Paying proper attention to the rhetoric and behavior of white segregationists has been a challenge for civil rights historians, but several studies have shown that it can be done (Arsenault 1996; Carter 1996). Even more important, civil rights scholars have finally begun to place the movement in an international context, exploring the racial implications of the Cold War and the decolonization of Africa and the Third World (Dudziak 2000; Borstelmann 2001). This broadened field of vision has the potential to make civil rights studies less parochial, though a strong sense of place is likely to remain an important part of the motivation to study the "strange career" Woodward identified a half century ago.

Even with the politics of black separatism and racial backlash swirling around him, the dean of southern historians could take some comfort in the knowledge that the fundamental changes brought about by the civil rights movement – from voting rights to civic equality – were irreversible. Despite continuing inequalities of economic and social conditions, the movement had exerted a profound influence on all aspects of southern life. From education and economics to politics and popular culture, regional institutions had adapted to new demands and expectations. Some institutions had adapted more rapidly and successfully than others, of course; and defiant resistance, shrouded as it was in code words and political indirection, was still a force to be reckoned with in the white South. But who could doubt that the worst elements of the "southern way of life," the welter of regional traditions that had limited and twisted the lives of so many millions, were living on borrowed time? Certainly not a man whose life had spanned most of the "strange career" that he had chronicled so faithfully.

Regional Identity

The historical analysis of southern regional identity is another area of inquiry pioneered by Woodward. During the first half of the past century, a wide variety of southern intellectuals, from novelists and poets to journalists and sociologists, explored the origins and evolution of regional distinctiveness. But Woodward was the first historian to offer extended commentary on the intellectual and cultural history of the modern South. *The Burden of Southern History* made a strong plea for taking the history of ideas seriously, something that few historians of the South had done to that point. The book's extraordinary impact on southern historiography stemmed from two suggestive essays: "The search for southern identity," and "The irony of southern history."

In the first of these, he laid out a theory of southern distinctiveness sharply contrary to the then-dominant consensus school of historiography. Writing against the backdrop of a nationalizing and homogenizing trend that he labeled "the Bulldozer Revolution," Woodward asked whether there was anything "about the South that is immune from the disintegrating effect of nationalism and the pressure of conformity." His answer would be elaborated during much of his remaining career: the history that the region had endured. He did not mean "written history and its interpretation, popular and mythical, or professional and scholarly," but rather "the collective experience of the Southern people." That included poverty, defeat, the guilt of slavery and racial oppression. The regional experience was therefore rather "un-American" (1960: 6, 15–17, 19–21).

In "The irony of southern history" in particular, Woodward located the usefulness of the regional past in a Cold War era beset by chauvinism. He offered the southern saga of economic desperation, political and military defeat, and racial guilt as a lesson for Americans tempted to believe that their nation was "somehow immune from the forces of history." Studied carefully, the South and its history had the power to reveal important truths about the American experience and perhaps even to help the nation avert the tragic consequences of trying "to compel history to conform to her own illusions." More broadly, he insisted, "it is not the South but America that is unique among the peoples of the world. This peculiarity arises out of the American legend of success and victory, a legend that is not shared by any other people of the civilized world." The United States "has a history. It is only that the tragic aspects and the ironic implications of that history have been obscured by the national legend of success and victory and by the perpetuation of infant illusions of innocence and virtue." Historians of the region were therefore positioned "to make a special contribution to the understanding of American history, as well as that of the South's history" (1960: 168–9, 173–4, 189).

Prior to the late 1970s modern southern intellectual history was limited, for the most part, to studies of the Fugitive-Agrarian writers associated with Vanderbilt University and the Southern Renaissance. The primary exception, aside from Woodward's essays, was Tindall, who discussed the evolution of regional consciousness among southern writers and social scientists during the interwar years (1967). His fascinating account of Chapel Hill sociologists Howard Odum and Rupert Vance, plus the "Regionalists" who "rediscovered" the South in the 1920s and 1930s, encouraged other scholars to investigate various aspects of modern southern thought. Morton Sosna's *In Search of the Silent South* profiled the contributions and limitations of Odum and other white southern liberals who tried to balance the values of regional heritage and racial tolerance (1977). But the book that raised southern intellectual historiography to a new level of sophistication and self-consciousness was by a Briton. In *The Idea of the American South, 1920–1941* (1979), Michael O'Brien probed the ambiguities in sociological and literary expressions of southern distinctiveness, identifying the "idea" of the South as a problematic cultural construction. He also explored the response to modernism, as did two complementary studies that appeared soon thereafter: Richard H. King's *A Southern Renaissance* (1980) and Daniel J. Singal's *The War Within* (1982). Employing psychoanalytic theory and emphasizing the power of patriarchal traditions, King traced the cultural awakening of southern writers and intellectuals from 1930 to 1955 and included a final chapter on "the new southern liberalism" of Woodward, Key, and Robert Penn Warren. Taking a somewhat different tack, Singal examined the cultural "war" waged between modernists and post-Victorian sentimentalists over the viability of the cavalier myth, white supremacy, and other sectional traditions.

This flurry of books fostered a new interest in the connections among ideas, literary expression, and social reality amid rapid economic and cultural change. A number of subsequent studies examined various aspects of the modern South's intellectual and ideological proclivities, including obsessive self-examination (Hobson 1983), racial conservatism (Kneebone 1985), and religious fundamentalism (Larson 1997). Other important studies, such as James Cobb's book on the Mississippi Delta (1992), used a geographically narrower focus and a mixture of social and intellectual history to explore patterns of identity. These works focus on the first half of the twentieth century, and as yet no comparable historical literature is extant on southern history of the second half of the century. Other than Pete Daniel's study of the 1950s, *Lost Revolutions* (2000), which pays more attention to popular culture than to intellectual or literary matters, the major analyses of post-1950 regional identity have been written by journalists. Like Daniel, the authors of these studies all take a decidedly "popular" or "low-brow" approach to the history of ideas. But the best of the journalistic accounts, John Egerton's *The Americanization of Dixie* (1974) and Peter Applebome's *Dixie Rising* (1996), provide a good introduction to the dramatic shift in regional consciousness generally known as the "Sunbelt."

The concept of a mega-region – encompassing the southern half of the nation and spanning the Southeast, the Southwest, and California – originated in the early 1930s, when Regionalist scholars called for a reorientation of traditional southern identity (Dorman 1993). While none of the Regionalists actually used the term "Sunbelt," their focus on the social benefits of economic and demographic growth, plus their willingness to transcend the traditional boundaries and cultural mandates of the ex-Confederate South, anticipated the arguments and observations of later Sunbelt enthusiasts. A conservative political analyst was the first to utilize the term "Sunbelt" in print. In 1969 Kevin Phillips forecast a southward and westward flow of political power in *The Emerging Republican Majority*. In 1976 the emergence of Georgia's Jimmy Carter as a national leader brought the phenomenon to center stage. By the beginning of the Carter administration, the mass media had made the "Sunbelt" a popularly accepted term and a common topic of discussion. Journalists found evidence of the Sunbelt's ascendance wherever they looked: in election returns, in census reports, in economic trend lines, and even in popular culture, which made southern self-expressiveness chic. Often focusing on southern California, Florida, Texas, and Arizona, pundits expounded on the benefits of an expanding economy based on high-tech commercialism and leisure-oriented consumption, a political structure that featured new faces and new ideas, and a warm climate that encouraged a casual, outdoor life-style. By contrast, the declining "Frostbelt" (or "Rustbelt") of the industrial Northeast and Midwest stimulated little enthusiasm.

The 1980 presidential election, which featured two Sunbelt candidates, Carter and Ronald Reagan, seemed to confirm the growing political power of the region. Nevertheless, during Reagan's presidency several high-profile media reports and academic studies uncovered the troublesome side of the Sunbelt. Profiles of Sunbelt cities such as Miami, Atlanta, and Houston suggested a regional pattern of violent crime and drug trafficking, substandard educational and cultural institutions, urban sprawl and environmental degradation, low wages, and endemic corruption among business and political leaders. Few observers questioned the growing importance of the Sunbelt, but many expressed concern that the new regional behemoth was leading the nation astray with an ethos of unregulated growth. Despite such misgivings, the growth patterns that had created the Sunbelt showed no signs of abating in the 1980s and

1990s. Metropolises continued to burgeon, as several factors present in limited form since World War II extended their influence. Prominent among these were the proliferation of technological innovations such as interstate highways, jet travel, personal computers, air conditioning, and pesticides; economic trends such as globalization, de-industrialization, and the decline of organized labor; federal policies that placed much of the military-industrial complex in southern and western states; the southward and westward spread of professional sports franchises; and civil rights and immigration legislation that opened both the biracial South and the Hispanic Southwest to new possibilities of racial equality and multicultural opportunity. Directly or indirectly, all of these factors fostered corporate relocation, year-round tourism, the skyrocketing popularity of Sunbelt retirement communities, and massive population growth that necessitated congressional reapportionment in 1990 and 2000.

As Applebome and others have observed, all of this continues to exert a powerful hold on popular perceptions of American regionalism. However, at the dawn of the twenty-first century, the Sunbelt concept was beginning to lose some of its currency and explanatory power, at least among academics. As early as the mid-1980s scholars were questioning the validity and utility of the Sunbelt as a regional category (Miller and Pozzetta 1988; Mohl 1990). Merging the South and much of the West, they argued, gives the impression of a consistent or coherent entity, belying the complexities of local and subregional variation. With the demographic, economic, and political power of the Sunbelt heavily concentrated in California, Texas, and Florida, the notion of a Sunbelt is inevitably misleading. Much of the South and West, especially rural areas and small towns, experienced the boom only barely or vicariously. The problem of regional definition is compounded by the absence of meaningful and definable borders, or even of certainty about which criteria to use in defining the region.

Perhaps so. But to date very few Sunbelt boosters are ready to jettison so popular a concept. How historians will ultimately handle the impact of the Sunbelt on southern identity remains to be seen. But one suspects that the questions of regional identity that engaged earlier generations of scholars will not be so pressing or important, when historians finally get around to an assessment of the late-twentieth-century South. As early as 1988, at a conference on "The Future South," James Cobb argued that it was time to halt the debate about distinctiveness. Amid rising globalism and multiculturalism, the quest for southern identity had lost much of its significance, because the traditional fascination with regional peculiarities presupposed a national mainstream that had vanished. While the southern history that Woodward deemed to be so instructive in the 1950s and 1960s may still be salient, Cobb urged his colleagues to consider a broader perspective that focuses on the common problems and prospects of the human condition (Dunn and Preston 1991).

REFERENCES

Applebome, Peter (1996) *Dixie Rising: How the South is Shaping American Values, Politics, and Culture.* New York: Times Books.

Arsenault, Raymond (1984a) "The end of the long hot summer: the air conditioner and southern culture," *Journal of Southern History* 50(4) (November), pp. 597–628.

—— (1984b) *The Wild Ass of the Ozarks: Jeff Davis and the Social Bases of Southern Politics*. Philadelphia: Temple University Press.

—— (1996) "The folklore of southern demagoguery," in Charles Eagles (ed.) *Is There a Southern Political Tradition?* Jackson: University Press of Mississippi.

Ayers, Edward L. (1992) *The Promise of the New South: Life After Reconstruction*. New York: Oxford University Press.

Bartley, Numan V. (1969) *The Rise of Massive Resistance: Race and Politics in the South During the 1950s*. Baton Rouge: Louisiana State University Press.

—— (1995) *The New South, 1945–1980*. Baton Rouge: Louisiana State University Press.

Bartley, Numan V. and Graham, Hugh D. (1975) *Southern Politics and the Second Reconstruction*. Baltimore, Md.: Johns Hopkins University Press.

Bass, Jack and De Vries, Walter (1976) *The Transformation of Southern Politics: Social Change and Political Consequence since 1945*. New York: Basic Books.

Billings, Dwight B., Jr. (1979) *Planters and the Making of a "New South": Class, Politics, and Development in North Carolina, 1865–1900*. Chapel Hill: University of North Carolina Press.

Black, Earl and Black, Merle (1987) *Politics and Society in the South*. Cambridge, Mass.: Harvard University Press.

Boles, John B. (ed.) (2002) *A Companion to the American South*. Oxford: Blackwell..

Boles, John B. and Nolen, Evelyn Thomas (eds.) (1987) *Interpreting Southern History: Historiographical Essays in Honor of Sanford W. Higginbotham*. Baton Rouge: Louisiana State University Press.

Borstelmann, Thomas (2001) *The Cold War and the Color Line: American Race Relations in the Global Arena*. Cambridge, Mass.: Harvard University Press.

Branch, Taylor (1988) *Parting the Waters: America in the King Years, 1954–63*. New York: Simon and Schuster.

Brundage, W. Fitzhugh (1993) *Lynching in the New South: Georgia and Virginia, 1880–1930*. Urbana: University of Illinois Press.

Bullard, Robert D. (1990) *Dumping in Dixie: Race, Class, and Environmental Quality*. Boulder, Colo.: Westview Press.

Carter, Dan T. (1969) *Scottsboro: A Tragedy of the American South*. Baton Rouge: Louisiana State University Press.

—— (1995) *The Politics of Rage: George Wallace, the Origins of the New Conservatism, and the Transformation of American Politics*. New York: Simon and Schuster.

—— (1996) *From George Wallace to Newt Gingrich: Race in the Conservative Counterrevolution, 1963–1994*. Baton Rouge: Louisiana State University Press.

Cash, W. J. (1941) *The Mind of the South*. New York: Alfred A. Knopf.

Cobb, James C. (1982) *The Selling of the South: The Southern Crusade for Industrial Development, 1936–1980*. Baton Rouge: Louisiana State University Press.

—— (1992) *The Most Southern Place on Earth: The Mississippi Delta and the Roots of Regional Identity*. New York: Oxford University Press.

Cowdrey, Albert E. (1983) *This Land, This South: An Environmental History*. Lexington: University Press of Kentucky.

Daniel, Pete (1972) *The Shadow of Slavery: Peonage in the South, 1901–1969*. New York: Oxford University Press.

—— (2000) *Lost Revolutions: The South in the 1950s*. Chapel Hill: University of North Carolina Press.

Davis, Jack E. (2001) *Race against Time: Culture and Separation in Natchez since 1930*. Baton Rouge: Louisiana State University Press.

Dittmer, John (1994) *Local People: The Struggle for Civil Rights in Mississippi*. Urbana: University of Illinois Press.

Dorman, Robert L. (1993) *Revolt of the Provinces: The Regionalist Movement in America, 1920–1945*. Chapel Hill: University of North Carolina Press.

Dudziak, Mary L. (2000) *Cold War Civil Rights: Race and the Image of American Democracy*. Princeton, NJ: Princeton University Press.

Dunn, Joe P. and Preston, Howard L. (eds.) (1991) *The Future South: A Historical Perspective for the Twenty-first Century*. Urbana: University of Illinois Press.

Eagles, Charles W. (2000) "Towards new histories of the civil rights era," *Journal of Southern History* 66(4) (November), pp. 815–48.

Egerton, John (1974) *The Americanization of Dixie: The Southernization of America*. New York: Harper's Magazine Press.

—— (1994) *Speak Now Against the Day: The Generation before the Civil Rights Movement in the South*. New York: Alfred A. Knopf.

Fink, Gary M. and Reed, Merl E. (eds.) (1994) *Race, Class, and Community in Southern Labor History*. Tuscaloosa: University of Alabama Press.

Fleming, Cynthia G. (1998) *Soon We Will Not Cry: The Liberation of Ruby Doris Smith Robinson*. Lanham, Md.: Rowman and Littlefield.

Foster, Gaines M. (1987) *Ghosts of the Confederacy: Defeat, the Lost Cause, and the Emergence of the New South, 1865–1913*. New York: Oxford University Press.

Franklin, John Hope (1947) *From Slavery to Freedom*. New York: Macmillan.

Garrow, David J. (1986) *Bearing the Cross: Martin Luther King, Jr. and the Southern Christian Leadership Conference*. New York: Morrow.

Gilmore, Glenda E. (1996) *Gender and Jim Crow: Women and the Politics of White Supremacy in North Carolina, 1896–1920*. Chapel Hill: University of North Carolina Press.

Grant, Joanne (1998) *Ella Baker: Freedom Bound*. New York: Wiley.

Grantham, Dewey W. (1958) *Hoke Smith and the Politics of the New South*. Baton Rouge: Louisiana State University Press.

—— (1983) *Southern Progressivism: The Reconciliation of Progress and Tradition*. Knoxville: University of Tennessee Press.

Green, Elna C. (1997) *Southern Strategies: Southern Women and the Woman Suffrage Question*. Chapel Hill: University of North Carolina Press.

Green, James R. (1978) *Grass-Roots Socialism: Radical Movements in the Southwest, 1895–1943*. Baton Rouge: Louisiana State University Press.

Hackney, Sheldon (1969) *Populism to Progressivism in Alabama*. Princeton, NJ: Princeton University Press.

—— (1972) "*Origins of the New South* in retrospect," *Journal of Southern History* 38(2) (May), pp. 191–216.

Hair, William Ivy (1991) *The Kingfish and his Realm: The Life and Times of Huey P. Long*. Baton Rouge: Louisiana State University Press.

Havard, William C. (ed.) (1972) *The Changing Politics of the South*. Baton Rouge: Louisiana State University Press.

Higgs, Robert (1977) *Competition and Coercion: Blacks in the American Economy, 1865–1914*. Cambridge: Cambridge University Press.

Hobson, Fred (1983) *Tell About the South: The Southern Rage to Explain*. Baton Rouge: Louisiana State University Press.

Holmes, William F. (1970) *The White Chief: James Kimble Vardaman*. Baton Rouge: Louisiana State University Press.

Honey, Michael (1993) *Southern Labor and Black Civil Rights: Organizing Memphis Workers*. Urbana: University of Illinois Press.

Kantrowitz, Steve (2000) *Ben Tillman and the Reconstruction of White Supremacy*. Chapel Hill: University of North Carolina Press.

Key, V. O. (1949) *Southern Politics in State and Nation*. New York: Alfred A. Knopf.

King, Richard H. (1980) *A Southern Renaissance: The Cultural Awakening of the American South, 1930–1955*. New York: Oxford University Press.

Kirby, Jack Temple (1972) *Darkness at the Dawning: Race and Reform in the Progressive South*. Philadelphia: Lippincott.

Kirwan, Albert W. (1951) *The Revolt of the Rednecks: Mississippi Politics, 1876–1925*. Lexington: University Press of Kentucky.

Kluger, Richard (1976) *Simple Justice: The History of* Brown v. Board of Education *and Black America's Struggle for Equality*. New York: Alfred A. Knopf.

Kneebone, John T. (1985) *Southern Liberal Journalists and the Issue of Race, 1920–1944*. Chapel Hill: University of North Carolina Press.

Kousser, J. Morgan (1974) *The Shaping of Southern Politics: Suffrage Restriction and the Establishment of the One-Party South, 1880–1910*. New Haven, Conn.: Yale University Press.

Kousser, J. Morgan and McPherson, James (eds.) (1982) *Region, Race, and Reconstruction: Essays in Honor of C. Vann Woodward*. New York: Oxford University Press.

Larson, Edward J. (1997) *Summer for the Gods: The Scopes Trial and America's Continuing Debate Over Science and Religion*. New York: Basic Books.

Lee, Chana Kai (1999) *For Freedom's Sake: The Life of Fannie Lou Hamer*. Urbana: University of Illinois Press.

Lichtenstein, Alex (1996) *Twice the Work of Free Labor: The Political Economy of Convict Labor in the South*. London: Verso.

Link, Arthur S. and Patrick, Rembert W. (eds.) (1965) *Writing Southern History: Essays in Historiography in Honor of Fletcher M. Green*. Baton Rouge: Louisiana State University Press.

Litwack, Leon F. (1998) *Trouble in Mind: Black Southerners in the Age of Jim Crow*. New York: Alfred A. Knopf.

McMillen, Neil R. (1989) *Dark Journey: Black Mississippians in the Age of Jim Crow*. Urbana: University of Illinois Press.

McWhorter, Diane (2001) *Carry Me Home: Birmingham, Alabama: The Climactic Battle of the Civil Rights Movement*. New York: Simon and Schuster.

Mandle, Jay R. (1978) *The Roots of Black Poverty: The Southern Plantation Economy after the Civil War*. Durham, NC: Duke University Press.

Manis, Andrew M. (1999) *A Fire You Can't Put Out: The Civil Rights Life of Birmingham's Reverend Fred Shuttlesworth*. Tuscaloosa: University of Alabama Press.

Marable, Manning (1984) *Race, Reform, and Rebellion: The Second Reconstruction in Black America, 1945–1982*. Jackson: University Press of Mississippi.

Meier, August and Rudwick, Elliott (1973) *CORE: A Study in the Civil Rights Movement, 1942–1968*. New York: Oxford University Press.

Miller, Randall M. and Pozzetta, George E. (eds.) (1988) *Shades of the Sunbelt: Essays on Ethnicity, Race, and the Urban South*. Westport, Conn.: Greenwood.

Mohl, Raymond A. (ed.) (1990) *Searching for the Sunbelt: Historical Perspectives on a Region*. Knoxville: University of Tennessee Press.

Mormino, Gary R. and Pozzetta, George E. (1987) *The Immigrant World of Ybor City: Italians and their Latin Neighbors in Tampa, 1885–1985*. Urbana: University of Illinois Press.

O'Brien, Michael (1979) *The Idea of the American South, 1920–1941*. Baltimore, Md.: Johns Hopkins University Press.

Oshinsky, David M. (1996) *"Worse Than Slavery": Parchman Farm and the Ordeal of Jim Crow Justice*. New York: Free Press.

Ownby, Ted (1990) *Subduing Satan: Religion, Recreation, and Manhood in the Rural South, 1865–1920*. Chapel Hill: University of North Carolina Press.

Payne, Charles (1995) *I've Got the Light of Freedom: The Organizing Tradition and the Mississippi Freedom Struggle*. Berkeley: University of California Press.

Phillips, Kevin P. (1969) *The Emerging Republican Majority.* New Rochelle, NY: Arlington House.

Phillips, Ulrich Bonnell (1928) "The central theme of southern history," *American Historical Review* 34 (October), pp. 30–43.

Rabinowitz, Howard N. (1978) *Race Relations in the Urban South, 1865–1890.* New York: Oxford University Press.

Ransom, Roger L. and Sutch, Richard (1977) *One Kind of Freedom: The Economic Consequences of Emancipation.* Cambridge: Cambridge University Press.

Roller, David C. and Twyman, Robert W. (1979) *The Encyclopedia of Southern History.* Baton Rouge: Louisiana State University Press.

Schulman, Bruce J. (1991) *From Cotton Belt to Sunbelt: Federal Policy, Economic Development, and the Transformation of the South, 1938–1980.* New York: Oxford University Press.

Simkins, Francis Butler (1944) *Pitchfork Ben Tillman, South Carolinian.* Baton Rouge: Louisiana State University Press.

Simon, Bryant (1998) *A Fabric of Defeat: The Politics of South Carolina Millhands, 1910–1948.* Chapel Hill: University of North Carolina Press.

Singal, Daniel Joseph (1982) *The War Within: From Victorian to Modernist Thought in the South, 1919–1945.* Chapel Hill: University of North Carolina Press.

Sitkoff, Harvard (1978) *A New Deal for Blacks: The Emergence of Civil Rights as a National Issue.* New York: Oxford University Press.

—— (1981) *The Struggle for Black Equality, 1954–1980.* New York: Hill and Wang.

Sosna, Morton (1977) *In Search of the Silent South: Southern Liberals and the Race Issue.* New York: Columbia University Press.

Sullivan, Patricia (1996) *Days of Hope: Race and Democracy in the New Deal Era.* Chapel Hill: University of North Carolina Press.

Thomas, Mary Martha (1992) *The New Woman in Alabama: Social Reforms and Suffrage, 1890–1920.* Tuscaloosa: University of Alabama Press.

Thornton, J. Mills, III (2002) *Dividing Lines: Municipal Politics and the Struggle for Civil Rights in Montgomery, Birmingham, and Selma.* Tuscaloosa: University of Alabama Press.

Tindall, George Brown (1967) *The Emergence of the New South, 1913–1945.* Baton Rouge: Louisiana State University Press.

—— (1995) *Natives and Newcomers: Ethnic Southerners and Southern Ethnics.* Athens: University of Georgia Press.

Wheeler, Marjorie Spruill (1993) *New Women of the New South: The Leaders of the Woman Suffrage Movement in the Southern States.* New York: Oxford University Press.

Wiener, Jonathan M. (1978) *Social Origins of the New South: Alabama, 1860–1885.* Baton Rouge: Louisiana State University Press.

Williams, T. Harry (1969) *Huey Long.* New York: Alfred A. Knopf.

Williamson, Joel (ed.) (1968) *The Origins of Segregation.* Boston: D. C. Heath.

—— (1984) *The Crucible of Race: Black–White Relations in the American South since Reconstruction.* New York: Oxford University Press.

—— (1997) "Wounds not scars: lynching, the national conscience, and the American historian," *Journal of American History* 83(4) (March), pp. 1221–53.

Wilson, Charles Reagan and Ferris, William (eds.) (1989) *Encyclopedia of Southern Culture.* Chapel Hill: University of North Carolina Press.

Wolfe, Margaret Ripley (1995) *Daughters of Canaan: A Saga of Southern Women.* Lexington: University Press of Kentucky.

Woodward, C. Vann (1938) *Tom Watson: Agrarian Rebel.* New York: Macmillan.

—— (1951) *Origins of the New South, 1877–1913.* Baton Rouge: Louisiana State University Press.

—— (1955) *The Strange Career of Jim Crow.* New York: Oxford University Press. Revised editions: 1966, 1974, 1990, 2002.

—— (1960) *The Burden of Southern History.* Baton Rouge: Louisiana State University Press. Revised editions: 1968, 1993.

—— (1971) *American Counterpoint: Slavery and Racism in the North–South Dialogue.* Boston: Little, Brown.

—— (1986) *Thinking Back: The Perils of Writing History.* Baton Rouge: Louisiana State University Press.

Wright, Gavin (1986) *Old South, New South: Revolutions in the Southern Economy since the Civil War.* New York: Basic Books.

Zieger, Robert H. (ed.) (1991) *Organized Labor in the Twentieth-Century South.* Knoxville: University of Tennessee Press.

—— (ed.) (1997) *Southern Labor in Transition, 1940–1995.* Knoxville: University of Tennessee Press.

CHAPTER TEN

The West

ANNE M. BUTLER

George Armstrong Custer guaranteed for the West a permanent place within the language of contest. Custer was certainly not the first person to bring conflict into the West. Nor was he the only historical actor on June 25, 1876, when Sioux people, camped near the Little Big Horn River, defeated the troops of the Seventh Cavalry. History, within and across cultures, had long constructed a legacy stoked by violence and racism, throughout the land today known as the American West. Yet Custer, in his fatal confrontation with the exasperated and enraged Sioux, carved for western history a singular space within the heritage of the United States. That space, now defined by a richly textured literature, remains, like the doomed Custer, as controversial in the twenty-first century as in the nineteenth.

"Custer's Last Stand," inflated by "nationalistic glory" and "righteous revenge," became part of America's popular vocabulary, often undergirding a nation's perception of a region's history. Somehow many Americans came to understand the West in descriptive terms that they appended to Custer's life and death. They saw the West as heroic, colorful, and bold, its brave figures pitted against fierce opponents: the harsh land and its harsher residents. Native people, with their colorful names – Crazy Horse, Sitting Bull, Gall, Wooden Leg, Spotted Calf – served as historical foils who, through exotic lives brought low by brutal defeats, contributed to the triumph of white society. As for the Little Big Horn battle itself, Americans – none more than the widowed Elizabeth Custer – chose to overlook the obvious: the colonel acted precipitously, violating his military orders and leading his troops to an unnecessary fate.

That aside, this tale of soldiers, outnumbered by mounted warriors and dead to the last man, appeared to infuse Americans with great pride and justify all behavior that resulted in dominance by the United States government and Anglo-European culture. Notions of conquest and destiny, democracy and freedom overtook the process of settlement and converted it into a national political rhetoric. If Custer and the troops, including his two brothers, brother-in-law, and nephew, died in what some insisted on calling a "massacre," it was not to be in vain. Whites intensified their regional claims, finishing off the nineteenth century in a burst of political and economic coups that embedded the power of the federal government in the West.

Others held to differing perceptions of what transpired near the banks of the Little Big Horn. The contrary accounts, preserved through a Native American oral tradition, remained largely muted. Though silenced or ignored, those voices nonetheless murmured that the Indian survivors of the battle had witnessed an event – indeed an era – differing in warp and woof from the mainstream legend. Across time, particularly after the 1933 death of the Widow Custer, the sounds of the counterpoint grew stronger, more insistent, and more convincing.

Yet from either perspective, the basics of the story appeared to be straightforward: white society, springing largely from European immigrant groups, had marched out of the forested East and across the continent, where, west of the Mississippi River, an arid world, inhabited in the main by nomadic people, produced catastrophic encounters. At every point on this landscape of mountains and valleys, deserts and prairies, opposing cultures fought emotional and physical battles. White settlers, fired by a series of economic opportunities, subdued the elements, extracted the resources, devastated the indigenous population, thus ensuring the triumph of Anglo-European institutions and values.

Everything seemed simplistic about the tale, but it yawed somewhat off-center with its white heroes always winning against a collection of ineffective natives. Frederick Jackson Turner, the dean of frontier historians, reframed the story in his famous address, "The Significance of the Frontier in American History," delivered at an 1893 Chicago meeting of the American Historical Association. Drawing on his professional training and his personal vision, Turner transformed Custer-like personalities into intellectual concepts, as he used the West to articulate the first formal definition of American national identity.

His patriotic message did not seem to be hard for anyone to understand; the frontier, with its vast stretches of land, explained the emergence of the nation's democratic traditions. Those who had gone to the West – mountain men, explorers, soldiers, pioneers – had done so as pro-active agents of democracy, repeatedly refined in the cauldron of frontier exigencies. The indigenous peoples of the West, with their "savage" ways and non-white countenances, sustained the Turnerian defense of cultural and institutional superiority and added just the right amount of dash and verve to make a historical era the stuff of popular appeal and civic pride.

Of course the problem was that this self-approving version short-changed itself. Turner tended to treat the West in a masculine-tinted fashion that neglected pertinent historical evidence and numerous human communities. Nor did some of his assertions match the record. Yet there was something viscerally attractive in his basic agrarian vision of "Americans made by America, America made by Americans," which – if flawed – still generated a fledgling enthusiasm for the academic study of the West.

The Turnerian celebration of a farm heritage confronted a West poised for a coming struggle between its agrarian roots and growing urban power. The nineteenth-century social and political focus on farm issues, especially as seen through the Grange and the Populists, yielded in the twentieth century to greater venture capitalism, more labor unrest, and intensified political maneuvering. While cities remained few and widely scattered, their potential as magnets for transforming the rural West made the writings of Turner especially poignant. The West would continue to ponder its place in the national scheme, uncertain whether to claim for itself a unique pioneer heritage or plunge when and where it could into an increasingly complex modern America driven by powerful urban forces.

This real-life dilemma in some ways mirrored the spirit of western historians who wanted to overcome the feeling among many academics that the region represented parochialism and antiquarianism. For example, James C. Malin, the scholar of the grasslands, led the way in defining the importance of western agricultural and rural studies. Malin concentrated on Kansas, and had begun by the 1930s to form his ideas about the regional nature of western history. He exploited other disciplines – geology, botany, geography – to understand how humans interacted with their environment, producing interdisciplinary studies long before they became fashionable. Yet titles such as *Winter Wheat in the Golden Belt of Kansas: A Study in Adaptation to Subhumid Geographical Environment* (1944) and *The Grassland of North America: Prolegomena to its History, with Addenda and Postscript* (1947) did not win the crusty author a large popular following, or even convince others, such as publishers, that his notions of the West as a region suggested something critical about American history in general.

The equally prickly Walter Prescott Webb attracted greater fame, not only through his writings, but also with his quotable, folksy Texas style. The son of a poor farmer, Webb drew on his own experience to illuminate the themes of land, water, and technology in *The Great Plains* (1931). He argued that vast open stretches, especially west of the 98th meridian, where aridity ruled, explained the national story of survival and innovation, both for the land and its inhabitants. Although Webb's ideas seemed derivative of Turner's agrarianism, the Texan emphatically insisted he was barely aware of the Wisconsinite's thesis.

While scholars with the interests of a Malin or a Webb tried to puzzle out the place of the environment in the emergence of Anglo institutions and practices in the West, others constructed a different path for its history. For example, Grant Foreman, an attorney who at mid-life shifted his energies to history, helped launch the distinctly important state component of the field. His passion for scholarly research unleashed, Foreman produced eighteen books and more than one hundred articles, essays, and reviews about the history of Oklahoma. His works, of varying interpretive merit, accomplished an unusual duality: documenting the formation of Oklahoma as a political entity and organizing its study as a scholarly subject. Foreman's monograph, *Indian Removal: The Emigration of the Five Civilized Tribes of Indians* (1932), contained presently outmoded advocacy for such Native goals as "progress" and assimilation. But on another level Foreman elevated the reputation of state history.

None of these scholars overlooked the harsh realities of life in the Depression West. They knew that for three decades westerners, living amidst rich natural resources – precious ores, timber stands, vast acreage, peculiar waterways – had quarreled over the place of the federal government in the management of these treasures. Westerners were suspicious of the moneyed entrepreneurs who swooped down on local resources, often with federal cooperation, in a process that funneled profits to outside investors. The Great Depression of the 1930s served to intensify this already burdened economic situation for westerners, especially people of color. The New Deal programs of President Franklin Delano Roosevelt loosened the grip of the regional poverty, perhaps the most lasting benefit being that of electricity, introduced through irrigation projects and dam building. By the end of the Depression, westerners, with or without electric lights, were no closer to resolving their uneasy perceptions of the federal government, but its agencies had infiltrated their lives in complex new patterns.

Not surprisingly, given the desperate times, the scholarship of western history pioneers, those studies of settlement and democracy, economics and cattle, water and environment, did not always resonate with the average American, who wanted to hear only the heroics of Wyatt Earp, Billy the Kid, or George Armstrong Custer. Still, because of the breadth of their writings and their emphasis on local history, these scholars drew attention to the West as a comprehensible region, with a distinct environment and a distinct identity. It occurred to some that the frontier of Minnesota had not been the frontier of New Mexico, nor that of California the same as Missouri or Idaho. Overall, the broad implications for the West of the work of these historians had yet to be sorted out. But rather than just a dusty location for lonely prospectors or singing cowboys, more than a setting for improbable adventures and legends, the West hinted of something with greater meaning, especially when placed against the backdrop of national events.

Like Turner, Malin, and Webb, these state historians made a decided impact with their personae, not only with their scholarship, on the growth of western history. Perhaps because so many emerged out of their local cultures, their personalities took on a certain celebrity status, usually colored in western hues. From Kansas to Texas, Montana to Arizona, this first wave of western historians was known as a unique and sometimes quirky collection of characters. More than one would agree with the comment, "I haven't taught history so much as I have lived it," a semi-witticism that captured part of the problem of western history: its champions could establish little distance from its events. Most had been born and raised on farms and in towns still mired in the rugged ambience of early rural conditions. Most pursued professional occupations as a way to escape that world, but memory and nostalgia held them prisoner. Overall, the original "new western history" acquired a highly personal tone along with its professional resonance. Western history has never entirely extricated itself from this oddly schizophrenic demeanor, an element that has been both its strength and its weakness.

Over the first half of the twentieth century western historiography, despite its bifurcated nature and uneven quality, appeared to steady itself. Scholars with university affiliations, as well as others, increasingly welcomed the West as a legitimate field for scholarly research. As the conversations multiplied, academic course offerings increased and interest deepened. A small cohort of historians moved to organize a professional association dedicated to the promotion of the scholarly study of the region. Acting on their sense of the West in academia and their regard for each other's scholarship, core supporters met in Santa Fe, New Mexico, in 1962 for the first meeting of what became the Western History Association. As this group took shape, the peculiar relationship between scholar and amateur solidified under the aegis of the Western History Association, in which the scholarship of the region came to be permanently centered, especially after the organization's official journal, the *Western Historical Quarterly*, began in 1970.

Concurrent with these developments and preceding their sharpest divisions, however, were national political storms destined to influence the practice of western history. The 1960s, with its fast-paced events tied to the civil rights movement, protests against the Vietnam War, and rush of political assassinations, unleashed cultural and political forces that uprooted long-held conventions. Government procedures, race relations, international policies, aging issues, economic development, religious structures, gender attitudes, penal management, educational institutions – all these and more felt the jolt caused by the rocking of tradition. Citizens of many persuasions wondered how a country proud to call itself a republic had come to be a haven for elitist government, racial injustice, entrenched poverty, and multifaceted discrimination. In an array of protests, Americans raised provocative questions that called for a re-examination of the country's origins and growth and an explanation for the modern conditions of such a democracy. Inevitably these questions fell to historians. No scholarly discipline was more appropriate to pick up this gauntlet than that of history, and no group more ready to engage the discussion. With their commitment to careful research, concern for detail, and love of the past, historians from many fields eagerly recast the questions asked of the national experience; they enjoyed the sense of urgency from a citizenry that suddenly saw its history in highly personal terms.

In this energized – even combative – arena, western historiography quickly arose as a natural forum for reassessment. Like its sister discipline of the American South, western history had leaned on widely recognized stereotypical characters as the important players in the regional experience. Mountain men, miners, loggers, soldiers, cowboys, farmers, outlaws, marshals: each appeared to have been sent from a Hollywood central casting office onto the western stage. Indeed, far too many Americans had learned such history from the flickering screens of darkened movie theaters. Yet just the quickest glance around this celluloid landscape suggested that its male, very white westerners could not have been the only historical actors. Of course a few white women, usually pioneer wives, schoolteachers, or prostitutes, could be found in a western script, but they rarely dominated the story line. These men of the West, with their John Wayne physiques and Clint Eastwood reticence, appeared to be the single active social force, even though they were clearly surrounded by and mingled with other people and other cultures. Native Americans, Mexicans, Mexican Americans, Asians, and blacks had also shaped the nineteenth-century West and their descendants. Women from all groups had carved out powerful cultural and economic lives in the region.

It did not take historians long to realize that the West, with its multiracial communities, could support drastically redesigned research. Once scholars were willing to recognize that the cowboy's story of adventure-filled roping and riding had mutated illogically into an epic tale of the love of freedom and the rise of democracy, the interpretive possibilities for the West could be grasped as limitless. Viewed through a different lens, that cowboy looked less like a romantic, unfettered hero on horseback and more like a migrant worker, whose political and economic power proved to be as problematic as his social acceptability. In a sudden analytical twist, the West lost its luster as a setting for anecdotal tales about lawmen and vigilantes, but gained as a laboratory for understanding fundamental issues in American history.

It seemed embarrassingly evident that while looking to the past, historians had skipped over critical events that had altered the configurations of twentieth-century western history. Crushed by the poverty of the Depression, partially resuscitated by the New Deal, the West rose to unprecedented power through the emergency needs of World War II. The remote spaces of the West took on new importance as industry and government looked to locate critical war plants in secure western locations. Industrialization, underwritten by federal money and staffed by local workers, inflated the standard of living in the West. Women and minorities found wartime employment in factories and urban areas. The West quietly appropriated America's military future with the establishment at Los Alamos, New Mexico, of the scientific laboratory that produced the first atomic bomb. When the 1960s and 1970s thrust themselves into the public mentality, many Americans wondered how they had missed the dramatic changes that gave the West a new place in the national mosaic.

With these decades, western history encountered the overlay of the personal and the professional in an entirely new way. Scholars inverted the volatile questions of modern America, placing them into the context of the past. Most especially the anguished clashes over race prompted historians to look for the origins of discrimination, not just in the slave society of the South, but also in what – according to Frederick Jackson Turner – was the breeding ground of democracy. These publications heralded a shift in research schemes, a shift that gained momentum through the decade. The scholarship moved away from biographical or institutional tomes and encompassed an ever larger assortment of people. In keeping with the themes of the 1960s and 1970s, western history dismantled its paradoxical "frontier elitism," based on rugged Anglo supremacy under "primitive" conditions, and turned to the nameless and the faceless, from whom little had been heard.

Issues of race in America, central to the national debate, pulsated through western history. As preferred racial language terminologies changed many times over the next three decades, western people of color and their communities began to step from the historical shadows. Charles M. Wollenberg bridged the chasm between historical origins and modern political awareness in his *All Deliberate Speed: Segregation and Exclusion in California Schools, 1855–1975* (1976). Although Wollenberg viewed his subject through the lens of legal history, his inclusion of Native Americans, African Americans, Asians, and Latinos suggested the broad sweep of materials about race and ethnicity to be extracted from the West. In 1977 Rudolph M. Lapp tied minority people to a landmark western event with *Blacks in Gold Rush California*, bringing African Americans to the very center of a major western episode. Crawford Kilian's *"Do Some Great Thing": The Black Pioneers of British Columbia* (1978) further pushed back the myth of a West "for whites only," documenting the black experience in the Pacific Northwest. In the same year Robert Athearn's *In Search of Canaan: Black Migration to Kansas, 1879–80* addressed the subject of African-American decision-making in a western context, showing the institutional and human outcomes for ethnic groups acting on their own behalf. Norman L. Crockett's *The Black Towns* (1979) refined the subject of community building by African Americans determined to leave their environment of enslavement and to capitalize on the promise of the post-Civil War West. The cumulative impact of these and other publications made it clear that black Americans owned a share in the western experience of settlement, a share tainted by national attitudes of discrimination.

The civil rights movement of black Americans also strengthened the public voice of Native Americans, more than ready to reclaim their place in the historical narrative of the West. Vine Deloria, Jr., with his popular and influential *Custer Died for Your Sins: An Indian Manifesto* (1969), and Rennard Strickland, with *Fire and Spirits: Cherokee Law from Clan to Court* (1975), launched a first wave of Native writings. University presses furthered the interest, publishing, in 1976 alone, William T. Hagan's *United States–Comanche Relations: The Reservation Years*, Gerald Thompson's *The Army and the Navajo*, Donald Parman's *The Navajos and the New Deal*, and H. Craig Miner's *The Corporation and the Indian: Tribal Sovereignty and Industrial Civilization in Indian Territory, 1865–1907*. In 1977 Roy W. Meyer's *The Village Indians of the Upper Missouri: The Mandans, Hidatsas, and Arikaras*, Gregory C. Crampton's *The Zunis of Cibola*, and in 1978 Robert Archibald's *The Economic Aspects of the California Missions* added to what the earlier works showed: a new Native history would explore tribal strategies for survival. Largely written by white scholars about people of color, some of these studies faltered, especially in presenting Native voices. Yet they demonstrated that an evolution was occurring in western history. Scholars no longer concentrated exclusively on the largest, most famous tribes, but examined some smaller groups, unearthed neglected federal records, and rearranged their point of view.

In the 1980s the emergence of a new cadre of scholars further deflected the conventional trajectory of western history, which had seemed for ten or fifteen years to be in step with the social impulses of the nation. The newcomers drove their research far from the American "glory" of the West, jettisoned Turner's celebratory claims, and stripped away most of the operative regional historical assumptions, starting with the word "frontier" as a vestige of colonialism. The resulting uproar produced an explosion within the historical literature, as well as within the community of scholars. In the early years of the Western History Association, the differing interests of the professional historian and the amateur fan appeared to divide the organization. Although those bickering foes remained unwilling to negotiate a full reconciliation, by the 1980s the warring sides somewhat realigned. The new camps, taking shape over a decade or more, split along intense ideological lines. The attitudes and the atmosphere of conflict, so evident at the site where Custer and his men died, made a comeback on an academic battlefield. Just as the language used about the Little Big Horn hung on extremes, so too did the conversations among historians. Just as the events of June 25, 1876, appeared tied to a single person, so did the history wars that erupted more than a century later.

The 1987 publication of *The Legacy of Conquest: The Unbroken Past of the American West* captured a restive mood within western history and even attracted the interest of a wider public. With her engaging narrative style, perceptiveness, and wit, Patricia Nelson Limerick reached deeply and broadly into the historical literature and reassessed what she found. She refocused the historical center away from traditionally celebrated western characters and onto the economic and political forces that gave them an existence. Too often, she complained, historians of the West couched their scholarship in one-dimensional language that celebrated "progress" and failed to consider the multilayered, inner regional forces that shaped events and lives. Limerick directed a spotlight onto the western past, questioning the scholarly advisability and national integrity of measuring a people's history by a yardstick of political and economic domination. The result was a brilliant synthesis that catapulted Limerick to fame inside and outside the scholarly community, energized western history, vindicated those who had argued against the emphasis upon conquest in their own monographs, and made the West a hot topic of news reporters, television producers, popular magazines, and the general public.

Western historians were astonished by the height to which the discipline ascended almost overnight. They gloried in the validation that Limerick's work appeared to bring to the entire field. Suddenly everyone wanted to talk about what had become the "new western history." The notion, however, of a new history presumed an old history of lesser currency. The "new western historians" defined the historical land-scape as a contested space, but no less a contest now dominated the academic conversations. Long-time scholars in western history went from a delight in the field's rising prominence to a sense that they were the targets of the criticism. In their view, they and their mentors were now dismissed as outdated, having demeaned western history by perpetuating the supremacy of Anglo culture or describing the region with patriarchal language.

Nor was it missed that several of the challengers, including Limerick (a woman at that) had been trained in eastern universities; some educational rivalry was added to the quarrel from those with roots in the West. A strong political tone appeared to pit "conservatives" versus "liberals" and "radicals," and some of the dispute rested on generational differences. The general public showed an insatiable appetite for the subject. University scholars became well-known media figures, appearing on one educational television program after another. Even the country singer Kenny Rogers, in the 1990s, hosted a long-running wildly popular series, *The Real West*, which made a serious commercial attempt to present the experience of westerners. The "new western history" may have been a product of the 1960s, or the work of a cohort of a few bright young thinkers, or the collective voice of emerging ethnics, or the natural evolution that could be traced in other works of intellectual history, or a combination of all four. But whatever its genesis, this western history joined the American conver-sation. Like the discipline at large, western history rested its new research framework on three elements: race, class, and gender. This trinity unlocked the door to a multicultural western past and unraveled the ways in which various groups living within the volatile borders of a unique topography negotiated cultural exchange and social accommodations.

For example, glib racist language, with its cheery myopia, could no longer gloss over the deeply complex matters of race, which made disunity and disharmony mild terms to describe the regional experience. From the nineteenth century, the earliest writers acknowledged the existence of ethnic groups, but in distorted terms that overlooked decision-making and group adjustment within cultures. Accordingly, in the Anglo writings about communities of color, cultural reputations had depended on submissiveness; contributions stemmed from defeats. The study of race, under the eye of the "new western history," abandoned that model, moving inside ethnic communities, finding their self-defining standards, and assessing their impact as builders of a regional heritage. An early work that set the discussion came with *They Called Them Greasers: Anglo Attitudes Toward Mexicans in Texas, 1821–1900* (1983). Not only did Arnoldo De León show how Anglo racism permeated every area of life, but also that prominent Texans (including Webb) depicted Mexicans as shiftless and dangerous. In this powerful, if depressing, work De León signaled the changed direction for race as a category of western historiography, and pointed to its tragic irony. Western life had been promoted by the scholarship and winning style of Walter Prescott Webb, but had also been weighed down by his own destructive racial epithets, often cast in "folksy" argot. De León's writing had implications that stretched far beyond the boundaries of Texas and encompassed the entire field of western history. His work became a springboard from which other scholars, especially a growing number of Latinos and Latinas, mapped out the rocky racial terrain of the West.

As they did so, scholars searched for their understanding of race inside their own cultures. For example, in 1987, Robert R. Alvarez stressed the importance of family values and networks for building immigrant life, in his *Familia: Migration and Adaptation in Baja and Alta California, 1800–1975*. Richard A. Garcia returned to the Texas experience, extending De León's work into the twentieth century, with *The Rise of the Mexican American Middle Class, San Antonio, 1929–1941* (1989). Erasmo Gamboa did the same with *Mexican Labor and World War II: Braceros in the Pacific Northwest, 1942–1947* (1990). Gilbert G. Gonzalez looked at children in his *Chicano Education in the Era of Segregation* (1990), linking school policy to economic goals. Emilio Zamora enriched labor history with *The World of the Mexican Worker in Texas* (1993). Although each was criticized for various shortcomings, these works collectively affirmed the importance of locating ethnicity in the twentieth century and buttressing the research through interviews with ethnic people, as well as using their records and newspapers.

In addition, through the 1980s and 1990s, ethnic scholars, some the educational heirs of 1960s and 1970s civil rights initiatives, established their presence. No longer would the history of people of color be written exclusively by those outside the community. The history of Latinos and Latinas would be forever changed by the names of Ramon A. Gutiérrez, Vicki L. Ruiz, Neil Foley, Mario T. García, George J. Sanchez, David G. Gutiérrez, Elizabeth Salas, Camille Guerin-Gonzales, Maria Montoya, and Roberto Trévino, as well as Irene Ledesma and Jeffrey Garcilazo (both of whom died at a tragically young age). The scholarship from a variety of Spanish-speaking cultures reached across centuries and embraced a range of subjects; the presence of the scholars of color adjusted the dynamics of the field, making it more vigorous, more sophisticated, and more authentic.

Likewise the field of Native American scholarship changed with the rise of a "new western history." The leading non-Native scholar of the field was Richard White, author of *The Roots of Dependency: Subsistence, Environment, and Social Change among the Choctaws, Pawnees, and Navajos* (1983) and *The Middle Ground: Indians, Empires, and Republics in the Great Lakes Region, 1650–1815* (1991). He conceived of the West in broad terms and decried the tendency of its historians to privilege one culture over the others. In White's "middle ground," the opposing interests of differing cultures forced a negotiated space, producing new social arrangements and structures over time. While Native American research flourished in the 1980s and 1990s, many of the practitioners continued to be non-Natives. R. David Edmunds, whose books included *The Potowatomis: Keepers of the Fire* (1978), *The Shawnee Prophet* (1983), and *Tecumseh and the Quest for Indian Leadership* (1984), made a strong presence for Native people, as did Donald Fixico, who acted untiringly on behalf of Native students. Choctaw Devon A. Mihesuah and a Choctaw-Cherokee-Chicana, Rebecca Bales, led the way for a still smaller group of Native women scholars.

Despite efforts by Native and non-Native historians, the future of Native American history remains uncertain. Tribal governing bodies, long vexed by white society, show themselves less willing to cooperate with scholars from outside the Native community. Among Native peoples, the "new western history" may be an ironic label, as a white community that only recently appears to have appreciated the importance of oral traditions and tribal memory. At the same time, scholars have been an important resource for Natives outside the academy, with some acting as strong public allies of Native American tribes.

Closely aligned with the reorganized concepts of race in western history, but not entirely removed from its emotional intensity, has been class. Among its many themes, the earlier history of the West, shaped by Turnerian notions, stressed the opportunity for anyone to be judged only by his accomplishment of the moment and not by social rank. John Mack Faragher questioned this assumption in *Sugar Creek: Life on the Illinois Prairie* (1986), which explored the interaction among tenant farmers, laborers, and large property holders, as class distinctions began to solidify on one frontier. This work followed Faragher's earlier study *Women and Men on the Overland Trail* (1979), which positioned pioneer gender roles against conventional ideas about domestic relationships. Faragher's works hold their place as seminal studies. In *No Separate Refuge: Culture, Class, and Gender on an Anglo-Hispanic Frontier, 1880–1940* (1987), Sarah Deutsch also considered the abrasive intersection of several different constituencies, and provided a well-constructed cross-cultural study. In that same year, Kathleen Underwood augmented Deutsch's book with *Town Building on the Colorado Frontier*, which examined local identity as well as class alignments. David M. Emmons's *The Butte Irish: Class and Ethnicity in an American Mining Town, 1875–1925* (1989) destroyed myths about an egalitarian West and documented the many ways class consciousness pervaded one town with expectant capitalists. Elizabeth Jameson built on Emmons's arguments with *All that Glitters: Class, Conflict and Community in Cripple Creek* (1998), which placed working-class issues into the context of social and economic change.

Other scholars, notably Donald Worster, made class an ingredient in environmental history, as well as in its neighbor, labor history. The two are so woven together as to be inseparable, and blend naturally into the themes of land use, land reform, and environmental activism. Worster's classic *Rivers of Empire: Water, Aridity, and the Growth of the American West* (1985), as well as his *Dust Bowl: The Southern Plains in the 1930s* (1979), and even *A River Running West: The Life of John Wesley Powell* (2001), annoyed some readers for their critical observations, undergirded with Marxist tones, about careless misuse of the land. But Worster could not be matched for his razor-sharp insights and passionate writing. He showed how environmental decisions, because of American power structures, have injured land and water resources in a cosmic manner. Like Worster, William Cronon wedded western environmental history to human decision-making that frequently chose short-term goals over long-range planning. *Nature's Metropolis: Chicago and the Great West* (1991) looked at the usual and unusual catalysts that brought about the hasty transformation of entire ecosystems, and Cronon tied those changes and uses to economics and politics. In its grand sweep, the historical writing of the new wave environmental studies saw disaster across the land, a vision that frequently included intensely political overtones.

Gender represented the final part of the historical triumvirate. Once thought to encompass only the domestic deeds of pioneer wives, at best to catalogue the daily production of bread, jams, and children to the benefit of males, gender history assumed a refreshing new identity. In its effort to reappraise the inexorable force of patriarchal social structures, its reach extended to women of all ages, cultures, and persuasions. It examined the wage earner and the unpaid laborer. It looked at secular pursuits and religious activity. It touched on political growth and educational development. It invaded the public sphere, as well as the private. It encouraged transgendered studies and supported the gay and lesbian discussion. Above all, regardless of the topic, it fully embraced race and class in its analysis. Women in the West thus became a centerpiece in the changed vocabulary and analytical vision of the "new western history."

The pioneers among women historians struggled for place and acceptance, both at their universities and in the Western History Association. Perhaps the life and career of Sandra L. Myres, who became president of the Western History Association in 1988, best encapsulated those experiences. While her scholarship shied away from feminist theory, she made important contributions, showing women as a legitimate part of western history and creating a female presence within its ranks. Despite the author's traditional gender views, Myres's *Westering Women and the Frontier Experience, 1800–1915* (1982) questioned stereotypes of western women and documented an array of ways that women experienced the region and challenged themselves. Western women's history further advanced with the scholarship of Glenda Riley, who sustained and expanded Myres's contributions. Launching her career with a modest study, *Frontierswomen: The Iowa Experience* (1981), Riley showed an early interest in the place of African-American women in the West. A prolific writer, Riley produced *Women and Indians on the Frontier* (1984), *The Female Frontier: A Comparative View of Women on the Prairie and the Plains* (1988), *Building and Breaking Families in the American West* (1996), and *Women and Nature: Saving the Wild West* (1999). With each monograph and article, her ideas deepened; and she, along with the New Mexico State University team of Darlis Miller and Joan Jensen, disputed the notion of western women as "gentle tamers" and spoke of African-American, Latina, and Asian women as central to western history, rather than merely attached to its scholarship. Riley summarized her own historical vision in the title of her book, *A Place to Grow: Women in the American West* (1992), and in her 1997 Western History Association presidential address, " 'Wimmin is everywhere': Conserving and Feminizing Western Landscapes, 1870–1940."

Drawing on the work of Myres, Riley, Jensen, and Miller, historians of women redesigned and strengthened the overall meaning of western history. They took as their rallying cry the title of the anthology edited by Susan Armitage and Elizabeth Jameson, *The Women's West* (1987), and set about to secure women a place in the literature. In her brilliant *Relations of Rescue: The Search for Female Moral Authority in the American West, 1874–1939* (1990), Peggy Pascoe convincingly demonstrated that all women from all cultures did not share the same gender values. D. Michael Quinn addressed the same subject from a different perspective in *Same Sex Dynamics among Nineteenth-century Americans: A Mormon Example* (1996), delving deeply into a religious culture to show its contradictions between public statement and private relationships. Benson Tong considered sexualized dynamics within the context of Asian culture in *Unsubmissive Women: Chinese Prostitutes in Nineteenth-century San Francisco* (1994). These themes were further reinforced with Albert

L. Hurtado's *Intimate Frontiers: Sex, Gender, and Culture in Old California* (1999), which illuminated the ways that sexual behavior and values overlay the power dynamics between men and women, as well as across competing cultures.

Individually and collectively, these works represent a body of literature that re-shaped the twentieth-century thrust of western historiography. They encouraged some scholars to think in broad regional language and to apply that thinking to major studies that serve to show the metamorphosis of western historiography. For example, Richard White's textbook, *"It's Your Misfortune and None of My Own"* (1991), flipped the success story on its head, setting its largest concepts within a national framework. For his perspective, White stood in the West and looked at its indigenous forces, human and natural, as well as the forces imposed from the outside. Not surprisingly, he formulated an epic notable for its tensions, but also for its capacity for change across time. In all his writing, but especially in this vast overview, White reminded readers that there have been many different Wests, many different experiences, for many different people.

In a similar fashion, Malcolm J. Rohrbough's *Days of Gold: The California Gold Rush and the American Nation* (1997) sharpened the image of western experience in the pantheon of national heritage. One cannot read this volume and remain unconvinced about the importance of region in shaping events from coast to coast, border to border, household to household. Rohrbough took a topic buffeted by overexposure and anecdotal treatment, and reworked it to reveal how a western event seeped into every nook and cranny of American life. In a magnificent retelling of the 1849 California Gold Rush, Rohrbough elevated local history to its best use: as an index of and contributor to national patterns. Elliott West's *Contested Plains: Indians, Gold-seekers, and the Rush to Colorado* (1998) likewise combined a sense of the West as place and process with a newer edge of cross-cultural perception. As a result, he produced a work, fueled by the currents of "new western history," that looked at changing power alliances to find the national implications resulting from the interaction between Plains Indians and whites. But perhaps no recent major work in western history equaled the impact of Walter Nugent's *Into the West: The Story of its People* (1999), which identified five forces that impelled people to move into the West. Nugent wove into a regional mural the many figures that traversed western rural and urban roads. He outlined his subject in its local, frontier, western, regional and national contexts, embracing the lands and the peoples in each part. His sweep across time showed the fundamental and far-reaching influence of the West on the United States as a sovereign whole, in each era of American history. *Into the West* demonstrates how scholars have refined western history and how the concept of a definitive study has matured in a century of historical scholarship.

Ultimately, however, what does this journey across the twentieth century, through the minds of scholars and across the lives of westerners, say about western history and scholarship? After its beginning in the early 1980s, what future lies ahead for a "new western history"? What, if anything, has this convoluted scholarly road meant for American history? What has happened to the place of George Armstrong Custer in this tale?

Regardless of decade or debate, it is impossible to understand western history without appreciating its twentieth-century organization as a discipline and the personalities that shaped its directions. Closely involved with its people, this historiography – unlike many other fields – lacks the grace of distance, the balance of time. Its roots lie within the lives and memories of its strongest voices; their vision, their biases, and their limitations accounted for much of the formation of the discipline. This is not to say that the work of the founders of western history was shallow or without merit, especially given their flashes of brilliance in a world far different from America of the twenty-first century. Indeed, a thinker such as James Malin or a teacher such as Frederick Merk, or a Ray Allen Billington, teacher and thinker, promoted the development of western history and advanced academic thinking. Turner also deserves credit for stimulating a forceful conversation that has endured for a century. Whether he was wrong or right seems far less important than the quantity and quality of the scholarship that he inspired.

Yet the more recent decades of western history have proven to be the most exciting and the most challenging. The "new western history," which owed its drama to an oddly textured past, enlivened the discipline and its formal organization, the Western History Association. It has particularly undercut the charges of provincialism, against which the field strained for so many years, and has forced other historians to grant the West a fuller place within the national heritage. These many forces culminated in 1994 with the publication of *The Oxford History of the American West*, edited by Clyde A. Milner II, Carol A. O'Connor, and Martha A. Sandweiss. Underwritten by a highly-respected press of international scope, this volume of nearly a thousand pages exemplified the vibrancy of western history. Its cover graced by a wash of Maynard Dixon art, the book gave twenty-eight historians the opportunity to write about the West in all its diversity.

Clearly the West infiltrated the collective mind of Americans, in the past and the present. How and why a world of such extreme geographic beauty and countless physical dangers, how and why a pioneer era of short duration, how and why a center of such cultural confusion and human misunderstanding so completely seduced the identity of a nation – these continue to be alluring questions. The scholars of western history have not been untouched by this force; but they have recently tried to place it on more manageable scaffolding, as they grapple with the core of the West in their own thinking. Perhaps they tarried too long in the nineteenth-century West, with its covered wagons and cattle drives, its mission churches and little schoolhouses. They may have been a bit slow to push the history of the region and themselves onto a modern stage; but they have finally done so, particularly since the early 1980s. Now they look across a West where life retains few connections to its pioneer history.

Instead they see a West that is the fastest growing region in the nation, host to industrial development and a complex federal bureaucracy, home to a new breed of pioneers, Spanish-speaking migrants from Mexico and well-to-do eastern retirees, each expressing scant connection to "western ways." These new Anglo newcomers care about taxes, health care, and golf courses. The new immigrants worry about jobs, education, housing, and discrimination. Can the West hold tight to an old identity that is daily challenged by these class-driven changing national demographics and shifting local priorities? The answers may be found in this new West, likely to become the arena for shaping the nation's political and economic future.

Ultimately, this saga circles back to George Armstrong Custer, who generated so much fodder for controversy and left such painful scars across cultures. Even this military man, however, could be moved – for all his bragging arrogance – by human insignificance when he gazed out over the majesty of western landscapes. Like Custer, the region and those who are awed by it will never be freed from its tensions. Too much was lost and too many wounded for the conflicts in the West and of western history to evaporate. Just as no one, not even western scoundrels, can escape that provocative beauty of the plains and valleys, neither will those who are its chroniclers abandon the effort to understand it more fully and more fairly, cherish it more dearly, use its disharmonies to reveal its textures. The enchanting embrace of the West has encircled many cultures and welcomed many visions across time. Its historians need to keep that in mind, as they unravel the tangled layers of a contentious past. It would seem that western history has a future, but not one of glory and conquest so entwined with Colonel Custer's legacy. Instead a maturing scholarship promises a kaleidoscope for the West, one colored with a desert sunset, a mountain range, and the many hues of many faces, perhaps able to soften the contested boundaries of the past and the present.

REFERENCES

Alvarez, Robert R. (1987) *Familia: Migration and Adaptation in Baja and Alta California, 1800–1975.* Berkeley: University of California Press.

Archibald, Robert (1978) *The Economic Aspects of the California Missions.* Washington, DC: Academy of American Franciscan History.

Armitage, Susan and Jameson, Elizabeth (1987) *The Women's West.* Norman: University of Oklahoma Press.

Athearn, Robert (1978) *In Search of Canaan: Black Migration to Kansas, 1879–80.* Lawrence: Regents Press of Kansas.

Crampton, Gregory C. (1977) *The Zunis of Cibola.* Salt Lake City: University of Utah Press.

Crockett, Norman L. (1979) *The Black Towns.* Lawrence: Regents Press of Kansas.

Cronon, William (1991) *Nature's Metropolis: Chicago and the Great West.* New York: W. W. Norton.

De León, Arnoldo (1983) *They Called Them Greasers: Anglo Attitudes Toward Mexicans in Texas, 1821–1900.* Austin: University of Texas Press.

Deloria, Vine, Jr. (1969) *Custer Died for Your Sins: An Indian Manifesto.* New York: Macmillan.

Deutsch, Sarah (1987) *No Separate Refuge: Culture, Class, and Gender on an Anglo-Hispanic Frontier, 1880–1940.* New York: Oxford University Press.

Edmunds, R. David (1978) *The Potowatomis: Keepers of the Fire.* Norman: University of Oklahoma Press.

—— (1983) *The Shawnee Prophet.* Lincoln: University of Nebraska Press.

—— (1984) *Tecumseh and the Quest for Indian Leadership.* Boston: Little, Brown.

Emmons, David M. (1989) *The Butte Irish: Class and Ethnicity in an American Mining Town, 1875–1925.* Urbana: University of Illinois Press.

Faragher, John Mack (1979) *Women and Men on the Overland Trail.* New Haven, Conn.: Yale University Press.

—— (1986) *Sugar Creek: Life on the Illinois Prairie.* New Haven, Conn.: Yale University Press.

Foreman, Grant (1932) *Indian Removal: The Emigration of the Five Civilized Tribes of Indians.* Norman: University of Oklahoma Press. Reprinted 1953.

Gamboa, Erasmo (1990) *Mexican Labor and World War II: Braceros in the Pacific Northwest, 1942–1947.* Austin: University of Texas Press.

Garcia, Richard A. (1989) *The Rise of the Mexican American Middle Class, San Antonio, 1929–1941.* College Station: Texas A&M University Press.

Gonzalez, Gilbert G. (1990) *Chicano Education in the Era of Segregation*. Philadelphia: Balch Institute Press.

Hagan, William T. (1976) *United States–Comanche Relations: The Reservation Years*. New Haven, Conn.: Yale University Press.

Hurtado, Albert L. (1999) *Intimate Frontiers: Sex, Gender, and Culture in Old California*. Albuquerque: University of New Mexico Press.

Jameson, Elizabeth (1998) *All that Glitters: Class, Conflict, and Community in Cripple Creek*. Urbana: University of Illinois Press.

Kilian, Crawford (1978) "*Do Some Great Thing*": *The Black Pioneers of British Columbia*. Vancouver: Douglas and McIntyre.

Lapp, Rudolph M. (1977) *Blacks in Gold Rush California*. New Haven, Conn.: Yale University Press.

Limerick, Patricia Nelson (1987) *The Legacy of Conquest: The Unbroken Past of the American West*. New York: W. W. Norton.

Malin, James C. (1944) *Winter Wheat in the Golden Belt of Kansas: A Study in Adaptation to Subhumid Geographical Environment*. Lawrence: Regents Press of Kansas.

—— (1947) *The Grasslands of North America: Prolegomena to Its History, with Addenda and Postscript*. Lawrence, Kan.: James C. Malin.

Meyer, Roy W. (1977) *The Village Indians of the Upper Missouri: The Mandans, Hidatsas, and Arikaras*. Lincoln: University of Nebraska Press.

Milner, Clyde A., II, O'Connor, Carol A., and Sandweiss, Martha A. (eds.) (1994) *The Oxford History of the American West*. New York: Oxford University Press.

Miner, H. Craig (1976) *The Corporation and the Indian: Tribal Sovereignty and Industrial Civilization in Indian Territory, 1865–1907*. Columbia: University of Missouri Press.

Myres, Sandra L. (1982) *Westering Women and the Frontier Experience, 1815–1915*. Albuquerque: University of New Mexico Press.

Nugent, Walter (1999) *Into the West: The Story of its People*. New York: Alfred A. Knopf.

Parman, Donald (1976) *The Navajos and the New Deal*. New Haven, Conn.: Yale University Press.

Pascoe, Peggy (1990) *Relations of Rescue: The Search for Female Moral Authority in the American West, 1874–1939*. New York: Oxford University Press.

Quinn, D. Michael (1996) *Same Sex Dynamics among Nineteenth-century Americans: A Mormon Example*. Urbana: University of Illinois Press.

Riley, Glenda (1981) *Frontierswomen: The Iowa Experience*. Ames: Iowa State University Press.

—— (1984) *Women and Indians on the Frontier*. Albuquerque: University of New Mexico Press.

—— (1988) *The Female Frontier: A Comparative View of Women on the Prairie and the Plains*. Lawrence: University Press of Kansas.

—— (1992) *A Place to Grow: Women in the American West*. Arlington Heights, Ill.: Harlan Davidson.

—— (1996) *Building and Breaking Families in the American West*. Albuquerque: University of New Mexico Press.

—— (1999) *Women and Nature: Saving the Wild West*. Lincoln: University of Nebraska Press.

Rohrbough, Malcolm J. (1997) *Days of Gold: The California Gold Rush and the American Nation*. Berkeley: University of California Press.

Strickland, Rennard (1975) *Fire and Spirits: Cherokee Law from Clan to Court*. Norman: University of Oklahoma Press.

Thompson, Gerald (1976) *The Army and the Navajo*. Tucson: University of Arizona Press.

Tong, Benson (1994) *Unsubmissive Women: Chinese Prostitutes in Nineteenth-century San Francisco*. Norman: University of Oklahoma Press.

Turner, Frederick Jackson (1920) *The Frontier in American History*. New York: Henry Holt.

Underwood, Kathleen (1987) *Town Building on the Colorado Frontier.* Albuquerque: University of New Mexico Press.

Webb, Walter Prescott (1931) *The Great Plains.* Boston: Ginn.

West, Elliott (1998) *Contested Plains: Indians, Goldseekers, and the Rush to Colorado.* Lawrence: University Press of Kansas.

White, Richard (1983) *The Roots of Dependency: Subsistence, Environment, and Social Change among the Choctaws, Pawnees, and Navajos.* Lincoln: University of Nebraska Press.

—— (1991a) *"It's Your Misfortune and None of My Own": A History of the American West.* Norman: University of Oklahoma Press.

—— (1991b) *The Middle Ground: Indians, Empires, and Republics in the Great Lakes Region, 1650–1815.* Cambridge: Cambridge University Press.

Wollenberg, Charles M. (1976) *All Deliberate Speed: Segregation and Exclusion in California Schools, 1855–1975.* Berkeley: University of California Press.

Worster, Donald (1979) *Dust Bowl: The Southern Plains in the 1930s.* New York: Oxford University Press.

—— (1985) *Rivers of Empire: Water, Aridity, and the Growth of the American West.* New York: Pantheon.

—— (2001) *A River Running West: The Life of John Wesley Powell.* New York: Oxford University Press.

Zamora, Emilio (1993) *The World of the Mexican Worker in Texas.* College Station, Tex.: Texas A&M University Press.

CHAPTER ELEVEN

The Environment

PAUL S. SUTTER

Questions and Issues

In their efforts to inject nature into narratives about the past, environmental historians generally ask three types of questions. The first centers on the agency of nature: how has it affected historical outcomes in ways heretofore unrealized by a profession focused on human actors, and how does including nature in the narratives of historians allow them to render the past in new ways? A second set of questions focuses on human impact: how have people acted upon nature, and what have been the environmental (and social) results of those actions? Finally, environmental historians ask, how have humans thought about nature, and how have those thoughts shaped human actions? At their best, environmental historians weave these questions together, crafting histories that are simultaneously ecological, economic, social, and cultural – and that move across these levels of analysis.

For environmental historians of the twentieth-century United States, some of these questions have been easier to address than others. Certainly the century was one of unprecedented human impact on the natural environment, and environmental historians have been busy – though perhaps not busy enough – detailing that impact. The past century also was a rich one for the history of ideas about nature and their manifestations in politics, law, and culture. Indeed the rise of environmentalism, broadly defined, was one of the most notable historical developments of the century.

Those seeking to establish nature as an historical agent have faced a more difficult task. The daily lives of most Americans no longer seemed so affected by the forces of nature. One might argue that the developments of the century meant that nature no longer shaped history as it once did, and that environmental historians – insofar as they are interested in nature's agency – would find more fruitful fields of inquiry in times (and places) where relationships between humans and nature were (and are) less mediated by machines, markets, corporations, states, genetic manipulations, and other techniques, systems, and institutions. There is some truth to this argument. The twentieth century was liberating in an environmental sense, as Americans mastered what were once major environmental constraints in food production, energy availability, and public health, for example.

Yet to see the twentieth century as one in which Americans achieved ecological escape velocity is to miss several important features of its environmental history. First, what has appeared to be escape has often been only obfuscation. The continuing agency of nature has been obscured by growing distances between production and consumption, by ubiquitous human meddling that has made it difficult to find a nature apart from human influences, and by a managerial approach to the environment whose supporters have claimed greater success than the historical and ecological records can support. Second, to the extent that Americans mastered environmental constraints and insulated themselves from nature's agency, they did so at the cost of amplifying the power of natural forces to shape human history in the century to come. Precisely because twentieth-century mastery may turn into twenty-first century maladaptation, understanding the history and fate of nature as agent is important.

I begin with an overview of the impact Americans have had on their natural environment during the past century, but first a few caveats. Environmental change is a constant. It exists on various temporal and spatial scales, and often it has little to do with humans. Measuring and assessing the century's human-induced environmental changes thus involves reckoning with background noise, and with the artificiality of separating the century from earlier and longer-term changes and trends. Second, while there has been profound degradation, there have also been significant examples of environmental aggradation. A third and related point: Americans have shifted many of the environmental (and social) costs of their production and consumption beyond the US, and some of this environmental aggradation within its borders has come as a result. While the focus of this essay is on the United States, it is important to recognize that the environmental impact of the American century was global.

Human Impact and Intervention

Let's look at the landscape. The history of America's forests has been a complex one. Prior to 1900, the major sources of deforestation were fuel wood harvesting and agricultural clearance, but industrial harvesting grew dramatically after the Civil War. Net clearing of forests for agriculture leveled off by about 1920, though it continued in pockets, while wood, which had provided 90 percent of the nation's energy in 1850, provided only 10 percent by 1910 (MacCleery 1993). The early transition to fossil fuels was one of the century's most important environmental and historical developments. Still, timber cutting continued apace, particularly in the South and the Pacific Northwest, as timber companies adopted the organizational structures of other industrialized sectors of the economy and as technological innovations allowed for a more thorough harvesting of the forested landscape. After World War II, as the private timber supply decreased, industrial timber cutters turned to the mature timber in the national forests. And federal foresters, guided by what Paul Hirt has called a "conspiracy of optimism," facilitated the reckless harvest of public timber (Hirt 1994). Thus while the traditional foes of the forest faded from view, ending a crucial chapter in the nation's environmental history, industrial producers continued to harvest mature forest ecosystems at alarming rates and on a wholly new scale.

The century's other major forest trend was reforestation. Much of this resulted from the abandonment of marginal or degraded farmland, the natural regeneration and replanting of cutover areas, conservation initiatives, and a century of fire suppression (plus timber cutting, since reforestation cannot happen without deforestation). The rebirth of the forest was most evident in the Northeast, although most of the states east of the Mississippi have recorded a significant net increase in forested land since 1900 (MacCleery 1993). Yet these quantitative measures did not always translate into qualitative improvements. In the South, for instance, much reforestation came in the form of intensively cropped commercial pine plantations that are more like the cotton monocultures they replaced than natural forests. Moreover, as Nancy Langston has shown, timber cutting – even under expert management – often brought with it unintended but devastating changes in the ecological structure of forests. Langston's is one among a growing number of environmental histories that have examined how ecological complexity confounded managerial attempts to rationalize natural systems for sustained production (1995). Roads and residential development also fragmented forests; and air pollution, pests, and pathogens degraded forest health. The forests are coming back; to say that the twentieth century brought unmitigated forest destruction is too simple. But the returning forest is immature, fragmented, and biologically impoverished, compared to what was lost. Finally, while destructive timber frontiers are becoming a thing of the past in the United States, they continue elsewhere in the world, fueled in part by American consumption (Tucker 2000).

If the nation's forests have shown some resilience, the same cannot be said for other ecosystems. Once a dominant part of the national landscape, grasslands became arguably the most endangered natural communities on the continent. Significant damage was done in the late nineteenth century by pioneer farmers with steel plows, but the early twentieth century saw a final fit of grassland transformation. The installation of tile drainage during the late nineteenth and early twentieth centuries allowed tilled acreage to expand dramatically across the wet prairies of the upper Midwest (Prince 1997). Mechanization, capitalization, and a bull market in wheat encouraged a vast expansion of agriculture onto the high plains between 1900 and 1930 and led to the catastrophic dust storms of the 1930s, the century's most dramatic instance of nature's agency. New farming techniques and the energy-intensive exploitation of ground water have kept high plains wheat farming viable, but that chapter in the region's history may be nearing an end (Worster 1979). And although the sparser desert grasslands of the West have largely been spared the plow, ranchers subjected them to grazing pressures that degraded them and opened them to invasives.

The banishment of fire was a potent force in shaping the American landscape during the century. Fire suppression allowed the colonization of grasslands by trees and other woody vegetation, and altered the structure of forest and scrub ecosystems to which fire had been an important sculpting force. In the absence of fire, many of the nation's landscapes have experienced dangerous fuel load increases that may lead to catastrophic fires. Fire suppression is a classic example of how environmental mastery achieved during the twentieth century may augment the power of nature's agency in the century just begun (Pyne 1982).

In 1780, what became the United States had more than 220 million acres of wetlands. Today there are only about 100 million acres left, and about half of that loss occurred during the past century (Vileisis 1997). Farmers traditionally have been the parties responsible for wetlands drainage; and they continued as major players in the twentieth century, though with new tools and support. Trenching machines made swift work of ditching, and government programs – drainage districts in particular – provided crucial assistance. Farmers were joined by federal agencies such as the Army Corps of Engineers, and by timber companies and real estate developers. Among the hardest hit areas were the prairie wetlands of the Midwest, southern bottomland forests, coastal marshes, California's Central Valley, and the Everglades. Public health concerns motivated some of this drainage early in the century, when malaria remained a problem in California and the South, but most drainage aimed to make what were considered wastelands useful agriculturally. Wetlands decline has meant the loss of rich wildlife habitat and the important ecological services that wetlands provide: from filtering runoff to buffering against flooding and coastal erosion (Prince 1997; Vileisis 1997; McNeill 2000; Rome 2001). Wetlands drainage deserves to stand with dam building and irrigation development in the history of large-scale water manipulation in the past century.

Arid lands and the rivers that flow through them were also transformed. Grazing, mining, urban sprawl, and off-road vehicle use affected large stretches of America's deserts; but dam building – mostly for irrigation and power development – has been the most studied trend in arid land transformation. The creation of the Bureau of Reclamation in 1902 marked the beginning of federal efforts to develop western water resources and to extend the homestead ideal onto lands that seemed to offer little agricultural promise. Moreover, ever since Los Angeles's water grab in the Owens Valley, cities exerted increasing control over scarce and distant water, particularly in arid regions. As the century progressed, dam building took on a life of its own. Dams grew in scale, and became associated with pork-barrel spending and regional economic stimulus. Americans also celebrated them as symbols of technological prowess. In the process, entire river systems, such as the Colorado and Columbia, were re-plumbed.

Few topics have been as pivotal to environmental historiography as the control of water, though scholars have disagreed over the nature and extent of such control. Donald Worster has argued that twentieth-century western water development produced a hydraulic society, in which a power elite dominated nature and labor alike. He also predicted that the costs of maintaining hydraulic systems – battling salinization and siltation, for instance – would eventually prove too burdensome to bear (1985). Donald Pisani has maintained that the politics of western water development have been more fractured than Worster's thesis allows, while Mark Fiege has argued that nature proved a resistant and resilient force in shaping and compromising irrigation regimes (Pisani 1992; Fiege 1999). Richard White has similarly insisted that we need to see developed rivers not as thoroughly dominated and denatured, but as "organic machines," hybrids of the natural and artificial (1995). Wherever one falls in this debate, it is undeniable that twentieth-century western water development had a transformative impact on the nation's arid lands and their rivers. And the West was not the only region so transformed; the South's waterways were also re-engineered, though environmental historians have paid less attention to that story. Finally, large-scale dam building became a staple American export to developing nations.

Agriculture

The history of twentieth-century agriculture deserves more attention, for the changes in farming practice and their ecological consequences were profound. A long agricultural expansion peaked early in the century and then declined; with the exception of an expansionary period in the 1970s, American farmland acreage contracted in during most of the century. At the beginning of this period, Americans had settled most lands suitable for agriculture. They then began pushing the limits of arability. Irrigation, wetlands drainage, the settlement of the Great Lakes cutover, and the move onto the high plains were all efforts to continue this expansion, as was the move of American agriculture into Latin America, the Pacific, Africa, and Asia. But the century's most important agricultural trend was the intensification of production on a limited farmland domain.

The traditional extensiveness of American agriculture was not only a product of population growth and land availability; it was also a de facto strategy for dealing with degraded soils. But with opportunities to move to "virgin" lands already constricted by the early twentieth century, farmers turned to machines, fertilizers, pesticides, and genetic manipulations to maintain soil fertility and increase production. Mechanization increased the labor efficiency of farmers (thus greatly reducing their numbers), and required capitalization, which meant that farming grew in scale and market orientation. Moreover, machine use favored monocultures planted hedgerow to hedgerow, which meant the ecological simplification of diverse agroecosystems and a subsequent decline in their ability to support wildlife and resist pests. Mechanization also exacerbated soil erosion, which plagued American agriculture during the century, and all those farm machines required significant fossil fuel inputs.

One of the dominant trends of twentieth-century environmental history was the transformation of soil chemistry achieved through fertilizer use. American farmers had long relied on ash, marl, various green and brown manures, imported guano, and even human wastes (or nightsoil) to maintain soil fertility. What set the century apart was industrial fertilizer production: the mining and refining of phosphate rock into super-phosphates and the Haber–Bosch process of extracting nitrogen from the air to create nitrates. As with mechanization, fertilizer use has been capital- and energy-intensive. Moreover, approximately half of all fertilizers missed their mark, polluting and eutrophying waterways (McNeill 2000).

The nineteenth century ended with a series of high-profile pest outbreaks, including the Rocky Mountain locust, the boll weevil, and various citrus scales, which both threatened and were the products of the simplified agroecosystems that came with agricultural intensification. Federal entomologists initially urged the use of biological and cultural controls, but such methods proved unpopular with farmers. Pesticides were more popular because they seemed to provide a quick technological fix. Before World War II, the most common pesticides were arsenicals and kerosene emulsions. The war introduced a miracle chemical, DDT, which was used successfully against the lice that spread typhus in the European theater and against the Anopheles mosquitoes that spread malaria in the Pacific. After the war, DDT and other synthetic chemicals gained momentum as agricultural technologies, in part because pesticide development had become tightly entwined with warfare itself. Indiscriminate use of pesticides had a marked effect on wildlife populations and untold human health effects, while the development of genetic resistance among pests shadowed pesticide development, turning what promised to be a total victory over pests into an escalating battle to maintain control (Dunlap 1981; Russell 2000).

Several other themes were important to the environmental history of agriculture. Like many other resource industries, agriculture became corporate and industrial in its organization (Igler 2001). Livestock raising moved away from the open range and toward a feedlot system of production, which created problems with concentrated animal wastes and the heavy use of antibiotics. Another important trend was genetic manipulation of crops and livestock, first through breeding and hybridizing efforts, and then through the direct manipulation of genes (Fitzgerald 1990). These activities raised profound questions about the ethical and ecological consequences of meddling with nature; but the more important results may have been socioeconomic, as corporations gained proprietary control over engineered plants and animals. Finally, this agricultural model was exported to developing nations under the auspices of the Green Revolution. While such efforts often increased production, they also privileged capitalized producers over subsistence farmers, contributing to the proletarianization of agricultural workers, rapid and disruptive urbanization, and human and environmental exposure to chemicals. Agricultural mastery was achieved at tremendous ecological and social cost, and may prove unstable as well.

Species: Human and Otherwise

The century began with a wave of concern about wildlife depletion and extinction; it ended more ambivalently. By the 1890s the American bison, whose population had once numbered in the millions, was reduced to a few hundred animals. A couple of high-profile bird species – the passenger pigeon and the Carolina parakeet – went extinct early in the twentieth century. All three species were symbols of an American natural abundance that appeared to be waning, primarily because of market hunting and habitat destruction. Moreover, organized extermination efforts targeted predators such as bears, wolves, mountain lions, and raptors well into the twentieth century. In the early 1900s even deer were scarce (Dunlap 1988; Price 1999; Isenberg 2000).

For many species – especially those that relied on endangered habitats or did not prosper in the presence of humans and the ecological disturbances they created – these trends continued throughout the century. As humans claimed more of the continent and its biological production for themselves, other species suffered. Moreover, events beyond our borders affected migratory species such as songbirds, whose numbers dwindled with changes in their tropical wintering grounds. For other species, however, the latter half of the century was a time of recovery and expansion. Forest regeneration and suburbanization allowed deer to rebound prodigiously, as did controls on human and non-human predators. Wild turkeys experienced a similar comeback; and coyotes thrived, spreading into niches left empty by the decline of other predators. Even those predators once targeted for extermination returned with the contraction of agriculture, the regeneration of forests, habitat preservation, and more favorable human attitudes towards them. The banning of DDT allowed for bald eagle, peregrine falcon, and brown pelican populations to return to health. And humans have been managing the recovery of wolves, whooping cranes, and other endangered species. The fate of wildlife during the twentieth century has been neither simple nor linear, though on balance there has been more loss than gain, particularly among those less charismatic species whose fates scientists are only beginning to understand.

Fisheries provide an important case study in twentieth-century environmental history. New technologies and expanding markets magnified the ability of Americans to harvest fish during the century, while pollution, siltation, and dams degraded habitat. The dominant pattern was one of boom, bust, and repeat, with industry shifting to new fishing grounds and newly defined fishery resources when traditional ones collapsed. But this simple narrative of decline does not tell the whole story. In their studies of key fisheries in California and the Northwest respectively, Arthur McEvoy and Joseph Taylor have shown how nature confounded efforts to understand and manage fisheries. Managerial visions of what a healthy fishery should look like foundered on misreadings of natural fluctuations in aquatic systems, while conservation measures often served to vilify and exclude users on the social and political margins, such as Native American and immigrant fishers. Finally, because healthy fisheries tended in their requirements to conflict with other sorts of economic development, resource managers embraced technological panaceas such as hatcheries to navigate through political conflicts. Without discounting the devastating impact of industrial harvesting, Taylor and McEvoy have shown how difficult it has been to define and explain the decline of fisheries, and how poorly conservation efforts have fared in trying to reverse it (McEvoy 1986; Taylor 1999).

The power of ecological invasion to reshape American ecosystems was central to North America's early history, providing one of the great examples of how nature has mattered in the course of human events. By the twentieth century, the effects of ecological invasion were perhaps less spectacular in terms of human mortality (pandemics from influenza to AIDS notwithstanding), but were more pervasive ecologically because of improved transportation and increased trade. Many biological introductions were both intentional and controlled. Most of our agricultural plants and animals, for instance, are exotic, as are many ornamental plants. But some of these intentional imports – and many unintentional ones – were not so easily controlled. The gypsy moth, imported for experiments in silk culture, and the chestnut blight, which arrived in a shipment of Asian nursery stock, altered eastern forest composition. Invasive plants such as kudzu (introduced from Japan as forage) and purple loosestrife (imported as an ornamental) overwhelmed the southern piedmont and the nation's wetlands respectively. Environmental historians are only beginning to give these phenomena the attention they deserve (Pauly 1996; Tyrrell 1999).

Pollution and the Urban Environment

The American atmosphere underwent profound changes during the century. Urban coal smoke was the major air pollutant in 1900. But domestic users soon shifted from coal to cleaner sources such as natural gas and oil, while industry opted for the technological fix of taller smokestacks. While some real improvements in air quality were registered in the post-World War II era, there was also a trend toward the regionalization of air pollution. Taller stacks made local air cleaner by ejecting pollutants into the upper atmosphere, where they were photochemically transformed and then returned to the earth, often in remote natural areas, as acid rain. As Americans became reliant on automobiles and moved to sprawling Sunbelt cities, smog replaced smoke as the nation's worst air pollution problem. Lead was also a significant air pollutant between 1921 (when it was first added to gasoline) and the 1970s (when its use was phased out). Finally, toward the end of the century it became clear that carbon emissions were contributing to global warming, and that chloro-fluorocarbons (CFCs) were eating away at the protective ozone layer. CFCs were banned in one of the century's great pieces of environmental diplomacy (a topic that deserves more attention), but carbon and other greenhouse gas emissions continue to increase. In sum, local air quality improved in many places over the course of the century, but the regional and global impact was magnified. The consequences of these atmospheric changes may become the dominant theme of twenty-first century environmental history (Tarr 1996; McNeill 2000).

Cities posed enormous environmental challenges. As William Cronon shows in his study of nineteenth-century Chicago, cities transform their hinterlands by pulling in raw materials and pumping out finished goods; and while cities have continued to do this in the twentieth century, environmental historians have been slow to follow Cronon's lead (1991). More common have been studies of urban metabolism and the infrastructures that support it. The century began with basic urban water delivery and waste water disposal systems in place, but because most sewers dumped waste water into local watercourses, downstream municipalities faced new challenges in acquiring potable water. As with air pollution, local water pollution problems were solved by regionalizing them, which in turn forced cities to look further afield for clean water. Early in the century, treatment of polluted water sources – through filtration and chlorination – emerged as a technological solution; only in the postwar years did efforts shift to treating effluent. Such treatment did not eliminate pollution, however, but only shifted its form and place of disposal. With both water and air pollution, twentieth-century Americans engaged in what Joel Tarr has called "the search for the ultimate sink." Attempts to solve pollution problems usually resulted in moving pollution around (Tarr 1996; Melosi 2000).

Before 1900 most Americans produced very little trash. They recycled wastes, and some of this recycling was crucial to various production processes. Americans saved food scraps or fed them to animals, used fat to make soap or candles, repaired clothing to maximize its usefulness, and, when that failed, sold the rags to peddlers who supplied papermakers. Most nineteenth-century Americans – and particularly women – practiced what Susan Strasser has called a "stewardship of objects." This economy of re-use faded in the twentieth century, and as disposal became disconnected from production and consumption, wastes proliferated. Mass production techniques made it cheaper to buy new goods than repair old ones; urbanization made space-intensive habits of re-use difficult to practice; municipal refuse collection made it easier to throw away things; health concerns and the desire for convenience led to more packaging and disposability; and municipal reformers regulated the scavenging trades out of business. While the World Wars and the Depression revived some of these practices, this old economy vanished as postwar markets were flooded with ever-cheaper goods, many of which were made of new materials, such as plastics, that did not degrade easily. At the beginning of the century, Americans still spent time to save money, which meant re-using and repairing. By the end of the century, Americans spent money to save time, which meant throwing things away. Paradoxically, recycling re-emerged during the last decades of the century as a seemingly new effort aimed at re-using the very materials whose cheap production had both doomed the older economy of re-use and contributed to the century's mounting piles of garbage (Strasser 1999).

A number of environmental historians have done important work on residential development. Mike Davis and Ted Steinberg have looked at the relationship between residential development and natural disasters, indicting human decisions to build in floodplains, hurricane-prone coastal zones, and urban-wildland interfaces where fire is a threat. Both authors argue that blaming catastrophes on nature has magnified rather than mitigated the likelihood of future disasters while serving the interests of the wealthy and powerful (Davis 1998; Steinberg 2000). Adam Rome has argued that postwar housing development was particularly destructive of the environment. Large-scale tract development involved bulldozing vast natural areas; powerful land clearing and grading technologies facilitated construction on hillsides and in wetlands; and a heavy reliance on septic tanks led to groundwater pollution. As the scale of residential development increased, builders turned to standardized designs that took little account of regional climate or site characteristics and instead substituted climate control technologies – particularly inefficient electric heat and air-conditioning – that made postwar houses energy guzzlers (Rome 2001). Air-conditioning alone had much to do with the staggering rates of development in the South and Southwest during the latter half of the century. American suburbs have also dictated a dependence on automobiles, which generated their own impact in terms of resource and energy consumption, pollution, and habitat destruction. Finally, postwar patterns of residential development were an important force in creating environmental inequalities. As Andrew Hurley has shown, working-class and African-American residents of Gary, Indiana often suffered disproportionate exposure to pollution and limited access to recreational nature; and those differences became more pronounced in the postwar years, as affluent whites fled to the suburbs (1995).

Profound changes in American bodies and disease environments also occurred in the twentieth century. The century began with a revolution in public health fueled by the germ theory of disease, important vector discoveries, and the effective sanitary interventions they made possible. Then, at mid-century, came "the antibiotic revolution." Diseases that were once a regular part of life – from typhoid, pneumonia, and tuberculosis to yellow fever and malaria – beat a steady retreat from our bodies and our collective consciousness. At the most basic level, Americans achieved a mastery over what were once significant environmental constraints, though AIDS, drug-resistant tuberculosis, and other emergent diseases provided an end-of-the-century intimation that such mastery may not be so complete (Tomes 1998). The public health advances of the early twentieth century also facilitated American commercial and military expansion into tropical regions. As the threats posed by this living world of microbes receded, a new set of toxicological and radioactive agents came to dominate concerns over human and environmental health, and tracing their paths through environmental systems and into human bodies became a major focus of the postwar environmental movement. Finally, Americans ended the century with a pronounced and unprecedented chemical body burden, and such chemical exposure may be altering human physiology (Sellers 1997).

The above has been a rough, general, and selective look at how Americans changed their physical environment, and how the natural world responded to such changes. More could have been written about industrial environments and their centrality to the twentieth century, though clearly industrial processes were behind many of the landscape changes already described. I have also been relatively silent about the military's environmental impact, though the World Wars and the Cold War were tremendous engines of environmental change, particularly in the South and the West. But this survey would not be complete without a look at how Americans have thought about nature. The rest of this essay will examine ideas and the actions they produced, and it will focus in particular on the rise of environmental concern.

Thinking about Nature

There were several meta-trends that made the century a distinctive one in terms of environmental thought and politics. First, popular American thought on the relationship between health and the environment changed dramatically. During the nineteenth century Americans commonly talked about the health of the land, and they perceived bodily and environmental health as inextricable conditions. During the early twentieth century the germ and vector theories of disease eroded such popular perceptions, with important results. For example, under this older paradigm, Americans generally saw unimproved land as sickly (though, importantly, there were landscapes deemed essentially healthy, such as beach and mountain resorts and hot springs). Making the land healthy meant improving it. During the twentieth-century, the environment polluted by humans became most associated with threats to health, with untouched rather than improved nature serving as the ideal landscape of health. This perceptual shift played a quiet but important role in shaping twentieth-century environmentalism (Bolton Valencius 2002).

Second, the century witnessed a long retreat from direct working relationships with nature, and the rise of environmental appreciation reflected that shift. At the beginning of the century, most Americans still knew nature through their labor, to paraphrase Richard White; they had a direct bodily relationship with a particular patch of earth, and they likely had a deeper knowledge, however vernacular and instrumental, of its constituent parts and processes. As rural Americans moved to towns, suburbs, and cities, and as immigrants – many of them from rural settings – joined them, a crucial intellectual reorientation occurred. By the end of the century most Americans knew and conceptualized nature as a place of leisure; and as a result they tended to idealize it as abstract, pristine, and distant. Environmental historians have long recognized a relationship between leisure, urbanity, and romanticized ideas about nature, but they have come to approach the intellectual and cultural implications of this shift more critically and with a greater appreciation of the paradoxes involved (White 1995; Cronon 1996).

Third, while the rise of environmental appreciation during the century paralleled growing government involvement in environmental regulation and management, the state was also a crucial force in environmental transformation, in large part through the development and deployment of state-sponsored scientific and technical expertise. While environmental historians have attended to certain strands of this developing expertise, such as forestry, there are other strands that deserve more attention. The growth of and contests over this environmental management expertise have been a signature feature of environmental thought and politics.

The rise of a significant body of conservationist and preservationist sentiment dates from the mid-nineteenth century, but the Progressive Era marked the rise of state conservation. The federal government extended itself as manager of natural resources, protector of wild nature, and guardian of worker safety and human health. It was the first step in the emergence of what Adam Rome has called the "environmental-management state" (2002). For instance, various presidents, under the authority granted by the Forest Reserve Act of 1891, set aside millions of acres of forest reserves; the Forest Management Act of 1897 dictated that they would be utilized for their resources; and the creation of the US Forest Service in 1905 institutionalized a utilitarian approach to forest management. Gifford Pinchot, the first head of the Forest Service, was the chief ideologue of utilitarian conservation, which emphasized the efficient management of resources by experts whose aim was to achieve the long-term public good. The Newlands Act (1902), which created the Bureau of Reclamation, represented a utilitarian approach to western water development; and there were important federal efforts to manage fisheries, inland waterways, and grazing lands. In the Progressive Era there was also a flurry of preservationist activity. Congress added numerous national parks to an embryonic system, the Antiquities Act (1906) allowed the president to set aside national monuments, and the Lacey Act (1900) prohibited interstate shipment of wild animals killed in violation of state game laws. Theodore Roosevelt inaugurated another important land preservation system when he created the first National Wildlife Refuge in 1903 – and more than fifty others before leaving office six years later. The century thus began with a burst of conservation and preservation activity, most of it in response to an unrestrained capitalist economy wreaking havoc on the natural world.

In the most scrutinized environmental episode of the era, conservationists and preservationists faced off over the Hetch Hetchy Valley in Yosemite National Park, which the city of San Francisco wanted to dam to create a public water source. Conservationists favored the plan for its promised public benefits. Led by John Muir, preservationists decried the invasion of a national park and the unwillingness of the dam's proponents – Pinchot among them – to appreciate the aesthetic value of the valley. The city of San Francisco won the battle in 1913, and the lines between conservationist and preservationist ideologies hardened. Preservationists got some satisfaction with the creation of the National Park Service in 1916, though it too would soon be charged with developmental biases.

Where did progressive conservation sentiment come from and what did it mean? The earliest historical interpreters saw the movement as a democratic and anti-corporate attempt to protect resources from industrial exploiters. Samuel Hays countered that the progressives' "gospel of efficiency" actually favored corporations and that it enshrined a model of politics that replaced the welter of democracy with the rule of apolitical experts. He focused on resource conservation, and his thesis has proven remarkably tenacious (Hays 1959). Peter Schmitt provided a thorough look at the Progressive Era's upswell of back-to-nature sentiment. In his classic account of popular attitudes towards nature, Roderick Nash similarly noted what he called a "cult of wilderness" that characterized the era. Both emphasized the urban, upper-class origins of this increasingly popular preservationist and back-to-nature sentiment (Schmitt 1969; Nash 1982).

More recently, environmental historians have used social and cultural analyses to rethink the rise of state conservation during the Progressive Era. Several scholars have taken a more critical look at how urban elites shaped conservation to serve their interests, while others have noted that nature preservation was often an economic proposition tied to the nation's burgeoning tourist economy (Sellars 1997; Taylor 1999; Isenberg 2000; Shaffer 2001). Still another group has examined conservation at the local level. Mark Spence has shown how national park preservation dispossessed Native Americans (1999); Louis Warren has noted that game laws often antagonized hunters accustomed to a local rather than a national commons (1997); and Karl Jacoby has provided an incisive look at the class biases of conservation (2001). By emphasizing the subaltern, these scholars have demonstrated how conservation efforts overrode local-use regimes and privileged recreational over working claims to nature. In a twist on these arguments, Richard Judd has noted that New England locals effectively shaped conservation policies and often initiated state intervention as a means of protecting traditional resource relationships threatened by commercial users (1997). Finally, there is growing appreciation that the rise of state conservation, and of environmental sentiment more broadly, needs to be understood in an international context and in relation to colonial and imperial conservation efforts.

Industrial pollution and the urban environment were also growing concerns during the Progressive Era, and women were particularly important to these movements. Middle-class women organized campaigns to improve public health, beautify cities, and reduce smoke pollution. Such "municipal housekeeping" represented an extension of the domestic sphere that allowed women to assert themselves politically (and publicly) while remaining true to prescribed gender roles (Hoy 1995). During the Progressive Era women also carved out professional niches by taking on urban industrial pollution. Building on her investigations of the "dangerous trades," Alice Hamilton pioneered the field of industrial hygiene, laying the groundwork for recognizing and responding to the toxicological concerns of postwar environmentalism (Sellers 1997). While most women reformers made fighting urban pollution a moral crusade, male physicians and engineers approached pollution largely as a technical problem to be dealt with by municipal and state bureaucracies to which women had only limited access. Gender was thus crucial to how Americans identified problems with urban life during the early twentieth century. As environmental historians pay more attention to gender (and they need to), they will discover its centrality to other aspects of environment history as well.

Interwar Environmental Thought and Politics

Because most students of environmental thought and politics have described the interwar years as transitional, the era has been largely ignored. That is a shame, for several developments mark the interwar years as distinctive. The growing influence of ecological science during the era has received the most attention. As a professional discipline, ecology in the United States was established at the turn of the century by Frederick Clements at the University of Nebraska and Henry Cowles at the University of Chicago. Each organized his work around the notion that a disturbed ecosystem would restore itself through a series of predictable successional stages to a climax state representative of equilibrium with environmental conditions. After World War I animal ecology grew in stature, as the work of Charles Elton and others stressed the complexity of predator–prey relations. Importantly, such ecological science gave preservationists a new set of arguments for protecting natural areas and challenging predator control policies (Dunlap 1988; Worster 1994).

Another distinctive interwar development was the rise of organized wilderness advocacy, most notably in the founding of the Wilderness Society in 1935. Many historians have assumed that ecology was central to this development, largely because Aldo Leopold, who first suggested wilderness preservation, later emphasized the ecological importance of wilderness. But there was another force more central to the birth of modern wilderness: the automobile. It transformed the recreational habits of Americans during the interwar years and spurred the construction of roads through previously roadless and remote areas. Wilderness advocacy arose largely in opposition to these trends, which reached a crescendo during the New Deal (Sutter 2002).

Despite the obvious centrality of the New Deal to twentieth-century environmental policy, and of environmental politics to the New Deal, there is no adequate overview of New Deal conservation. What themes might such an overview emphasize? First, restoration was an important component of New Deal environmental policy, as conservationists found themselves dealing with the consequences of failed settlement in marginal environments. Many of the areas protected during the 1930s were not pristine but degraded and abandoned lands. Second, the New Deal represented the culmination of a half-century of reckoning with the remaining unprotected public domain. The Taylor Grazing Act (1934) withdrew the nation's remaining public lands from homesteading and vastly expanded the permanent public landscape. Third, New Dealers embraced a modernist approach to environmental planning, which was best embodied by the Tennessee Valley Authority. Fourth, many New Deal initiatives were designed to integrate social and environmental policy. Through programs such as the Soil Conservation Service, New Deal policy also reached into the private agricultural landscape in unprecedented ways. Finally, federal agencies worked to open the public lands to outdoor recreation, while a therapeutic vision of nature served an important ideological function during the New Deal.

Most environmental historians have highlighted the World Wars as convenient points of demarcation, but the wars had their own intellectual and political effects that deserve attention. There were, for instance, connections between military camp life and the recreational camping about which Americans became increasingly enthusiastic as the century progressed. Indeed, throughout the century Americans connected outdoor recreation with nationalism and martial vigor. Moreover, war metaphors were crucial to the control of nature. And the most dramatic military achievement of the century, the atomic bomb, played a key role in raising postwar environmental consciousness. Yet despite the shock of the bomb, Americans entered the postwar years with an unbounded faith in their capacity to master nature. Postwar environmentalism emerged as a crisis in that faith (Worster 1994; Russell 2000).

Environmentalism Emerges

During the immediate postwar years, environmental politics focused on traditional conservation/preservation battles. The fight to keep a dam out of Echo Park, within Dinosaur National Monument, galvanized a new generation of wilderness activists. Preservationists won the contest, though at the cost of acceding to the damming of spectacular though unprotected canyon country downstream. This victory – and a sense of the cost at which it came – led to a campaign for passage of the Wilderness Act (1964), which created a system of wilderness areas on the public lands. The postwar success of wilderness activism drew on the dramatic increases in outdoor recreational activity, which was facilitated by automobiles and interstate highways, as well as the growth of the urban West during and after World War II (Harvey 1994).

In the immediate postwar years Americans began to couch environmental problems in global terms; this theme would be integral to the growth of environmental consciousness. William Vogt's *The Road to Survival* and Fairfield Osborn's *Our Plundered Planet* (both published in 1948) anticipated later works such as Paul Ehrlich's *The Population Bomb* (1968) in addressing the environmental implications of global development trends, and the relationship between population and resources in particular. All insisted that there were limits to growth that had to be respected.

No work was more important to the postwar environmental impulse than Rachel Carson's *Silent Spring* (1962). Her indictment of powerful new pesticides such as DDT was important in many ways. Carson successfully linked preservationist and human health concerns, a synthesis that defined modern environmentalism. She raised resonant questions about the relationship between science, technology, and progress, and about the unexpected consequences of controlling nature. Finally, she was a pioneer in mobilizing scientific expertise – traditionally the tool of the political and economic establishment – to inform popular environmental protest. Carson was vilified, often in harshly sexist terms; but her scientific critique prevailed. DDT was banned in 1972; so were several other dangerous pesticides, in 1976. More importantly, *Silent Spring* shook the technocratic faith of Carson's fellow citizens (Lear 1997).

By the end of the 1960s (and in the wake of several high-profile environmental disasters such as the Santa Barbara oil spill), tremendous political momentum propelled the passage of landmark environmental legislation that vastly expanded federal capacity in the areas of pollution control, the protection of wild lands (and waters) and wildlife, and occupational and consumer safety and health. The most far-reaching achievements of the era were the passage of the National Environmental Policy Act (1969), which created mechanisms for assessing the environmental impact of major development projects; the creation in 1970 of the Environmental Protection Agency, now the largest regulatory agency in the federal government; and the passage three years later of the Endangered Species Act, which prioritized species protection over economic development and unfettered property rights.

Pushing for such environmental protection was a growing and diverse group of environmental organizations. Traditional organizations such as the Sierra Club and the National Wildlife Federation expanded and professionalized their operations, while other groups, such as Earth First! and Greenpeace, adopted direct action tactics. From the 1960s on, grass-roots activism flourished, owing largely to the mechanisms for public input put into place by the environmental legislation of the era. Citizens also enjoyed new opportunities for litigation made possible by courts willing to give them legal standing in claims of environmental harm. Finally, environmental justice activism expanded and enriched postwar environmentalism by showing how the less powerful were disproportionately exposed to pollution, and by pointing out the blind spots of the mainstream movement.

Whence the dramatic upsurge in postwar environmental sentiment? Was it simply a reaction to progressive environmental degradation, or were other forces also at work? Samuel Hays has suggested that postwar environmentalism was the product of a broad set of demographic changes. As more Americans became affluent, educated, suburban consumers, they were presumably more inclined to support environmental protection for its amenity values. Environmentalism, Hays asserted, partook of a shift from a producer to a consumer society (1986). Other scholars, such as Adam Rome and Andrew Hurley, have complicated the role that suburbanization and postwar affluence played in raising environmental consciousness. Rome has suggested that the destructiveness of postwar suburban development (and postwar affluence more generally) was itself a potent force for generating environmental values, while Hurley has challenged the demographic specificity of the environmental impulse, suggesting that working-class and African-American constituencies developed distinctive environmental ideologies based in their own particular postwar circumstances. Hurley also has suggested the importance of women to postwar environmental activism, and other scholars are beginning to examine the important though tenuous relationship between environmentalists and the labor movement (Hurley 1995; Rome 2001). Finally, Robert Gottlieb has argued that, as the breadth of the postwar environmental impulse is acknowledged, so we need to appreciate its diverse roots. Postwar environmentalism was much more than the broadening of traditional conservationist and preservationist agendas, he has suggested (Gottlieb 1993).

Other scholars are tackling the complexity of postwar environmentalism by breaking open the black box of politics, with important results. Rather than simply responding to popular sentiment, state actors – members of Congress and federal administrators – often drove the creation of environmental policies and built constituencies for them (Milazzo 2001). Moreover, while environmentalists argued for a stronger federal regulatory presence, citizen challenges to the practices of expert-driven federal agencies (such as the Bureau of Reclamation, the US Forest Service, and the Atomic Energy Commission) were also decisive to the emergence of environmentalism. This happened in part because the prestige of federal experts, which had been central to progressive conservation politics, dissipated in the postwar era, as environmental activists marshaled scientific knowledge and expertise of their own (Balogh 1991). Finally, it's worth noting the connections between environmentalism and conservatism. Certainly the politics of environmental backlash were central to the conservative political ascendance during the final decades of the century, yet there were also conservative facets of the environmental impulse that deserve further exploration.

Environmental history was itself a product of postwar environmental sentiment, and this showed in the field's early dominant narratives: a declensionist story of environmental change and a whiggish story of the rise of environmental appreciation.

But as the century ended, these narratives were under revision on several fronts. As I have already mentioned, subaltern critiques have enriched the historiography of state conservation. Moreover, the discipline of ecology has moved in a more chaotic direction, prompting environmental historians to realize that ecological science might not offer the expected moral clarity and authority (Worster 1994). As their efforts to locate an objective, pristine, and pre-human nature against which to measure human impact proved chimerical, environmental historians often have turned to a more critical examination of environmental thought and advocacy, and of the very category "nature" that defines the field. In this spirit, William Cronon has offered a controversial critique of America's distinctive and peculiar attachment to the wilderness idea (1996); Jennifer Price has searched the mall, television, and other human artifacts for lessons about how modern Americans think about and value nature (1999); and Susan Davis has examined the commercialization of nature in the corporate environment of Sea World (1997).

These and other cultural studies of nature have performed a vital service. They have emphasized the "constructedness" of American ideas about nature, have under-scored the modern American propensity for idealizing nature in its purest forms, have illustrated how tightly intertwined nature appreciation and consumerism have become, and have insisted that environmentalists and environmental historians exam-ine their own ideals and values. Despite charges to the contrary, few of these scholars have questioned the existence of a physical nature capable of agency or in need of protection; but they have challenged colleagues to think critically about how that physical nature is defined and deployed. The irony of the pink flamingo, Price noted of one of her subjects, lies not in its apparent artificiality, but in our inability to see the nature in these birds: "nature that has been mined, harvested, heated, and shipped" (1999: 164). As her comment suggests, one promise of such cultural analysis is that it can foreground a real nature that we are not used to seeing.

Toward the New Century

The American century was also the environmental century, and environmental history must be central to twentieth-century US historiography. Certainly among the most important intellectual and political stories of the century were the rise of popular environmental sentiment and the birth of the environmental management state. These topics are being treated with increasing sophistication by environmental his-torians and deserve to be dominant storylines in broader historical narratives. Simi-larly, Americans transformed the natural world in unprecedented ways during the twentieth century, both within and beyond the United States. Historians can no longer afford to make the consummate twentieth-century error of externalizing the environmental costs of American development. As environmental historians have learned, exact costs are not always easy to calculate, but they nonetheless belong in our scholarly accounts.

Interpreters of twentieth-century America also must take seriously nature's agency, even though environmental historians still have work to do to clarify the complex twentieth-century career of nature as agent. A central theme of twentieth-century US history was human mastery of environmental constraints and the significant muting – at least temporarily – of nature's agency. Environmental historians must embrace this development, and not just its environmental costs, as a process that they are uniquely qualified to study and explain. A second task must be to reveal the cracks in this mastery: to show that human control over nature was never as complete as some have claimed, and that nature reshaped and resisted efforts to control it for human ends. Nature retaliated in various ways during the century. In disasters such as the Dust Bowl, its agency was clear and obvious; Americans ignored natural limits and paid for it. But there also were instances when nature responded in ways that have complicated the moral narratives that environmental historians have wanted to tell. Nature has been surprisingly resilient, and has often defied the well-intentioned goals of environmental managers. Nature has spoken with multiple and sometimes conflicting voices, and inevitably through the filter of culture. And speaking for nature sometimes has masked the exercise of power by certain social groups over others. Divining nature's agency, in other words, is a complex task. But as a new century begins, it is also a vital one, for there are ominous signs that nature is preparing a more far-reaching response to the various systems of environmental mastery that marked the American century.

REFERENCES

Balogh, Brian (1991) *Chain Reaction: Expert Debate and Public Participation in American Commercial Nuclear Power, 1945–1975.* New York: Cambridge University Press.

Bolton Valencius, Conevery (2002) *The Health of the Country: How American Settlers Understood Themselves and Their Land.* New York: Basic Books.

Cronon, William (1991) *Nature's Metropolis: Chicago and the Great West.* New York: W. W. Norton.

—— (ed.) (1996) *Uncommon Ground: Rethinking the Human Place in Nature.* New York: W. W. Norton.

Davis, Mike (1998) *The Ecology of Fear: Los Angeles and the Imagination of Disaster.* New York: Metropolitan Books.

Davis, Susan (1997) *Spectacular Nature: Corporate Culture and the Sea World Experience.* Berkeley: University of California Press.

Dunlap, Thomas R. (1981) *DDT: Scientists, Citizens, and Public Policy.* Princeton, NJ: Princeton University Press.

—— (1988) *Saving America's Wildlife.* Princeton, NJ: Princeton University Press.

Fiege, Mark (1999) *Irrigated Eden: The Making of an Agricultural Landscape in the American West.* Seattle: University of Washington Press.

Fitzgerald, Deborah (1990) *The Business of Breeding: Hybrid Corn in Illinois, 1890–1940.* Ithaca, NY: Cornell University Press.

Gottlieb, Robert (1993) *Forcing the Spring: The Transformation of the American Environmental Movement.* Washington, DC: Island Press.

Harvey, Mark (1994) *A Symbol of Wilderness: Echo Park and the American Conservation Movement.* Albuquerque: University of New Mexico Press.

Hays, Samuel (1959) *Conservation and the Gospel of Efficiency: The Progressive Conservation Movement, 1890–1920.* Cambridge, Mass.: Harvard University Press.

—— (1986) *Beauty, Health, and Permanence: Environmental Politics in the United States, 1955–1985.* New York: Cambridge University Press.

Hirt, Paul W. (1994) *A Conspiracy of Optimism: Management of the National Forests since World War Two.* Lincoln: University of Nebraska Press.

Hoy, Suellen (1995) *Chasing Dirt: The American Pursuit of Cleanliness.* New York: Oxford University Press.

Hurley, Andrew (1995) *Environmental Inequalities: Class, Race, and Industrial Pollution in Gary, Indiana, 1945–1980.* Chapel Hill: University of North Carolina Press.

Igler, David (2001) *Industrial Cowboys: Miller and Lux and the Transformation of the Far West, 1850–1920.* Berkeley: University of California Press.

Isenberg, Andrew (2000) *The Destruction of the Bison: An Environmental History, 1750–1920.* New York: Cambridge University Press.

Jacoby, Karl (2001) *Crimes Against Nature: Squatters, Poachers, Thieves, and the Hidden History of American Conservation.* Berkeley: University of California Press.

Judd, Richard (1997) *Common Lands, Common People: The Origins of Conservation in Northern New England.* Cambridge, Mass.: Harvard University Press.

Langston, Nancy (1995) *Forest Dreams, Forest Nightmares: The Paradox of Old Growth in the Inland Northwest.* Seattle: University of Washington Press.

Lear, Linda (1997) *Rachel Carson: Witness for Nature.* New York: Henry Holt.

MacCleery, Douglas W. (1993) *American Forests: A History of Resiliency and Recovery.* Durham, NC: Forest History Society.

McEvoy, Arthur (1986) *The Fisherman's Problem: Ecology and Law in California Fisheries, 1850–1980.* New York: Cambridge University Press.

McNeill, J. R. (2000) *Something New under the Sun: An Environmental History of the Twentieth-Century World.* New York: W. W. Norton.

Melosi, Martin (2000) *The Sanitary City: Urban Infrastructure from Colonial Times to the Present.* Baltimore, Md.: Johns Hopkins University Press.

Milazzo, Paul (2001) "Legislating the solution to pollution: Congress and the development of water pollution control policy, 1945–1972." PhD dissertation, University of Virginia.

Nash, Roderick (1982) *Wilderness and the American Mind*, 3rd edn. New Haven, Conn.: Yale University Press.

Pauly, Philip (1996) "The beauty and menace of Japanese cherry trees: conflicting visions of American ecological independence," *Isis* 87, pp. 51–73.

Pisani, Donald (1992) *To Reclaim a Divided West: Water, Law, and Public Policy, 1848–1902.* Albuquerque: University of New Mexico Press.

Price, Jennifer (1999) *Flight Maps: Adventures with Nature in Modern America.* New York: Basic Books.

Prince, Hugh (1997) *Wetlands of the American Midwest: A Historical Geography of Changing Attitudes.* Chicago: University of Chicago Press.

Pyne, Stephen (1982) *Fire in America: A Cultural History of Wildland and Rural Fire.* Princeton, NJ: Princeton University Press.

Rome, Adam (2001) *The Bulldozer in the Countryside: Suburban Sprawl and the Rise of American Environmentalism.* New York: Cambridge University Press.

—— (2002) "What really matters in history?: environmental perspectives on modern America," *Environmental History* 7, pp. 303–18.

Russell, Edmund (2000) *War and Nature: Fighting Humans and Insects with Chemicals from World War I to Silent Spring.* New York: Cambridge University Press.

Schmitt, Peter (1969) *Back to Nature: The Arcadian Myth in Urban America.* New York: Oxford University Press.

Sellars, Richard West (1997) *Preserving Nature in the National Parks: A History.* New Haven, Conn.: Yale University Press.

Sellers, Christopher (1997) *Hazards of the Job: From Industrial Disease to Environmental Health Science.* Chapel Hill: University of North Carolina Press.

Shaffer, Marguerite (2001) *See America First: Tourism and National Identity, 1880–1940.* Washington, DC: Smithsonian Institution.

Spence, Mark David (1999) *Dispossessing the Wilderness: Indian Removal and the Making of the National Parks.* New York: Oxford University Press.

Steinberg, Ted (2000) *Acts of God: The Unnatural History of Natural Disaster in America.* New York: Oxford University Press.

Strasser, Susan (1999) *Waste and Want: A Social History of Trash.* New York: Henry Holt.

Sutter, Paul (2002) *Driven Wild: How the Fight against Automobiles Launched the Modern Wilderness Movement.* Seattle: University of Washington Press.

Tarr, Joel (1996) *The Search for the Ultimate Sink: Urban Pollution in Historical Perspective.* Akron, Oh.: University of Akron Press.

Taylor, Joseph (1999) *Making Salmon: An Environmental History of the Northwest Fisheries Crisis.* Seattle: University of Washington Press.

Tomes, Nancy (1998) *The Gospel of Germs: Men, Women, and the Microbe in American Life.* Cambridge, Mass.: Harvard University Press.

Tucker, Richard (2000) *Insatiable Appetite: The United States and the Ecological Degradation of the Tropical World.* Berkeley: University of California Press.

Tyrrell, Ian (1999) *True Gardens of the Gods: California–Australian Environmental Reform, 1860–1930.* Berkeley: University of California Press.

Vileisis, Ann (1997) *Discovering the Unknown Landscape: A History of America's Wetlands.* Washington, DC: Island Press.

Warren, Louis (1997) *The Hunter's Game: Poachers and Conservationists in Twentieth-Century America.* New Haven, Conn.: Yale University Press.

White, Richard (1995) *The Organic Machine: The Remaking of the Columbia River.* New York: Hill and Wang.

Worster, Donald (1979) *Dust Bowl: The Southern Plains during the 1930s.* New York: Oxford University Press.

—— (1985) *Rivers of Empire: Water, Aridity, and the Growth of the American West.* New York: Pantheon.

—— (1994) *Nature's Economy: A History of Ecological Ideas*, 2nd edn. New York: Cambridge University Press.

CHAPTER TWELVE

The City

JON C. TEAFORD

During the twentieth century the concept of the city became increasingly obsolete as Americans fashioned a new pattern of metropolitan existence. At the beginning of the century commentators did not doubt the existence of something called "the city," a definable district of dense population with easily perceived boundaries and one pre-eminent business center as well as a single dominant government. By the century's close, however, settlement sprawled along freeways, engulfing a myriad of successive municipalities and school districts, each with separate governments, and with commercial hubs at each interchange. No one municipal government or single commercial center served the sprawling population. Instead, the whole was an amorphous expanse of roads, houses, apartment complexes, office buildings, and shopping malls that defied categorization as a city. Southern California was a densely populated region extending two hundred miles from north to south, and southeastern Florida was a sprawl of scores of municipalities stretching one hundred miles along the Atlantic coast. The region had supplanted the city; metropolitan development was a run-on sentence with little punctuation and no period.

This shift from city to region was evident in the changing focus of urban jeremiads. In 1900 critics perceived congestion as the pre-eminent urban problem; humanity was packed too densely into cities, producing a hellish existence. In 2000 the perceived sin was sprawl; Americans were spreading across the countryside, raping the land and destroying the environment. Over the course of the century, then, centrifugal forces triumphed over centripetal, creating a pattern of settlement that deviated from the traditional notion of the city.

In 1925 an early commentator on American suburbanization wrote that the city "has been so little a success that the quest of an alternative has become one of the primary concerns of our age" (Douglass 1925: 304). This observation sums up the trajectory of American development in the twentieth century. During these decades Americans sought something better than the city and ended up with a pattern of settlement that some believed was an even worse alternative. For better or worse, however, Americans were not indifferent to urban problems. They proposed improvements, pioneered new plans, challenged old ideas, and tore down and rebuilt expanses of real estate.

This spatial refashioning of the metropolis has been the pre-eminent theme in the works of urban historians and other students of the twentieth-century American city. Scholars have investigated the Progressive Era efforts to cope with the problems of the congested inner city and the suburban migration that seemed to promise a better life. They have examined the central-city reaction to this outward growth and the efforts of big-city boosters to revitalize the core and redirect investment back toward downtown. At the close of the twentieth century a new sensitivity to environmental issues led many scholars to join in the revolt against sprawl and question the consequences of decades of spatial revolution. Scores of monographs and articles have studied the causes and consequences of this revolution that transformed the American way of life.

The Congested Core

During the first decade of the twentieth century, the Lower East Side of Manhattan was reputed to be the most densely populated area in the western world, with some parts of the notorious district housing over a thousand residents per acre. Hundreds of thousands of immigrants jammed into five- and six-story tenements on narrow lots, and the district's crowded streets afforded only a modicum of open space. Eastern European Jews, Italians, and an array of other newcomers shared the congested space, a short distance from the financial hub of the nation's largest and richest city.

No other American metropolis was as crowded as New York City, but urban observers decried the debilitating pattern of congestion in other cities as well. Triple-deckers offered relatively inexpensive housing for thousands of urban New Englanders. These three-story wooden structures were ubiquitous in Boston, Providence, and Worcester, stacking New England families on top of one another and creating a compact pattern of urban settlement. West of the Appalachians the single-family dwelling was more common, but again space was often at a premium. Polish immigrants in Milwaukee helped finance the purchase of their frame cottages by renting basement apartments to newly arrived compatriots. Moreover, they built rear houses along their back alleys to earn additional rental income. In Chicago these alley structures were also commonplace, as working-class city dwellers sought to profit from their back yards.

According to many urban commentators of the age, these crowded working-class neighborhoods were breeding all manner of ills. Congestion seemed to foster crime and immorality, and middle-class observers viewed the densely packed immigrant districts as incubators of violence and gangs as well as prostitution and drunkenness. The scores of saloons in every working-class district were visible reminders of an intemperate way of life. Moreover, congested living was perceived as a threat to public health. An emerging corps of public health experts warned that the dark, narrow city streets and the unventilated tenements bred tuberculosis, whereas shared toilets and polluted water in the slum districts boosted the rate of typhoid fever.

Middle-class political reformers likewise attributed the problems of urban government to the benighted inner-city neighborhoods. These districts spawned the plebeian ward bosses who were the mainstays of the venal urban party organizations. The working-class saloon was the headquarters of these neighborhood overlords who profited from the bribes of franchise-hungry public utility companies as well as from the pay-offs of liquor sellers, prostitutes, and gamblers seeking to evade the law. During the first decade of the twentieth century, then, middle-class critics of city life viewed the congested tenement district and the working-class neighborhoods in general as the source of crime, vice, disease, and political corruption. The congested core was not only the heart of the city but the heart of American urban problems.

Overcrowding in the bustling commercial core of the city seemed to exacerbate the perceived urban dilemma. As the prices of downtown lots rose, developers sought to increase profits by erecting ever taller office towers. Iron- and steel-framed sky-scrapers first punctuated the skyline of Chicago in the 1880s; but, by the beginning of the twentieth century, many Americans deplored the advent of tall buildings. These office behemoths turned the narrow streets of the Lower Manhattan financial district into gloomy canyons and deprived workers in neighboring buildings of light and air. Moreover, by stacking office workers on top of one another, skyscrapers increased the congestion in the business district. At rush hour the transit lines leading into the skyscraper district were jammed with commuters, and at lunchtime the streets were carpeted with thousands of office workers. As early as 1891 the Massachusetts legislature mandated a 125-feet (38 meters) height limit for buildings in Boston, deterring skyscraper construction in New England's hub. Two years later Chicago's city council imposed a 130-feet cap, though in 1902 it raised this to 260 feet. Not until 1916 did New York City take action to regulate the height of skyscrapers, by which time gargantuan structures were casting shadows a quarter mile in length, engulfing thousands of Lower Manhattan office workers in a dark pall.

Crowding and congestion also stirred complaints among the many urban transit passengers. Electric streetcar lines converged on downtown areas, ensuring a centri-petal flow of workers, shoppers, and entertainment seekers. By the close of the first decade of the twentieth century, both Boston and New York City had constructed subway lines, and elevated rail systems offered an alternative to the streetcar in New York City and Chicago. Yet these lines further enhanced the flow of people to the central business district, their chief advantage being that they could deposit more people more quickly on the downtown streets than the smaller, slower streetcars. No matter what the form of transit, urban passengers complained about the crowding and lack of seats. Streetcar companies admitted that their profits were in the strap-hangers, the excess passengers who had to stand on the trip home from work or shopping. And urban dwellers understandably resented that their discomfort was a prerequisite for enriching transit magnates. In cities throughout America transit reform was a popular political issue. Mayors Tom Johnson of Cleveland, Samuel Jones of Toledo, and Edward Dunne of Chicago won a loyal following with their cries for lower transit fares and for the municipal ownership of streetcar lines. The tenement, the skyscraper, and the passenger-jammed streetcar were all symptoms of urban congestion; they were physical reminders to many urban dwellers that the American city was not proceeding along the correct course.

Responding to perceptions of an urban crisis, a number of reformers were working to improve conditions in the city. Settlement houses in the crowded working-class neighborhoods sought to bring some of the advantages of middle-class life to the least fortunate urbanites. Chicago's Hull House headed by Jane Addams and New York City's Henry Street Settlement House under the guidance of Lillian Wald were the two most famous examples, offering classes, recreation facilities, meeting rooms, and coffee houses for slum dwellers whose chief neighborhood gathering place had formerly been the corner saloon. Workers at the settlement houses also collected data on working-class life, for the new field of sociology was seeking "scientific" solutions to manifold urban problems. Housing reformers sought to enact housing codes that established minimum standards to protect the health and safety of working-class residents. In New York City Lawrence Veiller of the Tenement House Committee of the Charity Organization Society secured passage of the New York State Tenement House Law of 1901. It required a private toilet for each apartment, a window in every room, and adequate hallway lighting and fire escapes. Chicago's City Homes Association and Philadelphia's Octavia Hill Association likewise endeavored to upgrade housing conditions in the crowded urban core.

Meanwhile, urban political reformers campaigned to limit the power of ward political bosses and the party organizations, seeking to enhance the authority of mayors elected citywide and eliminate ward representation on city councils. Council members elected by voters from throughout the city would supposedly be less indebted to plebeian neighborhood bosses and better represent the opinion of the "respectable elements" of the urban population. Similarly, proponents of the city manager plan proposed shifting executive authority to an appointed, professional manager with no partisan ties. This expert was expected to impose a new level of efficiency on city government as professional management supplanted the amateur rule of party hacks.

An emerging corps of urban planners was lobbying for further action to improve the city core. Proponents of the city beautiful movement, led by Chicago architect Daniel Burnham, deplored the hodgepodge appearance of the nation's cities and the lack of any rational blueprint for future development. They believed that planning could impose a degree of harmony and order on polyglot metropolises that were divided by class and ethnic conflict and blighted by a cacophonous array of physical structures. Burnham and his ilk envisioned civic centers of neoclassical buildings, with uniform cornice lines and harmonious design, lined up along grassy esplanades. These centers expressed a new urban vision; rational planning would supplant individualistic, uncoordinated development. The helter-skelter, congested core would become a city beautiful. In 1909 the First National Conference on City Planning marked the beginning of a new profession dedicated to designing cities not for individual profit but to enhance the common welfare.

Basic to this new vision of a planned city was the concept of zoning. At the beginning of the twentieth century, no comprehensive zoning ordinances existed anywhere in the United States. Local governments did not mandate that certain zones remain exclusively residential, while others accommodate only retailing or manufacturing. In 1916, however, New York City adopted the nation's first comprehensive zoning ordinance, reserving two-thirds of the city for residential use and allocating the remainder for commercial development. Moreover, it established height and area zones, fixing maximum limits on the height and bulk of structures in the city's many districts. No longer would New Yorkers be able to build without providing adequate open space or ensuring some degree of sunshine and ventilation; no longer could factory lofts invade once fashionable shopping or residential areas. By 1920 in New York City and other municipalities across the country lawmakers were seeking to sort out the congested jumble at the core of the city and fashion a better urban existence.

The Suburban Trend

At the close of the nineteenth century, a leading student of urbanization concluded that "the 'rise of the suburbs' . . . furnishes the solid basis of a hope that the evils of city life, so far as they result from overcrowding, may be in large part removed." Though the "concentration of population seems destined to continue," he concluded: "It will be a modified concentration which offers the advantages of both city and country life" (Weber 1899: 475). Thus he summed up a solution to congestion that was to grow in significance throughout the twentieth century. Ultimately, the answer to urban ills was a dispersion of the population through suburbanization. Settlement houses, tenement reform, and zoning restrictions offered some relief, but the best answer to overcrowding was to create suburbs where residents could benefit from proximity to the core while still enjoying the fresh air and open space of the country. This possibility inspired millions of twentieth-century Americans, transforming metropolitan existence and producing a new pattern of settlement.

By the first decade of the twentieth century, some well-to-do Americans already lived in suburban manors along the lakeshore north of Chicago, on Long Island east of New York City, or in the towns ringing Boston. Commuter rail lines linked outlying areas to the core, permitting some to escape congestion and crowding at the end of each workday. As early as 1905 the Pacific Electric Railway operated nearly 500 miles of inter-urban lines in the Los Angeles area, encouraging a pattern of dispersed development that would remain characteristic of southern California throughout the twentieth century. In 1910 the federal census bureau first recognized the emerging suburban phenomenon, defining metropolitan districts that included both the core municipality and its populated environs. Already 23 percent of the residents of the nation's twenty-five largest metropolitan districts lived beyond the central city boundaries, and consequently the census bureau concluded that population figures for the central city alone did not adequately measure the magnitude of each urban area.

The suburban trend accelerated notably during the 1920s as the option of outward migration became accessible to an increasing number of Americans. During that decade the nation's suburban population soared 39 percent, compared to a 19 percent rise in the central cities. Fashionable communities such as Shaker Heights outside of Cleveland and Beverly Hills adjoining Los Angeles were among the most famous suburban magnets of the 1920s, but everywhere single-family homes were sprouting up along the metropolitan fringe. Harlan Paul Douglass, the most notable observer of this phenomenon, wrote with optimism of a new suburban civilization that might supplant the blighted urban past. Though he believed that suburbanization threatened community life because commuters spent only the evening hours in their outlying hometowns, Douglass concluded in 1925 that "a crowded world must be either suburban or savage" (1925: 327). In other words, there were pitfalls to suburbanization, but the alternative was the rough intensity of the congested big city.

Contributing to the suburban trend was the advent of the automobile. During the 1920s millions of Americans purchased their first automobile, giving them an unprecedented degree of freedom and mobility. No longer so dependent on the streetcar or commuter train, they could move away from the transit lines and seek a home in suburbia. Between 1920 and 1929 the number of registered automobiles in the United States soared from 8.1 million to 23.1 million. At the beginning of the decade there was one automobile for every 13 Americans; ten years later the rate was one to five. In some cities automobiles were especially numerous; by 1930 there was an automobile for every 1.5 residents in car-crazy Los Angeles. As early as 1924 nearly half of those entering downtown Los Angeles did so by automobile. Millions of Americans still rode the public transit systems, with ridership nation-wide peaking in 1926. By 1930, however, the number of riders had dropped 9 percent from this peak, despite an increase in the urban population. In the increasingly automobile-dependent southern California metropolis, per capita usage of the streetcar and electric inter-urban lines plummeted at a precipitous rate, anticipating later developments in other cities throughout the nation.

Some viewed the advent of the automobile as a possible answer to the troubling problem of the congested urban core. In 1925 Lewis Mumford, one of the century's most distinguished urban commentators and later a harsh critic of the automobile, wrote optimistically of "the tendency of the automobile . . . to disperse population rather than concentrate it" and noted that "any projects which may be put forward for concentrating people in greater city areas blindly run against the opportunities the automobile opens out" (Foster 1981: 61–2). Henry Ford, the nation's greatest automobile manufacturer, similarly envisioned the opportunities afforded by this new age of mobility, commenting that Americans would "solve the City Problem by leaving the City" (quoted in Duany et al. 2000: 135). Recognizing the possibilities of the motor age, the Kansas City real estate developer J. C. Nichols laid out not only suburban residential districts but also outlying retailing centers. In the 1920s he built Country Club Plaza, a shopping center on the southern edge of the city specifically designed to accommodate auto-borne customers. Though he normally assigned only a quarter of the land area of any subdivision to streets, in his Plaza development streets consumed more than half of the acreage. Nichols's wide thoroughfares permitted diagonal parking for automobiles on both sides of the streets; he also provided off-street parking. Moreover, he claimed tall commercial structures generated traffic congestion and thus preferred one-story shops. These low-rise structures would not cast lengthy shadows or impair the circulation of air, but would instead provide a bright and healthy shopping environment. Promoted as "an outlying business center planned in compliance with modern traffic demands," the low-rise, automobile-compatible Country Club Plaza seemed the very antithesis of the oft-criticized commercial core (Worley 1990: 245).

Meanwhile, the more idealistic followers of the British visionary Ebenezer Howard also deemed de-concentration of the congested metropolis as an increasingly real and desirable possibility. At the close of the nineteenth century Howard had devised his garden city scheme, envisioning a series of compact, self-contained cities of 32,000 people separated by greenbelts of farms and forests with all land communally owned. Garden city residents would enjoy both the social advantages of the city and the fresh air, open spaces, and sunshine of the country; communal land ownership would ensure that private speculators could not subdivide the greenbelt and destroy this utopia. During the first two decades of the twentieth century Howard created two garden cities in Great Britain, and by the 1920s some Americans were eager to apply his ideas in the United States. Most notably the Regional Planning Association of America (RPAA), founded in 1923, promoted the garden city idea, believing that it would relieve central-city congestion and yet avoid aimless suburban sprawl. In the late 1920s two RPAA architects, Clarence Stein and Henry Wright, designed Radburn, a model satellite town in northeastern New Jersey. Uniquely adapted to the motor age, the innovative community segregated people from traffic, locating residences along cul-de-sacs rather than arterial streets and providing pedestrian underpasses so that walkers would not have to face the dangers of speeding automobiles. It was, then, a community tailored to the automobile era, offering a supposedly superior alternative to both the central city and the unplanned suburb. Having welcomed its first residents in 1929, Radburn soon succumbed to the Great Depression, but this community remained an inspiration for later planners.

During the economically depressed 1930s the suburban trend slowed, though the suburban population growth rate of 17 percent far exceeded the 6 percent figure for the nation's central cities. With private developers unwilling or unable to invest in much new construction, the federal government got in the business of building suburban communities, incorporating the ideas of Howard and the planners of Radburn. The Roosevelt administration constructed three experimental communities: Greenbelt, Maryland, outside Washington, DC; Greenhills, Ohio, north of Cincinnati; and Greendale, Wisconsin, in the Milwaukee metropolitan region. Each was surrounded by a greenbelt, with all land owned by the federal government. Thus these communities seemed to promise an alternative to the congested jumble produced by private enterprise. Rexford Tugwell, the program's administrator, explained that his "idea was to go just outside centers of population, pick up cheap land, build a whole community, and entice people into them. Then go back into the cities and tear down whole slums and make parks of them" (quoted in Jackson 1985: 195). The greenbelt communities were intended, then, to replace the crowded, unhealthy slums of the urban core with outlying villages in sylvan settings. With only 2,100 dwelling units, the three communities, however, offered little relief; and in the 1940s the federal government backed away from a scheme that seemed too socialistic and too costly.

During the 1930s the most imaginative American proponent of population dispersion was the visionary architect Frank Lloyd Wright. His book, *The Disappearing City*, proclaimed that the city was dying – and good riddance. According to Wright, urban life was "outmoded" and the big city was "no longer modern." "Like some old building the city is inhabited only because we have it, feel we must use it and cannot yet afford to throw it away," Wright contended (1932: 20). He inveighed against the "congestion, confusion and the anxious spasmodic to and fro – stop and go" of the overgrown city, which was "as good an example of barbarism as exists" (pp. 22–3). "No longer do human satisfactions depend upon density of population," he argued, and suggested in place of existing urban hubs his Broadacre City scheme (p. 24). Broadacre City was, in fact, the negation of the city; it was a sprawling settlement without any perceptible center and with a maximum population density of only one family per acre. The line between urban and rural disappeared; each family could cultivate its large lot, thereby producing some of its food supply. Highways criss-crossed the low-density settlement, and automobiles ensured rapid transportation for all. Though Wright was never able to realize his scheme, as early as 1932 he recognized that the centrifugal forces of decentralization were becoming more powerful than the centripetal forces that had created the great urban hubs. Big cities were "already splitting up into several centers[,] . . . big mercantile establishments already building distributing centers on the edges of congestion[, and] new centers of distribution serving mobilization – the roadside service station an important one among them . . . everywhere rapidly growing in importance and range." With a dogmatic determinism, Wright announced: "Density of population must decline" (p. 87).

Not only was dispersion gaining the upper hand over centralization, big cities were increasingly sharing the governance of the metropolis with smaller municipalities and special districts. Despite the outward migration of the 1920s and 1930s, many older central cities failed to extend their boundaries. The city limits of Philadelphia remained unchanged after 1854, St. Louis did not add any new territory after 1876, New York City's municipal boundaries were fixed in 1898, and Boston and Baltimore annexed new territory for the last time in 1912 and 1918 respectively. Consequently, suburbanites had to fashion new governments to service their needs, creating an increasingly fragmented pattern of rule in the major metropolitan areas. Between 1920 and 1940 the number of municipalities in suburban St. Louis County rose from 15 to 41 and in Nassau County, bordering New York City on the east, the number of incorporated cities and villages soared from 20 to 65. In addition, between 1920 and 1933 the number of special district governments in 287-square-mile Nassau County increased from 87 to 173; by the latter date there were 53 lighting districts for the maintenance of street lights, 52 fire districts to combat the threat of fire, and 38 water districts charged with providing water for the county's residents. By the mid-1940s, 42 special districts provided water, drainage, fire protection, and sewerage services for St. Louis County; in addition there were 89 school districts. A study of Nassau County in the 1930s reported: "There are so many local jurisdictions that it was not possible to prepare a map of the county or even of one town showing local unit boundaries." According to this survey, there were 24 governmental units exercising authority within a single tract of 120 acres, "or one for every five acres of ground" (Teaford 1997: 25).

This proliferation of governmental units not only confused suburbanites; it also meant that a growing number of citizens in each metropolitan area were not central-city voters or participants in the government of the urban core. Nor were the property taxes on expensive suburban homes being paid into the central-city treasury. Many suburbanites viewed central-city problems as none of their business. Moreover, government fragmentation produced a heightened degree of hostility and suspicion between the central city and suburbs, fostering clashes over annexation, provision of services, and sharing of the tax burden. During the 1920s and 1930s there were a number of efforts across the country to unite the metropolitan fragments. Milwaukee's leaders conducted a vigorous and somewhat successful annexation campaign during the 1920s; boosters in Portland, Oregon, failed to secure passage of a state constitutional amendment to permit consolidation of Portland and surrounding Multnomah County; and "Greater Atlanta" and "Greater Newark" campaigns failed, blighting the hopes for governmental unity in the largest metropolises of Georgia and New Jersey. Meanwhile, civic leaders in St. Louis, Pittsburgh, and Cleveland backed unsuccessful schemes for federative rule in their metropolitan areas. Under these plans existing municipalities would continue to provide certain local services, but a new metropolitan government would have authority over broader regional functions. Proposals for such two-tier metropolitan schemes reappeared periodically during the remainder of the twentieth century. The metropolitan electorate, however, was unconvinced of the need for such innovative schemes, and government fragmentation remained the norm.

At the federal level the 1930s produced one lasting reform that had a marked impact on the decentralization of America's metropolises. In 1934 Congress authorized the Federal Housing Administration (FHA) to insure long-term, low-interest mortgages and thus boost home construction in the depression-plagued nation. Supplemented by Veterans Administration (VA) mortgage guarantees authorized by the GI bill in 1944, the FHA scheme enabled millions of American to purchase new homes in the years following World War II. The FHA, however, refused to insure high risk mortgages, and the agency's evaluation criteria defined high risk as any mortgage on an older home in a declining neighborhood. Moreover, the FHA regarded any neighborhood with African-American residents as declining. The effect was to encourage new, all-white subdivisions in the suburbs and discourage home purchases, construction, or repairs in the older, more racially heterogeneous central cities. In addition, the FHA fixed minimum requirements for housing eligible for insured mortgages, establishing standards for lot size and for distance of the house from the street and from adjacent houses. Density was discouraged and open space encouraged. During the suburban boom of the 1940s and 1950s, the federal government was, then, telling lenders and developers that the crowding of the past should yield to a new pattern of single-family dwellings with side yards and adequate light and air (Jackson 1985: 203–16).

Encouraged by the availability of FHA-VA insured mortgages and responding to a strong demand for new housing among returning veterans, post-World War II developers built housing at an unprecedented pace. The number of new houses being built peaked at almost 2 million in 1950, but in every year from 1947 through 1965 the number of new dwelling units in the United States exceeded 1.2 million. Most of these units were single-family houses, and many were in giant suburban subdivisions of the type made famous by the builder William Levitt. His first Levittown subdivision on Long Island, constructed between 1947 and 1951, comprised more than 17,400 houses, and originally harbored 82,000 residents. Levitt mass produced the houses at the rate of 150 a week, or one every sixteen minutes. In the 1950s he built a second Levittown north of Philadelphia with 16,000 houses, as well as a third development in New Jersey. As Levitt and other builders provided millions of new homes along the suburban fringe, the share of the metropolitan population living in suburbia soared. Whereas in 1940 less than one-third of America's metropolitan residents lived in the suburbs, in 1970 more than one-half did so. By the 1970s the United States was a suburban nation, with the largest portion of the citizenry living neither in central cities nor in rural areas but in suburbia.

Meanwhile the construction of superhighways was encouraging the outward flow not only of residents but also of stores and factories. In 1956 Congress passed the

Federal-Aid Highway Act, authorizing 41,000 miles of limited-access, high-speed interstate highways. The interstate highway system was designed to include peripheral expressways intended to divert through traffic, especially trucks, from the urban core and thus relieve congestion in the central city. Along these peripheral superhighways, however, shopping malls, industrial parks, and office campuses soon arose, shifting commerce from the traditional urban hub to the metropolitan fringe. The planners of the interstate highway system had promised that the new superhighways would "disperse our factories, our stores, our people; in short . . . create a revolution in living habits" (Whyte 1958: 144). By 1970 their prediction had come true. Decentralization was triumphing, and dispersion rather than concentration was the prevailing trend. The suburban trend of the twentieth century had created a metropolis without a single dominant commercial, governmental, or social focus.

Reviving the Central City

Not everyone was pleased by the triumph of the edge over the center. Throughout the second half of the twentieth century, urban policy-makers were obsessed with reviving the central cities. Older urban centers repeatedly declared their renaissance, and chambers of commerce loudly proclaimed their hometowns as comeback cities. Yet during the late twentieth century, it was clear to any unbiased observer that the central cities were not as central to American life as they had once been.

Hard times in the 1930s had made many central-city leaders aware of the challenges facing their communities. Boston, Philadelphia, Cleveland, and St. Louis all lost population during the 1930s, a humiliating fate in a nation that had always valued growth. Many other cities grew slowly, and local business leaders feared the impact of the automobile and suburbanization on downtown retailers who were largely dependent on streetcar-borne customers and who lacked adequate parking facilities. During the first half of the 1940s, the legislatures of New York, Michigan, Illinois, and Missouri all passed Acts that authorized cities to use their powers of eminent domain to condemn slum sites and assemble tracts for private redevelopment. Moreover, some states offered tax incentives for inner-city rebuilding. Then in Title I of the Housing Act of 1949 Congress authorized a federal urban redevelopment program; the federal government would pay up to two-thirds the net cost of purchasing and clearing slum properties, which would then be sold to private developers who would rebuild the blighted urban core.

Contributing to the perceived need for urban renewal was the massive migration of African Americans to most of the nation's leading cities. During the 1940s and 1950s millions of blacks moved from the rural South to northern cities that seemed to offer greater economic opportunities. In 1940 blacks constituted 8.2 percent of Chicago's population; by 1970 this was up to 32.7 percent. During the same period the proportion of African-American residents rose from 9.2 percent to 43.7 percent in Detroit and from 9.6 percent to 38.8 percent in Cleveland. Yet many whites, including FHA administrators, viewed blacks as synonymous with blight. In white eyes a black neighborhood was a bad neighborhood, one that posed a threat to the economic and social welfare of the city.

Indicative of the racial fears and tensions were all-too-frequent incidents of racial violence in mid-twentieth-century American cities. During World War II race riots erupted in New York City and Detroit, and during the late 1940s and the 1950s racial incidents were commonplace in northern cities. In 1949 rioting erupted among whites in Chicago's Englewood district owing to rumors that blacks were about to move into the neighborhood. Four years later, when the first black family moved into Chicago's Trumbull Park public housing project, racial violence ensued, as white residents resorted to arson, window smashing, and rock throwing. According to historian Thomas Sugrue, between 1943 and 1965 white Detroit residents organized at least 192 neighborhood organizations, dedicated to improving and protecting their share of the urban turf (1996). In fact, protection and improvement often meant keeping African Americans out of the neighborhood, and some members were not adverse to stoning the houses and slashing the tires of black "invaders." In Detroit whites also opposed construction of public housing that would attract black newcomers and thus "ruin" the neighborhood. Meanwhile, Chicago's housing authorities built thousands of public units, largely intended to contain African Americans within their traditional neighborhoods. Gargantuan high-rise projects provided shelter for thousands of African Americans who might otherwise have moved into white areas. By the 1960s, in cities throughout the country, public housing was becoming increasingly an African-American ghetto, a place to segregate poor blacks and keep them out of the way of their fellow metropolitan residents.

During the 1960s a series of highly publicized riots brought attention to the seething racial unrest in the nation's cities. In the summer of 1964, black mobs rampaged through the streets of Harlem and Bedford-Stuyvesant in New York City. The next summer an estimated 31,000 to 35,000 black adults engaged in a rampage of looting and arson in Los Angeles's Watts neighborhood; the toll was 34 persons killed, at least 1,032 injured, and almost a thousand buildings looted, damaged, or destroyed. In 1966 Cleveland's Hough district was the scene of angry African Americans taking to the streets; and in 1967 riots in both Newark, New Jersey, and Detroit grabbed the headlines, though in the Motor City both blacks and whites engaged in looting. Much of the anger in the 1960s was aimed at the police, and each of the major riots began with a clash between black residents and white police. Embittered by discriminatory law enforcement practices, some inner-city residents resorted to gunfire and arson. The violence made the nation aware of African-American grievances, but it also tarnished the already grim reputation of older central cities. The inner city was not only shabby; it was dangerous.

Urban renewal efforts only partially compensated for the bad publicity. Though the Title I redevelopment projects produced some glittering high rises on the site of former slums, they also stirred some blistering criticism. Some residents of neighborhoods slated for renewal fought displacement, viewing themselves as victims of planners' dreams of a revitalized city. Italian Americans in Boston's West End protested the destruction of their close-knit ethnic community; and Croatian Americans in Portland, Oregon, mobilized to fight plans for the redevelopment of the Vaughan Street area. By the 1960s African Americans throughout the country were criticizing urban renewal as "Negro removal," a means for eliminating black neighborhoods that seemed to threaten downtown real estate values. Moreover, redevelopment often proceeded slowly, leaving large tracts of the central city vacant for years. Ten years after authorization of redevelopment, there were only six new single-family homes on the 161 acres of Buffalo's Ellicott project; and much of the land in Los Angeles's

Bunker Hill project was used as parking lots as buildings only gradually arose on the cleared acreage. Some ambitious schemes proved at best modest successes. Luxury high-rise apartments in the redevelopment areas did not necessarily attract the upper-middle-class tenants who were expected to bring money and renewed respectability to the inner city.

There were some success stories. The Society Hill project in Philadelphia restored an eighteenth-century neighborhood adjacent to the central business district and proved that central cities could profit from the rehabilitation of older structures. Charles Center in Baltimore was hailed as a triumph over blight and improved the appearance and reputation of that city's downtown. Boston's Government Center won applause for its planning and architecture, though its windswept plaza facing the new city hall was a bleak reminder of the aridity of many renewal projects. And local renewal authorities joined with the University of Chicago to upgrade the neighborhood surrounding the university by carefully removing any deteriorating dwellings, thus evicting poor African Americans who were inhabiting them.

In the end, however, urban renewal proved incapable of stemming the suburban trend that continued to sweep the nation in the 1950s and 1960s. The much-publicized projects were actually minor phenomena compared to the centrifugal force transforming metropolitan America. The rehabilitation of a few thousand structures and the clearance of a few hundred acres paled in comparison to the building of one million new suburban dwellings each year and the wholesale removal of much central-city commerce to outlying malls and industrial parks. The census returns reported a persistent decline in population. In 1950 Baltimore's population peaked at 949,708, and then dropped every decade for the next fifty years; at the end of the century 651,154 residents remained in the city. Detroit's population likewise declined steadily from 1,849,568 to 951,270, and the pattern in Cleveland was similar. It recorded a drop from 914,808 in 1950 to 478,403 in 2000. No city seemed to hemorrhage population more rapidly than St. Louis, declining from 856,796 in 1950 to 348,189 fifty years later. Some older central cities fared better; New York City and San Francisco had almost the same population in 2000 as in 1950. But throughout the nation downtown department stores closed their doors, and nearby movie palaces went out of business. By the 1970s relatively few suburbanites were going downtown to shop, and the central business district no longer was the pre-eminent focus of metropolitan life. Downtown had lost its magnetic appeal.

Also disheartening to boosters in the older northeastern and midwestern cities was the loss of business and people to the new metropolises of the Sunbelt. The southern tier of states garnered the largest share of the nation's growth during the second half of the twentieth century, and a new line-up of metropolitan areas boomed in a region devoid of large cities at the beginning of the twentieth century. In some states such as Texas, permissive annexation laws allowed these newer cities to add territory, enabling them to avoid a noose of suburban municipalities choking off growth. Consequently, they moved up the list of American cities, displacing the giants of an earlier age. Between 1950 and 2000 Dallas almost tripled in population, and moved from twenty-second to eighth rank among the nation's largest cities. Holding the thirty-first position in 1950, San Diego rose to seventh rank with 1.2 million residents at the end of the century, and Phoenix soared from a humble ninety-eighth rank to sixth position, increasing in population from 107,000 in 1950 to 1,321,000 in 2000. The new Sunbelt giants conformed to the expansive settlement patterns of the automobile age, and unlike older cities were from their beginning adapted to the motor age. They were sprawling rather than compact; built around multi-lane expressways rather than narrow, tenement-lined streets. These sunny, sprawling behemoths appeared to represent the America of the future. Americans were not only spreading out from the city center to the suburb; they were also moving out from the densely-populated industrial Northeast and Midwest to the less developed South and West. The dispersion of urban America was evident in the migration from the metropolitan hub to the rim and from the North to the South.

The Age of Sprawl

In 1958 William H. Whyte, Jr., an editor of *Fortune* and a leading urban commentator, opened his attack on urban sprawl by observing: "Already huge patches of once green countryside have been turned into vast, smog-filled deserts that are neither city, suburb, nor country, and each day – at a rate of some 3,000 acres a day – more countryside is being bulldozed under" (1958: 133). With considerable prescience Whyte recognized the emergence of a new world – neither urban, nor suburban, nor rural – that was to become increasingly evident in the late twentieth century. The age of the city was passing; the traditional upper-middle-class suburban residential haven was likewise becoming a relic of the past. The pattern of settlement was sprawl: mile after mile of housing subdivisions, garden apartment complexes, strip-mall retailing, fast-food eateries, and ample expanses of pavement to facilitate the movement and storage of the ubiquitous automobile. It bore no more resemblance to Manhattan in 1900 than to rural Kansas. It was a new phenomenon, which neither Whyte nor others liked.

Across the nation amorphous sprawl was supplanting the single-centered city of the past. In 1991 journalist Joel Garreau analyzed this new world in *Edge City*, an account of the many centers of commerce that had developed along what was formerly the metropolitan periphery. Garreau reported that the freshly minted edge centers arising around freeway interchanges or extending for miles along peripheral expressways were the "new hearths of our civilization – in which the majority of metropolitan Americans now work and around which we live." He found that two-thirds of all office space in the United States was in the edge cities (1991: 3, 5). This was especially true in the booming metropolises of the South and West. In Dallas and Houston the amount of office space outside the central business district (CBD) was almost three times as great as that in the CBD. By 2000 office parks lined Interstate 25 south of Denver; and this zone, known as the Southwest Corridor, had surpassed Denver's central business district in both office space and employment. Tyson's Corner, southwest of Washington, DC, the lengthy strip of development along Interstate 494 south of Minneapolis, and the Schaumburg area northwest of Chicago were other well-known edge cities. Perimeter Center outside of Atlanta was perhaps the pre-eminent symbol of how the new world defied traditional notions of cities. Its very name was a seeming contradiction. But in the age of sprawl, centers were on the perimeter; and the traditional core was increasingly on the fringe of American life.

Commerce and housing were eating up thousands of acres of countryside in this new world of multiple centers and expansive growth. No wonder that urban planners and scholars in general identified sprawl, not congestion, as the great demonic force threatening the metropolis. At the close of the century, policy-makers and commentators were calling for anti-sprawl legislation to curb the apparently ceaseless outward flow of humanity. Led by architects Andres Duany and Elizabeth Plater-Zyberk, the New Urbanism movement declared war on sprawl and battled for a return to compact settlement and traditional neighborhoods. In their manifesto *Suburban Nation*, Duany and Plater-Zyberk presented a new end-of-the-century litany for sprawl fighters: "No more housing subdivisions! No more shopping centers! No more office parks! No more highways! Neighborhoods or nothing!" (2000: 243).

Foes of sprawl invariably identified the automobile as the chief corrupter of American life. Proposals for new mass transit lines won plaudits from observers throughout the nation, and some cities constructed "light-rail systems," the fashionable late-twentieth-century term for streetcars. Yet transit patronage did not soar, and at the close of the century few Americans were abandoning their automobiles. Meanwhile, there were calls for "regional governance" to facilitate the fencing-in of the outward flowing masses. The fact that "regional" had supplanted "metropolitan" as the preferred term describing supra-municipal cooperation was indicative of the growing awareness that many sprawling areas were less metropolises than densely-populated regions. Portland, Oregon, was hailed for its regional growth limits that seemed at least to slow the centrifugal pace. But regional governance, like earlier metropolitan federative schemes, faced opposition from many voters and local officials throughout the country.

Whereas the century began with cries of too much city, it closed with complaints of too little. At the beginning of the twentieth century, crowded, narrow streets, tightly-packed tenements, behemoth skyscrapers, and jammed transit systems seemed to represent a new barbarism that could only be dispelled by the decentralization of population and business. At the end of the century, expansive asphalt, tract houses on grassy plots, low-rise malls, and commodious automobiles were blamed for having destroyed urbanism and the community and culture associated with it. In the course of one hundred years, the term "city" had grown increasingly anachronistic; it no longer described actual American settlement. The supposed "cities" of 2000 bore little resemblance to those of 1900, and the maladies of the congested core had yielded to a plague of sprawl.

This transformation has dominated the work of urban historians, planners, and social scientists. Scholars have produced an extensive literature on twentieth-century suburbanization, and even studies of older central cities have focused on decentralization and efforts to counter it. Works on "white flight" and racial succession in neighborhoods as well as studies of central-city decline and revitalization all recognize and confront this dominant theme. In the minds of planners, historians, political scientists, and sociologists, the shift from city to region was the primary legacy of twentieth-century metropolitan development.

REFERENCES AND FURTHER READING

Arnold, Joseph L. (1971) *The New Deal in the Suburbs: A History of the Greenbelt Town Program, 1935–1954.* Columbus: Ohio State University Press.

Bottles, Scott L. (1987) *Los Angeles and the Automobile: The Making of the Modern City*. Berkeley: University of California Press.

Douglass, Harlan Paul (1925) *The Suburban Trend*. New York: Century.

Duany, Andres, Plater-Zyberk, Elizabeth, and Speck, Jeff (2000) *Suburban Nation: The Rise of Sprawl and the Decline of the American Dream*. New York: North Point Press.

Fishman, Robert (1977) *Urban Utopias in the Twentieth Century: Ebenezer Howard, Frank Lloyd Wright, and Le Corbusier*. New York: Basic Books.

—— (1987) *Bourgeois Utopias: The Rise and Fall of Suburbia*. New York: Basic Books.

Fogelson, Robert M. (2001) *Downtown: Its Rise and Fall, 1880–1950*. New Haven, Conn.: Yale University Press.

Foster, Mark S. (1981) *From Streetcar to Superhighway: American City Planners and Urban Transportation, 1900–1940*. Philadelphia: Temple University Press.

Garreau, Joel (1991) *Edge City: Life on the New Frontier*. New York: Doubleday.

Gelfand, Mark I. (1975) *A Nation of Cities: The Federal Government and Urban America, 1933–1965*. New York: Oxford University Press.

Jackson, Kenneth T. (1985) *Crabgrass Frontier: The Suburbanization of the United States*. New York: Oxford University Press.

Rome, Adam (2001) *The Bulldozer in the Countryside: Suburban Sprawl and the Rise of American Environmentalism*. New York: Cambridge University Press.

Sugrue, Thomas J. (1996) *The Origins of the Urban Crisis: Race and Inequality in Postwar Detroit*. Princeton, NJ: Princeton University Press.

Teaford, Jon C. (1979) *City and Suburb: The Political Fragmentation of Metropolitan America, 1850–1970*. Baltimore, Md.: Johns Hopkins University Press.

—— (1990) *The Rough Road to Renaissance: Urban Revitalization in America, 1940–1985*. Baltimore, Md.: Johns Hopkins University Press.

—— (1997) *Post-Suburbia: Government and Politics in the Edge Cities*. Baltimore, Md.: Johns Hopkins University Press.

Weber, Adna Ferrin (1899) *The Growth of Cities in the Nineteenth Century*. New York: Macmillan.

Whyte, William H., Jr. (ed.) (1958) *The Exploding Metropolis*. Garden City, NY: Doubleday.

Worley, William S. (1990) *J. C. Nichols and the Shaping of Kansas City*. Columbia: University of Missouri Press.

Wright, Frank Lloyd (1932) *The Disappearing City*. New York: William Farquhar Payson.

PART III

People

CHAPTER THIRTEEN

Immigration

ROGER DANIELS

While I was in London in the summer of 1999 a gregarious Nigerian gypsy cab driver asked me what I did in the United States. When I told him that I taught the history of immigration, he smiled broadly and said, "Ah, immigration history, that *is* America."

Not all, of course, share his perception. Most history textbook writers, judging from the amount of space they devote to immigration, do not regard it very highly, and many Native Americans and their politically correct supporters speak as if immigration destroyed an Edenic civilization. We can see this new tendency in the successive commemorations of the 400th and 500th anniversaries of Columbus's "discovery" of America.

The 1892 celebration was a gala affair. The Genoese navigator was hailed as the man who had transported "Christ across the sea" for "the salvation of the world," an image that was aided both by his first name, Christopher or "Christ bearer," and by the propaganda of the Knights of Columbus. This Catholic men's organization had been founded just ten years previously, and habitually referred to the admiral as "a prophet, a seer, an instrument of Divine Providence." Cities all over America vied for the honor of a Columbian Exposition, a prize won by Chicago, which staged, although a year late, an epochal world's fair. This greatly influenced American architecture and gave us such cultural icons as Dvořák's "New World" symphony, Frederick Jackson Turner's seminal essay on the significance of the frontier, and the hootchy-kootchy dancer, "Little Egypt," really an immigrant from Syria named Fahrenda Mahzar.

What a difference a century can make. Two years before the 1992 Quincentennial the National Council of Churches of Christ in the United States declared that "for the descendants of the survivors of the subsequent invasion, genocide, slavery, 'ecocide' and exploitation of the wealth of the land, a celebration is not an appropriate observation"; rather, the Council said, "repentance would be more appropriate" (quoted in Thernstrom 1992: 24). One of Mark Twain's entries in Pudd'nhead Wilson's calendar read: "October 12, the Discovery. It was wonderful to find America, but it would have been more wonderful to miss it" (quoted in Clemens 1980: 113). Twain was kidding, but these folks were deadly serious. That many Native Americans looked somewhat askance at the Quincentennial is understandable, but surely the reaction of the member of the American Indian Movement who announced at a press conference that

"Columbus makes Hitler look like a juvenile delinquent" was overkill and foolish overkill at that. Similarly, but with less excuse, the city council of Berkeley, California officially voted to rename Columbus Day "Indigenous Peoples Day." Interestingly, no city in America hosted a major celebration – these took place in Genoa and Seville – and even the executive director of the official Christopher Columbus Quincentenary Jubilee Commission described the year-long multi-continent event as a "commemoration" or "encounter" rather than a celebration. Some historians, who should know better, have gone so far to describe Columbus and his successors as "conquerors of paradise" (Sale 1990). The New World, even at its best, was far from paradise. No one who has seriously studied the remarkable civilizations that had developed in the New World – those of Mexico and Peru for example – can believe that their societies were "perfection" any more than the ancient civilizations of the old world were. They were based on slavery, human sacrifice, and other practices for which we today have little sympathy.

While it is clear that the "discovery" of America, like every significant event in history, has had both positive and negative aspects, this trashing of Columbus was at least puerile and perhaps worse. As both a son of immigrants and a historian of immigration, I cannot accept the notion that the "discovery" of the New World and the subsequent bringing to it of peoples and cultures from four other continents was an essentially negative event. While the Nigerian cab driver surely overstated the case, immigration has been crucial to the development of the United States and other societies in the New World. The United States may not be "the last best hope of earth," as Abraham Lincoln put it, but this immigrant nation does represent one of the more successful examples of human society in the modern world.

During the last four centuries immigration has been responsible for the presence of almost all of the 285 million persons who presently inhabit the United States. The 2 million Native Americans excepted, all are immigrants and the descendants of immigrants. This essay will largely ignore the descendants of immigrants – some 90 percent of the population at the beginning of the twenty-first century – and focus on the process of immigration and on the immigrants themselves. But readers should keep in mind Franklin D. Roosevelt's often noted and usually misquoted 1938 admonition to the Daughters of the American Revolution: "Remember, remember always that all of us, and you and I especially, are descended from immigrants and revolutionaries." (quoted in Daniels 2002: 296).

By the dawn of the twentieth century perhaps 25 million persons, the vast majority of them Europeans, had immigrated to America. During the twentieth century some 47 million have come, almost twice as many as in all of our previous history. A convenient periodization of the century's immigration is:

I. High immigration, increasing restriction, 1901–24.
II. Low immigration, high restriction, 1925–45.
III. Increasing immigration, decreasing restriction, 1946–2000.

High Immigration, Increasing Restriction, 1901–24

Although during most of the nineteenth century immigration was almost totally unrestricted, by 1900 what would become a powerful anti-immigrant or nativist movement was building up a head of steam. Effective immigration restriction had begun with the passage of the Chinese Exclusion Act of 1882, and it is now apparent that its passage was the hinge on which all American immigration policy turned. But contemporary observers, and many later historians, could only see that immigration was continuing to grow. Immigration which had hit a nineteenth-century high of 5.8 million in the 1880s, slumped to 3.7 million in the depression-scarred 1890s, and rose rapidly in the new century, until the onset of World War I seriously disrupted the flow of immigration from Europe (see Table 1).

Table 1 Immigration, 1901–24

1901–10	8,795,386
1911–20	5,735,811
1921–4	2,344,599
Total	16,875,796

This immigration was uneven: 12.9 million – more than three-quarters – came in the period before the outbreak of World War I.

In the entire period more than 80 percent were Europeans, primarily those from southern and eastern Europe, as Table 2 indicates. Most of the rest were from the New World, chiefly Canada, Mexico, and the Caribbean, while Asians – chiefly Japanese and Chinese – accounted for less than 2 percent.

Table 2 European immigration, major sources, 1901–24

Nation/region	1900–10	1910–24	Total
Britain	525,950	522,952	1,048,902
Scandinavia	505,234	309,240	814,474
Germany	341,498	291,204	632,702
Ireland	339,065	219,046	558,111
W. Europe	1,711,747	1,342,442	3,054,189
Italy	2,045,877	1,475,023	3,520,900
Austria-Hungary	2,145,266	1,069,512	3,214,778
Russia	1,597,306	993,373	2,590,679
Poland*		177,881	177,881
Southern and eastern Europe	5,788,449	3,715,789	9,504,238
Europe, 8 sources	7,500,196	5,058,231	12,558,427
Europe, all sources	8,056,040	5,862,895	13,918,935
All sources	8,795,386	8,080,410	16,875,796

* Immigrants from Poland before 1920 are included in the numbers for Austria-Hungary, Russia, and Germany.

The 9.5 million southern and eastern Europeans – largely Italians, Jews, and Poles – seemed particularly alien to most established Americans, just as western European Catholics – largely Irish and Germans – had seemed in the decades before the Civil War. In its well-known 1911 report the United States Immigration Commission stigmatized the southern and eastern Europeans as "new immigrants who have no intention of permanently changing their residence, their only purpose in coming to America being to temporarily take advantage of the greater wages paid for industrial labor in this country" (United States Immigration Commission 1911: I, 24).

By 1911 "new immigrant" was already a code phrase for "undesirable." Historians habitually use the term today, often not realizing its pejorative origins. What is almost never noticed is that, despite the great increase in their numbers, the incidence of immigrants – the percentage of foreign-born in the population – was remarkably constant between 1860 and 1920. That percentage did not vary significantly in any of the seven censuses of that period, a period justly characterized as one of rapid change in almost every other aspect of American life. Both the 1860 and 1920 censuses recorded foreign-born as 13.2 percent of the population, while those in between reported percentages of 14.0, 13.3, 14.7, 13.6, and 14.7. Yet contemporaries perceived that the amount of immigration was overwhelming. These perceptions have been repeated by historians who have persisted in using what I call hydraulic metaphors to describe the immigration process. Immigrants are described as coming to the United States in "waves," "floods," "torrents," and "streams." One does not have to be a specialist in semiotics to understand that the habitual use of such language tends to stigmatize immigrants as the "other," rather than as the ancestors of large numbers of Americans.

But numbers alone cannot tell the full story of immigration. Use of the so-called "immigrant paradigm" can help to give substance to the numbers. That paradigm asks, in addition to "Where did immigrants come from?," other questions: "Why did they leave?"; "How did they come?"; "Where did they settle?"; "What did they do?"; "How did they live?"; "In what ways did their culture change/not change?"; and "How did they interact with their environment?"

Although the answers to these questions will vary, not only between groups but also over time and within groups, it is possible to make some generalized responses to them. Most of those who left Europe in the early twentieth century were young adult males who did so chiefly for economic reasons. The industrial jobs for immigrants were unskilled or, at best, semi-skilled. They were dirty, dangerous, and low paid. One Polish immigrant wrote home that, "in America Poles work like cattle. Where a dog does not want to sit, there the Pole is made to sit, and the poor wretch works because he wants to eat" (quoted in Buckowczyk 1987: v). Immigrant industrial workers of dozens of ethnicities could have made similar complaints. These workers were not only mistreated by their bosses, they were also slighted by American trade union leaders, most of whom were themselves immigrants or children of immigrants from western Europe. Only with the organizing drives of the labor federation the Congress of Industrial Organizations (CIO) in the 1930s did industrial workers become organized, by which time there were more second-generation ethnics than immigrants in the mass production industries.

Many of these immigrants came intending to work for a time and return home, a phenomenon called "sojourning." Since the United States did not begin to record emigration prior to 1909 we have no specific data, but most authorities believe that perhaps one emigrant in three returned home in the years between 1820 and 1920, although many of those later returned to America. In one survey of incoming Italians at Ellis Island early in the twentieth century one in ten reported having been in the US before. Sojourners were typically young adult males hoping to earn enough money to buy a new farm back home or to be able to purchase more land for an existing one. A Hungarian-language newspaper published in Cleveland wrote of Hungarian sojourners in 1901, "The majority of our people do not want to adjust to the conditions here, do not like it here, yet do not want to return home [because they have not saved enough money]" (quoted in Hoerder and Rossler 1993: 185). Yet, whatever they intended, many thousands of Hungarian immigrants did stay in Cleveland, which became one of the centers of Hungarian-American life. The same would be true for members of many other ethnic groups all over industrial America.

As near as we can tell, sojourning was least prevalent among immigrants who had been "pushed" out of Europe, such as the Eastern European Jews and the Armenians, and was most prevalent among immigrant groups in the early years of their migration to America and among groups, such as the Chinese, who felt particularly unwelcome in America. It was almost standard procedure for those, such as Mexicans and Quebeckers, for whom return migration was quite easy. Both came and departed over the land borders largely unimpeded by regulations or regulators until well into the twentieth century. Many of the latter groups engaged in what is called "circular migration" because the people involved come and return on a more or less regular basis, often a seasonal one attuned to cycles of agricultural employment.

Large numbers of urban immigrants lived in ethnic enclaves, usually in the run-down areas of city centers close to their work places. Anachronistically many now refer to them as "ghettos," but immigrants were not confined to these places by external restraint: they clustered together largely for convenience. One historian of American Catholicism, Jay P. Dolan, refers to the immigrant church as a "fortress" which protected its parishioners (1975). The urban turf that constituted the church's parish was also a kind of fortress, whether or not its inhabitants were religious. Those inside these "fortresses" tended to live surrounded by kith and kin in Chinatowns and Little Italies. But in what seemed to be an undifferentiated Little Italy to the outsider, the insider knew that in such and such a block, or even tenement, Neapolitans lived; while over there one found mostly Calabrians, and, across the street there were mostly Sicilians.

Like most immigrants, those within the fortresses tried to recreate a familiar social milieu; but "Little Italy" and "Chinatown" could never be Italy or China. Added to the fundamental environmental differences – differences which were most pronounced for those who came from rural societies – was the impact of the second generations, who eventually helped to tear down the communities' defenses. The differences and conflicts between generations were profound. An Italian immigrant boy who grew up on New York's Lower East Side remembered that he never met any of his non-Italian neighbors: "The household my parents established on Mott Street was typical of those of little Italy. We spoke only Italian, ate Italian food, celebrated Italian holidays, and on Sundays entertained relatives and friends. We knew nothing of the outside world" (quoted in La Sorte 1985: 148). Mario Cuomo (b. 1932), a native-born son of a later immigrant generation, recalled: "I can cry now when I think about the time when I was fourteen years old and embarrassed to bring my father to St. John's Preparatory School to meet the teachers and other parent because he didn't speak English well" (quoted in Italian American Historical Society 1977: 6).

The immigrant generation understood – and resented – the erosion of the cultures that it tried to nourish and sustain. Nothing better epitomizes this well-nigh universal phenomenon than the wistful realization of some observers of Jewish immigrant culture that "the grandfather believes, the father doubts, and the son denies." One could ring dozens of changes on that sad tune from a whole variety of ethnic groups, and, of course, the point of view of older generations is often (nearly always?) that their successors have, somehow, lost touch with "ancient ways."

But however stressful the tensions within the immigrant communities were, they were dwarfed by the attacks that came from outside. Even the most positive of support groups from the larger society – the friendly Americanizers such as social workers and school principals – usually urged or even insisted that the immigrants and their children shed all or almost all of their original cultures. Julia Richman (1855–1912), herself the daughter of German-Jewish immigrants who rose to become district superintendent of schools on New York's Lower East Side early in the twentieth century, was one such Americanizer. In an effort more fully to acculturate her charges, she forbade children from speaking foreign languages in school, even during recess, and encouraged her teachers to wash out the mouths of any offending pupils with soap. Later in the century the "flivver king," Henry Ford, staged a ceremony as part of the indoctrination of his workers that epitomized the acculturationist ideal. During a patriotic pageant for his workers, a procession of persons in old world garb, bearded men and head-scarfed women, entered stage left and seemed to climb into a huge cauldron labeled "melting pot," only to emerge clean-shaven and garbed in "American" clothes.

Other reactions to immigrants were antagonistic and sometimes violent. There has almost always been a strain of nativism in modern American life, ranging from mild resentment of folks who seemed "not like us" to assaults that occasionally became murderous, particularly in the period from the 1840s to the 1890s. During World War I a German American was lynched in Illinois and non-fatal violence against immigrants was widespread.

Those seeking to extend the legislative restriction of immigration beyond Chinese focused on a literacy test for more than two decades. Passed four times by Congress and vetoed by presidents as diverse as Grover Cleveland, William Howard Taft, and Woodrow Wilson, a 1917 version became law over Wilson's second negative. Although most of the literacy test's staunchest proponents wanted the law to specify literacy in English, as enacted the statute specified only an ability to read a brief text in any "language or dialect, including Hebrew or Yiddish" by immigrants over 16 years of age. In addition, wives, mothers, grandmothers, widowed or unmarried daughters of a literate male alien, or one already living here, need not be literate. The law seemed to have little effect. In the last year in which it was the major bar to general immigration – 1920–1 – only about 1.5 percent of the more than 800,000 immigrants who arrived at the borders seeking admission were rejected for all causes. Just over a tenth of these, 1,450 persons, were barred for illiteracy. However the enactment of the literacy test, along with the hyper-nationalism of the World War I era and the general xenophobia of the postwar era, prepared the way for the drastic curtailment of immigration in the 1920s. In addition, by the end of 1917, immigration had been restricted by Congress in six other major ways: most Asians, criminals, persons who failed to meet certain moral standards, persons with various diseases, persons "likely to become a public charge," and certain radicals had been denied admission.

These restrictions, plus the war, caused short-term changes in American immigration patterns, some of which had long term consequences. The most significant of these was surely the so-called "great migration" of southern African Americans to northern cities, an ongoing migration that was stimulated by the wartime shortages of fresh European immigrant workers. But it was the postwar reaction which demonstrated that the era of mass immigration had ended.

Low Immigration, High Restriction, 1925–45

In 1921 and 1924 the US enacted the first two "quota laws," the first avowedly "temporary," the second allegedly "permanent." A persistent myth has developed that these laws drastically reduced immigration to almost nothing. This myth is epitomized by a contemporary cartoon, which is reproduced in many textbooks, showing Uncle Sam forcing large numbers of prospective European immigrants into the large end of a funnel with only a very few being allowed to enter. The actual numbers of immigrants, while reduced, were still substantial even after the more restrictive 1924 Act. As Table 3 shows, it was only the depression-scarred 1930s and war years of the 1940s that fit that description. In two years of the 1930s, for the only time in United States history, more persons were recorded as leaving the country than entered it.

Table 3   Immigration, 1925–45

	Total	Per annum
1925–30	1,762,610	393,768
1931–5	220,209	44,042
1936–40	308,222	61,644
1941–5	170,952	34,190

In no year between 1930 and 1946 did as many as 100,000 immigrants enter the country, something that had not happened since 1862. Thus the forces of economics and war were more effective in inhibiting immigration than was the power of nativism, although the impact of the latter was important, both in its demographic and psychic impacts.

The quota system begun in 1924 and continued until 1965 was based, after 1930, on a national origins system which purported to calculate "the number of inhabitants in continental United States in 1920 whose origin by birth or ancestry" was attributable to each eligible nation. The law denied the right to immigrate to "aliens ineligible to citizenship" – i.e. Asians – whatever their nationality, and excluded from consideration in determining quota numbers descendants of "slave immigrants" and "American aborigines." The quota system privileged, as it was intended to do, immigrants from the British Isles, Germany, and Scandinavia and deliberately discriminated against immigrants from southern and eastern Europe. The privileged group got more than three-quarters of the quota spaces; in 1913, the last pre-World War I year, those nations had accounted for just over 10 per cent of all immigrants.

That the privileged group of nations was predominantly Protestant and those from the disadvantaged group predominantly Catholic, Jewish, or Orthodox, was not an accident. The contemporary congressional debates and pamphlet literature show overt and often vitriolic religious and ethnic bias against persons of color, persons from the "wrong" parts of Europe, and, in fact, against anyone who could not be described as "Anglo-Saxon."

But the law also set up categories of persons who could enter "without numerical restriction." The most significant groups thus affected were wives and children under 18 years of age of American citizens and natives of independent nations of the western hemisphere and Canada. Thus, although the quota limit was some 150,000 annually, pre-depression admissions under the 1924 law averaged more than twice that. The western hemisphere exception, largely owing to pressures from legislators speaking for southwestern agricultural interests, was significantly modified by administrative decisions begun in the Hoover administration. It expanded the use of the "likely to become a public charge" clause to bar immigrants who seemed poor. Originally the clause had been applied only to persons who seemed unlikely to be able to work. Earlier in the century it had been used to keep out able-bodied Asian Indians; the Hoover administration used it largely against Mexicans. The western hemisphere exception would last, like the quota system, until 1965. But the family unification provisions, significantly expanded, have remained a cornerstone of American immigration policy.

Despite his immigrant-friendly rhetoric, Franklin Roosevelt's New Deal had no program for immigration. This was not of much import in the early 1930s. However the now notorious failure of American immigration policy even to try to make adequate provision for the refugee crisis stemming from the rise of Hitler and other totalitarians to power in Western Europe is a great moral policy stain on FDR's administration. Nothing better demonstrates this than the President's failure to lift a finger in support of the Wagner–Rogers Bill of 1939, which would have admitted 20,000 German refugee children outside of the German quota. Despite important bipartisan support, including that of Herbert Hoover, the bill never came to a vote. Roosevelt told his wife, in February, 1939, that "it is all right for you to support the child refugee bill, but it is best for me to say nothing [now]." Now became never, as FDR remained publicly silent. In June, as the bill was dying, the President annotated a memo asking for his support "File No Action, FDR." Some members of his administration, most notably Secretary of Labor Frances Perkins, publicly supported the bill, but Secretary of State Cordell Hull pointed out the difficulties in administering such a law. One member of FDR's own family – Laura Delano, wife of his Commissioner of Immigration and Naturalization, James Houghteling – told people at cocktail parties that the "20,000 charming children would all too soon grow up into 20,000 ugly adults" (quoted in Stewart 1982: 532).

On the other hand, FDR took unpublicized administrative steps to make life simpler for refugees who had managed to get to the US. In late 1938 he "suggested" to Frances Perkins that she allow refugees who were in the country on a six-month visitor's visa, to renew them as they expired. This enabled some 15,000 refugees to remain. Once war came the President ordered other administrative actions, for example, enabling German refugees outside Germany to use spaces in the now undersubscribed German quota, and arranging with Canada for refugees in the US on temporary visas to make a pro-forma entry to that country in order to change their status, which the law said could not be done without leaving the country.

Two other actions, the first of which was secret, brought some refugees to the US during the war. After the fall of France FDR authorized sending a secret agent to Marseilles with authority to issue visas to cultural luminaries. More than a thousand such visas were utilized and brought a galaxy of cultural stars to the US. They included Lion Feuchtwanger, Heinrich Mann, Franz Werfel, Anna Mahler Werfel, Marc Chagall, Jacques Lipchitz, Marcel Duchamp, and Wanda Landowska.

Little else was done to facilitate refugee entry to the US before 1944, although after the 1942 invasion of North Africa the government was actively involved in refugee camps there and later in occupied Europe. Then, on January 16, 1944, Secretary of the Treasury Henry Morgenthau handed FDR a report prepared by his staff originally titled "Report to the Secretary on the Acquiescence of this Government in the Murder of the Jews." This report triggered a flurry of activity. From its blunt first sentence, "One of the greatest crimes in history, the slaughter of the Jewish people in Europe, is continuing unabated," to its end, it was a damning indictment of American policy in general and of the State Department in particular (quoted in Blum 1967: 220). Just six days later FDR issued an executive order setting up the War Refugee Board whose bills were paid out of the President's discretionary funds and by Jewish organizations. The Board was not designed to bring refugees to the US but to rescue and succor refugees in camps in neutral and occupied Europe and North Africa.

In 1944 FDR did authorize one boatload of 987 refugees – what Sharon Lowenstein (1986) has aptly called a "token shipment" – from camps in Italy to a camp in Oswego, New York. With that administrative ingenuity for which he was famous, FDR explained to Congress that he was simply "paroling" them into the US and that they would have to return after the war. In the event, only 69 went elsewhere, since FDR's successor allowed them to change their status in December 1945. While this single event was clearly a "token" for Holocaust survivors, the "parole" precedent would be used by later presidents and was eventually enacted into law. Hundreds of thousands of Cold War refugees became its beneficiaries.

Clearly, the United States, as Vice President Walter Mondale would later observe, simply "failed the test of civilization" as far as its prewar and wartime refugee policies were concerned (quoted in Daniels 1983: 61). But, it is important to note, perhaps 150,000 refugees, the overwhelming majority of whom were Jews, did manage to reach the United States before Pearl Harbor. This was more than were admitted by any other nation, but many more could have been saved by a more resolute policy.

Increasing Immigration, Decreasing Restriction, 1946–2000

The war years brought one other seemingly small change in immigration policy: the repeal of the fifteen statutes that comprised the Chinese Exclusion Acts. The gesture was not considered a major departure at the time; Roosevelt in a message to Congress endorsed repeal as a good behavior prize for China's struggles against Japan. Yet it is now clear that this was a turning point in American immigration policy. Not only were other ethnic barriers soon dropped, but the volume of immigration began to rise. In the more than half century since World War II the volume of immigration has risen steadily, as Table 4 shows.

By the 1990s the numbers of arriving immigrants were approaching the level – a million a year – reached in the years before the outbreak of World War I, but the incidence of foreign-born in the population was greatly reduced. In the ten years before 1914, 10.1 million immigrants came to a nation of just under 100 million. The 9 million immigrants of the 1990s came to a nation of 285 million. The incidence of foreign-born, 11.1 percent in 2000, while up dramatically from the

Table 4   Immigration, 1941–2000

	Immigrants	The foreign-born as a percentage of total population
1941–50	1,035,034	6.8 (1950)
1951–60	2,515,479	5.4 (1960)
1961–70	3,321,677	5.4 (1970)
1971–80	4,493,314	6.2 (1980)
1981–90	7,338,062	7.9 (1990)
1991–2000	9,095,417	11.1 (2000)

record lows in the 1950s and 1960s, was well under the 13–14 percent range that prevailed between 1860 and 1920. What changed even more significantly than the volume of immigration was its composition in terms of race, national origin, gender, and class distribution.

By the 1950s Europeans, who had dominated immigration to the United States from its beginning, were only a bare majority: 52.7 percent. In the 1960s Latin Americans outnumbered Europeans, in the 1970s both Latin Americans and Asians outnumbered Europeans, and in the 1980s, more than twice as many persons migrated from Mexico alone (1,655,843) as from all of Europe (761,550). The 1997 Census Bureau estimate of the nativity of all the foreign-born then living in the United States showed an absolute majority (51.3 percent) of the nearly 26 million foreign-born as coming from Latin America, with 27.5 per cent from Mexico. More than a quarter, 26.8 percent, came from Asia, and just over a sixth, 16.9 percent, from Europe.

While traditionally immigration had been predominantly male – perhaps two out of three during the nineteenth century – since the late 1940s females have constituted a slight majority, in some years about 54 percent. Immigrants have always tended to be young adults and that remains true. If one compares the age structure of contemporary immigrants with that of the United States as a whole, one finds a smaller proportion of the immigrant population under 10 and over 40 years of age than is found in the general population. Thus the continuing infusion of young immigrants has retarded significantly the "greying" of the American population and minimizes the inevitable problem that is being created by a population with an increasing percentage of persons above the traditional retirement age. Most other "modernized" nations, for example Germany and Japan, are greying much more rapidly.

But the most startling difference between contemporary immigrants and their predecessors is in their class and occupation. The vast majority of the immigrants in the pre-Civil War decades had been drawn from rural populations, had little education, and few industrial skills, although there had always been some artisans in the mix. The generalization made by a British social scientist, E. G. Ravenstein (1834–1913), that most immigrants, anywhere, had educational and occupational levels that were intermediate between those prevailing in the country of origin and the country of destination, held true for the American experience into the 1930s. The largely Jewish refugee migration before and during World War II represented the largest one-time increment, in both absolute and relative terms, of professionals and highly educated persons to immigrate to the United States. This was not just the case of a few cultural and scientific "superstars" (Albert Einstein, Enrico Fermi, and

Thomas Mann immediately come to mind), but also of thousands of professionals, especially physicians, lawyers, and educators.

Much of the post-World War II migration has been of highly qualified individuals, what is sometimes called a "brain drain." This phrase became common in the 1960s and may have been coined then, but the phenomenon it described had been occurring, especially with regard to Canadians, since the later nineteenth century. In the post-World War II era, the phrase was applied to both other immigrants from the first world, especially Great Britain, and immigrants from the third world, especially students trained at American universities who initially entered on student visas but stayed on in the United States. While both of these trends continued in the latter decades of the twentieth century and in the twenty-first, a third kind of brain drain developed, that of Asian scientists and professionals who emigrated shortly after receiving their education and training. They ranged from Indians and Chinese with PhDs to physicians and nurses, chiefly from India and the Philippines.

Very large numbers of these highly trained immigrants have been concentrated in the information technology complexes, particularly California's Silicon Valley, where Chinese, Indian, Korean, and Israeli scientists and engineers are not only key employees but increasingly entrepreneurs starting their own companies. These imports of what some call "human capital" have been a significant factor in the continuing dominance of American computer and computer-related industries. Since sometime in the 1980s recent immigrants have been much more likely to have doctorates than are native-born Americans.

On the other hand, large numbers of recent immigrants come with little or no education. Many of these are refugees, or relatives of refugees, from Southeast Asia and immigrants from Latin America and the Caribbean, particularly Mexico. (However, a significant minority of the immigrants from all these places bring a high level of education and professional experience.) Thus the educational levels of most post-World War II immigrants can be described as bi-polar. That is, if the educational achievements of these immigrants, as measured by years of school attended, are arranged graphically, many more will be clustered at both ends of the spectrum than would be in the middle, while most native-born Americans will be found in the middle, with fourteen to sixteen years of education.

A vast array of immigration legislation has facilitated these changes, although some of the changes were what political scientists call "unintended consequences": statutes that had results undreamt of by most of the legislators who voted for them. At least five major factors have motivated the most significant changes.

(1)   First and foremost has been the Cold War. The United States consciously strove for a kind of hegemony most often described as a desire to be or become "the leader of the free world." Since it was difficult to be such a leader when American law barred most members of most of the world's peoples from either immigrating, or becoming naturalized citizens, Congress was persuaded to drop all racial and ethnic bars to immigration and naturalization. Begun piecemeal with the 1943 repeal of Chinese exclusion, and the passage of 1946 statutes permitting the naturalization of Filipinos and "natives of India," all remaining such bars were removed by 1952.

(2)   A continuing diminution of statutory discrimination of all kinds and a growing awareness of American failures to provide havens for Jewish and other refugees during

World War II sparked the passage of a series of statutes and executive actions, beginning with the Displaced Persons Acts of 1948 and 1950 and ending with the Refugee Act of 1980. The latter firmly established a positive refugee policy, including the right of asylum. American membership in the United Nations was a factor here, as American law, on more than one occasion, adopted or adapted standards first established by the UN and its refugee arms.

(3)   American participation in military actions, most notably the wars in Korea and Vietnam and "fighting Communism" in the Caribbean and Central America, created refugees for whom the United States felt some responsibility.

(4)   An increasing need for labor of all kinds was evinced first during World War II by passage of legislation enabling the "temporary" entrance of agricultural and railroad workers from both Mexico and the Caribbean. While such needs continued, other legislation in the 1960s and 1970s facilitated the immigration of doctors, nurses, and paraprofessional medical personnel largely from the Philippines and India, and in the 1980s and beyond for highly trained computer professionals, chiefly from India and Taiwan.

(5)   Greater American concern for a growing, if limited egalitarianism, stimulated by an increasingly pervasive legal activism, spread into every area of American life. This included immigration decisions that had previously been decided almost completely by immigration bureaucrats.

The increasingly numerous and complex immigration legislation of the later twentieth century – an absolute majority of all the general immigration legislation ever enacted has been passed since 1950 – cannot possibly be treated here. Four pieces of legislation are fundamental to understanding the legal basis of immigration in the last half-century: the McCarran–Walter Act of 1952, the Immigration Act of 1965, the Refugee Act of 1980, and the Immigration Reform and Control Act of 1986.

The McCarran–Walter Act was, essentially, a modification of the 1924 Act. Apart from its lifting of racial and ethnic bars, noted above, the 1952 law retained the essentially discriminatory national quotas of the 1924 Act, and added particularly stringent provisions barring Communists, real and imagined, from even visiting the United States. Hotly contested, it was enacted over a strident veto by President Truman. In practice, however, the Act was less discriminatory than either its proponents intended or opponents claimed. Because it stressed family reunification as well as quotas, and since all immigrants could be naturalized, relatively large numbers of Asians were able to enter legally as close family members of American citizens, despite tiny quotas of about a hundred or so for all Asian nations. The struggle over the immigration act impelled Truman to establish a presidential commission whose report, *Whom We Shall Welcome* (1953), became a template for immigration reform.

That reform came twelve years later as part of the massive legislative agenda pushed through Congress to execute Lyndon Johnson's vision of a Great Society. Little noticed at the time and in the following decade, we can now see that, along with the Voting Rights Act and Medicare in the same year, the Immigration Act of 1965 was the high-water mark of postwar American liberalism. Even Johnson, never one to minimize his accomplishments, said, in a signing ceremony, "This bill . . . does not affect the lives of millions. It will not reshape the structure of our daily lives" (Johnson 1967).

Johnson, and most of those who supported the bill, saw it as a redress of grievances dating back to 1924 and nothing more. Its congressional opponents feared chiefly that there would be too many immigrants from southern and eastern Europe. The major Asian American civil rights organization, the Japanese American Citizens League, attacked it as still too discriminatory against Asians. If any contemporary foresaw its chief unintended consequences – the dominance of immigration by Latinos/Hispanics and Asians – I have found no record of it.

The Refugee Act of 1980, enacted at the end of Jimmy Carter's administration without significant dissent – it passed the Senate 85–0 – is the last major artifact of traditional twentieth-century liberalism. It sought to stabilize refugee immigration, which, under a complex variety of separate programs, had constituted a significant share of American immigration since the end of World War II. Although much in the legislation was, as noted below, chimerical, its uncontroversial passage shows clearly how much had changed in the thirty-five years since the end of World War II. As we have seen, then any refugee admissions at all were controversial. By 1980 it was axiomatic that the nation would have a refugee policy.

The Carter administration bill, passed in March, 1980, was a combination of conservatism, liberalism, and hocus-pocus. It was conservative because it sought to freeze the number of refugee admissions at about what was then the current level: 50,000 per year. (See Table 5.) It was liberal because, for the first time, it provided a procedure for asylum, whereby a person illegally in the US, or at a port of entry, might apply for asylum, based on "persecution or a well-founded fear of persecution," and have a legal right to have that asylum request evaluated by the Immigration and Naturalization Service (INS). It was hocus-pocus because it promised something for nothing. The worldwide ceiling for immigrants was reduced by 50,000, allegedly to compensate for the spaces reserved for refugees. This ignored the fact that, in the 1970s, a third or more of immigrants had been family members "not subject to numerical limitation" and that one could expect refugees, once settled, to institute new migration chains.

Table 5 Refugees, 1946–80

	Refugees	*Percent of total immigration*
1946–50	213,347	24.7
1951–60	492,371	19.8
1961–70	212,843	6.4
1971–80	539,447	12.0

But hopes for an orderly, planned refugee policy were soon in ruins. A month and four days after President Carter signed the bill, Fidel Castro set off the Mariel boatlift which developed out of a three-cornered argument between Cuba, Peru, and the US over the fate of some 3,500 Cuban dissidents who had taken sanctuary in the Peruvian Embassy in Havana. The US was willing to accept them, but only after a screening and only if they went first to Costa Rica. Castro was willing to let them leave, but only if they went directly to the US. When the negotiations stalled, Castro announced that anyone who wished to leave Cuba could do so, but only if they went directly to the US from the tiny Cuban port of Mariel, which was roughly opposite

Key West. After a few boatloads had arrived from Mariel, Cuban exiles in the US bought, borrowed, or hired small- to medium-sized boats and went, in violation of US law, directly to Mariel to pick up relatives and anyone who wanted to come. Within just over a month, some 125,000 Cubans – two and a half years worth of refugees – had arrived.

The Carter administration was trapped. On the one hand, Cold War imperatives and presidential politics made it imperative to accept anyone fleeing Communism. On the other hand, American law was supposed to be respected and orderly refugee limits observed. The result was strenuous vacillation. At first the government tried to stop the flow by arresting and fining the boat operators. When this produced adverse public reaction the administration reversed itself and Carter himself proclaimed that the US would welcome all with "an open heart and open arms." Then, when it seemed that Castro was opening Cuba's jails and mental institutions on condition that the inmates leave from Mariel, American public opinion turned against the "Marielitos" and US authorities again imposed fines and, more effectively, began seizing boats. Castro had again thumbed his nose, effectively, at the US, and Carter's refugee policy was a shambles. Between April and September 1980 the government approved 89,000 refugee applications. This does not count what the INS, then and later, denominated "Cuban-Haitian Entrants (Status Pending)" and did not include the 180,000 persons thus labeled in official refugee statistics. (The vast majority were Cubans; most Haitians were administratively adjudged to be fleeing poverty rather than persecution, but thousands were able to stay in the US.) Every year since 1980 the President of the United States has gone through the charade of proclaiming an annual upper limit for refugees, but, in fact, actual refugee entries have almost invariably exceeded that number. In no year since 1980 have as few as 50,000 persons classified as refugees entered the US.

The numerical provisions for asylum in the 1980 law were quite small: 5,000 per year was the estimate. By the mid-1990s, 12–13,000 asylum applications were being granted annually, about one-fifth of the applications. The number of both refugee and asylum applications approved has been markedly increased by the tendency of many federal judges to look behind the once inviolate administrative decisions of the INS. The famous Elián Gonzales case of 1999–2000, although eventually supportive of the initial INS decision, is an extreme example of the lengths to which such cases can now go. Elián was the 6-year-old sole survivor of an ill-fated attempt by Cuban escapees to reach Florida. Although the Cuban community of Miami wanted him to receive asylum, the law was that minors could not make such a decision; and his father was allowed to come to the US and take him back to Cuba, to the delight of Fidel Castro and the rage of the exile Cuban community.

The Reagan and Bush administrations (1981–93) clearly represented a turn to the right, but a turn, as far as immigration was concerned, that was more rhetorical than actual. Ronald Reagan, in a metaphor intended to frighten, spoke of the dangers of countless "feet people" from Mexico and Central America crossing the southern border. Increasing concern about illegal immigrants, and sometimes highly exaggerated notions about their number and incidence, came to dominate the immigration debates of the 1980s and early 1990s. The legislative result was the Immigration Reform and Control Act of 1986, hereafter IRCA. A compromise measure, IRCA neither reformed nor controlled immigration, but, in the final analysis, actually expanded it, although its bipartisan sponsors and the Reagan administration promised otherwise. One often-repeated promise was that it would enable the United States "to regain control of its borders," although America's borders have always been permeable. Raiding Native Americans from north and south in one era, and immigrants from all points of the compass in another, have always managed to cross.

The complex law's most vital part was its "amnesty" provisions, although that term does not appear in the law. Immigrants who had either entered the country illegally or had entered legally on tourist or other visas and overstayed their authorized stay, *and* had been in the United States since January 1, 1982, could legalize their stay and eventually be eligible to become naturalized citizens of the US. Under its provisions 2,684,892 persons had legalized their status and become naturalized citizens by 1996. Just over 2 million of those thus naturalized – 74.7 percent of the total – were natives of Mexico. Other significant provisions of IRCA included sanctions against employers employing aliens not authorized to work, sanctions that have been utterly ineffective because only "knowingly" hiring such persons was illegal, and special provisions gave a privileged position to farm workers.

As immigration continued to grow in the early and mid-1990s, its congressional opponents, with the eventual acquiescence of the Clinton administration, passed a series of measures designed to make life miserable for recent legal immigrants if they happened to be poor. They were denied a whole array of government benefits normally available to all Americans. Other statutes increased the size, but lowered the quality, of the border patrol, particularly along the southern borders. Many authorities believed that a major result of such border tightening was to make many immigrants illegally in the United States think twice before returning to Mexico since it might become more difficult to return. This interrupted what had been a largely circular migration flow. A longer-term result was to raise the political consciousness of much of the Latino population so that both voter registration and naturalization increased markedly. By the end of the century there was a distinct reversal of what David Reimers had perceptively called "the turn against immigration," as both courts and Congress struck down, modified, or even reversed many of the punitive measures of the mid-1990s, measures that considerable portions of the American public had come to see as unfair.

Opponents of immigration, as they always had, stressed cultural, economic, and demographic factors as reasons for curtailing immigration more or less severely, but the naked ethnic and racial prejudices of the past were no longer uttered. Proponents of immigration tended to argue for continuing a relatively high level of immigration by praising the cultural values of diversity, the strengths brought by highly educated immigrants, and the buffer that continuing migration of relatively young immigrants provided against a greying population.

At the beginning of the twenty-first century there was every reason to believe that, as long as the economy remained robust and no major external crisis occurred, immigration would continue at relatively high levels and that it would continue to be dominated by migrants from the southern parts of the western hemisphere and much of Asia. The likely effects on the American population were fairly clear. Hispanic migrants would, early in the twenty-first century, replace African Americans as the largest minority of color. Whether large numbers of them would move into at least the lower levels of the middle class, as members of previous immigrant generations had, was an open question. It was clear that most members of the smaller but growing immigrant groups from Asia, and particularly their American-born children, had already done so, although large numbers of Asian Americans remained poor.

REFERENCES AND FURTHER READING

Archdeacon, Thomas (1983) *Becoming American: An Ethnic History*. New York: Free Press.

Bao, Xiaolan (2001) *Holding Up More than Half the Sky: Chinese Women Garment Workers in New York City, 1948–1992*. Urbana: University of Illinois Press.

Barkan, Elliott R. (1992) *Asian and Pacific Islander Migration to the United States: A Model of New Global Patterns*. Westport, Conn.: Greenwood.

Blum, John Morton (1967) *From the Morgenthau Diaries: Years of War, 1941–1945*. Boston: Houghton Mifflin.

Breitman, Richard and Kraut, Alan M. (1987) *American Refugee Policy and European Jewry*. Bloomington: Indiana University Press.

Buckowczyk, John J. (1987) *And My Children Did not Know Me*. Bloomington: Indiana University Press.

Butler, Jon (2000) *Becoming America: The Revolution before 1776*. Cambridge, Mass.: Harvard University Press.

Chan, Sucheng (1991) *Asian Americans: An Interpretive History*. Boston: Twayne.

Clemens, Samuel Langhorne (1980) *Pudd'nhead Wilson and Those Extraordinary Twins*, ed. Sidney E. Berger. New York: W. W. Norton.

Daniels, Roger (1983) "American Refugee Policy in Historical Perspective," in Jarrell C. Jackman and Carla M. Borden (eds.) *The Muses Flee Hitler*. Washington, DC: Smithsonian Institution Press.

—— (1997) *Not Like Us: Immigrants and Minorities in America, 1890–1924*. Chicago: Ivan R. Dee.

—— (2002) *Coming to America: A History of Immigration and Ethnicity in American Life*, 2nd edn. New York: HarperCollins.

—— (2003) *Guarding the Golden Door: American Immigration Policy and Immigrants since 1882*. New York: Hill and Wang.

Daniels, Roger and Otis, Graham (2001) *Debating American Immigration*. Lanham, Md.: Rowman and Littlefield.

Dinnerstein, Leonard (1982) *America and the Survivors of the Holocaust*. New York: Columbia University Press.

Dolan, Jay P. (1975) *The Immigrant Church: New York's Irish and German Catholics, 1815–1865*. Baltimore, Md.: Johns Hopkins University Press.

Foner, Nancy (ed.) (1987) *New Immigrants in New York*. New York: Columbia University Press.

Freeman, James M. (1990) *Hearts of Sorrow: Vietnamese-American Lives*. Stanford, Calif.: Stanford University Press.

Gabaccia, Donna (1995) *From the Other Side: Women, Gender, and Immigrant Life in the US, 1820–1990*. Bloomington: Indiana University Press.

Garcia, Maria Christina (1996) *Havana USA: Cuban Exiles and Cuban Americans in South Florida, 1959–1994*. Berkeley: University of California Press.

Gjerde, Jon (1997) *The Minds of the West: Ethnocultural Evolution in the Rural Middle West, 1830–1917*. Chapel Hill: University of North Carolina Press.

Haines, David W. (ed.) (1996) *Refugees in America in the 1990s: A Reference Handbook.* Westport, Conn.: Greenwood Press.

Handlin, Oscar (1941) *Boston's Immigrants, 1790–1865: A Study in Acculturation.* Cambridge, Mass.: Harvard University Press.

—— (1951) *The Uprooted: The Epic Story of the Great Migrations that made the American People.* Boston: Little, Brown.

Hein, Jeffrey (1995) *From Vietnam, Laos, and Cambodia: A Refugee Experience in the United States.* New York: Twayne.

Higham, John (1988) *Strangers in the Land: Patterns of American Nativism, 1860–1925,* 2nd edn. New Brunswick, NJ: Rutgers University Press.

Hoerder, Dirk and Rossler, Horst (eds.) (1993) *Distant Magnets: Expectations and Realities in the Immigrant Experience, 1840–1930.* New York: Holmes and Meier.

Hutchinson, E. P. (1981) *Legislative History of American Immigration Policy, 1798–1965.* Philadelphia: University of Pennsylvania Press.

Italian American Historical Society (1977) *The Urban Experience of Italian Americans.* Staten Island, NY: The Association.

Jacobson, Matthew Frye (1995) *Special Sorrows: The Diasporic Imagination of Irish, Polish and Jewish Immigrants in the United States.* Cambridge, Mass.: Harvard University Press.

Johnson, Lyndon B. (1967) *Public Papers, 1965,* vol. 2. Washington, DC: Government Printing Office.

Jones, Maldwyn A. (1992) *American Immigration,* 2nd edn. Chicago:University of Chicago Press.

La Sorte, Michael (1985) *La Merica.* Philadelphia: Temple University Press.

Lowenstein, Sharon R. (1986) *Token Refuge: The Story of the Jewish Refugee Shelter at Oswego, 1944–1946.* Bloomington: Indiana University Press.

Mitchell, Christopher (ed.) (1992) *Western Hemisphere Immigration and United States Foreign Policy.* University Park: Pennsylvania State University Press.

Owen, Irma Watkins (1996) *Blood Relations: Caribbean Immigrants and the Harlem Community, 1900–1930.* Bloomington: Indiana University Press.

Posadas, Barbara M. (1999) *The Filipino Americans.* Westport, Conn.: Greenwood Press.

President's Commission on Immigration and Naturalization (1953) *Whom We Shall Welcome.* Washington, DC: Government Printing Office.

Reimers, David M. (1992) *Still the Golden Door: The Third World Comes to America,* 2nd edn. New York: Columbia University Press.

—— (1998) *Unwelcome Strangers: American Identity and the Turn Against Immigration.* New York: Columbia University Press.

Sale, Kirkpatrick (1990) *The Conquest of Paradise: Christopher Columbus and the Columbian Legacy.* New York: Alfred A. Knopf.

Sánchez, George J. (1993) *Becoming Mexican American: Ethnicity, Culture and Identity in Chicano Los Angeles, 1900–1945.* New York: Oxford University Press.

Schrag, Philip G. (2000) *A Well-Founded Fear: The Congressional Battle to Save Political Asylum in America.* New York: Routledge.

Stewart, Barbara McDonald (1982) *United States Government Policy on Refugees from Nazism, 1933–1940.* New York: Garland.

Swierenga, Robert P. (1994) *Dutch Jewry in the North American Diaspora.* Detroit: Wayne State University Press.

—— (2000) *Faith and Family: Dutch Immigration and Settlement in the United States.* New York: Holmes and Meier.

Tatalovich, Raymond (1995) *Nativism Reborn: The Official English Language Movement and the American States.* Lexington: University Press of Kentucky.

Thernstrom, Stephan (ed.) (1980) *The Harvard Encyclopedia of American Ethnic Groups.* Cambridge, Mass.: Harvard University Press.

—— (1992) "The Columbus Controversy," *American Educator* 16, pp. 24–32.

United States Immigration Commission (1911) *Reports of the Immigration Commission*, 41 vols. Washington, DC: Government Printing Office.

Vecoli, Rudolph J. and Sinke, Suzanne (eds.) (1992) *A Century of European Migrations, 1830–1930.* Urbana: University of Illinois Press.

Vickerman, Milton (1999) *Crosscurrents: West Indian Immigrants and Race.* New York: Oxford University Press.

Weber, David J. (1992) *The Spanish Frontier in North America.* New Haven, Conn.: Yale University Press.

Wokeck, Marianne S. (1999) *A Trade in Strangers: The Beginnings of Mass Migration to North America.* University Park: Pennsylvania State University Press.

Wyman, Mark (1993) *Round-Trip to America: The Immigrants Return to Europe, 1880–1930.* Ithaca, NY: Cornell University Press.

Yans-McLaughlin, Virginia (ed.) (1990) *Immigration Reconsidered: History, Sociology, and Politics.* New York: Oxford University Press.

Yung, Judy (1995) *Unbound Feet: A Social History of Chinese Women in San Francisco.* Berkeley: University of California Press.

Zucker, Norman L. and Zucker, Naomi F. (1987) *The Guarded Gate: The Reality of American Refugee Policy.* San Diego, Calif.: Harcourt Brace Jovanovich.

Academic journals: *Journal of American Ethnic History, Immigrants and Minorities* (Great Britain), *International Migration Review: IMR.*

CHAPTER FOURTEEN

Ethnicity

Hasia R. Diner

The concept of ethnicity, like that of race, has metamorphosed several times. Each historical transformation in usage and meaning has reflected new directions within the world of historical scholarship. Each stage or incarnation of the term has also refracted the currents of the political moment, the cultural context in which scholars have used it. Because the category of ethnicity has functioned so centrally at the meeting point between the scholarship on the nation's past and the practice of politics, it has been used both as an analytic category as well as a statement of deep meaning for group identities and policy formation. To assess how "ethnicity" has been used in the realm of the former cannot be accomplished without cognizance of its power in the latter.

Before exploring the current "state of the subject," I would like to sketch a few of the component parts of the concept of ethnicity as it evolved historically and as it is conventionally understood. Some elements of that definition have seemed, at least heretofore, unassailable, while other elements are now undergoing serious revision. First, ethnicity has always been understood as a matter of identity, but one that encompassed groups of people endowed with some level of group consciousness. Individuals have it by virtue of their belonging to, or feeling a part of, some collectivity. Second, it has by and large been assumed to have some connection to ancestry. Occupational groups, for example, have been excluded from it, as have regional and religious ones. Third, ethnicity exists in relationship to consciousness of, and contact with, others who appear to be different.

But within this relatively vague set of principles, the issue of ethnicity, what it is, who has it, and what it means, has been a shifting terrain, informed by both scholarship and politics. From a technical, linguistic perspective it is a relatively new term, with its origins going no further back in time than the 1940s. Used initially by sociologists W. Lloyd Warner and Paul S. Lunt in their study of Newburyport, Massachusetts, ethnicity emerged as a concept of convenience. It seemed to Warner and Lunt to be an appropriate category by which to understand the behavior, attitudes, and various social positions of the Irish, Italian, Greek, Polish, and French Canadian residents of "Yankee City." The sociologists did not include under the ethnic umbrella the community's oldest residents, those who constituted its best-off, most powerful element, the "Yankees" whose presence gave Newburyport its pseudonym. As such in this debut of the word, we can see one of the most important elements in the initial formulation of the concept of ethnicity (Warner and Lunt 1941).

Ethnicity as a concept had been, from its earliest formulation, linked to some kind of marginality or otherness. The neologism "ethnicity," drawn from the Greek root, *ethnos*, refers to people, but not to everyone. This in part grew out of the sociologists' recognition that for centuries the prefix "ethno" had been used to refer to people, usually those defined as primitive or uncivilized. While the sociologists who coined the term in the 1940s, and those who followed them, did not use it for its reference to primitivity, they did use it to indicate the distinctiveness of those people who were considered to have ethnicity. That distinctiveness was measured against the dominant, mainstream group whose culture was assumed to be the same as the culture as a whole. In its modern form, as presented by the historians and sociologists who employed the term, "ethnicity" assumed that a community's stable, long-standing, and powerful core population – here, the New England Yankees – lacked ethnicity. Their behavior and values were one and the same as the basic practices and beliefs of the normative society. They constituted the society. They shaped the public agenda. Those who carried ethnic labels were different, subordinate, and of more recent origin to the place in question.

Those who had ethnicity as such were the "others." Indeed the statement made repeatedly by those who wrote and taught about ethnicity was that a group of people received its ethnicity only in relationship to its becoming an "other." The French in France, Italians in Italy, Japanese in Japan, the conventional assumption explicated, were not ethnic groups. They were merely the "people." But individuals from those places could be understood as having ethnicity when they migrated to Canada, Argentina, the United States, or any place where they stood out as different.

The *ethnos* in this sense are not the same as people in general, but people notable for having undergone a journey, almost always a geographic one, by which they achieved their alterity. This element of Warner and Lunt's neologism has been relatively enduring, at least until recently. The people whom they considered to have ethnicity had come to Newburyport from elsewhere, beyond the geopolitical boundaries of the United States. These were the women and men who had left Quebec, Ireland, Italy, Greece, and Poland to try to make a living in America. By coming to "Yankee City," they confronted a Protestant establishment of English origins which set the terms of the culture and dominated the economic, political, and social structure.

Therefore it was not surprising that sociologists like Warner and Lunt did not include in that category of ethnicity the relatively poor hard-scrabble white, Protestant, native-born women and men of New England who increasingly in the late nineteenth century could not succeed on their small farms. Unable to hold on to agriculture, the poor turned to the industrial cities of their region, including Newburyport, where they might find jobs and rebuild their homes. How that group saw itself in relationship to the powerful and wealthy power elite of Newburyport, Warner and Lunt did not explore. This set a key tone to the literature of ethnicity, which as a concept tended to involve people in the working class, however different the entities of ethnicity and class are. Over time scholars of ethnicity would pay some attention to ethnic elites, to those individuals within ethnic communities who had achieved some wealth and contacts in the larger society. They served as the ethnic communities' brokers and the intermediaries to the larger society.

This key element in the conventional use of the concept of ethnicity owed some of its intellectual underpinnings to the great debates in American society which, from the end of the nineteenth century onward, speculated about the meaning of the mass migration from Europe, which between 1880 and 1924 sent over 25 million people westward across the Atlantic. Americans concerned with the nature of civil society debated among themselves the implications of this tremendous, polyglot diversity and welter of loyalties (Higham 1963). Could the nation endure such differences, they wondered. Would immigrants and their children "become" American, and what did "becoming" American really mean? How might they best be molded into Americans? When the immigration from Europe was at its height, the term "ethnicity" did not as yet exist. Before its sociological coinage, such words as "race" and "nationality" implied a similar concept. Women and men had come to America speaking languages, subscribing to value systems, and behaving in particular ways that seemed to be alien to the prevailing patterns of communication, belief, and practice in America. They were women and men of other races and other nationalities.

That tidal wave of immigration not only stimulated public policy discussions, but also helped fundamentally to shape the emergence of the social sciences within the newly formed university system of the late nineteenth century. Sociology in particular owed much of its early history to the immigration crisis. In its first generation, such notable practitioners as Edward A. Ross, Ernest Burgess, Robert Park, and Louis Wirth explored the impact of American culture on the immigrants and their children, and the ways in which the newcomers structured communities in response to American conditions (Thomas 1921; Wirth 1928). Immigration, and what followed in its wake, loomed large as social problems, and early sociologists believed that they needed to be studied so that the US could cope better with them.

The nexus between the scholarship on the immigrants and the ranging policy debates about them focused on the question of exactly how much they differed from the "real" Americans and the depths to which the roots of those differences went. One segment of social scientists, represented by Ross of the University of Wisconsin, worked on the assumption that those differences were fundamentally inherent and ineradicable. Little could be done to change the basic, and inferior, temperaments of the Latins, Slavs, Semites, Celts, and other "types" who were inundating America. The Immigration Restriction League, founded in 1894 in Boston, echoed this sentiment. Some peoples were inherently unsuited for the republic because of the fixed nature of their defective characteristics. But Park and Wirth posited those differences as more superficial and as likely to become muted, because of the positive influence of the institutions of Americanization upon the children of the immigrants. In general the Chicago school of sociology aligned themselves, both intellectually and politically, with the settlement house movement and other agencies of benevolent assimilation (Steven J. Diner 1980).

The 1924 National Origins Act, complex though its legislative history was, favored the intellectual consensus of the former bloc. Differences were simply too great between the newcomers and a clearly understood entity defined as American culture.

Yet the restrictionists lost the intellectual battle. By the 1930s and 1940s, social scientists had almost entirely rejected the notion that culture and biology were linked variables. The emerging notion of ethnicity was understood as a matter of culture, which individuals had a great deal of power to shape. By the 1940s a new generation of sociologists was partly inspired by the Chicago school, and indeed Wirth himself continued to address this issue until his death in 1952. The new generation studied the immigrants and their children partly in reaction to the anti-immigrant paradigm of Ross. Their work emerged in tandem with the rise of mid-century liberalism, inspired by a deep revulsion against the racism that Nazism had thoroughly discredited. The idea of difference as inherent was demolished. Such social scientists rebelled against the theory that biology produced behavior, and against the notion that some people could never assimilate into the American mainstream because "nature" decreed them to remain what they were (Gossett 1963).

But in the process of de-racializing ethnicity, these scholars articulated a deep discomfort with talking about difference. Implicitly and explicitly, they identified obvious differences in behavior and beliefs as problems, which could not be of any value in and of themselves. When they focused on the ethnic communities of Newburyport and the other ethnic enclaves that were subjected to investigation, they did so as a way to understand the structural relationships between those in the center, the Yankees, and those on the periphery, the ethnics. Scholars asked a series of questions about how standing on the margins shaped access to jobs, influence, and power, and how the ethnic communities derived their characteristics from their relationships to those who dominated the larger community. Ethnicity as a bundle of beliefs, practices, and institutions had no inherent value to those who clung to it.

Ethnicity came to be the same as foreign birth or ancestry; and those who were understood by means of this term, had somehow to be "different" in part by virtue of having come from some place other than the United States. This in turn reflected one of the major paradigms in the study of ethnicity: the concept of culture. Ethnicity, as a subject of inquiry, assumed a tension between the universality of human needs, and place and time as specific ways of fulfilling them. The particular ways in which people satisfied basic needs, or culture, came to be objects of study for anthropologists from the turn of the century onwards. Anthropology also provided a core element in the concept of ethnicity. Taking their cue from Franz Boas, the father of American anthropology, and his students, such as Margaret Mead, Ruth Benedict, Ruth Bunzell, Robert Lowie, and their students in turn, scholars of ethnicity accepted the idea of "traditional" culture. What immigrants brought with them to the United States – their family ideals, food, language, education, religion, and work ethic – were seen as elements of a traditional cultural repertoire. Immigrants and their parents and grandparents and their great-grandparents, and beyond, to time immemorial, had always behaved and believed in particular ways.

Thus the stuff of the study of immigration and ethnicity involved the shock of transplantation, or – as the most important early historical works on the subject emphasized – uprootedness of those traditional patterns (Handlin 1941, 1951). Ethnicity as a field of inquiry rested on the question stated repeatedly, in different guises: how did traditional patterns of culture withstand the shocking move to a radically different environment? What if immigrants came from a place where, for example, children were viewed as economic assets, who participated in the toil of their family? When they arrived in America they found that its laws forbade child labor, and children were viewed as impressionable twigs, to be bent by the beneficent forces of education. What happened to the family system of groups who had traditionally viewed the normative parent–child relationship as based upon the deference and respect that the latter owed the former? In America children were expected to improve upon their parents' status, and were encouraged to do better. The idea of Oscar Handlin's 1951 classic, *The Uprooted*, emanated from the emotional crises generated by the inhospitality of the American soil to most of these traditional roots, however appropriate they had been to other places. The ethnic experience that Handlin so lyrically described involved the emotional turmoil and ultimate readjustment needed in order to narrow the gap between tradition and the New World.

Scholars of ethnicity of the earlier eras focused primarily on the first American-born generation, the children of the immigrants. This cohort of the population was understood to be the most torn between the world of traditional culture, as lived by immigrant parents, and that of American society. The immigrant generation had been mostly understood to have felt little connection to American institutions and to the native-born citizenry. As depicted in the scholarship, they lived out their lives in immigrant enclaves, learned little English, and worked in relatively homogeneous settings, where they rarely mixed with people different from themselves. The fact that many went back to their places of origin, or hoped to do so, made them less interesting to the scholars of ethnicity, who found the dilemma of marginality compelling. The immigrants did not in this context really have ethnicity. What they had was immigrant identities, a repertoire of practices and beliefs imported largely intact from abroad.

Studies of ethnicity rarely went beyond the first generation born in America either. Partly this resulted from timing. By the time the field of ethnic history (as distinct from sociology) took off, in the 1950s and 1960s in particular, those who were born in America from parents of the "great wave" were adults. They made up the majority of the ethnic communities. They represented those communities to the American public, but their children had not as yet constructed identities for themselves that could be studied. Nor did data from the US Census make it easy to determine nativity beyond that of one's parents. It was then virtually impossible to track the grandchildren and great-grandchildren of the immigrants. So the first American-born generation captured the scholarly imagination. Here were women and men who lived in two worlds, the immigrant cosmos of their parents and the American streets. Here were women and men who felt the tug-of-war between identities and the cross-pressures of institutions. The subjects of their academic inquiry were people who had a host of choices. They could be American *or* they could be Italian, *or* Greek, *or* Polish. How they negotiated between these loyalties and demands constituted the stuff of the scholarship of ethnicity.

Because of this fundamental interest in culture and its fate in the aftermath of immigration, students of ethnicity had a complicated relationship with the concept of social class. They understood that it and ethnicity were closely intertwined. Immigrants arrived relatively poor. Lacking appropriate skills, they were denied well-paying jobs. Being uncertain how to navigate a modern society, speaking little more than a broken English, kept them locked into the lower rungs of the economy. As long as the immigrants stayed at the bottom of the economic scale they had to depend on middlemen, whom scholars have usually depicted as unscrupulous political bosses or exploitative labor agents, such as the Italian *padrone* who made deals with the American elites. Analysts linked the upward mobility of the children of the uprooted to the gradual acquisition of insider's knowledge of America. The children did well economically in proportion to their exposure and education. As they moved closer to the middle class their need for intermediaries lessened. They could free themselves of the political machines that had thrived on their parents' marginality, poverty, and ignorance. In the process, movement into the middle class eroded the power of those who had dominated the communities. And by definition the communities lost their internal cohesion.

Until well into the 1970s the generations of social scientists and historians also tended to make "race" and "ethnicity" separate analytic categories. Scholars hoped to prove that the behavior of the ethnics was not biologically determined. Scholars of ethnicity who focused primarily on the children of the European immigrants were also fascinated by the choices that their subjects made. Because of their white skins, the newcomers had the potential to blend into the American mainstream. A change of name, an immersion course in manners, an unaccented English, a pew in a prestigious Protestant church – and the child of an impoverished Greek immigrant, for example, could "pass" as a New England Yankee, a southern gentleman, a midwestern native. Even when not seeking to escape the ethnic community completely, the option of sometimes acting like "ordinary" Americans, of being unidentifiable as a person whose family roots lay outside of North America, gave the children of European immigrants a set of formative experiences even when such anonymity was not entirely necessary.

Given the range of possibilities theoretically available to them, the immigrants' children, the bearers of ethnicity, involved themselves in the process of identity negotiation. They weighed and measured what to keep of their ancestral cultures and what to shed. They could reshape practices and institutions to their own tastes, and develop forms of behavior that allowed them to be "ethnic" in private but "typically" American in public. To the historians and sociologists of ethnicity this possibility differentiated them from African Americans, Chinese Americans, Japanese Americans, and Mexican Americans. However often nativists and bigots had portrayed Italians as "swarthy," Jews as "hook-nosed," or Irish as "simian," the offspring of the immigrants (as well as the immigrants themselves) from Palermo, Minsk, or County Clare always had the right to be naturalized, gain citizenship, hold office, and participate in the political process. The children of the immigrants from these places as well as from everywhere else in Europe understood that what was demanded of them in America was a cultural renegotiation rather than an (impossible) phenotypic remaking.

Scholars of ethnicity have by and large stood with Warner and Lunt in understanding the legacy of foreign birth as not only an important difference, but as a selective one. Warner and Lunt, plus the early scholars of ethnicity who followed in their wake, considered ethnicity to be different from the category of "race." Just as only those people who through their foreign ancestry stood out as different from the mainstream had "ethnicity," so too only blacks, Asians, Hispanic, and Native Americans had race, that is, recognizable, and stigmatized, physical characteristics, usually defined by skin color. The category of ethnicity made room for these Americans. But the fact that they were the bearers of phenotypical markers that "white" Americans disliked, or considered to be the signs of inferiority, complicated their ethnicity. Put simply, from the perspective of the literature on ethnicity, Italian Americans, Greek Americans, and Hungarian Americans could, with varying degrees of effort, disassociate from their ethnicity, and shed that first element of their identity. With a few idiosyncratic exceptions to the rule, those who had "race" could not. The larger, mainstream society would never let them forget who they were, should they have wanted. The profoundly embedded racism of the society made their identities less, or indeed never, negotiable.

But for the "ethnics" (a collective noun that seemed to have emerged in the late 1960s) identity always had a degree of choice. Early in the twentieth century, Robert Park had depicted the marginal man; and the pioneer immigration historian Marcus Hansen had echoed the Chicago sociologist's sense that ethnicity had within it some element of active consent on the part of those who want it. Park understood ethnicity (without using the word) as a border identity. The marginal man, the member of the ethnic community, stood with one foot in the American world and one foot in the ethnic one. He (or she) functioned simultaneously in the two worlds, or serially, and could be an American in the American setting, and an Italian (Greek, Jew, Pole, Norwegian) in the other. In 1937 Hansen proposed the "three generation" law. The immigrant, he wrote, is, or was, consumed with the details of survival, and practiced the details of the traditional culture in relatively automatic and uncomplicated ways. The newcomer lived within relatively limited ethnic enclaves and experienced few meaningful, or challenging, contacts with American society. The second generation on the other hand had ample opportunity to learn about the larger world, and yearned to become part of it. That generation functioned as a liminal one, which sought to shed much of the parental baggage, and to forget practices that highlighted the distance between it and the American mainstream. Only in the third generation, Hansen asserted, was the value of memory reasserted; the grandchildren of the immigrants sought to relearn and to revive what had been surrendered (Hansen 1940).

Both of these formative ideas assumed volition. Hansen's child of the immigrant can, at will, choose to forget. The grandchild, on the other hand, has the option of recreating. Park's marginal man derived some level of his angst from the fact that he could slip in and out of the two worlds. Either way, and unlike the minorities stigmatized by their physical characteristics, ethnic identity involved an active process in which individuals could largely chart their paths. Not so those whom social scientists depicted as having race, rather than ethnicity. Regardless of the polish of their English, the reserve of their manners, or the depths of their roots on American soil, African Americans, Native Americans, and Hispanics of the Southwest endured civil liabilities because of their ineffaceable physical characteristics. By congressional legislation, the Chinese were even specifically excluded from ever immigrating to the United States after the 1870s; and their physiognomy, like that of the Japanese and other Asians, could not be subjected to a learning process that might eliminate stigmas. The element of volition informs early scholarship on ethnicity. Once on American soil, all immigrants and certainly their children *chose* to maintain affiliations, loyalties, and practices that set them apart from native-born whites. How and why new Americans chose what they did offers us the core of the body of research and writing on ethnicity.

Moreover, much of what constituted the practice of ethnicity occurred in a realm of life that was understood by scholars to be private. Ethnicity involved family ritual, food in particular, but also intimate relations between spouses and between parents and children. Much of ethnicity played itself out in voluntary associations and in the sanctity of religion and religious practice, two areas of American life that not only took place behind closed doors, but that the state had no interest in and that much of the general public knew nothing about. Language loyalties were variably maintained in private institutions such as homes, places of worship, parochial schools, ethnic theaters, and other sites of sociability.

Ethnicity was also manifested in civic life, however. Scholars, like office-seekers, recognized the existence of ethnic voting patterns. Leading political scientists defined politics in terms of group interest, and described it as a constant jockeying within the society for "who gets what, where, when, and how," in V. O. Key's definition of politics. The divergences of Italians, Greeks, Jews, and the Irish in their voting patterns were an expression of ethnic distinctiveness, to be taken into account along with differences of age, gender, region, and occupation. That various ethnic groups met under the tent of the two parties, and wheeled and dealed for patronage and influence, made sense in light of the mid-century academic analyses of consensus politics (Key 1942; Dahl 1965).

The first serious challenge to ethnicity studies as shaped by sociologists like Warner and Lunt came in the form of the emergence of ethnic history in the 1960s. This shift, which proclaimed the positive value of difference, had several origins. Set amidst the cultural criticism of the 1960s and the civil rights movement, scholars of ethnicity, particularly historians, took up the study of immigration and the fate of immigrant cultures in America. The evolution of ethnic history in this decade was facilitated by two specific but related political phenomena. First, in 1965 Congress emended the immigration legislation that since 1924 had divided the world into racial zones. The earlier and hated system set quotas based on national origins. The new one eliminated the previous invidious distinctions and instituted a system that encouraged family reunification and assigned quotas on the basis of jobs and skills. This legislative change itself had several consequences. Initially it unleashed a new wave of immigration from a number of countries that had sent large numbers of immigrants before 1924, but that had suffered from severely low quotas, particularly Italy, Greece, Poland, and Portugal. Secondly, beginning in the early 1970s, immigrants began to flood to America from places that heretofore had not been represented in the American "mosaic," particularly places in Asia, the Middle East, Africa, and the Americas. Immigration historians had before their eyes the living examples of the processes of migration, settlement, social adaptation, and the shaping of cultures.

The passage of the 1965 legislation, as part of the civil rights juggernaut, also represented the legitimization of difference. While its impact upon most ethnics may have been largely symbolic, the legislation rode the cultural wave that made it possible, indeed affirmative, for Americans to talk about who they were, where they – metaphorically – had come from, and how those roots made them unique and unlike the American mainstream. This played itself out in the ethnic revival of the 1960s, when women and men of one ethnic community after another involved themselves in the recreation (or, more accurately, the creation) of ethnic cultural institutions and practices. Particularly in artistic expression and in the open displays of group pride, the "ethnics" publicly and exuberantly announced their distinctiveness.

In the public presentation of the humanities, the subject of ethnicity became prominent. In 1976, as part of the Bicentennial of the United States the Smithsonian Institution's National Museum of American History, with the cooperation of a team of ethnic historians, opened the long-running exhibit, "A Nation of Nations: The People Who Came to America." In the years following the centennial of the Statue of Liberty in 1992 and the opening of a museum at the major immigrant receiving station, Ellis Island, the ethnic experience was enshrined as one of the nation's most hallowed characteristics.

The historians who helped make these public ventures possible and who wrote the key works that informed the study of ethnicity reflected the public mood in their scholarship. In the paradigm of this era, they depicted ethnicity as a constant in American history. Everywhere immigrants settled, they recreated the worlds of "back home." This act of recreation, they asserted, could only be understood by producing a body of literature on a group-by-group basis. Many, although not all, of the historians were themselves the products of ethnic communities. The children and grandchildren of the immigrants who came of age in the middle of the twentieth century had received their American education in the 1960s, and entered the academy in the 1970s, when the public culture privileged difference. That new ethos increasingly sanctioned behavior and attitudes that departed from earlier efforts at consensus. Nor did the academic enterprise itself force scholars to shy away from focusing on issues close to their own experiences and emotions. Indeed the general assumption was that insider status conferred upon the scholar a level of knowledge and a depth of understanding unobtainable by the outsider who had to learn the ethnic repertoire from the ground up. The idea of scholars studying their own groups and heritages had been nearly unthinkable in an earlier generation, which had been suspicious of dangerously subjective ethnic explorations. There had been one notable exception, in that descendants of the native-born white Protestant elite could certainly study their heritage without being accused of parochialism and bias.

The late 1960s pushed the historical enterprise beyond such boundaries. Historians interested in ethnicity benefited from not only the greater openness of American culture, but from the growth of the sub-field of social history, whose youngest practitioners asserted that history ought in part be written from "the bottom up." More specifically a whole generation of historians who began their careers in the late 1960s took their cues from the monumental work of British historian E. P. Thompson, whose 1963 book, *The Making of the English Working Class*, introduced the concept of "agency." Human beings, including slaves, industrial workers – or immigrants and their children – were not just mere victims of mammoth social forces. However much oppression was inflicted by those who exercised obvious power, ordinary people had the ability – the agency – to shape their own lives, circumstances, and cultural products. History was not just about what happened to the poor and how the powerless endured, but also how they resisted and adapted, and how they gained power for themselves.

In this cultural moment, as shaped by the turmoil on the streets and the new paradigm in the scholarship, ethnicity emerged as a radically different construct.

While it was still posited as a phenomenon that resulted from migration from abroad, and remained relatively locked into discussions of European immigrants, increasingly newer groups were folded into the study of ethnicity. Mexicans, Puerto Ricans, Central Americans, Chinese, and Japanese Americans started appearing as the subjects of inquiry in the field of ethnic history. Indeed, with a degree of trepidation, historians of ethnicity began to include under their intellectual aegis the experiences of the descendants of native peoples and more importantly, the descendants of forced migrants. The trepidation came from two sources. Not only did black history emerge at exactly this moment as a separate, and significantly larger field of study; but also neither of these two groups had chosen migration to America. Historians of ethnicity were still focused on the voluntary nature of the migrations and the contingent nature of identities. No wonder that experiences of forced migration, extirpation, and colonization so vastly complicated their histories. But those scholars who used the concept of ethnicity as the core of their work found ways to broaden the scope of their endeavor. For example, they began to write about the migration of southern blacks to the urban North as fitting the immigration-ethnic paradigm. They looked at black institution-building in the cities as analogous to the process among immigrants and their children.

Students of ethnicity still maintained assumptions about the voluntary nature of ethnic identities. Ethnicity emerged from transplantation, from culture contact, and from the decision of immigrants to leave one place and settle elsewhere. Ethnicity, and the migrations that produced it, grew out of choice; and within those terms historians found ways to talk about African Americans after emancipation, after they left the plantations. As a category of analysis, ethnicity also served as the immigrants' tool of resistance against the encroachment of a threatening and powerful national culture. The immigrants did not just react to the power of established cultural elites, according to scholars of the Italians (Yans-McLaughlin 1977), of the Romanians and Slavs (Barton 1975); of the Germans (Conzen 1976); of the Cape Verdeans (Halter 1993); and of the Jews (Hasia R. Diner 1977) and the Irish (Hasia R. Diner 1983). Such minorities constructed their own priorities, picking and choosing among the new options at their disposal and the elements of their traditional repertoire. The products of those negotiations led to the creation of particular communal institutions which the immigrants and their progeny wanted. The structure of their communities and the elements of their subcultures grew out of their own preferences and did not merely bear the impress of the native-born elites who had exercised hegemony.

The period from the middle of the 1960s through the end of the 1980s represented a kind of golden age for the study of ethnicity. Universities and history departments recognized it as a legitimate subject of inquiry, and began to hire professors who defined their specialty as "ethnicity." Sometimes they broadened the label to "immigration and ethnicity." Likewise the panels of professional historical associations, like the American Historical Association and the Organization of American Historians, began to showcase at their annual meetings individual papers and panels on immigration and ethnicity. Yet even when scholars defined themselves as students of both immigration and ethnicity, or included in the titles of their courses both analytic categories, ethnicity elicited greater interest than immigration – which was a given. People became ethnics as a result of migration from one place to another. But in fact the real source of the historians' interest and inspiration was the later phase of the process:

how immigrants became ethnics. Limited pedagogical and scholarly attention was paid to the motives for immigration, and a fleeting glance was given to the migration process itself. But what was most dear to scholars was the actual transplantation of various foreign cultures, the creation of ethnic communities in the United States.

Without attending much to the conceptual implications of ethnicity, scholars launched a mighty enterprise of research and writing. They wrote about the Irish in Butte, the Poles in Johnstown, Mexicans in Los Angeles, French Canadians in Manchester, Italians in Buffalo, Jews in New York, Norwegians in Minnesota, Germans in Milwaukee, Chinese in San Francisco, and so forth. Historians studied the housing patterns, work experiences, political encounters, and cultural works of these ethnic groups – and many more – throughout the nation. Every one of these studies operated on the assumption, as in the earlier paradigm, that the immigrant and ethnic cultures were one and the same, with some minor fine-tuning to accommodate the national setting. The immigrants arrived with "baggage"; and among the feather beds, copper pots, and straw suitcases were ideas fixed in the ageless past about language, family, religion, and authority, plus a set of rituals that permeated life. Once settled in their tenements, cottages, or sod-huts on the prairie, they opened up their baggage and recreated traditional practices, without so much as missing a beat.

What was contained in those pots or suitcases was, however, finite. At some point, in the third generation, possibly a bit later than that, the traditional resources, the stuff in the baggage, would be spent. Only something unforeseen, like a new and sizable influx of immigrants from the same place, could replenish the ethnic pot. Therefore ethnicity and immigrant status, or ethnic culture and immigrant culture, were posited as the same. Because of this notion that ethnicity stood as the American variant of some transplanted culture, scholars confronted the dilemma of the vibrant mid-twentieth-century manifestations of ethnic identity. If, as historians asserted, the immigrants brought intact cultures which over time lost their salience, how was persistence to be evaluated? In 1979 sociologist Herbert Gans dubbed such remnants "symbolic ethnicity" (Gans 1979; Alba 1990). This presumably differed from what had once been present; its opposite was an ethnicity that was real or concrete. Indeed much of the scholarly writing about the behavior and cultural artifacts of the second and third generations tended to dismiss their ethnicity, to see it as lacking authenticity, as shallow and derivative.

In this period, from the 1960s through the end of the 1980s, some of the key texts of the field were nevertheless written; and key institutions were founded. In 1965 a group of social historians, including Rudolph Vecoli and Philip Gleason, formed the Immigration History Society. Its purpose was to promote understanding of the history of immigration to North America from elsewhere in the world, to heighten appreciation of the role of various ethnic minorities in the United States, and to enhance the status of immigration-ethnic history itself. In 1980 this society launched the publication of its journal, the *Journal of American Ethnic History*. In that same year the *Harvard Encyclopedia of American Ethnic Groups*, edited by Stephan Thernstrom and Ann Orlov, was published, and became canonical. This compendium of information largely defined ethnicity. In 1983 the Immigration History Society created the Theodore Saloutos Prize, an award for the outstanding book in the field, further testifying to the growth in the size of the profession, and the stature of the enterprise.

In 1985 John Bodnar published *The Transplanted*. Subtitled *A History of Immigrants in Urban America*, it was nevertheless, like the sub-field as a whole, really more about ethnicity than about immigration. The heart of Bodnar's narrative lay in what took place in America, as immigrants and their children built institutions to suit their needs, or transformed existing ones, in order to accommodate their particular concerns. *The Transplanted* stood as a culmination of a challenge, running several decades, to the idea of ethnicity as articulated in the "Yankee City" series, and in Handlin's *The Uprooted*. Bodnar's ethnic Americans, whoever they were and regardless of where they lived, were creators of their subculture and agents of their own communal life, not passive and dislocated victims, as the earlier paradigm suggested.

The Transplanted contained within it a concept which would ultimately serve as a stepping stone to the next paradigm of ethnicity. Like Barton before him, Bodnar challenged the notion that what immigrants brought to America was indeed "traditional" culture. Rather, migrations occurred in the context of modernization, and the women and men who migrated had already been involved in a complex process of cultural renegotiation. Indeed the very act of migration represented innovation, Bodnar said. *The Transplanted* amply proved that immigrants ought not to be thought of as traditional people relocated to new spaces. By describing immigrants as modern people who created cultures, Bodnar's book challenged the prevailing orthodoxy of the field. If they recreated themselves once before migration, and then again in America, there was essentially no limit to how often and how many ways they switched identities and rebuilt institutions. According to *The Transplanted* and to the emerging paradigm of the sub-field, all of ethnicity was symbolic; all of it entailed a degree of invention. Virtually all of the institutions of these communities were new: ethnic newspapers, ethnic social clubs, ethnic benevolent associations, ethnic theaters, even ethnic food. The religious practices of the immigrants and their children also were not, and could not be, the exact replication of the sacred rituals of ancestral homes.

Indeed even the very terms used to label and categorize people, "Italian," "Polish," "Czech," "Mexican" were recent inventions. The immigrants had come from specific towns, villages, and regions, and defined themselves as denizens of these units. Loyalties, at least initially, focused on these local and specific places. Over time, however, back home changed, and underwent the process of nation-formation. As the newcomers interacted in America with others from different parts of that same "nation," they redefined their identities, and began to subscribe to new, nationally charged allegiances. A group of immigrants from a village in Calabria maintained, before migration, a deep sense of themselves as the sons and daughters of that town. They may have maintained some social relations with individuals in neighboring towns. By the end of the nineteenth century, however, while the migration was in process, villagers came increasingly under the influence of the state; and the concept "Italy" as a larger entity began to inform their lives and identities. In America, however, they went through two encounters that shaped the emergence of Italian ethnicity. They lived in enclaves made up of Neapolitans, Sicilians, and Abruzzians, and others who seemed more like the Calabrians of back home, than did the other peoples they were meeting in America. In the cities of the United States, Eastern European Jews lived near the former Calabrian villagers, while Polish, German, and Irish Americans, with whom they may have interacted through the Catholic Church were rivals for institutional control. In such encounters the immigrants from the Calabrian village went through the process of renegotiating their identities, and became comfortable with the idea of being Italian. They defined themselves as Italians, to distinguish themselves from the Jews, Poles, Germans, Irish, and other American strangers around them.

Certainly ethnic practices and institutions founded in America, and the loyalties forged there as well, could be traced to pre-migration experiences. But they were products of constant change and constant elaboration. This theme emerged repeatedly in the scholarly literature. Consider, for example, one monograph on the many incarnations of a particular devotional practice associated with a group of Genoese immigrants to Italian Harlem. While the Madonna, Our Lady of Carmel, remained the same, the ways she was venerated, the reasons for the veneration, and the implications for the participants in the act changed over time. Those changes were part of a dynamic process of cultural invention (Orsi 1985).

As ethnicity moved from a fixed entity and shifted to a constantly evolving product of fusion, groups once thought to lack ethnicity were increasingly brought under its rubric. In this process two works were decisive. Sarah Deutsch studied Hispanics in the Southwest who had once been almost exclusively the only occupants of a broad swath of territory. International politics, particularly the vast expansion of the United States into land once owned by Mexico, as well as the exploitation of that land for new commercial purposes, transformed these women and men into members of an ethnic group, without the journey across an ocean, or a movement across a border. They stayed put. The border changed. And in the process they became "others" (Deutsch 1987). Likewise David Hackett Fischer's *Albion's Seed* examined the British immigrants of the seventeenth and eighteenth centuries, the original white settlers of what would become the United States. Here too, a group once assumed to have a singular culture that would over time come to be synonymous with American culture manifested many idiosyncratic patterns, shaped by the counties in England where they had originated. Fischer's immigrants became America's first ethnics. Wherever they settled, whether in New England, the middle colonies, the back country, or the southern piedmont, they transplanted the housing stock, the foodways, and other social patterns of the English regions from which they had come (Fischer 1989). Deutsch and Fischer dramatically enlarged the category of who might be an ethnic.

In their work, and much of the other scholarship of the 1980s, the emphasis shifted to the process of creating ethnic consciousness. The word "ethnicity" came to be replaced, or used alternatively, with "ethnicization." This neologism has replaced older terms like "Americanization" and "acculturation," and refers to the various ways in which the immigrants set upon the process of creating cultural forms, so that "old" world tropes were blended with novelties in the United States. To "ethnicize" a practice meant, for example, to adapt, invent, and adjust practices to the American situation (Morawska 1985, 1996). The implications for the study of ethnicity were startling. If, as Bodnar asserted, the newcomers to America were constantly creating and recreating forms of behavior and structures of values, then the whole edifice of ethnicity needed to be reinvestigated. That scholarly enterprise had assumed a finite repertoire, which had been transmitted in America in place and then had lessened. But the idea of the construction of ethnicity implied the possibility of infinite iterations, and it launched the idea of ethnicity as invention. Ethnicity was re-conceived: a fixed identity that weakened over time became a constantly evolving, boundless invention. A given, a fact of culture, became something amorphous and constructed. It was, by the late 1980s, no longer reified. It ceased to be recognizable as an entity at all. Like other categories such as gender, race, and even nationality, ethnicity became a process, and at the same time a project (Sollors 1986; Waters 1990).

The earlier paradigm of ethnicity scholarship had emerged out of a confluence of political and cultural forces and changing orthodoxies in the academy. The latest mode is indebted to forces that are both internal to the academy and outside of it. Postmodernism and poststructuralism, for example, both questioned the previously fixed boundaries of scholarly categories. If previously scholars had felt comfortable labelling some identities as "ethnic" and others as something else, postmodernism challenged analysts to defend – or, preferably, reject – those labels. Historians began to think of geographic locations as borderlands, where multiple peoples interacted with each other, influenced each other, and in the process invented new identities.

The political climate of the end of the twentieth century also profoundly affected how scholars thought about ethnicity, and about the general use of the concept. As American society has struggled with the enduring burden of past (and indeed present) discrimination based on color, policies were devised to level out the playing field and to foster greater equality. Affirmative action, which has meant preferences in hiring, contracting, and admission to universities and professional schools, has been instituted in order to ensure that African Americans, Hispanic Americans, Native Americans, and sometimes Asian Americans get a chance to compete in the quest for economic resources and professional access. Universities have likewise created, often in response to student pressure, programs or departments of "ethnic studies." These academic programs have been intended to broaden the canon and enrich the base of knowledge which universities transmit to their students. A comfortable niche was also intended to be provided in the universities for groups which had previously been underrepresented and understudied in the academy.

In the 1990s ethnic studies programs rarely studied, nor did they include, the experiences of European immigrants. Immigrants from, say, Italy, Norway, Ireland, Poland, and Greece, and their descendants, were labelled either "Euro-American" or just plain "white folks." Their histories have appeared as examples of multiculturalism only when they were "racialized," that is, oppressed as members of a despised and physically identifiable group. A number of books at this time asked how European immigrants "became" white, and how they used the privilege of skin color to participate in the exploitation of African Americans. Those who identified with specific European heritages, and with their immigrant ancestors, were analytically expelled from the ethnic fold.

These programs and social policies have focused on the experience of America's blacks, Latinos (sometimes labelled Hispanics), Asians, and native peoples. This iteration of the category "ethnicity" has in part stemmed from problems associated with another category: "race." Ethnicity carried with it the emphasis on culture and its artifacts, while a term such as "race" carries with it the burden of thinking about physical type and biology. Yet such programs emphasize and celebrate cultures, therefore making ethnicity an appealing term to use. Likewise, people from Latin America cannot be said to constitute a race. They have no phenotypical characteristics which have united them, and marked them off, as a group. If anything does, it has been language. But that is itself a problem. If preference categories specified language as a determinant for inclusion into the group "Hispanic," then what would happen to those individuals who were native speakers of English, but who are the children and grandchildren of immigrants from Spanish-speaking countries? Immigrants from Brazil do not even speak Spanish, yet are lumped with immigrants from the Dominican Republic and Honduras as "Hispanic." No wonder that Franz Boas, at the beginning of the twentieth century, argued that all racial categories were inventions, without any basis in scientific fact. The many people, he declared, whom the law put into a single racial category, had as much that separated them from one another, as they did between themselves and the people who were inserted into some other typological box.

So the term "ethnicity" has come to be widely used to refer not to many, or all, the national origins represented within the American population, and not to the range of cultural differences – past or present – that have been exhibited in America. In the common encounters that many Americans have with this term, whether on US Census forms, or on papers in the workplace and at school, or in the ethnic studies programs at colleges and universities, ethnicity refers to identification with, and self-inclusion into, those minority groups that bore the fiercest brunt of racism. Those who are neither "African American," "Asian American," "Native American," nor "Hispanic American" must check a box labelled "White."

By the end of the twentieth century, there was certainly a degree of irony in the evolution of the concept of ethnicity. What was coined and constructed to de-racialize the way that scholars and the general public understood the experience of the millions of people who had chosen to immigrate and to create new lives in the United States, has come to be rejoined to a concern with color and color difference. What was coined and elaborated upon to identify the cultural works and processes of identity formation of people who had made a dramatic geographic journey and then experienced a complex cultural journey to becoming Americans, came to be removed from the context of culture. Those women and men whose lives spawned to the concept "ethnicity" seem to be in the process of losing their connection to it.

REFERENCES

Alba, Richard (1990) *Ethnic Identity: The Transformation of White America*. New Haven, Conn.: Yale University Press.

Barton, Josef (1975) *Peasants and Strangers: Italians, Rumanians, and Slovaks in an American City, 1890–1950*. Cambridge, Mass.: Harvard University Press.

Bodnar, John (1985) *The Transplanted: A History of Immigrants in Urban America*. Bloomington: Indiana University Press.

Conzen, Kathleen N. (1976) *Immigrant Milwaukee, 1836–1860*. Cambridge, Mass.: Harvard University Press.

Dahl, Robert (1965) *Who Governs?: Democracy and Power in an American City*. New Haven, Conn.: Yale University Press.

Deutsch, Sarah (1987) *No Separate Refuge: Culture, Class, and Gender on an Anglo-Hispanic Frontier in the American Southwest, 1880–1940*. New York: Oxford University Press.

Diner, Hasia R. (1977) *In the Almost Promised Land: American Jews and Blacks, 1915–1935*. Westport, Conn.: Greenwood Press.

—— (1983) *Erin's Daughters in America: Irish Immigrant Women in the Nineteenth Century.* Baltimore, Md.: Johns Hopkins University Press.

Diner, Steven J. (1980) *A City and its Universities: Public Policy in Chicago, 1892–1919.* Chapel Hill: University of North Carolina Press.

Fischer, David Hackett (1989) *Albion's Seed: Four British Folkways in America.* New York: Oxford University Press.

Gans, Herbert J. (1979) "Symbolic ethnicity in America," *Ethnic and Racial Studies* 2, pp. 1–20.

Gossett, Thomas (1963) *Race: The History of an Idea in America.* Dallas: Southern Methodist University Press.

Halter, Marilyn (1993) *Between Race and Ethnicity: Cape Verdean American Immigrants, 1860–1965.* Urbana: University of Illinois Press.

Handlin, Oscar (1941) *Boston's Immigrants, 1790–1865: A Study in Acculturation.* Cambridge, Mass.: Harvard University Press.

—— (1951) *The Uprooted: The Epic Story of the Great Migrations that Made the American People.* Boston: Little, Brown.

Hansen, Marcus Lee (1940) *The Immigrant in American History.* Cambridge, Mass.: Harvard University Press.

Higham, John (1963) *Strangers in the Land: Patterns of American Nativism, 1860–1925.* New York: Atheneum.

Key, V. O. (1942) *Politics, Parties, and Pressure Groups.* New York: T. Y. Crowell.

Morawska, Ewa (1985) *For Bread with Butter: The Life-Worlds of East Central Europeans in Johnstown, Pennsylvania, 1890–1940.* Cambridge: Cambridge University Press.

—— (1996) *Insecure Prosperity: Small-Town Jews in Industrial America, 1890–1940.* Princeton, NJ: Princeton University Press.

Orsi, Robert A. (1985) *The Madonna of 115th Street: Faith and Community in Italian Harlem, 1880–1950.* New Haven, Conn.: Yale University Press.

Sollors, Werner (1986) *Beyond Ethnicity: Consent and Descent in American Culture.* New York: Oxford University Press.

Thomas, W. I. (1921) *Old World Traits Transplanted.* New York: Harper and Brothers.

Warner, W. Lloyd and Lunt, Paul S. (1941) *The Social Life of a Modern Community.* New Haven, Conn.: Yale University Press.

Waters, Mary (1990) *Ethnic Options: Choosing Identities in America.* Berkeley: University of California Press.

Wirth, Louis (1928) *The Ghetto.* Chicago: University of Chicago Press.

Yans-McLaughlin, Virginia (1977) *Family and Community: Italian Immigrants in Buffalo, 1880–1930.* Ithaca, NY: Cornell University Press.

CHAPTER FIFTEEN

Labor

JOSEPH A. McCARTIN

In the twentieth century both the lives of US workers and the nature of their work changed spectacularly. As the century began, more than 40 percent of Americans still labored on the land; by the end of the century that number had shrunk to less than 3 percent. As the century began, industry was in the midst of an economic transformation ushered in by electrical power, the internal combustion engine, and the formation of vast, integrated corporations that came to dominate critical sectors of the domestic economy. By the century's end, the manufacturing sector had been supplanted by the service and information technology sectors. The computer, the Internet, and expanding international markets were refashioning the economy. And conglomerates that spanned several sectors of the economy and exercised truly global reach had all but completely replaced the old manufacturing goliaths as the economy's driving engines. As the century began, non-agricultural wage workers were overwhelmingly white and traced their ethnic origins to Europe. By the century's end, government estimates indicated that 23.6 percent of the work force was African American or Hispanic; and the number of Asian workers was rising rapidly, owing to immigration reforms enacted in the 1960s.

Despite these discontinuities, however, certain trends proved stubbornly persistent over the course of the century. At the end of the twentieth century, as at its beginning, economic booms distributed their fruits unequally. The well-being of workers greatly depended upon their race and national origin; belief in the beneficence of the free market dominated political debate; unions struggled to retain their tenuous holds in sectors of the economy transformed by new technologies; and no national consensus existed regarding the proper basis of labor relations.

Like the history of labor over this past century, interpretations of that experience have been marked by continuities and discontinuities. The most evident caesura in the historiography of American labor arose in the late 1960s and early 1970s. A young cohort of scholars, including David Brody, Melvyn Dubofsky, Herbert G. Gutman, and David Montgomery, then broke with the focus on unions and collective bargaining. That emphasis had defined labor history since its origins, during the Progressive Era, in economics departments that were under the influence of the University of Wisconsin's John R. Commons and his students. The "new labor historians" broke with the "Commons school" in both subject and interpretation. The revisionists attempted to understand the unorganized as well as organized labor, and gave greater attention to changing work processes as well as to the cultures and communities of workers. Some of these historians also broke with the assumption of the Commons school that US labor was destined from the beginning to integrate itself into industrial capitalism rather than to challenge any of its basic premises. Though the revisionists expanded their research beyond the realm of unions and collective bargaining, and discarded the ideological commitments of the Commons school, the new labor historians nevertheless confirmed their predecessors' belief that the collective struggles of workers were central to a proper understanding of the changing shape of labor and production in the twentieth century.

The Nineteenth-century Inheritance

One of the most important contributions of scholarship in the late twentieth century has been the attention that it has given to the ways in which nineteenth-century developments shaped labor in the following century. Three areas in particular elicited historians' attention: the ways in which the working class took shape; the role that government played in labor relations; and the organization, membership, and orientation that the labor movement took.

The formation of the working class took place under conditions made unique by the entry of unprecedented numbers of immigrants into a work force deeply divided along racial lines. A population explosion, poor agricultural conditions, and political turmoil in Europe – combined with industrial growth, western geographical expansion, and the establishment of millions of new farmsteads in America – drew more than 17 million European immigrants between 1820 and 1900. At the same time, the failure of Reconstruction after the Civil War resulted in the entrapment of millions of former slaves in debt peonage in the cotton culture of the South. As the century began, more than two-thirds of the nation's 10 million African Americans lived under oppressive conditions as sharecroppers or tenant farmers. And blacks who did hold skilled jobs lost ground as white workers fought to replace them. Other non-whites also fared poorly. In 1882 the US Congress passed the first of a series of acts excluding Chinese immigrants; fewer than 370,000 Asian workers entered the United States in the nineteenth century. The result was that, by 1900, white workers of European heritage dominated industrial jobs, racializing the process of class formation in ways that held profound and lasting significance.

The role that government played in labor relations early in the twentieth century was also rooted in trends set in the previous century. Workers enjoyed no legally recognized right to join trade unions, which operated under precarious legal status; and their activities, particularly strikes, were frequently limited by judicial injunctions. The Supreme Court almost always ruled against the interests of workers. *In re Debs* (1895), for example, upheld an injunction issued under the Sherman Antitrust Act that subverted the Pullman strike, which Eugene V. Debs of the American Railway Union led. Nor did unions receive better treatment from the executive branch of the federal government. US troops were called out against strikers on a number of occasions in the late nineteenth century, from the Great Railroad Strike of 1877 to the bitter 1892 strike of miners at Coeur d'Alene, Idaho.

Historians now argue that the unfavorable legal and political climate in which unions organized in the late nineteenth century had much to do with the craft union structure, exclusive membership, and the "pure-and-simple" business union approach of the labor movement at the turn of the century, which focused narrowly on achieving better wages, hours, and working conditions. In the mid-1880s a different sort of labor movement had seemed possible. Founded in 1869, the Noble and Holy Order of the Knights of Labor became the dominant organization of workers. The Knights sought to organize nearly all wage workers: skilled and unskilled, black and white, men and women. By the mid-1880s, after a strike victory over the railroad interests of Jay Gould, the Knights may have had as many as 750,000 members. But the Knights soon fell victim to internal factionalism, failed political initiatives, and staunch employer opposition, which the courts fortified.

By the mid-1890s the Knights had been eclipsed by the American Federation of Labor (AFL). This craft union federation, founded in 1886, was headed by Samuel Gompers, an immigrant cigar maker. A shrewd and pragmatic leader, he headed the AFL for all but one of its first 38 years. The federation over which Gompers presided was dominated by craft unions, which limited workers' entrance into their trades, charged high initiation fees and monthly dues, and – because of their members' scarce skills – conducted strikes more effectively than prior labor organizations had managed to do. When the economy revived after the depression of 1893–7, craft unions enjoyed explosive growth, rising from approximately 350,000 members in 1897 to more than 2 million by 1904. Yet craft unions never enrolled more than 10 percent of the total industrial work force prior to World War I. Organized labor also lost ground quickly in industries in which new technologies made craft production obsolete and in which massive corporations easily rebuffed union challenges. That was the fate of labor organizing in steel, auto, and electrical manufacturing.

Where they were organized, however, AFL craft unions exerted a great degree of control over work processes and production. Craft unionists sought to buttress that control by seeking limits on immigration and by opposing production methods that would improve productivity at the cost of jobs. Most AFL unions effectively banned blacks from membership. (The United Mine Workers of America was the chief exception to this rule.) And male craft unionists sought a "living wage" that would allow women to remain at home to be supported by their husbands, fathers, and brothers. While ensuring that the AFL would represent only a minority of workers, such practices also help explain why AFL-style "business unionism" survived economic downturns and employer opposition in the early twentieth century.

The Progressive Era

Recent interpretations have tended to see the period immediately before World War I as crucial to the formation of both modern labor and management. New technologies, mass production, and the advent of scientific management mixed with political reform, the arrival of millions of immigrants, and an upsurge in radicalism combined to create explosive conflicts that would influence the course of labor and industry for decades.

The assembly line introduced at Henry Ford's Highland Park plant in 1913 was only one of several developments that were redefining production in the Progressive

Era. By 1910 the "scientific management" theories of consultant Frederick Winslow Taylor were being disseminated widely among manufacturers. Although few adopted Taylor's ideas in their entirety, a growing number of employers introduced new techniques, including time-and-motion study, differential piece rates, and the "dilution" of skilled workers' jobs (which allowed semi-skilled workers to perform tasks that were once reserved for craftsmen). Increasingly employers could turn to immigrants to fill their growing need for less skilled labor.

The surge of immigration during this period was dramatic. An average of over one million arrivals disembarked annually between 1900 and the outbreak of World War I in Europe in 1914. Significantly, roughly 62 percent of those arriving between 1900 and 1920 came from Italy, the Austro-Hungarian empire, Russia, and the Baltic states. These regions far outdid western Europe as a source for new arrivals. Many of these "greenhorns" arrived in industrial America directly from peasant societies. Whether or not they were familiar with industrial labor and trade unionism, however, these new Americans were not easily assimilated into a union movement that focused on organizing skilled workers and that fought to limit further immigration. Yet immigrants translated their own native traditions of militancy into American labor organizations, most effectively in the garment trades unions. In the International Ladies Garment Workers Union (ILGWU) and the Amalgamated Clothing Workers of America (ACWA), Jewish and Italian immigrants played the leading roles. In 1909, thousands of immigrant women in New York's sweated garment trades staged an effective strike (the "Uprising of the Twenty Thousand") through the ILGWU. Overwhelmingly, however, the new immigrants who entered mines and mills learned that unions feared them as competition with native-born workers, instead of recognizing them as potential recruits.

The task of assimilating immigrants into mainstream culture was but one part of the "labor question" that was a central concern of the middle-class reformers known as "Progressives." They were also deeply troubled by the level of labor violence that erupted in the prewar period. That violence began to escalate after 1903, when the National Association of Manufacturers (founded in 1895) launched an attack on unions. Its aim was to achieve what employers called the "open shop," a workplace not governed by union contracts, so that employers could hire or dismiss workers freely without respect to union membership. (In practice, "open shops" did not tolerate union sympathizers.) Employers used labor spies, blacklists, and "yellow-dog contracts" (in which workers signed away their right to join a union as a condition of employment). By such means the AFL's growth between 1905 and 1910 was halted. Bitter conflicts erupted periodically between 1910 and 1917. Perhaps the most infamous occurred in 1914, when militiamen gunned down striking coal miners in the vicinity of Ludlow, Colorado, torching a tent village where they and their families had taken refuge.

The explosive conflicts touched off by the reorganization of production and the struggle of unions to hold on to their limited power sparked a series of government investigations of the labor problem in this period. Beginning with the US Industrial Commission (created in 1898) and concluding with the US Commission on Industrial Relations (1913–15), investigations probed the sources of labor violence. But no consensus emerged to resolve these conflicts. When unions did win legislative protection during this period, as in the clause banning the yellow-dog contract on the nation's railroads contained in the 1898 Erdman Act, courts generally overturned those protections. In *Adair* v. *United States*, for instance, the Supreme Court gutted the Erdman Act in 1908. When President Theodore Roosevelt intervened in 1902 to foster a negotiated settlement between coal operators and striking miners in Pennsylvania, his involvement was significant because it was such an aberration from the history of presidential hostility to union efforts. But Roosevelt's gesture betokened no lasting change in Washington's approach to labor.

To reverse the consistently hostile actions of government, the AFL increasingly abandoned its official non-partisanship and plunged into politics. In 1906 the AFL drafted a "Bill of Grievances," and lobbied both major parties for legislation that would restrict the power of judicial injunctions. Led by William Jennings Bryan, who would campaign in vain for the White House for the third time in 1908, the Democrats responded more warmly to this initiative. And by 1912 most AFL unions worked hard to elect Democrat Woodrow Wilson. But until the eve of US entry into World War I, when Wilson signed several bills favored by labor, unions achieved little through their lobbying; and labor was by no means unified in its political strategy.

The failure to realize meaningful reform in industrial relations, the fierce resistance of employers, and the entry of millions of immigrants into burgeoning industries created a serious challenge for the movement during the years before World War I. By no means was it obvious that the AFL's brand of unionism would survive this crisis, since opposition to business unionism emerged from several sources. The Socialist Party of America (SP), founded in 1901 and led by Debs, grew in influence during the first decade and a half of the century. The SP attracted strong support in immigrant communities, and exerted control over such AFL unions as the Brewery Workers. The SP criticized the AFL's craft structure and attempted to transform the AFL into an industrial union federation open to all workers. The Socialist Trades and Labor Alliance, which was the union arm of the rival Socialist Labor Party of Daniel DeLeon, broke with the AFL completely and organized its own unions to compete with the AFL's.

The most significant challenge to the AFL in this period, however, came from the Industrial Workers of the World (IWW), or "Wobblies." The IWW traced its lineage back to the struggles in the 1890s of the Western Federation of Miners (WFM), a union of hard-rock miners in the mountain west. Bloody battles with copper, gold, and lead mine owners radicalized the leaders of the WFM and provoked a break with the cautious AFL. In 1905 the WFM helped give birth to the IWW, whose members aspired to organize all workers without respect to race, religion, gender, nationality, or level of skill. The Wobblies eschewed political action, believing that "bourgeois politics" would never yield lasting gains to workers, and espoused a version of syndicalism, holding that one great strike by "One Big Union" would end capitalism. Wobblies were also skilled practical organizers who won significant short-term victories. On the west coast the IWW flooded such towns as Spokane in 1909 to campaign for the right to speak freely on street corners. In 1912 Wobblies led a successful strike of polyglot textile workers in Lawrence, Massachusetts, and, on the eve of the entry into World War I, successfully organized farm workers in the Midwest, loggers in the Northwest, and copper miners in the Southwest. The IWW's "Big Bill" Haywood was perhaps Gompers's most effective critic.

Wartime Upheaval and Aftermath

If scholars have judged the progressive era as a time of labor's ordeal, they are increasingly viewing the Great War as a turning point in labor history. Mass production methods spread widely in wartime, and craft labor was further "diluted." Immigration came to a temporary halt, and the federal government effectively intervened for the first time in labor relations. The results were dramatic. By 1919 the IWW had been almost completely destroyed, the AFL was ascendant, and the open shop status of mass production industries was under serious threat.

Among the most significant changes that the war wrought was to affect the composition of the working class. By cutting off immigration from Europe for nearly five years, the war set in motion the Americanization of immigrant workers. The shortage of labor created by the disrupted flow of immigrants in turn provided an opportunity for those historically excluded from industrial employment. The African Americans of the "Great Migration" left the South to take jobs in northern steel mills, packing houses, and rail yards. Some 300,000 trekked north during the war. Mexican immigration also jumped during the war, while women gained access to well-paying jobs – from streetcar conducting to machine tool operating – that previously were deemed "male."

Besides fostering the transformation of the wage labor force, the war also provided unions an opportunity to capitalize on the labor shortage. In 1917 some 4,450 strikes, involving more than a million workers, swept across industry, particularly in sectors connected to war production. During the war the AFL gained more than a million new members, enrolling some 4.1 million by 1919. And, by early 1917, membership in the IWW had also ballooned. But the surge of strikes and organizing set in motion the formation of a federal labor policy that would have far-reaching consequences for both the AFL and the IWW.

Amid the strike wave of 1917, the Wilson administration crafted a series of war labor policies that culminated in the formation of the National War Labor Board (NWLB) in April 1918. The government recognized workers' rights to organize unions and fostered collective bargaining between workers and employers, in return for the AFL's promise to limit disruptive strikes. Under this arrangement the AFL prospered, even though Washington did not require that employers bargain directly with unions. Government policies helped account for the AFL's early wartime successes in organizing meat-packers, railroad mechanics, steelworkers, and electrical workers. At the same time, however, the Wilson administration moved (with the AFL's approval) to crush the IWW, whose leaders criticized the war. In August 1918 the government began to crack down on the Wobblies. Hundreds of their leaders were arrested, the organization's records were seized, and its field offices were closed. By 1919 the IWW was virtually dead; and the Socialist Party of America, which had refused to endorse US entry into the Great War, was fractured and marginalized. Debs, the SP's perennial presidential candidate, was imprisoned for denouncing conscription.

Federal intervention in wartime labor relations left a lasting mark on American labor politics, the AFL, workers' expectations, and employers' behavior alike. The war decisively changed the course of US radicalism. Although repression shattered the SP, labor radicalism was not altogether doomed. Inspired by the Bolshevik Revolution, elements of the SP reconstituted themselves in 1919 into two rival Communist parties. By the early 1920s these parties would unite to form the Communist Party of America. The CPUSA would influence the labor movement through the late 1940s, far beyond the narrow boundaries of its membership. The war also changed the AFL, planting the seeds for industrial unionism in its ranks through successful wartime organizing in steel, meat-packing, and electrical manufacturing, even as the industrial unionism of the IWW was being crushed. The war to "Make the World Safe for Democracy" also encouraged workers to demand "industrial democracy" on the job. Although most union gains were reversed after the war, management was less likely thereafter to ignore completely employees' desires for a voice in the determination of their working conditions. Most large-scale employers responded by linking reformed personnel practices to the continuing reorganization of production after the war.

More immediately, however, the changes initiated by the war instigated a backlash. When the war ended in 1918, federal agencies such as the NWLB were dismantled. Freed from federal interference and capitalizing on a glutted labor market, employers launched a postwar counterattack, the "American Plan," against union gains. Insisting that only the open shop was consistent with the nation's values, large-scale employers coordinated union-busting drives in industrial cities across the country. In 1919 there were unprecedented levels of labor conflict, as some 4 million workers went on strike. In the Great Steel Strike alone, hundreds of thousands walked out. The strike wave panicked middle-class Americans, who feared that revolution was imminent and whose paranoia stoked the postwar Red Scare. Hundreds of aliens and radicals were arrested and deported during the frenzy. When the dust had settled it was clear that unionism had been dealt a terrible blow. Unions were driven out of mass production industries and lost many wartime gains. Organized labor's malaise was compounded by a recession in 1921, as well as a disastrous strike of 400,000 railroad shop mechanics the following year. The Republican administration of Warren G. Harding returned to pre-Wilsonian form by siding with employers to break that strike.

In part owing to the shift to the right that Harding's election represented, the 1920s were lean years for the AFL. Membership declined from over 5 million during the tumultuous year of 1919 to 3.4 million a decade later. Employers meanwhile made great strides toward winning the loyalty of their workers through the sorts of benefits that historians have come to term "welfare capitalism." Profit sharing, job promotion ladders, sickness benefits, and recreation opportunities were offered by the largest welfare capitalist employers. In an effort to grant workers a semblance of industrial democracy, many large employers also created company unions. By 1926 over four hundred such unions claimed nearly 1.4 million workers as members, which was almost half the membership of the AFL. Although such unions did not have the power to strike, they often responded to workers' grievances just enough to deflect interest in the AFL. Stymied by employer opposition and deprived of the leadership of Gompers, whose death in 1924 led to the ascendancy of the less capable William Green, the AFL could not capitalize on tightened labor markets when the economy revived in the mid-1920s. Craft unions still protected skilled workers in some sectors. But the vast expansion of mass production and the continued electrification of factory machinery in this decade made craft unionism look increasingly anachronistic.

Nor could the unions expect much help from government. Progressivism fell into decline after Harding's election. A 1924 effort by the AFL and its allies to resurrect reform politics through Robert M. LaFollette's third-party campaign for the White House did rouse significant support, but ultimately failed. And the courts once again took the lead in defining labor policies to the detriment of labor. In 1923, for example, *Adkins v. Children's Hospital* struck down a minimum wage for working women. The one bright spot for unions in the decade was the passage of the 1926 Railway Labor Act, which recognized the right of railroad workers to join unions without interference from employers. It would be another nine years, however, before industrial workers in general gained that right.

Depression, New Deal, and Industrial Unionism

Had it not been for the Great Depression that began in 1929, most historians have claimed that many more years might have passed before workers won the right to organize. But the economic crisis undermined the labor stability that employers had painstakingly constructed after World War I. Workers who relied on their employer-bestowed benefits became disillusioned, the reform impulse in American politics was revived, radicals were energized, and reforms within the AFL itself were encouraged. These reforms would ultimately give birth to mass industrial unionism. The combination of these developments transformed labor relations.

In the short term, though, the Great Depression brought cruel deprivation. Approximately 15 million workers were jobless by 1932, more than a quarter of the work force. Many others worked fewer hours or suffered pay cuts, as employers suspended welfare benefits and scrambled to protect shrinking profits. Industrial production was halved during this period, as was aggregate national income. The network of fraternal, ethnic, and religious organizations to which workers turned for relief was overwhelmed by the crisis. Nor did state, local, and national governments prove equal to the task of relief. By 1932 union membership fell to 3 million (roughly the size of the prewar labor movement), and the number of strikes dropped to a new low in 1930. Understandably unionists proved reluctant to strike when long lines of the jobless waited in vain for work. Depression, meanwhile, bred a sense of desperation. In the South, unemployed white workers organized to demand the jobs of working blacks. In California and the Southwest, a systematic deportation of Mexican workers was launched. And all levels of government showed reluctance to hire married women so long as men lacked jobs. Neither the administration of Herbert Hoover nor the nation's employers had a remedy for the agony of the Depression.

But the tide began to turn in 1932, when two significant events occurred. Congress passed the Norris–LaGuardia Act, which declared yellow-dog contracts illegal and limited the issuance of judicial injunctions in labor disputes; and Democrat Franklin D. Roosevelt was elected President, promising Depression-weary Americans a "New Deal."

In his first months in office in 1933, Roosevelt signed an unprecedented volume of legislation, much of which directly affected workers. Among his most noteworthy actions was the creation of relief agencies designed to employ the jobless and to feed and clothe the needy. The Public Works Administration, the Civilian Conservation

Corps, and the Federal Emergency Relief Authority dwarfed into insignificance the voluntary relief measures that President Hoover had attempted to coordinate. But the most important law of 1933 affecting workers was the National Industrial Recovery Act (NIRA), which created the agency charged with driving the economy out of depression: the National Recovery Administration (NRA). The NIRA resulted largely from demands made by business leaders, who wanted to halt cutthroat competition and to codify price and wage guidelines, thus removing the pressures on employers to slash wages and employment rolls further. But Section 7(a) of the NIRA put into law workers' right to organize as well as employers' obligation to bargain collectively with workers. Like the NWLB during World War I, however, the NIRA did not compel employers to bargain directly with unions.

Yet the NIRA's promises triggered a massive wave of unionization in 1933–4, especially in the mass production industries from which unions had been excluded since 1919. Within months some 100,000 auto workers joined unions, as did 90,000 steelworkers and 60,000 rubber workers. Indeed, so quickly did industrial workers clamor for union cards that the AFL could not decide the jurisdictional boundaries of the craft unions that claimed them. The AFL's confusion contributed to rising discontent among workers, which employers in turn exacerbated by aggressively promoting company unions (legal under the NIRA) as substitutes for the AFL. Where workers insisted on organizing AFL unions, employers simply flouted Section 7(a) by firing union leaders. And when the government attempted to settle the rising number of disputes by creating labor boards to investigate these conflicts, the boards proved too weak to enforce settlements. In 1934 growing frustrations led to nearly two thousand strikes, involving a million and a half workers; especially bitter conflicts erupted in San Francisco, Minneapolis, and Toledo. In September 1934 some 400,000 textile workers struck textile centers on the east coast.

Amid this tumult the Supreme Court struck down the NIRA in 1935. The court's action created an urgent need for new labor legislation, which Democratic Senator Robert Wagner of New York offered. It was destined to become the legal foundation for American industrial relations in the post-New Deal era. The National Labor Relations Act (NLRA), or Wagner Act, signed into law on July 5, 1935 restated in clear terms workers' rights to organize. Unlike previous measures, however, the Wagner Act outlawed collective bargaining by company unions; and it created a powerful National Labor Relations Board (NLRB) to enforce the Act. In 1937, when the Supreme Court upheld the constitutionality of the Wagner Act in *NLRB v. Jones and Laughlin*, US labor entered a new era. Now legally protected, unions also enjoyed wide public support.

Such a favorable legal and political climate presented unprecedented opportunities for the AFL to organize workers. The question remained, however, whether the organization had the will and the determination to do so. Although workers had flooded into unions in 1933–4, disillusionment with the ineffectual efforts of the AFL soon followed. Powerful craft union leaders, meanwhile, remained so ambivalent about organizing unskilled workers that the AFL could formulate no clear policy on how to organize manufacturing industries. John L. Lewis of the UMWA, Sidney Hillman of the ACWA, and other reformers demanded that the AFL charter industrial unions to pursue this task. But the AFL did not act. Disgusted with the AFL's timidity, Lewis and Hillman joined with David Dubinsky of the ILGWU and a few other like-minded union leaders in 1935 in launching – over the objections of the AFL's Green – the Committee on Industrial Organization. The CIO immediately laid plans to organize mass production workers. When Green attempted to obstruct this process, the CIO disaffiliated from the AFL and renamed itself the Congress of Industrial Organizations.

Almost immediately the CIO experienced significant breakthroughs that were to have profound implications for manufacturing. In 1936 rubber workers gained union recognition, and steelworkers moved in that direction. After Roosevelt's landslide re-election in 1936, thanks in no small measure to the CIO, its organizers were poised to seize the initiative. They did so on the night of December 30, 1936, in Flint, Michigan, where a group of militant members of the CIO's United Automobile Workers sat down and occupied the Chevrolet No. 1 plant of General Motors. The "Flint Sit-Down Strike" lasted until February 11, 1937, when GM finally gave in and signed a union contract. The excitement of the Flint victory soon spread to other industries and regions. By June 1937 some half a million workers had launched their own sit-down strikes. In this heady atmosphere, the CIO achieved its largest victory without even having to call a strike. On March 2, 1937, US Steel signed with the CIO's Steel Workers' Organizing Committee (SWOC). By the end of the year, the CIO claimed 3.7 million members, surpassing the AFL's 3.4 million.

Almost overnight the CIO began to redefine the role of labor in American life. Not only did the CIO plunge into the organization of industrial unions, unlike the cautious AFL. It made serious efforts to organize workers historically neglected by AFL unions, especially women, African Americans, and Latinos. The CIO's more inclusive vision was in part influenced by radicals, especially Communists, who played a prominent role in CIO unions. Fortuitously, the launching of the CIO coincided with international Communism's inauguration of the "Popular Front." That move saw Communists abandon their own sectarian unions and join the CIO, in many cases becoming its most effective organizers. Finally the CIO charted an aggressive political strategy, making itself a central component of Roosevelt's elect-oral machinery. Indeed, his 1936 landslide marked the arrival of organized labor as the single most potent organizational constituency of the Democrats – the anchor of the party's liberal wing. The unions held this position for most of the rest of the century.

But the CIO's early successes were soon followed by critical defeats that weakened its power in the workplace. After the victory at US Steel, the CIO called a strike against the smaller Little Steel companies that year. That strike failed amid violent clashes on the picket lines. In the most brutal episode, police fired on unarmed strikers near Republic Steel's South Chicago plant on May 30, 1937. Ford Motor Company likewise used violent intimidation to thwart a UAW organizing drive among its employees. And the AFL, shocked out of its dormancy by the CIO's victories, began to challenge its rival by mounting its own organizing drives among industrial workers. Between 1938 and 1940, as AFL and CIO unions battled each other, and the economy continued to sag, employers became more effective at fighting both federations. Not until the mobilization preceding US entry into World War II did unions manage to follow up on the breakthroughs of 1937.

World War, Cold War, and the Consolidation of a New Order

If historians generally agree that the Depression set loose forces that remade the labor movement, there is also agreement that World War II and the early Cold War consolidated the new place of labor in American society. These years also saw limits set on organized labor's control over industrial production.

The war set in place trends that would in the postwar era define both the labor force and the role of unions within it. Besides ending the decade-long economic slump that had caused so much misery for workers, the war also contributed to the further transformation of labor force demographics. Continuing the Great Migration, as many as 5 million African American workers moved to industrial jobs in the North and West during the war. The number of working women, meanwhile, jumped from 11 million to nearly 20 million by the summer of 1945. But the most lasting legacy of World War II may have been that unions were further allowed to organize basic industries. When the war ended, labor would be too deeply entrenched to be dislodged from its gains.

Critical to both the unions' success during the war and the limited nature of their gains was the labor policy of the Roosevelt administration. In return for the cooperation of both Philip Murray, who succeeded Lewis as CIO president in 1940, and the AFL's William Green, the Roosevelt administration gave unions a role in war preparedness planning. After the Japanese attack on Pearl Harbor both the AFL and CIO offered the government a no-strike pledge. The administration responded by creating a National War Labor Board (NWLB) to protect the interests of war-production workers and to ensure labor peace for the duration of the conflict.

In all, both workers and unions prospered under the wartime regime. Ford, the Little Steel companies, and the meat-packing corporations all signed contracts with unions. The total union membership rose in wartime from 10 million to 15 million, as the NWLB actively encouraged union membership and provided for the dues check-off in unionized settings. Labor leaders also emerged as important players in the wartime bureaucracy.

Yet the entente between labor, employers, and government during World War II was not without tensions, nor were labor's gains without costs. Workers chafed at some of the decisions of the NWLB, especially its effort to limit wage gains during the war. Rank-and-filers were less willing than their leaders to surrender the right to strike during the war, and staged thousands of unauthorized "wildcat" strikes. Such militancy could backfire, as happened when Lewis's UMWA refused to abide by the no-strike pledge and staged walkouts in 1943 that turned public opinion against labor. Unions also lost a measure of accountability during the war, as the rank-and-file autonomy that characterized the early CIO was replaced with the growing bureaucracy necessary to represent huge, far-flung constituencies in their negotiations with government and with employers. Although union leaders used this new bureaucracy to deliver on their promises of full-scale production, efforts to secure equal power with management in wartime workplaces were rebuffed. Finally, the continued dependence on federal support also threatened the long-term independence of the labor movement. By 1945, the CIO especially had tied itself so closely to the Democrats that it risked being taken for granted as a captive constituency.

Undeniably, however, wartime developments so ensconced unions within the nation's power structure that their survival was all but assured after 1945. As in the era immediately after World War I, demobilization in 1945–6 made labor relations volatile. A wave of strikes swept over steel, auto, electrical, meat-packing, and other industries, and some 2 million workers were out on strike as 1946 began. But post-World War II strikes were held not over the survival of unions, but over the details of postwar union contracts. Unions were unsuccessful at widening their role in the management of industry, as many radicals and progressives had hoped to do. But unions did succeed in winning hefty wage increases while holding on to the member-ship gains they had made in wartime.

Postwar gains were overshadowed, however, by ominous political developments destined to erode organized labor's strength in years ahead. After eighteen years in the minority, Republicans capitalized on President Harry Truman's unpopularity, plus the strife associated with the 1946 strikes, to win control of both houses of Congress in the elections of that year. In 1947 the 80th Congress promptly passed (over Truman's veto) the Taft–Hartley Act, which amended the Wagner Act in ways that weakened union power. The President was given the power to invoke a cooling-off period to avert strikes that threatened to disrupt the national economy. The new law allowed states to pass laws banning union-controlled "closed shops" from workplaces ("right to work laws"), and required labor officials to sign oaths asserting that they were not Communists if their unions were to avail themselves of the services of the NLRB. Even as unions protested this "slave labor act," the CIO's most important postwar organizing drive, an effort to unionize southern industry called "Operation Dixie," collapsed under the attack of oppressive local authorities and red-baiters.

The enactment of Taft–Hartley in 1947 coincided with the onset of the Cold War between the United States and the Soviet Union. Both developments became pivotal to the history of organized labor. Although most AFL and CIO leaders supported the Cold War, an influential minority faction within the CIO did not. With strong ties to the Communist party, these left-wingers criticized Truman's anti-Soviet foreign policy as warmongering. They supported the third-party presidential candidacy of Henry Wallace in 1948, and refused to sign the Taft–Hartley Act's anti-Communist affidavits. Their split with CIO leaders resulted in the expulsion of eleven left-wing unions (which contained one-fifth of all members) from the CIO in 1949–50.

The CIO's purge, the deaths in 1952 of the CIO's Philip Murray and the AFL's William Green, as well as the consensus politics bred by the Korean War (1950–3) and McCarthyism, created conditions favoring the reunification of a labor movement that had been divided for nearly two decades. Negotiations begun in 1953 between George Meany of the AFL and Walter Reuther of the CIO resulted in the creation of a unified AFL-CIO under Meany's leadership in 1955.

The birth of the AFL-CIO occurred in a mood of great optimism. Unions had not only survived the postwar tumult, the Red Scare, and the purging of the left from the CIO; they had also experienced growth in their size and influence. In 1954 unions could claim 18 million members, which was 35 percent of the non-agricultural work force. Union power meant collective bargaining gains. Auto workers, for example, won not only hefty pay increases, but supplemental unemployment benefits in times of layoff, annual pay increases tied to productivity, paid vacations, and company-funded health care. Workers generally experienced rising real incomes, improved diets, better health and living conditions, and expanded educational opportunities in the two decades after World War II. Nor could labor's political influence be denied. In 1955, the AFL-CIO created the Committee on Political Education. Through the late 1960s COPE served as the Democratic Party's most vital electoral machine. There was every reason to believe that the newly united labor movement would see its size, influence, and power grow in coming decades. But that did not happen.

The Origins and Onset of Labor's Crisis

At the very moment that the AFL-CIO was created in 1955, unions began a long slide downward in the share of the work force that they claimed as members. That decline would become a near free fall during the economic crises and political defeats of the late 1970s and 1980s. In 1962 union membership fell to 16.8 million (30 percent of the non-agricultural work force). By 1978 only 20.3 percent of non-agricultural workers belonged to unions. In 1982 the figure was 17.7 percent. Why did this slide occur? Historians have focused on several factors to account for this: the decline of the manufacturing sector in relative terms, along with the continuing transformation of manufacturing production by technology; the expansion of the service economy; the transformation of the work force; the skill with which employers learned to manipulate labor law as well as the political process, thus frustrating union organization and weakening union political power; and the inability of AFL-CIO leaders to craft effective responses to these trends.

After World War II the manufacturing sector experienced dramatic changes, as the introduction of new technologies altered the manufacturing work force. Between 1955 and 1963 the auto industry expanded production while reducing the work force by 17 percent. The US steel industry lost more than half of its jobs in the three postwar decades. Overall, the growth of high-paying blue-collar jobs was barely noticeable. Meanwhile manufacturers increased their investments in overseas plants, while reducing the level of domestic investments; and competing foreign-based manufacturers of autos, steel, textiles, garments, and electronics gained larger shares of the US consumer market. The result of such trends was that primary sector blue-collar employment fell from 41 percent of the total work force at the end of World War II to less than 27 percent by 1980. In the 1970s the decline of employment in manufacturing became precipitous, with disastrous effects for organized labor. Between 1974 and 1978 manufacturing unions lost more than a million members. Amid such conditions employers easily mastered the art of intimidating organized workers with the threat of a plant closing in order to wrest concessions in collective bargaining. Contracts signed during a recession in the early 1980s actually reduced real wages by an average of more than 7 percent.

As the manufacturing economy stagnated or declined in relative importance, the service sector expanded robustly. Non-manufacturing employment grew by 37 percent in the decade after 1968, led by such sectors as health care and food service. By the early 1980s more workers were employed in fast foods than the auto industry. Although unions expanded their membership in the service sector, particularly among the ranks of government workers, keeping up with the growth of service employment was much harder. Membership in this sector increased by only 13 percent in the decade 1968–78. Worse still for labor, as technology sector employment burgeoned, beginning in the late 1970s, unions were virtually shut out from this sector. Large technology-related firms such as International Business Machines or Eastman Kodak kept workers content with a revamped version of welfare capitalism.

In part the unions experienced difficulty organizing in the service sector because of the composition of its work force. In the decades between 1950 and 1990 job opportunities increased dramatically for women, African Americans, and immigrants. After a brief decline following World War II the labor force participation of married women steadily increased through the rest of the century. Roughly 30 percent of married women worked for wages in 1950; by 1970 the figure was closer to 40 percent; and by 1990, it was 60 percent. The pace of the African-American exodus from the rural South quickened after the mechanization of cotton farming following World War II. In the early 1950s, 2,000 blacks were arriving in Chicago every week. The 1965 Immigration Reform Act ended a forty-year-old quota system, opening a new era in immigration history. Between 1970 and 1990, roughly 80 percent of all legal immigrants came from Asia and Latin America. Many other immigrants came illegally. Immigration from Mexico especially contributed to the explosive growth of the Latin American population. Between 1950 and 1968 the Mexican-American population of Los Angeles, for example, tripled, reaching nearly a million. Across the country these new immigrants were overwhelmingly urban dwellers employed in service occupations. Organized labor had generally (though often warily) supported the struggle for civil rights waged by African Americans in the 1950s and 1960s. But the unions of the AFL-CIO, almost all of which were led by white men, were as slow to organize the increasingly non-white workers of the new service industries as the AFL unions once had been to organize in mass production.

The general drift of labor law in the postwar era did not make the jobs of union officials any easier. Though unions seemed to enjoy legal advantages at the end of World War II, the situation had clearly changed by 1980. The Taft–Hartley Act, as well as the Labor-Management Reporting and Disclosure Act (LMRDA) of 1959, provided employers with legal advantages they had not enjoyed in the original Wagner Act. Not content, employers went on the political offensive in the early 1970s, organizing the Business Roundtable in 1972 to seek further changes in labor law. By then professional labor consultants already had developed sophisticated methods for defeating union organizing drives, whether by defying existing labor laws, or by willingly paying the none-too-punitive penalties, or tying up cases in appeals for years. Unions won more than 75 percent of NLRB elections before the Taft–Hartley Act. As employers learned how to operate in the post-1947 legal atmosphere, however, union advantages evaporated. After 1975, unions fared poorly in NLRB elections and the negotiations of new contracts.

Politically, too, the tide had turned. Unions had been a critical bloc in the dominant electoral coalition in the first decades after World War II. But the Democrats' electoral strength weakened in the wake of the turbulent 1960s. Richard M. Nixon's narrow 1968 election in the face of an all-out effort by the AFL-CIO on behalf of Democrat Hubert H. Humphrey signaled the advent of a new political era. The daunting levels of inflation in the 1970s, meanwhile, helped convert many workers to the cause of tax relief championed by conservatives such as Ronald Reagan. Rising prices caused a rift between the AFL-CIO and the inflation-wary administration of

Democrat Jimmy Carter, elected in 1976. Although labor unions continued to exert a powerful influence in the political field through the remainder of the century, they found it increasingly difficult to marshal their rank-and-file as a bloc. Many of their members subscribed to the social conservatism championed by Reagan's Republican Party, while others grew disillusioned with the Democrats' retreat from liberalism in the post-Reagan era. Even under Democratic administrations, unions suffered severe disappointment. They were stymied by the Congress in seeking labor law reforms in 1977 (under Jimmy Carter) and in 1994 (under Bill Clinton). At the same time both presidents broke with labor on decisive questions, as Clinton did in obtaining free trade agreements with Mexico and China over the unions' strenuous objections that such agreements would end up exporting American manufacturing jobs.

Nothing better symbolized the eclipse of union power, however, than President Reagan's decision to fire 11,000 striking members of the Professional Air Traffic Controllers' Organization (PATCO) in 1981. Reagan easily broke the strike against the Federal Aviation Administration, while his union-busting caused no drop in his approval ratings. The significance of this victory did not escape private employers. Taking advantage of the failure of US labor law to forbid the permanent replacement of strikers, Phelps Dodge, Hormel, and other firms defeated strikes in the 1980s by bringing in replacement workers.

As organized labor stagnated as a social force by the 1980s, AFL-CIO leaders seemed incapable of bucking the trends with which unions now contended. Lane Kirkland, who succeeded Meany as president of the AFL-CIO in 1979, created a Committee on the Evolution of Work in 1983 to study labor's plight and to recommend solutions. But this study came to little, and Kirkland seemed helpless to arrest the AFL-CIO's steady decline. The lone exception was public employment. Between 1955 and the mid-1970s the number of organized public employees leaped from 400,000 to over 4 million. That growth continued even as industrial unions suffered sharp losses in membership. In the decade 1968–78, public employee unions gained 2 million members. By the mid-1970s the American Federation of State County and Municipal Workers (AFSCME) was larger than the AFL-CIO's industrial unions. From sanitation workers to teachers, public employees took advantage of the new federal and state policies that allowed for union organization. Embracing more women and minorities than typical industrial or craft-based unions, public employee unions also began to change the face of the labor movement. But public employee unions too fell on hard times in the late 1970s and early 1980s, when the widespread fiscal crisis, growing opposition to taxes, and calls for downsizing government weakened the bargaining power of these unions and led to cuts in government employment.

Times of Flux, Signs of Change

Beginning in the early 1980s, the explosive growth of information technology began to refashion the economy. At least initially, the growth of the technology sector continued a bifurcating trend in the labor force that had been underway since the 1960s. Even as well-paying, semi-skilled industrial jobs were replaced by low-wage, part-time jobs that lacked benefits, highly remunerative jobs for highly trained technicians burgeoned. Income inequality grew steeply between 1980 and 1995, as the real incomes of most wage earners stagnated while corporate profits climbed at a healthy rate. Thus, as the last decade of the century unfolded, a number of voices argued that organized labor was a spent force. Unions may have been appropriate to the era of mass production, these voices argued. But they were anachronisms in an age of global markets, specialized batch production, and high technology. As if to confirm such criticisms, union membership failed to grow during the economic boom of the late 1990s (unlike previous periods of low unemployment).

This continuing crisis led to an unprecedented development in the AFL-CIO. Increasingly dissatisfied with the leadership of Lane Kirkland, a group of union leaders headed by Gerry McEntee of AFSCME succeeded in electing John Sweeney of the Service Employees International Union (SEIU) to the presidency of the federation at the 1995 AFL-CIO convention. Sweeney's SEIU had been one of the few unions boasting of unimpeded growth, and he made organizing new workers a priority of the labor federation. As the 1990s drew to a close, the AFL-CIO put more of its resources into organizing campaigns than ever. The "Justice for Janitors" campaign spearheaded by the SEIU made progress among mostly minority building service workers from Los Angeles to Washington, DC. In 1999 unions experienced their largest single organizing victory in half a century, when 74,000 home health care workers in Los Angeles County joined the SEIU. The union movement also made a special effort to revamp its image as a progressive social movement by seeking support among college students and leftist intellectuals. "Union Summer" campaigns attracted thousands of idealistic college students to volunteer in organizing drives across the nation; and in 1997 the formation of Scholars, Artists, and Writers for Social Justice (SAWSJ) gave intellectuals an institutional forum through which to support the revamped labor movement. Symbolic of the energy and potential of the movement was the protest mounted against the World Trade Organization in Seattle, Washington, in December 1999. There AFL-CIO leaders marched arm-in-arm with environmentalists, church groups, trade unionists from other lands, leftists of varying persuasions, and advocates of social justice for developing nations.

Yet in struggling to redefine itself, labor faced enormous obstacles at the end of the twentieth century. Labor could derive little solace either from Democratic Party leaders' defiance of the AFL-CIO's wishes on the matter of free trade, or from the election of anti-labor Republican George W. Bush, despite a massive union mobilization during the 2000 presidential election. The trans-national mobility of capital and the consolidation of international conglomerates made effective organizing against colossal global enterprises daunting. Nor was there much reason to believe that the union movement would soon make inroads in the technology sector that was fast transforming the US economy. Meanwhile the appeal of unions to younger workers, who were more likely to be women or non-white than ever before, remained largely untested. In short, as the century that marked the ascent of organized labor as a central social institution came to an end, the union movement looked ahead toward an uncertain future.

FURTHER READING

Brody, David (1993) *Workers in Industrial America: Essays on the Twentieth Century Struggle*, 2nd edn. New York: Oxford University Press.

Cohen, Lizabeth (1990) *Making a New Deal: Industrial Workers in Chicago, 1919–39.* New York: Cambridge University Press.

Commons, John R. et al. (1921–35) *History of Labor in the United States,* 4 vols. New York: Macmillan.

Dubofsky, Melvyn (1988) *We Shall Be All: A History of the Industrial Workers of the World.* Urbana: University of Illinois Press.

—— (1994) *The State and Labor in Modern America.* Chapel Hill: University of North Carolina Press.

Dubofsky, Melvyn and Van Tine, Warren (1977) *John L. Lewis: A Biography.* New York: Quadrangle/New York Times.

Faue, Lizabeth (1991) *Community of Suffering and Struggle: Women, Men, and the Labor Movement in Minneapolis, 1915–1945.* Chapel Hill: University of North Carolina Press.

Forbath, William E. (1991) *Law and the Shaping of the American Labor Movement.* Cambridge, Mass.: Harvard University Press.

Fraser, Steve (1991) *Labor Will Rule: Sidney Hillman and the Rise of American Labor.* New York: Free Press.

Greene, Julie (1998) *Pure and Simple Politics: The American Federation of Labor and Political Activism, 1881–1917.* New York: Cambridge University Press.

Jacoby, Sanford (1997) *Modern Manors: Welfare Capitalism since the New Deal.* Princeton, NJ: Princeton University Press.

Kelley, Robin D. G. (1994) *Race Rebels: Culture, Politics, and the Black Working Class.* New York: Free Press.

Kessler-Harris, Alice (1982) *Out to Work: A History of Wage-earning Women in the United States.* New York: Oxford University Press.

Lichtenstein, Nelson (1982) *Labor's War at Home: The CIO in World War II.* New York: Cambridge University Press.

—— (1995) *The Most Dangerous Man in Detroit: Walter Reuther and the Fate of American Labor.* New York: Basic Books.

—— (2002) *State of the Union: A Century of American Labor.* Princeton, NJ: Princeton University Press.

McCartin, Joseph A. (1997) *Labor's Great War: The Struggle for Industrial Democracy and the Origins of Modern American Labor Relations, 1912–1921.* Chapel Hill: University of North Carolina Press.

Mink, Gwendolyn (1986) *Old Labor and New Immigrants in American Political Development: Union, Party, and State.* Ithaca, NY: Cornell University Press.

Montgomery, David (1987) *The Fall of the House of Labor: The Workplace, the State, and American Labor Activism, 1865–1925.* Cambridge and New York: Cambridge University Press.

Moody, Kim (1988) *Injury to All: The Decline of American Unionism.* New York: Verso.

Roediger, David (1991) *The Wages of Whiteness: Race and the Making of the American Working Class.* New York: Verso.

Sugrue, Thomas J. (1996) *The Origins of the Urban Crisis: Race and Inequality in Postwar Detroit.* Princeton, NJ: Princeton University Press.

Tomlins, Christopher (1985) *The State and the Unions: Labor Relations, Law, and the Organized Labor Movement in America, 1880–1960.* New York: Cambridge University Press.

Zieger, Robert H. (1995) *The CIO, 1935–1955.* Chapel Hill: University of North Carolina Press.

CHAPTER SIXTEEN

Race

REED UEDA

The Paradox of America's Racial Patterns

The role of race in the twentieth century changed according to public conceptions of collective identity and intergroup relations. When ethnic groups were assumed to have impermeable boundaries and a homogeneous core, race was seen as a key determinant of collective identity. The racialization of identity coincided with a politics of exclusionary group solidarity. The de-racialization of collective identity occurred when public policies promoted weak ethnic boundaries and intergroup mixing.

Intergroup relations in the twentieth century were shaped by two different public spheres for representing race. The sphere of an open, democratic pluralism of weak group boundaries and strong individual identity sprang from the nation's founding charters. The Declaration of Independence and the constitutions of the revolutionary era institutionalized a republican form of self-government recognizing the capacity of all persons to become citizens regardless of the "accident" of birth. What was common among all individuals was more important than the differences existing between them as members of groups.

The revolutionary founding, however, had been preceded by a colonial founding: an encounter across great cultural distances in which English settlers marked a social boundary between civilized and savage, between whites and the Indians and Africans. The coming of the Industrial Revolution that spurred the growth of cities and the manufacturing economy filled the minds of Anglo-Protestant natives with new anxieties. They saw the rise of a new social order filled with alien newcomers as a force for destroying their local worlds, which were based in small towns and rural life. Reacting to these threats, Anglo-Saxon elites searched for new ways to secure their hold on the nation. Those who believed in their hegemony over other groups tried to shore up their position with an ideology verifying that ethnic cultures corresponded to a ranked order of distinct races, and assumed it was proper for public policies to draw racial boundaries and divisions among ethnic groups.

Nativism and Racism

At the turn of the twentieth century, nativist social thinkers in America drew upon European scholarship to argue that the population of Europe was constituted out of three races: the northern European Teutons, the central European Alpines, and the southern European Mediterraneans. These racial theorists contended that measurable physical features, such as the shape of the skull, allowed the three races to be identified scientifically. American scholars and opinion-makers argued that European immigrants naturally reflected these racial divisions. The forty-two volume report of the United States Immigration Commission published in 1911 traced the origins of European races on the continental margins to infusions of Asiatic or African stock at earlier historical junctures. A University of Wisconsin sociologist, Edward A. Ross, emphasized the racial primitivism of southern and eastern Europeans. He claimed that their hereditary inferiority predisposed them to pervasive forms of dysfunctional behavior, which set them apart from Americans of Teuton ancestry and made them "beaten members of beaten breeds . . . that . . . lack the ancestral foundations of American character." Ross postulated "that the blood now being injected into the veins of our people is 'sub-common.' . . . . These oxlike men are descendants of those *who always stayed behind* . . . To the practiced eye, the physiognomy of certain groups unmistakably proclaims inferiority of type" (Ross 1914: 285–6). Other academics besides Ross subscribed to the doctrine that inherent biological traits separated Italians, Jews, and Poles, as well as Chinese and Japanese, into different races.

Congressional debates and deliberations on admissions and naturalization policy gave formulation to a set of labels for collective racial identities of immigrants. Terms such as "Southern Italians," "Hebrews," and "Asiatics" were officially normalized in the discourse on immigration controls. Federal bureaucrats and expert consultants designed a scheme for classifying immigrants according to racial groupings, which lawmakers employed as a guide to patterns of assimilability. Legislators who crafted immigration policy referred to "the English, Irish, Germans, Scandinavians, and Swedes, the light-haired, blue-eyed Anglo-Saxons, or Celts" as "pure Caucasians," in contrast to the "mongrelized" Italians, Greeks, Jews, Poles, Hungarians, Romanians, Ukrainians, Russians, and Armenians.

Racial categorization was a convenient tool for policy-makers wishing to manage the unfamiliar groupings of foreigners in a time of rapidly shifting social and cultural boundaries. The assumption of the fixed and racially predetermined character of ethnicity was revealed in many important policy documents. Throughout the first half of the twentieth century, the US Bureau of Immigration employed a classification of immigrant "races or peoples" for purposes of enumerating immigrants arriving each year. The US Immigration Commission submitted summary reports that interpreted the social data on immigrant life according to racial differences and stereotypic categories. The belief that racial factors primarily caused differences in collective behavior and traits was widely accepted during the Progressive Era (Gerstle 2001). Irrespective of regional, social, or educational background, the native-born indulged in crude generalizations about racial distinctiveness. In a classic historical study of nativist attitudes, John Higham quoted a construction boss who was asked, "You don't call an Italian a white man?" and replied: "No, sir, an Italian is a Dago" (quoted in Higham 1955: 66). A historian of the Pennsylvania steel industry noted that, when a labor investigator requested to work at the blast furnace, he was told: "Only Hunkies work on those jobs, they're too damn hot for a 'white' man" (quoted in Brody 1960: 120).

Gino Speranza, an Italian American, proclaimed that "American civilization" was Anglo-Saxon to its core. The "task and call for us all – Old Stock and New," as he saw it, "was to keep America as it was," or to risk losing it. Keeping America as it was included drawing national boundaries to exclude racial diversity. Speranza complained about the "tendency in certain . . . 'intellectuals[,]' aided and abetted by 'internationally minded' Americans, to theorize about a future amalgamated or mongrelized Americanism." He himself feared the "Synthetic America" that might result (Speranza 1925: 32–3). Some nativist thinkers even concluded that the assimilation of the "New Immigrants" from southern and eastern Europe was unfeasible on biological grounds alone. In his brief for restriction submitted to the House Immigration Committee, a eugenicist named Harry Laughlin stated that the newcomers generally exhibited more "inborn socially inadequate qualities" than did immigrants who came earlier (quoted in Higham 1955: 314). Anthropologist Madison Grant of the American Museum of Natural History argued in a best-seller, *The Passing of the Great Race* (1916), that an iron law determined that racial intermingling among immigrants would lead to the degradation of the intellectual stock of the population. The United States would be undermined from within by biological degeneration, and would lose the ability to compete with other nations. Grant's student, Lothrop Stoddard, echoed this alarm call to Nordics to avoid the undesirable breeds, and even made apocalyptic predictions of worldwide racial conflicts, in books such as *The Rising Tide of Color against White World-Supremacy* (1920) and *The Revolt against Civilization: The Menace of the Under Man* (1922).

Since 1790 naturalization had been confined to "white persons"; that federal law covering applicants for citizenship fell under new scrutiny after the Civil War. The racial eligibility for citizenship of immigrants from the Middle East and Asia was debated by federal attorneys who had to enforce this requirement of the law of naturalization, by judges who interpreted it, and by experts who were consulted to determine its conceptual basis (Ueda 1980). Despite legal challenges and inconsistent court decisions, the right to naturalization of the vast majority of immigrants from the Middle East and western Asia was upheld. As a result, naturalization policy ultimately consolidated Armenians, Turks, Syrians, Palestinians, and other Arabs into a community defined as "white" with respect to citizenship. But this chapter in the history of American nationality was not completed without serious legal debates over the character of their racial eligibility. Immigrants from the eastern and southern regions of Asia became targets of far more potent challenges to their racial eligibility for naturalization. By federal statute and by judicial rulings that reached the Supreme Court, such newcomers were classified as "aliens ineligible for citizenship." Citizenship was available to blacks, American Indians, mestizo Mexicans, and other racially defined groups; immigrants from east and south Asia alone suffered the burden of permanent disenfranchisement enforced by the state.

An all-encompassing framework for racial sorting began to develop after Reconstruction and, by the 1920s, had developed into a pattern of hegemonic pluralism. Lawmakers attempted to separate the rights of whites, blacks, Asians, and Hispanics by treating them as permanent members of racial and ethnic groups. These racialized boundaries were situated within regional patterns of ethnic relations (Glazer 1982: 128–33). In the South, a bi-modal caste system of white dominance and black subordination succeeded slave society and received judicial sanction in 1896, when the Supreme Court decided in *Plessy v. Ferguson* that "separate but equal" public facilities were constitutionally valid. In western states and territories, a multiracial, caste-like hierarchy placed white settler populations over socially subordinate Hispanic immigrants, Asian immigrants, and American Indians. The national government did not intervene in localities where social boundaries were racialized. At times, violent and destructive acts were committed to protect and monitor boundaries. The need to express white dominance underlay lynching, a ritualistic form of organized racial violence in the post-bellum South. From Reconstruction until the middle of the twentieth century, in the border states as well as the Deep South, lynching was used to terrify, demean, and control the African-American population. Between 1882 and 1931, over 3,300 blacks died by lynching, mostly in the South (Raper 1933; Woodward 1966). Even in the North, white mob attacks against blacks occurred in the urban centers and involved issues of racial territorial dominance (Brown 1975: 211–12).

The legislative efforts to bring about racial equality had been eclipsed by the structure of hegemonic pluralism that dominated intergroup relations in the early decades of the twentieth century. Nevertheless, the pursuit of racial equality continued through a long and difficult struggle in which black Americans were centrally involved. The National Association for the Advancement of Colored People (NAACP) became the vanguard of the antidiscrimination movement for American blacks. Founded in 1908, the NAACP worked in its early years toward the ending of lynching, but became a general advocacy group to promote equality of opportunity for blacks (Zangrando 1980). The NAACP supported civil rights suits that led to the expansion of judicial intervention into race relations to create new opportunities for blacks in jobs, education, and voting.

National leadership on race issues emerged in the 1930s, when the New Deal and black advocacy organizations began to build a framework for integrationist policies, marking the beginnings of the modern, federally-led movement for civil rights. Black victims of discrimination began aggressive new efforts to obtain redress through the judiciary system. From the 1930s to the 1940s, legal theorists began to chart a new relationship between laws and cultural systems, and abandoned the concepts of social scientists like William Graham Sumner, who held that the law was subordinated to mores and customs. Under the influence of "legal realism," scholars came to view law as an instrument for shaping moral and customary codes. Roscoe Pound, the dean of the Harvard Law School, argued that legal codes could actually change moral codes, that the welfare of society required that law reinforce beneficial habits and attitudes. In one way or another, he asserted, law expresses a set of values. Studies of prejudiced personalities indicated that although law could not in the short term extirpate prejudice, especially among deeply disordered personalities, it could aid in controlling discriminatory behavior by reinforcing a new conformity that mitigated such behavior. Studies of prejudice also demonstrated the tendency of people to conform readily to new consensual or normative environments engineered from without. One sociologist insisted that the impact of the law was often indirect, and the private realm could be affected and changed (Berger 1950).

The movement for a public policy of anti-discrimination sparked new interest in the processes that created stereotypical constructions of negative group qualities. In the aftermath of the Nazi defeat, a diverse group of psychologists, educators, sociologists, and therapists initiated experimental research on the social and interpersonal dynamics that created ethnic miscommunication and misperception. Psychologist Kurt Lewin, who had lost most of his family in the Holocaust, studied how destructive and dehumanizing ethnic antagonisms were generated, and how they could be neutralized in workplaces, classrooms, and public institutions. As systematic findings emerged in this field of applied social psychology, social reformers were encouraged to believe that ethnic and racial discrimination might be ended. If the prejudiced attitudes that underlay acts of ethnic discrimination might be causally understood, then prejudice could be undone and discrimination eliminated (Lewin 1947, 1948; Jackson 1990).

The Assault on Racial Discrimination

From World War II to the Eisenhower era, federal, state, and local governments began new initiatives to bring race relations into alignment with the democratic ideology used to justify America's new international leadership during these years. Opinion-makers and statesmen realized that the nation would be judged according to the caliber of its domestic race relations. Southern black leaders united with northern reformers to petition for new executive initiatives. They successfully pressured President Franklin D. Roosevelt to issue an executive order creating a federal Fair Employment Practices Commission (FEPC) and President Harry S. Truman to start the desegregation of the armed forces. The NAACP and ethnic advocacy groups submitted civil rights suits that enlarged the scope of judicial intervention into race relations to promote equality of opportunity.

The pursuit through government action of equal opportunity – irrespective of ethnic and racial background – was an outgrowth of a long political struggle in which blacks had been centrally involved since the very beginnings of free African-American communities. During the post-Reconstruction era, when the federal government withdrew from the field of civil rights activism, state legislatures assumed new responsibilities for establishing the rights of minorities to public accommodations and facilities. Black citizens' organizations were instrumental in lobbying for these protections. In the early twentieth century, lawmakers seeking to protect the rights of minorities moved into the unprecedented field of employment opportunity (Ruchames 1953). The breakthroughs in occupational antidiscrimination policy occurred in New York state, where Jewish, black, and labor leaders formed a vigorous alliance. Other states were quick to follow New York. Before the end of World War II, thirteen other states passed laws prohibiting racial discrimination in employment (Berger 1950).

New York state took the lead in the development of antidiscrimination by administrative agencies. Its employment antidiscrimination law called for a state commission to monitor and protect equal employment opportunity. The New York state commission represented a new conception of the purpose of government services. The responsibilities of government to the public included regular surveillance, intervention, and enforcement of conditions for maintaining equal civil rights to opportunity.

No longer would individuals have to seek recourse in the courts as lone appellants; they could apply to a permanent regulatory agency that specialized in prevention of civil rights violations. The operation of the New York state commission against employment discrimination spawned a widening pattern of regulatory intervention. By 1960, sixteen other states established their own versions of an antidiscrimination commission. State agencies extended their work to include education and housing. Their omnibus coverage marked a wholesale transformation of the relationship between private rights and state regulation concerning the rights of minorities to individual opportunity. Administrative action against discriminatory practices became a valid exercise of the state's police power to ensure universal citizenship rights, which reached into the private control of jobs, schooling, and housing (Mayhew 1968). Pioneering efforts in controlling and monitoring discrimination promised to make the scope of citizenship rights wider and more inclusive.

Until the early 1960s, the evolution of antidiscrimination social policy aimed at the negative goal of preventing harm to an individual based on national, racial, or religious discrimination. The goal of reform in race relations was to prevent the rights of the individual citizen from being undermined by discrimination based on racial identity. Achieving this goal required dismantling the structures of legalized discrimination and segregation in the public sphere. Black plaintiffs supported by the NAACP and its independent legal aid wing, the NAACP Legal Defense and Education Fund, played a key role in launching new legal challenges to segregation. In 1948 the Supreme Court decided in *Shelley* v. *Kramer* that racially restrictive covenants in housing markets were unconstitutional. In 1954 the Supreme Court began the process of ending the system of segregated public schools when *Brown* v. *Board of Education of Topeka, Kansas* overturned the "separate but equal" precedent of *Plessy* v. *Ferguson*.

Legal advocacy and self-defense organizations from the Hispanic and Asian communities also joined historic black civil rights organizations in the fight for the equality of minorities. The League of United Latin American Citizens (LULAC), a national civil rights organization founded by Mexican Americans just before the Great Depression, supported legal challenges to discrimination and prejudice. The Japanese American Citizen League (JACL), founded in the 1920s, also supported the quest for civil rights for racial minorities through court action and political lobbying. Both LULAC and the JACL, like the NAACP, aimed to increase opportunities that would promote racial integration.

The institutionalization of the principle of antidiscrimination – whether in legislation, jurisprudence, or in bureaucratic administration – was one of the most important shifts in race relations after World War II. The Civil Rights Act of 1964 barred discrimination in public facilities, in federally assisted programs, in employment, on the grounds of race, color, national origin, or sex. Title VII of the 1964 Civil Rights Act also established a federal Equal Employment Opportunity Commission. In 1965 Congress passed the Voting Rights Act to give federal protection to the exercise of the right to vote by racial minorities. During the presidency of Lyndon B. Johnson, the antidiscrimination policies of federal, state, and local governments promoted equal citizenship for minority citizens.

Immigration policy paralleled the race relations policies of the middle decades of the twentieth century. Beginning in World War II, congressional legislation abandoned the racial standards used to judge admissibility and naturalization. In 1943 federal lawmakers repealed the Chinese Exclusion Act, which had prohibited the immigration of Chinese workers since 1882 and which had excluded Chinese immigrants from naturalized citizenship. In 1946 the Philippines and India received token admissions quotas, and immigrants from these countries were allowed the right of naturalization. In 1952 the passage of the McCarran–Walter immigration act abolished all exclusions in admissions and naturalization based on racial origins, but continued the discriminatory allocation of visa quotas that favored immigrants from northern and western Europe. Finally, in 1965, Congress passed the Hart–Celler Immigration Act, which completely dismantled national origins as the criterion of admissions, and instead installed a worldwide system of equal "per-country" visa allocations. By transforming its admissions and nationality system to conform with globalism and universalism, the United States exorcised national origins discrimination from this domain of public policy. By the postwar years, mainstream public opinion moved toward accepting the idea that many immigrant populations, once regarded as unassimilable, had indeed become American, and thus their countrymen should also be welcomed as immigrants.

After World War II the children and grandchildren of the impoverished Italians, Jews, Slavs, Asians, and Mexicans – who had possessed few skills and little education – began to catch up with the descendants of earlier immigrants and old-line native-born Americans in occupational status, earnings, and property ownership. Occupational and property mobility closed economic gaps, so that social class cut across ethnic lines instead of reinforcing them. Nearly all immigrant communities after two or three generations included a group of entrepreneurs, a middle class, and an industrious working class (Lieberson 1980; Sowell 1981). Popular and elite views of southern and eastern European immigrants as "mongrelized" white races dissolved and were replaced by a new set of public images as fully white "ethnics" (Jacobson 1998). The mid-twentieth century thus marked a turning point in ethnic relations. From World War II to the Great Society, public policy-makers retreated from the view of American society as a hierarchy of unequal groups; and the nativism that dominated the first quarter of the century declined sharply. The Anglo-supremacist conception of national identity began to lose ground, as immigrant and racial minorities were increasingly seen as potentially equal members of society. Political leaders and opinion-makers re-envisioned American identity as the product of democratic ideology, an "American Creed," as the Swedish economist Gunnar Myrdal wrote in his landmark study of race relations, *An American Dilemma* (1944). The shift toward the democratizing of American identity prepared the way for the decline of fortress America (Gleason 1992).

In the postwar decades, social policy institutionalized the negative liberal imperative to protect the individual from harm due to national, racial, or religious discrimination. The glaring negative example of European nationalistic fascism and its destructive consequences during World War II reinforced the public will to prevent racist movements from achieving a similar impact in the US. And the return of prosperity after World War II lessened the fear of competition with outsiders and allowed the public to focus on mutual patterns of progress toward material betterment. The trend toward social tolerance and coexistence accelerated, thanks to the open conditions afforded by limited government and free institutions. A robust civil society produced areas for action and association by groups pressing for equal treatment and undermined the ability of exclusionary movements to use government to further their agenda. These trends supplied a powerful forward thrust to the democratic quest for a nationhood based on equality of individual opportunity rather than on racial categories.

The Return to the Primacy of Race

The growth of antidiscrimination policy occurred in a time of national economic expansion and unprecedented social mobility by African Americans. The outlawing of racial discrimination and segregation by new civil rights laws and judicial decisions opened new opportunities. The rise of a black middle class, which had roots in the postwar years, accelerated in the 1950s and 1960s. In 1940, only 5.2 percent of black men and 4.3 percent of black women held white-collar occupations; by 1970, 21.7 percent of the former and 36.1 percent of the latter were in these jobs. The rates of high school and college education among blacks also showed steady movement toward the national norm.

From the New Deal to the New Frontier, antidiscrimination policy had a steadily rising effect on equalizing opportunity for individuals regardless of racial background. The high point of national leadership for this movement was marked by a special presidential address to the nation in 1963. John F. Kennedy declared that "race has no place in American life or law." The moral mandate of racial equality, he added, "is as old as the Scriptures and is as clear as the American Constitution" – which was held to be color-blind (quoted in Fuchs 1990: 165–6). By 1965, however, a national politics based on "race-blind" and integrationist principles began to be abandoned in favor of a new agenda of social regulation. Makers of regulatory public policy in the Johnson and Nixon administrations redefined ethnic equality as proportional representation of a minority group in social and institutional structures equal to the proportion of a group in the population, not the uneven patterns of representation arising through equality of individual opportunity.

Supporters of affirmative action wanted public policy to take into account ethnic or racial background to achieve the goal of ethnic proportionality. These policy advocates referred to the goal of ethnic proportionality with terms such as "racial balance" or "diversity" and eschewed overt use of the terminology of "quotas." The first minority hiring formulas were developed as a result of the Department of Labor's "Philadelphia plan" in 1969 and developed into simple minority proportionalism in 1970. In the 1970s courts managing the school desegregation ordered by federal regulators employed "mathematical ratios," the Federal Office of Contract Compliance set "goals and timetables" for hiring minorities in firms receiving federal contracts, and federal statutes required special funding for minority educational programs. Racial discrimination was redefined in terms of "disparate impact." Any institutional policies that produced racial representation patterns diverging from racial proportions in the population caused a disparate impact on minorities that, by law, had to be remedied.

The division of the nation into new official racial groups advanced by devising government programs to target collective categories instead of individuals. The adoption of various preferential policies, described officially as affirmative action, necessitated the formulation of official identities as an entry pass to coverage. Census bureau counts and classifications of government agencies had the effect of preserving the separate racial identity of whites, Asians, blacks, Hispanics, and so forth. The relocation of ethnic identity around official ethno-racial categories required definitional shortcuts that oddly reduced and homogenized nationality groups. Incongruent combinations occurred. Samoans and Pakistanis merged into an Asian Pacific bloc; Hispanics of a variety of national and racial origins became a unitary Hispanic bloc. "The new immigrant categories," Lawrence H. Fuchs observed, "veiled the diversity within them" (1990: 285). The creation of official non-white groups implicitly created an official white group and exaggerated its historical unity. The rubric "people of color" tended to overlook the history of racial differentiation and discrimination against European immigrants such as Greeks, Jews, Armenians, Sicilians, and Slavs. In the search for new categories for the new politics, these ethnic groupings were lost in a monolithic Eurocentric mass. No individual and no group escaped reduction and homogenization in the new corporate ethnicities.

The Black Power movement was the model for organizing a new politics of anti-integration and separatism with many facets and involving many groups. Hispanic militants took their cue from black power and discovered Cuban, Maoist, and third-world alternative models of national liberation which moved in the train of black power. Asian-American militancy also rested on the belief that, to carry on the struggle against racism, it was necessary to organize around racial identity. Post-Great Society Hispanic and Asian advocacy leaders favored a group agenda replacing assimilation; immigrant ethnic groups were thus compartmentalized as disadvantaged racial minorities. They, therefore, sought a parallel to the model of black oppression in their framework for group history. This reorientation of identity required a categorical rejection of the democratic pluralist vision of pan-immigrant American identity. They sought to convey to the American public the existence of separate racial experiences that profoundly divided the nation, rather than a universal assimilation or integration that unified all. Because blacks had been historically excluded from the path toward assimilation as ethnic Americans, the new model of oppression denied that African Americans were merely "the last of the immigrants" (Thernstrom 1973: 176–8).

If blacks were not the "last of the immigrants," it followed that special public measures were needed to treat "people of color" as permanently disadvantaged groups. In the wake of the breakdown of the immigrant paradigm, advocacy leaders claimed that all racial minorities required strong state action to achieve equality of opportunity. Leading black advocacy groups such as the NAACP and the Urban League began to argue for affirmative action to end discrimination. In doing so, they called for benign racial preferences, and facilitated the perpetuation of the principle of the color line rather than the universalist rights of citizenship. From the late 1960s, the multiracial coalition represented people of color as state minorities. Because of the pervasiveness of racial prejudice and discrimination, minorities had a claim upon the liberal democratic state for special protection.

The minority coalition claimed that, as they were represented functionally in politics, employment, education, residency, and the media, minorities would diversify and enrich American culture. In 1978 legal backing for the goal of institutional diversity came from the Supreme Court decision in *Regents of the University of*

California v. *Bakke*. Speaking for the majority, Associate Justice Lewis Powell held that racial criteria for admission were legitimate so long as they furthered the goal of achieving institutional diversity (Belz 1990). Federal courts played a crucial ancillary role in the policy-making structure for group empowerment. Through judicial decisions from the 1970s to the 1990s, equal results remedies for discrimination in employment, education, and electoral representation were established within acceptable norms of constitutionality. The courts, therefore, played a central role in shifting the meaning of equal treatment from individual rights toward group preference (A. Thernstrom 1987; Belz 1990; Graham 1990).

According to historian David A. Hollinger, "enlightened anti-racism" in the form of group empowerment policies led to the re-creation of the "popular color-consciousness of the past: black, white, red, yellow, and brown," an ethno-racial "pentagon" whose "architecture has its unmistakable origins in the most gross and invidious of popular images of what makes human beings different from one another" (1995: 32). Ethnic groupings received official racial status as disadvantaged minorities or people of color, as they became subjects for programs and entitlements. Those who became subjects to be excluded from outreach were blended into the undifferentiated mass of whites. Hollinger described how the most telling instance of racialization proceeded among Hispanics, who were usually seen until the 1970s as white: " 'Brown' remained only a colloquial designation, although it served to mark lines of discrimination in many communities, especially in California and Texas. As late as the 1990 census," he added, "more than half of the Mexican American population continued to classify itself as white." Yet he also noted "the increasing frequency with which the people in this Latino bloc are being called a 'race' in popular discourse" (1995: 31–2).

Electoral redistricting to create "safe" voting districts for minority candidates for political office presupposed that a member of a racial community would act in its best interests in representing it politically. The creation of set-aside minority voting districts to assure the selection of black or Hispanic elected officials had a funneling or homogenizing effect that heightened racialized politics. Those who advocated racial re-districting were establishing conditions for making electoral behavior into a byproduct of different racial blocs (Thernstrom 1987). Private-sector institutions also developed parallels to such racialized policies. The commercial and journalistic mass media marketed issues in racialized forms of advertising and image "packaging." A consultancy- and poll-driven political culture constructed collective issues for targeted racial constituencies. Pressures for the creation of homogeneous racial classifications also came from industrial, institutional, and business managers. Corporate personnel offices realized that racial and multicultural programs were useful instruments for recruiting and organizing the work force. Such personnel programs could be cited to maintain a favorable relation with government offices with the power to bring suits against businesses that did not conform to targets for hiring and promotion of members of "under-utilized" minority groups.

In the 1980s, the presidential campaigns of Reverend Jesse L. Jackson made the rainbow a new symbol of group diversity in the United States. The rainbow, unlike the melting pot or the mosaic, possessed separate colors as its distinctive quality. It signified the idea that color or race, a fixed and inherited factor, was the defining characteristic of individuals. By symbolizing race, it downgraded the role of non-racial aspects of identity in determining how Americans acted and represented themselves.

In 1980 and 1990, the United States Bureau of the Census broke significantly with past practices in counting ethnic populations. The changes revealed much about the new construction of ethnic identity under the pluralism of the regulatory state. From 1850 to 1970, the census bureau had extensively enumerated the ethnic character of the population according to the country of birth and race of individuals. From 1870 onwards people were also counted and identified according to the birthplace of their parents. Hispanics were by and large counted according to the same rules applied to European ethnic groups, resting on identification by country of origin of individuals and their parents. Blacks, American Indians, and Asians were tabulated separately as racial categories in published census reports. Even among Asians and blacks, however, distinctions of foreign and native birth were made.

The Bureau of the Census kept track of European ethnic identity only in the first two generations, unlike other countries such as Canada and South Africa, which continued to categorize descendants of European ancestors to third, fourth, and subsequent generations. By the late decades of the twentieth century, the enumeration of European ethnic groups was featured less and less in the cross-tabulations of the federal population census reports, as the numbers of immigrants and their children shrank and those of succeeding generations rose. In 1980 and 1990, tabulations based on differentiated European first- and second-generation identity were replaced by the catch-all classification of "white."

Concurrently the federal census continued to enumerate non-white and Hispanic ethnic categories that had been derived from preferential and multicultural policies. In effect the census became a demographic mirror and an empirical base for establishing quotas for group-allocation policies. In the 1990 census, this shift in enumeration procedure became clearly crystallized. More consistently than ever before, in the summary tables for the nation and individual states that identified ethnic groups, ethnic sub-populations descended from the historical migrations from Europe and parts of the Middle East such as Lebanon and Armenia were homogenized into a monolithic "white" category. In New York City, which possessed an enormous and vibrant array of European ethnic groups, none appeared in the new summary tables because they were all collapsed into the totality of the white enumeration column.

Separate tabulations were entered for blacks, Hispanics, and Asians/Pacific Islanders. Hispanic and Asian groups were tabulated in detail, but as separate "minority" categories. For these groups, extensive and detailed breakdowns were made for sub-populations such as "Laotian" or "Cuban." The census was re-imaging the American population not upon a universal grid of ethnic characteristics such as country of birth, country of ancestry, or linguistic community, but rather upon political formulas for separating ethnic groups into super-categories. European ethnicity was marginalized. All descendants of Europeans were reduced to a "white" bloc, as all other ethnic groups were apportioned into African, Hispanic, and Asian/Pacific Islander blocs.

The nation's racial boundaries were drawn tighter, as the census increasingly responded to political and administrative needs for ethnic identification (Petersen 1987). In 1978 the US Office of Federal Statistical Policy and Standards announced that the categories for ethnic population counts "have been developed in response to needs expressed by both the executive branch and Congress to provide for the collection and use of . . . racial and ethnic data by federal agencies." Policy analyst Ira Lowry determined that the census bureau sacrificed "gathering valid and reliable information about the population of the United States," under the aegis of bureaucratic directives, administrative needs, and political pressures stemming from advocates of ethnic groups (Petersen 1987: 204).

In 1990 the census bureau established a "racial classification" system not on the tenets of anthropology or social science but by "the guidelines in Federal Statistical Directive No. 15, issued by the Office of Management and Budget." Although operating on the procedure of "self-identification" (which had replaced the judgment of census interviewers since 1960), the 1990 census was administered from the premise of "self-classification by people according to the race with which they most closely identify." The census presupposed that individuals belonged to a single homogeneous racial category and would define their identity in terms of it. Respondents who were of Asian ancestry were told to report a single racial identity, even though a substantial number were of mixed ancestry. Hispanics were encouraged to choose a single Hispanic subgroup identity, although they, too, had experienced much intermarriage into the historic native core population. The census bureau eliminated ambiguous answers by follow-up interviews. In these interviews, an uncertain responder "was asked to select, based on self-identification, the group which best described his or her racial identity." When the interview process did not yield a single racial identification, the following rule for ultimate resolution was used: "If a person could not provide a single race response, the race of the mother was used. If a single race response could not be provided for the person's mother, the first race reported by the person was used" (US Bureau of the Census 1993: B-29).

In another set of tables, the 1990 census displayed a seemingly more subtle approach to ethnic identity by taking into account ethnic ancestries of respondents. Nevertheless the 1990 census publications only reported the data according to single ancestry categories. For example, a person who reported his primary ancestry was Irish and his secondary ancestry was Italian appeared twice, once in the Irish ancestry group and another time in the Italian ancestry group. Thus the actual number of those with mixed Irish and Italian ancestry disappeared. Furthermore, Asian and Hispanic groups were completely left out of the ancestry reports. Only individuals descended from European ancestors or from African ancestors from the Caribbean or Africa were recorded in the public reports. The ancestry of Asian or Hispanic respondents was apparently presumed to be sufficiently homogeneous and obvious (notwithstanding the substantial intermarriage in these sub-populations) to exclude them from the ancestry table. Thus the ancestry tabulations in the 1990 census were reported in a way that downplayed or completely concealed the large categories of respondents with mixed ancestry. By doing so, the 1990 census conveyed the impression of much sharper boundaries separating groups. The amorphous areas of population mixing had to be ignored to convert the complex American population into a simplistic racial mosaic that yielded the exact counts required by preferential policies.

The use of census enumeration to reinforce politically and administratively defined collective identities was not unique to the United States in the era of multicultural state policies. In turning India into a colonial dominion, the British took censuses that oversimplified its complex and crisscrossing network of plural sub-communities. The imperial census reformatted this dense and historically evolved social composite into a schematic hierarchy of caste and ethnic sub-populations. This approach may have introduced artificial distinctions that aggravated status tensions among India's sub-populations. In the late twentieth century, the reification of ethnic politics into the form of the new multicultural census risked producing similar problems for American group relations. No wonder that the demographer William Petersen located the US and Indian approaches as part of a global pattern. He explained: "With the development of a welfare state, the financing of many local or private functions was shifted to the national capital and, with it, the same means of seeking preferment. It is the supreme paradox of our time," he added, "that, not only in the United States but generally, the greater state control over the economy and society has brought about not the growing indifference to nationalism and ethnicity . . . but precisely the opposite" (1987: 230).

Race at the Crossroads of State-managed Pluralism

By the 1990s, what had been a liberal project to promote social democracy had created a more ethnically divided and racially conscious society. In the late twentieth century as in its early decades, racialized collective identities overshadowed individual identities. The state attempted to treat immigrant minorities within the same framework of racialized public policy as that created for native American blacks. Through race-based principles of inclusion, immigrants from non-European societies received government-managed access to opportunity structures not as individual citizens but as members of descent-defined political groups. The salutary social goal of ethnic intermingling was achieved only by creating and reinforcing racialized spheres of rights.

The movement toward a state-managed pluralism based on preferences for racialized collective groups had been gaining momentum since the late 1960s. Within three decades, however, a reversal occurred in the nation's political currents that touched both conservative and liberal poles. Leading policy-makers and opinion-makers began to take stock of policies that dealt with social inequality through racial preferences. The emerging opposition to racial preferences in public policy also moved increasingly from intellectual critique to political advocacy. In 1995 the Regents of the University of California abolished racial and gender preferences in the state's public programs. In 1998, the state of Washington approved a similar referendum. A counterattack occurred in the courts, the political arena, and journalism. Even the US Department of Justice filed a challenge against the constitutionality of Proposition 209. In applying the principle of race in public policies, the republic stood at a new crossroads.

Perhaps the most fundamental problem for the movement to classify the American population in racial terms was the rise of mixed ancestry in the latter half of the twentieth century. National intermarriage data from the US Bureau of the Census, as well as other sources, demonstrated that ethnic groups from Asia and Latin America showed substantial and growing rates of mixed ancestry. A Bureau of the Census population survey in 1979 showed that 31 percent of Filipinos, 23 percent of Chinese, and 22 percent of Japanese reported having multiple ancestry. Nearly 22 percent of the Spanish ancestry population claimed multiple ancestry (US Bureau of the Census 1982: 7). The rates of intermarriage among Asians and Hispanics reflected much interracial exogamy (Harrison and Bennett 1995). They were especially striking when taking into account their historic group sanctions toward endogamy, plus many state laws barring miscegenation, which were not completely stricken until the 1960s. The majority of intermarrying Japanese had white spouses, thus showing that their exogamy was primarily interracial (Kikumura and Kitano 1973). Furthermore, by the 1960s one out of three third-generation Mexican Americans were intermarried, often with white partners (Grebler et al. 1970).

Hollinger remarked in 1995 how the "authority of descent-defined categories" was being placed "under severe pressure by the rate of intermarriage and by the greater visibility of mixed-race people" (pp. 41–2). He interpreted the striking spread of racial intermarriage as a ratification of the principle of letting individuals themselves determine how intensely or casually they wish to associate themselves with an ethnic or racial group. The intermarried and their interracial offspring provided a kind of renewed social support to a basic American civic ideal of voluntary social relations. The rising rate of racial intermarriage symbolized the political crossroads on matters of race emerging with the arrival of the twenty-first century. On the one hand, the rapidly increasing population of interracial Americans broke down the simplistic racial compartments created under state pluralism. On the other hand, advocates of racial classification urged that a new "multiracial" official identity should be recognized in public policy and enumerated as a separate population category (Skerry 2000; Perlmann and Waters 2002).

Racial intermarriage and mixed ancestry thus signified the contradictory processes at work in American race relations at century's end. Americans were still trying to decide whether to support policies that treated the population in terms of collective racial categories or as individuals who did not represent fixed racial identities.

Racialization in the Twentieth Century

US history in the twentieth century was shaped by two contradictory structures of group relations: a diversity pattern of open boundaries and a diversity pattern of constricted boundaries. The pattern of open diversity was deeply rooted in the nation's constitutional history. It possessed a political and civic framework derived from the era of the American Revolution, with its conception of cosmopolitan citizenship and nationality. It was expressed in policies that situated group life in a civil society affording a dynamic, self-regulated, and consensual balance between group solidarity and intergroup intermixing, between group membership and individualism.

By contrast, the diversity pattern of constricted boundaries hinged on public policies and ideologies that established separate racialized spheres of collective identity. Since its founding, the republic also created a public sphere that sought to separate and harden groups, that presupposed racial differences were self-evident, predetermined, and natural states, which government was bound to represent. This diversity pattern of constricted boundaries encouraged a politics of enforced group membership. A formal corporate pluralism could be promoted both for inegalitarian purposes (as in the case of Jim Crow segregation), and for democratizing outcomes (as in group empowerment policies under affirmative action). In either case policymakers introduced a potential into public life for reducing group life to an extension of pre-existing ethno-racial divisions, hierarchies, and separations. As people defined themselves as "Anglo Saxons," "people of color," "Euro-Americans," "Latinos," "African Americans," and "Asian and Pacific Islander Americans" at various moments in the twentieth century, they created a pluralism on the basis of their racialized identities. But it was pluralism that created a problematic and sometimes irreconcilable tension with a classical liberal pluralism founded on the primacy of the individual and fluid communities.

REFERENCES AND FURTHER READING

Allport, Gordon W. (1958) *The Nature of Prejudice*. Garden City, NY: Doubleday.

Bell, Derrick A., Jr. (1973) *Race, Racism and American Law*. Boston: Little, Brown.

Belz, Herman (1990) *Equality Transformed: A Quarter-Century of Affirmative Action*. New Brunswick, NJ: Transaction.

Berger, Morroe (1950) *Equality by Statute: The Revolution in Civil Rights*. New York: Doubleday.

Brody, David (1960) *Steelworkers in America: The Nonunion Era*. Cambridge, Mass.: Harvard University Press.

Brown, Richard Maxwell (1975) *Strain of Violence: Historical Studies of American Violence and Vigilantism*. New York: Oxford University Press.

Fredrickson, George M. (1981) *White Supremacy: A Comparative Study in American and South African History*. New York: Oxford University Press.

Fuchs, Lawrence H. (1990) *The American Kaleidoscope: Race, Ethnicity, and the Civic Culture*. Hanover, NH: Wesleyan University Press.

Gerstle, Gary (2001) *American Crucible: Race and Nation in the Twentieth Century*. Princeton, NJ: Princeton University Press.

Glazer, Nathan (1975) *Affirmative Discrimination: Ethnic Inequality and Public Policy*. New York: Basic Books.

—— (1982) "The politics of a multiethnic society," in Lance Liebman (ed.) *Ethnic Relations in America*. Englewood Cliffs, NJ: Prentice-Hall.

Gleason, Philip (1992) *Speaking of Diversity: Language and Ethnicity in Twentieth-Century America*. Baltimore, Md.: Johns Hopkins University Press.

Graham, Hugh Davis (1990) *The Civil Rights Era: Origins and Development of National Policy, 1960–1972*. New York: Oxford University Press.

Grant, Madison (1916) *The Passing of the Great Race, Or The Racial Basis of European History*. New York: Scribner.

Grebler, Leo, Moore, Joan W., and Guzman, Ralph C. (1970) *The Mexican-American People: The Nation's Second Largest Minority*. New York: Free Press.

Greenberg, Jack (1959) *Race Relations and American Law*. New York: Columbia University Press.

Handlin, Oscar (1957) *Race and Nationality in American Life*. Boston: Little, Brown.

Harrison, Roderick J. and Bennett, Claudette E. (1995) "Racial and ethnic diversity," in Reynolds Farley (ed.) *State of the Union: America in the 1990s*, vol. 2: *Social Trends*. New York: Russell Sage.

Higham, John (1955) *Strangers in the Land: Patterns of American Nativism, 1860–1925*. New Brunswick, NJ: Rutgers University Press.

Hing, Bill Ong (1993) *Making and Remaking Asian America through Immigration Policy, 1850–1990*. Stanford, Calif.: Stanford University Press.

Hollinger, David A. (1995) *Postethnic America: Beyond Multiculturalism*. New York: Basic Books.

Jackson, Walter A. (1990) *Gunnar Myrdal and America's Conscience: Social Engineering and Racial Liberalism, 1938–1987*. Chapel Hill: University of North Carolina Press.

Jacobson, Matthew Frye (1998) *Whiteness of a Different Color: European Immigrants and the Alchemy of Race*. Cambridge, Mass.: Harvard University Press.

Kikumura, Akemi and Kitano, Harry H. (1973) "Interracial marriage: a picture of the Japanese Americans," *Journal of Social Issues* 29, pp. 67–82.

Konvitz, Milton R. (1946) *The Alien and the Asiatic in American Law*. Ithaca, NY: Cornell University Press.

Lewin, Kurt (1947) "Frontiers in group dynamics," *Human Relations* 1, pp. 5–41.

—— (1948) *Resolving Social Conflicts*. New York: Harper and Row.

Lieberson, Stanley (1980) *A Piece of the Pie: Blacks and White Immigrants since 1880*. Berkeley: University of California Press.

Mayhew, Leon H. (1968) *Law and Equal Opportunity: A Study of the Massachusetts Commission against Discrimination*. Cambridge, Mass.: Harvard University Press.

Myrdal, Gunnar (1944) *An American Dilemma: The Negro Problem and Modern Democracy*. New York: Harper and Row.

Perlmann, Joel and Waters, Mary C. (2002) *The New Race Question: How the Census Counts Multiracial Individuals*. New York: Russell Sage.

Petersen, William (1987) "Politics and the measurement of ethnicity," in William Alonzo and Paul Starr (eds.) *The Politics of Numbers*. New York: Russell Sage.

Raper, Arthur F. (1933) *The Tragedy of Lynching*. Chapel Hill: University of North Carolina Press.

Ross, Edward A. (1914) *The Old World in the New: The Significance of Past and Present Immigration to the American People*. New York: Century.

Ruchames, Louis (1953) *Race, Jobs and Politics: The Story of FEPC*. New York: Columbia University Press.

Skerry, Peter (2000) *Counting on the Census? Race, Group Identity, and the Evasion of Politics*. Washington, DC: Brookings Institute Press.

Solomon, Barbara Miller (1956) *Ancestors and Immigrants: A Changing New England Tradition*. Cambridge, Mass.: Harvard University Press.

Sowell, Thomas (1981) *Ethnic America: A History*. New York: Basic Books.

Speranza, Gino (1925) *Race or Nation: A Conflict of Divided Loyalties*. Indianapolis, Ind.: Bobbs-Merrill. Reprinted 1975, New York: Arno Press.

Stoddard, Lothrop (1920) *The Rising Tide of Color against White World-Supremacy*. New York: Scribner.

—— (1922) *The Revolt against Civilization: The Menace of the Under Man*. New York: Scribner.

Thernstrom, Abigail (1987) *Whose Votes Count? Affirmative Action and Minority Voting Rights*. Cambridge, Mass.: Harvard University Press.

Thernstrom, Stephan (1973) *The Other Bostonians: Poverty and Progress in the American Metropolis, 1880–1970*. Cambridge, Mass.: Harvard University Press.

—— (1992) "American ethnic statistics," in Donald L. Horowitz and Gerard Noiriel (eds.) *Immigrants in Two Democracies: French and American Experience*. New York: New York University Press.

Thernstrom, Stephan and Thernstrom, Abigail (1997) *America in Black and White: One Nation, Indivisible*. New York: Simon and Schuster.

Ueda, Reed (1980) "Citizenship and naturalization," in Stephan Thernstrom (ed.) *Harvard Encyclopedia of American Ethnic Groups*. Cambridge, Mass.: Harvard University Press.

United States Bureau of the Census (1982) *Current Population Reports*, Series P-23, no. 116, *Ancestry and Language in the United States: November 1979*. Washington, DC: Government Printing Office.

—— (1993) *1990 Summary Population and Housing Reports.* Washington, DC: Government Printing Office.

United States Immigration Commission (1911) *Reports of the Immigration Commission*, vol. 1. Washington, DC: Government Printing Office.

Woodward, C. Vann (1966) *The Strange Career of Jim Crow*, 2nd edn. New York: Oxford University Press.

Zangrando, Robert L. (1980) *The NAACP Crusade Against Lynching, 1909–1950.* Philadelphia: Temple University Press.

CHAPTER SEVENTEEN

Women

JUNE SOCHEN

Women historians and women's history grew up together in twentieth-century America. Before, there were women and men writing about women's lives and experiences, but they were few and far between. The definition of "history" rarely included women, thus making it unnecessary to have a discipline in the subject. Rather, political leaders, generals, and businessmen occupied the pages of history books. Only the so-called great events in the public arena warranted the attention of historians. By definition, then, women who lived in the private sphere – or so it was believed – did not make history. This neat syllogism existed in the minds of most people until well into the twentieth century. By the same token, ordinary people, including men, as well as minority peoples, did not exist in the eyes of historians.

Since men were the writers of history for most of recorded time, and women's lives were seen as unworthy of documentation, women were invisible to historians. The domestic world – the environment in which children were raised, food was cooked, and clothing was made – was seen as insignificant daily activities. Even when women entered the public world as volunteers in hospitals, Sunday School teachers, and as petitioners for worthy causes, their work was not defined as important because there was no monetary award attached to it. All cultures have celebrated motherhood, child raising, the cultivation of the garden, weaving, and all of the other women's roles. But such experiences have usually been seen as trans-historical, reproduced in each generation and therefore ignored in historical texts. Women communicated their behavior to their daughters and demonstrated the tasks needed for adulthood. Though cultures varied, and circumstances changed over time, women's roles in all cultures were more similar than different. Careful records of female activities become superfluous under this cultural system, or so it seemed to the writers of history for a very long time.

Many factors came together in the twentieth century to change this scenario; and it was in the United States that the discipline of women's history began and then established the pattern followed in most western countries since. An active women's reform movement early in the century, during the progressive era (roughly the first fifteen years), included workers for suffrage, birth control, and children's welfare; these reform efforts brought together an impressive number of white and African-American women in urban America who made history in the public arena. They all believed in the importance of their work and kept good records. In some cases, they became their own historians, publishing the proceedings of their activities, keeping copies of the speeches they gave, and documenting their correspondence.

A rising rate of education among women and the growth of a significant middle class in industrial America also contributed to the creation of a later-to-be-critical mass of women interested in their own history. Indeed, throughout the twentieth century, external forces played major roles in preparing the groundwork for a professional discipline called women's history. The academy did not pioneer; male historians teaching largely men until the 1960s had little motivation or interest in integrating women's experiences into the narrative of history. Rather, it was major changes in the culture that eventually brought together disparate groups of women demanding the telling of their stories.

The women's suffrage movement of the early twentieth century worked for the passage of a constitutional amendment to grant women the right to vote. While petitioning, campaigning, and marching, the women reformers also kept documents on their conventions, their speeches, and their resolutions. This material was published and became one of the key primary source collections for later researchers on the subject of women's reform. Women's activities outside the home received more attention from historians than their work in the home, accurately reflecting the generally low esteem with which domestic work was held. It would take many decades before the everyday lives of women became a subject of historical research.

During the Progressive Era, historian Mary Beard began a career of researching and writing about women's accomplishments. While writing prolifically on American history with her husband Charles, an eminent historian at Columbia University, she also wrote a study of women's work in municipalities in 1915. Her particular interest in women's lives led her, in the 1930s and 1940s, to write about women's work, which she viewed as essential for civilization. During the Depression, Mary Beard predicted that scholarship would turn from its narrow focus on specialties toward a general integration of subject areas. She reasoned that men, as specialists, had been unable to deal with the economic catastrophe of the 1930s, while women, as generalists, had exhibited resilience in coping with life's multiple tasks. Beard's keen interest in the interaction of the past with the present, the ordinary with the extraordinary, and women and men's lives, convinced her that women's history would receive a lot of attention in this more enlightened environment. The skills displayed by women at home could heal a sick community (Beard 1976).

Beard collected women's records and writings with the intent to create an archive for future researchers. World War II interfered with her efforts, but they were not in vain. In 1942, Smith College created the Sophia Smith Collection as an offshoot of Beard's work; the following year the Schlesinger Library at Radcliffe College was established. Though not the World Center of Women's Archives, as originally envisioned by Beard, it was a sturdy beginning for research into women's history. A pioneer historian of the next generation, Eleanor Flexner, worked as an independent scholar, and used these resources as well as the Library of Congress and the National Archives to produce the first major synthesis of US women's history, in 1959: *Century of Struggle: The Women's Rights Movement in the United States.*

The period after the passage of the Nineteenth Amendment (women's suffrage) in 1920, however, did not lead to continued interest in female experiences; nor was it an equally active period for women reformers. To be sure, organization women in every community as well as on a national level continued to work for the betterment of the society and to keep records of their respective organization's work. But the 1920s and on did not maintain the momentum created by the Progressive Era. Young women in the 1920s, for example, may have joined the newly formed League of Women Voters but did not run for office. They remained behind the scenes. The campaign to end child labor met with defeat during the decade; and the Shepherd–Towner Act, the first major piece of legislation benefiting mothers and children, was born and died during the 1920s.

In the thirties figures such as Eleanor Roosevelt played a prominent public role, but the enormous challenge of keeping families stable and solvent preoccupied most women. Exceptional women like Roosevelt's friend, Florence Allen, became a judge; and Hollywood actresses achieved great celebrity. But the National Woman's Party failed to get the Equal Rights Amendment (ERA) passed, feminists split on various issues, and most women focused upon their private lives. The federal government, in fact, passed a law denying women employment if their husbands worked for the government. The primary breadwinner, or so it was assumed, was always the man, who was favored when unemployment was so severe.

Much research has concentrated on the role of women during World War II. For the first time in American history, married women in great numbers were recruited into the labor force to meet the extraordinary needs of military production. Women with small children, never a major part of the labor force, were brought into the factories; some private industries created day care centers to accommodate this new constituency. The US Congress passed the Lanham Act in 1942 to provide federal child care centers; but only 10 percent of defense workers' children were enrolled. Historians have debated whether the large numbers of working women constituted progress or not (Chafe 1972). Women as wage earners experienced an unprecedented sense of independence. While older women wished to remain in the work force after the war, large numbers of young women were happy to go home and become mothers. The resulting baby boom reflected the new optimism in postwar America. Accompanied by a long period of prosperity and the move to the suburbs, the growing middle class raised the largest families in twentieth-century history.

Life in 1950s America has been described as blissful, boring, or banal, but all Americans experienced a rising standard of living. Women continued working in record numbers, including middle-class women with older children, in order to maintain this new prosperity. But they returned to traditionally female jobs. Few women retained their high-paying, technical jobs. In 1945, Rosie the Riveter was replaced by the returning GIs. A consensus seemed to emerge that the veterans, and men in general, required the high-paying jobs. While on the surface women appeared to accept this reality, signs of discontent, though rarely interpreted as such, were beginning. The introduction of tranquilizer drugs in the mid-1950s, and particularly Valium in 1960, marketed for women's nervousness, indicated a new malady, though one unnamed.

Women's History Comes of Age

The existence of the preserved voices and documents concerning women's lives – both prominent and ordinary – did not, and does not, insure the flowering of a scholarly field called "women's history." While one of the patterns begun early in the century continued during the middle years – the increased education for girls – the goals of women's education remained traditional. Women in college studied domestic science and were told that their education would be useful in raising good children, a message that had been inculcated to women for many generations. The overwhelming majority of women college graduates (a percentage of women that remained low) may have worked for a few years before marriage, but either quit upon marriage, or when their first child was born. Only working-class women with children remained in the work force. If ambitious middle-class women wished to enter a profession, nursing, teaching, and librarianship were recommended, not the more demanding fields of doctoring or management. Combining a compatible career with marriage may have been a middle-class goal, but few envisioned themselves as a single career woman enjoying single adulthood forevermore.

The 1950s offered college women the same old message, but the circumstances were changing. The middle class expanded dramatically during the period, with the postwar baby boom and prosperity creating a new generation that came of age in the 1960s and 1970s. The women's liberation movement, born in the late 1960s out of the civil rights and antiwar movements, had, among its goals, to recreate its history. In an atmosphere of questioning, women activists began to insist that the colleges of America teach women's history as well as courses on women's psychology, culture, and society. The temper of the times was to categorize people by their shared grievances; and no constituency was larger than that of women.

These reformers, usually young college students, were joined by suburban wives awakened by Betty Friedan's *The Feminine Mystique* (1963) and by professional women. They had worked behind the scenes throughout the 1950s to achieve women's equal rights in the government and the courts. Together, they created a major reform movement dedicated to improving women's rights while learning about their past. In order to show present discrimination, evidence of past oppression had to be uncovered. New words entered the public vocabulary. "Sexism," "patriarchy," and "the personal is political" became slogans for both the ills of society and the solutions. Feminists defined women's traditional roles as oppressive and as handed down by a male-dominated power structure. A central message, communicated on platforms, in the streets, and on television, was sexual inequality: the consequence of custom, tradition, and historic discrimination. In order to redress contemporary grievances, however, it was necessary to know the past.

Women activists insisted upon learning about women's experiences in other historical periods so as to plan a future of women's equality. A generation of female and male historians in graduate school in the 1960s and 1970s answered the call, thereby becoming the first generation of researchers, teachers, and writers in the emerging field of women's history. They joined another new emerging discipline, social history, to study the lives of everyday people of all classes and colors. In the heady atmosphere of the late 1960s and early 1970s, diverse groups announced their grievances and their demands for redress. Many feminists in the university consciously modeled their plans after the Black Studies programs, asking for Women's Studies to enjoy equal status as a major in the university curriculum.

While initial reaction was often negative and doubtful, with few universities creating majors in Women's Studies, acceptance increased over time, so that specialized courses in women's history, psychology, and literature became common in the curricula by the 1980s. To fill the material vacuum, publishers began including important women and their accomplishments into their textbooks; no longer was Betsy Ross the only woman in discussions of the era of the Revolutionary War. No longer did Eleanor Roosevelt alone speak for all outstanding women. Incorporating all of the new fields and approaches – black history, social history, and women's history – elementary, high school, and college students read about people of color, about working-class leisure activities, and about the similarities and differences between women of different colors and classes. But the need for separate courses in women's history remained. Women's perspectives still required separate treatment.

The first generation of historians who specialized in women's history published their findings in the 1970s and began an ongoing process that has continued to this date. The output has been impressive; the first generation has been joined by a younger generation who came of age in the 1980s and 1990s. Both generations continue to research and write, and ranged from individual biographies to group studies and analyses of feminism. Local, regional, and national women's organizations have received attention, as well as the work of ordinary women in various communities. Key reform groups such as the nineteenth-century women abolitionists and the early twentieth-century feminists have received considerable attention, because the documentary record is extensive. Studies of extraordinary individuals continue to be produced as do biographies of little-known figures.

One of the main goals of the first generation of historians of women (which included male historians) was to introduce women and their perspectives into the historical record. They often raised questions about traditional historical topics; for example, what does war mean to women? What roles did they perform under such trying circumstances? Did it affect their postwar lives? Historians of women asked and answered these questions about the American Revolution and every subsequent war. By raising the question of female roles during wartime, they shone a light upon other participants too. No longer is the soldier and the battlefield the only focus in studies of war. Thanks to this re-evaluation, military history was humanized; and new studies highlighting the lives of ordinary soldiers have been produced.

Besides raising questions about old material, many historians asked new questions. For example, what were the turning points in women's history? How important was the sewing machine in the life of women (Lerner 1979)? What role has birth control played in women's lives? Indeed, a renewed interest in demography accompanied the new interest in women. The size of families became a significant factor in analyzing women's lives and those of other members of religious groups, classes, and regions. The meaning of the Industrial Revolution, which historians have long addressed, took on novel meanings under the influence of feminism. For instance, to study women's lives as garment workers – first in the home and then in the factory – enlarges the picture of industrializing America. Too often had scholars concentrated exclusively on male coal miners or male auto workers. The formation of labor unions, and their attitudes toward young and often single women workers, also received attention (Kessler-Harris 1982).

Both generations of women historians have devoted much research to the large subject of women's work. Who are women workers? Where do they work? Are they paid equally with men for their labor? These are all questions raised by historians

(Kessler-Harris 1982). The enormity of the subject has resulted in numerous studies examining particular groups of women: African-American domestics, white professionals, and Hispanic farm workers among others. The field has become a sub-field of women's history, sometimes blending into labor studies, sometimes remaining separate. It is a good example of Mary Beard's wish, half a century earlier, for disciplinary lines to blur and to unite present concerns with history. Contemporary issues drive much of the research into wage equality as well as racial and gender inequality. The perspective of the female economists and historians who study this subject varies as well, reflecting the diversity of interests of the researchers.

Women historians, then, were among the first intellectuals to raise the bar and admit women into the official portrait of America. They also brought the subject of gender, that is to say, the importance of culturally constructed values and behaviors in how women and men act, to public attention. They created a new consciousness that has become an integral part of American public discourse, a truly enormous contribution to cultural discussions. Some women historians also took an explicitly feminist perspective: they were intent on demonstrating how women's rights had been denied in the past and how the agenda for equality remained unfinished (Cott 1987). Some second-generation historians, as feminist-socialists, added another dimension: a conscious focus upon the lives of working-class and minority women (Kessler-Harris 1982). These historians emphasized the ways in which women had been exploited by capitalism and the patriarchal system.

As scholarship has increased, and diverse points of view have been welcomed, some recent historians have concentrated on the differences between groups of women, rather than their similarities. Previously, it had been the shared traits and experiences of all women – marriage and motherhood being the most obvious – that received the most attention. Ironically, male domination of women's lives, regardless of class or color, became a preoccupying concept for both the historians who emphasized similarities and those who concentrated on difference. Studies of nineteenth-century women abolitionists, for example, had noted how the white women reformers identified with black women slaves because they too were under the thumb of masters: their husbands. So while they recognized the severity of slavery, they wished to emphasize how all women suffered, slave and free.

Current historians, who mark off the differences between groups of women rather than searching for their commonalities, may also discuss how men possessed all of the power in the family and the society. But voice is given to the rejected women and to note their particular oppression. Women historians (often members of the minority about which they write) who subscribe to the difference point of view devote themselves exclusively to the recreation of their group's history and do not offer comparisons with the dominant white group; nor do they deal with possible interactions between white women reformers and minority women reformers. The need to resurrect the separate histories of different groups of women continued to be a research project to the end of the century. The possibility of an ambitious synthesis of majority and minority women's history remains on the agenda.

Beginning in the 1980s, with more minority women, particularly black women, attending graduate school, those who chose history researched their own group's past and wrote about their distinctive oppression (Yung 1995; Hine and Thompson 1998). African-American women's clubs, suffrage groups, and welfare organizations entered the historical record, often for the first time. A new cast of characters joined the well-known figures in the history textbooks. Feminist historians' emphasis on middle-class women had ignored working-class women's perspective, a situation minority women are correcting.

As a result of this continuing reappraisal, all accepted judgments became suspect. For example, male historians studying minorities had often concentrated only on the achievements of men. African-American women historians observed that the women's movement studied white women, and the civil rights movement scholars studied black men. It became their task to uncover the activities of African-American women in diverse activities including the civil rights movement. Impressive field workers such as Ella Baker and Joanne Robinson now received attention alongside narratives of the well-known Rosa Parks and the better known Reverend Martin Luther King, Jr. Indeed, the role of ordinary women doing ordinary tasks, such as teaching illiterate southern blacks to read in their homes and mimeographing news-letters to report on the progress of the Montgomery bus boycott in 1955, became a major contribution of these minority women historians (Hine and Thompson 1998).

No End of Ideology

Clearly, ideological considerations affect the historical enterprise. Contemporary women historians differ according to their personal views and predilections, as their work reveals. The public interest in multiculturalism beginning in the 1980s encour-aged many women historians to consider the variety of female experiences. A recent study of Chinese women in San Francisco (Yung 1995) is a good example of this newer scholarship. Yet it must be quickly added that publications cannot always be distinguished by generations. Historians' writings are rarely neat and predictable, nor do all members of a generation share a point of view. Gerda Lerner, the dean of modern women's history, for example, published a ground-breaking collection of documents on African-American women early in the period (Lerner 1972). She also wrote a major series of essays conceptualizing the field (1979), while publishing work on mainstream women's experiences.

Lerner established the first doctoral program in women's history at the University of Wisconsin in the 1980s, and in 1981 became the first female president of the Organization of American Historians in half a century. She continued to write, expanding her range to include women's history from the ancient world to the present. She exemplified a pioneer in the field who anticipated many of the themes and concerns of the second generation of women historians. Further, Lerner's work fits into the category of reinserting important women into the historical record as well as describing the lives of both minority and majority women. As both a practicing historian and a frequent lecturer to general audiences, she became a role model to women interested in their history as well as in pursuing graduate studies in the field.

More typical of the first generation's scholarship, Allen F. Davis's *Spearheads for Reform: The Social Settlements and the Progressive Movement, 1890–1914* (1967) demonstrated the importance of women, largely middle-class white women, to the settlement houses where newly arriving immigrants attended English classes, cooked their ethnic foods, knitted, and learned American ways. Jane Addams of Chicago and Lillian Wald of New York appeared as critical reform leaders, whose interests and activities reached beyond the home into every aspect of the community. Addams became the garbage collector in her ward in order to become more involved in the community; Wald started a visiting nurses' unit for the tenement dwellers on the Lower East Side. Parallel African-American women's organizations became the subject of many second-generation texts (Hine and Thompson 1998), and Ida Wells-Barnett and Mary Church Terrell became especially known, both as the subjects of feminist histories and the documenters of their own stories. The combined scholarship of both generations offers a rich and comprehensive record of women reformers bettering their communities throughout the twentieth century.

Indeed, the role of women as institution builders and preservers has been pivotal to many studies of the last three decades. There is no school, church, hospital, or social welfare agency that has not been started or staffed (or both) by women, often volunteers. Women historians have pointed out the importance of *all* work in a culture that only recognizes and rewards paid labor. The unpaid labor of women as Sunday school teachers in the white and African-American communities, for example, is now appreciated as well as the women's auxiliaries of most men's organizations. Historians have published numerous studies of YWCAs in various cities as well as the work of the National Council of Negro Women, the National Council of Jewish Women, and a myriad of other women's clubs and organizations. They brought benevolent, welfare, and philanthropic activities to every community in the country (Cott 1987; Hine and Thompson 1998). Prior to the New Deal, no federal protection was available for vulnerable women, whether widows or single mothers. And volunteer organizations were crucial to the survival of many of the beleaguered.

In the 1960s, when the feminist movement was reborn, *The Feminine Mystique* became both a rallying cry for contemporary women and a summation – from a feminist perspective – of women's twentieth-century experience, particularly that of white middle-class suburbanites. Friedan's enormously popular book, based partly on interviews with Smith College graduates, articulated individual grievances while suggesting that they were shared by countless others across the generations. While both contemporary critics and later commentators questioned her analysis of women's history (Sochen 1973), her study struck a popular chord and made Friedan an avidly sought speaker on the subject of women's issues throughout the 1970s and 1980s. *The Feminine Mystique* legitimated heretofore unspoken frustrations. It gave intellectual heft to discontented housewives and in 1966 contributed to the formation of a multi-generational women's organization, the National Organization for Women (NOW). Friedan served as its first president. While she was not a professional historian, her success encouraged everybody interested in the field to continue their research and to explore in many directions. Indeed, by the 1990s, historians had produced biographies of Friedan, organizational studies of NOW, and various analyses of the women's liberation movement. The Equal Rights Amendment, passed by the US Congress in 1972, died a decade later, when too few states ratified it. This was the most conspicuous failure of the political organization that Friedan helped to found.

While acknowledging that women historians' personal philosophies, their individual temperament, and often unplanned circumstances shaped their scholarly work during the last three decades, it is also important to note that most histories of women fell into one of two categories: "womanist" or "feminist." The former concentrates on the accomplishments of women, sees women as active agents on their own behalf, and generally lauds their efforts (Flexner 1959; Sochen 1973). The latter notes the many ways in which discrimination and prejudice have prevented women from fulfilling their human potential (Kessler-Harris 1982; Cott 1987). The two viewpoints are not mutually exclusive; after all, it is possible to record women's successes while also noting the obstacles in their paths. But the bridge between the two is not often crossed. Cott discusses the split in the feminist movement after 1920 in somewhat different terms, noting that the ERA feminists insisted upon legal equality, while the "protectionists" argued that women's differences must be protected in the workplace.

The ideological divide occurred earlier in the century when some women reformers followed Alice Paul and the National Woman's Party and worked for the ERA, which was first introduced in Congress in 1923. Not all women activists agreed with the ERA assessment. Florence Kelley, who had worked long and hard for protective labor laws for women throughout the Progressive Era (Sklar 1995), insisted that women in the work force had to be treated differently because their situations differed significantly from men's. Not until the home, the factory, and the office treated women the same as men would true equality come into being. Since equity had not been reached, Kelley and the subsequent generations of women who shared her views believed that special treatment for women was essential.

In the late twentieth century, the nature of the disagreement between "womanists" and "feminists" shifted. The former lauded and celebrated women's differences, while the latter continued to work for equal rights. While Kelley's view of difference was based upon the understanding of women as mothers, potential mothers, and workers, the contemporary commentators emphasize, often in mystical terms, women's moral superiority, and in rare cases, the belief that they should separate from men, living communally with other women. This is a distinctly minority position, but it divided the women's movement by the end of the twentieth century. The feminists continued to work for equal rights under the law, though further complications erupted among feminists. Some of them held that the First Amendment protected pornography; others sought to restrict it as harmful to women.

In 1980, historian Carl Degler took a different approach. His study discussed the inherent conflict that exists in every time period between woman as an autonomous individual and as a family member. This seemingly irreconcilable difference is the primary reason for an inability to live fully in both the private and public worlds. As a built-in cultural problem, it can only be ameliorated by the acknowledgment of both realms and by the creation of provisions for women to be wives, mothers, workers, and volunteers. To overcome patriarchy, a major shift in cultural values, values held by most men and women, is required (Degler 1980). The traditional belief that each mother should raise her own children in her own home must be analyzed and evaluated as a cultural choice; women should decide for themselves whether to follow it. But as Degler and others have noted, the legitimacy of this position is not yet widely recognized; nor have taxpayers shown any willingness to provide adequate day care facilities for all children.

Degler's perspective is not that cultural arrangements are a one-sided, male-dominated arrangement, but rather a shared value system in which both men and women collaborate. While recognizing the importance of male power, Degler also considered the ways in which both women and men shape the outcome. In his analysis, individualism (and the woman's wish to be defined as an individual) invariably clashes with communalism, which requires a mother in the home who cares for her family and the larger community. Role conflicts, evident during all periods of American history, result in incremental social change but not in revolutionary transformations. Rather than use the vocabulary of Marxism or a patriarchal frame-work, Degler's cultural frame encompasses much of the historical debate in less ideologically-charged language.

Hine and Thompson's synthesis of African-American women's history embraces both the womanist and feminist positions. They demonstrate that African-American women lived in both the public and private spheres. Black women were community builders while also caring for their own homes and working as domestics in other people's homes. They displayed extraordinary strength in the face of continual adver-sity, thereby earning the admiration of all womanists; they petitioned for the right to vote and to attend quality schools, winning the support of feminists. Their successful adaptations provide important evidence of women preserving family under extremely difficult circumstances. Both in slavery and in freedom, these women kept both families and communities together and defied the dichotomous view held by some historians. Because African-American men were also oppressed, the women did not choose between marking off women's differences from men, but rather worked for civil rights alongside African-American men, while also fighting for women's rights. They lived as mothers and workers all at the same time.

Let Us Now Praise Un-famous Women

While public activities have received much attention, they have not been the exclusive focus of historians, particularly those writing in the 1980s and 1990s. Researchers at the end of the twentieth century have cast their eyes upon the experiences of ordinary women. Such scholars have shown that all subjects have a history. Women historians have also contributed mightily to the democratizing of historical studies, bringing daily lives into the textbooks, and boldly asserting that the obscure deserve as much attention as the famous. Alongside social historians, African-American historians, and labor historians, women historians have elevated the accomplishments of heretofore nameless women into the history books. In so doing, they have implicitly expanded the definition of history, removing its elite label. No longer can history textbooks offer students a select and slim version of the past, ignoring the everyday occurrences, the popular pastimes, the women's clubs, and the sewing circles. All subjects became appropriate studies for historians.

For example, David Katzman's study (1988) of domestic workers in the late nineteenth and early twentieth centuries highlighted an important but often neg-lected subject. As America industrialized, and more people lived in cities and worked in the new offices, the middle class expanded and housewives relied on cheap immigrant labor (most notably Irish) and then African-American women from the South to clean their houses and do the laundry. The reluctance of black women to live in employers' homes led to day labor for domestics. This refusal highlighted the difference between married black women workers and single Irish immigrant women.

Home workers were not included in labor statistics and were therefore invisible to traditional historical studies of workers. Labor that is paid for in private escapes public scrutiny, a phenomenon that persists. And women's work, often done for lower pay than men's wages, has always received less consideration. Further, the mistresses of the household playing the role of employer often exposed tensions that were previously unexamined. The employer-woman was often uncomfortable in her role as boss and treated the servant badly. The sexual exploitation of the domestic worker by the master of the household also became a subject worthy of historical examination. Indeed, by examining diaries, correspondences, and reminiscences, a dramatic, usually difficult world was uncovered.

Housework, of course, was a chore all women knew about, even if they were fortunate to have domestic help. This subject, like all others, has a history, and Susan Strasser's monograph (1982) put the subject into a context that enabled readers to compare and contrast their contemporary experiences with past ones. This is a good example of the constant interaction between studies of the past and concerns of the present. Susan Porter Benson's work (1986) on the new group of saleswomen in the growing department stores of America (her study covers 1890–1940) offers a fascinating glance not only at the sales clerks, but at their managers and the customers as well. The interaction, and often the tension, between these three groups opens a window into the new roles of women in the twentieth century. The growing popularity of consumerism and the multiple lives women led as workers and consumers received attention from historians as part of this new evaluation of all of women's activities.

Working in a department store was viewed as one step above working in a factory and parallel with office work. Wearing a white collar and not engaging in physical work gave working-class and lower-middle-class women an opportunity to earn more money and enjoy more autonomy. Progress in women's work, of course, is a relative term. Farm girls working in textile mills in the mid-nineteenth century saw their wages and working conditions as better than farm chores, although the later sweatshops were miserable places for young women to work. Relative to the economic possibilities available to working-class or middle-class men, women's work was low paid. Female school teachers received half the salary given to men in the early years of the twentieth century. Women were not offered the most lucrative jobs in the factory, the office, or the department store either.

As women's lives became an appropriate subject for study, every aspect came under scrutiny. Women in popular culture, a seemingly pleasant but unworthy topic for the historian's attention, captured the interest of film critics and women historians. Beginning with critic Molly Haskell's seminal study, *From Reverence to Rape* (1974), scholars have studied the images of women in film, music, and television. Borrowing from literary theory and the new field of cultural studies (and thanks to the newly awakened consciousness of the 1970s women's movement), how women were portrayed, who did the portraying, and how the audience received the portrait all became subjects for study. Both the female performer and the performance became the text. From Mae West to Marilyn Monroe, writers have commented on the cultural images of women as presented through popular film stars, singers, and television personalities (Sochen 1999).

Women entertainers have been among the most visible and successful women. While the glass ceiling still prevails in the corporate world, twentieth-century show business had a place (often prominent, though not equal) for women. Though boundaries clearly existed – women as film producers and directors, for example, remained a rarity – women became highly-paid performers. When the movie industry was young, women dominated screen writing. When the field was unionized and movies became profitable, women lost out. Women historians have produced biographies of individual women performers, as well as analyses of television situation comedies and dissections of Madonna's lyrics and persona. With studies proliferating, a consistent picture emerged, demonstrating how stubborn cultural images are. Woman as victim or as sexual temptress, for example, has long existed in literature, film, and music. While a few male and female writers for popular culture have tried to break the traditional image pattern, the stereotypical formulas persist.

What these studies have demonstrated, among other things, is that there is no area of American culture that does not have something to say about women's real or ideal lives. Indeed, popular cultural material is an inviting pathway for those seeking to fathom enduring values and prejudices. Asking questions of popular figures as well as popular institutions shows a new awareness of the meaning invested in all aspects of culture. If women are absent from adventure movies, what message is being sent by the filmmakers? Furthermore, how is the audience receiving it? If women always have to be saved from villains, what is being said about the treatment and value of women? Unexpected questions are raised by the younger generation of college students who regularly take courses in popular culture.

Women scholars examine all material as appropriate for analysis of cultural values. Since the 1970s, a new awareness has taken hold; and though not everyone enjoys the interrogation (nor engages in it), clearly two generations of young women and men watch movies and television programs with a heightened consciousness. Furthermore, the active participation of the entertainer in creating the roles she plays becomes another variable in the mix. Contemporary actresses share their personal lives with their fans and try, when they can, to select screen roles that harmonize with their personal philosophy. In the 1930s and 1940s, actress Katharine Hepburn's career was unique in her careful choosing of roles. She characteristically played an independent woman who was often married, but was rarely a mother. Most actresses during Hollywood's golden era (1930s to 1950s) had been under long-term contract to a film studio, and lacked the power to choose.

But the upper-class Hepburn had advantages unknown to most struggling actresses; examining her career from a feminist perspective gives viewers an opportunity to study the ways in which the men of Hollywood shaped the careers of women and insisted upon the perpetuation of old stereotypes. Marilyn Monroe's physical beauty denied her the opportunity to stretch herself dramatically. The male screen-writers, directors, and producers would not consider it. A womanist interpretation of women's roles in popular culture might focus upon the spunky roles played by Hepburn, Joan Crawford, Rosalind Russell, Bette Davis, and others during the Depression. In sharp contrast to the action movies starring men, the women portrayed survivors and adapters during the crises of economic distress and war. Greer Garson as Mrs. Minniver during World War II epitomized the woman preserving family and humane values under pressure.

The subject of scholarship expands considerably once the climate permits questions about all parts of a woman's life. Women's sexuality only became an acceptable subject after the opening of the public discourse on heretofore forbidden themes.

Gender studies enabled historians to consider how both men and women have expressed their sexuality in the course of American history (D'Emilio and Freedman 1988). The emergence of the gay rights movement in the 1970s also led to new studies of lesbianism. Again, the contemporary scene influenced research rather than the other way around. Historians began to examine laws written from the colonial era and thereafter, to discover the dominant expectations of proper sexual behavior. Lawmakers often passed laws to inhibit what was perceived to be immoral actions. While other evidence noted that the laws were inconsistently enforced, their presence on the law books suggested social ideals. Researchers on this subject have also studied prescriptive literature, the self-help books and advice literature offered to nervous people on how to court, how to be a good lover, and how to prevent conception. The gap between the ideal and the real, of course, remains wide in all eras. Studies of women's sexuality intersect with family history, social history, and women's history and therefore demonstrate the interdisciplinary nature of much of the scholarship on women's lives.

Among the many sub-specialties that have been spawned by women's history is the interdisciplinary field of women in sports. No phenomenon illustrates the cultural divisions between men and women more dramatically. Indeed, high school and collegiate women who began to take physical education classes in the 1880s and 1890s had to fight the dominant prejudice against women behaving like men. Many of the women athletic leaders shared the view that competition was an evil to be overcome. As Lucille Eaton Hill, the director of physical training at Wellesley College, announced in 1903: "We must avoid the evils which are so apparent to thoughtful people in the conduct of athletics for men." Senda Berenson, who invented women's basketball in the 1890s, created special rules acknowledging women's physical differences. She emphasized intramural activities at Smith College, where she was athletic director, and studiously avoided the rough-and-ready view that winning was everything (Riess 1984).

While team sports could be played in school, no professional opportunities were available for talented women athletes, though in individual sports (such as tennis, golf, track and field, and ice skating) women could distinguish themselves. During the course of the twentieth century, many moved from amateur to professional status. As sport became part of popular culture, attractive and capable women athletes received media attention. Babe Didrikson Zaharias became the first famous woman athlete. In the 1932 Olympics in Los Angeles she broke three women's world records: in javelin throwing, in the high jump, and in the 80-meter hurdles. In the 1930s and 1940s, she became a champion golfer as well. Zaharias offered admirers a new view of a strong and self-assured woman, though her so-called masculine appearance was gradually altered by media-wise promoters to include a softer hairstyle and makeup. The stereotypical view that muscular women must be lesbians remained a somber cloud hanging over women in sports.

Billie Jean King's career in tennis coincided with the emerging women's liberation movement in the 1960s and 1970s. To promote her agenda, she consciously took advantage of the growing awareness that women were not treated equally with men in the sports arena, the schools, and the workplace. In 1967 King publicly insisted that women tennis players receive equal prize money as well as an equal number of professional endorsements. Three years later she and tennis magazine publisher

Gladys Heldman began the Virginia Slims tournament, which was the first professional tour for women. Television also became an ally of women athletes. In 1973 King's match against Bobby Riggs was televised before over 30,000 spectators in the Houston Astrodome. Though Riggs was an older, over-the-hill player, sports writers and feminists invested considerable emotion and hyperbole in King's victory over him.

In 1972 the US Education Amendments included a provision for all elementary gym classes to be integrated; separate sports programs at the high school and college level were required to receive equal funding. Advocates of women's sports were elated, though their optimism has so far not proven warranted. Though little girls and boys have taken physical exercise and gym classes together in elementary school, college athletic programs have in particular been loathe to provide as much funding for women's sports programs as, say, varsity football. The power of men's college teams to attract alumni funds continues to prevent realization of the goal of equal funding. In the professional arena, the Women's Basketball Association has experienced a rocky history, in contrast to the National Basketball Association. Individual women athletes in track and field, tennis, and ice skating have nevertheless become prominent figures in popular culture.

No aspect or dimension of women's lives escapes the scrutiny of contemporary historians. In the early twenty-first century, universities regularly offer courses on the subject and students major in Women's Studies. Furthermore, in all aspects of public life, be it government, the professions, or the business world, women's past is considered in determining present policies. In this sense, the popular cry of the women's liberation movement in the early 1970s – the personal is political – has become the guideline for both scholarship and public policy. Recognizing women's impressive contributions to American history, in the private and public spheres, has become accepted wisdom. Indeed, the distinctions between the two realms has diminished with the recognition that all human activities are important and that the skills learned in the home are applicable elsewhere. The constant interaction of the past, the present, and the future has become a vital ingredient in the study of women's history.

REFERENCES AND FURTHER READING

Bailey, Beth (1999) *Sex in the Heartland*. Cambridge, Mass.: Harvard University Press.
Beard, Mary (ed.) (1976) *America Through Women's Eyes*. New York: Greenwood Press.
Benson, Susan Porter (1986) *Counter Cultures: Saleswomen, Managers, and Customers in American Department Stores, 1890–1940*. Urbana: University of Illinois Press.
Cahn, Susan K. (1990) "Coming on strong: gender and sexuality in women's sport, 1900–1960." PhD dissertation, University of Minnesota.
Chafe, William H. (1972) *The American Woman: Her Changing Social, Economic, and Political Role, 1920–1970*. New York: Oxford University Press.
Cook, Blanche Wiesen (1992, 1999), *Eleanor Roosevelt*, 2 vols. New York: Viking Press.
Cott, Nancy F. (1987) *The Grounding of Modern Feminism*. New Haven, Conn.: Yale University Press.
Davis, Allen F. (1967) *Spearheads for Reform: The Social Settlements and the Progressive Movement, 1890–1914*. New York: Oxford University Press.

Degler, Carl N. (1980) *At Odds: Women and the Family in America from the Revolution to the Present*. New York: Oxford University Press.

D'Emilio, John and Freedman, Estelle B. (1988) *Intimate Matters: A History of Sexuality in America*. New York: Harper and Row.

Flexner, Eleanor (1959) *Century of Struggle: The Women's Rights Movement in the United States*. Cambridge, Mass.: Harvard University Press.

Friedan, Betty (1963) *The Feminine Mystique*. New York: W. W. Norton.

Gordon, Linda (1976) *Woman's Body, Woman's Right: A Social History of Birth Control in America*. New York: Grossman.

Haskell, Molly (1974) *From Reverence to Rape: The Treatment of Women in the Movies*. New York: Penguin.

Hine, Darlene Clark and Thompson, Kathleen (1998) *A Shining Thread of Hope: The History of Black Women in America*. New York: Broadway.

Katzman, David (1988) *Seven Days a Week: Women and Domestic Service in Industrializing America*. Champaign: University of Illinois Press.

Kessler-Harris, Alice (1982) *Out to Work: A History of Wage-Earning Women in the United States*. New York: Oxford University Press.

Lerner, Gerda (ed.) (1972) *Black Women in White America*. New York: Pantheon.

—— (1979) *The Majority Finds its Past: Placing Women in History*. New York: Oxford University Press.

Riess, Steven A. (ed.) (1984) *The American Sporting Experience*. West Point, NY: Leisure Press.

Rupp, Leila and Taylor, Verta (1987) *Survival in the Doldrums: The American Woman's Rights Movement, 1945 to the 1960s*. New York: Oxford University Press.

Sklar, Kathryn Kish (1995) *Florence Kelley and the Nation's Work*. New Haven, Conn.: Yale University Press.

Sochen, June (1973) *Movers and Shakers: Women Thinkers and Activists in America, 1900–1970*. New York: Quadrangle.

—— (1999) *From Mae to Madonna: Women Entertainers in Twentieth Century America*. Lexington: University Press of Kentucky.

Strasser, Susan (1982) *Never Done: A History of American Housework*. New York: Pantheon.

Yung, Judy (1995) *Unbound Feet: A Social History of Chinese Women in San Francisco*. Berkeley: University of California Press.

PART IV

The Polity and the Economy

CHAPTER EIGHTEEN

The Military

JERRY COOPER

From their origins to the early twentieth century, America's armed forces have existed on the periphery of national life. Safety rested within the confines of the North American continent for most of the nation's history. That reality shaped America's approach to world affairs and profoundly influenced military policy and institutions. Changing relationships with the world in the twentieth century involved the nation in increasingly complex economic and diplomatic affairs far beyond the western hemisphere and altered dramatically the status of the military.

Continental security until 1900 allowed the United States to follow policies of non-intervention overseas and defense of the homeland. Consequently the US rarely used military force outside the western hemisphere before 1898 other than to protect overseas citizens and assist in extending American commercial interests. The policy of continental defense allowed the maintenance of remarkably small armed services, given the geographic size, population, and wealth of the nation. Moreover, from the colonial era, Americans had viewed military forces with suspicion, seeing large standing armies and navies as possible sources for political interference and graft, if not outright threats to republican liberty. Public indifference replaced anti-militarism in the nineteenth century, yet ensured the continuance of a small army and navy as surely as did any lingering anti-militarism.

A changing relationship with the world after 1898 moved the armed forces from the periphery to the heart of national affairs, as policy-makers fitfully redefined America's defensive frontier. Early in the twentieth century, President Theodore Roosevelt extended the frontier into the Caribbean basin. By 1917 President Woodrow Wilson defined the frontier as the northeastern Atlantic, where German submarines roamed at will. A quarter of a century later, President Franklin D. Roosevelt identified the River Rhine as the eastern limits of the US line of defense. After victory in 1945 the defensive frontier became a global one, encompassing all of western Europe on the one hand, and the 38th parallel in Korea on the other. Where US defense might begin in the post-Cold War years remains unclear. But its locus surely will lie beyond the North American continent.

Until the late 1960s, military historians devoted most of their work to relating and analyzing American participation in the two world wars and the Korean War. Even before the Vietnam conflict ended in 1975, historians began to treat it similarly. Books and articles on these wars continue to appear regularly, with a renewed interest in the Korean conflict evident of late. Military accounts of World War II and Vietnam remain perennial favorites with publishers. Interpretive disputes in these works center on strategy, generalship, and operations. Historians have argued, for example, over the virtues of Dwight D. Eisenhower's broad front strategy in Europe, wrangle about the efficacy of strategic bombing in World War II, Korea, and Vietnam, or quarrel about whether there was an acceptable strategy that could have produced victory in Vietnam. The conduct of war, of course, is the ultimate reason why nations maintain armed forces; and an emphasis on wartime leadership, strategic decision-making, and operational effectiveness surely belongs in the domain of the military historian.

Military organizations exist in peace as well as in war, and spend far more time carrying out peacetime duties than they ever engage in combat. Historians working in military affairs gave little attention to the peacetime history of the armed forces until the mid-1960s. Military history then broadened its purview to examine the institutional development of the services, the social composition of the officer corps and enlisted ranks, the professional development of the officer corps, the nature of civil–military relations, and the economic importance of military spending (among many topics long neglected). This new emphasis on the institutional and social history of the military largely began at the beginning, dealing first with eighteenth- and nineteenth-century developments. These accounts often bristle with historiographical contentions. For the most part, historical assessment of the twentieth-century military off the battlefield and outside headquarters tents and wardrooms is not fully developed. The reader of military affairs during peacetime in the twentieth century will not find sharp interpretive disagreements. Historians have yet to complete the institutional, social, political, and economic history of the military since 1900. Consequently their accounts lack distinctive, contrasting interpretations. This essay reflects the current state of the historical literature for the period.

The acquisition of overseas holdings after 1898, followed by intervention in World War I two decades later, shaped America's rise to world power. Although the Senate refused to accept the Treaty of Versailles by the necessary 2/3 vote, the US in fact became an international power during the years between the two world wars. The need to defend a small overseas empire, participate in the Great War, then meet the nation's security needs in the interwar period fostered significant changes in the army and navy between 1899 and the late 1930s. The total strength of the armed forces grew significantly in the aftermath of the Spanish-American War. The army, a mere 28,000 officers and men in 1898, roughly quadrupled from 1899 to 1916. Growth in the navy paralleled that of the senior service, increasing nearly five times between 1898 and 1916, from 12,000 to just over 58,000. The Marine Corps expanded as well, growing from just below 4,000 in 1897 to 10,600 in 1916. Military expenditures grew proportionately to the increase in the size of the services after the Spanish-American War. Between 1897 and 1916 the combined budgets of the army and navy rose from $82 million to $370 million.

More men and more money aided the services in meeting increased responsibilities. Traditionally the army's major missions were to defend the United States from invasion and to preserve domestic order. The navy served to prevent invasion and to attack enemy commerce in war while representing US overseas interests in peace.

Acquisition of an overseas empire required the services to take on new duties, including the establishment of overseas army garrisons. (Roughly 30 percent of the army served overseas to 1917.) When President Theodore Roosevelt redefined the nation's frontier to include the Caribbean basin, the navy and marines assumed the task of insuring American dominance in the region, with the marines spearheading major interventions on the island of Hispaniola and in Nicaragua.

Professional military men, who were unhappy that colonial responsibilities absorbed so many of the new soldiers, sailors, and marines joining the ranks, appealed for military reform. The precipitate alteration in the US role in the world affected how officers perceived the status of their services and the nature of national security. To these men, the new role created distinct possibilities that the US might become involved in war with one or more of the great powers. By any measure, they believed, the nation was woefully unprepared to take on the mass armies and battle fleets of these powers. From the early twentieth century to the Japanese attack on Pearl Harbor in December 1941, military leaders lamented unpreparedness, and labored – with limited success – to convince presidents and congressmen to support further expansion and modernization of the armed forces.

The pleas for reform suggest that the most significant change in the American armed forces after 1898 took place in the minds of army and navy officers. Military professionals wanted well-equipped, well-trained active forces, supported by reliable ready reserves, to confront potential foreign enemies. Their calls failed to win civilian political support. Presidents and congressmen had no desire to become embroiled in international conflict and were content to keep forces sufficient only to defend the nation and support its unilateralist and non-interventionist foreign policy.

Congress did approve increases in manpower and budgets to meet the new colonial responsibilities, and adopted measures that incrementally improved the effectiveness of the services. Army reformers had long sought a general staff system that would give the service an agency to make contingency war plans, coordinate training and education, develop a reliable reserve, and evaluate world military activities. Secretary of War Elihu Root convinced Congress to approve a general staff act and a militia reform law in 1903. He also reorganized the army's education system by reviving the service school at Fort Leavenworth and by establishing the Army War College. Army leaders damned the National Guard as an unreliable reserve force, arguing that the localized state soldiery could not be made into reliable troops. Chief of Staff Leonard Wood (1910–14) spoke for ardent reformers in urging army expansion and replacement of the National Guard with a federally controlled reserve system. Wood's efforts failed because adoption of his ideas would mark too sharp a break from traditional military practice.

Substantive reform came when Congress approved the National Defense Act of 1916. In equal parts a reaction to the war in Europe, to deteriorating German–American relations, and to the fervor of the 1916 presidential campaign, the law partially met the demands for preparedness. Army strength was increased to a maximum of 175,000; it established greater federal control over the National Guard and created a separate army reserve system as well. For the first time in American history, Congress adopted a peacetime military policy governing how the nation would mobilize an army for war. The 1916 law marked the triumph of military professionalism, ensuring general staff control of the next war's army and relegating the National Guard to minority status.

At the dawn of the twentieth century, the navy also sought to abandon traditional policy. Naval officers embraced the ideas of Alfred Thayer Mahan, who asserted that national security depended upon a large battleship fleet that was fully manned, trained, and ready to take offensive action against an enemy on the high seas. Like their army counterparts, naval reformers sought to win professional control of policy, strategy, and force structure. Their ideas had made inroads on traditional policy before the Spanish-American War. But the postwar service still lacked the requisite ships and internal professional control to create a sea force capable of matching the fleets of the major naval powers.

An impressive performance against Spain in 1898, and Theodore Roosevelt's succession to the presidency in 1901, gave the navy the opportunity to build a Mahanian force. Roosevelt won substantial increases in naval appropriations, added fifteen new battleships to the fleet, and acquired the Panama Canal Zone. The navy also gained greater control of operations, planning, and strategy. In 1900 Secretary of the Navy John D. Long established the Navy General Board, which – in conjunction with the Naval War College and the Office of Naval Intelligence – carried out contingency war planning that was more sophisticated than army planning was. Belatedly, in 1915, the navy acquired a more sophisticated staff system, when Congress created the office of the Chief of Naval Operations.

The navy wanted more. As early as 1903, the General Board urged creation of a two-ocean navy with 48 battleships and another 250 combat vessels, which would equal if not outclass the British fleet. More realistically, the board continually but fruitlessly requested the craft needed to join battleships in a properly balanced fleet. Moreover a modern navy needed overseas bases to refuel and refit while far from home. Congress and presidents, however, refused to fund globe-straddling naval bases, and therefore approved only modest bases at Pearl Harbor, Hawaii, and Subic Bay in the Philippines. Nonetheless naval supporters convinced Congress to approve an act in 1916 that revolutionized naval affairs. The law provided for a navy, to be completed in 1925, that was theoretically the equal of any in the world. As with the National Defense Act of 1916, the Naval Act was not connected to a specific foreign policy, and did not anticipate American intervention in the Great War.

America sent untrained soldiers into the trenches in 1918. Despite unpreparedness and a secondary role in the war, the intervention of the US ensured Allied victory. Participation in the war deeply affected army, navy, and marine officers who remained in service thereafter. Having been unprepared to cope immediately with the complex demands of world war, armed service leaders insisted after 1918 that the United States had to be fully prepared for the next conflagration. In 1920 the army's general staff offered a bill that called for an army of 500,000, for the elimination of the National Guard, and for the adoption of universal military training (UMT). Just as boldly, the navy urged Congress to resume funding of the Naval Act of 1916, which had been suspended during the war so that ships to combat German submarines could be acquired. Both soldiers and sailors would be sadly disappointed in their quest for military strength and respectability.

Congress refused to approve the army's proposal and instead enacted the 1920 National Defense Act. The law authorized the enlargement of the army to 280,000 men, the retention of a beefed-up Guard, and the creation of an Organized Reserve for the army. Finally, the law gave the general staff more authority to prepare contingency plans, especially to mobilize a war army. The navy suffered an even greater defeat. After initially appropriating funds to resume a 1916 building plan, Congress approved the treaties signed at the Washington Naval Conference of 1921–2. The treaties imposed limits on the number and size of major combat vessels maintained by the treaty signatories: the United States, Great Britain, Japan, France, and Italy. Treaty limits governed naval policy until 1938, and denied the navy its long-sought two-ocean fleet that the General Board had envisioned in 1903.

While the army and navy lost much of what they hoped to win in the early 1920s, they increased their prewar strength. The 4-million-man war army demobilized rapidly; from 1925 to 1935, the army never exceeded 140,000. The service grew slowly from the mid-1930s and reached 269,000 in 1940, as the nation began to rearm. Although the general staff believed that the army was far too small, its average size in these years reflected a 38 percent increase over the 1906–15 strength of 90,000. The navy also experienced a sharp drop from its wartime strength of nearly 500,000 sailors. Until the naval expansion of the late 1930s, the sea service kept 90,000 to 95,000 men in uniform, 37,000 more than served in 1916. The marines achieved a postwar gain of between 18,000 and 19,000 in the interwar years, a 55 percent increase from 1916.

Interwar defense spending also exceeded prewar figures. Army expenditures for 1923 alone totaled $7 million more than what had been appropriated for both services in 1916, while the navy expended another $378 million in 1923. The services faced financial stringency throughout the interwar period, yet both received funding far more substantial than that appropriated in the five years before entrance into World War I. Army spending before the war peaked in 1914 at $208 million. Its lowest budget during the 1920s was $357 million, in 1924. Despite the onset of the Great Depression, army spending never fell below $400 million during the 1930s. Navy expenditures reveal similar patterns. The navy's highest pre-1917 budget was $170 million in 1916; its lowest after the war came in 1926, at $311 million. From 1934 onward, the New Deal provided extra funds for the navy, especially in 1935 and 1936.

Historian Russell Weigley, among others, stressed the severe neglect in military affairs between the wars, and argued that the army "may have been less ready to function as a fighting force than at any time in its history" (1984: 402). Other scholars view the interwar years more favorably, noting that until the mid-1930s military policy adequately met national defense needs. The US adhered to its fundamental foreign and military policies after World War I, emphasizing defense of the continent and overseas possessions, suzerainty in the western hemisphere, and limited efforts to uphold the Open Door and preserve Chinese sovereignty. Congress provided the services with the means to meet those basic responsibilities until the disruption of international order in the mid-1930s.

Moreover, the services could determine how they spent much of the money Congress gave them. In some instances they used their admittedly sparse resources wisely, and sometimes not. The army, for example, spent more money on personnel than on the procurement of weapons and equipment, thereby neglecting crucial technological developments. Although the officer corps was twice the size of the pre-1918 army corps, too many combat units were woefully undermanned. In addition, the army neglected its reserve components, treating the National Guard indifferently and ignoring the Organized Reserves. The navy put too much of its faith and money in battleships, while relegating aircraft carriers and fleet submarines to secondary status. The general staffs of both services were sometimes wrong, even myopic.

At the same time, the services made wise decisions that would serve them and the nation well in World War II. Since well before World War I, for example, the navy had pressed the Marine Corps to develop doctrine and tactics to provide an advanced base force which could seize and defend island bases in the Pacific. Until the late 1920s the conservative marine officer corps neglected the idea; but innovative officers then began to develop the theory and doctrine of amphibious warfare. The navy supported experimental exercises to test the doctrine and established the Fleet Marine Force in 1933 as a permanent organization, with divisions and air groups assigned to it for wartime duty.

Neither the army nor the navy neglected aviation as severely as some historians have asserted. More than a few infantry generals and battleship admirals opposed extensive development of military aviation, especially in an era of limited defense spending. Nonetheless, aviation found a place not only in the army and navy, but in the marines as well. Despite early resistance, the army came to accept military aviation by the mid-1920s. Congress created the Army Air Corps in 1926, elevating flyers to institutional equality with the other combat arms. Establishment of the General Headquarters, Air Force in 1935 gave aviation semi-autonomy within the army. Support for the Air Corps came directly from army funding and manpower allotments, and by the 1930s aviation absorbed 10 percent of army personnel and nearly a quarter of its budget.

Naval aviation also found a niche. The navy began testing carrier-launched aircraft techniques immediately after World War I. Under treaty limits, it built two of the world's best attack carriers, which joined the fleet in 1927. By then naval regulations required that only qualified aviators could command carriers, seaplane tenders, and naval air stations. The navy remained first and foremost a battleship force. When naval building resumed in the late 1930s more battleships were built than carriers. Nonetheless, the service attempted to establish a balanced fleet within treaty limits that included aircraft carriers and that provided naval and Marine Corps aviators full promotion opportunities.

The record of contingency war planning is mixed. World War I demonstrated the necessity for long-term contingency planning and for inter-service cooperation. During the interwar years, however, the services largely worked separately on contingency planning. In part this was to due to the starkly different approaches taken by the army and navy in their planning. The army emphasized the mobilization of manpower and industry, assuming it would be asked again to raise and equip a mass army. Army planners, even as late as mid-1940, could only guess where they might be asked to fight, and so worked on mobilization plans and generally ignored strategic planning.

On the other hand, the navy stressed strategic planning by focusing on imperial Japan. Naval planners spent the interwar years assessing and fine-tuning War Plan Orange, which first appeared in 1911. The plan called for a powerful naval offensive across the central Pacific with the intent of finding, then destroying, the Japanese fleet. Plan Orange dominated Naval War College courses, shaped annual naval maneuvers, and spurred development of the Marine Corps advanced base function. Immediately after the signing of the Treaty of Versailles, the Department of the Navy broke thirty years of practice by stationing the bulk of the battleship fleet in Pacific ports as an expression of its commitment to Orange.

A final strength of the interwar services was their emphasis on the professional education of officers. The army and navy had developed post-baccalaureate schools before World War I; the marines would do so after 1918. Military education peaked at the Army and Naval War Colleges, and at the Army Industrial College. But such training began at the army combat branch and technical schools, or at naval schools for surface officers, aviators, and submariners. The Army Air Corps and Marine Corps operated their own schools and sent their officers to the war colleges. Military education in the interwar years gave large numbers of junior officers the opportunity to prepare for command responsibilities they were not likely to obtain for years in the course of normal careers. Historians Allan Millett and Peter Maslowski partly refute the older notion that interwar policy left the military unfit to defend the nation. They contend that the service schools allowed the ablest officers to develop doctrine and war plans, "rich in ideas" about the use of "naval aviation, amphibious forces, mechanized ground armies, and strategic air power" (Millett and Maslowski 1994: 407).

Yet the military was ill-prepared to wage a major war in the late 1930s. Restricted in budgets and manpower, hampered by senior officers who were rarely imaginative, and bereft of strategic direction from its civilian superiors, the military awaited direction. America belatedly began partial mobilization in 1940, first in the name of hemispheric defense and then in preparation for intervention in World War II, though that effort fell well short when Japan bombed Pearl Harbor in December 1941. The lack of preparedness in 1941 was a national failure and not exclusively a military one. Throughout the interwar years, the armed services remained largely marginal to American society. Rarely did the White House or the State Department seek their advice, and civilians seldom came into contact with service men. The social structure of the military hardly mirrored the society it served, because the officer corps was almost exclusively middle-class, white, and Christian. The army included four segregated black regiments, led by white officers. But the marines and Air Corps were lily-white, and the navy enlisted blacks only as stewards for officers. Men enlisted in the army and marines when no other employment was available, although the Great Depression forced many high school graduates to enlist.

Other than Brian Linn's recent work on what he calls the "Pacific Army," historians have yet to examine military life in these years – of which fiction continues to provide the best picture. Novels such as James Jones's *From Here to Eternity* (1951) and Richard McKenna's *The Sand Pebbles* (1962) depict an insular military life cut off from mainstream America. These books portray soldiers and sailors enmeshed in a male subculture punctuated frequently by violence and alcohol abuse. African Americans in the army's segregated regiments and navy stewards suffered a double segregation, isolated from civilian life and from the full opportunities of the military as well.

Participation in World War II brought military affairs into national life on a scale unseen in American history. If the United States was not fully prepared to fight in late

1941, it eventually met the challenge by drawing on strategic ideas and leadership, qualities fostered at the interwar service schools. America placed over 15 million people in uniform and, however reluctantly, enlisted far more women and blacks than ever before. By 1945 the United States reached a pinnacle of war production unprecedented in world history, dispatched its armed forces to the four corners of the earth, and harnessed nature itself to produce the atomic bomb. The nation organized itself for the sole purpose of prosecuting war, by adopting a wartime draft, by mobilizing the economy, and by granting the armed forces the sort of political and economic power which they had never before exercised. Such mobilization allowed the United States to play a major role in the Western European and Pacific theaters of the war. A prodigious capacity to manufacture war *matériel* truly made the United States the arsenal of the Allies. Ironically, the need for industrial works and service troops to sustain this technical force condemned infantrymen, especially in Europe, to unrelieved combat duty.

In late 1945 the nation stood transformed, a victorious global military power possessing atomic weapons and a powerful economy unmatched by any other power in the world. But the rise to global power precipitated a forty-year rivalry with the USSR. The adoption of a policy of containment – to prevent Soviet expansion – and deterrence – to prevent total war through the threat of nuclear retaliation – provided the broad outlines of a global strategy. Congress supported containment by approving military aid to nations presumed to be threatened by totalitarian movements (the Truman Doctrine in 1947) and economic assistance to help rebuild the war-shattered economies of Western Europe (the Marshall Plan in 1948). In 1949 Congress also committed the United States to collective, forward defense in approving the North Atlantic Treaty Organization (NATO). Commitment to NATO required stationing American troops in Western Europe for an indeterminate duration. Cold War policies ended a traditional continental, non-interventionist foreign policy.

Congress also altered the place of the military in American government and society. The National Security Act of 1947, as amended between 1949 and 1958, established a centrally-controlled military system in the Department of Defense. At the same time, the law authorized the formation of the US Air Force as an independent armed service, and gave the Joint Chiefs of Staff (JCS) statutory authority. Moreover, the law created a Central Intelligence Agency (CIA) to collect and assess information on real and potential foreign foes, plus a National Security Council (NSC) to advise the President on strategic planning. In theory the 1947 law provided an effective system able to assess national security threats and to develop plans and forces as responses to the threats. Finally Congress also reversed tradition in 1948 by adopting a peacetime selective service law, which would endure for twenty-five years.

The general outlines of Cold War policy and strategy were in place by 1950. But which specific form containment, deterrence, and collective security might take remained undetermined. Despite a firm intent to confront Communism, the Truman administration was reluctant to fund armed forces at the levels the JCS recommended. Although military spending in the late 1940s exceeded 1939 levels tenfold, standing at just under $14 billion in fiscal year 1950, the armed services quarreled bitterly over the allocation of defense dollars. The Department of Defense failed to quell inter-service bickering over the scant allocations. A top secret NSC study of early 1950 calling for annual defense spending of $40 billion a year went unheeded. Funding at NSC-recommended levels came only when the Korean War extended containment to Asia.

From the early 1950s through the collapse of the Soviet Union four decades later, Congress generously appropriated funds for national security. Even in retrospect it is not easy to answer the late 1960s question: "How much is enough?" In the mid-1950s, military allocations exceeded $55 billion and consumed over 60 percent of total federal spending. Military costs as a proportion of total federal spending declined slowly from Dwight D. Eisenhower's inauguration into the 1990s, although the Pentagon continued to account for a significant proportion of an ever-growing federal budget. Military allocations absorbed half of national budgets in the Eisenhower years, 35 to 40 percent in the 1960s, and under a third in the mid-1970s.

Inflation distorts dollar amounts for any given period; but suffice it to say that, after 1951, the military was never seriously underfunded, despite its complaints. Military problems were rarely due to sparse funding. The core of the institutional history of Cold War military affairs concerned not budgetary shortfalls but conflicts over allocation of defense funds and the concomitant assignment of service roles and missions that those allocations dictated. Roles and missions determined the place each service held in overall defense strategy, and thus governed how much money each service received. Arguments over the function of the separate services in executing Cold War strategy and nuclear deterrence shaped the perennial budget arguments and their accompanying squabbles. Senior Department of Defense civilian leaders never could rein in the endless inter-service budget battles.

World War II proved the absolute necessity of joint service cooperation when waging global war. Containing Communism around the world and deterring the Soviet Union would require the same kind of interservice cooperation. However, as during World War II, the services did not readily surrender their particular interests to the necessity for interservice cooperation. The army and navy were reluctant to abandon traditions of semi-independence in controlling their own budgets and shaping their own missions, and the newly independent air force quickly adopted this stance. Though the Department of Defense was created so that a single agency could define national security threats, devise strategies to meet those threats, and allocate funds to the services according to their assigned roles and missions, no President or Secretary of Defense could overcome service rivalries or convince the joint chiefs of staff to make budget recommendations based on strategic needs rather than the desires of their own services.

The centrality of nuclear weapons to American defense policy shaped the unseemly service competition for money. The air force easily claimed the central role in nuclear deterrence. Its manned bombers and intercontinental ballistic missiles, the latter operational in 1960, provided two parts of the nuclear triad. In the mid-1950s, for example, the air force claimed nearly half of the defense budget but accounted for only one-third of active-duty personnel. Until the end of the 1970s, the air force received at least a third of annual defense spending while fielding only a fourth of the total armed forces. Over the same quarter-century, second in budgeting was the navy, which had also had garnered a nuclear role: first in carrier-launched fighter-bombers, and then more securely after perfecting submarine-launched ballistic missiles. Subs armed with missiles joined the fleet in 1960. The army was always the largest service in total personnel, but, lacking a direct strategic deterrence role, consistently finished third in Cold War budgeting.

During Eisenhower's administration, the army protested its serious losses both in the money scramble and in the centrality the service had traditionally held. The Eisenhower Cold War strategy, labeled the "New Look," sought to limit defense spending and to avoid military interventions like the Korean War. Nuclear deterrence, infelicitously dubbed massive retaliation, served as the core of the New Look policy. As a consequence, the army fared poorly in defense budgeting and lost 530,000 soldiers (40 percent) between 1954 and 1960. Bitterly objecting to the policy, two successive army chiefs of staff, Matthew Ridgway and Maxwell Taylor, retired to protest the New Look.

Defense spending rose under President John F. Kennedy, as did support for the army. Kennedy's "flexible response" military policy sought to lessen reliance on nuclear weapons by increasing conventional forces. Flexible response reflected the beliefs of Taylor and Ridgway that massive retaliation was simultaneously a rigid strategy, which gave the initiative to the enemy, and a morally bankrupt approach, which condemned millions to nuclear destruction. Army strategists argued that expanding conventional forces gave national security leaders multiple policy options. When used wisely, flexible response would avoid total nuclear war but would permit limited conventional wars and brief interventions in order to apply military force as an instrument of policy. Military spending under Kennedy rose 13 percent, but army strength grew by 20 percent, while the navy and air force gained only 8 percent increases in personnel.

Pentagon budget and strategic battles, which were vitally important to the armed services, their supporters in Congress, and defense industry lobbyists, made little impression on the general public. Military affairs nonetheless affected American society during the Cold War in ways never before experienced. After 1945 "war and national security became consuming anxieties," historian Michael Sherry claimed. National security issues assumed a permanent presence and established the lowest common denominator for political discourse. National security offered something for nearly everyone: employers, labor, civil rights advocates, educators, and even highway contractors. Militarization provided "metaphors that shaped broad areas of national life," Sherry observed, not only to fight Communism but also to wage "wars" against poverty, inequality, illiteracy, and drugs. He may have overstated his case. Nevertheless national security and policies did profoundly affect major segments of national life, for better or worse (Sherry 1995: xi).

Defense spending made the most direct impact, accounting for 5.5 percent of gross domestic product (GDP) in 1948 and soaring to 15 percent in 1953. Until the end of the Vietnam War, the proportion hovered near a tenth of a steadily growing GDP. The effects of defense spending filtered through the economy, affecting the income of major manufacturers, the well-being of specific regions, labor union membership and employment patterns, and research funding at prestigious universities. The fear that defense spending might come to benefit only vested interest groups prompted retiring President Eisenhower to warn of the dangers of an enduring "military-industrial complex."

More directly, the Cold War touched two generations of young, physically fit men through selective service. Despite historic resentment against conscription (even in wartime), Congress approved a peacetime draft in 1948 that lasted until 1973. Conscription became a teenage rite of passage, motivating thousands of young men to marry early or to attend college to avoid the call-up. Others enlisted before the draft board called. The low annual conscription rates of the 1950s and early 1960s masked the decisions of hundreds of thousands who were impelled by the draft to enlist. Compulsory military service included a reserve obligation following active duty. The size and efficiency of the reserves varied greatly during the Cold War, but never approached the nearly 3 million ready reservists whom Congress authorized in 1955. Nonetheless, for the next two decades, some 2 million men and some women served annually in the ready reserve. The greatest impact of the reserve forces was not in the conduct of the war but in the towns and neighborhoods that served as home stations for their armories. Reservists brought their military pay and their presence in uniform to myriad places that before World War II were wholly unfamiliar with – and probably even hostile toward – men in uniform.

Long-term compulsory military service and the pressing need for qualified personnel altered the composition of the armed forces after 1945 by ending racial segregation. African Americans challenged segregated service during World War II but failed to smash a tradition that had endured since the Civil War. Partisan politics and Cold War rhetoric led President Harry S. Truman to order the end of military segregation in 1948. The armed services reluctantly complied with the order, and only the desperate need for an efficient manpower policy in the Korean War compelled them to end segregation decisively. Desegregation began in Korea when the army integrated its field forces in 1951. Elsewhere the army and the other services were slower to act. By 1955, however, all the forces had ended segregation and opened up all military occupational specialties to blacks. Compulsory military service brought tens of thousands of black and white Americans together every year – to live, work, eat, and sleep together in barracks and ships across the globe. The commingling of large numbers of blacks and whites in such intimate circumstances could not have occurred anywhere else in Cold War America. Black servicemen re-enlisted at twice the rate of whites; and in the early 1960s the armed services offered African Americans integrated economic opportunities and leadership roles that were rarely available in civilian society.

From the onset of the Cold War, strategists viewed Western Europe as the likeliest place where Americans and Soviets would fight a hot war. Mutual fears of total war and nuclear annihilation, however, restrained the superpowers. Open conflict came in Asia, where the two antagonists fought each other indirectly in two so-called "limited wars." The wars in Korea and Vietnam remained localized, but compelled two generations of American servicemen to give a year of their lives to fight wars that most of their countrymen came to ignore or oppose. The Korean War ended in stalemate, before public opposition to the struggle had reached a boiling point. However, the United States fought its fiercest open battle against Communism in Indochina, and lost. Despite awesome power, the US failed to find the proper balance of military force and political persuasion to end the war in its favor. Vietnam thus engendered direct opposition to a national military effort unseen since the Civil War. As the armed forces seemingly foundered in the conduct of the war, young men defied the draft; and undiscipline and sinking morale plagued the forces fighting the war. In 1969, Richard M. Nixon's new administration began to withdraw ground troops from Vietnam and to reduce defense spending, hoping to lessen public disgust with the war, to counter massive war debts, and to rehabilitate a foundering economy. Between 1968 and 1974 military appropriations dropped 37 percent, and fell by nearly 20 percent as a proportion of the total national budget.

The budgetary trends that Nixon established persisted into the early 1980s. Defense costs dropped to a quarter of total federal spending, while slowly declining as a proportion of GDP, absorbing 8.7 percent in 1970, 6.2 percent in 1975, and only 5.5 percent in 1980. Moreover defense dollars in the later 1970s lost purchasing power as inflation soared. Ronald Reagan's administration reversed the trend, increasing defense allocations by a third and expending billions of dollars to modernize weaponry. Costly items, including cruise missiles, stealth aircraft, new nuclear submarines, and armored vehicles consumed most of the new money. With the end of the Cold War in the early 1990s, military spending has steadily declined both in dollar amounts and as a percentage of federal spending. In 1995, for example, defense costs accounted for only 18 percent of the national budget.

Spending reductions meant decreases in the number of active-duty armed forces. Nixon began withdrawing ground troops from Vietnam as soon as he entered office. He also reduced draft calls, introduced a draft lottery, then ended conscription altogether in 1973, not only to stymie protest but also to cut costs. Active military forces fell from 3.2 million to 1.9 million between 1968 and 1972. Through the 1970s, active military forces held steady at around 2 million men and women. Despite substantial increases in spending, the active forces grew by only 8 percent during the Reagan years, to 2.2 million in 1988. By 1995 some 1.5 million served on active duty, a figure smaller than the force on duty in 1949. The end of the draft prompted a precipitate drop in the ready reserves, which lost over a million men between 1972 and 1979, and which did not rebound until the Reagan years.

Reductions in the strength of the standing forces led to dramatic changes in the composition of the armed forces. Social turmoil during the 1960s and the demoralizing war in Vietnam brought to the surface black resentments toward institutional racism within the armed services and toward blatant discrimination when black servicemen left military bases. Black protests and sporadic black–white violence on ships and bases wracked the services in the early 1970s. Belatedly the Department of Defense reduced discriminatory treatment of blacks and educated white servicemen on racially sensitive issues. Despite the turbulence of the late 1960s and early 1970s, blacks continued to see the armed forces as venues for good jobs and promising careers. At the end of the Vietnam War, blacks composed nearly 10 percent of the armed forces. In 1976, three years after the draft ended, blacks accounted for 17 percent of the total forces and a fifth of the army alone.

Women found it more difficult than blacks to pursue military careers. Over 300,000 women experienced military service during World War II. All except army and navy nurses served in temporary organizations, which disbanded when the war ended. In 1948 Congress approved the Women's Armed Forces Integration Act, which created a system by which women could follow a military career outside of nursing. However, only a few occupational specialties – largely clerical and administrative jobs – were open to female personnel. As late as 1960, only 32,000 women served as part of a 2.5 million active-duty force. The end of the draft in 1972 and the difficulties of recruiting men after the Vietnam War opened doors for women, however. Females in the armed services quadrupled between 1970 and 1979. In the early 1990s, women accounted for nearly 12 percent of the total forces. Women remained excluded from most combat specialties, but otherwise served in many military roles that were unthinkable just two decades earlier. By the 1980s, the armed forces had been transformed into an amalgam of men and women, whites and blacks, Hispanics and Asian Americans and Native Americans. Men and women of varying ethnicity served as both officers and enlisted personnel, as graduates of the service academies, as drill instructors, as general officers, even as chairmen of the Joint Chiefs of Staff. The military at the dawn of the twenty-first century differs most significantly from its counterpart a century ago in its social composition.

The Vietnam War also altered national strategy, despite the persistence of the Cold War into the early 1990s. Vietnam highlighted the enduring strategic dilemma. American policy sought to avoid a large conventional war as well as a nuclear conflict. Flexible response offered strategies for confronting Communism militarily, but on a limited basis. However, the "limited" wars fought in Korea and Vietnam demonstrated that flexible response could be both expensive and indecisive. President Nixon's foreign policies reflected that reality. First with Vietnamization and then with the Nixon Doctrine, he proclaimed that in the future the US would provide arms and advisors to aid nations in fighting Communism – but not troops. Eisenhower's New Look policy was revived.

Nixon's partially successful quest for détente with the Soviet Union and the People's Republic of China sought to alter the course of the Cold War by relying on diplomacy and balance of power arrangements rather than military force. Critics left and right often blasted Nixonian policy as either cynical or immoral. Two of Nixon's successors, Jimmy Carter and Ronald Reagan, increased defense spending and escalated Cold War rhetoric, especially the latter. However, they adhered to Nixon's basic policy of avoiding direct confrontation with the Soviet Union and its allies. From the late 1970s to the end of the Cold War, American presidents used American military power cautiously and then only on the periphery of great power relations. Michael Sherry detects "an oddly hollow Cold War" in the mid-1980s when anti-Soviet rhetoric and military spending soared. Sherry's observation could easily apply to the last two years of Carter's term as well. In retrospect, neither Jimmy Carter nor Ronald Reagan had any intention of using a big stick against the Soviet Union, whether or not it was an "evil empire" (Sherry 1995: 365).

The post-Vietnam years left the military in dire straits. In the 1970s, military leaders feared a vulnerability to Soviet military threats, unless the services could be modernized and heavily rearmed. The fears were largely misplaced, although sometimes echoed by historians. Despite large increases in Soviet military expansion in the 1960s and 1970s, the United States alone possessed genuinely global naval and air forces; and the US nuclear arsenal remained the most efficient and technologically advanced in the world. Nonetheless the services faced serious problems, such as recruiting, weakened morale, and *matériel* depletions.

Manpower issues loomed largest. The end of the draft forced the military to face an old problem, which was how to recruit volunteers from a society that again viewed the armed services with suspicion if not animosity. Compelled to find ways to attract youth to enlist, the armed forces needed to allocate an increasing segment of their budgets to enlistment bonuses, college scholarship funds, and the employment of civilians to perform the menial chores (like kitchen police, latrine duty, yard work), which was once assigned to low-ranking enlisted men. For a time in the 1970s the services found it difficult to recruit reliable, high school-educated young men and women. A worsening economy, however, impelled thousands of qualified recruits to sign up for an increasingly attractive occupational opportunity through the 1980s.

Military leaders also eagerly sought new institutional and doctrinal directions. An emphasis on future roles and doctrines served three interrelated purposes. The first, and most important, function was to provide each service with a viable mission statement to use in allocation struggles in an era of declining defense spending. Secondly, the services needed to restore morale and a sense of professionalism in the aftermath of the Vietnam debacle. Finally, service leaders believed that institutional reassessment would return the armed forces to their proper function, deterring and containing the Soviet Union through conventional warfare and would thus avoid a nuclear holocaust. The quest for new roles and doctrines in the 1970s and early 1980s precipitated a renaissance in military education and thinking.

The new military intellectualism virtually ignored Vietnam, both as a military experience and as a means of containing Communism. Vietnam was viewed as a disastrous aberration, a journey into unconventional war and nation-building that left the United States gravely weakened militarily. Such a perspective allowed the armed forces to forget the war in Indochina. Most military thinkers looked to the educational experience of the interwar years and the conduct of World War II. In a search for a new doctrine for ground warfare, the army, for example, studied how the Germans and Soviets conducted armored war in World War II. In their equivalent search for new doctrines, the navy and marines respectively reviewed the role of carrier-based air power and amphibious operations of World War II. By the early 1980s, each service had adopted doctrines premised on the assumption that the Soviet Union could be defeated somewhere in central Europe without escalation to nuclear war. Much of the military equipment acquired in the Reagan years, such as highly technological "force multipliers," was to be used to execute the new doctrines and compensate for smaller US forces when combating the bigger Red Army.

Fortunately the central European battle never took place, as the Soviet Union and its satellite states fell apart in the early 1990s. Instead the major test of post-Vietnam military reform came in the Persian Gulf War of 1990–1. The conventional doctrines adopted by the armed forces worked superbly against the Soviet-trained and-equipped, but poorly led, Iraqi forces. Efforts to align reserve components more closely with active forces proved successful as well. Little euphoria attended victory in the Gulf War, however, for budget cuts and reductions in force that came with the end of the Cold War continued despite success against Iraq. It was nevertheless disturbing that military dislike for civilian leadership lingered, as did open distaste for the media. These legacies of the Vietnam War reappeared during Operation Desert Shield and Operation Desert Storm. Since then the services have come to see themselves as a band of warriors increasingly isolated from a civil society that neither understands nor cares much about the demands and sacrifices required of professional military life. The soldiers and sailors of the early twentieth century would have found those feelings the most familiar aspect of their end-of-century counterparts. As was true at the beginning of the twentieth century, the United States still lies largely secure within the bastion of the North American continent. Much changed during the twentieth century. But civilian society continues to look askance at the military, its needs, and its ethos.

REFERENCES AND FURTHER READING

Bacevich, A. J. (1986) *The Pentomic Era: The US Army between Korea and Vietnam.* Washington, DC: National Defense University Press.

Baer, George W. (1994) *One Hundred Years of Sea Power: The US Navy, 1890–1990.* Stanford, Calif.: Stanford University Press.

Dunnigan, James F. and Macedonia, Raymond M. (1995) *Getting It Right: American Military Reform after Vietnam to the Gulf War.* New York: William Morrow.

Goldman, Nancy L. (ed.) (1982) *Female Soldiers: Combatants or Noncombatants.* Westport, Conn.: Greenwood Press.

Grandstaff, Mark R. (1997) *Foundation of the Force: Air Force Enlisted Personnel Policy, 1907– 1956.* Washington, DC: Air Force History and Museums Programs.

Griffith, Robert K., Jr. (1982) *Men Wanted for the United States Army: American Experience with an All Volunteer Army Between the Wars.* Westport, Conn.: Greenwood Press.

Hagan, Kenneth J. and Roberts, William R. (eds.) (1986) *Against All Enemies: Interpretations of American Military History from Colonial Times to the Present.* Westport, Conn.: Greenwood Press.

Hewes, James E. (1975) *From Root to McNamara: Army Organization and Administration, 1900–1963.* Washington, DC: US Army Center for Military History.

Howarth, Stephen (1991) *A History of the United States Navy, 1775–1991.* New York: Random House.

Jones, James (1951) *From Here to Eternity.* New York: Scribner.

Linn, Brian (1997) *Guardians of Empire: The US Army and the Pacific, 1902–1940.* Chapel Hill: University of North Carolina Press.

McFarland, Stephen L. (1995) *America's Pursuit of Precision Bombing, 1910–1945.* Washington, DC: Smithsonian Institution Press.

McKenna, Richard (1962) *The Sand Pebbles.* New York: Harper and Row.

Mershon, Sherie and Schlossman, Steven (1997) *Foxholes and Colorlines: Desegregating the US Armed Forces.* Baltimore, Md.: Johns Hopkins University Press.

Millett, Allan R. (1991) *Semper Fidelis: The History of the United States Marine Corps,* rev., expanded edn. New York: Free Press.

Millett, Allan R. and Maslowski, Peter (1994) *For the Common Defense: A Military History of the United States of America,* rev., expanded edn. New York: Free Press.

Nalty, Bernard C. (1986) *Strength for the Fight: A History of Black Americans in the Military.* New York: Free Press.

—— (ed.) (1997) *Winged Shield, Winged Sword: A History of the US Air Force,* 2 vols. Washington, DC: Air Force History and Museums Program.

Neilson, Keith and Haycock, Ronald G. (eds.) (1990) *The Cold War and Defense.* New York: Praeger.

Nenninger, Timothy K. (1994) "Leavenworth and its critics: the US Army Command and General Staff School, 1920–1940," *Journal of Military History* 58, pp. 199–231.

Pogue, Forrest C. (1963) *George C. Marshall: Education of a General, 1880–1939.* New York: Viking.

Sherry, Michael S. (1995) *In the Shadow of War: The United States since the 1930s.* New Haven, Conn.: Yale University Press.

Vlahos, Michael (1980) *The Blue Sword: The Naval War College and the American Mission, 1919–1941*. Newport, RI: Naval War College Press.

Weigley, Russell F. (1972) *The American Way of War: A History of United States Military Strategy and Policy.* New York: Macmillan.

—— (1984) *History of the United States Army,* enlarged edn. Bloomington: Indiana University Press.

CHAPTER NINETEEN

Foreign Policy

JUSTUS D. DOENECKE

From one vantage point, the course of American foreign policy in the twentieth century can be stated quite simply. The first half of the century marked a steady trend away from insularity, at least as far as binding alliances were concerned, to sweeping commitments manifested in the United Nations Charter in 1945 and the North Atlantic Treaty Organization (NATO) in 1949. The second half was signified by a global anti-Communism. After a series of mishaps and blunders bordering at times on the tragic, the United States could witness the dissolution of the Soviet empire. Throughout the past century, Americans have themselves been ambivalent about the role that their nation should play, and such uncertainties have often limited the power of leadership to influence international events in a way commensurate with the nation's enormous resources. Seeking to expand commercial opportunities at the dawn of the twentieth century, the republic suddenly found itself with an empire – a taste that had to be acquired. By the end of the century, the US possessed a unique superpower status; what had been achieved was unique, due in no small measure to its dynamic prosperity.

From Empire to Neutrality

The acquisition of colonies came quickly and easily, on the cheap, so to speak, as the result of war with Spain that lasted about four months. Beginning in 1898, the US picked up virtually all of what remained of the decrepit Spanish empire (Puerto Rico, the Philippines, and Guam), except for the island that had instigated the conflict: Cuba. Formally independent, Cuba became an American protectorate. During the Spanish-American War, the US also annexed Hawaii, which for five years had been ruled by an American junta that had overthrown the indigenous monarch and had sought US annexation. A republic that had been born in an eighteenth-century colonial rebellion against a distant empire had itself become an imperial power. In the immediate aftermath of the conflict with Spain, the US was obliged to reconcile the ideal of consent of the governed with the cruelties of colonial rule. That the ruled tended to have darker skins than the white majority in the US only intensified domestic anxieties, and some prominent foes of American expansion – such as political leader and reformer Carl Schurz – based their arguments on racism, on separating peoples of color as much as possible from the scope of US politics and law.

The electoral test came in 1900. The Democratic nominee for the presidency, William Jennings Bryan, had sought to stress strong opposition to imperialism. But the issue did not resonate among the voters, and he soon downplayed his criticism of overseas expansion. The Republicans favored expansion on patriotic as well as economic terms. They got full mileage out of their vice-presidential nominee, 41-year-old Theodore Roosevelt, who had become famous for leading the charge up San Juan Hill in Cuba two years earlier. TR personified the gusto of imperial and military ambitions. When he became President in 1901, after the assassination of President William McKinley, the conversion of the United States to a nation with international commitments could not be thwarted.

How those commitments might be understood was to be tested when war erupted in Europe in 1914. For the next three years, public ambivalence was most evident in the struggle for neutrality. In an address to the US Senate on August 19, President Woodrow Wilson wanted his countrymen to be "neutral in fact as well as in name during these times that try men's souls." He asked the public to "exhibit the fine poise of undisturbed judgment, the dignity of self-control" (quoted in Commager 1948: 276–7), so that eventually the US could play the role of peacemaker respected by both the Triple Alliance and the Triple Entente. The President himself believed that all belligerents shared some responsibility for the horrors of battle; hence the dividing line between aggressors and victims was blurred. He personally abhorred violence and, like many progressives, feared that war overseas would short-circuit the reform movement within the United States. To Wilson, US military involvement would be only a last resort, to uphold the rights essential to civilization.

Like most Americans, he traced his ancestry to the British Isles. Both a historian and a political scientist, Wilson also admired the economic and cultural achievements of the Germans. As late as the autumn of 1916, he did not want to see Germany crushed but to remain a stabilizing force on the European continent.

Nevertheless Wilson did not challenge the illegal naval blockade that the British imposed upon the Germans. In one sense the US was in a bind. If the President attempted to crush the British blockade, he would favor the Central Powers. If no such attempt were made, their enemies would be favored. The huge loans made to the British and the French tied the US economy to their fate. Great Britain, its ambassador wrote from Washington, had become America's best customer. Indeed, for the first time in its history, the US became a creditor nation.

An increasingly choked and desperate Germany could only crack the British blockade by unrestricted submarine warfare, and that policy provoked Wilson to invoke a rather special right. He insisted that American citizens sailing on British ships were entitled to be immune from attack by German submarines. The President was adamant even when those ships carried munitions, like the *Lusitania*, sunk in May 1915. Civilization was presumably at stake were the U-boats to sink British merchant ships that happened to have American passengers on board. The situation was peculiar. Wilson was asserting the right of a few of his fellow citizens to travel in a war zone, on munitions ships owned by a belligerent. He would not acknowledge that Americans ought to accept the inconveniences of war and might restrict their right to transatlantic travel without loss of dignity or honor (Devlin 1975). But

Wilson insisted on that right; such was the inexorable logic by which Wilson asked Congress for a declaration of war on April 2, 1917: "We will not choose the path of submission and suffer the most sacred rights of our nation and our people to be ignored or violated." He added that "the right is more precious than peace" (quoted in Commager 1948: 310, 312). A year and a half later, after the loss of 112,432 American lives, Germany surrendered.

From Victory to Versailles

In asking for a declaration of war, Wilson had envisioned "a concert of free peoples as shall bring peace and safety to all nations and make the world itself at last free" (quoted in Commager 1948: 312). At Paris, Wilson got the opportunity to persuade the other victors that such a concert was not only possible but necessary. What Britain, France, and the United States in particular wrought in 1919 was not quite what had been integral to the Fourteen Points that he had promulgated in January 1918. The peace treaty was not an "open covenant, openly arrived at." Instead it was drawn up, behind locked doors, by such statesmen as Britain's David Lloyd George and France's Georges Clemenceau. Nor did the peace treaty settle colonial claims in a "free, open-minded, and absolutely impartial manner." Little weight was given to "the interests of the populations concerned," as opposed to those of the colonial powers.

Perhaps even more problematic and consequential was the violation of the principle of self-determination. Some Germans found themselves under Polish or Czech or French rule. Italy took over German-speaking Tyrol. Japan was given temporary control of Shangtung peninsula, whose inhabitants were Chinese, though Tokyo promised to restore full political sovereignty to China in the near future. Wilson's ideal of self-determination, his own Secretary of State, Robert Lansing realized, "is simply loaded with dynamite. What a pity it was ever uttered!" (Lansing 1921: 97). Nor did the Versailles treaty guarantee freedom of the seas (though Wilson had cherished that particular right of civilization), nor the removal of barriers to free trade. So many compromises to "realism" (or cynicism) had been made that even Lansing conceded that the treaty was a bad one (Cooper 2001: 170–1).

Wilson had told his confidant, Colonel E. M. House, on the day of the triumphant presidential arrival in Paris, that once the League of Nations was established, major global problems would eventually be solved. The President's Fourteenth Point, centering on a "general association of nations," therefore became the most significant of all the promises that were designed to vindicate the bloodshed on the battlefield. Two months before the Versailles conference opened, however, the Republican Party regained control of Congress as a result of elections that Wilson himself claimed would be a test of his leadership. In effect the President had been repudiated. The new chairman of the Senate Foreign Relations Committee, Henry Cabot Lodge of Massachusetts, insisted upon his mandate to oppose the foreign entanglements that the covenant of the League of Nations entailed. Lodge was an imperialist and a navalist; in fact he was far from being an isolationist. But the Republicans made themselves the champions of those citizens who declined to accept the sorts of responsibilities for peacekeeping that the League of Nations was meant to accomplish. People who recoiled in horror at the unprecedented human costs that the Great War had imposed wanted as little to do with Europe as possible.

Wilson was forced to defend a treaty that bore little resemblance to his own Fourteen Points. He suffered from declining health that impaired his political judgment, was resistant to negotiations with his partisan foes, and remained inflexible in his faith in the redemptive dream of a League of Nations. He certainly was no match for Lodge and the rising spirit of isolationism and nativism that much of the Republican Party represented. In March 1919 a senatorial "round robin" had been issued, declaring that the covenant was unacceptable "in the form now proposed," and the 37 senators who signed it were more than enough to defeat Wilson's dream of League membership. This manifesto was a clear signal that the White House had to compromise with the senatorial opposition, but Wilson stubbornly refused to conciliate the "irreconcilables."

Many of their questions were quite legitimate, however. How did a moral obligation differ from a legal one? When it came to the implementation of collective security, how could the League promote change (for example, permitting greater self-determination) while still maintaining order? Above all, how could membership in the League be consistent with national sovereignty? Even a healthier Wilson might not have won over irreconcilable senators. But the Senate also contained reservationists, who favored joining the League but who sought compromise with the President on details. Wilson would not agree to engage in such give-and-take.

Instead Wilson sought to rally popular support, travelling 8,000 miles in 22 days, delivering 32 major speeches, in an effort to bring overwhelming public pressure to bear upon the Senate. He saw no alternative to the end of American isolation,

> not because we choose to go into the politics of the world, but because, by the sheer genius of this people, and the growth of our power, we have become a determining factor in the history of mankind, and after you have become a determining factor, you cannot remain isolated, whether you want to or not. (quoted in Baker and Dodd 1924: II, 18)

He denied that American sovereignty would be undermined, as the US would have a permanent seat on the League's Council and would hence be able to veto any decision to achieve collective security by military means. (The Council's decision required unanimity.) But in late September 1919, in the midst of the tour to rally the public, he suffered a severe stroke and could not muster the strength to bring his dream to fruition. A majority of the Senate was willing to endorse membership in the League of Nations in some form, but not the two-thirds necessary for ratification. For the next two decades, while the League of Nations veered toward enfeeblement and self-destruction, the US distanced itself from the European efforts at collective security upon which peace depended.

The Roosevelt Myth – and Reality

Even today most historical treatments of Franklin Roosevelt remain positive. As the architect of major domestic reforms and the single most important figure in maintaining the wartime alliance, FDR retains his esteemed place in world history. One historian has asserted that "no president in our history has faced such critical problems with the courage, vision and stamina that Roosevelt displayed" (McJimsey 2000: 295).

Admittedly FDR always had his critics and, because of the wide-ranging scope of his policies, they have often been impassioned ones. For well over half a century, certain foes have claimed that the President maneuvered the United States into World War II because, they believed, the New Deal was such a miserable failure. A best-seller published three years after Roosevelt's death argued that he had found in war "a glorious, magnificent escape from all the insoluble problems of America, and he strode forward not like a man running away from the falling fragments of his shattered temple but as one going to a festival" (Flynn 1948: 293).

Indeed the most vehement critics of FDR asserted that he knew in advance that Japan would attack Pearl Harbor and thereby willingly sacrificed the over two thousand servicemen who died in the attempt to defend the Hawaiian naval base. In 1954 Rear Admiral Robert A. Theobald accused Roosevelt of deliberately withholding vital intelligence from on-scene American commanders, a charge echoed a year later by another rear admiral, Husband E. Kimmel, who commanded the US Pacific fleet at Pearl Harbor at the time of the attack. The accusation has never died (Theobald 1954; Kimmel 1955; Toland 1982; Stinnett 2000).

Opponents also point to the President's role in the various wartime conferences, finding them resulting in the betrayal of Eastern Europe and nationalist China. In 1950, for example, one foreign correspondent referred to "the Munich called Yalta" (Chamberlin 1950: ch. 9). Roosevelt has also been charged with abandoning European Jewry during the Holocaust, remaining indifferent, as one book title phrased it, "while six million died" (Morse 1967). Even the more scholarly Frederick W. Marks III could write that "FDR accumulated the largest overseas credibility gap of any president on record" (Marks 1988: 287).

Yet these critics remain very much in the minority, and their more sweeping accusations are certainly unfounded. The folly of the more extreme charges, however, does not mean that Roosevelt's leadership did not manifest major defects.

During his first term, much of his foreign policy was blatantly isolationist. In campaigning for the White House in 1932, he turned against the very League of Nations that, in 1920, he had so fervently backed as vice-presidential candidate on the Democratic ticket. In the summer of 1933 he "torpedoed" the London Economic Conference, a move that, according to a leading historian of the era, "sapped the morale of the democratic opponents of fascism" (Leuchtenburg 1963: 203). Although FDR had long sought to gain US membership on the World Court, he waited until 1935 to submit his proposal to Congress. Woefully underestimating the opposition, he lost by seven votes. Hardly a scholar finds anything to praise in Roosevelt's frustrated effort. In March 1936, Germany invaded the Rhineland – an egregious violation of the Versailles Treaty of 1919 as well as the multinational Locarno agreements of 1925. The President did nothing. With elections only seven months away, he was not about to challenge the anti-interventionist sentiment of the public.

In July 1936 Spanish army officers launched a revolt against their Republican government. Led by General Francisco Franco, the army rebels were backed by landowners and by the Roman Catholic Church. The opposing Loyalists drew their support from peasants, laborers, and much of the middle class. The next month the

Roosevelt administration reinforced a non-importation agreement by which the European nations hoped to contain the conflict by suspending delivery of all war materials to both sides. Nazi Germany, Fascist Italy, and Communist Russia made no secret of violating the understanding. But FDR cooperated with the sponsors of non-importation – Britain and France – and announced a voluntary "moral embargo" on arms shipments. On his recommendation, Congress voted overwhelmingly a non-discriminatory arms embargo in January 1937, thereby banning munitions shipments to either force. The move helped cripple the resistance of the Spanish Republic. A public opinion poll showed two-thirds siding with neither faction. Thereafter FDR blocked all efforts to repeal the embargo.

In the spring of 1937 Roosevelt was facing a major battle with the Supreme Court, which had outlawed some major New Deal legislation and was threatening such social welfare policies as Social Security. It would have been difficult to split the country further over so tangled an issue as the Spanish Civil War (Dallek 1979: 136). By March 1939 General Franco had victory, as he approached the gates of Madrid, well within his grasp. Only late that January did Roosevelt admit that his embargo was "a great mistake" (quoted in Ickes 1954: II, 569). Yet while the Spanish Republic lay desperate and dying he had remained passive.

On September 1, 1939, German armored divisions knifed into Poland's frontier. Within two days, Britain and France declared war on the Third Reich. World War II had officially begun. FDR immediately offered tacit support for the Allied cause, while promising that "every effort" would be made to keep the US "out of this war" (quoted in Jones and Myers 1940: II, 3–5). By early November Congress had acceded to Roosevelt's urging to repeal an existing arms embargo, thereby allowing American arms to reach the beleaguered democracies.

Barely a year later, after France had surrendered and Britain was alone in withstanding the German onslaught, the Roosevelt administration transferred to Britain fifty destroyers of World War I vintage. The US simultaneously leased British bases scattered over four thousand miles of ocean, such as the Bahamas, Jamaica, St. Lucia, Antigua, Trinidad, and British Guyana. To Roosevelt's surprise, no congressman introduced legislation to nullify the agreement, which was mutually advantageous (especially for the US). The precedent was not encouraging, however. In the wake of surreptitious presidential commitments much later (including the Gulf of Tonkin resolution of August 1964 and the Iran-contra scandal of the mid-1980s), the subtitle of one book on the destroyer-bases deal was *How FDR Twisted Churchill's Arm, Evaded the Law, and Changed the Role of the American Presidency* (Shogan 1995).

By October 1940 Britain was losing 400,000 tons at sea. British naval power was at risk of disappearance. Roosevelt responded with the lend-lease bill, which reached Congress on December 30. So sweeping was the proposal that, according to *Newsweek*, he would be able to lend "anything from a trench shovel to a battleship" (January 20, 1940: 16). The magazine was not exaggerating. By the terms of H. R. 1776, the President could provide military articles and information to any country "whose defense the president deems vital to the defense of the United States" (quoted in Commager 1948: 635). If he so desired, the terms "defense article" and "defense information" could cover virtually everything, military secrets included. No limits were set on the quantity of weapons loaned or the sums to be allocated. Friendly belligerents could use American ports. The debate over H. R. 1776 was intense, but in March 1941 the President signed the legislation.

Lend-lease forged a genuine Anglo-American alliance, in the process taking the country to the very edge of the European conflict. The US now possessed a major material stake in British victory and Axis defeat. Scholars do not quarrel with the stated purpose of the bill, although historian Warren F. Kimball noted that Roosevelt's assurances of its "unwarlike" intent were shockingly lacking in candor (Kimball 1969). In June 1941 the Third Reich invaded the Soviet Union, triggering the greatest single onslaught in all of military history. Roosevelt believed that Stalin could hold out. In October, with congressional authorization, he made lend-lease aid available to the USSR.

The Soldier of Freedom

With the US drawing ever closer to armed conflict, Roosevelt attempted to define his postwar aims. His views could be cosmic indeed. In the very speech in which he proposed lend-lease to Congress, FDR claimed to envision a world founded on "four essential freedoms." He defined them as follows: "speech and expression"; the right of "every person to worship God in his own way"; "freedom from want," which the President further defined as "economic understandings which will secure to every nation a healthy peacetime life for its inhabitants"; and finally "freedom from fear," based on "a worldwide reduction of armaments." Such aims, he went on, could be obtained "everywhere in the world . . . in our own time and generation." Were these freedoms achievable? In a press conference held on March 15, 1941, the President conceded: "They may not be immediately attainable throughout the world" (quoted in the *New York Times*, March 16, 1941: 42).

In August 1941 Roosevelt and the British Prime Minister, Winston Churchill, met off the coast of Newfoundland. In addition to conferring, along with their staffs, on how best to confront the Axis, the two leaders signed Eight Points, subsequently known as the Atlantic Charter. Echoing the Fourteen Points, the charter announced that the US and Britain desired no additional territory. The framers favored "the right of all peoples to choose the form of government under which they will live." They endorsed "no territorial changes that do not accord with the freely expressed wishes of the people concerned." They favored "the enjoyment by all states, great and small, victor or vanquished, of access, on equal terms, to the trade and the raw materials of the world which are needed for their economic prosperity." At the same time, the two nations adhered to "due respect" for "existing obligations." Point Eight spoke of "the final destruction of Nazi tyranny," after which it envisioned "the establishment of a wider and permanent system of general security" that would guarantee such blessings of peace and freedom of the seas. Pending the establishment of this new system, aggressor nations would be disarmed ("Eight Points," *New York Times*, August 15, 1941: 1).

Admittedly the Eight Points promised nothing. Verbs like "hope" and "desire" indicated intent. Nations that already controlled a major share of the earth's resources could, one might argue, well afford to offer a disclaimer concerning additional territory. By hinting at plebiscites, a favorite panacea of FDR, the document ignored their proven inadequacy in resolving the complicated problems of nationality. The assurance of equal access to raw materials would have required a revolutionary transformation of the world economy that neither the US nor Britain had the will, much less the power, to establish. As for the eighth point, who would identify would-be aggressors? How might the two allies disarm such powerful nations as the Soviet Union, which was then bearing the bulk of fighting the Third Reich? Would other powers remain willing to accept permanent disarmament while the United States and Britain kept massive quantities of weapons? The British and Russians quickly issued disclaimers, denying that the document necessarily applied to their spheres of influence. Furthermore FDR was, like Wilson, creating a credibility gap that would render his legacy vulnerable to criticism long after his death. Certainly subsequent Soviet claims in Eastern Europe could never be reconciled with the Atlantic Charter.

By the fall of 1941, it was becoming obvious that some form of US participation in the conflict was likely, particularly as the Roosevelt administration was involved in an undeclared naval war in the Atlantic. On September 11, FDR told Congress that a German submarine had fired on the American destroyer *Greer*, though he neglected to note that the US ship was spotting German submarines for the British Navy. Roosevelt announced that in response he was ordering the American fleet to "shoot on sight." Misleading the public "in its own interest," he had, according to historian Robert Dallek, created a dangerous precedent (1979: 289). Within two months FDR had secured the arming of merchant ships and congressional authorization to send them all the way to Britain.

All this time, he was engaged in risky diplomacy with Japan. In response to its seizure of South Indochina in July 1941, he issued "freezing orders," which soon became an instrument for severing all trade between the two countries and cutting Japan off from vital oil supplies. Roosevelt had hoped that his move would face Tokyo down. Instead a time limit was placed on peace in the Pacific (Utley 1985). Oil-starved Japan saw armed attack as the only way to secure access to the petroleum of the Dutch East Indies, not to mention the rubber, tin, rice, manganese, bauxite, and iron ore of southeast Asia. Most citizens, including many leading figures in the Roosevelt administration, felt little sense of emergency – until December 7, when Japan attacked not only Pearl Harbor but also Singapore, Wake, Midway, and the Philippines.

Immediately after the Japanese strike, Roosevelt was in a quandary. Germany was under no obligation to honor the Tripartite Pact, a defensive agreement that Germany, Italy, and Japan had signed in September 1940. Mutual support was specified only if one party to the agreement was attacked. On December 7, Japan was not the victim of aggression. By declaring war on the US four days after the Pearl Harbor attack, the Führer had inadvertently come to Roosevelt's rescue. Without Hitler's declaration of war, public sentiment would undoubtedly have forced the administration to focus upon Japan rather than upon an Axis power nominally at peace with the US. American planners, who had long adhered to a "Europe first" strategy, would have remained even more frustrated, for the military focus would necessarily have been on the Pacific (Doenecke and Wilz 2003).

Once the US entered the conflict, Roosevelt speculated upon the shape of the postwar order. In March 1943 he spoke of his desire to establish a security organization in which the Big Four (the US, the USSR, Great Britain, and China) would exercise major responsibility for "all the important decisions" and would wield "police powers" for "the United Nations." (His use of the last term did not refer to any international body but simply to the wider anti-Axis coalition.) The new entity would include an advisory council to settle the less volatile international questions and would consist of the Big Four, plus six to eight smaller powers representing smaller regions. A general assembly would meet annually. It would lack any real power but would permit the smaller nations "to blow off steam" (quoted in Kimball 1997: 202). According to one diplomatic historian, the plan required the "little countries to keep quiet and take orders" (Smith 1985: 16). The concept of the four policemen might have given Roosevelt flexibility, while ensuring that the US remained dominant in the western hemisphere and that both Soviet expansionism and British imperialism might be checked.

Yet the scheme might have been quite unworkable, reproducing the very spheres-of-influence system that he had come to believe had so plagued the world before 1914. Roosevelt's wife Eleanor herself found the scheme "fraught with danger," because the machinery that was envisioned could not restrain the major nations, "drunk with power," from imposing their will on the weak (quoted in Kimball 1997: 202). By citing the Good Neighbor policy as an example of what was intended, her husband did not mollify his critics, who regarded US hegemony as a prime case of informal hemispheric colonialism.

Moreover, the inclusion of China only revealed FDR's naïveté. The very president who wanted to exclude France from the ranks of the leading postwar powers, considering it a feckless and unworthy ally, would have made China – among the weakest states in the entire Allied coalition – a major player, even in European affairs (Smith 1985). Not until mid-1944 did he reconsider his faith in Chiang Kai-shek, the Chinese leader who always retained FDR's support.

Early in 1943, Roosevelt and Churchill met in Casablanca, in French Morocco, to announce one of the most controversial decisions of the war: to require Germany's unconditional surrender. At a press conference, FDR defined the policy as the "total elimination of German and Japanese war power." He added that the policy did "not mean the destruction of the population of Germany, Italy and Japan," but rather "the destruction of the philosophies in those countries which are based on conquest and the subjugation of other people" (quoted in Jacobsen and Smith 1979: 249–50). Late in August 1944, over a year after Italy had surrendered, Roosevelt admitted to his Secretary of State, Cordell Hull, that "whatever words we might agree on would probably have to be modified or changed the first time some nation wants to surrender" (quoted in Bennett 1990: 122).

How have historians evaluated this policy? The British military scholar B. H. Liddell Hart claimed that it stiffened the resistance of German troops, while giving the Third Reich an unmatched opportunity to rally the populace behind the regime. The policy similarly discouraged Germans from trying to overthrow Hitler and negotiating a separate peace that, had it been achieved in time, might have prevented the Soviet occupation of Eastern Europe (Liddell Hart 1970). Defenders of the unconditional surrender policy stress that, contrary to their reaction in 1918, Germans would be unable to believe that they had been "stabbed in the back" by civilian traitors, because it would be obvious that the Reich had been vanquished in battle. The policy also served to reassure the Soviet Union, which as early as 1943 was bitter with the West for having failed to launch a second front. Because the demand for unconditional surrender promised Stalin that his major allies would fight to the finish, the Grand Alliance was cemented (O'Connor 1971). The efforts to overthrow Hitler were flimsy at best. As for the claim that a powerful postwar Germany would somehow have prevented the Soviet domination of Eastern Europe, Kimball retorted: "That was just what the world needed: a strong, armed Germany led by the same wonderful set of military characters that had destroyed peace and stability in Central Europe since the 1860s" (Kimball 1997: 189).

Yet the matter cannot be left here. Unconditional surrender meant hazards. For Roosevelt, it became a substitute for long-range planning. Too many Americans believed that somehow a just and lasting peace would automatically arise from the ruin of the Axis, so that the Anglo-American "special relationship" would easily triumph after the war.

If the President exhibited one dominant trait, it was optimism. Shrewd leadership, if combined with deft manipulation, was expected to be equal to any task; and FDR prized his role as "Mr. Fix-It." He gave the impression of being able to achieve just about anything if he could establish a one-on-one relationship, even with Stalin. Roosevelt's wheeler-dealer style usually proved effective in the arena of domestic politics.

But in foreign policy, in which vital interests are at stake, such a style carried with it tremendous drawbacks. Personal charm could go only so far. In February 1940, when he condemned the Soviet invasion of Finland, Roosevelt accused the Kremlin of running "a dictatorship as absolute as any other dictatorship in the world" (quoted in the *New York Times*, February 11, 1940: 44). Yet the President was ludicrously confident of his capacity to bond with Stalin. "I can personally handle him better than either your Foreign Office or my State Department," the President assured Churchill in March 1942. Why? "Stalin hates the guts of all your top people. He thinks he likes me better" (quoted in Kimball 1997: 145). But the Stalin whom Roosevelt fancied himself capable of charming did not exist.

Late in 1943, the Big Three met at Teheran. Although historians have given Yalta far more attention, the capital of Iran was the site of more crucial decisions, particularly on grand strategy. The conference devised the essential victory strategy in Europe, centering on a cross-channel invasion of the European continent (OVERLORD) initially scheduled for May 1944. (In fact D-Day took place on June 6.) Stalin reaffirmed his intention of entering the war against Japan, made first in October 1943, in exchange for territories and privileges the Tsarist regime had possessed. The Soviet dictator left Teheran confident that the western allies would not challenge his control over Eastern Europe. Two months before the meeting, Roosevelt had confided to Archbishop Francis Spellman of New York that the US had indeed written off eastern Poland, the Baltic states, Bessarabia, and Finland: "So better give them [up] gracefully. What can we do about it?" (quoted in Freidel 1990: 479). The President also surmised that Austria, Hungary, and Croatia would end up as Soviet protectorates, because the advancing Red Army was bound to dominate those areas.

Despite the significance of Teheran, the greater fascination of historians with the Yalta conference, held on the Black Sea early in February 1945, is understandable. Samuel Flagg Bemis, once the dean of American diplomatic historians, called Yalta "one of the most dramatic parleys in modern history, rivalling in that respect the memorable meeting of Napoleon and Alexander I on a raft in the middle of the Niemen River" (Bemis 1955: 896). Soviet-occupied Poland headed the agenda and was, as Churchill wrote in his memoirs, "the most urgent reason for the Yalta Conference." When the Prime Minister stressed that he wanted Poland to be "mistress in its own house," Stalin retorted that Poland must serve as a barrier against any future German invasion of his country; this was "a matter of life and death" (Churchill 1953: II, 314–17). With Roosevelt unwilling to adjudicate this dispute, the conferees equivocated, calling vaguely for "free and unfettered elections." Yalta endorsed the expansion of the Communist-dominated Lublin government, so that it might be reorganized "on a more democratic basis with the inclusion of democratic leaders from Poland itself and from Poles abroad" (quoted in Jacobsen and Smith 1979: 415). No arrangements were made for the supervision of the promised elections.

Such crucial issues as the future borders of Germany were postponed. By giving Poland hundreds of square miles of German territory, the Big Three created close to 9 million refugees. Even Churchill was troubled: "It would be a pity to stuff the Polish goose so full of German food that it got indigestion" (quoted in Byrnes 1947: 30). The US and Britain were no longer committed to their scheme of German dismemberment but had not yet come up with any substitute. In the end the Big Three gave themselves permission to use German labor as a source of reparations, a policy without precedent in modern history. Large numbers of German war prisoners thus served as forced laborers in the Soviet Union, Britain, and France.

At Yalta Roosevelt indicated his increasing faith in collective security, as manifested in a new international organization, the United Nations. Stalin accepted the American formula for voting in the new UN Security Council. By its terms a permanent member could veto any resolution but never block consideration of an issue. In return a reluctant FDR acceded to Stalin's bid for two additional seats in the General Assembly: for the Ukraine and for Byelorussia (White Russia). Like Woodrow Wilson, Roosevelt hoped that, with the passage of time, the sheer existence of a new international organization might manage to cushion the severity of any immediate settlement.

As with his predecessor, Roosevelt's faith proved futile. Moreover FDR was a dying man at Yalta, where his very appearance was cadaverous. As the needed blood was not reaching his brain, he was subject to occasional forgetfulness, what physicians call "secondary metabolic encephaloathy." Yet it is dubious that his condition significantly affected the conduct of diplomacy at Yalta. A robust FDR would not have acted very differently; troop dispositions gave him little leverage. The Red Army was dominant in Central and Eastern Europe (except for Czechoslovakia) and was only 44 miles (nearly 71 km) from Berlin.

The health problem lay deeper, however. A politician subject to congestive heart failure had chosen to run again for the office that happened to be the most powerful one in the world. In the final months of life, he was scarcely working more than an hour a day. His mind was unaffected, but concentration for long periods was impossible. He was, according to historian Robert H. Ferrell, "in no condition to govern the Republic" at war (1998: 4). Having been re-elected the previous November 1944, FDR did not inform – much less consult – his Vice President about crucial policies. Hence Harry Truman knew nothing about secret accords made at Yalta to induce the USSR to enter the war against Japan. Nor was he told that an atomic bomb was being developed. He knew less about the US progress in nuclear weaponry than Stalin did. Only twice since becoming Vice President had Truman even met with his commander-in-chief. Few if any presidential successors were so unprepared.

By the time of Roosevelt's death in April 1945, the United States had become the world's dominant power. Its wealth was of a magnitude that could scarcely have been imagined when he had taken office at the nadir of the Great Depression. Of the leading countries in the world, only the US and Canada had emerged from the Second World War unscathed. By all available economic indices (gross national product, industrial production, standard of living), the US was experiencing an unrivaled prosperity. Roosevelt had not only presided over this abundance at home. More than any other world leader, FDR had also kept the Big Three together until the Axis was defeated. Neither Churchill nor Stalin had the skills needed to do so. The American President was truly the Architect of Victory.

But he paid a price. At crucial junctures foresight was lacking. He failed to aid the Spanish Republic, underrated Japan, overestimated the power of Nationalist China, and made irresponsible promises to the Poles. He handled his serious health problems recklessly. He postponed the resolution of vital issues, such as the postwar treatment of Germany, while taking refuge in amorphous platitudes concerning the postwar order. He never prepared the public for the inevitable tensions that would follow the military victory, and to that degree Franklin Delano Roosevelt contributed significantly to them. His legacy is therefore more ambiguous than many Americans realize.

The Cold War

It was left to his immediate successor to try to keep the Grand Alliance intact after V-E Day and V-J Day, though the failure to do so cannot be blamed upon Harry Truman. In retrospect there is something inevitable about the tensions and conflicts associated with the Cold War, a term coined by publicist Herbert Bayard Swope and put into circulation by the pundit Walter Lippmann (Safire 1968: 83–4). Bolshevism had defined itself largely in opposition to capitalism and to the evils that Vladimir Lenin, his revolutionary comrades, and his successors ascribed to the exploitation of the toiling classes by the owners of capital: imperialism, militarism, racism, chauvinism. Marxist doctrine could not envision anything but class conflict as long as the bourgeoisie existed, and could not imagine peace except through the achievement of a classless society. The nation-states of the West that had been formed in the era of industrial capitalism were inevitably and even instinctively committed to defining Communism as a dangerous threat to the existing order. Generally both conservatives and most liberals, reactionaries, and even some radicals shared an animosity to both Communist ideology and Communist practice, however much westerners differed from one another in their own motives, their own values, their analyses and their policy preferences. Even if Roosevelt had lived, it is hard to imagine that the Cold War could somehow have been avoided.

Truman bears responsibility, however, for the particular form that US foreign policy took. His presidency was punctuated by some of the most consequential acts of anti-Communism: the political and economic rescue of regimes in the eastern Mediterranean (Greece and Turkey) that Communism was imperilling either by subversion or pressure (the Truman Doctrine); the massive credits and other forms of financial aid to facilitate the economic recovery of Western Europe after the devastation of the Second World War (the Marshall Plan); the protection of West Berlin through air supplying and the first stages of incorporating West Germany into the anti-Soviet system; the forging of a military alliance designed to protect Western Europe against attack from the East (the North Atlantic Treaty Organization, or NATO); the defense of South Korea (which Truman called a "police action" in enlisting the participation of other UN members) against attack from North Korea; the development of a hydrogen bomb frighteningly more powerful than the atomic weapons that had eviscerated Hiroshima and Nagasaki.

All of these policies enjoyed considerable bipartisan and public support; all were presented as necessary shows of strength in resisting what was understood to be Communist aggression (or what was believed to be the threat of aggression). All were justified (if only retroactively) to achieve "containment" of the Soviet Union, a formulation that the Sovietologist George F. Kennan, who served as director of the Policy Planning Staff of the Department of State, presented (as "X") in the July 1947 issue of *Foreign Affairs*. Kennan called for containing the Soviet Union within its own borders, by making it clear that any Soviet advances would be met with resistance. Western recalcitrance and patience would eventually "promote tendencies which must eventually find their outlet in either the break-up or the gradual mellowing of Soviet power" (Kennan 1951: 127). To reward aggression, as Britain and France had done in the 1930s, would not avoid war, the advocates of containment argued, but would make collective violence inevitable.

In his initial presentation of what soon became the official foreign policy of his government, Kennan had Europe in mind. On that continent two world wars had already been fought to devastating effect in the first half of the century, and he believed that a strong defensive posture had a good chance of avoiding a third catastrophe. What worried Kennan were Soviet designs on Western Europe, where the geopolitical conflict did indeed become manageable and was prevented from bursting into a hot war. In Asia, however, the clash between Communism and the US turned bloody, with the loss of 54,000 American lives during the Korean War and 58,000 dead in the Vietnam War. (No one knows exactly how many Vietnamese died during the conflict, but perhaps 4 million were killed or wounded.) The Korean War ended in a stalemate, and with the realization that in the nuclear age a substitute for victory had to be discovered and accepted. However costly the sacrifice of life on the Korean peninsula from 1950 until 1953, however frustrating a result that left the Communist dictatorship of Kim Il Sung in power in Pyongyang, the concept of containment was not seriously affected. But a decade later, military intervention in Indochina would shatter faith in the applicability and efficacy of containment and Kennan himself would become a vocal critic of the US policy. The Vietnam War would also prove to be the most divisive episode of the century, and the most searing domestic conflict since the Civil War itself. "The American Century foundered on the shoals of Vietnam," sociologist Daniel Bell observed (quoted in Karnow 1991: 16).

The Catastrophe of Vietnam

Posterity will undoubtedly be mystified by the extent and the durability of the military objective of blocking the Communist effort to unify Vietnam. "Why should the United States have concerned itself for so long, and at such a heavy cost, with the internal affairs of a new Asian state, over 10,000 miles away, [a state] without a navy or air force, and with exceedingly limited ground forces?," diplomatic historian Norman Graebner asked. "And why should a small, backward, jungle-ridden country embarrass the US militarily when this country possessed more destructive power than any nation in history?" (Graebner 1984: 223).

The answers have varied. By 1971 the public rationales were exposed as divergent from what officials secretly believed, thanks at first to the *New York Times*, which published excerpts of the top-secret Pentagon Papers. Perhaps the most common justification was given by Secretary of State Dean Rusk, who served both Presidents John F. Kennedy and Lyndon B. Johnson. Rusk defended US policy in terms of containment: Hanoi was attempting to replace the anti-Communist regime in Saigon, which needed American protection from such aggression. Adding to the memory of the capitulation to Nazi Germany in Munich in 1938 was the domino theory: the collapse of South Vietnam would produce repercussions throughout southeast Asia and the momentum of Communism incursions might become unstoppable. As one critical historian sought to fathom the policy, "Empires were of a piece, and the loss of one member affected the organic health of the whole" (McCormick 1989: 149).

The justifications of the Republicans were continuous with the preceding Democratic administrations. According to Henry A. Kissinger, who served as national security adviser and then secretary of state under Richard M. Nixon (and then Gerald Ford), the presence of thousands of American troops "has settled the issue of the importance of Vietnam. What is involved now is the confidence in American promises," he said in January 1969. "Other nations can gear their action only if they can count on our steadiness" (quoted in Isaacson 1992: 160). A superpower's credibility would be undermined unless a conspicuous military involvement could somehow stave off the defeat of an independent Republic of South Vietnam.

But as the Pentagon Papers revealed, the concerns of both elected officials and bureaucrats were more immediate. The odds on defeating Ho Chi Minh – an anti-colonialist and nationalist leader as well as a Communist – were long. But a loss to Vietnamese Communism had to be postponed, at least until another US administration or the rival political party could take office and take the blame for failure. It is doubtful whether US foreign policy was animated by the hope of reforming the autocratic and corrupt rule emanating from Saigon. Indeed one Pentagon official explicitly (if secretly) deprecated the importance of stopping Communism in order to achieve democracy in the Republic of South Vietnam. According to a 1965 memo by John McNaughton, the Pentagon's chief civilian representative, 70 percent of the justification was to avoid a humiliating military loss (that is, to maintain international credibility); 20 percent was to keep China from taking over South Vietnam; and the need of its people "to enjoy a better, freer way of life" accounted for only 10 percent of American intervention (quoted in Gardner 1995: 595).

But whatever the answers to the questions that historians like Graebner have posed, there is no doubt about the formidable resources deployed. The explosives dropped from the air were more than three times the power of all of the explosives that all belligerents dropped during the Second World War on three continents. US bombers unleashed $17 billion worth of explosives, most of which was destined for South Vietnam itself, the very nation that the US was supposed to be defending. Yet such awesome pounding from the air had no demonstrable effect on Hanoi's morale, resilience, and resupply efforts, and may well have turned South Vietnamese peasants into supporters of the Communists. Not even half a million American troops in Vietnam could stem the tide of northern infiltration or fortify the will of demoralized South Vietnamese soldiers, whose indifference to the patriotic claims of their own government was palpable.

Containment ran aground in Vietnam, not because the US did not apply sufficient force but because there nationalism and Communism were entwined. Having successfully led the Viet Minh movement to expel the French colonialists, Ho Chi Minh had achieved a heroic status that itself testified to the Wilsonian ideal of "self-determination," even though the regime in Hanoi was scarcely less despotic than in most of the other nations where Marxist-Leninists had seized power. What had animated US foreign policy under the auspices of containment was a binary assumption – us versus them – with neutrals eventually having to choose sides. According to this Cold War dichotomy, no populace would freely prefer "them"; the aspiration to live unbound by the shackles of foreign oppression could be honored and promulgated only by "us." Yet the Americans were the foreigners in Indochina, because the Republic of South Vietnam owed its fragile existence to US underpinning, which eventually involved US military protection. Vietnamese yearning for national liberation was inevitably linked to the Communist struggle against the Americans. Such a contest had not been anticipated in the strategy of the Cold War; and because after all the Vietnamese Communists had a greater commitment to evicting the Americans than the foreigners had in remaining in Indochina, the US suffered an ignominious defeat, the worst in the history of American arms.

Yet after Saigon changed its name to Ho Chi Minh City, no dominoes fell elsewhere; no other country in southeast Asia converted to Communism as a result of the national humiliation that Kissinger had feared. Indeed little more than a decade after Vietnam was unified under Communism, its Soviet version was clearly losing ground economically and politically to an increasingly unified and prosperous Western Europe, a dynamic Japan, and a United States where the masses were not becoming immiserated. History was evidently not following the Marxist script; the capitalist camp was showing few signs of decay, at least in contrast to an increasingly sclerotic Soviet system.

The End of the Cold War

The momentum of events and actions that brought the Cold War to an end will remain subject to investigation and dispute among historians and may never be settled with exactitude. But during the 1980s, President Ronald Reagan was instigating a massive rearmament program for the United States, aiming for supremacy on the seas, not to mention superiority in strategic nuclear weapons. Much stress was also placed on advanced technology, which put the USSR at a competitive disadvantage. Because the Soviet economy had also slowed down significantly in that decade, the superpower that had posed such a challenge to the US for nearly four decades was not well-positioned for a competitive high-tech race.

In November 1985 Reagan met his counterpart in Geneva. Mikhail Gorbachev had become General Secretary that March, at the age of 54. This summit conference was long on symbolism, short on substance. The personal rapport between the two leaders seemed to be most significant, and the desire to reduce tensions seemed uppermost. Nevertheless Reagan continued to promote the building of a costly, complicated defensive shield against incoming missiles (the Strategic Defense Initiative (SDI) or "Star Wars"), which was his solution to the Cold War.

But their next encounter, in Reykjavik, Iceland, in October 1986, might well have been the most extraordinary summit meeting of the postwar era (Gaddis 1992). Gorbachev proposed 50 percent cuts in both Soviet and American strategic weapons. The US countered with a proposal that would have cut ballistic missiles to zero within a decade. At the same time both countries would invoke the right to deploy strategic defenses against the bombers and cruise missiles that would remain in the arsenals of the superpowers. The Soviet leader responded with the most sweeping proposal ever made at a disarmament conference: the abolition of all nuclear weapons within a decade (that is, by 1996). Reagan replied: "That's exactly what I've been talking about all along. That's always been my goal" (quoted in Gaddis 1992: 128). Gorbachev insisted however on one condition: a ban on laboratory testing of Star Wars. Reagan demurred; and "the meeting broke up in disarray, acrimony and mutual disappointment," wrote historian John Lewis Gaddis. "It was probably just as well," since the proposals were so hastily advanced. "It was as if Reagan and Gorbachev had been trying desperately to outbid each other in a gigantic but surrealistic auction, with the diaphanous prospect of a nuclear-free world somehow on the block" (Gaddis 1992: 129). But the two leaders did sign an agreement in Washington in December 1987, so that an entire category of nuclear missiles could be dismantled and destroyed.

Gorbachev soft-pedalled Soviet opposition to Star Wars thereafter, first because he realized how the huge budget deficit in the US was threatening the schedule of the laboratory tests anyway. Second, he saw how opposed many American scientists were to a program they dismissed as unfeasible, indeed even wacky. SDI may have had its problems as a missile shield, but initially it did work to unsettle the Soviets and make them more amenable to arms control. The American public generally expected toughness, and the perception that Reagan would not yield on Star Wars gave him significant domestic support.

The impression of American resoluteness was matched by the vigor of the economy. Reagan's Secretary of State, economist George Schultz, noted the impact of the "information revolution. We have entered a world in which the important capital is human capital, what people know, how freely they exchange information and knowledge, and the intellectually creative product that emerges" (Schultz 1993: 893). In the Soviet Union, photocopying machines were often put under lock and key, and access to computers was equally limited. Not surprisingly, the habits of a closed society were impeding the capacity to sustain Soviet power.

Gorbachev soon found himself presiding over the dissolution of the Soviet empire. By 1989 the military withdrawal from Afghanistan was completed; it was a humiliating defeat. That year also began the fragmentation of the Eastern and Central European parts of the empire. Poland broke away successfully when Gorbachev refused to intervene. Then Hungary did the same. In November 1989 the Berlin Wall, the supreme symbol of what was known as the Iron Curtain, came down. The old regimes collapsed in Czechoslovakia and Bulgaria; and by the end of the year a firing squad in Romania took care of the most feared of Communist tyrants, Nicolae Ceaucescu. By 1991, after more than half a century of rule from Moscow, the Baltic states also separated. Then the USSR itself imploded, beginning in the south, as Georgia, Armenia, and Uzbekistan declared themselves to be "sovereign" republics. The Cold War was essentially over when there was no more USSR; on December 7, 1991, it had "ceased to exist." The next day a confederation was created, the Commonwealth of Independent States. It posed no serious challenge to American interests.

The end of the Cold War was as decisive as its origins were ambiguous. In March 1946, when Churchill announced in Fulton, Missouri that an Iron Curtain had descended upon the continent ("from Stettin in the Baltic to Trieste in the Adriatic"), no one could have anticipated how resoundingly (and peacefully) that barrier would be smashed in less than half a century. The determination to apply constant pressure upon the Soviet Union – the very policy advocated by George F. Kennan in 1947 – had been vindicated. The finale also meant a victory for open societies and a defeat for command economies; even Gorbachev, out of office, ended up making a commercial for Pizza Hut.

Obviously, over the past century, the United States had often acted irresponsibly, as was evident in such matters as indifference to human rights and reluctance to engage in collective action. However, the extinction of two forms of totalitarianism – first Nazism, then Communism – was part also of the legacy of US statecraft as well; and the elimination of these terrible tyrannies deserves to be central to any retrospective reckoning.

REFERENCES AND FURTHER READING

Baker, Ray Stannard and Dodd, William E. (eds.) (1925) *The Public Papers of Woodrow Wilson*, vol. 2. New York: Harper.

Bemis, Samuel Flagg (1955) *A Diplomatic History of the United States*, 4th edn. New York: Holt, Rinehart, and Winston.

Bennett, Edward M. (1990) *Franklin D. Roosevelt and the Search for Victory: American–Soviet Relations, 1939–1945*. Wilmington, Del.: Scholarly Resources.

Byrnes, James F. (1947) *Speaking Frankly*. New York: Harper.

Chamberlin, William Henry (1950) *America's Second Crusade*. Chicago: Henry Regnery.

Churchill, Winston S. (1953) *The Second World War*, vol. 2. New York: Bantam.

Commager, Henry Steele (ed.) (1948) *Documents of American History*. New York: Appleton-Century-Crofts.

Cooper, John Milton, Jr. (2001) *Breaking the Heart of the World: Woodrow Wilson and the Fight for the League of Nations*. New York: Cambridge University Press.

Dallek, Robert (1979) *Franklin D. Roosevelt and American Foreign Policy, 1932–1945*. New York: Oxford University Press.

Devlin, Patrick (1975) *Too Proud to Fight: Woodrow Wilson's Neutrality*. New York: Oxford University Press.

Doenecke, Justus D. and Wilz, John E. (2003) *From Isolation to War, 1931–1941*, 3rd edn. Wheeling, Ill.: Harlan Davidson.

Ferrell, Robert H. (1998) *The Dying President: Franklin D. Roosevelt, 1944–1945*. Columbia: University of Missouri Press.

Flynn, John T. (1948) *The Roosevelt Myth*. New York: Devin-Adair.

Freidel, Frank (1990) *Franklin D. Roosevelt: A Rendezvous with Destiny*. Boston: Little, Brown.

Gaddis, John Lewis (1992) *The United States and the End of the Cold War: Implications, Reconsiderations, Provocations*. New York: Oxford University Press.

Gardner, Lloyd C. (1995) *Pay Any Price: Lyndon Johnson and the Wars for Vietnam*. Chicago: Ivan R. Dee.

Graebner, Norman (1984) *America as a World Power: A Realist Appraisal from Wilson to Reagan*. Wilmington, Del.: Scholarly Resources.

Ickes, Harold L. (1954) *The Secret Diary of Harold L. Ickes*, vol. 2. New York: Simon and Schuster.

Isaacson, Walter (1992) *Kissinger: A Biography*. New York: Simon and Schuster.

Jacobsen, Hans-Adolf and Smith, Arthur L., Jr. (eds.) (1979) *World War II – Policy and Strategy: Selected Documents with Commentary*. Santa Barbara, Calif.: ABC-Clio.

Jones, S. Shepard and Myers, Denys P. (eds.) (1940) *Documents on American Foreign Relations*, vol. 2. Boston: World Peace Foundation.

Karnow, Stanley (1991) *Vietnam: A History*. New York: Penguin.

Kennan, George F. (1951) *American Diplomacy, 1900–1950*. Chicago: University of Chicago Press.

Kimball, Warren F. (1969) *The Most Unsordid Act: Lend-Lease, 1939–1941*. Baltimore, Md.: Johns Hopkins University Press.

—— (1997) *Forged in War: Roosevelt, Churchill, and the Second World War*. New York: William Morrow.

Kimmel, Husband E. (1955) *Admiral Kimmel's Story*. Chicago: Henry Regnery.

Lansing, Robert (1921) *The Peace Negotiations: A Personal Narrative*. Boston: Houghton Mifflin.

Leuchtenburg, William E. (1963) *Franklin D. Roosevelt and the New Deal, 1932–1940*. New York: Harper and Row.

Liddell Hart, B. H. (1970) *History of the Second World War*. New York: Putnam.

Link, Arthur S. (1979) *Woodrow Wilson: Revolution, War, and Peace*. Arlington Heights, Ill.: AMH Publishing.

Marks, Frederick W., III (1988) *Wind Over Sand: The Diplomacy of Franklin Roosevelt*. Athens: University of Georgia Press.

McCormick, Thomas J. (1989) *America's Half-Century: United States Foreign Policy in the Cold War*. Baltimore, Md.: Johns Hopkins University Press.

McJimsey, George (2000) *The Presidency of Franklin Delano Roosevelt*. Lawrence: University Press of Kansas.

Morse, Arthur D. (1967) *While Six Million Died: A Chronicle of American Apathy*. New York: Random House.

O'Connor, Raymond G. (1971) *Diplomacy for Victory: FDR and Unconditional Surrender*. New York: W. W. Norton.

Safire, William (1968) *The New Language of Politics*. New York: Random House.

Schultz, George P. (1993) *Turmoil and Triumph: My Years as Secretary of State*. New York: Scribner.

Shogan, Robert (1995) *Hard Bargain: How FDR Twisted Churchill's Arm, Evaded the Law, and Changed the Role of the American Presidency*. New York: Scribner.

Smith, Gaddis (1985) *American Diplomacy during the Second World War, 1941–1945*, 2nd edn. New York: Alfred A. Knopf.

Stinnett, Robert B. (2000) *Day of Deceit: The Truth about FDR and Pearl Harbor.* New York: Touchstone.

Theobald, Robert A. (1954) *The Final Secret of Pearl Harbor: The Washington Contribution to the Japanese Attack.* New York: Devin-Adair.

Toland, John (1982) *Infamy: Pearl Harbor and its Aftermath.* Garden City, NY: Doubleday.

Utley, Jonathan G. (1985) *Going to War with Japan, 1937–1941.* Knoxville: University of Tennessee Press.

CHAPTER TWENTY

Consumption

CHARLES McGOVERN

During the twentieth century the United States conclusively became a consumer society. Its citizens found their daily lives defined by getting and spending in a commodity system that sold everything from food and entertainment to the most intimate feelings and perceptions. The US economy came to rest upon the fulcrum of commodity production and distribution; and culture increasingly centered on consumer products, rituals and relations. Over the course of the century, national domestic politics came to focus broadly and at times decisively on consumer issues. The significance of the commodity system was manifest in major issues of national import. Whatever their divisions and differences in politics, culture, and outlook, long before the close of the twentieth century, Americans viewed consumption firmly (although ambivalently) as a significant index of national health. Despite venerable traditions celebrating workers and farmers – the linchpins of nineteenth-century democratic politics – as producers, and despite equally enduring and in-grained suspicions of wealth, ostentation, and accumulation, by the century's end full participation in the mass consumption system helped define culture and citizenship. Consumer goods and privileges marked and reinforced social divisions even as they promised to overcome them. Though debates over the consequences and purposes of consumption would be divisive, Americans supported personal economic growth measured in consumption.

How did this happen? What were the forces that enmeshed American life in spending for daily life? How did the ascent of a consumer and commodity system affect the basic structures of everyday life, politics, or culture? How did this consumer society change over the century? Although interested in those changes from the outset, scholars and commentators chronicled them only in fits and starts throughout the century. Since the 1970s historians have studied the United States as a consumer society and culture more intensively. As a result we have a better – though by no means comprehensive – understanding of its origins, structures, and consequences. This essay will address critical episodes in which the consumption system had the greatest impact upon life in the United States (Agnew 1990; Lebergott 1993; Glickman 1999; Cross 2000).

The Origins of Consumer Culture, 1880–1930

Americans had participated in the marketplace for manufactured goods since the eighteenth century, when there was a brisk, if limited, international trade in such goods and in some household staples. Yet only in the late nineteenth century did the United States develop a full-fledged consumer economy. In this period, Americans turned to purchasing and using most of the commodities and tools with which they made and understood their world: their daily experience along with their material needs. In this era the American economy dedicated its surpluses to consumer goods and turned decisively to making consumer products (Livingston 1994). In the half-century after Reconstruction, the agricultural economy of the antebellum years was outstripped by a new urban industrial system that made available a staggering variety of retail goods. By 1920, when the consumer system was largely in place, much of the populace still lived in small villages and made their living from the land. But the agrarian antebellum republic had yielded to a majority urban nation characterized by new technologies, institutions, values, and experiences. In the twentieth century Americans lived in a commercial system in which anything – not only food, clothing and furniture but even ideas, perceptions and emotions – could and did become a commodity. The United States became a consumer society, its economy one of mass consumption, its culture centered around commodities and spending.

A series of related structural changes in the economy and society made possible a consumer civilization. The advent of widespread mechanized mass production and managerial capitalism allowed industry to develop a plethora of new goods. A mass industrial labor force operating new technologies and processes manufactured this abundance of goods, environments, and experiences that made up the new consumer world. Those workers, their families and communities of course formed a key base of customers for those goods. Emerging ideas and beliefs about the fluid and contingent nature of the self in turn proved critical to widespread adoption of consumption in everyday life. Mass-circulation media, including newspapers, popular magazines, radio, film, electrical signs, and billboards, all featured the local and national advertising and stories that hawked products and entertainment. New institutions and modes of distribution – from national advertising and marketing to department stores, chains, and mail order firms – revolutionized selling by remaking relationships of producers, vendors, and consumers.

In the general reconstruction of American politics and economy during the Depression and World War II, consumption became the province of government and the state, seemingly for good. Prevailing morality as well as some laws had regulated aspects of consumption since the eighteenth century, but only in the twentieth century would the federal government enter into wholesale regulation and promotion of consumption. In the Progressive Era workers, farmers, and small entrepreneurs attacked monopolies. Muckraking exposés set the stage for national regulation of food and drug production and local oversight of utilities. During the New Deal the state redefined its policies to promote consumption and to manage citizens as consumers. Conversely, Americans themselves used the rituals and activities of consumption to claim and renegotiate their rights as citizens. While classical republican as well as liberal political thought shared a belief in the incompatibility of consumption and citizenship, Americans fused the two in their daily lives. Examining in brief each of these changes should help understand the ways in which the consumer order built upon and altered the nation.

Making Consumers

Although consumption took root in both the country and the city, urbanization was crucial in bringing about the consumer regime in the late nineteenth century. Massive migration, both domestic and foreign, dramatically remade America. Young people especially left rural homesteads and areas to seek new lives in the industries and businesses of urban America. The same cities simultaneously took in millions of immigrants from abroad, particularly from southern and eastern Europe. These diasporas placed millions of the foreign-born – all of different cultures, religions, and nationalities – together in urban enclaves and ghettos. The two distinct groups of migrants formed the core of the industrial working class that built modern America and constituted immense markets for goods of all kinds.

The consumer economy hinged upon mass industrial production along with standardized bureaucratic white-collar jobs that served corporations and the new organizations of capital. Massive industrial enterprises eclipsed (but did not destroy) the small factories and shops populated by the skilled artisans, semiskilled workers, and proprietors of the antebellum era. The new factory system combined dozens of different jobs in complex mechanized arrangements, centrally coordinated and powered. In these often giant production centers, thousands of workers performed mechanized, standardized, and repetitive jobs. The largest industries – energy, transportation, machinery, chemicals, metals and rubber, foods and tobacco – dominated the economy. The success of such enterprises symbolized both productive might and national dependence on the products and processes that enabled the consumer regime (Chandler 1977; Hounshell 1984). Eclipsed by the great corporations' scale, market dominance, and capital resources, small firms survived by relying on batch production, diversified lines, and rapid responses to market shifts (Scranton 1997). The rationalization and resource manipulation of both large and small firms established profit and price margins as the overarching concerns of the new economy with a corresponding disregard for human capital. The interchangeable parts of the industrial system now expanded to include the human workers at the machines and offices.

These industrial workers comprised a large constituency of consumer markets. From 1880 to 1930 (with some notable exceptions), the real wages of workers rose, unevenly but unmistakably. The middle class – consisting of small entrepreneurs and landowners, highly skilled workers, professionals (such as lawyers, engineers, educators, physicians and scientists), bureaucrats, managers, and educated white-collar workers (writers, accountants, analysts) – enjoyed an even greater rise in fortunes and salaries. Workers as well – factory hands, unskilled day and agricultural labor, clerks, tellers, office operatives – all took part in the new consumer abundance. Historians disagree on the extent to which the consumer regime opened to the working class before the Great Depression, yet it is clear that workers did participate enthusiastically if incompletely in the new market relations and culture. Their lives were most often characterized by constraint and struggle, yet by the 1920s even working people had become consumers of more than the bare necessities of food, clothing, and basic shelter. More importantly, workers fashioned a critique of the uneven and inequitable distribution of goods and abundance that they endured under industrial capitalism. They demanded justice in wages and working conditions by claiming their rights to consumer goods and entertainment (Olney 1991; Glickman 1997).

Mass consumption was structured not only by class but by race and ethnicity. Migrating to cities in great numbers after 1900, African Americans not only survived economic and social discrimination, but built a substantial middle class. They created separate businesses, institutions, and economies to serve their communities. From retail establishments to entertainment venues and media to financial, insurance, and funerary services, these businesses served the specific needs and interests of African Americans when white commerce selectively but systematically excluded them (Weems 1998; Ownby 1999). Most often shunned by the large national advertising, marketing, and retailing firms, African Americans ultimately created a place for themselves as consumers. They used their economic power and interests to enhance their rights and civic standing under law.

Other ethnic groups similarly found themselves ghettoized in the marketplace as well as in neighborhoods. They used the consumer system paradoxically both to become Americanized and to cling to their heritage. While brand-name goods, new clothes, and entertainments helped mark such immigrant consumers as "American," the consumer system also provided the goods and services to support and maintain ethnic cultures and folkways. Thus major corporations and small businesses each sought ethnic patronage for both mass market items and specialized lines. Ethnic identities were addressed and only partly remade in American consumer culture (Ewen 1985; Heinze 1990).

By virtue of their labor as homemakers, as well as the power of domestic ideals, women were the key figures in American consumption. Marketers and advertisers long believed that women either directly spent or influenced the spending of 85 percent of all consumer dollars. While men made many home consumption decisions, the labor of shopping and purchasing largely fell to women. Accordingly, women were the targets of most advertising and marketing campaigns. Spending was gendered both as women's work and avocation. Even as the suffrage campaign to win full voting rights for women culminated in the Nineteenth Amendment (1920), advertisers and marketers depicted consumption and spending as women's proper public roles and communal service (Strasser 1982, 1989; McGovern, forthcoming). While suffragists themselves used the tools of consumption to promote their cause, commercial spokesmen offered a vision of women's true public and civic role as one of consumption. In likening women's civic rights to their satisfaction within the marketplace, merchants, manufacturers, and advertisers all reduced the significance of women attaining full citizenship. Women were instead expected to play the role of choosing among competing brands.

Yet the consumer economy represented opportunities and new avenues of expression and agency for women. From the turn of the century, those purveying goods used politically charged language to argue that consumption helped realize greater independence, individuality, and freedom. Throughout the nineteenth century access to the franchise and to labor had constituted the principal conditions of full citizenship. That access was denied to most Americans (Smith 1997; Livingston 2001). Consumption, located in a very different public arena, was potentially much more inclusive. A material basis of self-expression was both liberating from previous bourgeois gender roles and often subversive, especially when wedded to a political or social critique of economic relations. Consumption appealed to middle-class women, providing them with access to inviting and opulent public spaces (the department store in particular), with autonomy within that space, with deference, and with the imaginative allure of goods, light, color, and fashion. Seen this way, consumption not only gratified the senses but allowed women to imagine themselves differently from the roles laid out for them by tradition, convention, or male pressure (Leach 1993; Scanlon 1995). Conversely, politically active women used the issues affecting family and consumption to anchor an emerging agenda that shaped American politics throughout the twentieth century (Sklar 1995).

The consumption regime also enabled women to become active participants in many businesses and occupations that flourished in the consumer system. They won jobs in marketing, magazines, and radio; in retailing (particularly as buyers), fashion, and dry goods; and in fields like home economics and advertising, which educated women to be consumers. If consumption channeled women into spending, consumer businesses needed women as workers and consultants.

The Realization of a Consumer Culture

The consumer economy rested upon the production and use of new goods and technologies, but Americans attained a consumer culture only through access to those goods in revolutionary modes of distribution. Massive mail order catalog retailers, such as Sears, Roebuck and Montgomery Ward, enjoyed government subsidies by the establishment of parcel post, rural free delivery, and second-class postal rates. They could ship thousands of goods to the remotest corners of the republic. These merchants pioneered in selling mass-manufactured goods, introducing standardized products virtually everywhere. Large urban-based department stores, led by A. T. Stewart, Wanamaker's, Marshall Field's, and Macy's, combined under one roof the same items as seen in catalogs and dream books, and thousands more besides. By 1910 department stores exerted an extraordinary influence in the American city. They offered a cornucopia of goods, but even more significantly purveyed visions and values of luxury, desire, and unbounded abundance. Here was a source of the almost limitless appetite for accumulation still familiar a century later (Leach 1993; Lears 1994).

Other emporia competed with department stores for influence and markets. Spearheaded by F. W. Woolworth, five-and-ten-cent chain stores brought cheaper goods within the reach of millions of more Americans. Through high-volume purchasing and a standardized, focused line of goods, the chains made inexpensive products socially respectable and broadly attainable. The chains perhaps most of all made consumption national. With avid markets for such goods, the chains eventually penetrated into every city and hamlet in the United States. Ready-made clothing and accessories, home furnishings (from wallpaper and rugs through sofas and chairs, pillows, bureaus, and bedding), kitchen and household equipment, musical instruments, artwork and prints, books, cosmetics, sports equipment, food stuffs, cigarettes, stationery, farm equipment, and tools: all found places on the shelves of chains, just as they had in mail order as well as tonier department and specialty stores.

Goods drew millions of consumers into the pages of copious catalogs, the palatial department stores, and ubiquitous chains. In 1927, R. L. Polk estimated that nearly 40 percent of America's 3.5 million businesses were devoted to retail selling and consumption. Between 1880 and 1920 retailers, manufacturers, and wholesalers all fought over what goods would fill the shelves and retail stores. Groceries, pharmacies, five-and-dime chains, department, hardware, and cigar stores, all served as front lines in the battle. Extensive advertising to create product demand allowed manufacturers of branded goods (those marked with a distinct proprietary name) to circumvent the established relations of customer and merchant and to assume greater control over consumer preferences. By 1920 the brand name system dominated marketing in the United States, and few alternatives have arisen since to challenge the overall prominence of branded goods (Strasser 1989; Tedlow 1990; Laird 1998).

The brand name system made winning the consumer the most important factor in sales. To that end, firms sought and often achieved national and international distribution of their wares. New technologies and processes – refrigeration, corrugated cardboard, vacuum packaging, for example – made possible shipping and selling throughout the United States. Besides their nationally advertised brands, manufacturing firms sold still more to other manufacturers or retailers under "private label" and generic (unadvertised) names. Most importantly, producers, advertisers, and marketing specialists all collaborated and competed to identify and address specific markets within the general populace, as the preferred or likely customers for their wares. With the rationalization of production methods for goods well under way before World War I, many American firms attempted a similar streamlined production of consumers.

In pioneering methods of marketing, advertisers began to identify consumers as elements of a civic "public," an association with far-reaching consequences. They equated the idea of markets with political publics and social communities, thus conflating the private interests of marketing with the common public interest inherent in politics and civics. Additionally, in cataloguing consumer tastes, behavior, and demographic information, marketers would fragment the population so thoroughly as to nearly abandon modes of address that spoke to the populace as a whole (Turow 1997). The result was a blurring of very distinct social realms and the promotion of the idea that commerce and consumption, not civic beliefs, are predominant unifying national interests (Habermas 1989; McGovern, forthcoming).

Dependent upon advertising were the many forms of media that conveyed commercial messages along with entertainment and diversion. Hundreds of cheap magazines, plus thousands of local and rural newspapers (heavily underwritten by advertising revenue and subsidized with low postal rates), brought visions of new products into homes. In their features as well as the ubiquitous advertisements that ran beside them, *Ladies' Home Journal, Saturday Evening Post, Women's Home Companion, Collier's, Good Housekeeping* and many others provided the vision of a good life. Such magazines emphasized that the purchase and use of new products were appropriate and attractive activities. By 1900, widespread use of advertising indeed made a national culture of magazines that was unimaginable fifty years before (Ohmann 1996; Scanlon 1995). Billboards and electric signs now joined posters and placards – those staples of antebellum commerce – to promote every conceivable product, thoroughly commercializing urban spaces (Nye 1990; Jakle 2001). Subsequent new media, most prominently radio and later television, would turn to commercial messages and advertising for financial feasibility, forging enduring links between the entertainment and selling goods.

From Work to Leisure

The new forms of entertainment emerging at the dawn of the century were critical to consumer culture. The nickelodeon, movies and radio, vaudeville and burlesque, spectator sports, dance halls, roller skating rinks, and amusement parks all attracted immigrants as well as older stock Americans. These new institutions sanctioned experiences and images rooted in spending. In particular they promoted new forms of sociability between men and women, along with spectacles that emphasized sexuality and gratified the senses. Linking such experiences to the commodity system (away from other forms of social authority) only hastened their acceptance. In both the silent and sound eras, movies were a chief conduit of consumer values. Films featured individual products, while portraying getting and spending with glamorous settings and exciting plot lines, and decisively linked goods, leisure, sexuality, and consumption (May 1980).

Entertainment offered leisure and play for adults as well as young people, and presented itself as an antidote to the rigidly enforced disciplines of rationalized factory and office work. The impulse of relaxation undergirded a multitude of commercial amusements and pursuits, from spectator sports and social dancing to amusement parks, carnivals, arcades, and expositions; movies, pleasure gardens, theaters, and vaudeville; boat rides, excursions, and ultimately, the paid vacation as a regular component of employment (Nasaw 1993; Aron 1999). For working- and middle-class women, commercial leisure held its own attractions as welcome release from a seemingly boundless toil of home-making. For the young working and immigrant women who made up the ranks of garment, domestic, and clerical workers, avid participation in commercial leisure activity was critical in gaining freedom from the patriarchal power of their parents' homes, and in establishing their own independence (Ewen 1985; Peiss 1986).

For working people in general, commercial leisure and amusements offered a critical terrain in which to claim independence from supervision and control from either political elites or their own bosses, who often sought to control not only conditions of their work but also the rest of their lives. Amusement parks and resorts such as Coney Island or Euclid Beach offered crowds of patrons a whole series of pleasurable diversions that brought together men and women in a physical proximity that would have been embarrassing or forbidden in conventional society. Dance halls and beer gardens allowed crowds of young patrons to dance physically close and to engage in courtship, flirting, and sexual experimenting away from the watchful eyes of chaperones. Professional sports (especially baseball) attracted thousands of spectators in mass spectacles (Kasson 1978; Rosenzweig 1983).

All these turn-of-the-century enterprises were highly successful commercially, and they each brought forth both criticism and praise. Precisely through their intimate connections to immigrants, working classes, and to the public mixing of women and men on very different terms than typical Victorian leisure, all these forms of entertainment drew the ire of reformers and social critics (Boyer 1978; Nasaw 1993; Gorman 1996; Kammen 1999). At the same time, the exuberance and energy of these popular entertainments made them attractive to many in the middle classes. That simultaneous allure and fear of commercial entertainments has colored the twentieth-century experience of consumption.

These commercial attractions promoted values and habits central to the new culture. Up through the Victorian era, pundits and authorities had championed "useful" didactic recreation intended to improve the minds of workers while occupying otherwise free time. In this era workers now successfully fought to gain control of their non-work time and to direct it toward community and commerce-based activities of their own making and choosing. The commercialization of entertainments saw the remaking of leisure as an end in itself, with no reference to moral probity, individual salvation, or communal good. Secondly, advertisers and purveyors of leisure celebrated novelty and youth as important markers of cultural authority in a society that had venerated age and experience. Already important as consumers, young people by the 1910s now found themselves in the narratives of popular fiction, movies, dancing, and hit songs.

But while young adults figured more as both symbols and consumers of these cultural institutions, experts championed amusement and play for older adults as well. Victorian culture had celebrated children for their innocence and purity, even as the idea of childhood as a separate stage of life had taken firm hold in the nineteenth century. In the consumer era, commentators began to see children as differing from adults through the precise qualities celebrated in the new leisure: energy, boundless enthusiasm, imagination. Advertisers and marketers thus came to conceive of children as ideal consumers: ready for any experience, easily amused, with limitless appetites, ruled by emotion and not reason. Conversely, marketers urged adults to imitate and seek the emotional habits and activities of children and youth. The result was a blurred conception of boundaries between children and adults that has continually reshaped American culture and generations ever since.

But who were consumers, and how should they behave? What would be their relationship to this new economy? How were Americans to be educated to new behavior, and who would take responsibility for the task? Which institutions were dependent on the proper behavior of consumers? In a world in which domestic and productive identities were paramount, could people learn to think of themselves as consumers? These questions – as much as the productive might of the economy, the spending capacities of workers, and the clash and accommodation of divergent values – would shape consumer culture and society.

A culture that centered around commodities in effect privileged individual experience unmediated by traditional authorities: family, religion, elders, bosses. In this sense, traditional notions of individuality derived from political liberalism easily fit the form, content, and feeling of new entertainments and goods. Advertisers and salesmen celebrated consumption as pivotal to maintaining individuality in a shrinking urban world. Yet the new modern social order hinged upon a "therapeutic" ethos which, while praising individuality, paradoxically looked to outsiders for education, guidance, and validation in virtually all areas of daily living (Lears 1981; Marchand 1985; Higham 2001). With communal authority now diminished, people sought out more distant sources of wisdom, drawn from an emerging professional class: the experts. Such authorities presented other Americans with an ever more complex body of lore and advice to bolster their individuality, and even maintain the fragile illusion of freedom from such expertise. While neither determining nor dictating what Americans experienced, these experts abetted the commercial interests that often employed and trained them. They continually shaped understandings and practices of consumer culture. Such experts were critical in identifying and addressing consumers, in announcing the advent of consumer society, and in maintaining, defending, and sometimes criticizing the consumer system (Horowitz 1985; Lears 1994).

Experts were advocates and interpreters, but they were hardly sovereign. The values of consumption that they announced and the commercial interests they represented did not reign unopposed. Leisure and play, youth and novelty, possession and accumulation, individuality and desire gained great influence in American life as cornerstones of the new culture. But they co-existed with older, perhaps even more cherished values: love of family and loyalty to community; pride in and respect for work as the measure of the individual, in the home as well as the workplace; deeply held religious and spiritual convictions; local, racial, ethnic, and class pride; patriotism, sacrifice, and generosity to friend and stranger. While money and the goods it bought served as a measure of almost any experience, relationship or thing, most Americans simply did not accept the absolute rule of the dollar over their lives. To be sure, the United States operated a consumer economy by 1920, and the citizenry lived in a consumer society. An undiluted consumer culture might fully embody values of commodity exchange and ideas of marginal utility in which value was only determined by the money generated in exchange. But unchecked self-interest, unmitigated acquisitiveness, and unregulated pursuit of material gratification – the practical results of an unconstrained consumer ethos – remained far off, a dream of free-market apologists and a nightmare of moral critics.

Throughout the twentieth century Americans debated and fought over the nature of consumption in their lives. Over several eras they redefined the role of consumers in the state and the government's relationship to consumption. While Americans undeniably pursued material abundance, symbolized by "more and better," they remained unwilling to cede their culture or social lives fully to marketplace logic. But even as they debated over the limits and extent of consumption, they could never fully embrace an alternative either. Indeed, consumption became both a sign and an instrument of the social divisions within America. At the same time the ability to consume goods represented individual and collective freedom for people marked by those social divisions. To those debates, struggles, and policies we now turn.

From Depression and War to Prosperity, 1930–1970

In the first decades of the twentieth century, defenders and architects of the consumer system – most notably corporate advertisers, merchants, salesmen, and some economists – defined consumption in the explicit political language of citizenship. In this thinking, consumption granted freedom, consumers "voted" for corporations and goods through their dollars, and indeed the mass availability of inexpensive goods constituted a material democracy and social equality (McGovern forthcoming). All Americans were presumably equal in their access to breakfast cereals and floor wax, a vision that historian Roland Marchand called the parable of "the democracy of goods" (1985: 217–22, 233–4, 290–5). Citizenship was thus defined and realized in broad access to consumer goods.

But the Great Depression created new meanings of consumption and citizenship, by bringing consumers fully under public scrutiny and decisively politicizing their status. The near collapse of capitalism brought forth seismic social and economic tremors: massive job loss, homelessness, and poverty, curtailed production and reduced investment. A resurgent labor politics, which was based in the union movement but with strong alliances beyond, broadly focused not only on hours and wages, but also on issues of economic equity and social justice. After the inauguration of Franklin D. Roosevelt in 1933, consumption slowly but inexorably emerged as a public and national political issue. In programs and policy, the federal government recognized that citizens were necessarily consumers, and that consumption was essential to daily life. Conversely consumers themselves made claims for their rights as citizens to affordable and reliable goods. Under the New Deal the abstractions of economic policies, once measured in tariffs and balance of payments, now became familiar domestic issues. Workers claimed the right to a living wage: a wage that could be converted into the consumer goods, entertainments, and services necessary to fashion daily life in the commodity system. They sought a standard of living that ensured broad democratic access to consumer goods (Cohen 1990; Glickman 1997). The New Deal tacked from fostering cartels and oligarchies in the interests of restoring production, to intervening in fiscal and regulatory policies to shore up purchasing power and shield consumers from monopolistic practices (Hawley 1966; Brinkley 1995; Barber 1996). Such shifts in policy reflected the politicization of consumption, as policy-makers, politicians, corporate lobbyists, labor activists, and voters all identified the citizen's individual economic interest with consuming.

The early New Deal identified consumers as stakeholders in the economy and polity, but their concerns took a back seat to corporate and business interests in both legislation and policy-making. The National Industrial Recovery Act and the Agricultural Adjustment Act (1933) both sought federal control over production in their respective sectors. Both brought together large-scale producers, small entrepreneurs and, to a lesser extent, workers to shape production. Consumers were putatively included in deliberations in setting productions levels, prices, and working conditions. Yet in both the NRA and AAA, consumers' voices counted for little to nothing, as these regimes focused on rationalizing profits and production at the expense of consumer prices or quality (Hawley 1966). The federal Food and Drug Administration, which was charged with regulating the manufacture and contents of medicinal products, received its first overhaul since its advent in 1906. An early proposal drafted by brain trust member and Assistant Secretary of Agriculture Rexford G. Tugwell would have brought wide-ranging governmental oversight not only to medicines, but to cosmetics, tobacco, and advertising. The bill provoked a firestorm of counter-lobbying from business, pharmaceutical, and publishing interests. Bitter wrangling for over four years resulted only in a modest bill (Jackson 1970).

The first New Deal's emphasis on commercial reorganization and cartelization ended in political stalemate and constitutional defeat as both the NRA and AAA were overturned in 1935. The later New Deal institutionalized a fiscal approach to consumption. Roosevelt's 1937 and 1938 adoption of Keynesian deficit financing attempted to promote individual spending; enhancing consumer purchasing power would revive the recession-slowed economy. Such policies decisively committed the federal government to managing demand rather than directing production. Politically it made the connections of consumer, voter, and citizen inextricable. Institutionally, this new equation created a dynamic and sometimes unstable political economy which linked national economic health with consumer activity, regulated in a relatively weak state. Although by the 1990s the government had abandoned most attempts to influence demand, the emphasis upon consumer activity as the index of a healthy economy has remained powerful and influential.

Challenge and Response

But even as the government took these sustained steps to meet its obligations to citizens, consumers themselves were organizing. Americans made claims upon the state to acknowledge their interests and defend their rights as consumers. The consumer movements that emerged in the 1930s constituted a shifting coalition of civic, women's, and buyers' groups. They shared a belief in an active government role in consumption: setting minimum standards for goods, and enforcing stricter regulations in the marketplace, including advertising, packaging, quality, safety, and performance. These groups all demanded that the government provide the consumer protection from the excesses of the marketplace and enforce a minimum compliance by manufacturers and retailers of their social contract with consumers. An early inspirational voice in the movement was Consumers' Research, the first non-partisan, non-profit product testing organization. Founded in 1929, CR provided specific comparative information to members on the performance, qualities, and values of name-brand goods, wedding a fierce anti-market critique to specific pragmatic recommendations. By "naming names" in direct brand comparisons, CR directly challenged dubious and deceitful claims made in advertising and gave consumers clear recommendations easily applied in the marketplace. CR offered an alternative vision, derived from Jeffersonian ideals of independence from the market, to counter business encomiums of consumer democracy as freedom of choice. The group's chief, physicist F. J. Schlink, based the organization's reports and methods firmly in scientific testing, using government reports, a wide network of technicians, and its own labs to make its recommendations. With colleague Arthur Kallet, Schlink penned a sensational best-selling exposé, *100,000,000 Guinea Pigs* (1933), which ignited a second wave of muckraking literature that persisted throughout the Depression. Such "guinea pig" books all focused on the dangers in everyday life to consumers in certain goods and retail markets. Whether targeting canned goods or autos, such books denounced excessive commercialism, and portrayed business as rapacious and reckless, as well as dangerous to common public health, the environment, and morality. In the trough of the Depression, CR gained notoriety and influence well beyond its membership numbers. Its revelations of health hazards and deceptive market practices, along with its willingness to name offenders and defend its charges, brought the group influence with consumers and government activists, and earned it the implacable opposition of Madison Avenue (McGovern forthcoming).

Women's clubs, civic groups, housewives' and community associations all championed consumer rights and product standards during the 1930s. Mainstream groups such as the General Federation of Women's Clubs, government agencies such as the Bureau of Home Economics, and radical organizations like the League of Women Shoppers all campaigned against high prices and shoddy goods, and sought greater government regulation in local and regional campaigns. The National Consumers' League, a holdover of progressive-era activism, generated vigorous campaigns to urge buyers to demand better working conditions and wages for those who made consumer products. Consumers' Union, a splinter group from Schlink, took up the banner, fusing union movement concerns with product standards. CU offered information on working conditions as well as test results and brand recommendations (Silber 1983; Storrs 2000). Popular Front coalitions of leftists, Communists, and Democrats all joined the interests of workers and consumers. These activists claimed that higher wages and improved working conditions not only produced better consumer goods but also strengthened the economy; the strength of the consumer's dollar was the health of the state.

Without posing a serious threat to established business interests, the consumer movement nevertheless gained powerful enemies. Discredited by the Depression, disgraced by opposition to Roosevelt's programs and isolated by their own intransigence, most corporate leaders bitterly opposed the New Deal and the labor movement. Consumer advocates criticized both business practices and underlying assumptions that manufacturers and merchants knew best how to protect consumers' interests. Businessmen retaliated by organizing campaigns to re-establish their unquestioned legitimacy and influence. Stung by FDR's 1936 landslide re-election, corporate spokesmen developed systematic strategies both to discredit government and to win back public allegiance from the New Deal to "free" enterprise.

Businesses soon began underwriting such campaigns, not only in direct advocacy but more pervasively in entertainment, with radio programs such as *The DuPont Cavalcade of America* and the *American Family Robinson* (sponsored by the National Association of Manufacturers), plus attractions such as the barnstorming *General Motors Cavalcade*, a traveling exhibition of new products. Business showered workers and consumers with pamphlets defending free enterprise, short sponsored films that linked consumption with business interests (such as Jam Handy's 1937 *From Dawn To Sunset*), and advertising, campaigns all aimed at restoring public confidence in business. All these portrayed a consumer interest – abundant, new, and better products – made possible only through private enterprise, not government (Fones-Wolf 1994; Marchand 1998; Bird 1999; McGovern, forthcoming). Business argued that government could never fulfill popular desires, and only unfettered enterprise would give consumers what they wanted.

The battle for consumers' allegiance openly erupted in World War II. The era directly pitted government planning and the corporate counter-revolution against state regulation. The war years saw Americans faced with competing obligations: their individual welfare and freedom as consumers clashed with the material sacrifices and socialized economic decisions required in wartime planning. Consumer freedom squared off against the common needs of a society facing enforced scarcity. Americans thus endured rationing and shortages to maintain war production, even as they experienced a recovering economy for the first time since 1930.

The war marked the high point in government intervention in consumption. The needs of fighting the war prompted FDR to assert control of both production and consumption. The Office of Price Administration (OPA) administered domestic rationing of consumer goods, and set and maintained rent and price controls. Consumers themselves were recruited by the government to be active participants in voluntary cooperation with rationing and price levels of thousands of goods, from foodstuffs to clothing, utensils to playthings. Yet firm government commitments to wage controls, along with business and merchant resistance to reducing profit levels, combined to force an inflationary spiral that angered workers and consumers and discredited central planning among the populace. In the postwar year of 1946, the largest wave of wildcat strikes ever seen in the US exploded, even as a prolonged and deliberate corporate meat packers' strike undid the OPA. Broadly underlying these two phenomena was an unmet demand for consumer goods. Clearly Americans had come to feel entitled to a steady supply of goods, along with the wages to purchase them (Lipsitz 1994; Brinkley 1995; Jacobs 1998).

Workers for many years had linked wages, jobs, and goods with what became known as the American standard of living. Yet during World War II leaders and citizens framed understanding of the war effort not as political abstractions of freedom but in the familiar terms of consumption, goods, and home. The American Way of Life that emerged as the object of the war effort was portrayed precisely in consumerist terms that corporate spokesmen were only too happy to echo in their product advertising. The Office of War Information (OWI) coordinated the campaigns of public education on war aims and home front participation. Initially headed by the poet and Librarian of Congress, Archibald MacLeish, the staff's internationalism stressed opposition to fascism. But by 1943 the OWI largely had abandoned such views in favor of anti-Nazi, anti-Japanese simplicities. Staffed by advertising and publishing executives along with other businessmen, the OWI continually emphasized the private and local aspects of war aims. Even as it was unseemly and unpatriotic to stress the interests of business, commerce, or sales during the war, advertisers found no difficulty in fitting the broadest military aims to a vision stressing political freedom as freedom of choice (Winkler 1978; Horten 2002).

The wartime contradictions of consumption were prismatically focused during the 1940s. During the decade Americans embraced several enduring landmarks of the modern American Christmas, including Irving Berlin's "White Christmas" (1942), Frank Capra's film *It's a Wonderful Life* (1946), and Valentine Davies' 1947 story and George Seaton's film of the same year, *Miracle on 34th Street*. The uncertainties and the material constraints of war fed a popular hunger for films, songs, and stories on Christmas themes. Most linked the celebrations of abundance and gifts with community and home, the places where "more and better" mattered less than love and loyalty. Overseas servicemen made Bing Crosby's 1942 recording of "White Christmas" a hit, and fueled its rise to the best-selling record of all time (Waits 1994; Restad 1995; Marling 2000).

Miracle on 34th Street especially used Christmas and consumption to fuse the private interests of home and family with the public concerns of the state. Kris Kringle, the Macy's Santa Claus who believes that he is the one true Santa, gains fame in his dealings with the public. Putting consumer interest ahead of commerce, he sends Christmas shoppers away from Macy's to stores all over New York to find their ideal gift purchases.

The altruism is hailed by grateful consumers and quickly adopted throughout the marketplace. Macy's business increases along with its competitors'. The state, represented by a ward healer and a politically-minded judge presiding at Kringle's sanity hearing, recognizes the public economic and political stake in a vigorous Christmas shopping season. The federal government – the postal system – endorses Kringle as the one and only Santa and ratifies Christmas in the national interest by delivering thousands of letters to Kringle at the New York courthouse. And his greatest gift is revealed in the finale: a suburban home, complete with swing set, for the city-bred little girl whose divorced and disillusioned mother is Kris's boss. Thus Christmas joins and heals the family, state, and economy. Business, political, and familial interests all converged in the great festival of consumption.

An Affluent Society

Kringle's gift of a "real" house was the harbinger of the postwar consumer regime. Prosperity entailed the fulfillment of the entitlements to consumption for vast members of the populace. Postwar consumers saw the Gross National Product grow fivefold from 1945 to 1970, from $200 billion to over $1.1 trillion. The war's conclusion unleashed the pent-up demands not only of five years of rationing and sacrifice but of a decade of worry and privation before that. Purchasing on household goods and appliances rose over 200 percent before 1950, while the number of new homes rose from an average of 237,000 a year during the war to 1.3 million annually from 1946 to 1950. That trend continued throughout the following decade.

Returning veterans married in record numbers, and their families brought forth the largest American generation ever: the baby boom. Indeed, the consumer economy recovered fully. In this era the phrase "the American Way of Life" came into widespread use, and was practically synonymous with high levels of consumption and abundance (Potter 1954; Samuelson 1995; Nickles 2002). This prosperity rested on new relationships of workers, capital, and the state. The New Deal efforts to enhance consumption through collective means and appeals gave way to a privatized corporate definition of public interest. The federal government abandoned price and production controls but made other, quieter commitments to enhance consumption. Government policies made consumption a "state project" through programs that promoted private, family-centered consumption to enhance the economy and manage social conflict. The Federal Housing Administration subsidized mortgages for veterans (especially whites), thus underwriting family amenities. Simultaneously dismantled (through targeted blight, neglect, and segregationist lending policies) were infrastructures friendly to collective trans-racial groups or minorities. Banks and insurance companies followed suit, racially redlining neighborhoods, defining mixed-race residence patterns as de facto economic blight, and heavily targeting investment in newer suburbs in the interests of class and racial homogeneity (Lipsitz 1998; Cohen 2003).

Older spaces and syatems such as mass transit – subways and streetcars – and urban ethnic enclaves had nurtured the collective identities of workers and consumers who challenged government and business for economic justice and political empowerment. But postwar economic growth, government-sponsored suburbanization, and subsidies to corporate interests helped undo this social formation. The postwar American republic was built upon a consumption-driven political economy, which placed the white middle-class family at the center of policies and benefits. Thus enacting and symbolizing inequalities, consumption neither concealed nor healed social divisions, which were aggravated by the unequal distribution of and subsidies for postwar consumer benefits. The promises of abundance were made, but not granted, to all (May 2000; Cohen 2003).

The flight from city to suburb was the central social movement of the postwar years. Promoted by (and requiring) the growing ownership of automobiles, new federally subsidized highways and interstates, as well as the population boom itself, the suburbs became the locus of new families and the new middle class. The family was the focus of the consumer boom. Housing developments and subdivisions filled the agricultural perimeters of cities; William Levitt's famous "towns" offered the most streamlined and well-known version of these subdivisions. His homes were small, 800-square-foot (just under 75 square meters) models set on concrete slabs; yet along with dozens of other similar developments, these houses found eager young families ready to move in. The suburbs offered not only partially prefabricated and identical homes but also new communities. Migration from the city sundered old neighborhoods that sheltered extended family and ethnic enclaves; the new suburban communities were communities of choice, in which residents made their new lives often with people of very different backgrounds. Yet in critical ways many of these communities were more alike than different. While many suburbs had specific ethnic, religious, and class concentrations, racial integration was rare. Indeed many new developments had restrictive covenants; either by code or custom, segregation was a feature of the suburbs (Jackson 1985).

Critics fretted that the suburbs, the cascade of inexpensive goods, and the opening up of new leisure time would foster an anemic and mediocre culture and a dull citizenry. For example, Clement Greenberg and Dwight Macdonald warned that mass-produced kitsch would debase perceptions and tastes, while the platitudes of pseudo-intellectual "midcult" would crowd out vigorous debate or challenging ideas (Rosenberg and White 1957). For many thinkers on the Left and Right, the postwar era ushered in a civilization typified by comfort and conformity. Sociologist David Riesman and journalist William Whyte produced influential studies that portrayed the American middle class (especially men) as ominously susceptible to external pressures and influences. The bureaucratic "organization" stultified thinking and crushed initiative, while suburbs and the demands of family life posed a similar challenge outside work. Whether "other-directed" (Riesman) or conformist (Whyte), such critiques argued that the American middle-class worker-consumer inhabited a world that made individuality difficult and a vibrant culture elusive.

Such comments conflated consumer abundance with the overall quality of American life. Many an anxious intellectual querulously criticized, or occasionally defended, American civilization solely in terms of the consumer plenty of two-tone Plymouths, living room sectionals, and TV dinners (Kammen 1999). Such observers need not have fretted. Even as high wages and cheap goods allowed industrial workers to own goods once reserved for an economic elite, and as working-class aesthetics now influenced the mass market, consumption still marked barriers of class and caste for celebrants and critics alike. When the civil rights movement occupied national attention in the 1950s and 1960s, African-American demands for equal rights addressed not only voting and schooling, but full access to the fruits of the consumer system, whether a cup of coffee at a Woolworth lunch counter or the right to patronize department stores, mass transit, and movie theaters.

The new abundance was a principal feature of these suburban towns. Consumer plenty highlighted not only goods, but systematically featured a spending based both on novelty and accumulation – new and more. While values of thrift and deferred gratification persisted in popular practice, they began to fade from postwar advertising and marketing. Manufacturers and merchants would certainly continue their appeals to consumers' sense of savings, economy, durability, and efficiency. Yet the overall consumer ethos decisively turned to novelty, modernity, and obsolescence. In the postwar era, many goods that are today standard were introduced or widely adopted. Dishwashers, blenders, and garbage disposals joined electric mixers, washing machines, and vacuum cleaners as common features of middle-class homes. Reclining chairs came into use, alongside sofas and easy chairs in living rooms. New materials (principally plastics) offered a cheap, durable, and ultimately disposable medium for thousands of products, from melamine tumblers and tupperware storage bowls to ash trays, picture frames, and toys. Postwar working-class women challenged and influenced the mass market. They preferred goods whose designs incorporated an enthusiastic abundance rather than the "restraint" associated with refined middle-class or elite taste. Thomas Hine's memorable term captures the ideal of the era: "populuxe." This luxury for the masses embodied goods that saved time and labor, transformed living spaces, and supported the belief that "more and better" was within universal reach. This ethos was cheerily presented in an aura of growth without limits (Hine 1986; Nickles 2002).

An Age of Ambivalence

At the heart of postwar affluence were two consumer goods that became the centerpieces of suburban family life. Introduced at the 1939 New York World's Fair, television did not reach many Americans until the mid-1950s. But by 1960, 90 percent of homes had TV sets. Television was essentially an advertising system that made its money by delivering the millions of consumers to sponsors who paid for unmediated access to viewers. While businessmen, broadcasters, audiences, educators, and politicians had struggled for nearly a decade over the nature and extent of radio's commercial focus, no such uncertainty clouded the course of the new medium. From the start, broadcast television was created, structured, and run to sell goods, not the least of them television sets themselves (McChesney 1993; Smulyan 1994; Samuel 2001). Television soon drew most national advertising dollars, with sponsors, networks, and broadcasters all made giddy by endlessly rising sales curves.

Television was the medium that promoted and made possible the scope and fervor of the postwar consumer boom. Families gathered for their nightly rituals of television viewing, each program framed by inevitable commercial messages. Cultural critics assailed broadcasting's continuous stream of low-brow offerings (even in the medium's so-called "Golden Age"), while magazines, designers, and experts saw television as a key ingredient in unifying the family and providing a focal point within the home (Boddy 1990; Tichi 1991; Spigel 1992). Like the movies, television promoted consumption by featuring products and leisure almost endlessly, in the programs along with the commercial spots that paid for them. Daytime service programs, led by the NBC *Today* show, offered women advice on household chores; game and quiz shows showered contestants with goods and prizes (donated by sponsors to gain maximum publicity at minimum expense); variety and dramatic shows often featured and plugged goods. Situation comedies often took consumption as the departure point of story lines. Sponsors even enjoyed veto power over scripting, and they regularly prohibited unflattering portrayals of their goods or mentions of competitors' products.

Beginning most spectacularly with the Howdy Doody series (1947–60) and the Walt Disney "Davy Crockett" phenomenon (1955), television's successful cultivation of the baby boom generation tapped an undreamt-of market for toys and other juvenile items. Televison not only taught children to consume but created a powerful marketing model. Manufacturers created a wide interwoven array of goods from apparel to breakfast foods, all sold through the trademarked cartoon character or toy. In this manner breakfast cereal, toy, and book manufacturers built upon radio's successful socialization of children to the consumer system; television reached children without the mediation of parents and taught them to be consumers well before they reached adolescence (Seiter 1993; Cross 1997).

Automobiles were the other key to postwar abundance. Car ownership increased substantially after World War II, through accessible pricing and financing options. Along with homes, the car was the principal consumer purchase in most families. Designed to embody purported aerodynamic innovations, by the mid-1950s American cars sported tail fins reminiscent of aircraft, bright colors, two-tone finishes, and bountiful chrome. The suburbs necessitated automobiles as well, owing to an overall scarcity and decline of public transport. While it was possible perhaps to commute to city jobs by rail or bus, travel within and between suburbs was severely hampered without a car; suburban homemakers increasingly came to rely on cars for shopping and daily chores outside the home. By the mid-1950s Detroit was selling matching "his and hers" models for the growing number of families that could afford or desired two cars. The models produced by the "Big Three" firms of Chrysler, General Motors, and Ford (along with smaller competitors Hudson, De Soto, Packard, and Rambler) were widely viewed as the great symbols of American manufacturing capacity, engineering, and opulence.

The automobile saved labor and promoted freedom, leisure, and family togetherness (symbolically, the capacious station wagon lost its trappings as a work vehicle to become the typical family car). But there was a hidden and high after-sticker price. As government subsidized the highway system and neglected mass transport, Americans had fewer alternatives to the car. With an ethos of limitless personal freedom, drivers were also unwilling to entertain constraints on the use and enjoyment of automobiles (Bottles 1987; Kay 1997). By the 1960s the car would come to symbolize the problems of consumer culture, including the costs of growth, problems of safety and corporate neglect, environmental damage and pollution, and the real limits on natural resources.

Buyers' Remorse

In the 1960s, as consumer spending and accumulation accelerated, persistent critical voices offered a devastating portrait of the costs of affluence and consumption.

Dormant since the war, such critiques found vast audiences in these years of high prosperity and unquestioned American power. A growing unease with the costs and dimensions of abundance united these critics with their audiences, and these voices set the stage for much of the dissidence that characterized the 1960s and 1970s. Vance Packard, Rachel Carson, Michael Harrington, Betty Friedan, and Ralph Nader each offered fundamental critiques of the pillars of American abundance, especially the alliance of technology, corporate and government power on the one hand, and on the other the unquestioned assumption that the wealth, ease, and comfort of American life were universally shared, admired, or beneficial. Carson's *Silent Spring* (1962) passionately revealed the devastation wrought by pesticides in the natural world, galvanizing a modern environmental movement that aimed to reduce or eliminate the harm done by human economic growth and technology to nature. Nader's *Unsafe at Any Speed* (1965) accused automobile companies of putting profits ahead of lives, and charged that manufacturers systematically sabotaged efforts to introduce any safety features. Not since the first widespread consumer movement of the Depression had citizens confronted charges that their consumer abundance was perilous and flawed, and that corporations were in fact hazardous to health, safety, and happiness.

Michael Harrington's *The Other America* (1962) offered an overwhelming critique of the assumptions of national affluence, by showing that abject and systemic poverty persisted throughout America. People of color, migrants, children, and the elderly, Harrington charged, lived in misery and privation, hidden from the gaze of mainstream media and society. He charged that the plight of the poor was even more noxious and indefensible in light of an affluence that had reached undreamt-of levels. *The Other America* came as both a challenge to the conscience of citizens and policy-makers, and sowed the seeds of social programs and the war on poverty of the 1960s and beyond.

Finally, Betty Friedan's *The Feminine Mystique* (1963) provided the most potentially revolutionary critique of consumerism of all. She offered a collective portrait of the effects upon middle-class women, who were contained within the domestic sphere and confined to a routine of child-rearing, shopping, and house work. The "problem that has no name," as Friedan called it, had devastating consequences: depression, frustration, misery. The postwar suburbs were little more than "comfortable concentration camps," with endless rounds of homemaking and child-care duties, breeding isolation and alienation from a wider world. If a woman's principal duties were to be homemaker, mother, wife, and consumer, the social price was too great. Millions of women were trapped, torn from their own dreams of achievement, of careers, of individuality undefined and unencumbered by responsibility to others. The consumption regime was deadly to the spirits and lives of women, those who for sixty or more years had been seen as its major beneficiaries.

These brief summaries can hardly do justice to four critical texts that served as wellsprings for the modern environmental, consumer, anti-poverty, and women's movements respectively. Yet they all revealed a conviction that consumer abundance had costs and consequences far greater than those determined in any calculation of prices, wages, costs, and purchasing power. Business, media, science, and government together concealed, mystified, or marginalized the processes and consequences of consumption.

Conclusion: Attention Shoppers

If consumers did not know the implications and social costs of their desires and actions in 1960, events in the next decades would oblige them to confront those costs repeatedly. Americans had long been encouraged to view their spending choices as individual actions, and they had grown accustomed (although with resistance) to seeing their lives as workers and consumers separately. Individuals' interests were divorced from those of their communities at large. While World War II had taught consumers to think and behave with collective ends and concerns in mind, the postwar economic restoration sealed that earlier era of communal effort in a veil of both relief at its passing and nostalgia for its loss. But those individualized and specific habits were indeed part of broader, more systemic, and perhaps intractable problems. In the decades after the 1960s, Americans confronted material limits and checks upon their consumption. While they did not abandon the optimistic expectations for endless and painless growth, of more and better without cost or consequence, such appetites had to coexist with knowledge of shortages, of global interdependence, and limited resources. While citizens have repeatedly turned to politicians and presidents who share those postwar assumptions for reassurance, they have also continually encountered a world that does not concur with or sustain those beliefs. Postwar baby boomers especially have been torn, as different members of this generation (now fully in public and economic power at the turn of the new century) either cling to an ethos of unchecked growth or espouse the alternative of sustainable, renewable, or limited development.

Neither politics nor economics can fully address the questions underlying these tensions. Can a country that monopolizes so much of the world's resources and plenty continue on such a course? Can a society in which 1 percent of its population controls 40 percent of its wealth remain free and democratic? What is the true purpose of consumption? What really is the pursuit of happiness? Throughout the twentieth century, Americans believed that consumption was key to that pursuit, and that their independence, freedom, and indeed their distinct culture and nationhood were bound up in consumption. Those beliefs will undoubtedly shape their decisions in the decades to come, as consuming will inform but never fully contain American life and culture.

REFERENCES

Agnew, Jean-Christophe (1990) "Coming up for air: consumer culture in historical perspective," *Intellectual History Newsletter* 12, pp. 3–21.

Aron, Cindy S. (1999) *Working at Play: A History of Vacations in the United States.* New York: Oxford University Press.

Barber, William S. (1996) *Designs Within Disorder: Franklin D. Roosevelt, the Economists, and the Shaping of American Economic Policy, 1933–1945.* New York: Cambridge University Press.

Bird, William L. (1999) *Better Living: Advertising, Media and the New Vocabulary of Business Leadership, 1935–1955.* Evanston, Ill.: Northwestern University Press.

Boddy, William F. (1990) *Fifties Television: The Industry and its Critics.* Urbana: University of Illinois Press.

Bottles, Scott L. (1987) *Los Angeles and the Automobile: The Making of the Modern City.* Berkeley: University of California Press.

Boyer, Paul (1978) *Urban Masses and Moral Order in America, 1820–1920.* Cambridge, Mass.: Harvard University Press.

Brinkley, Alan (1995) *The End of Reform: New Deal Liberalism in Recession and War.* New York: Alfred A. Knopf.

Chandler, Alfred D., Jr. (1977) *The Visible Hand: The Managerial Revolution in American Business.* Cambridge, Mass.: Harvard University Press.

Cohen, Lizabeth (1990) *Making a New Deal: Industrial Workers in Chicago, 1919–1939.* New York: Cambridge University Press.

—— (2003) *A Consumer's Republic: The Politics of Mass Consumption in Postwar America.* New York: Alfred A. Knopf.

Cross, Gary S. (1997) *Kids' Stuff: Toys and the Changing World of American Childhood.* Cambridge, Mass.: Harvard University Press.

—— (2000) *An All-Consuming Century: Why Commercialism Won in Modern America.* New York: Columbia University Press.

Ewen, Elizabeth (1985) *Immigrant Women in the Land of Dollars: Life and Culture on the Lower East Side, 1890–1925.* New York: Monthly Review Press.

Fones-Wolf, Elizabeth (1994) *Selling Free Enterprise: The Business Assault on Labor and Liberalism, 1945–1960.* Urbana: University of Illinois Press.

Glickman, Lawrence B. (1997) *A Living Wage: American Workers and the Making of Consumer Society.* Ithaca, NY: Cornell University Press.

—— (ed.) (1999) *Consumer Society in American History: A Reader.* Ithaca, NY: Cornell University Press.

Gorman, Paul R. (1996) *Left Intellectuals and Popular Culture in America.* Chapel Hill: University of North Carolina Press.

Habermas, Jürgen (1989) *The Structural Transformation of the Public Sphere: An Inquiry into a Category of Bourgeois Society,* trans. Thomas Burger. Cambridge, Mass.: MIT Press.

Hawley, Ellis M. (1966) *The New Deal and the Problem of Monopoly: A Study in Economic Ambivalence.* Princeton, NJ: Princeton University Press.

Heinze, Andrew R. (1990) *Adapting To Abundance: Jewish Immigrants, Mass Consumption and the Search for American Identity.* New York: Columbia University Press.

Higham, John (2001) *Hanging Together: Unity and Diversity in American Culture.* New Haven, Conn.: Yale University Press.

Hine, Thomas (1986) *Populuxe.* New York: Alfred A. Knopf.

Horowitz, Daniel (1985) *The Morality of Spending: Attitudes Toward the Consumer Society in America, 1875–1940.* Baltimore, Md.: Johns Hopkins University Press.

Horten, Gerd (2002) *Radio Goes to War: The Cultural Politics of Propaganda during World War II.* Berkeley: University of California Press.

Hounshell, David A. (1984) *From the American System to Mass Production, 1800–1932: The Development of Manufacturing Technology.* Baltimore, Md.: Johns Hopkins University Press.

Jackson, Charles O. (1970) *Food and Drug Legislation in the New Deal.* Princeton, NJ: Princeton University Press.

Jackson, Kenneth T. (1985) *Crabgrass Frontier: The Suburbanization of the United States.* New York: Oxford University Press.

Jacobs, Meg (1998) "How about some meat?: The Office of Price Administration, consumption politics, and state building from the bottom up, 1941–1946," *Journal of American History* 84, pp. 910–41.

Jakle, John A. (2001) *City Lights: Illuminating the American Night.* Baltimore, Md.: Johns Hopkins University Press.

Kammen, Michael (1999) *American Culture, American Tastes: Social Change and the Twentieth Century*. New York: Alfred A. Knopf.

Kasson, John F. (1978) *Amusing the Million: Coney Island at the Turn of the Century*. New York: Hill and Wang.

Kay, Jane Holtz (1997) *Asphalt Nation: How the Automobile Took Over America, and How We Can Take It Back*. New York: Crown.

Laird, Pamela Walker (1998) *Advertising Progress: American Business and the Rise of Consumer Marketing*. Baltimore, Md.: Johns Hopkins University Press.

Leach, William (1993) *Land of Desire: Merchants, Power and the Rise of a New American Culture*. New York: Pantheon.

Lears, T. J. Jackson (1981) *No Place of Grace: Antimodernism and the Transformation of American Culture, 1880–1920*. New York: Pantheon.

—— (1994) *Fables of Abundance: A Cultural History of Advertising in America*. New York: Basic Books.

Lebergott, Stanley (1993) *Pursuing Happiness: American Consumers in the Twentieth Century*. Princeton, NJ: Princeton University Press.

Lipsitz, George (1994) *A Rainbow at Midnight: Class and Culture in the 1940s*. Champaign: University of Illinois Press.

—— (1998) *The Possessive Investment in Whiteness: How White People Profit from Identity Politics*. Philadelphia: Temple University Press.

Livingston, James (1994) *Pragmatism and the Political Economy of Cultural Revolution 1850–1940*. Chapel Hill: University of North Carolina Press.

—— (2001) *Pragmatism, Feminism, and Democracy: Rethinking the Politics of American History*. New York: Routledge.

McChesney, Robert W. (1993) *Telecommunications, Mass Media, and Democracy: The Battle for the Control of US Broadcasting, 1928–1935*. New York: Oxford University Press.

McGovern, Charles F. (forthcoming) *Sold American: Inventing the Consumer, 1890–1945*. Chapel Hill: University of North Carolina Press.

Marchand, Roland (1985) *Advertising the American Dream: Making Way for Modernity, 1920–1940*. Berkeley: University of California Press.

—— (1998) *Creating the Corporate Soul: The Rise of Public Relations and Corporate Imagery in American Big Business*. Berkeley: University of California Press.

Marling, Karal Ann (2000) *Merry Christmas! Unwrapping America's Greatest Holiday*. Cambridge, Mass.: Harvard University Press.

May, Lary (1980) *Screening Out the Past: The Birth of Mass Culture and the Motion Picture Industry*. New York: Oxford University Press.

—— (2000) *The Big Tomorrow: Hollywood and the Politics of the American Way*. Chicago: University of Chicago Press.

Nasaw, David (1993) *Going Out: The Rise and Fall of Public Amusements*. New York: Basic Books.

Nickles, Shelley (2002) "More is better: mass consumption, gender and class identity in postwar America," *American Quarterly* 54, pp. 581–622.

Nye, David E. (1990) *Electrifying America: The Social Meanings of a New Technology, 1880–1940*. Cambridge, Mass.: MIT Press.

Ohmann, Richard M. (1996) *Selling Culture: Magazines, Markets, and Class at the Turn of the Century*. New York: Verso.

Olney, Martha L. (1991) *Buy Now, Pay Later: Advertising, Credit, and Consumer Durables in the 1920s*. Chapel Hill: University of North Carolina Press.

Ownby, Ted (1999) *American Dream in Mississippi: Consumers, Poverty and Culture, 1830–1998*. Chapel Hill: University of North Carolina Press.

Peiss, Kathy Lee (1986) *Cheap Amusements: Working Women and Leisure in New York City, 1880 to 1920*. Philadelphia: Temple University Press.

Potter, David M. (1954) *People of Plenty: Economic Abundance and the American Character*. Chicago: University of Chicago Press.

Restad, Penne L. (1995) *Christmas in America: A History*. New York: Oxford University Press.

Rosenberg, Bernard and White, David Manning (eds.) (1957) *Mass Culture: The Popular Arts in America*. Glencoe, Ill.: Free Press.

Rosenzweig, Roy (1983) *Eight Hours For What We Will: Workers and Leisure in an Industrial City, 1870–1920*. Cambridge: Cambridge University Press.

Samuel, Lawrence R. (2001) *Brought to You By: Postwar Television Advertising and the American Dream*. Austin: University of Texas Press.

Samuelson, Robert J. (1995) *The Good Life and its Discontents: The American Dream in the Age of Entitlement, 1945–1955*. New York: Times Books.

Scanlon, Jennifer (1995) *Inarticulate Longings:* The Ladies' Home Journal, *Gender, and the Promises of Consumer Culture*. New York: Routledge.

Scranton, Philip (1997) *Endless Novelty: Specialty Production and American Industrialization, 1865–1925*. Princeton, NJ: Princeton University Press.

Seiter, Ellen (1993) *Sold Separately: Children and Parents in Consumer Culture*. New Brunswick, NJ: Rutgers University Press.

Silber, Norman Isaac (1983) *Test and Protest: The Influence of Consumers' Union*. New York: Holmes and Meier.

Sklar, Kathryn Kish (1995) *Florence Kelley and the Nation's Work*. New Haven, Conn.: Yale University Press.

Smith, Rogers M. (1997) *Civic Ideals: Conflicting Visions of US Citizenship in History*. New Haven, Conn.: Yale University Press.

Smulyan, Susan (1994) *Selling Radio: The Commercialization of American Broadcasting, 1920–1934*. Washington, DC: Smithsonian Institution Press.

Spigel, Lynn (1992) *Make Room for TV: Television and the Family Ideal in Postwar America*. Chicago: University of Chicago Press.

Storrs, Landon R. Y. (2000) *Civilizing Capitalism: The National Consumers' League, Women's Activism, and Labor Standards in the New Deal Era*. Chapel Hill: University of North Carolina Press.

Strasser, Susan (1982) *Never Done: A History of American Housework*. New York: Pantheon.

—— (1989) *Satisfaction Guaranteed: The Making of the American Mass Market*. New York: Pantheon.

Tedlow, Richard S. (1990) *New and Improved: The Story of Mass Marketing in America*. New York: Basic Books.

Tichi, Cecelia M. (1991) *Electronic Hearth: Creating an American Television Culture*. New York: Oxford University Press.

Turow, Joseph (1997) *Breaking Up America: Advertisers and the New Media World*. Chicago: University of Chicago Press.

Waits, William B. (1994) *The Modern Christmas in America: A Cultural History of Gift Giving*. New York: New York University Press

Weems, Robert E. (1998) *Desegregating the Dollar: African American Consumerism in the Twentieth Century*. New York: New York University Press.

Winkler, Allan M. (1978) *The Politics of Propaganda: The Office of War Information, 1942–1945*. New Haven, Conn.: Yale University Press.

CHAPTER TWENTY-ONE

Law

NORMAN L. ROSENBERG

The Dawn of the Twentieth Century

Social activities considered "law," in the formulation of the sociologist Pierre Bourdieu, take place inside a "field of specialized practice" set off from other fields, particularly the political. The specially trained professionals who work within the "field of law" assert a monopoly over the performance of certain tasks, such as the settlement of individual disputes and the legal oversight of many political decisions. As a consequence, they must repulse challenges to their claims of lawful authority. Similarly, guardians of the legal field need constantly to reassert their claim to perform the myriad tasks of "governance," the art and practice of controlling people's conduct and channeling their expectations.

The boundaries of the twentieth-century legal field continually shifted. By 1900, for example, work by secular courts had already made the field of religion, including its church-run tribunals, marginal to everyday dispute settlement. In contrast, at the century's end, professionals in other fields of social practice may have performed certain tasks, such as settling accident claims or giving tax advice, as skillfully (and more cheaply) as judges or lawyers. Throughout the century, the boundaries that separated different institutions within the legal field itself, such as courts and administrative agencies, constantly changed.

The twentieth century's field of law has produced three important, distinctively legal products.

(1) Over the course of the century, the *judicial rulings* that concluded court room adjudication remained in the forefront of both the popular and professional images of law. In 1900, rulings by local, state, and federal courts still dominated daily governance in the United States. Courts employed a rule-grounded vision, a special judicial "gaze" that the legal historian Tim Murphy calls an early form of "social science" expertise. Judges looked at arguments by opposing attorneys, at evidence these lawyers offered, and finally at earlier court decisions or "precedents" (Murphy 1997).

By surveying precedent, judges proceeded *as if* the legal rulings of the past, collected in written accounts of previous cases, provided a special, legalistic expertise that could still govern in the present. They thus assumed that the subject matter of these earlier cases mirrored, or at least closely resembled, contemporary disputes. Confidently invoking venerable common law rules, such as the liberty of individuals to make private contracts that public authorities would enforce, judges decided the specific cases before them and also made broader social and economic policies, a practice called "adjudicative governance." By applying rules grounded in precedent, courts could underscore the theoretical claim that judges did not govern by political expediency but by "the rule of law."

Theory aside, the daily practice of adjudicative governance faced intense challenge at the beginning of the twentieth century. Decision-making through the judicial gaze, critics argued, was hardly the only legitimate kind of governance. Legislatures and administrative agencies, such as the Interstate Commerce Commission (established by Congress in 1887), were already doing the kind of law-like work, such as determining the "fairness" of railroad rates, that courts had claimed for themselves throughout much of the nineteenth century.

Still, early twentieth-century courts peered into nearly every corner of social and economic life. Prevailing legal wisdom warned judges to fear legislation, the kind of law-related work done by popularly elected majorities, because it too easily threatened individual liberties, especially economic rights. Judges who heard cases on appeal came to view the overruling of illegitimate and unwise legislation as central to their job description. In practice, however, courts generally accepted legislation that affected individual conduct, even in the economic realm, but only after they had subjected legislative action, through the practice of "judicial review," to their own supposedly unique and elevated gaze. An important line of precedent supported the judicial upholding of legislation regulating private economic activities, such as the setting of railway rates, if courts themselves could see that these activities were "affected with a public interest." Judicial rulings did protect private property and contract rights, historian William Novak concludes, but relatively, not absolutely. Economic life was "governed by the overarching principle that private interest must be made subservient to the public welfare" (1996: 112).

(2)   The field of law generated an increasing number of *judicial opinions*, the written justifications that accompanied court rulings. A private company, West Publishing, disseminated the public opinions of state and federal courts to a constantly growing legal profession. West also developed a patent-protected Key Number System, a print-based search engine that allowed judges and attorneys to locate the ruling in virtually any appellate court decision. The non-professional legal consumer, likely interested in only the most spectacular cases, particularly those involving sex and murder, could ignore West's system and law libraries. The early twentieth-century press featured the arguments and opinions of celebrated cases such as the 1905 trial of socialite Harry Thaw, accused of murdering the prominent architect Sanford White. This was the first of many spectacles termed "trials of the century."

(3)   Finally, the field's most prominent lawyers, law professors as well as judges, already played a significant role by supplying *legal commentary*. The leading law schools published student-edited law reviews. The *Harvard Law Review* began in 1887, and the *Yale Law Journal* contained brief "case notes" about specific court

decisions and articles on broader topics such as contract law. Most important, law reviews increasingly featured "advocacy" or "prescriptive" scholarship in which law professors, assuming a quasi-judicial stance, advised courts on which legal rules to apply in particular cases. Using law review articles as their primary vehicle, law professors became "super-judges" whose commentaries surveyed the entire field of law.

Judicial rulings often addressed fiercely debated political, economic, and social issues. How could anyone be sure that the courts adjudicated questions – such as the fate of public legislation affecting private contractual relationships – on the basis of a distinctly legal rather than an ordinary political – or, worse, partisan political – vision?

At the dawn of the century, the dominant gaze, which historians now call "legal classicism," answered this question by envisioning the field of law as marked off, like a checkerboard, by clearly defined, easily discernable boundaries. Law, in this view, consisted of a logical pattern of rules that laid out objective, bright-line boundaries that clearly separated one set of rules from another and ultimately law from politics. Judges trained in legal classicism, commentators maintained, could recognize and abide by these neutral boundaries much better than either legislators or administrators. Law professors handed down the gospel of legal classicism, sometimes called "boundary jurisprudence," to students (and future attorneys) through a regimen, "the case method," introduced at Harvard Law School toward the end of the nineteenth century.

This legal-academic gaze looked at empirical data. During the nineteenth century, law professors had simply lectured students about general principles, grounded in natural law, that supposedly dictated the particular legal rules that courts used to decide specific cases. The case method reversed the process. Faculty engaged law students in a kind of Socratic dialogue that dissected judicial opinions in order to get to the specific rulings that, taken together, illustrated general rules. Thus, the law-school classroom became a kind of scientific laboratory in which professors guided students through a microscopic examination of judicial opinions. The case method spread to every other law school in the country. This style of instruction facilitated production of the ever-greater number of attorneys that daily life apparently required. The law professor's job description expanded to include the collection, editing, and annotation of the leading cases that were said to illuminate how courts employed the rule of law, decision-by-decision, to adjudicate individual cases.

The Legal Field at Work: The Era of *Plessy* and *Lochner*

Two controversial cases around the turn of the twentieth century suggested how classicism's approach could produce rulings and opinions that seemed, to their critics, anything but distinctively legal in nature. They also illustrated how the practice of seeing law and life divided by objective, neutral, bright-line rules could justify legal decisions that, seen in almost any other way, looked highly partisan.

In *Plessy* v. *Ferguson* (1896), the Court upheld a Louisiana law requiring segregated railroad passenger cars for persons of African and those of European descent. This state-legislated racial separation would not violate the equal protection clause of the

Fourteenth Amendment, the Court's majority insisted, if the public facilities remained of same quality. Responding to the charge that this "separate but equal" rule meant that the law relegated persons of African descent to an inferior status, the same majority invoked one of legal classicism's basic boundaries, splitting the "public" and "private" spheres of both life and law. If some people purported to see a public segregation law implying a "badge of inferiority" for people of African descent, "it is not by reason of anything found in the [public] act but solely because the colored race [privately] chooses to put that construction on it" (163 US 537, 551). Critics, in other words, were viewing the social relationships at issue in *Plessy* through an inappropriate non-legal lens when they entered the field of law.

The majority opinion also claimed that it could not see how private "social prejudices might . . . be overcome" by any public law that required persons of different ethnic backgrounds to share the same facilities. Here, the opinion in *Plessy* envisioned racial prejudice as a matter of voluntary private choice with which the public ideal simply could not deal. Though heavily criticized and adroitly sidestepped by the anti-segregationist opinions of some courts, this ruling remained the law of the land until the middle of the twentieth century.

The public/private distinction helped to structure the response to issues involving gender. Although older rulings, such as those that subordinated a married woman's legal status to that of her husband, did not survive the nineteenth century, the men who dominated the legal field rarely looked very closely at the legal implications of most "private," gendered relationships. What, by the end of the twentieth century, feminist lawyers had successfully labeled as "spousal abuse" or "sexual harassment" were a century ago examples of conduct – such as Jim Crow – that occurred in the purely private arena.

The public/private distinction also became central to the legal controversy that dominated roughly the first third of the twentieth century: attempts by legislatures and administrative agencies to regulate economic relationships. *Lochner* v. *New York* (1905), in which the Supreme Court overturned a law that limited the hours that bakers could work on the grounds that it violated the Constitution, came to symbol-ize this issue. Though called a public safety measure, this law "necessarily interferes with the [private] right of contract between employer and employees, concerning the number of hours that the latter may labor in the bakery of the employer," a 5/4 majority ruled (198 US 45, 53). The Fourteenth Amendment's guarantee of liberty protected the right of private citizens to make contractual agreements among themselves.

Although *Lochner* remained the leading precedent on economic relationships for the next three decades, courts never used the power of judicial review to strike down all economic legislation. Judges often ruled, for instance, that the law did permit some legislative regulations on matters such as safety conditions and working hours in businesses "affected with a public interest." Even so, the continued invocation of bright-line categories signaled that legal classicism remained the dominant gaze. Courts, their celebrants continued to claim, could legitimately oversee the entire legal field and, when necessary, overrule the actions of people from other fields of practice (particularly the political) when they violated the rule of law.

Lochner remained at the center of ongoing, bitter struggles over the field of law. The way in which the majority opinion in *Lochner* used the concepts of coercion and freedom ignited a firestorm of dissent that helped to light several ultimately divergent paths away from legal classicism.

Roscoe Pound of the Harvard Law School condemned *Lochner* as an example of how the classical legal gaze could degenerate into a "mechanical jurisprudence." By relying on the image of a freely bargained contract, this ruling failed even to glimpse the context in which labor/management relations operated. Jurists must expand their gaze, Pound argued, and see that the claim of workers bargaining freely with employers was a "fallacy to everyone acquainted first hand with actual industrial conditions" (quoted in Fisher et al. 1993: 27). He urged a "sociological jurisprudence," a broader vision that looked at current social conditions and did not apply old legal precedents by rote.

The dissenting opinion of Justice Oliver Wendell Holmes, Jr., in *Lochner* criticized the majority opinion from a somewhat different angle. He claimed that this ruling really made a partisan appeal to the theory of laissez-faire. The holding in *Lochner* turned on the contested political claim that legislative regulation of the terms of labor contracts was coercive – not on any clear, neutral, or distinctively legal rule. The issue of working hours, according to the dissent of Holmes, involved a political battle over public policy rather than a uniquely legalistic view of contractual liberty.

Policy-makers interested in realigning the legal field itself did make some headway early in the century. Claiming that adjudicative court procedures treated youthful criminal defendants too harshly, for example, people associated with the progressive movement successfully pressed for the creation of separate, specialized juvenile courts. Here, judges could deal with young people through paternalistic norms and flexible procedures that seemed anything but "lawful" when judged by the strict requirements of adjudicative governance. Meanwhile, use of administrative agencies, such as the Federal Trade Commission (created in 1914) and worker's compensation courts, also became a more prevalent kind of legal practice during the progressive period.

The Legal Field in the 1920s and 1930s

In the interwar period, more ambitious efforts to restructure the legal field emerged. The "Restatement Movement" of the American Law Institute (ALI), an enterprise that continues into the twenty-first century, tapped the wisdom and experience of leading lawyers, judges, and academics. Largely satisfied with the institutional role of the courts, the ALI's "Restaters" saw judges burdened by a mass of uncertain, overly complex rules. Their solution, represented in works such as *The Restatement of Contracts*, was to reconcile – primarily through the case method and discussion of hypothetical problems – ambiguities within existing rules and thereby to improve, in an evolutionary way, the practice of adjudicative governance.

A second, more radical attempt to re-envision the legal field during these decades became associated with a diffuse movement called "legal realism." The figures now considered "realists," as the historian Morton Horwitz has noted, "shared one basic premise – that the law had come to be out of touch with reality," a claim earlier associated with Roscoe Pound's sociological jurisprudence (Horwitz 1992: 187). Why, then, did legal realism spark so much controversy, even among lawyers who embraced Pound's vision?

Sociological jurisprudence and legal realism took different views of adjudicative governance, for example. Pound saw judges generally doing better legal work than realist law professors, and he credited courts with doing an increasingly better job of recognizing social needs. Although Pound recognized a role for legislatures and administrative agencies, his vision of sociologically informed judicial governance saw case-law precedent continuing to provide courts with valuable, rule-based wisdom with which to address economic problems, even during the Great Depression. Legal realists found such judgments far too Pollyannaish and overly solicitous of judicial governance. Viewing the field of law very differently, they worked to empower other legal actors, especially legislators and administrators, to take the reins of governance away from judges.

Realism also rejected the image of objective, bright-line boundaries and ridiculed any legal gaze that purported to see clearly demarcated private and public realms. Given the disparity in effective bargaining power between employers and workers, a labor contract without any legislatively imposed limits on matters such as hours would likely involve more coercion by private corporations than free negotiation between equally situated bargainers. *Lochner* was condemned because governmental regulation, even if seen as "coercion," might actually enhance "freedom," at least for less powerful bargainers such as industrial workers.

Most subversively, a group of iconoclastic realists assailed rival legal gazes as lacking grounding in the theories of cognition now being used in other fields of social practice. On what basis, they asked, could judges and commentators "really" claim to know, and be able to represent, the social world? Why should anyone accept the particular angle of sight through which legal classicism envisioned legal work? Felix Cohen, a prominent realist and an ardent New Dealer, criticized any vision that saw a legal field that was staked out, neat and tidy, like a checkerboard. "Legal systems, principles, rules, institutions, concepts and decisions can be understood only as functions of human behavior," he insisted (Cohen 1960: 72). Turning to cultural psychology, another prominent realist who supported the New Deal, Jerome Frank, dismissed the whole ideal of the rule of law as a childish fantasy. People who looked to The Law as a "body of rules apparently devised for infallibly determining what is right and wrong and deciding who should be punished for misdeeds," he wrote in *Law and the Modern Mind*, were unconsciously seeking "a partial substitute for the Father-as-Infallible-Judge" (Frank 1930: 19).

These styles of legal commentary, while providing enduring models for enlivening academic discourse, appeared to offer scant guidance for the practitioners who worked in other areas of the field of law. Ambitious attempts to dethrone the case method by introducing law students to the latest research in fields such as behavioral psychology gained little support from practicing attorneys. After his appointment as a federal judge, Jerome Frank sought to extend the ideas of *Law and the Modern Mind*, but little of this iconoclastic commentary found its way even into his own judicial opinions. Rejecting this style of commentary, other realists, such as Karl Llewellyn of the University of Chicago Law School, joined projects aimed at changing the day-to-day operations of the legal field. Llewellyn played a central role in the drafting of the Uniform Commercial Code (UCC). Begun during the 1930s, this effort aimed at simplifying and systematizing the legal rules on commercial transactions by taking into account how businesses actually dealt with one another. Less indebted to case-law precedent than the work of the ALI, the European-modeled UCC – which virtually every state adopted by legislative statute during the 1950s and 1960s – tried to provide flexible guidelines for a new form of adjudicative governance. Its framers hoped to help judges resolve commercial disputes in light of a set of commonsense rules based on actual business practices.

"Process jurisprudence" became the most influential way of re-envisioning the legal field to emerge during the 1920s and 1930s. Even the earliest legal commentary in this frame, such as Benjamin Cardozo's *The Nature of the Judicial Process* (1921), has remained influential within the legal field. Sometimes seen as a direct reaction to legal realism, this process vision can also be viewed, historian Neil Duxbury has argued, as paralleling it. Though acknowledging realism's claim that external forces, such as politics and economics, helped shape work done within the legal field itself, the process vision retained clearly discernible traces of classicism's reverence for the field's internal dimensions, particularly the practice of adjudicative governance. As the appeal of legal realism waned, process jurisprudence became the dominant way of imagining the field of law.

The process vision shared several of realism's key claims. It appreciated the innovative work of legislatures, valued the flexible techniques of administrative agencies, and acknowledged the policy-making nature of adjudicative governance. Moreover, process jurisprudence shared realism's contempt for how "conservative" courts had used the claims of legal classicism to block political change, especially during the New Deal. Albert Sacks and Henry Hart, Jr., who championed process jurisprudence at Harvard Law School, urged lawyers to seek the kind of knowledge that would be needed to solve particular problems and "*affirmatively to advance* the larger purposes of the society" (quoted in Duxbury 1995: 256, emphasis added).

Process jurisprudence also stressed two important themes largely absent from legal realist commentary. First, it focused on a question occasioned by the changing shape of the legal field. As the amount of work done by legislatures and administrative agencies increased, the process gaze seemed an appropriate way for the commentators at leading law schools to judge *which institutions*, including the judiciary, best addressed *what kinds* of policy issues. Process jurisprudence came to feature elegant theories of "institutional competency," which urged limiting the scope of adjudicative governance and acknowledging that legislation and administrative agencies were becoming increasingly important to the regulation of the economy.

Second, process jurisprudence revisited a familiar question: How could the work of judges be seen as any different, let alone more elevated, than that done by people in other fields of social practice such as politics? Legal realism had made old answers seem hopelessly naïve. Once it was conceded that adjudicative governance, like legislation and administration, involved at least some degree of policy-making, with partisan origins and political implications, who and what safeguarded the rule of law?

The process-oriented answer, in retrospect, seems all too obvious: reason. Although the realists interested in psychology and the non-rational had tried to push reason to the sidelines, it had long been part of the legal field's shared discourse. Process jurisprudence returned reason to the center of the field. When courts adjudicated economic disputes, for example, they were not merely working with logical rules, as the legal classicists had claimed, nor simply selecting from competing policy options, as realists emphasized. Rather, the process vision saw judicial work involving a difficult, precise, and always reasoned process of balancing competing sets of rules. Commitment to a reason-based approach, according to proponents of process jurisprudence, kept adjudicative governance contained within the boundaries of the legal field and out of the political arena. Advocates of process jurisprudence saw reason operating in every part of the legal field and especially at all levels of adjudicative governance. Reason was embedded, for instance, within familiar legal rules, such as "nobody should be allowed to profit by fraudulent activities," or "no one should escape liability for negligent actions." When considering if administrative agencies and legislatures had made "proper" choices when issuing orders or passing laws, courts must only look at the "reasonableness" – rather than the ultimate wisdom – of the decisions made by these non-judicial bodies.

Most important, reason seemed absolutely central to the process of adjudicative governance itself. Simply stating a rule, no matter how clearly, and citing a precedent, no matter how well-established, would no longer suffice, claimed supporters of the process vision. A legitimate judicial holding demanded a carefully crafted opinion that featured a "reasoned elaboration" of the legal rule that it announced. In this sense, process jurisprudence offered another way of undermining *Lochner*. It had been not only a case of poor policy-making but, worse, an example of utterly failing to articulate, in a way commensurate with the highest standards of judicial craftsmanship, the reasons for its own holding.

Challenges to classicism, especially when framed within the process mode, triumphed. By the mid-1930s only the most traditional of jurists managed to cling to an entirely inward gaze in which legal rules unfolded logically, outside of the pull of social, economic, and political forces.

The Demise of *Lochner*

Legislation such as the National Industrial Recovery Act (NIRA) of 1933 and Agricultural Adjustment Act (AAA), part of the New Deal's remedy for the Great Depression, raised highly charged issues. Critics insisted that both the Roosevelt-controlled Congress and state legislatures, while claiming to address social and economic disarray, were trampling the rule of law, especially when granting broad discretion to administrative agencies such as the National Recovery Administration (NRA). Celebrants of adjudicative governance urged courts to uphold legal principles, especially the public/private and the legal/political distinctions that had long been central to the protection of economic liberties in the classical legal vision that *Lochner* had come to symbolize. For a brief time, some courts, led by the Supreme Court, did invalidate Depression-era legislation, such as FDR's NIRA, on the claims that they violated the private liberty of contract and/or illegally delegated undefined legal authority to administrative agencies. By the end of the 1930s, however, the situation began changing dramatically. With the Supreme Court in the spotlight, judges now invariably upheld economic legislation such as the Wagner Labor Relations Act. The standard story of this change claims that pressures from outside the legal field, such as President Roosevelt's "court-packing" plan of 1937, prompted judges suddenly to switch their view of economic legislation. More recently, revisionist accounts see factors connected to the field of law itself, such as new, lawyer-drafted legislation and more carefully crafted legal arguments, producing a less abrupt, more evolutionary shift in judicial vision.

Both the standard and revisionist accounts, despite their differences, see the *Lochner* era ending by the early 1940s, and courts beginning to embrace a post-classicist legal view of economic legislation and regulatory activity. In *Wickard* v. *Filburn* (1941), for example, the Supreme Court ruled that a federal administrative agency could coerce farmers into limiting purely private crop production if such a regulation might reasonably be expected to stabilize and to regulate better the public market for agricultural products. More broadly, the legal process vision came to dominate commentaries about the field of law. As Nazism and then Communism seemed to endanger national security, celebrations of the legal field – particularly that offered by process jurisprudence – advanced the ideal of the rule of law as the antidote to totalitarianism. Indeed, commitment to this ideal became one of the markers, if not the central marker, of a "free" and "democratic" society. With quasi-religious fervor, prominent commentators hailed the work of institutions within the legal field, particularly courts. Emphasis on rule-bound adjudication and reasoned elaboration within the field of law, hallmarks of the process view, could support an even broader vision in which legal-political principles, such as majority rule and respect for dissent, distinguished America's democratic system from that of totalitarian regimes.

The Legal Field, 1940s to 1973

The shape of the field of law in the United States continued to change significantly during the middle of the twentieth century. First, the portion of the field occupied by state law expanded. The important Supreme Court decision of *Erie Railroad* v. *Tompkins* (1938) held that, in cases where no constitutional issue was at stake, federal courts must apply state law – as interpreted by state courts – rather than a federal common law, which they had used since 1832. Second, courts continued to play a role in adjudicating economic matters, but the surrounding political cacophony of the early twentieth century faded away. The primary focus of adjudicative governance, signified by rulings such as that in *Wickard* v. *Filburn*, shifted away from the concern with the wisdom of economic policy that courts had displayed during the *Lochner* era. The continued expansion of administrative agencies and a dramatic increase in legislative work, at all levels of governance, meant that courts might still clarify disputed administrative orders or contested legislative commands. In line with the process gaze, however, judges were to avoid second-guessing the legitimacy or the policy implications of apparently reasonable economic regulations by Congress, state legislatures, or administrative agencies. Law schools introduced new courses on the legislative process and the administrative process that supplemented, without totally overthrowing, the case method's focus on appellate court opinions. Attorneys began to specialize in new types of legal practice, such as administrative or tax law, that brought them into daily contact with the work being done by legislatures and regulatory agencies.

Changing forms of legal commentary, which departed from the prescriptive or advocacy model, sought to highlight everyday legal work involving economic relationships and explain how most of this activity produced only intermittent and low-level political controversy. The research of legal commentators who claimed to illuminate the relationship between law and society, by employing new social-science insights, argued that people in overlapping areas of social-legal practice, say insurance or contractual bargaining, viewed the legal implications of their activities in similar ways. Very often, it seemed, many businesses routinely operated at the fringes of the legal field, having only a general notion of what specific legal rules might require of them and yet amicably dealing with one another without seeking judicial or administrative intervention.

In contrast, debates over other activities of the legal field raged every bit as fiercely as during the *Lochner* era. Much of this conflict stemmed from the fact that the job description of major legal actors, particularly judges, changed considerably during the middle of the century. The Supreme Court, in a famous footnote to its *Caroline Products* decision of 1938, anticipated this shift by suggesting what became known as the doctrine of "preferred freedoms." In this view, certain non-economic liberties, particularly those mentioned in the Bill of Rights, deserved emphatic judicial attention and protection, especially when the people claiming the violation of a right were members of "discrete and insular minorities" (304 US 144, 152–3).

Although courts did not always rule favorably on behalf of claimants alleging violations of their rights, the preferred freedoms doctrine did signal a coming "rights revolution." This revolution rested on "strict scrutiny," by courts, of possible infringements on preferred freedoms, such as those protected by the First Amendment. It also turned on a cultural shift in which people readily turned to the field of law to vindicate "rights claims." Here, organizations such as the American Civil Liberties Union (ACLU) spearheaded a new form of legal practice later called "cause lawyering." They aggressively litigated particular cases, such as local disputes over city ordinances that limited political leaflets in the name of preventing litter, in order to give precise legal content to broad, abstract, legal-political principles such as freedom of speech. By the early 1940s, political dissenters (especially those on the left), black citizens (supported by the NAACP's Legal Defense Fund), and members of unpopular groups (such as Jehovah's Witnesses) pressed rights claims alleging violations of fundamental freedoms that lawyers and judges could locate in the Bill of Rights. Most legal commentators initially expressed optimism that courts could adjudicate such rights-claims in a clear, rule-based manner. Commitment to the rule of law, after all, distinguished the United States from totalitarian regimes. Addressing disputes over the meaning of non-economic rights, especially when the controversies involved racial discrimination or the First Amendment, became a major task for the mid-century legal field. But could daily legal practice in these areas, skeptical legal commentators and citizens asked, ever match celebratory visions of the rule of law that stressed reason, clear-cut rules, and well-crafted opinions?

The system of racial segregation in the South, which combined brute coercion and terrorism with the legal authority of *Plessy* v. *Ferguson*, provided an important test for the preferred-freedoms version of the rule of law ideal. Increasingly challenged by an organized, inter-racial civil rights movement during World War II and the Cold War era, segregation became an acute embarrassment to the political elites who directed a globalist foreign policy. Led by the cause lawyering of the NAACP, civil rights activists went to court to contest the legality of segregation.

World War II and the Cold War raised other important questions that affected the legal field. Were preferred freedoms to work as robust, independent checks that could be aggressively asserted, even during times of domestic discord and international upheaval, against governmental claims of the need for reasonable restraint? Or should rights such as freedom of speech and association better be seen as contingent, contextual claims, whose meanings pragmatically varied during times of perceived internal or external crisis?

Few clear answers emerged. During the Second World War, for example, legal commentators rarely worried about the thousands of German and hundreds of Italian aliens whom the Roosevelt administration interned on grounds of national security. Even limitations on the daily activities of tens of thousands of people of Italian descent, such as rules against working or living in certain areas, produced little commentary. In contrast, the 1942 presidential Executive Order 9066 forcibly relocating 120,000 persons of Japanese descent on the West Coast to internment camps for the duration of the Second World War, without trials or even formal charges, raised considerable controversy. Citizens lost homes, property, and their personal liberty. To the despair of commentators who urged an expansive preferred-freedom vision, a majority of the Supreme Court in the *Korematsu* case (1944) upheld the order and accepted the government's claims of military necessity and of its inability to distinguish "the disloyal from the loyal" (323 US 214, 219). To celebrants of the rule of law, *Korematsu* seemed a tragic exception, one that Congress repudiated in 1988 when it voted $20,000 payments to survivors of the camps. To critics, then as now, *Korematsu* (which has never been formally repudiated by another court) symbolized the great difficulty of distinguishing law from politics whenever the legal field confronted issues of race and political dissent, particularly in times of widely-perceived peril. The job of protecting rights increasingly tested the resources and cultural capital of the legal field.

Several broad areas eventually became the most politicized and the most contested aspects of the mid-century rights revolution: (1) litigation over the kind of race-based rules at issue in *Plessy*; (2) adjudication involving First Amendment claims; (3) rulings on the rights of criminal defendants; and (4) judicial decisions affecting gender issues.

(1) Courts had been chipping away at *Plessy* v. *Ferguson* before the Supreme Court unanimously repudiated it in *Brown* v. *Board of Education* (1954). In 1946, for example, the Court adroitly sidestepped the public/private distinction used in *Plessy* by holding that public officials could not lawfully enforce, through "state action," restrictive covenants. These were provisions in private property deeds that prevented the sale of a house or land to people of certain ethnic and religious backgrounds. The Court later ruled that separate graduate and professional schools for the descendants of former slaves could never be judged equal to the institutions from which they were legally barred on account of racial categories. Drawing on research in behavioral psychology about the impact of legal segregation on students of African descent, the Court in *Brown* finally reached the same conclusion about all segregated educational institutions. Although the subsequent attempt to integrate schools proceeded slowly, if at all, *Brown* did signal the demise of legally imposed apartheid in virtually every area of public activity.

By the mid-1960s, with Lyndon Johnson's Great Society temporarily dominating the political field, the legal field tried to work out the judicial and administrative implications of legislation such as the Civil Rights Act of 1964, the Voting Rights Act of 1965, and their state-level counterparts. The most controversial legal remedy for past discrimination, "affirmative action" programs, produced bitter controversy. The idea of these plans was that government and private institutions act affirmatively to ensure that people from racial groups once underrepresented be admitted and hired, and then graduated or promoted, in nondiscriminatory ways. But affirmative action proved difficult to implement. If progress in undoing previous discrimination were, for example, to be measured by comparing the number of people admitted or advanced in accordance with their percentage in the total population, might not the result be a "quota system" or, worse, "reverse discrimination" against people identified with other groups? In the political field, did the drawing of electoral districts that promised to guarantee the selection of office-holders from groups long pushed to the margins provide a legally appropriate remedy, or reintroduce, in the name of promoting racial justice, new forms of race-conscious discrimination? Proponents of affirmative action insisted that it provided a means by which the legal field could gauge progress in undoing past wrongs; its opponents saw it using a distorted legal gaze, similar to the one the *Plessy* court had earlier employed, to justify race-based decision-making.

(2)   At the same time, courts throughout the legal field were joining legislatures and administrative agencies in considering First Amendment claims. Debate became intense during the late 1940s and the 1950s when the specter of Communist espionage and domestic subversion complicated the attempt to find reasoned rules or to balance apparently incommensurable claims about safeguarding the right to dissent and defending the nation from foreign enemies.

Not surprisingly, the dominant political view during the post-World War II era, embodied in the Cold War foreign and domestic policies of both political parties, saw Communism as evil: as despotic rule by corrupt people whose Marxist ideology mocked the ideal of the rule of law. Why, on the basis of what fundamental principle, should the law work to provide tolerance for supporters of a totalitarian movement that stood for intolerance? Civil libertarians offered an answer, also based on principle. Tolerance for expression by the intolerant, unless they were committing acts that directly and immediately threatened public safety, provided the real test of reverence for the rule of law.

A series of cases during the 1950s prompted leaders from many areas of social practice, not simply those in the field of law, to consider how to balance these conflicting principles. The results satisfied neither libertarians nor defenders of national security. The Supreme Court, in *Dennis* v. *United States* (1951), ruled that the grave evil posed by the Communist Party of the United States of America (CPUSA) would sustain a prosecution against its leaders even if the government could not clearly demonstrate any imminent threat to national security. Several years later, however, the Court overturned a conviction against lower-level members of the CPUSA on the grounds that the government was prosecuting them for their political ideas and associations, rather than for any immediately dangerous activities. Guardians of national security hailed the first and reviled the second decision, while civil libertarians made precisely the reverse judgments. Conflicting judicial decisions involving persons who charged that they had been illegally dismissed from government employment because of their political associations produced similar legal/political division.

Perhaps the most difficult issue for the legal field, and its rule-of-law ideal, came from the surveillance activities undertaken during the Cold War era by the Federal Bureau of Investigation, the National Security Agency, and other intelligence-gathering institutions. In the name of collecting information about potential threats to national security, and about people who would never formally be charged with a violation of the law, FBI operatives sometimes committed acts that seemed akin to burglary, illegal entry, blackmail, and character assassination. Evaluating activities undertaken by the FBI's COINTELPRO division, one civil liberties lawyer saw "a deliberate intent to punish" people who had neither been convicted nor were even suspected of committing a crime (Donner 1980: 180). In the 1970s, in response to COINTELPRO and other intelligence-gathering efforts, Congress passed legislation that charged the legal field with limiting surveillance activities, such as wiretapping, by the FBI and other policing agencies.

Meanwhile, as more lawyers committed to the political agenda of the New Deal and Great Society became judges and legal commentators, the case for broad judicial protection of political and cultural expression gained increased visibility. Although opinions invariably justified legal protection on the basis of the public's need for a free flow of information and ideas, most also implicitly acknowledged the individualistic, almost private nature of most First Amendment claims. This amendment, courts held, protected people carrying a "Fuck the Draft" sign, preaching the doctrines of white supremacy, dancing nude at a strip club, and burning Old Glory or a KKK cross. One of the few exceptions to the (reasoned) rule that the law could only limit dangerous "action," and not simply "offensive expression," came in judicial rulings dealing with child pornography.

(3)   Although First Amendment cases, especially on flag-burning and sexually explicit materials, produced controversy within and without the legal field, emotions here rarely matched those generated by rights rulings made on behalf of criminal defendants. During the 1950s large philanthropic institutions like the Ford Foundation funded social scientific research that looked at how the criminal justice system operated and at how better to protect the rights of people accused of a crime. By the next decade, commentaries in this law-and-society vein generally criticized the existing system. Even if low-income criminal defendants received legal counsel, their lawyers generally viewed their primary job as helping the criminal-justice bureaucracy run as smoothly as possible, without tearing up the legal field on behalf of indigent clients. Studies also suggested that long before most criminal defendants ever met a lawyer, skilled or abusive police interrogators had already effectively undercut the real value of formal legal rights by "coercing" a confession. This claim helped justify rulings such as *Gideon* v. *Wainwright* (1963) and *Miranda* v. *Arizona* (1966). As viewers (in both the United States and other nations) of post-*Miranda* television shows and movies saw, police officers had to inform suspects of their rights to consult with an attorney and to remain silent once they were taken into custody. The state would provide lawyers for persons unable to hire their own attorneys. Critics of the rights revolution, however, dismissed the law-and-society commentary that saw no clear connection between a rise in criminal activity and opinions like *Miranda*. Consequently, calls for rules that did not handcuff the police helped fuel the conservative political movements that emerged during the late 1960s and 1970s and ultimately "blew back" on the legal field.

(4)   Even the controversy over criminal justice issues such as the *Miranda* warning could not match the one produced by *Roe* v. *Wade* (1973), in which the Supreme Court validated a woman's access to legal, medically-supervised abortion procedures.

Roe built on an earlier decision, *Griswold* v. *Connecticut* (1965), which had struck down a state law inhibiting access to birth control measures. Both legal rulings rested on a right to privacy, which was said to cover the relationship between a woman and her physician. Justice Harry Blackmun's opinion in *Roe* conceded the difficulty of specifying where the right of privacy might be found in the Constitution but insisted that it was nevertheless "broad enough to encompass a woman's decision whether or not to terminate her pregnancy." Although "the right of personal privacy includes the abortion decision," *Roe* continued, it was "not unqualified and must be considered against important state interests in regulation" (410 US 113, 177–8). Blackmun's opinion went on to detail, much as a legislative statute might do, a complicated "tri-semester" formula, which tracked the normal nine-month pregnancy cycle. *Roe*, in short, concluded that the state's duty to safeguard individual privacy rights could outweigh other legitimate interests, including that of protecting unborn fetuses.

Roe seemed the "new *Lochner*." Critics portrayed it, particularly after state legislatures and Congress enacted legislation to overturn or limit its impact, as antimajoritarian. This view had first (very cautiously) surfaced during the academic response to the Warren Court's opinion in *Brown* by some adherents of the process vision. In it, *Roe* looked to be the rights-revolution equivalent of an economic-rights decision like *Lochner*. Were not judges using the practice of adjudicative governance to overrule (now through an avowedly political, policy-balancing process) laws passed by popularly elected legislatures? Even some commentators who supported a woman's "right to choose" came to see *Roe* as part of a broader trend often called "liberal legalism." This form of adjudicative governance, in the words of historian Laura Kalman, rested on a "confidence in the ability of courts to change society for what judges think is better" (1996: 4). Decisions such as *Roe* also revealed sharp differences over how participants in the legal field should view the law. By the early 1970s, faith in a process-based craft of balancing principles was increasingly scrutinized. How could any legal gaze that retained the ideal of the rule of law pretend to balance, in any wholly legally-informed manner, a woman's "right" to a safe abortion against the unborn child's "right to life"?

Here, as with so many other contested questions, such as those raised by affirmative action programs, First Amendment claims, and criminal justice matters, process jurisprudence seemed an increasingly cloudy lens. Would any type of reasoned elaboration convince one side of the dispute to yield, as a matter of legal reasoning alone, to the vision of the other? Could two conflicting rights really be balanced? If so, how? As a matter of "principle versus principle"? Or should the balancing proceed on a more pragmatic and case-by-case basis? What institutions – legislatures, administrative agencies, or courts – provided the appropriate forums for doing what kinds of balancing? Because *Roe* crystallized long simmering questions such as these, it might be seen as the legal field's equivalent of the Big Bang; everything seemed to fragment and sail in every direction at once after about 1973.

The Field of Law, 1973 to 2000

Controversies that recalled the heyday of legal realism rocked the leading law schools and the intellectual ground on which prominent legal commentators purported to stand. The proliferation of competing legal gazes paralleled the flux found in other parts of academic life, such as literary studies or political science, during the last quarter of the twentieth century. Commentators tried to view the legal field through frameworks informed by structuralism, post-structuralism, rational choice theory, neo-pragmatism, moral theory, and the other theoretically related gazes that found support in the academic culture. At the same times, as a more diverse group of lawyers became professors, their commentaries often stemmed from their non-legal identities rather than any uniquely legal vision. Thus commentators wrote from the standpoint of gender (producing not only different kinds of "legal feminism" but eventually "queer legal theory") and race (generating "critical race theory" and later Latino/ Latina, Asian-American, and other ethnically-informed legal gazes). By the end of the century, as cross-disciplinary enterprises such as cultural studies emerged, new forms of legal commentary turned on recently articulated relationships between law and economics, law and culture, and eventually law and just about every other academic inquiry.

The growing list of "law ands" meant that legal commentary was dramatically changing. More than at any other time in the twentieth century, legal commentary more closely resembled academic practice in fields such as political theory or even the sciences. As had been the case with legal realism, judges and practitioners invariably dismissed new forms of commentary as useless to their daily jobs. But the system of academic rewards (and penalties) for law professors, and a sense that older frames no longer adequately represented a complex social practice, helped to sustain scholarly discourses about the law.

Several other broad trends might be highlighted. The composition of the legal profession changed, especially as more women and members of non-European ethnic groups entered the field of law. As late as the mid-1960s, for example, relatively few women even enrolled in law school – Harvard admitted no women until the 1950s; and even fewer could hope to join a top-rung law firm. According to one attorney, who later became a law professor at Harvard, a (male) partner in a New York City firm rejected her job application because he could no more bring "a girl" into a corporate board room "than I could bring a Jew" (quoted in Posner 1999: 198).

The boundaries among institutions within the legal field, as always, continued to shift. Much as the people who worked within the legal field during the 1960s and early 1970s had looked favorably toward policies associated with the Democratic Party, the political conservatism that marked the final quarter of the twentieth century helped to reshape the field of law. Most obviously, this translated into increasing sympathy for shrinking the size of the field. Faith in administrative regulation had remained strong enough to sustain a flurry of environmental and health-and-safety regulation (such as the law creating the Environmental Protection Agency) during the early 1970s. But legal commentary indebted to conservative economic theories, together with right-leaning changes within the political field, increasingly affected legal practice. Economic regulation, conservatives claimed, destroyed inherently efficient marketplace mechanisms. In addition, even many commentators on the left agreed that regulation rarely advanced any larger public good, because private businesses seemed able to tilt the administrative process their way.

Although cause lawyers such as Ralph Nader called for making regulation stricter and more extensive, the growing strength of political conservatism, along with the proliferation of market-worshiping legal-economic commentary, powered a "deregulation" impulse, first evident during the late 1970s in the transportation industry. Congress eventually abolished the Interstate Commerce Commission (the oldest administrative agency) and the Civil Aeronautics Board. Legislative deregulation of other major industries, such as banking, steadily gained ground; meanwhile, courts, using their authority to review the reasonableness of agency decisions, rolled back the scope of administrative governance. Richard Posner, a prominent conservative legal theorist who became a federal judge during the 1980s, later spoke for the deregulators in insisting that even much safety and environmental regulation appeared to be "regressive, ineffectual, perverse, needlessly expensive, or all four at once" (1999: 238).

The backlash against a broadly defined field of law gained visibility as the twentieth century was ending. A series of spectacle-laden trials, such as the case of former football star O. J. Simpson, acquitted of murder, exposed the litigation process to popular, often critical examination. Most broadly, one commentator talked of "jurismania," a kind of cultural "madness" that could elevate a petty dispute – such as whether or not a professional basketball player might refuse to stand for the national anthem – into an important rights issue for the legal field. More commonly, differences over the extent of the field of law surfaced in debates over an excess of litigation, especially in areas such as liability for defective products and accident claims. In one popular view, too many lawyers were entering the legal field in pursuit of excessive monetary damages for wrongs allegedly suffered by their (too numerous) clients. By the mid-1990s, attorneys were estimated to be filing 50,000 different lawsuits every day of the week. Other observers insisted that the cost of litigation threatened to bankrupt businesses and professional operations and to drive up the price that consumers paid for goods and services. On the other hand, competing studies downplayed any litigation explosion and depicted the existing system as working better than it might seem at first glance. Among those 50,000 lawsuits that were begun each day, only the smallest fraction of these ever moved toward the litigation stage, let alone resulted in a formal courtroom trial. Still, a growing number of participants within the legal field itself urged mediation or arbitration instead of more traditional forms of lawyering.

Impulses to re-map the legal field also surfaced in the area of rights litigation. Both courts and commentators looked skeptically at rulings that supported new rights claims, except perhaps when based on the First Amendment. For example, Christian groups asserted the right to freely exercise their religious beliefs. Following the example of the ACLU and the NAACP, conservative legal organizations embraced cause lawyering. As the federal judiciary became more conservative, a leader of the Federalist Society (whose membership included two Supreme Court Justices) predicted that the next century would bring a "revolutionary" legal transformation. During the 1990s many lower federal and states courts seemed hospitable to conservative activism and issued rulings, particularly in cases involving the rights of criminal defendants, directly aimed at overturning those from the era of the rights revolution.

The highest court in the legal field, most commentators agreed, was following a more circuitous path. Seen in one way, for example, the Supreme Court appeared engaged in a project that could be called "constitutional minimalism." It began to limit the number of cases on which it ruled and to avoid sweeping holdings by issuing narrow, technical opinions. This meant forgoing direct assaults on rights-revolution precedents in favor of rulings that chipped away at their reach without directly overruling them. Thus, to the consternation of conservative activists, both *Miranda* and *Roe* managed to survive the end of the twentieth century. But police officers had the right to stop and arrest motorists only on the basis of a suspected seat-belt violation, and it became more difficult for women to obtain a safe abortion.

Thus, seen from another perspective, the conservative majority on the Supreme Court appeared anything but minimalists. Its attitude toward Congress's view of legal matters, for instance, recalled the classical era of the early twentieth century. The end-of-the-century Supreme Court struck down a congressional measure, in *Lopez* v. *United States* (1995), that had made areas around local school buildings "gun-free zones," and later invalidated part of a Handgun Control Law. Subsequently, the Court declared that employees of state governments could not sue under Americans with Disabilities Act (ADA) and held the Violence Against Women Act of 1994 unconstitutional. One prominent legal commentator argued that, at the end of the century, conservative judges were doing more than using judicial review to roll back the rights revolution and to restore power to the states. Viewed more broadly, courts at all levels were implicitly claiming that the practice of adjudicative governance should, once again, dominate the legal field and that the judicial gaze, though no longer as all-encompassing as it had been in 1900, could still scrutinize the wisdom of the work done by elected legislatures.

This last trend seemed evident during the last great legal spectacle of the twentieth century, the contested presidential election of 2000. In theory, as would have likely happened in other democratic electoral systems, political officials – with minimal judicial intervention – could have orchestrated an ending to the contest between George W. Bush and Al Gore. Concluding the election, however, quickly became a matter reserved for judicial governance. Old questions reappeared. Could courts easily distinguish the rule of law from the practice of politics? Would any judicial ruling that went beyond clarifying the process for re-counting votes in Florida's disputed balloting improperly invade the political field? Claiming to find federal constitutional principles at stake, the five most conservative Justices of the Supreme Court – all Republicans – handed down *Bush* v. *Gore* (2000). They did not, of course, make a blatantly partisan call for Bush, but their ruling – justified by opinions that four other Justices and most commentators rejected – ensured his election by asserting the superiority of their legal-constitutional gaze to any competing view of the political issues at stake in *Bush* v. *Gore*.

Contests over the nature and practice of the rule of law ideal, then, punctuated the end of the twentieth century, just as analogous disputes had marked its beginning. Despite continued claims that a distinctively legal gaze could see issues in ways that embodied truth, logic, and reason, the legal field remained an arena in which competing visions of social organization, of individual liberties, and of proper mode of governance continually clashed. At the same time, the majority of legal profession-als continued to pursue the task of convincing those outside the legal field, and perhaps themselves, of the legitimacy and efficacy of the rulings, opinions, and commentaries that taken together constructed twentieth-century versions of the rule of law.

REFERENCES AND FURTHER READING

Bourdieu, Pierre (1990) *The Logic of Practice*. Palo Alto, Calif.: Stanford University Press.

Campos, Paul (1999) *Jurismania: The Madness of American Law*. New York: Oxford University Press.

Cohen, Lucy (ed.) (1960) *The Legal Conscience: The Collected Papers of Felix S. Cohen*. New Haven, Conn.: Yale University Press.

Delgado, Richard and Stefancic, Jean (2001) *Critical Race Theory: An Introduction*. New York: New York University Press.

Donner, Frank J. (1980) *The Age of Surveillance: The Aims and Methods of America's Political Intelligence System*. New York: Alfred A. Knopf.

Duxbury, Neil (1995) *Patterns of American Jurisprudence*. New York: Oxford University Press.

Feldman, Stephen (2000) *American Legal Thought from Premodernism and Postmodernism: An Intellectual Voyage*. New York: Oxford University Press.

Fisher, William W., III, Horwitz, Morton J., and Reed, Thomas A. (eds.) (1993) *American Legal Realism*. New York: Oxford University Press.

Frank, Jerome (1930) *Law and the Modern Mind*. New York: Brentano's.

Friedman, Lawrence Meir (2002) *American Law in the Twentieth Century*. New Haven, Conn.: Yale University Press.

Horwitz, Morton J. (1992) *The Transformation of American Law, 1870–1960: The Crisis of Legal Orthodoxy*. New York: Oxford University Press.

—— (1998) *The Warren Court and the Pursuit of Justice*. New York: Hill and Wang.

Hull, N. E. H. (1997) *Roscoe Pound and Karl Llewellyn: The Search for an American Jurisprudence*. Chicago: University of Chicago Press.

Hull, N. E. H. and Hoffer, Peter Charles (2001) *Roe v. Wade: The Abortion Rights Controversy in American History*. Lawrence: University Press of Kansas.

Kahn, Paul W. (1999) *The Cultural Study of Law: Reconstructing Legal Scholarship*. New Haven, Conn.: Yale University Press.

Kalman, Laura (1986) *Legal Realism at Yale, 1927–1960*. Chapel Hill: University of North Carolina Press.

—— (1996) *The Strange Career of Liberal Legalism*. New Haven, Conn.: Yale University Press.

Kennedy, Duncan (1997) *A Critique of Adjudication (Fin de Siècle)*. Cambridge, Mass.: Harvard University Press.

Kramer, Larry D. (2001) "The Supreme Court 2000 term: Foreword: We the Court," *Harvard Law Review* 115, pp. 4–168.

Kutler, Stanley I. (1984) *The American Inquisition: Justice and Injustice in the Cold War*. New York: Hill and Wang.

Murphy, W. Tim (1997) *The Oldest Social Science?: Configurations of Law and Modernity*. New York: Oxford University Press.

Novak, William J. (1996) *The People's Welfare: Law and Regulation in Nineteenth-Century America*. Chapel Hill: University of North Carolina Press.

Posner, Richard A. (1999) *The Problematics of Moral and Legal Theory*. Cambridge, Mass.: Harvard University Press.

Post, Robert C. (ed.) (1998) *Censorship and Silencing: Practices of Cultural Regulation*. Los Angeles: Getty Research Institute.

Powe, Lucas A., Jr. (2000) *The Warren Court and American Politics*. Cambridge, Mass.: Harvard University Press.

Purcell, Edward A., Jr. (2000) *Brandeis and the Progressive Constitution: Erie, the Judicial Power, and the Politics of the Federal Courts in Twentieth-Century America*. New Haven, Conn.: Yale University Press.

Sarat, Austin D. and Kearns, Thomas (eds.) (1996) *Legal Rights: Historical and Philosophical Perspectives.* Ann Arbor: University of Michigan Press.

—— and—— (eds.) (1998) *Law in the Domains of Culture.* Ann Arbor: University of Michigan Press.

Schlag, Pierre (1998) *The Enchantment of Reason.* Durham, NC: Duke University Press.

—— (2002) "The aesthetics of American law," *Harvard Law Review* 115, pp. 1047–118.

Shamir, Ronen (1995) *Managing Uncertainty: Elite Lawyers in the New Deal.* Durham, NC: Duke University Press.

Steele, Richard W. (1999) *Free Speech in the Good War.* New York: St. Martin's Press.

Sunstein, Cass R. (1999) *One Case at a Time: Judicial Minimalism on the Supreme Court.* Cambridge, Mass.: Harvard University Press.

Sunstein, Cass R. and Epstein, Richard A. (eds.) (2001) *The Vote: Bush, Gore, and the Supreme Court.* Chicago: University of Chicago Press.

Tushnet, Mark V. (1997) *Making Constitutional Law: Thurgood Marshall and the Supreme Court.* New York: Oxford University Press.

Van Burkleo, Sandra, Kaczorowski, Robert J., and Hall, Kermit (eds.) (2002) *Constitutionalism and American Culture: Writing the New Constitutional History.* Lawrence: University Press of Kansas.

White, G. Edward (1993) *Justice Oliver Wendell Holmes, Jr.: Law and the Inner Self.* New York: Oxford University Press.

—— (2000) *The Constitution and the New Deal.* Cambridge, Mass.: Harvard University Press.

CHAPTER TWENTY-TWO

Business

DAVID B. SICILIA

In 1900, and again in 2000, the United States commanded the largest economy in the world. Giant corporations dominated many key industries and evoked both fear and admiration among political leaders, social critics, small entrepreneurs, and consumers. Although not the world's purest capitalist society (a distinction probably held by Hong Kong or Singapore), the United States was, at the turn of both centuries, the world's quintessential business society. Skyscrapers, not cathedral towers or (outside of the nation's capital) government buildings, dominated the skylines of leading cities; meritocracy rather than nepotism ruled when it came to staffing key managerial positions; and millions of Americans gauged their success chiefly in terms of wealth and material comfort. Enterprise so dominated American culture that leading purveyors of popular culture – journalists and novelists in 1900, filmmakers, television producers, and, again, popular writers in 2000 – felt business important enough to portray it as a threat to democracy, liberty, creativity, and "the little guy."

In spite of these striking continuities, a great deal about the scale and character of American business changed in the twentieth century. Although the US economy remained the world's largest and grew considerably in the 1900s, it suffered two major slumps (in the 1930s and the 1970s) and lost position relative to several other industrialized nations, particularly Germany and Japan, in the last quarter of the century. Second, the power and reach of the state as a regulator of American business grew dramatically during three major stages – the Progressive Era, the New Deal, and the era of New Social Regulation in the late 1960s and early 1970s – and as a partner with American business in the Cold War "mixed economy" from the late 1940s through the 1970s. Third, managers developed new strategies and managerial methods, from the multidivisional firm, to the conglomerate, to "lean" organizations in the 1980s and 1990s. Fourth, business became increasingly focused on consumer goods and services rather than on producer goods, and became much more sophisticated about and committed to marketing those goods and services to a growing American middle class. Fifth, the relationship between the firm and its employees traced a broad arch over the course of the century, as union power and an implicit corporate-worker "social contract" rose during the late 1930s, peaked in the 1950s, and declined from the 1970s onward. Finally, American business became more diverse in the twentieth century, as African Americans, Hispanics, Asians, and other minority groups founded businesses in growing numbers, and as women did the same, while also moving into the middle (and occasionally upper) ranks of big business.

Big Business and Progressive Reform

In 1900, nine out of ten Americans still lived in rural areas and worked in agriculture. Yet in the previous generation the nation's business sector had undergone a series of dramatic transformations that gave rise to a new core of powerful firms that dominated the transportation, telecommunications, and industrial sectors, setting the stage for further consolidation in the early twentieth century. As business historian Alfred D. Chandler, Jr. has shown (1977), industrial corporations in several industries, often borrowing techniques from the railroads, grew to unprecedented size and geographical reach by exploiting new mass production technologies and by serving national and sometimes international markets. These big businesses – in petroleum and chemicals, primary and fabricated metals, machinery, food processing and tobacco, brewing and distilling, machinery and transportation equipment – shared several characteristics, most notably: capital intensity, high fixed costs, large economies of scale, and a hierarchical management structure organized into functional or geographic departments or divisions and staffed with professional managers.

Chandler posited a model for how and why firms grew to become dominant players in their sectors. By merging with rivals in the same transportation or manufacturing business, they gained control over wages, prices, and output. By buying suppliers (a process known as backward integration), they better insured reliable sources of raw materials and semi-processed goods. And by acquiring wholesalers and retailers (forward integration), they gained control over the distribution and marketing of their products. These steps led to oligopolies in core industries, that is, consolidation to the point where only a few very large producers survived to serve the national market. Chandler was quick to point out that such consolidation did not occur in most industries because they lacked "high throughput" technologies and vast markets.

While Chandler's seminal work changed the way a generation of business historians understood the dynamics of industrial capitalism in the Gilded Age and early twentieth century, his framework was hardly all-encompassing. As Philip Scranton has shown (1997), giant enterprises in this period not only mass produced uniform commodities, but quite often custom produced goods individually or in limited batches for specialized niche markets as well. Mansel Blackford (1991) chronicled the history of small business in American in this period, and showed that the vast majority of sectors remained dominated by small and medium-size firms that competed in an atomized market, although many adapted to the rise of big business by cultivating symbiotic relationships with the giants. Taken together, these accounts offer a rich portrait of turn-of-the-century business that encompasses the many small family firms and partnerships serving local markets as well as the multinational behemoths with both standardized mass production and flexible batch production.

The dominance of giant firms in transportation, telecommunications, and manufacturing had powerful and diverse effects on a variety of groups in American society.

Contrary to classical monopoly theory, consumers typically benefited from falling prices. Oligopoly insured some degree of competition, but mostly the mass producers reduced selling prices because they could afford to do so while still, thanks to the great efficiencies of their giant factories, amassing vast fortunes. Industrialists nevertheless remained anxious about competition and economic downturns. Whereas smaller firms had considerable flexibility in how they could respond to falling sales, the giants had to service the debt on their capital intensive networks or factories regardless of sales volume.

Politicians for the most part viewed the rise of big business with trepidation. Losing power relative to the new moguls, some simply went on the take, while others built political careers by attacking the new generation of "robber barons." For their part, industrial laborers lost considerable control over their jobs, as work was routinized and "deskilled" through mechanization and the techniques of efficiency experts such as scientific management guru Frederick W. Taylor. With heavy industrialization came walkouts, strikes, and other forms of worker resistance on a sometimes massive scale.

The captains of the new giant firms did not represent a cross section of American society, but were overwhelmingly white Protestant men. And very few actually climbed from "rags to riches," as portrayed in popular lore and in the Horatio Alger success novels of the day. Rather, most industry leaders were well educated and came from comfortable or affluent homes. Wall Street, dominated by blue blood firms such as J. P. Morgan & Company, effectively excluded Jews until after World War II.

Women participated in the new corporate economy in new but limited ways. The vast corporate bureaucracies required armies of clerical workers; and this occupation, as Angel Kwolek-Folland has explained, was re-defined as a women's domain. Some women exploited new entrepreneurial opportunities by establishing training schools for typists, stenographers, and secretaries. Because prevailing attitudes about gender assigned women to largely domestic roles – as mother, wife, and caregiver – their participation in business was largely confined to home economics, nursing, teaching, dressmaking and millinery, banking, and retail sales. A few women became managers in department stores, cosmetics companies, advertising, and other businesses, where they were expected to leverage the "female point of view" to boost sales. Apart from clerical positions, there were more businesswomen proportionally outside of large firms, where women operated and often owned small dry-goods and grocery stores. Nor was it uncommon for women to operate a family business successfully, after the death of the husband (Kwolek-Folland 1998).

Inspired by colorful exposés of corporate misdeeds penned by Gilded Age muckrakers, most Americans were at best uneasy about the meteoric rise of the captains of industry and their sprawling empires. It was plain to see that once an industry was consolidated by the likes of John D. Rockefeller (who controlled 90 percent of US petroleum refining) or Andrew Carnegie (the nation's most powerful steelmaker), there was little or no room for small producers or newcomers. Moreover, Americans never before had witnessed disparities of wealth and income of such magnitude. At a time when Rockefeller's workers earned the standard $1 a day, he was worth nearly $1 billion. In these and other ways, the new breed of industrial behemoths raised fundamental questions about American opportunity, individualism, and liberty in the face of the unprecedented concentration of economic power.

At the turn of the century, the "trust" (or monopoly) problem was the pre-eminent issue of the day. Some politicians and reformers sought to block the advance of big business and industry consolidation, the latter particularly glaring in the wake of the great merger movement of the late 1890s, which swallowed up some 1,200 firms. Competition and liberty could not survive in the face of such concentration of economic power, argued these reformers; corporations that grew very large could have done so only through improper and illegal means – the latter defined, albeit vaguely, by the Sherman Anti-Trust Act of 1890. Armed with this legislation, anti-trusters attempted to roll back the clock by dismantling trusts and other near monopolies. But at the same time, other reformers and prominent political leaders, most notably Theodore Roosevelt, saw some advantages in the huge new producers at the core of the economy. They particularly valued their great efficiency, and called for expanded government powers to monitor and, if necessary, rein in giant firms that might abuse their power.

Along with government reform, corporate reform was the centerpiece of the progressive movement of the late nineteenth and early twentieth centuries. Most business-related progressive reforms were intended to increase the accountability of corporations, compel them to take greater responsibility for the health and welfare of both employees and customers, and endow the state with greater powers to police and enforce the competitive behavior of firms. In these policies, federal reformers borrowed liberally from their counterparts on the state level, who, as Grangers, Populists, and state utility commissioners, had pioneered an array of regulatory modes in the mid- and late nineteenth centuries.

During Theodore Roosevelt's presidency (1901–9), Congress passed the Hepburn Act (1906), which strengthened federal power to set railroad rates; the Pure Food and Drug Act and the Meat Inspection Act (both also in 1906); and the first employer liability laws for federal workers. After an interlude of relative federal inactivism during William Howard Taft's presidency, the Woodrow Wilson administration (1913–21) further expanded federal regulatory powers through the Federal Reserve Act (1913), the Clayton Act (1914), and stronger railroad regulation. The Clayton Act established the Federal Trade Commission, which outlawed interlocking directorships, selling and tying contracts, and price discrimination and (unlike the weaker Sherman Anti-trust Act of 1890) could issue "cease and desist" orders against corporations. The Federal Reserve Act created a central banking system with twelve district banks governed by both public and private officials, a system that helped stabilized the currency and limit the reckless practices endemic among many state and "wildcat" banks.

Meanwhile, the Department of Justice – which broke apart Standard Oil and American Tobacco in two high-profile decrees in 1911 – and the US Supreme Court – through a series of key rulings – increasingly discriminated between "good" and "bad" (i. e., anti-competitive) trusts. As historian Thomas K. McCraw has argued, the emergence of federal business regulation was a halting and protracted process that did not take on its modern form until well into the early twentieth century. For McCraw (1984), regulation truly began to benefit society (especially consumers) when regulators started to grasp the internal economic dynamics of the industries they were regulating, rather than taking ideological stands against bigness per se, as (according to McCraw) Louis Brandeis did in attacking utility companies and advising Woodrow Wilson.

Business in War and Depression

The First World War ushered in a new era of business–government relations. The Wilson administration remained firmly isolationist long after the fighting erupted in Europe in August 1914, although US mobilization began in earnest in mid-1916, nearly a year before the Congress declared war. In the early months of the war, shortages and misallocations of critical raw materials, transportation bottlenecks, and confused priorities plagued the mobilization effort. In response, the Wilson administration centralized powers for setting priorities and coordinating production in the hands of the War Industries Board (WIB), created in July 1917. Many business leaders opposed the measures, some claiming that the WIB lacked clear constitutional authority over the private sector. The turning point came in 1918, when Wilson appointed Wall Street tycoon Bernard Baruch as the new head of the WIB. Baruch staffed the WIB with business executives and reorganized it along functional lines like a business corporation. The WIB ultimately took over the operation of the nation's railroad, telephone, telegraph, and shipbuilding industries.

It was the first formal attempt at centralized economic planning in US history. But by the end of the war, business leaders accepted and even welcomed the partnership. Corporate profits during the war outstripped those in prewar years, and industry leaders were pleased with their direct influence in setting production priorities. Too, the government relaxed anti-trust enforcement during the war. Wartime economic controls were rapidly dismantled after armistice, but a decade later many government and business leaders would again turn to business–government cooperation when confronted with another national crisis, the Great Depression.

The 1920s is remembered as a decade of prosperity; and, indeed, the economy expanded more than 40 percent. This was due to a combination of forces: the rapid and widespread diffusion of automobiles, radios, and other consumer durables; the spread of electrification from one-third to two-thirds of the nation's homes; the dramatic expansion of advertising and consumer credit; and a pro-business White House under Warren G. Harding (1921–3) and Calvin Coolidge (1923–9). The Coolidge administration cut taxes, raised the tariff, staffed the Federal Trade Commission with business-friendly regulators, and eased anti-trust enforcement. Coolidge's oft-repeated remark that "the chief business of the American people is business" exemplified an era when business leaders where held in high regard as the stewards of progress and material wealth. He went on to say that "the man who builds a factory builds a temple . . . The man who works there worships there" (Leuchtenburg 1958: 188). And indeed, business was regarded with almost religious fervor, as in the best-selling book *The Man Nobody Knows* (1925) by advertising expert Bruce Barton. He portrayed Jesus Christ as a charismatic salesman who "picked up twelve men from the bottom ranks of business and forged them into an organization that conquered the world" (quoted in Leuchtenburg 1958: 189).

In the early 1920s, Du Pont and General Motors (GM) pioneered a new organizational structure called the M (for multidivisional) Form. Large corporations had previously been organized by function, with departments for marketing, manufacturing, finance, research, and so on. The new structure combined these functions into divisions devoted to product lines or geographical regions. Thus, GM's Pontiac

Division handled all aspects of making and selling the Pontiac line, rather than a single marketing department selling all of GM's automobile lines from posh Cadillacs down to inexpensive Chevrolets. Balancing centralization with decentralization, the M Form helped GM overtake the Ford Motor Company in the middle of the decade. While Ford continued to offer only reliable workhorses, GM changed its models annually and offered a growing array of styles, colors, and accessories.

Sophisticated new advertising techniques helped GM and other consumer product companies mass market their goods. Roland Marchand's study of advertising in the 1920s and 1930s shows that admen saw themselves as "apostles of modernity" as they promoted a vision of consumerist society that largely reflected their values as young, urban professionals. Exploiting Freudian and behaviorist psychology for the design of advertisements, they strived to exploit "basic human drives" such as insecurity, envy, and greed. Their advertisements highlighted or even invented maladies related to urban life, then offered a consumer product as the solution. Many former luxury items were democratized for mass consumption. As business executives or housewives or children, the individuals depicted in mainstream advertisements conformed to a narrow definition of their roles, with virtually no space devoted to people of color or other marginal groups (Marchand 1985).

Not all Americans prospered in the 1920s, and the gap between rich and poor expanded dramatically. Farmers especially suffered severely from plummeting prices and widespread bankruptcy due to wartime overexpansion. Women's participation in business continued to be confined largely to a limited range of lower-paying occupations such as teaching, clerical work, and domestic work, although a few women built very successful careers in advertising and fashion and in the new silent film industry. African Americans faced even stiffer barriers to broad participation in business; many owned and operated small, local shops, but only a few built large companies, and then only to serve black consumers in a handful of businesses such as publishing, hair care products, and life insurance. In his study of the black-owned Chicago Metropolitan Assurance Company, Robert E. Weems showed how racism caused the mainstream insurance industry to spurn black customers, which created a large entrepreneurial opportunity for African Americans to serve their own community. At the same time, these and other large black insurance firms grew out of the strong tradition of African-American fraternal and benevolent societies. Weems's work (1996) implicitly challenges neoclassical notions of "economic man" as invariably profit-maximizing, and reveals the family- and community-based character of many minority owned enterprises.

The 1920s ended inauspiciously with the spectacular collapse of the Wall Street bull market. And with the onset of depression in the early 1930s, the reputation of American business seemed to plummet as precipitously as the Dow. Although margin buying (borrowing most of the money to purchase stock) was commonplace during the 1920s, according to Robert Sobel (1968) most stocks were not overvalued until late in the decade. Few historians believe that the Wall Street crash caused the Great Depression. There are many explanations for why the Depression lasted so long, among them: the maldistribution of wealth and income (which weakened middle-class purchasing power); historically high trade barriers; weaknesses in banking, housing, railroads, and other key sectors; and an international debt crisis. An emerging consensus among economic historians, as exemplified by the work of

Barry J. Eichengreen (1992) points to the efforts of US central bankers to preserve the gold standard, which in turn had a severely deflationary effect on the economy.

Franklin Roosevelt's New Deal was a complicated and far-reaching constellation of economic and social reform programs instituted through a blizzard of legislation and administered by scores of "alphabet agencies." On many fronts, the New Deal shaped and was shaped by business interests. Initially, Roosevelt, like "associationalist" President Herbert Hoover before him, tried to forge a partnership between business and government interests in order to maintain wages, prices, and output in the face of severe deflation and depression. The centerpiece of this approach was the National Industrial Recovery Act (NIRA) of 1933, which put into place an elaborate system of industry codes, most voluntary, some legally enforceable. The New Deal also attempted to reform several key economic sectors: finance, manufacturing, agriculture, communications, transportation, and utilities. Several of the reforms were aimed specifically at eliminating financial practices then held responsible for the economic collapse. The Public Utilities Holding Company Act of 1935, for example, pronounced a "death sentence" on pyramid ownership structures which had been common in the 1920s. The most important legislation of this kind was the Banking (or Glass-Steagall) Act of 1933, which separated investment banking from commercial banking, empowered the Federal Reserve to adjust reserve requirements, created federal deposit insurance, and otherwise tightened government regulation of banking. The Securities Exchange Act of 1934 created the Securities and Exchange Commission, which set rules and procedures to govern members of exchanges and issuers of securities.

After the Supreme Court struck down the NIRA in 1935, the Roosevelt administration became more adversarial toward big business, as reflected in its shift from associationalism to anti-trust and in its rising anti-business rhetoric. As historian Ellis W. Hawley has shown (1966), advocates of three long-standing ideologies toward business monopoly competed for dominance during the New Deal: central planners, business rationalizers (or partial planners), and anti-trusters. Initially, partial planners held the day, but their influence was eclipsed by anti-trusters after the NIRA's demise. And no group or ideology ever dominated completely. Hawley's framework highlights the simultaneous and often contradictory streams of ideology about the thorny problem of business concentration, and can be usefully projected backward toward the age of industrialism and forward to our own time.

Historians now emphasize the revolutionary dimensions of the New Deal as well as its powerfully conservative undercurrents. Although Roosevelt increased executive power substantially, he never attempted to fundamentally transform American capitalism. New Dealers did not, for example, attempt to nationalize the banking system; rather, they sought to eliminate its major weaknesses and abuses. From this perspective, the business community's fear and antagonism toward the Roosevelt presidency was largely misplaced.

World War II resurrected the business–government partnership, dormant since the First World War. In many ways, the pattern was similar: "dollar-a-year men" from corporate America volunteered their services to head the nation's key war administration agencies such as the War Production Board; large corporations were privileged over small and medium-sized firms; women and African Americans took plant jobs normally reserved for white men; and wartime corporate profits were generous.

Inflation was better controlled than in World War I, and labor unions maintained a no-strike policy throughout most of the war, although Congress passed the War Labor Disputes Act in 1943, which strengthened executive power to halt strikes at government war plants. US industrial might proved to be a decisive factor in the Allied victory, as the wartime economy churned out an astonishing volume of arms and *matériel*. Giant corporations converted quickly and applied methods from car manufacturing and other mass production industries with great efficiency. The reputation of the nation's business leaders, tarnished by the Great Depression, regained much of its luster. For its part, the US government spent lavishly on the war (some $300 billion), racking up a massive national debt.

Partner in the Postwar Mixed Economy

Heavy government spending during the war had a strong Keynesian effect on the economy. That is, the New Deal effectuated the relatively new theory of the British economist John Maynard Keynes that government deficit spending was needed to end depression. Many business leaders and economic policy-makers concluded from the wartime experience that the federal government should play a large and *permanent* role in the economy in order to prevent the return of economic recession. And, indeed, after the war the US government assumed responsibility for the economic health of the nation as never before. In 1946, Congress passed the Employment Act, which declared it the "continuing policy and responsibility of the federal government to . . . promote maximum production, employment, and purchasing power." Originally called the Full Employment Act, the proposed legislation met stiff opposition from business leaders who feared that government jobs programs would impair business confidence, compete with the private sector, foster inflation, and cost too much. The compromise legislation created the Council of Economic Advisors, which was charged with advising Congress and the White House on macroeconomic policy.

Rather than taking charge of the economy, the federal government supported private corporate interests throughout the 1950s and 1960s. The result was a mixed economy, foreshadowed as far back as the First World War but now permanent and on a much larger scale than before. Large corporations were deemed the primary drivers of economic growth, while the government's proper role was to create a favorable climate for corporate expansion. Kim McQuaid's insightful study of postwar business–government relations emphasizes the close, symbiotic relationship between the two. From energy policy to labor relations, from tax reform to trade policy, business and government leaders collaborated closely to the point where, as McQuaid put it, "businessmen are politicians and politicians are businessmen" (1994: xiii). In a book that surveys the history of American business and public policy throughout the twentieth century (1988), Louis Galambos and Joseph Pratt see the period from 1940 to 1969 as one in which corporate America flexibly accommodated the rising power of state and citizen interests to forge an effective "corporate commonwealth."

The federal government played a direct Keynesian role in the immediate postwar era through programs that, in effect, amounted to forms of industrial policy. The Serviceman's Readjustment Act (or GI Bill) of 1944 paid to send a generation of World War II veterans to college, thereby boosting the nation's technical skills and wealth-producing capacity, and guaranteed first mortgage loans for home purchases. The Federal Highway Act of 1956 allocated more than $30 billion for construction of 41,000 miles (about 66,000 km) of interstate highways. The largest public works project in world history, the interstate highway program created tens of thousands of jobs and added a basic component to the nation's transportation infrastructure.

But the two most important forms of Keynesian economic stimulus in the postwar period were spending for the Cold War and for social welfare programs. The Department of Defense funneled billions of dollars into aerospace and electronics defense contractors and major research universities. In 1961 President Dwight D. Eisenhower memorably dubbed this nexus of relationships the "military-industrial complex." In the same period Congress vastly expanded the Social Security program in the 1950s, and added other major programs for the elderly (Medicare and Medicaid) as part of President Lyndon Johnson's Great Society in the 1960s. Military and social welfare spending continued at high levels regardless of whether the nation was at war or in a business recession.

As in the 1920s, corporate American enjoyed a heyday in the 1950s and 1960s. Automobile manufacturing again played a central role, as the United States produced larger and larger passenger cars loaded with luxury extras. Approximately one in seven working Americans earned a living directly or indirectly from the automotive industry. The computer industry became a darling of Wall Street, led by International Business Machines (IBM), which marketed its massive Model 360 mainframe computers to corporations and government agencies. Petrochemical (petroleum-based) plastics were another high-growth industry. Mass produced by Du Pont, Monsanto, Dow, and other chemical giants, they were fashioned into seemingly indestructible carpeting, toys, kitchen appliances, and "miracle" fabrics (such as polyester) for "wash and wear" clothing.

The chemical industry was the most science-based sector in the economy. More than ever, US industry was applying scientific expertise in its research and development (R&D) efforts. The first corporate R&D laboratories dated back to the General Electric, Bell, and Du Pont facilities established at the turn of the century. During the interwar decades, American corporations opened some 1,200 new R&D labs that employed 27,700 researchers. According to Alfred D. Chandler, Jr., science-based innovation between 1914 and World War II centered on electrical, chemical, and internal combustion technology, while the postwar period was an era of "intangible capital" driven by great advances in aerospace, computers, consumer electronics, polymer chemistry, and telecommunications (1997).

It was the age of the Company Man. White-collar and blue-collar workers alike routinely expected to hold their jobs for life. In corporations, new personnel experts screened applicants to identify those most likely to rise steadily through the ranks of the organization. Middle managers were invariably male, with their wives playing key supporting roles, as laundress, errand runner, and social hostess. Office clerical work remained gendered as a female occupation, and the only wage category in the economy where women held the majority of positions.

American big business expanded internationally and evolved organizationally in the generation following World War II. Many of the largest corporations opened their first overseas branches in the 1950s and 1960s. Typically they began with a foreign sales office, followed by one or more manufacturing facilities. Part of this trend reflected the popularity of American products in Canada and overseas, but often foreign expansion was defensive as well. Following the establishment of European economic communities in the 1950s, scores of US firms built plants on the continent to jump over the new tariff barriers and to redress foreign exchange imbalances. The multidivisional structures pioneered decades earlier by GM and Du Pont easily accommodated such foreign expansion, and became commonplace among the nation's largest firms.

The M Form also was well suited for diversification into related areas of business (that is, product lines developed from the same technical base or relying on the same marketing channels). But many firms carried the strategy further by acquiring companies or business units in completely unrelated lines of business. Early examples of such firms, known as conglomerates, could be found as far back as the 1920s, if not earlier. The strategy gained great momentum and reach in the 1960s, when several well-publicized conglomerates – Textron, Litton Industries, Ling-Temco-Vought, ITT, and others – gobbled up thousands of firms and became glamour stocks on Wall Street. Conglomerate builders exploited tax laws to their advantage, swapped their firms' high-priced stock to acquire other firms, and avoided anti-trust prosecution by operating in several industries at once. Many other firms that did not become conglomerates nevertheless began to expand into unrelated businesses as well, usually moving from mature, slow-growth industries into younger ones with higher rates of innovation and higher returns on investment.

A new breed of management consultants played a central role in the trend. With MBA (Master of Business Administration) degrees in hand, young, confident, and aggressive staffers from the Boston Consulting Group (BCG), McKinsey & Company, and other leading management consulting firms counseled board members with new strategic plans and econometric models for measuring business unit performance. BCG's "growth share matrix," for example, advised firms to sell "dogs" (low profits, low prospects), hold "question marks" (low profits, high prospects), and milk "cows" (high profits, low prospects) to fund "stars" (high profits, high prospects). Large corporations increasingly were buying and selling business units, and thus entering and leaving lines of business like stock speculators who buy and sell shares in their portfolios. It was a business culture infused with enormous confidence that general management principles and practices would succeed, whatever the industry.

New Constraints: Global Competition and Social Regulation

In 1941 publisher Henry Luce (*Time, Life*) proclaimed that the twentieth century would prove to be "The American Century," economically, diplomatically, and culturally. For the first postwar generation, his prediction appeared to come true. But by the late 1960s and early 1970s, there were signs that the American century already was coming to a rapid and untimely end. Much of this concern centered on the failing vitality and competitiveness of corporate America.

The counterculture that critiqued many of the nation's mainstream values and behaviors leveled some of its most scathing criticisms at business. The so-called military-industrial complex was seen as an unhealthy partnership that fostered arms dealer profiteering and corrupted the intellectual independence of major research universities that held large government contracts, such as the University of California at Berkeley and the Massachusetts Institute of Technology. Many business critics in the 1960s drew inspiration from sociological writings of the 1950s such as David Riesman's *The Lonely Crowd* (1950) and William H. Whyte's *The Organization Man* (1956), both of which decried the intense pressure for conformity in thought, dress, and action within the nation's vast business bureaucracies. Such pressure, Whyte warned, was stifling creativity and independent thought in favor of "group think."

In their most radical incarnations, the attacks on big business in the 1960s and early 1970s took the form of strident Marxist rhetoric combined with various forms of collective action. As Charles Perrow (1972) demonstrated in his chronicle of New Left anti-corporate writings in the 1960s, such critiques often emphasized the imperialistic drives of American corporate global interests as well as their stultifying effects on the human spirit. The latter was a central theme in Theodore Roszak's classic 1969 book, *The Making of a Counter Culture*. In this view, American society was a "technocracy" exemplified by its leading military and corporate institutions and dominated by reductionist, positivist thinking alienated from humanistic thinking and values.

Some of these institutions became the targets of collective action. The Dow Chemical Company – because it manufactured both Agent Orange (a toxic defoliant) and napalm for the US military effort in Vietnam – was the target of hundreds of demonstrations, mostly at its university campus recruiting offices. Anti-business forces also devised new techniques, such as disrupting shareholder meetings. In fundamentally questioning the rights of large corporations to exist, the radicals never found a large audience. However, anti-business collective action sometimes made a great difference, especially against the nuclear power industry in the 1970s. Large, well-organized protests to stop the construction and licensing of the Seabrook nuclear power station in New Hampshire caused long delays that cost the utility billions of dollars. Cost overruns already were plaguing the industry; but the protests heightened the problem, so that, for the rest of the century, no new reactors were ordered.

Along with the cultural challenges to its legitimacy, business faced three structural challenges in the late 1960s and early 1970s: eroding competitiveness in the face of foreign competition, new social regulation, and the onset of economic stagflation. Together, this confluence of forces marked the end of the business community's robust growth and confidence in the postwar period.

The so-called "Japanese invasion" of American consumer markets had become a *cause célèbre* in the 1980s, when the rapid erosion of US market share in consumer electronics, machine tools, steel, automobiles, and a few other key sectors burst into the national consciousness. But the transformation had begun much earlier. Imports of consumer textiles and steel exceeded exports as early as the 1950s, while auto products imports had outstripped exports by 1968. In his examination of one of these sections (steel manufacturing) (1988), Paul Tiffany indicted business management, government policy-makers, and organized labor alike for the decline of American competitiveness. While managers became complacent about innovation and ignored crucial warning signals, the federal government attacked domestic producers with anti-trust prosecutions while supporting cartels abroad. For its part, organized labor pursued too narrow a range of interests, centered on job security and pay hikes. Other scholars have offered similar explanations, although managers most often have been faulted for the nation's eroding global market share. Max Holland's (1989) vivid account of the decline and fall of a Los Angeles-based machine tool maker (Burg Tool) encapsulates in one case study many of the travails of postwar American business, from the breakdown of relations between bosses and workers under conglomerate management to appeals for protectionism against the Japanese.

In the late 1960s and early 1970s, business encountered another wave of regulatory legislation and government agency for the third time in the twentieth century. Often referred to as the "new social regulation," this expansion of state regulatory power affected business behavior on many fronts, in relation to the safety of consumer productions, the protection of the environment, and the health and safety of workers. The impetus behind the new social regulation was both positive and negative. On the one hand, it reflected postwar optimism that many if not all major social problems – poverty, crime, racism, and the like – could be ended by an activist state and a robust economy. On the other hand, the new wave of regulation was animated by a series of highly publicized harms to individuals and to the environment caused by unsafe products such as the Corvair and Ford Pinto automobiles, DDT, and cigarettes, as well as chemical and nuclear accidents and pollution.

Between 1964 and 1977, ten major federal regulatory agencies were created, including the Environmental Protection Agency (1970), the Occupational Safety and Health Administration (1970), and the Consumer Product Safety Commission (1972). These were joined by a host of private citizen organizations, many devoted to protecting the rights of consumers (such as Ralph Nader's Public Citizen). In the environmental field, new organizations such as Friends of the Earth (1969) and the Environment Defense Fund (1970) splintered from century-old conservation groups such as the Sierra Club and the Audubon Society. Unlike progressivism and the New Deal, the new social regulation cut across industry boundaries. It, too, was opposed by business interests, who increasingly cited the costs of meeting the new regulations as a prime reason for failing US industrial competitiveness.

The new social regulatory state was put in place just as the global economy entered a long economic slowdown. The precipitating event was the OPEC oil embargo and first energy crisis of 1973, although that served mainly as a shock to a system already suffering from structural weaknesses. As the 1970s unfolded, the US economy struggled under the double burden of high inflation and stagnation (dubbed "stagflation" by economist Herbert Stein). Struggling to rein in inflation and restore growth, a Republican president, Richard M. Nixon, took the unorthodox step of instituting wage and price controls in 1972. His successor, Jimmy Carter, a Democrat, was equally unpredictable; he began to deregulate financial services, electricity, railroads, trucking, airlines, petroleum and natural gas, and telecommunications. By that time, many economists and policy-makers were calling for the dismantling of the regulatory regime put in place during the early 1930s. Richard H. K. Vietor's study (1994) of twentieth-century US regulation and deregulation shows clearly the "market-structuring" impact of regulatory regimes, as well as how they often led to unintended, and sometimes unwanted, consequences. This was true in the 1970s, as many attributed corporate ailments to the New Deal regulatory regime; and it would be true again in the 1980s and 1990s, when many blamed deregulation for excesses in the financial sector.

The 1970s was a confusing and unpredictable time for American business. As the decade came to a close, many expected deregulation to ease the costs of environmental and other kinds of social regulation while removing long-standing constraints to open competition. But big business hardly spoke with a single voice. The managers at AT&T warned that service would degrade and rates soar if its century-old sanctioned monopoly was broken up, while challengers at MCI lobbied hard for telecommunications competition. Most business leaders, however, hoped and expected that Ronald Reagan's presidential victory in 1980 would bring much-needed revival.

Excess and Innovation in the 1980s and 1990s

The "Reagan revolution" indeed offered much that was applauded by managers and entrepreneurs. Within months of his taking office, the AT&T monopoly was ordered dismantled, and a long-standing suit against IBM was settled in favor of the company. When the Professional Air Traffic Controllers Organization (PATCO) struck for higher wages and shorter hours in the summer of 1981, Reagan issued an ultimatum that led to the firing of some 11,000 union members, a move that sent a strong message to labor unions of all stripes. Meanwhile, the Reagan administration's economic policies brought on a severe recession in the early 1980s, one that nevertheless helped bring inflation under control. As promised, Reagan and his successor, President George H. W. Bush (1989–93), cut taxes for individuals and corporations, eased anti-trust enforcement, and reduced the number of health, safety, and environmental regulators (from more than 51,000 to fewer than 47,000). But Reaganomics also tripled the national debt (as a percentage of gross domestic product), which made investment capital scarcer for private firms. And in the 1980s the economy expanded at about the same pace as it had the previous decade.

Wall Street in many ways defined the business culture of the 1980s. For better and worse, the decade brought enormous financial innovation. This took several forms. Banking deregulation broke down the barriers between commercial and investment banking that had been erected a half century earlier under the New Deal. Commercial banks now could compete in the interest paid to depositors, and could move into other financial arenas. Buttressed by a massive wave of consolidations, financial institutions began to offer a full range of services. Mortgage lenders especially welcomed deregulation because the cost of buying a home had put homeownership well out of reach of the average family. In response, lenders devised a host of new products (variable-rate mortgages and balloon payments) to replace the traditional 30-year fixed mortgage. Deregulation brought creative destruction to banking as well. As deposit interest rate ceilings were removed in the early 1980s, savings and loans were squeezed by the low rates they were earning on fixed mortgages. Nearly a third of the "thrifts" collapsed, and the Federal Savings and Loan Insurance Corporation was forced to pay some $12 billion to depositors in failed savings and loans.

Finance also defined the decade because of a massive wave of mergers and acquisitions and the often innovative motives and methods behind them. Many of these deals occurred when conglomerates or unrelated diversified firms decided to divest business units they had acquired in earlier postwar decades. The conglomerate movement had collapsed at the end of the 1960s, as managers discovered that unrelated diversified firms lacked focus and "synergy," not to mention profitability.

Since then the trend among corporate strategists was to focus firms more sharply on core competencies. Thus, "deconglomerization" was an effort to undo the errors of the past. According to Galambos and Pratt (1988), the conglomerate movement exemplified the general failure of corporate managers during this period to balance innovation, efficiency, and control over their social and regulatory environment.

At the same time, many of the decade's mergers and acquisitions were driven by more purely financial considerations. Most of these were friendly takeovers, but many were "hostile." In those scenarios, "raiders" calculated that a target firm's real value was worth more than its market value (as reflected in the current price of its stock), and then secretly or openly acquired a controlling share in the company in order to sell off its assets piece by piece for a substantial profit. Such practices generated a new vocabulary on Wall Street, with terms like "greenmail" (the premium paid by a target company to a raider to call off the raid), "white knights" (a third-party investor who rescues a raided firm from a raider), and "poison bill" (changes in a corporation's by-laws that make it unattractive to raiders).

Often corporations were taken over from within, by a small group of current or former managers disgruntled with current management. Whether internal or external, such takeovers were made possible by new forms of debt financing, most notably the high-yield or "junk" bond financing made popular by bond trader Michael Milken at Drexel Burnham. As a brilliant student of finance, Milken calculated that markets for low-rated bonds typically underpriced them, even factoring in total losses from defaults. With junk bond financing he raised billions of dollars of new investment capital for corporate financings, refinancings, and takeovers, and became a billionaire in the process. Takeovers financed with junk bonds or higher quality debt were known as leveraged buyouts, because they left firms with a heavy load of fixed debt to be serviced month by month.

These high-flying financial dealings were controversial and became fodder for the mass media. Tom Wolfe's novel about arrogant Wall Street bond traders, *The Bonfire of the Vanities* (1987), became a best-seller. Movies such as *Wall Street* and *Other People's Money* portrayed corporate raiders as heartless manipulators who wrecked companies and destroyed the livelihoods of their workers. "Greed is good," intoned the raider in *Wall Street* played by Michael Douglas, parroting a comment attributed to Ivan Boesky, who had been convicted of insider trading. The reality, of course, was somewhat more complex. As often as leveraged buyouts and takeovers destroyed good companies, they imposed new discipline and reinvigorated firms whose managers had become complacent and ineffective. Milken paid $200 million in fines and served 22 months in jail for several technical securities violations, though he was never convicted of insider trading. He had become the symbol for an age of financial excess.

Corporations also changed shape, often dramatically, by "downsizing" and restructuring. A euphemism for massive layoffs, downsizing struck middle managers and plant workers alike. Some firms shed workers when they lost market share to foreign competitors, others in order to boost efficiency and profits by operating with far fewer workers. Millions of well-paying blue-collar jobs were eliminated during the 1980s, leaving the economy more based on services and less on manufacturing than ever before. At the same time, the rate of small business start-ups surged in the 1980s. The Company Man of the 1950s and 1960s had become an anachronism.

Along with entrepreneurs, women made important strides in business in the 1980s. The biggest drivers were the changes in the legal standing of women as workers, owners, and creditors enacted during the 1960s and 1970s, and the spread of professional business education among women. While women earned only 6 percent of MBAs in 1977, a decade later they earned nearly a third. As women streamed out of the MBA pipeline, they began to populate the ranks of corporate middle management at historically record levels, although not at the same pace that they were earning business degrees. And few went on to become Chairwomen or CEOs of major corporations. Enduring cultural attitudes that characterized women as nurturing caregivers proved to be a double-edged sword. Such views allowed women to excel in business professions such as finance, consulting, health care, education, hospitality services, domestic work, and the arts, while at the same time limiting their opportunities in most other domains, where they were often sidelined on a "mommy track." Business ownership became an even greater option for women in the 1980s, as the number of all firms owned by women jumped from 7 percent in 1977 to 30 percent a decade later. Businesses owned by minority women also proliferated during the 1980s, reaching 13 percent of all female-owned firms by the late 1990s.

Conclusion

From the late 1980s until about 2000, the economy grew at a robust pace similar to that of the 1950s, while sustaining historically low unemployment levels and very low rates of inflation. The decade also saw an enormous stock market run-up, with heavy participation by ordinary investors (many trading on the Web), followed by a spectacular collapse that wiped out most of the gains. Much of this new investment capital was funneled by venture capitalists into start-up firms somehow or other related to the Web, especially the hundreds of "incubators" situated in the Silicon Valley region of southern California. All of these developments are sometimes lumped under the rubric "new economy," which after the collapse of the "dot.com bubble" and the slowdown of the US economy became a term of derision.

The 1990s stock market boom and bust bore all the hallmarks of a classic speculative mania, from prognostications that the business cycle and inflation had been defeated forever to securities prices that far outstripped the value of their firms' assets or earning potential. Journalist John Cassidy captured much of the flavor and complexity of the phenomenon. According to Cassidy (2002), Federal Reserve Chairman Alan Greenspan contributed to the euphoria by revising his inflation expectations as the decade wore on. After warning of "irrational exuberance" on Wall Street early in the boom, he went on to tout the contributions of high technology to economic productivity and became more optimistic about low-inflation growth possibilities.

But there are dimensions to the 1990s economy (whether "new" or not) that reach well beyond the dot.com bubble. Globalization clearly has acted to restrain inflation as capital and labor circulate more and more rapidly. Web-based retailing has not become the juggernaut once predicted, yet traditional firms are employing more and more Web-based tools to streamline their operations, shorten delivery times, and reach customers. A new wave of business consolidation has raised new questions about the viability and desirability of anti-trust law. Corporate scandals

– touched off by the collapse of energy trading giant Enron in late 2001 and quickly spreading to others, as well as to a stalwart accounting firm, Arthur Andersen – have ushered in a new wave of public mistrust of big business.

In the late 1990s a growing number of corporations became defendants in class action tort lawsuits brought by attorneys representing asbestos workers, cigarette smokers, and victims of man-made environmental toxins such as groundwater chemicals and lead paint. Some have produced settlements in the billions of dollars. The rise of corporate tort litigation may signal a shift away from the kind of regulatory control of business that emerged and grew in the twentieth century and a return to court enforcement of corporate behavior as prevailed when the century began.

REFERENCES AND FURTHER READING

Blackford, Mansel G. (1991) *A History of Small Business in America*. New York: Twayne.

Cassidy, John (2002) *Dot.con: The Greatest Story Ever Sold*. New York: HarperCollins.

Chandler, Alfred D., Jr. (1977) *The Visible Hand: The Managerial Revolution in American Business*. Cambridge, Mass.: Harvard University Press.

—— (1997) [1977] "The United States: engines of economic growth in the capital-intensive and knowledge-intensive industries," in Alfred D. Chandler, Jr., Franco Amatori, and Takashi Hikino (eds.) *Big Business and the Wealth of Nations*. Cambridge: Cambridge University Press.

Eichengreen, Barry J. (1992) *Golden Fetters: The Gold Standard and the Great Depression, 1919–1939*. New York: Oxford University Press.

Galambos, Louis and Pratt, Joseph (1988) *The Rise of the Corporate Commonwealth: US Business and Public Policy in the Twentieth Century*. New York: Basic Books.

Hawley, Ellis W. (1966) *The New Deal and the Problem of Monopoly: A Study in Economic Ambivalence*. Princeton, NJ: Princeton University Press.

Holland, Max (1989) *When the Machine Stopped: A Cautionary Tale from Industrial America*. Boston: Harvard Business School Press.

Kwolek-Folland, Angel (1998) *Incorporating Women: A History of Women and Business in the United States*. New York: Twayne.

Leuchtenburg, William E. (1958) *The Perils of Prosperity, 1914–32*. Chicago: University of Chicago Press.

Marchand, Roland (1985) *Advertising the American Dream: Making Way for Modernity, 1920–1940*. Berkeley: University of California Press.

McCraw, Thomas K. (1984) *Prophets of Regulation: Charles Francis Adams, Louis D. Brandeis, James M. Landis, Alfred E. Kahn*. Cambridge, Mass.: Harvard University Press.

McQuaid, Kim (1994) *Uneasy Partners: Big Business and American Politics, 1945–1990*. Baltimore, Md.: Johns Hopkins University Press.

Perrow, Charles (1972) *The Radical Attack on Business*. New York: Harcourt Brace Jovanovich.

Scranton, Philip (1997) *Endless Novelty: Specialty Production and American Industrialization, 1865–1925*. Princeton, NJ: Princeton University Press.

Sklar, Martin J. (1988) *The Corporate Reconstruction of American Capitalism, 1890–1916: The Market, the Law, and Politics*. New York: Cambridge University Press.

Sobel, Robert (1968) *The Great Bull Market: Wall Street in the 1920s*. New York: W. W. Norton.

Tiffany, Paul A. (1988) *The Decline of American Steel: How Management, Labor, and Government Went Wrong*. New York: Oxford University Press.

Vietor, Richard H. K. (1994) *Contrived Competition: Regulation and Deregulation in America*. Cambridge, Mass.: Harvard University Press.

Vogel, David (1989) *Fluctuating Fortunes: The Political Power of Business in America*. New York: Basic Books.

Walker, Juliet E. K. (1998) *The History of Black Business in America: Capitalism, Race, Entrepreneurship*. New York: Macmillan Library Reference USA.

Weems, Robert E. (1996) *Black Business in the Black Metropolis: The Chicago Metropolitan Assurance Company, 1925–1985*. Bloomington: Indiana University Press.

Zunz, Olivier (1990) *Making America Corporate, 1870–1920*. Chicago: University of Chicago Press.

Part V

Images and "isms"

CHAPTER TWENTY-THREE

Journalism and Broadcasting

JAMES L. BAUGHMAN

Although few deny the importance of journalism and broadcasting in twentieth-century America, these fields have engaged relatively few historians. The bulk of scholarly study has been conducted by those, outside of history, who have been trained in sociology, political science, journalism, and communication.

The Golden Age of the American Newspaper, 1900–30

The first three decades of the twentieth century represented a pinnacle for American journalism, certainly for the nation's newspapers. A higher percentage of the citizenry read papers than at any time in the country's history. Just over 95 percent of those surveyed in 1918–19 reported reading a newspaper (Stedman et al. 1991: 169, 172). The popularity of newspapers owed much to their broad definition of "news." Indeed the nation's dailies only became a mass medium after many editors redefined their product. Until then, newspapers had a narrow agenda, which included political, governmental, and financial information, but not much more. In larger cities and towns, crime reportage began to receive significant display. And it was in the biggest metropolitan areas that the newspaper underwent a re-invention. The news agenda grew. More pages went to the coverage of sports, fashion, society, and show business. In what proved to be an American innovation, many dailies began pouring resources into large Sunday editions, with the greatest number of special sections, including comic pages, to attract young and old. Finally, innovations in publishing allowed for bigger, attention-grabbing headlines; and more illustrations attracted still more consumers, especially those newer immigrants struggling with written English.

The extraordinary reach of the newspaper between 1900 and 1930 thus can be explained largely by its capacity both to entertain and to inform. Especially on Sundays, most newspapers were likely to carry something of interest to the vast majority of Americans, and, in the case of comic sections, even children. On a given Sunday, families eagerly fought for different sections, the consumption of which might devour the better part of a morning or afternoon.

Some historians have attached great importance to the hold of newspapers over urban readers. Reviving an argument first posited by the sociologist Robert E. Park

(1925), historian Gunther Barth deemed the new daily one of four city institutions that helped to create an identification with the burgeoning urban culture (Barth 1980). In the late nineteenth and early twentieth centuries, cities had grown rapidly, with the result that newcomers from the countryside and overseas formed the majority of their populations. By appealing across class lines and neighborhoods, the mass newspaper helped to craft a common identity (Nord 1985). Yet the Park–Barth thesis is not entirely convincing. Did foreign-born Americans in fact consume newspapers? Relatively few could read English, or have the time for reading that others enjoyed.

Journalism history has slighted smaller communities. Only a few outstanding studies have examined the country weeklies and small-town dailies that served, despite the pronounced trend to urbanization, the great majority of Americans in the early twentieth century. In the late nineteenth century smaller papers developed their own set of "rules" for capturing and holding readers. The most mundane occurrences – whether relatives visiting someone, or a barn-raising – received coverage, thus flattering local residents and assuring their continued support of the paper. Small-town residents were also given a prominence and dignity they could never have achieved in the large city (Atherton 1954). The most valuable study of a small-town paper, Sally Griffith's *Home Town News*, nevertheless suggested that some of the same technological and economic forces transforming the big-city paper affected the *Gazette* of Emporia, Kansas. In the 1920s the *Gazette* and other smaller dailies came to depend on syndicated features and wire services, led by the Associated Press (AP). These provided papers across the country with entertaining filler a small-town paper would be hard put to produce. A modest daily found it far cheaper to run an AP story about Washington than to employ a correspondent in the capital. Gradually, papers in smaller cities and towns surrendered more content to national syndications – at the loss, Griffith noted – of community identity (1989).

Thus business considerations essentially accounted for the transformations of the twentieth-century newspaper. In the late nineteenth century, a new generation of newspaper owners recognized the profits that could be earned from a massification of their product. Urban centers were growing, as were the number and size of their retail outlets. Department stores played a special role. These enterprises needed high and constant sales to offset the costs of their high inventories of goods and services. Newspapers were by far the most efficient conduit to potential consumers, especially women. To reach them, however, retailers pressured editors to downplay their past partisanship while offering features that would attract female readers. Editors and their patrons assumed that women were less interested in politics and government (Baldasty 1992). This is not say that newspapers abandoned partisanship altogether. Most newspapers continued to endorse candidates, and tended to favor one party – the Republican – over the other. Then, too, party ties could still affect how newspapers covered certain stories. Newspapers were nevertheless gradually stepping away from the fierce party commitments characteristic of the press earlier in the nineteenth century (Schudson 1978).

In a sense, editors had substituted one master for another. In the nineteenth century a variety of party subsidies (not all of them publicized) sustained individual newspapers. This dependency often left editors at the mercy of party bosses. Retailers and others assumed this role. Some editors, Griffith and others suspected, found this shift liberating. But many contemporary critics decried the influence of advertisers. Still, the nation's dailies were hardly free of controversy. Yet the same system gave primacy to the circulation leadership in a given community and fostered intense rivalries for news "scoops" or exclusives. As a result, reporting could be very aggressive. *The Front Page* (1928), written by two former Chicago reporters, is the best and most hilarious theatrical testament to this tendency. Editors and publishers understood that a reputation for sustained reporting could cement reader loyalties. And papers poured considerable resources into investigative pieces that might run for days. Such exclusives, which usually targeted local or state government officials or monopolies like urban transit lines, carried vital secondary messages. In a community portrayed as the victim of "corrupt" officials, party bosses, and big businessmen, the newspaper cast itself as the people's champion.

Some historians argued that such investigative instincts and the shift to objectivity may have had unintended effects on the political culture. Although journalism schools and traditional histories of the profession bemoaned the partisanship of the nineteenth-century newspaper, Gerald Baldasty (1992) and Michael McGerr (1986) have defended the party press as an important agency for mobilizing the electorate. Voter turnouts were far higher in the age of partisan journalism. The party sheet treated readers as citizens. The "objective" daily regarded them as spectators or, worse, as mere consumers. By distancing themselves from politicians and parties, and occasionally attacking them as hopelessly venal, the less partisan newspaper may have discouraged participation in the civic culture. So also did a news agenda that appeared to give as much weight, if not more, to a bizarre murder or to a college football game as to a major candidate's speech.

Like newspapers, magazines had begun to seek larger circulation by widening their agendas and, benefiting from new printing technologies, by carrying more illustrations. At the same time, editors cut the price of individual issues and annual subscriptions, which lower postal rates helped to subsidize. Although many magazines were sold at or below per issue cost, a huge increase in advertising sales provided publishers with their profit margins. Advertisers had little choice. At the turn of the century, producers of goods and services increasingly combined and sought nation-wide audiences, and turned to advertising in magazines, which until the late 1920s constituted the only national medium.

Despite higher circulation, periodicals ranked well behind newspapers as mass media. This would remain true throughout the century. Magazine audiences tended to be middle class. Circulation grew because more of the middle class, especially the new class of clerical professionals moving to cities between 1880 and 1920, began subscribing to periodicals. The working class lacked the time to consume magazines. This class division hardly upset publishers and advertisers, most of whom deliberately cultivated better-off consumers. It also helps explain why magazines aimed at women had such a traditional, middle-class orientation, emphasizing the home and fashion above all else (Schneirov 1994; Scanlon 1995; Garvey 1996; Ohmann 1996).

For a decade, beginning with *McClure's Magazine* in 1902, a wide range of magazines practiced an advanced version of the crusading journalism first seen in many dailies in the 1880s and 1890s. *McClure's* writers Lincoln Steffens, Ida Tarbell, and Ray Stannard Baker led a generation of reporters investigating a wide range of political, social, and economic injustices (Wilson 1970). It was the most sustained period of investigative journalism in the nation's history. One series, David Graham Phillips' highly critical portrait of the US Senate, incensed President Theodore Roosevelt, who likened Phillips and his colleagues to the eyes-cast-down muckraker in John Bunyan's *Pilgrim's Progress*. The moniker stuck. Yet the muckrakers, with a few exceptions, posed no threat to the established political and economic order. Most were the publicists of the progressive movement. When the Progressive Era in effect ended around 1912, so did muckraking. Many readers believed the great problems besetting the nation in the wake of industrialization had been resolved. Some had simply tired of the genre. Perhaps the muckrakers were even too effective, so that their highly critical reportage of politics fostered voter apathy (Leonard 1986).

The end of muckraking had larger implications for both periodicals and newspapers. In the later half of the 1910s and 1920s, both news media cast less critical glances at politics, government, and business. Indeed, for many journalists, the economic expansion of the twenties made the big businessman a hero. No less a muckraker than Ida Tarbell, whose elaborate exposure of Standard Oil had rendered owner John D. Rockefeller into a modern-day Shylock, found herself writing an admiring biography of the head of US Steel. Then, too, companies like Standard Oil began employing modern public relations agents to manipulate corporate images in the press. At the same time, the moral exhaustion that followed the Progressive Era and World War I, as well as the banality of political leadership, caused many citizens to lose interest in politics and government in favor of crime, sports, and mass entertainment (Lowenthal 1944; Brazil 1981). Moreover, newspapers expanded their coverage of various "stunts," notably Charles A. Lindbergh's solo flight across the Atlantic in 1927, as well as extraordinary murder trials. Even many readers in smaller towns demanded stories on crimes committed half way across the country. By 1925 the AP began offering its members feature material.

The 1920s marked several major changes in the newspaper industry. Although newspapers expanded in size and many profited immensely in the decade, in many smaller cities and towns competing dailies ceased operation. More and more Americans lived in "one-newspaper towns," a trend that persisted through the remainder of the century. Newspaper competition had become a deadly business. Failing to win the circulation war could be fatal. Advertisers overwhelmingly preferred the winner, and their patronage covered the otherwise prohibitive cost of publishing a paper. Between 1923 and 1982 the number of communities with competing dailies fell from 503 to 49. The surviving paper enjoyed a virtual monopoly, both for readers and for advertisers, and proved a money-maker for several generations of owners (Bogart 1982).

After World War I several important periodicals were born that greatly affected all of journalism. *The New Yorker*, established in 1925, offered self-consciously sophisticated views of urban life and, eventually, became the country's leading repository of literary journalism. More influential on journalism itself was *Time*, founded two years earlier by two young Yale graduates with the slimmest of journalistic credentials. A news magazine, *Time* anticipated a shift to synthesis that characterized much of the news media for the remainder of the century (Baughman 2001). *Time* seized upon Walter Lippmann's argument of the previous year (1922) that the modern world had become too complex. The reader needed guidance. Deliberately playing that role, *Time* sought to synthesize in entries of no more than 400 to 500 words every important news story that week. The omniscient and – for a couple of decades – quirky style of this news magazine would inspire countless journalists. And younger, middle-class readers began to rely on *Time*'s guided synthesis. By the late 1930s many dailies had introduced special Sunday sections that aspired to the kind of analytical journalism of summary that *Time* had invented. Another sign of its influence, according to one analysis of newspaper accounts of presidential addresses, was an increasing mediation by reporters (Schudson 1995).

The Advent and Triumph of Radio, 1922–48

In the early 1920s improvements in the over-the-air transmission and reception of radio waves created a new mass medium. It quickly gained favor, especially among the middle class and in more populated areas. A drop in the cost of receivers in the early 1930s encouraged still more households to acquire radios. By 1940, just over 80 percent of all homes had one or more receivers. There were biases in set ownership. The very poor were less likely to own radios, as were rural residents who were without electrical service or who lived near mountainous areas that disrupted the transmission of signals. These distortions became less pronounced in the 1940s. By the end of the decade, just under 95 percent of all households had radios.

In contrast to services that developed in most other nations, the so-called "American" system of broadcasting was largely free of governmental oversight. The nation's political leaders never seriously considered creating a federal network similar to the British Broadcasting Corporation. Instead the government through an independent agency awarded relatively scarce radio frequencies (all on the AM dial until the late 1940s) for three-year periods. Although universities and other non-profit groups obtained some licenses, most went to commercial ventures. Revenues came from advertisers sponsoring individual programs. With due regard for dominant social norms, radio consequently offered fare intended to attract the largest possible audience (Rosen 1980; McChesney 1993).

The task of programming largely fell to national networks: the National Broadcasting Company (NBC), which was a subdivision of a set-manufacturer, the Radio Corporation of America (RCA); and the Columbia Broadcasting System (CBS). Pledging to provide so many hours of programs, each network established affiliate agreements with stations across the country. (The government limited the number of stations that each network could own.) The networks compensated affiliates for surrendering their broadcast time; the stations in turn saved money by not having to produce their own programs. And network shows, with very few exceptions, proved to be immensely popular, far more so than what most individual stations could offer. By the early 1930s, radio executives and advertisers had developed programming practices that would dominate the medium – and then television – for the remainder of the century. Essentially this model involved the daily or weekly "series" organized around a set of characters. Advertisers sought to build and hold audiences by sponsoring programs at specific times. Another inspiration came from newspapers' continuity comic strips like *Little Orphan Annie*. In theory, listeners would develop the habit of tuning in specific programs (underwritten by specific sponsors). The formula was first and most effectively demonstrated in the late 1920s with Sam 'n' Henry, a daily comedy show highlighting two black characters (played by white performers). Renamed *Amos 'n' Andy* and broadcast on NBC, the series developed a vast following. Although very few programs approached *Amos 'n' Andy* in popularity, its success validated the emphasis on the series (Smulyan 1994; Hilmes 1997). Indeed a mid-1940s survey indicated that, if forced to chose, Americans were more reluctant to give up radio than any other mass medium (Lazarsfeld and Field 1946).

Relatively few historians have dealt with radio. Broadcast historians have tended to come from film programs or communication departments. For a generation, the single best history of broadcasting was Erik Barnouw's three-volume series (1966, 1968, 1970). Although possessed of many insights, he organized his histories episodically, and yielded to the biases of a former insider angered by the direction of the industry. A series of important work started appearing in the 1980s. Several significant studies, for example, have examined the impact of radio in the 1930s. Most politicians, with the exception of President Franklin D. Roosevelt and Louisiana Senator Huey P. Long, failed to master the new medium (Craig 2000). Radio did aid the efforts of Long and his allies to create a national political movement that ended with his assassination in 1935 (Brinkley 1982). A more intriguing, if ultimately speculative argument, is found in Lizabeth Cohen's study of working-class Chicagoans. They were divided by strong ethnic loyalties, which contributed to the frustration of the budding labor movement. But popular programs like *Amos 'n' Andy* appealed to listeners regardless of ethnic identity. Working-class Chicagoans suddenly had something in common, an association that helped them to establish their class interests (Cohen 1990).

However profitable their enterprise through the 1940s, broadcasters had to reckon with the prospect of greater regulation. The refusal of the federal government to follow Britain or Canada in creating a state broadcasting authority did not give, as some scholars led by Robert W. McChesney have implied, commercial radio a free hand. Stations and networks had to live constantly with the possibility of interference from radio's overseer, called from 1927 to 1934 the Federal Radio Commission (FRC), and then from 1934 the Federal Communications Commission (FCC). Although virtually toothless, the FCC could induce pain on occasion. In 1943 the Commission forced NBC to sell off one of its two networks, which became the American Broadcasting Company (ABC). Then, too, members of Congress occasionally complained about the new medium, all but forcing otherwise somnambulant regulators to review programming. At the same time, although radio proved profitable for most commercial operators and the networks, much air time went unsold or undersold.

Radio was able to reconcile these challenges to its advantage. From the beginning, the FRC, then the FCC, refrained from mandating that specific programs be aired or dropped. Yet the overseers did set minimum, "public interest" standards for all licensees. Stations were expected to air "minority interest" fare, including news and religious programs that might only attract minorities of listeners. This expectation had to be honored, if only because license-holders were subject to renewal every three years. Although the FCC rarely revoked a license, the possibility of a "death sentence," or a probationary, one-year renewal, loomed. Satisfying this requirement in the 1930s was less onerous, however, because some broadcast time went unsold. Comparatively inexpensive public interest programs, usually "sustaining" or unsponsored, designated at such hours would placate regulators and members of Congress. Stations might air religious services on Sunday mornings, a time of scant interest to advertisers. Much of the earliest news programming was, indeed, sustaining. And CBS, which was long the more anxious about government intervention, poured many resources into the creation of a news division.

CBS News helped to transform public perceptions of radio. Until the late 1930s, most listeners turned to the medium for entertainment; it was more like going to the movies than reading a newspaper. The prospect of another world war beginning in Europe in 1938 and 1939 caused many more Americans to turn to their radio for updates; and CBS provided the most extensive, continuous coverage (Douglas 1999). More and more of those polled regarded radio as their most important news source. Compared to newspapers, radio had an obvious advantage of immediacy. Americans did not have to wait for their morning or afternoon paper to learn the latest news. A 1946 survey indicated that 67 percent of those interviewed believed radio had done the best job "of serving the public during the war" of any major medium; newspapers ranked second, at 17 percent (Lazarsfeld and Field 1946: 99). Research also suggested that many listeners trusted the individual voice of a radio news reporter or commentator, "speaking to them," as opposed to the relatively impersonal, group-written and edited newspaper account (Stott 1973). Television news came to enjoy the same advantage over newspapers later in the century. An individual broadcast newsperson might be fairly incompetent, and his or her report incomplete or simply wrong-headed. Yet many individuals had come to know and trust the messenger as a person over and above the corporately constructed (albeit more complete) newspaper version.

All of the news media covered World War II. Radio, notably CBS, provided gripping coverage of battles and air raids as they occurred. Newspapers and many magazines invested even more into reportage. Coverage was uniformly supportive of the US and its allies. Sharing the national consensus on behalf of the war, correspondents cooperated with military and naval leaders. Blundering and battlefield brutalities went unreported (Honey 1984; Fussell 1989; Adams 1994). Fearful of complacency midway through the conflict, the government relaxed some visual representations of the dead. Still, the overall portrait left Americans strikingly innocent about the horror of the battlefield, leaving them ill-prepared for the costs of intervention in Vietnam (Roeder 1993). Historian John Fousek has suggested that World War II encouraged in Americans and their news media an expansive sense of national destiny in world affairs (Fousek 2000). Then, too, the war left a legacy of trust in the federal government that deeply affected coverage of national security matters well into the 1960s. Touched by their wartime experiences, reporters tended to give the government the benefit of the doubt. For its part, Washington skillfully used war analogies to win the backing of newspapers, newsmagazines, and radio networks after 1945. Seeking support first for foreign aid and then for a permanent military establishment, the administration of Harry Truman likened the Soviet Union in the late 1940s and 1950s to Germany before 1939. America must not return to its prewar isolationism. Few in the fourth estate dissented from this logic (Adler and Paterson 1970; Paterson 1979; Bernhard 1999).

V-J Day also signaled several significant changes in radio. Networks and stations thereafter reduced their news programs in favor of more entertainment shows.

Increasing advertiser demand caused a reduction in sustaining hours. At the same time, the number of radio stations increased as the FCC began issuing more licenses, including for the first time some on FM frequency. Between 1945 and 1950, the number of radio stations rose from 973 to 2,867.

The Coming of Television

A long-anticipated television invasion commenced in the late 1940s. Television sets received visual and aural images in black and white. War-related perfections in the construction of receivers improved reception and lowered costs. Led by NBC, which was anxious to promote the sale of RCA sets, national television networks began operations after the war, joined by Du Mont, another set manufacturer. (Du Mont shut down in 1955.) By 1960, just under 90 percent of all homes had one or more televisions. Several factors explained the rapid diffusion of television, including the prosperity that followed the war. Not to be overlooked was the extraordinary baby boom that roughly coincided with the introduction of television. Young parents found television to be superior to radio in entertaining children and, after they were put to bed, themselves. It was also cheaper than attending a movie, which necessitated hiring baby-sitters. Children themselves clamored for television, especially as the networks produced daytime and early evening series, like *Howdy Doody*, which were specifically aimed at the very young. No wonder that virtually the last demographic sub-group to purchase a television set consisted of couples without children (Spigel 1992).

The programs did, in fact, greatly encourage the securing of a television set. As in the case of radio, the networks cultivated large audiences. Many popular radio programs and performers, including briefly *Amos 'n' Andy*, moved to the newest medium, as did such tried-and-true program genres as the soap opera and quiz program (later renamed the game show). Advertisers and networks offered numerous appealing programs. Watching some shows, like *Texaco Star Theater* and *I Love Lucy*, became national habits. Like radio, television originally concentrated on live broadcasts, on the basis of the long-held assumption that Americans preferred a live to a recorded performance. Simultaneous transmission also justified the networks' existence. Yet the success of *I Love Lucy*, which was filmed, as well as a host of action dramas on ABC starting in the mid-1950s, suggested that viewers would accept filmed fare. They would also, much to the shock of some station managers, watch "re-runs" of filmed series in the summer. (Conventional wisdom among broadcasters had contended otherwise.) The introduction of videotape in the late 1950s gradually wiped out live performances except for some newscasts.

The growing reliance of the new medium on film changed television in several ways. In its first years, New York was the center of television production. The city's legitimate theater as well as its night clubs became sources for programs and performers. A viewer in 1953 could sample original drama influenced by Arthur Miller and starring a Broadway actor, or could encounter the slapstick antics of a former night-club MC, Milton Berle, who hosted the Texaco program. As television production shifted to Hollywood in the mid-1950s, however, that choice ended. A middle ground was secured as programs came to be manufactured in assembly-line fashion by small and large movie studios. Some provided memorable entertainment.

But many more conveyed the half-hearted investments of their producers, whose preoccupation remained the production of feature films. Although contemporary critics, mainly based in New York, decried Hollywood's takeover of the industry, at least one scholar has recently dismissed their concerns as "tendentious and their anti-Hollywood biases constricting" (Boddy 1990: 8). Hollywood's relationship to broadcasting has inspired several other scholarly studies. Film historians Tino Balio (1976) and Michele Hilmes (1990) disputed the once-common view that movie-makers and broadcasters had a deeply antagonistic relationship. Both Balio and Hilmes argued the opposite, and stressed the extent to which each industry depended on the other. Broadcasters found film stars to be popular guests on programs. The studios recognized the potential of broadcasting for promoting new theatrical re-leases. Television plainly posed the greatest threat to the movie industry. Yet United Artists and some smaller concerns were producing programs for television from the very beginning of regular telecasts (Balio 1990).

Advertisers at first exercised enormous influence over programming. Individual series frequently had single sponsors, which in turn contracted to independent producers the actual production of programs. This system gradually broke down in the late 1950s and early 1960s. Contemporary observers blamed the fallout accompanying the revelations in 1959 that popular quiz shows had been fixed; some sponsors had been deeply involved in rigging the contests. But the change was inevitable. Rising production costs encouraged advertisers to surrender their control over programs to the networks. This shift permitted advertisers to sponsor (though only in part) more programs and thus limit their financial risks. In exchange, however, the networks promised advertisers to maximize their potential audiences by giving even greater emphasis to the broad appeal of the programs. Less time was left to series with higher cultural aspirations – even if they had potential sponsors (Baughman 1997).

News programs generally lagged behind entertainment. Most consumers bought their first sets to watch situation comedies or comedy variety hours. News programs were initially a "loss leader" for networks and stations, something aired to placate federal regulators and opinion leaders. Beginning in 1948, the airing of the quadren-nial national political conventions proved a relatively cheap concession to politicians; summer demand for air time among advertisers was relatively soft. As total advertiser interest in the medium grew in the 1950s and 1960s, some public interest programs disappeared. Then, too, the networks redirected their energies into a smaller number of informational programs, such as *The Today Show* on NBC and the early evening newscasts on NBC and CBS. In time these shows became money-makers for the networks, and their hosts or "anchors" were turned into national celebrities.

The impact of television on politics has preoccupied several generations of scholars. Popular writers with no formal training in communication effects long asserted that the mass medium and especially its advertising had enormous influence over voters. John F. Kennedy's election in 1960 has been commonly – and overly – attributed to his performance on the first televised debates between the major party presidential candidates. For many of his critics, Ronald Reagan's subsequent political success was wholly due to his mastery, as a former film and television star, of the "home screen." Historians have shared many of these assumptions, but have generally avoided coming to terms with the role of television in modern politics. This is probably the better part of wisdom. While acknowledging that it can affect some voters, most specialists in media effects will not grant television sovereignty over the electorate. Nevertheless, by the 1980s politicians had intuited the power of television, and especially of its advertising; and much of the waking hours of candidates were spent raising money to purchase air time for campaign advertisements. Thus the political class – whether Republican or Democratic – became all the more dependent on interest groups able to donate vast sums.

The effects of television on rival mass media are less open to dispute. No other mass medium was more quickly or adversely affected than radio. Between 1946 and 1960, daily hourly use of the radio per household fell by more than 50 percent. Only the increasing number of car radios prevented greater audience losses. Yet radio survived the arrival of television largely by being the first mass medium to respond effectively to the new media environment. Rather than continue to compete for the largest possible audience, radio stations began appealing to specific sub-groups of listeners. Long ignored by broadcasters, teenagers suddenly became desirable; and individual stations began carrying teen-oriented rock 'n' roll music. This trend accelerated with the expansion of FM radio in the 1970s. In the mid-1960s, some stations shifted to "all-news" or "talk" formats. The economic logic was obvious: enough advertisers would support a radio station which could promise a targeted (as opposed to a mass) audience. In many ways, radio's emphasis on sub-groups anticipated trends noticeable in much of the rest of the mass media at the end of the century (Baughman 1997; Douglas 1999).

Television had little initial impact on the circulation of newspapers and magazines. Many big city papers concentrated their energies on a series of costly but, in most cases, successful battles with unionized employees. The disappearance of some competing dailies in larger markets, especially the well regarded New York *Herald Tribune* in 1966, disguised the basic robustness of newspaper publishing. Throughout most of the century, the *New York Times* ranked as the nation's single most influential newspaper. In purchasing it in 1896, Adolph Ochs deliberately determined to render the *Times* the newspaper of record. No other daily invested more in reporting national and international affairs. Its accounts were extensive and generally balanced. Although the editorial page tended to be moderately liberal, completeness in news coverage made the newspaper indispensable to opinion leaders regardless of party affiliation. More prominent Americans, a careful survey indicated in the late 1950s, regularly read the *Times* than any other newspaper or magazine (Rosenau 1963). In establishing their news agendas, the national television networks and newsmagazines heavily relied on the paper (Gans 1979).

In the late twentieth century only two other newspapers rivaled the *Times* in national influence. In the 1960s, after decades of mediocrity, the *Washington Post* began to emerge as one of the nation's leading dailies. As the federal government expanded, and more news organizations (including television news), shifted more resources in the capital, the *Post* gradually helped to shape the national news agenda. The political and journalistic elites based in Washington read the *Post*. The impact of the newspaper was first evident in its heavy coverage in 1972–4 of the Watergate scandal involving President Richard M. Nixon. A third newspaper of national impact in the late twentieth century was the *Wall Street Journal*, which focused on financial and economic news. In the 1950s and 1960s the *Journal* was the first daily to create a national publication and distribution system. Readership was at first limited mostly to business and financial leaders. But beginning in the 1970s, the paper's forcefully conservative editorial page started attracting readers with little or no interest in the economic reportage that filled the rest of the paper. In the process, the *Journal* helped to popularize the "supply-side" economics that informed the fiscal policies of Presidents Reagan and George H. W. Bush. Yet the ideological stridency of the newspaper largely restricted its audience to like-minded conservatives.

Other dailies underwent substantial changes in the 1970s, 1980s, and 1990s. One striking phenomenon was the growth in the number of "chain" newspapers. Between 1960 and 1986 the percentage of independently owned daily newspapers dropped from 68 to 30 percent. The locally owned and operated daily was becoming an anachronism (Busterna 1988: 835). Most of the new, absentee owners prized maintaining or increasing quarterly profit margins over keeping their properties' editorial quality (Roberts et al. 2001). At the same time, newspapers were losing readers. Circulation per household had been falling; the ratio to newspapers per household dropped from 133:100 in 1946 to 70:100 in 1981 (Rykken 1989: 23). The estimated percentage of adults reading a weekday paper fell from 77.6 percent in 1970 to 58.7 percent in 1997 (Newspaper Association of America, 1998). So too had the amount of time readers devoted to newspaper reading. Although this change had many causes, most editors blamed the growing popularity of television, especially local newscasts. Assuming (not always correctly) that readers had attentively watched television news the night before, dailies allotted more space to analyzing than to presenting the news. Opinion and predictions took up more of the newspaper. At the same time, many smaller dailies simply jettisoned their coverage of state government and local events. Instead came more nationally syndicated material, much of which attended to the ever-growing celebrity culture, largely based in Hollywood (Bogart 1985; Gamson 1994).

An increasing number of newspapers surrendered some of their editorial authority to focus groups. Popularized by market researcher Ruth Clark, focus groups consisted of a small body of readers who met to discuss what they wanted in their newspapers. Clark located a disturbing and growing gulf between readers and their newspapers. Most focus group members preferred information more "relevant" to their daily lives such as health news. Moreover, her findings, Thomas Leonard wrote, indicated that "distant events and complicated stories were found to endanger circulation" (Leonard 1995). Most editors took notice. Clark's report became "probably the single most influential statement ever made about the news reader," Leonard added. Editors, one media critic complained, "have become focus-group groupies" (Leonard 1995: 141, 142).

Trying to retain readers was not the same as expanding circulation. Like their counterparts in radio, publishers slowly granted the obvious: television had become the most popular mass medium. Advertisers were no longer as impressed with the size of a newspaper's readership as its composition. Some dailies and newspaper chains began what a generation earlier had been unthinkable; they cut back on circulation (Leonard 1995). Big dailies such as the Atlanta *Constitution* and the Des Moines *Register* eliminated delivery to distant counties, where readers rarely patronized the local advertisers in these papers. The decision of many dailies to reduce distribution to the inner city distressingly suggested that many newspapers were content to become middle-class organs. Media critic William A. Henry III wrote "of the end of the newspaper as a mass medium. It is becoming a class medium, ideal for advertisers. The masses are left to television, to suburban localism, and to ignorance" (Henry 1982: 23).

Magazines underwent a re-invention as well. Anxious to make younger adults subscribers, *Time* and its major competitor, *Newsweek*, began in the mid-1970s to reduce the number of individual stories, especially from overseas. Instead came longer features meant to scoop competing media and, inevitably, more celebrity-driven journalism. Still, the most successful magazines played to fairly narrow, specialized tastes (Abrahamson 1995).

Indeed the largest single dilemma facing all of the news media was the changing sensibility of the audience. The baby-boomers, the large generation of Americans born after World War II, did not possess their parents' appetite for "serious" journalism, that is, news about government. Some boomers suffered from an excess of narcissism; many entering adulthood beginning in the 1970s nurtured interests in hobbies and sports that bore little connection to larger public concerns. Others never overcame the mistrust for government that was born of the Vietnam War and the Watergate scandal. Their children, the so-called "generation X," appeared even less interested in traditional news agendas. Finally, the end of the Cold War in 1989 caused many Americans to lose interest in international reportage.

Perhaps the news media had done their job too well. Beginning with the latter stages of the Vietnam War, much of the national journalistic community – that is, reporters with the largest papers, news magazines, and television networks – had begun to cover the federal government and national politics with greater skepticism. Although some critics accused the press of becoming the "adversary" of the political elite, in truth most reporters were simply abandoning the uncritical, stenographic approach that had been taken earlier in the century. This change was partly explained by their growing autonomy and greater self-esteem (Boylan 1986). Moreover, in treating foreign policy, reporters came to convey the growing divisions, especially in Congress, over America's world role. As the national consensus surrounding the military intervention in Vietnam and then the logic of the Cold War itself began to unravel, reporters essentially described rather than manufactured that breakdown. Cynicism increasingly marked the tone of national news reportage, notably on television (Hallin 1986, 1994). Thus journalists unintentionally fostered the more jaded inclinations of the citizenry, especially younger Americans.

The Explosion of Media and the End of the Mass

Another communication revolution came at the century's end. For more than a generation, most Americans had relied on over-the-air reception of their television signals. But beginning in the 1970s, they began subscribing to cable systems. The percentage of households with cable television increased from 7.6 percent in 1970 to 49.4 percent in 1988. By the late 1990s up to 70 percent of all homes had cable, which greatly augmented the choices of signals. At the same time, more non-network, independent stations commenced operations in many markets. New national cable services slowly challenged the old network oligopoly. Some national cable channels, like those controlled by media entrepreneur Ted Turner, relied heavily on re-runs of network series. Others targeted audiences divided by gender, age, or hobby. Even pet fanciers had a channel. In 1980 Turner himself helped usher in a new information medium by creating the all-news Cable News Network (CNN). Others eventually followed. Their presence notwithstanding, the ultimate effect of cable television on the nation may not have been beneficial to self-government. Most cable subscribers used the far larger array of choices in programs to escape the responsibilities of citizenship. The percentage of the national audience viewing the presidential debates, with one exception, steadily declined. The most watched 2000 debate drew 42 percent fewer viewers than the Carter–Reagan confrontation twenty years earlier (Rutenberg 2000: A22). More and more viewers abandoned those network and news channels carrying the debates in favor of options promising only entertainment.

As the networks' hold on the national audience began to slip, new rules emerged. First NBC, then ABC recognized that programs had to be more daring, and less respectful of small-town moralism, to win viewers. This signaled a relaxation of decades-old edicts against treatments of violence or sexuality. Offended viewers were likely older and less desirable to advertisers, and could always repair to one of Ted Turner's re-run channels. By the 1990s the dominant programming strategy at all three networks emphasized situation comedies and dramas that were intended to appeal to younger adults – and to the advertisers who coveted these viewers. The new rules failed to hold the networks' share of the audience, however. Even counting a new and appealing rival, Fox, the four-network percentage of the evening audience was 62.1 percent for the 1996–7 season (Carter 1997). Before cable the established three networks commanded over 90 percent of the nighttime viewership. What constituted a "hit" series in the 1990s signalled this transformation. NBC's *Seinfeld* was one of the most watched network programs of the 1997–8 season. Two decades earlier, however, the series' total viewership would not have ranked it in the top 25 in audience size. By 2002, the networks' share of the evening audience had fallen below 50 percent.

Second only to cable in annoying the established networks was Rupert Murdoch. In the mid-1980s, after creating an international chain of newspapers (most of them cheap tabloids), the Australian billionaire entered television. The Fox Network, which he founded, specialized in situation comedies, cartoons, and science fiction programs that drew many teenage and young adult viewers. Fox's following among young adults was reinforced by the network's reliance on the medium's newest genre, "reality" programs. Reality shows ran footage of real police raids or pets gone berserk, as well as tests of survival skills or sex appeal among physically isolated contestants. Fox comedies, like some of Murdoch's newspapers, banked heavily on their capacity to offend propriety. After a series of missteps, his Fox network became a legitimate rival to NBC, CBS, and ABC. Its competitiveness was aided by Murdoch's expensive acquisition of stations and affiliates, plus a National Football League television contract in the mid-1990s.

Nevertheless even the wily Murdoch could not arrest the larger tendency of the mass media. At the close of the twentieth century, the mass media had virtually lost their mass. Although Fox's broadcast of the 1999 All-Star Baseball game was the audience ratings leader for the week of July 12, it was the second lowest rated in television history. Each mass medium had to settle for smaller percentages of consumers' time. The newest technology, the Internet, allowed those with personal computers to avoid the established media in favor of new websites and "chat rooms." The trend was liberating – and alienating. Far more than cable, the Internet was dividing the national audience not by class or national interest, but by hobbies and fetishes. For all the failings of journalism and broadcasting in the twentieth century, the new world of privatized media consumption portended a nation of strangers, disengaged from the rites of citizenship and from the company of their neighbors.

REFERENCES

Abrahamson, David (1995) *Magazine-Made America: The Cultural Transformation of the Postwar Periodical*. Cresskill, NJ: Hampton Press.

Adams, Michael C. C. (1994) *The Best War Ever: America and World War II*. Baltimore, Md.: Johns Hopkins University Press.

Adler, Les K. and Paterson, Thomas G. (1970) "Red fascism: the merger of Nazi Germany and Soviet Russia in the American image of totalitarianism, 1930's–1950's," *American Historical Review* 75, pp. 1046–64.

Atherton, Lewis (1954) *Main Street on the Middle Border*. Bloomington: Indiana University Press.

Baldasty, Gerald (1992) *The Commercialization of News in the Nineteenth Century*. Madison: University of Wisconsin Press.

Balio, Tino (1976) *United Artists: The Company Built by the Stars*. Madison: University of Wisconsin Press.

—— (ed.) (1990) *Hollywood in the Age of Television*. Boston: Unwin Hyman.

Barnouw, Erik (1966) *A Tower in Babel: A History of Broadcasting in the United States, to 1933*. New York: Oxford University Press.

—— (1968) *The Golden Web: A History of Broadcasting in the United States, 1933–1953*. New York: Oxford University Press.

—— (1970) *The Image Empire: A History of Broadcasting in the United States, from 1953*. New York: Oxford University Press.

Barth, Gunther (1980) *City People: The Rise of Modern City Culture in Nineteenth-Century America*. New York: Oxford University Press.

Baughman, James L. (1997) *The Republic of Mass Culture: Journalism, Filmmaking, and Broadcasting in America since 1941*, 2nd edn. Baltimore, Md.: Johns Hopkins University Press.

—— (2001) *Henry R. Luce and the Rise of the American News Media*, rev. edn. Baltimore, Md.: Johns Hopkins University Press.

Bernhard, Nancy E. (1999) *US Television News and Cold War Propaganda, 1947–1960*. New York: Cambridge University Press.

Boddy, William F. (1990) *Fifties Television: The Industry and Its Critics*. Urbana: University of Illinois Press.

Bogart, Leo (1982) "Newspapers in transition," *Wilson Quarterly* 6, pp. 58–70.

—— (1985) "How US newspaper content is changing," *Journal of Communication* 35, pp. 82–90.

Boylan, James (1986) "Declarations of independence," *Columbia Journalism Review* 25, pp. 30–45.

Brazil, John (1981) "Murder trials, murder, and twenties America," *American Quarterly* 33, pp. 163–84.

Brinkley, Alan (1982) *Voices of Protest: Huey Long, Father Coughlin, and the Great Depression.* New York: Alfred A. Knopf.

Busterna, John C. (1988) "Trends in daily newspaper ownership," *Journalism Quarterly* 65, pp. 831–8.

Carter, Bill (1997) "The networks lose viewers to cable, again," New York *Times,* May 22, p. B3.

Cohen, Lizabeth (1990) *Making a New Deal: Industrial Workers in Chicago, 1919–1939.* New York: Cambridge University Press.

Craig, Douglas B. (2000) *Fireside Politics: Radio and Political Culture in the United States, 1920–1940.* Baltimore, Md.: Johns Hopkins University Press.

Douglas, Susan J. (1999) *Listening In: Radio and the American Imagination.* New York: Times Books.

Fousek, John (2000) *To Lead the Free World: American Nationalism and the Cultural Roots of the Cold War.* Chapel Hill: University of North Carolina Press.

Fussell, Paul (1989) *Wartime: Understanding and Behavior in the Second World War.* New York: Oxford University Press.

Gamson, Joshua (1994) *Claims to Fame: Celebrity in Contemporary America.* Berkeley: University of California Press.

Gans, Herbert J. (1979) *Deciding What's News: A Study of CBS Evening News, NBC Nightly News,* Newsweek, *and* Time. New York: Pantheon.

Garvey, Ellen Gruber (1996) *The Adman in the Parlor: Magazines and the Gendering of Consumer Culture, 1880s to 1920s.* New York: Oxford University Press.

Griffith, Sally Foreman (1989) *Home Town News: William Allen White and the Emporia* Gazette. New York: Oxford University Press.

Hallin, Daniel C. (1986) *The "Uncensored War": The Media and Vietnam.* New York: Oxford University Press.

—— (1994) *We Keep America on Top of the World: Television Journalism and the Public Sphere.* London: Routledge.

Henry, William A., III (1982) "The decline and fall of the New York *Daily News," Washington Journalism Review* 4, pp. 18, 20, 22–3.

Hilmes, Michele (1990) *Hollywood and Broadcasting: From Radio to Cable.* Urbana: University of Illinois Press.

—— (1997) *Radio Voices: American Broadcasting, 1922–1952.* Minneapolis: University of Minnesota Press.

Honey, Maureen (1984) *Creating Rosie the Riveter: Class, Gender, and Propaganda during World War II.* Amherst: University of Massachusetts Press.

Lazarsfeld, Paul F. and Field, Harry (1946) *The People Look at Radio.* Chapel Hill: University of North Carolina Press.

Leonard, Thomas C. (1986) *The Power of the Press: The Birth of American Political Reporting.* New York: Oxford University Press.

—— (1995) *News for All: America's Coming-of-Age with the Press.* New York: Oxford University Press.

Lippmann, Walter (1922) *Public Opinion.* New York: Macmillan.

Lowenthal, Leo (1979) [1944] "Biographies in popular magazines," in Paul F. Lazarsfeld and Frank N. Stanton (eds.) *Radio Research, 1942–1943.* New York: Arno Press.

McChesney, Robert W. (1993) *Telecommunications, Mass Media, and Democracy: The Battle for the Control of US Broadcasting, 1928–1935.* New York: Oxford University Press.

McGerr, Michael E. (1986) *The Decline of Popular Politics: The American North, 1865–1928.* New York: Oxford University Press.

Newspaper Association of America (1998) "Facts about newspapers 1998" (www.naa.org/info/facts).

Nord, David Paul (1985) "The public community: the urbanization of journalism in Chicago," *Journal of Urban History* 11, pp. 411–41.

Ohmann, Richard M. (1996) *Selling Culture: Magazines, Markets, and Class at the Turn of the Century.* New York: Verso.

Park, Robert E. (1925) "The natural history of the newspaper," in Robert E. Park, Ernest W. Burgess, and Roderick D. McKenzie, *The City.* Chicago: University of Chicago Press.

Paterson, Thomas G. (1979) *On Every Front: The Making of the Cold War.* New York: W. W. Norton.

Roberts, Gene, Kunkel, Thomas, and Layton, Charles (eds.) (2001) *Leaving Readers Behind: The Age of Corporate Newspapering.* Fayetteville: University of Arkansas Press.

Roeder, George H., Jr. (1993) *The Censored War: American Visual Experience During World War II.* New Haven, Conn.: Yale University Press.

Rosen, Philip T. (1980) *The Modern Stentors: Radio Broadcasters and the Federal Government, 1920–1934.* Westport, Conn.: Greenwood Press.

Rosenau, James N. (1963) *National Leadership and Foreign Policy: A Case Study in the Mobilization of Public Support.* Princeton, NJ: Princeton University Press.

Rutenberg, Jim (2000) "Number of debate viewers rises from the first but remains low," *New York Times,* October 19.

Rykken, Rolf (1989) "Readership decline brings newspapers to crossroads," *Presstime* 11, pp. 22–4.

Scanlon, Jennifer (1995) *Inarticulate Longings:* The Ladies' Home Journal, *Gender, and the Promises of Consumer Culture.* New York: Routledge.

Schneirov, Matthew (1994) *The Dream of a New Social Order: Popular Magazines in America, 1893–1914.* New York: Columbia University Press.

Schudson, Michael (1978) *Discovering the News: A Social History of American Newspapers.* New York: Basic Books.

—— (1995) *The Power of News.* Cambridge, Mass.: Harvard University Press.

Smulyan, Susan (1994) *Selling Radio: The Commercialization of American Broadcasting, 1920–1934.* Washington, DC: Smithsonian Institution Press.

Spigel, Lynn (1992) *Make Room for TV: Television and the Family Ideal in Postwar America.* Chicago: University of Chicago Press.

Stedman, Lawrence C., Tinsley, Katherine, and Kaestle, Carl F. (1991) "Literacy as consumer activity," in Carl F. Kaestle et al., *Literacy in the United States: Readers and Reading since 1880.* New Haven, Conn.: Yale University Press.

Stott, William (1973) *Documentary Expression and Thirties America.* New York: Oxford University Press.

Wilson, Harold (1970) McClure's Magazine *and the Muckrakers.* Princeton, NJ: Princeton University Press.

CHAPTER TWENTY-FOUR

Religion

CHARLES H. LIPPY

At the dawn of the twentieth century mainline Protestant denominations, broadly evangelical in their emphasis on personal experience and conversion, dominated American religious life, even though for half a century Roman Catholics had constituted the largest single religious body in the nation. Until World War I disrupted the pattern of over three decades, immigration had been swelling the ranks of Catholicism, Eastern Orthodoxy, and Judaism. By the middle of the twentieth century Protestantism, Catholicism, and Judaism seemed to have become functionally equivalent in providing a socially acceptable religious identity (Herberg 1960). By the twenty-first century a more expansive pluralism had become entrenched, however. Islam, Buddhism, and Hinduism had become commonplace in the nation's cities; and home-grown religions such as the Church of Jesus Christ of Latter-day Saints (the Mormons) were growing faster than any mainline group. What illuminates American religious life in the twentieth century is the changing influence of mainline Protestant demoninations as the basic structure of American religion; a more diffuse pluralism became the norm.

Movements transcending denominational boundaries have remained vital to American religious culture. One dynamic instance has been fundamentalism; another is Pentecostalism. Both were embryonic at the start of the century, when most denominational leaders and theologians dismissed these phenomena as anachronistic. By the end of the century, however, fundamentalism and Pentecostalism represented thriving ideological approaches to worship and religious identity that deeply affected American Christianity. It has also both shaped and been shaped by social forces that may at first seem totally secular. At the very end of the nineteenth century, rapid industrialization and urbanization helped spawn the Social Gospel movement; Social Christianity sought to transform society into the kingdom of God on earth. Cresting in influence when World War I erupted, the Social Gospel fused with progressivism in politics. But world war, global depression, and then another world war shattered the optimism undergirding these political and religious movements. The civil rights movement – the most influential social movement of the century – mattered as much to religion as to every other institution.

Religion harbors an essential dimension that denominations or religious institutions, trans-denominational movements like fundamentalism, and the impact of social currents such as the civil rights movement do not capture. Earlier generations called this more personal side piety, a term assuming negative connotations in the twentieth century. Some students of religion speak of popular religion or popular religiosity to suggest the side of religion that comes from ordinary people, rather than from churches or priests. Other analysts write about lived religion, trying to grasp the ways personal experience is organized into a meaningful whole, often in an eclectic fashion. By the end of the century even the word "religion" to describe these impulses had fallen into disfavor. Religion reflected institutions and creeds, belief systems and doctrine. In its stead was "spirituality," a term devoid of such baggage. Appraising twentieth-century faith requires probing this elusive dimension of religion, whatever label one uses for it.

Scrutinizing religion from these four perspectives and also examining changes within each provide one way to trace the story of American religious life. Denominations and sects highlight the public structures of organized religion, even when undergoing transformation. Trans-denominational movements such as fundamentalism and Pentecostalism (even though both have some denominational expression) accentuate phenomena with a vitality that standard structures cannot contain. Social movements, from civil rights to feminism, show that religion interacts with other forces and never exists apart from the world around it. Spirituality, lived religion, popular religiosity – all lift up that highly personal nature of faith beneath all institutional and social expression.

Other approaches also illuminate the dynamism characteristic of American religion. One might focus on religious thought. Protestant theologian Reinhold Niebuhr, for example, exerted an influence in intellectual circles that went beyond his impact on believers; and Abraham J. Heschel offered some of the most creative Jewish philosophical writing in generations, even as he sought to engage his tradition in social action. Another approach might examine civil religion, those broadly-based constructs existing alongside of denominations, spirituality, and other expressions of religion that endow American history with meaning and address national identity. There are other strategies as well, each with its own questions and interpretations. The range of interpretive approaches itself suggests much about the vigor of religion throughout the past century.

The Structures of American Religion

From the colonial period on, denominational expressions of Protestant Christianity have dominated American religion. In the nineteenth century, thanks to camp meetings and revivals, evangelicalism came to prominence. Some historians have called the nineteenth century "the Methodist century," because of the spectacular growth of that group and its stunning ability to follow Americans wherever they went. When the twentieth century opened, however, only about 12 percent of the US population were church members identified with the mainline Methodists, Baptists, Presbyterians, Lutherans, and Episcopalians. A century later that proportion would drop to around 8.5 percent. Yet Presbyterians and Episcopalians exercised an influence exceeding their numbers, thanks to their prominence in business and government. Lutherans owed their strength primarily to ethnic ties. A century ago the numerous Lutheran bodies reflected cultures of origin more than differences in belief. There were Swedish Lutherans, German Lutherans, Finnish Lutherans, and more. For all the major Protestant bodies, allegiance or affiliation spanned generations; until mid-century, the denominational switching occurring so often after World War II was rare.

The tenacity of denominations early in the century reflected the varied historical circumstances that gave them birth as well as theological differences. In 1900 such distinctions mattered more than in 2000. Infant baptism or believer's baptism for many had a direct bearing on one's eternal destiny. The divisions among Protestants were real. Presbyterians and other groups in the Calvinist heritage asserted that one was chosen by God for salvation. Methodists and other Arminians countered that one had to make a decision to accept the gift of salvation offered by God to all. These debates became less heated – so much so that, by the end of the twentieth century, sociologists portrayed the "changing shape" of mainline denominations (Roof and McKinney 1987), and a powerful case was advanced for a more dramatic "restructuring" of American religion (Wuthnow 1988). Indeed mainline denominational leaders had become virtually obsessed with perceptions of erosion of influence and numerical decline.

To a large extent, social transformations resulting from the impact of World War II were responsible. Geographic mobility soared after the war, as business and industry struggled to incorporate millions of military personnel into the civilian work force. Suburban growth skyrocketed as families sought to establish a place for themselves after the interruption of the war years. The GI Bill allowed hundreds of thousands of veterans to pursue higher education, which was once the virtual monopoly of a social elite. Educational opportunities brought exposure to new ideas, to persons from different social and ethnic backgrounds, and to different religious denominations and beliefs. Marriage across religious lines increased dramatically. While popular culture celebrated the nuclear family, with mothers not employed outside the home, in wartime women had entered the labor force in unprecedented numbers. Some did withdraw from it after the war, but the trend for women to work outside the home continued. Political fears also became pervasive. Communists replaced Nazis and Fascists as the major menace to democracy, and the introduction of "the bomb" sparked anxieties that another global confrontation would lead to the annihilation of humanity itself.

As suburbs grew, denominations established new congregations where members actually lived. Although often accused of abandoning the inner cities where "downtown" churches once featured "princes of the pulpit" whose spellbinding oratory dazzled audiences, the denominations were simply responding to market pressures. Limited resources for expansion fostered a spirit of cooperation rather than competition. The roots of that cooperation among mainline Protestants stretched back to 1908, when the Federal Council of Churches sparked ecumenical endeavors nationwide. The FCC was reorganized in 1950 as the National Council of Churches, prompting formation of cognate bodies on state, regional, and local levels. The most visible symbol of the enthusiasm for cooperation was the Interchurch Center in New York City, built adjacent to the interdenominational Riverside Church and the interfaith Union Theological Seminary. Ecumenical advocates failed to appreciate, however, the extent to which cooperation further eroded distinctions among denominations. As mainline groups began to resemble each other, denominational switching lost its opprobrium.

This homogenizing process crossed boundaries among faith traditions. In 1955 sociologist Will Herberg demonstrated how all three faith traditions functioned equivalently to identify followers as decent citizens. The particular religious label one had mattered less than having a label. He also posited that a more fundamental faith, a secular faith, had penetrated these three faith traditions, so that a religion of the American way of life – oriented around conspicuous consumption – had replaced authentic faith in a transcendent reality (Herberg 1960). Another force challenged the hegemony of denominations and cognate religious institutions. The "baby boom" generation, born in the two decades after World War II, came to maturity in a social climate that fostered short-term commitments more than long-term obligations. Mobility meant that people were less likely to remain in one place long enough for enduring commitments to take hold. The erosion of denominational distinctiveness lessened affective ties to any one faith community. Marriage across religious lines frequently resulted in a family's seeking out a new religious identity different from that of either marriage partner or, increasingly, none at all. Different dimensions of a "free market" religious economy increasingly took hold, as individuals tried one approach for a time and then moved on to another. Dean Hoge and his associates found all of these trends among boomers reared as Presbyterians (Hoge et al. 1994). Indeed the religious odyssey of the baby boomer generation had generated an entirely new spiritual marketplace (Roof 1999).

One response apparent among Protestant bodies was to start congregations offering what the baby boom generation claimed it wanted in a religious group. In the last two decades of the century, this approach gave birth to the "megachurch," which offered countless small groups. Many were based on the twelve-step model first advanced by Alcoholics Anonymous, so that everyone would find something appealing. Often participants developed a greater loyalty to the small group than to the congregation. Many of the megachurches that attracted 10,000 to 15,000 to weekend services counted only a fraction of that number – often not more than 10 or 15 percent – as actual members. The authors of *Habits of the Heart*, a landmark study from the mid-1980s, emphasized the hesitancy of the baby boom generation to make firm commitments of any sort. Robert Bellah's research team had a rather grim forecast for religious institutions, if the reluctance to become committed endured (Bellah et al. 1985).

By the close of the twentieth century individuals were less likely to let religious institutions be the sole determinants of personal religious identity. Roman Catholicism, for example, for centuries insisted that the faithful were obligated to follow the moral teachings of the church. That teaching included a ban on the use of artificial means of birth control, reaffirmed in the papal encyclical *Humanae Vitae* of 1968. Yet devout Catholics were as likely as the non-Catholic population to use contraceptive devices. Believers were thus affirming a Catholic identity on their own terms, not those set by the church. The same held true for virtually all religious institutions. Likewise, congregations themselves reflected the same concerns in terms of their relationships with the larger denominations with which they were affiliated. A century ago denominations had been eager to adapt business models and methods for structuring their bureaucracies. By the end of the twentieth century localism was strident in individual congregations in almost every denomination, though astute students of congregational life still found enough vitality to insist that congregations remained alive and well as the core unit of Christianity.

Patterns in motion by the middle of the twentieth century continued into the opening years of the twenty-first. Americans moved freely among denominations, if they affiliated permanently at all, and refused to allow denominations to control or even define personal religious identity. What made the mix all the more difficult to analyze was the way so many religious currents crossed denominational lines, blurring old distinctions. A reconfiguration in the structures of religious life might well transpire in the twenty-first century.

Movements without Boundaries

The sight of worshipers lifting hands toward heaven in praise, singing choruses with words flashed on screens rather than printed in hymnals, and sometimes bursting into tongues or experiencing seemingly miraculous healing – such versions of faith were increasingly common at the end of the twentieth century. All were rare at its beginning. The surge of Pentecostal and charismatic phenomena across all denominational lines, taking in both Protestant and Catholics, represents one of the key developments in American religious life.

A revival in 1906 in a mission church on Los Angeles's Azusa Street found those attending caught up in ecstatic religious experience, usually manifested in glossolalia or speaking in tongues. Under the powerful preaching of African-American William J. Seymour, this revival marks one strand in the origin of modern Pentecostalism. Earlier, though then less widely publicized, similar experiences transpired in North Carolina, both in the mountains near Camp Creek and in the area around Dunn. Mainline Protestants, who thought reports of tongues and healing represented emotionalism run amok, consigned to the periphery believers who found a vibrant religion in charismatic experience. Pentecostal expression disrupted other cultural patterns. The Azusa Street revival and those following in its wake challenged prevailing patterns of racial separation, since both black and white Christians worshiped together and encountered the same supernatural power together. As Pentecostalism attracted greater interest and formal groups began to emerge, however, embryonic denominations like the Assemblies of God and the Church of God (in Cleveland, Tennessee) tended to be racially separate.

For several decades Pentecostalism remained marginalized. In the 1940s and 1950s, healing revivals revitalized one form of charismatic experience, although individual healers such as Aimee Semple McPherson and Oral Roberts were often regarded with disfavor; and their detractors insisted that healings were rigged. Astute observers recognized that Pentecostalism and its charismatic manifestations had become pivotal to Christianity. In 1958 Henry Pitney Van Dusen, the president of the Union Theological Seminary, dubbed Pentecostalism a "third force," alongside the standard Protestant denominations and Roman Catholicism. That force was about to erupt. In the next year Episcopal rector Dennis Bennett related to his flock in Van Nuys, California that he had received the baptism of the Spirit. Soon reports came from Roman Catholic Duquesne University of prayer groups characterized by glossolalia. Pentecostal experience quickly penetrated Christianity of all types. By the 1970s annual charismatic gatherings were held in cities such as Ann Arbor, Michigan; and schools such as Steubenville University in Ohio were known as centers for Pentecostalism, which had joined the mainstream.

Several features set this later-twentieth-century Pentecostal surge apart from that
rooted in the Azusa Street revivals. While independent charismatic congregations
cropped up, few new denominations formed. Those for whom the gifts of the Spirit
were part of religious life tended to remain within their own religious groups,
operating more as a leaven within rather than breaking away. Catholic charismatics
remained Catholic; Methodist charismatics remained Methodist. Yet persons from
different denominations who shared Pentecostal experience often evidenced a greater
affinity for each other than with non-charismatics from the same denomination.
Boundaries were shattered.

Shortly after the Azusa Street revivals a series of pamphlets called *The Fundamentals* were distributed to most Protestant clergymen in the country; and another
movement that ignored boundaries took its name: fundamentalism. Its heritage
stretches back in theological circles to the later nineteenth century, when professors
at schools such as Princeton Theological Seminary, considering the ramifications of
Darwin's evolutionary theory, feared for the Christian faith. Nor could the challenges
to traditional interpretation of scripture, resulting from use of historical-critical
methods pioneered largely by German theologians, be long ignored. What gave
fundamentalism its prominence, however, was the Scopes "Monkey Trial" in Dayton,
Tennessee in 1925. The trial, intended to challenge a state law prohibiting the
teaching of evolutionary theory in public schools, pitted well-known Democratic
politician and religious conservative William Jennings Bryan against the shrewd
criminal attorney Clarence Darrow, who represented the teacher, John Scopes.
Scopes was convicted. But most onlookers believed that Darrow had succeeded in
making the emergent fundamentalist position – symbolized by Bryan – seem out of
step with modernity.

Fundamentalist inroads in mainline denominations fared little better. Conventional
wisdom makes the South the bastion of fundamentalism. But in the 1920s northern
denominations, especially Presbyterians and Baptists, were at the center of the controversy, as fundamentalists battled so-called modernists for control of denominational bureaucracies and agencies. Fundamentalists generally failed in their
endeavors and, like Pentecostals, found themselves on the fringes of Protestantism.
But a vast network linked fundamentalists together, regardless of denominational
label, paving the way for a resurgence before century's end (Carpenter 1997).

A theological orientation known as premillennial dispensationalism sustained the
formal thinking of fundamentalists. According to this perspective, human history was
divided into seven large time blocks or dispensations, in each of which God had
established a particular mode of revelation or salvation. The present (the church age)
was the sixth and last before the physical return of Christ, who would rule for a
thousand years (the millennium), prior to the final confrontation between good and
evil and the end of time as we know it. This mode of thinking undergirded an edition
of the Bible prepared by C. I. Scofield in 1909; generations of Protestants absorbed
fundamentalist presuppositions through use of this wildly-popular reference edition
of the King James Version. Schools such as the Moody Bible Institute and Dallas
Theological Seminary became centers for training both clergy and lay workers who
espoused a fundamentalist perspective. Publishing firms such as David C. Cook
produced a steady fare of fundamentalist literature for use in Sunday schools and
other local church study programs. Prematurely buried by pundits in the aftermath of

the Scopes Trial, fundamentalism did not die. It moved into a subculture that kept its own institutions and agencies alive and well.

Shortly after the Pentecostal-charismatic renewal blossomed at mid-century fundamentalism likewise experience a significant rebirth. Propelled by such best-selling works as *The Late Great Planet Earth* by Hal Lindsey and Carole C. Carlson (1970) fundamentalism once again became a vital feature of religious life. Within what became the nation's largest Protestant denomination after 1960, the Southern Baptist Convention, a bitter struggle ensued between fundamentalists and moderates for control of denominational machinery in the late 1970s and 1980s. Unlike the conflicts among northern Baptists and Presbyterians half a century earlier, this time fundamentalists reaped success. Within its ranks virtually every Protestant denomination faced a fundamentalist caucus or similar unofficial body emerging. Frequently congregations inclined towards fundamentalist ways attempted to split off. Sometimes new denominational clusters arose. While not strictly fundamentalist, the Presbyterian Church in America owed its genesis to controversies over orthodox and presumably liberal ways among southern Presbyterians in the decade or so prior to the merger of the main northern and southern Presbyterian bodies.

Both Pentecostalism and fundamentalism were manifestations of a broader phenomenon called evangelicalism. Notoriously difficult to define with precision, evangelicalism by the end of the century had become identified with trends toward orthodoxy in theology and a generally conservative posture in articulating the social implications of religious faith. Not every conservative stance wore the label of evangelicalism, however. Yet it almost always denoted an emphasis on some deeply personal, inner religious experience as the springboard for vital faith and a greater certainty about the exact meaning of scripture, especially when applied to social issues such as abortion, feminism, or homosexuality. Evangelicalism penetrated deeply into Protestantism, and more subtly than did Pentecostalism and fundamentalism. Widespread were the proliferation of parachurch movements that by definition were not limited to a particular denomination and the explosion of what in the last two decades of the century was called contemporary Christian worship. Parachurch groups generally targeted a particular audience or interest group. Women's Aglow, for example, brought evangelically and Pentecostally-inclined women together for worship, fellowship, and mutual support. The Full Gospel Business Men's Fellowship International did the same primarily for white-collar males of a Pentecostal bent. The Fellowship of Christian Athletes, Campus Crusade for Christ for college students, Youth for Christ for high schoolers, and InterVarsity Christian Fellowship provide other examples. Various congregations started groups and programs to target single adults, those recently divorced, or those grieving the loss of a spouse or partner. Even if one congregation sponsored such a group, membership generally cut across denominations and faith traditions.

Contemporary Christian worship was more a direct outgrowth of the Pentecostal surge, as it intersected with popular culture, and of the religious counterculture of the 1960s and 1970s. Market research also helped determine which worship style would appeal to the population cohorts who were, according to most surveys, "unchurched." Rock bands and electronic keyboards, for example, replaced pipe organs in contemporary Christian worship. Pop music was part of the lived experience of baby boomers and Generation X; pipe organs were seen as icons of a religious style dismissed as archaic and irrelevant. So, too, with traditional church structures filled with hard-backed pews. Cushioned theater seats to which one might bring a cup of coffee were thought to be more in tune with contemporary mores. Drama sketches and skits supplanted the reading of scripture; seeing rather than just hearing somehow made faith appear more directly related to daily life. Adapting worship to patterns prevalent in the larger culture was historically nothing new. The frontier camp meetings and revivals of the nineteenth century arose as adaptations of traditional religious institutions to prevailing cultural conditions, and hymn writers had for generations set their lyrics to secular tunes. Contemporary Christian worship, as it moved across traditions from Catholic folk masses with guitar accompaniment to evangelical megachurches with rock trios belting out songs praising Jesus, pushed beyond borders and revolutionized what worship meant in America.

The aspect of evangelicalism associated with reclaiming orthodoxy was manifested well beyond American Protestantism. In 1962, when Pope John XXIII inaugurated the church council known as Vatican II, major transformation came to Catholicism. In the United States English replaced Latin as the language of the Mass, the laity assumed some responsibilities along with priests for parish programs, scholars left behind a centuries-old commitment to Thomistic thought, and countless individuals began making moral decisions for themselves without the sanction of the church. As such changes took hold, the numbers of those taking religious vocations as priests and nuns dropped drastically. The severe shortage of professional leadership was exacerbated by the loss of thousands who relinquished their orders for life in the secular world. Some saw the shifts as marking a Protestantizing of Catholicism, and others regretted the transformations. By the end of the twentieth century calls for a renewed orthodoxy were coming from the top ranks of Catholic leaders. Occasionally the Latin Mass could be heard. In innumerable local communities Catholics worked to limit abortion rights because of the moral teaching of the church. At the same time Catholics had to deal with a steady presence of charismatics who remained devoted to the faith but who found in ecstatic experiences like glossolalia vivid signs of spiritual power. By the end of the century Catholicism struggled to accommodate yet other ways of expressing the faith, as the proportion of Hispanic Americans mushroomed. Catholicism was thus subject to the same pressures that lowered barriers among Protestant denominations.

The Impact of Social Forces

Social currents that at first glance seem wholly secular had a profound impact on religion. Over the course of the century immigration may well be the most significant. Already the largest single religious group in the nation by the mid-nineteenth century, Roman Catholics came by the millions from southern, central, and eastern Europe between the Civil War and World War I. That same wave of immigration also implanted Judaism more firmly in the United States, and also assured the survival of various strands of Eastern Orthodox Christianity.

At the end of the twentieth century immigration patterns had changed dramatically. After World War I Congress set quotas on immigration, which favored immigration from areas in northern and western Europe that were overwhelmingly Protestant. Immigration from parts of Asia remained subject to severe limits as well. But by the mid-1960s congressional legislation facilitated greater immigration from South America, the Middle East, and Asia than ever before. In the last third of the century new Americans who brought with them their Hinduism, Islam, and Buddhism exceeded the total number of immigrants of those religious backgrounds prior to that time, and thus altered the character of religious pluralism in the United States.

In the early part of the twentieth century the massive numbers of arrivals brought an extraordinary boom to Catholic institutions. New churches had to be built. The parochial school system blossomed not only because of the distinctly Protestant (if not anti-Catholic) flavor of the public schools, but also because schools attached to a particular parish could celebrate the ethnic heritage of the immigrant community there, and could help mediate the transition into a new cultural setting. So rapid was the growth of Catholicism in the last decades of the nineteenth century that in 1908 church authorities in Rome ended the missionary status of the church in the United States, despite abiding concerns that a democratic environment pervaded by Protestant influence might not be a viable context for Catholicism. During World War I Protestant suspicion of Catholicism began to wane, as the church mustered support for the cause through the National Catholic War Conference. A potent, residual anti-Catholicism surfaced in the 1928 presidential campaign, when the Democratic Party nominated the first Catholic for President, New York Governor Alfred E. Smith. He lost. A generation later, when another Roman Catholic Democratic nominee, John F. Kennedy, was elected, analysts believed that anti-Catholic sentiment had finally dissipated.

The ethnic pluralism of American Catholicism continued to influence the practice of the faith. Thanks to earlier immigration, Irish Americans dominated the ranks of the priesthood and hierarchy. But individual parishes often took on a special cast that reflected the ethnic origins of congregants. For example, parishes serving a primarily Italian-American constituency included celebrations that evoked the village festivals of Italy and often served as the symbol of an ethnic identity long after the neighborhood around the parish changed. An Italian-American parish in East Harlem remained the center for Italian cultural and religious festivals. Hundreds came from suburbs and other parts of the city to join in the celebration, thanks to family and ethnic ties to the parish (Orsi 1985).

The impact of immigration on the shape of Judaism differed somewhat. For centuries European Jews had suffered political disabilities and often outright persecution because of their religious faith. Jews committed to observing law and practice would inevitably stand out in a society dominated by Christianity, because synagogue services were held on the Sabbath (from sundown Friday to sundown Saturday) rather than on Sunday and because of adherence to a kosher diet. This public dimension of Jewish identification was also evident when men wore the *yarmulke* (skullcap). Legally, however, thanks to the First Amendment to the US Constitution, such disabilities did not exist in the United States, though anti-Semitism did.

Most Jewish immigrants in the nineteenth century had come from German-speaking central Europe, and transplanted and adapted Reform Judaism. Eager to avoid overt discrimination because of their religious identity and aware that some aspects of practice reflected ancient cultural ways and therefore might not be compatible with rationality, Reform Judaism encouraged assimilation into American culture. The kosher diet, for example, was widely ignored. Prayer books for use in synagogues were printed in English as well as Hebrew. Rabbis took on a role akin to that of the minister or priest rather than that of a teacher of Torah. Reform Jews thus adapted both faith and practice to absorb the culture dominated by Protestantism.

The Jewish identity of those who came to American shores between 1880 and the outbreak of World War I was quite different. For hundreds of thousands, being Jewish wedded aspects of eastern European agrarian folk culture with biblical precept. Some were aghast at Reform, convinced that the essence of Judaism was irrevocably compromised. Intent on adhering more strictly to tradition, many who shunned Reform finally set up their own institutions as Orthodox Jews. Others believed that some adaptation was unavoidable to preserve Jewish life in a new environment, but felt that Reform had gone too far. They formed the nucleus of what became known as Conservative Judaism, because they wanted to conserve the essentials of the tradition but leave to individual choice what was not integral. By mid-century Conservative Judaism became the largest strand of the tradition in the United States. Other Jews began to see their religion more as an ethical heritage or a style of civilization bereft of supernaturalism. Under the leadership of Mordecai Kaplan, they formed the core of Reconstructionism. Of course some imbibed the freedom that was thought a hall-mark of American culture and abandoned religious practice altogether, although many frequently retained some of the cultural trappings of Jewish life.

Hence, by the 1930s, Judaism had developed something like the denominations that marked Protestantism. Sharing some features in common, all the various strands had their unique emphases or their own understanding of what was integral to Jewish identity and faith. Some mirrored Protestant understandings of religious groups, as the architecture of temples and synagogues sometimes even resembled Christian churches. Perhaps because of the history of persecution in Europe, Jewish immigrants – from the most Orthodox to the Reconstructionist – wanted to gain acceptance and chose to do so by allowing the dominant Protestantism to define which structures were appropriate and, in some cases, which practices were emphasized.

Immigration patterns in the last third of the century had a rather different impact. The primary change within Catholicism came with the increasing Hispanic presence, whether along the borders with Mexico, or in states such as Florida where Cuban immigrants had flocked when Fidel Castro came to power in 1959, or finally in every city where Puerto Ricans and immigrants from across Latin America settled. Hispanic-American Catholicism developed its own history and style. Centuries of Catholic ways fused with the traditions of the indigenous peoples conquered by the Spaniards and with ways of being religious brought by other Europeans and Africans who found their home in Latin America. The Hispanic-American worship style was sometimes more exuberant. It could also reflect an amalgamation of pre-Christian modes with rituals of the Spanish and Portuguese conquerors of the sixteenth century. By the end of the twentieth century Catholic parishes were offering Sunday Mass in Spanish as well as in English; and new Catholic immigrant communities – perhaps most con-spicuously in Miami – were also creating their own shrines to help sustain an ethnic heritage (Tweed 1997).

For immigrants coming from Asia and the Near East, the construction of religious institutions and the preservation of their native traditions became paramount. So Hindu temples, Muslim mosques, and Buddhist meditation and retreat centers were formed not only in the large cities that had been the points of entry for earlier generations of immigrants, but also in every region of the nation. Even in the South, widely perceived to be a bastion of conservative Protestantism, cities boasted a Hindu temple and often more than one mosque. A large Buddhist retreat center was nestled in the mountains just outside Asheville, North Carolina.

Those who planted these traditions on American soil had rather different attitudes about how to fulfill such obligations than had earlier immigrants. The contrast with Judaism at the start of the twentieth century is instructive. If Jewish immigrants sought to fit into the religious culture around them by modelling their own institutions and even their practices after the dominant Protestant denominations, the new immigrants at the end of the century no longer felt the need to mimic what existed around them. Immigrants from India unapologetically built Hindu temples and celebrated Hindu festivals, often bringing priests from India to oversee temple operations. Muslims held prayer services on Fridays, rarely if ever considering a change to Sunday, and thus ignored the Protestant norms fixed a century earlier.

To be sure there were some moves at adaptation, as well as some efforts to gain Euro-American or African-American adherents. After the World's Parliament of Religions, held in Chicago in 1893, some Hindu spokesmen had remained in the United States, seeking to promote a modified Hinduism. They favored adaptation. The Vedanta Society, for example, long operated primarily as a lecture agency and offered little at all by way of Hindu religious practice. Such practice would presumably not appeal to Americans. When the San Francisco Zen Center began operations in 1959, benefiting from the interest in Zen of beat writers like Jack Kerouac, the traditional Japanese meditation schedule had to be modified to accommodate American mores. Perhaps the most obvious sign of adaptation came in the 1960s, when practitioners of Transcendental Meditation abandoned meditation halls and sitting for hours at a time. TM adherents meditated while riding the subway or during a fifteen-minute break at work. TM aimed to attract an American following more than to provide religious expression primarily for persons of Asian descent.

Among the earliest signs that Asian religious expressions could maintain their integrity came with the International Society for Krishna Consciousness (Hare Krishna). It insisted that converts wear traditional Indian garb, take up a vegetarian diet, chant in Sanskrit, and even take a Sanskrit name. The attraction was more than a countercultural fascination with Asia during the Vietnam War. Krishna Consciousness based much of its teaching and practice on authentic Hindu modes of religiosity. Most adherents were converts rather than Asian Americans of Hindu background, proving that a religious style close to authentic Asian practice could take root in the United States.

In the twentieth century Islam has had an equally rich, if somewhat divergent, history. The number of practicing Muslims coming to the United States to study, to engage in business, or to remain permanently has skyrocketed in the last few decades (Haddad and Smith 1994). Attracting a few converts, Islam at the dawn of the twenty-first century may number more adherents than America's traditional "third faith," Judaism. If there are not now more American Muslims than American Jews, then there will be by 2025.

Next to immigration, the social factor most affecting religious life in the twentieth century has been the civil rights movement. In 1955, when black bus riders in

Montgomery, Alabama, began their prolonged boycott to protest segregated seating, the Reverend Martin Luther King, Jr., emerged as the leader of a massive social movement and dominated it until his assassination in 1968. A master of African-American preaching style, King drew on powerful biblical analogies to articulate his vision of a nation rid of distinctions – *de jure* and *de facto* – based on race. He combined the technique of nonviolent resistance advocated earlier in the century by Mahatma Gandhi in India's struggle for independence with aggressive action to promote social justice. King's understanding of justice derived from the prophets of ancient Israel and from the ethical teachings of Jesus.

King knew that black churches had long been incubators of leadership for a people legally excluded from participation in the larger society in many states. From the days of slavery, when the "invisible institution" sustained a lively hope of freedom, through the emergence of independent African-American denominations in the early nineteenth century, to the creative adaptation of southern rural ways in the storefronts of northern cities during the age of the Great Migration, black religion and its institutions were always more than merely places for worship. As the center of the black community, the church fostered a sense of identity and pride among a people whom racism had forced to the margins. It was natural that the churches provided not only the leadership of the civil rights movement, but also the thousands of ordinary men and women who engaged in sit-ins, marches, and other peaceful demonstrations.

By the mid-1960s, however, some African Americans felt that King was too moderate and that the Christianity he espoused too much a mirror of a white religion of oppression. The Nation of Islam called for a rejection of Christianity altogether. King himself offered a rejoinder, arguing that, while buttressing slavery and racism, Christianity had also offered the promise of liberation through suffering. Black theologians such as James Cone interpreted the black experience of suffering as the key to restoring all of Christianity to its authentic base.

From the civil rights movement came a renewed sense of pride in the African heritage. It was a short step from black pride to ethnic pride movements of all sorts. Noteworthy were efforts to rekindle the tribal religiosity that has sustained generations of Native Americans, but that had been brutally crushed as the United States extended its conquest from ocean to ocean. Ideas of liberation were connected with cognate movements among Latin American Catholics, who were engaged in their own quest for economic and social justice in an environment that too often allied the church and tyrannical regimes against the masses. In the United States women soon recognized that a liberation theological perspective directly applied to their exclusion not only from positions of leadership in business and government, but also from positions of leadership in the churches and other religious bodies. The United Methodist Church's predecessor body had sanctioned the ordination of women to the professional ministry as early as 1956. But few religious groups ordained women until feminists called for the inclusion of women at all levels of religious leadership. Just as the civil rights movement had generated a black theology that emerged from the lived experience of African Americans, the women's movement that crested in the 1970s and 1980s stimulated a feminist theology that resounded among all faiths.

These movements of pride and liberation brought controversy in the religious sphere as well as in society at large. But none was as rancorous in the religious realm as the demands of gay, lesbian, bisexual, and transgendered Americans for full acceptance – and the response to such appeals. At the dawn of the twenty-first century virtually every religious body was debating not only whether homosexuality was compatible with religious doctrine, but also whether to admit practicing homosexuals into the ranks of the clergy, and whether justice demanded sanctioning of same-gender relationships on a par with heterosexual marriage.

Countless other social issues and movements in the twentieth century had ramifications for religious life. The national experiment with Prohibition would never have occurred had not leaders in several Protestant denominations endorsed total abstinence enforced by law. The Red Scare after World War I, and then the fear of the Soviet Union for over four decades after World War II, received much grass-roots support because religious institutions identified Communism with supernatural powers of evil. Yet however much religious currents reflected passions coursing through the larger culture, individuals continued to draw on their own private sets of beliefs and practices to give meaning to their personal lives.

Popular Religion or Lived Religion

Students of American religious life have understood that, alongside the religious institutions and the public apparatus of religion, run more vital currents that actually do the work usually assigned to religion. This religiosity gave the masses some sense of direction in their lives, by endowing the vagaries of daily experience with some overarching purpose. Springing directly from the people and their experience, rather than from the denominations and their leaders, this has been called "popular religion." More recently, scholars have labelled this stratum "lived" religion, because it reflects how people go about the business of life. Regardless of definitional nuance, however, lived religion has taken many cues from the popular culture that shapes the perceptions of all Americans, whether or not they have any formal religious affiliation or identification.

Three arenas where this popular or lived religion comes to the fore must suffice to illustrate its significance: the impact of communications media such as radio and television; the continuing heritage of revivalism; and the recovery of pre-industrial ways of being religious in New Age movements, wicca, and cognate endeavors.

When commercial radio invaded the daily lives of millions in the 1920s, religious broadcasting was part of its story. The same held for the rise of television as a medium of popular entertainment in the 1950s. While both media initially favored the dominant Protestant traditions, as networks sought programming assistance from the Federal Council of Churches and then the National Council of Churches, few regular religious programs trumpeted the particular denominations in the background. From the start those willing to buy air time could generate their own programs. In the late 1930s and early 1940s, for instance, evangelist Charles E. Fuller's *Old Fashioned Revival Hour* garnered the largest audience of any program on commercial radio. Few listeners knew Fuller's denominational affiliation; he was first a Presbyterian and then an independent Baptist. What mattered was that he spoke with authority and conviction in such a way that listeners looked to his preaching to guide them in their own lives.

The same held with the only religious personality to win an Emmy award. On his television program, *Life Is Worth Living*, Roman Catholic Bishop Fulton J. Sheen appeared in clerical garb. But his homespun approach and the practical nature of the television dramas seemed to capture eternal truths, rather than specifically Catholic doctrines. When religious telecasts combined preaching with entertainment, as with the wildly popular *PTL Club* of the 1970s and 1980s, few viewers cared about the religious background – which was Assemblies of God – of Jim Bakker and his then-wife, Tammy Faye. Televangelists offered an indefinable access to spiritual power that resonated with millions. Ordinary men and women took the religious cues offered, perhaps combining them with doctrines and creeds of one of the denominations or faith traditions, and then molded them all into an idiosyncratic worldview that allowed them to give their lives some coherence. Lived religion or popular religion may thus have become more vital than formal membership in any religious body.

In the 1950s pundits spoke of a national revival of religion, as Americans were adjusting to a peacetime threat of imminent global conflict. Among the public personalities who symbolized this revival of religion were Norman Vincent Peale and Billy Graham. Peale influenced millions through his best-selling *The Power of Positive Thinking* (1952), which combined psychological precepts with religious ideas in a triumphant formula that anyone could use in seeking happiness and success. The monthly magazine associated with Peale's ministry, *Guideposts*, intentionally cut across faith traditions to offer examples of Protestants, Catholics, Jews, and even the unaffiliated. A particular religious label was unnecessary.

Graham became the premier revivalist of the second half of the twentieth century. He consistently made lists of the "most admired Americans" while perpetuating an American heritage stretching back at least to the mid-eighteenth century. He was a Southern Baptist. But in launching a crusade or revival, Graham insisted on support from congregations across the religious spectrum and often garnered endorsements from prominent political officials. Never did he impose tests of religious affiliation or membership. On the platform at crusades could be found Catholics sitting next to Methodists – signalling not only that any label was functionally equivalent to any other, but even more that individuals could find meaning in their own personal mix of beliefs and practices. Graham was unapologetically Christian. But he offered a spirituality that could be adapted to individual needs. Lived religion, not denominational or institutional religion, was primary.

The various liberation movements of the last third of the twentieth century unwittingly enriched countless strains of popular religion. Women, for example, who felt excluded or marginalized by male-dominated religious communities began to look not only to experiences unique to women to give meaning to their lives, but also to some pre-Christian fertility expressions and to wicca for components in building a personal religious worldview that might give meaning to their lives. Female and male baby boomers, who saw the standard religious institutions buttressing racism and an increasingly rusty morality, began to define themselves as spiritual rather than religious. The latter term was too associated with arid institutions to breathe vitality into personal life. Many dabbled with what became called New Age spirituality, frequently combining a highly personal style with aspects of traditional religion to create an eclectic spirituality. One might attend a Christian church, but practice some form of Buddhist meditation in the confines of one's home, before an altar adorned with crystals, candles, and incense. As the cultural climate weakened taboos against interfaith marriage, families drew on multiple religious heritages that each brought into the family, sampled some others, and crafted a personal religious style that defied easy categorization. The penchant for self-help that marked the last quarter of the century produced thousands of books and guides that individuals could use in carving a personal, idiosyncratic way of being religious. To be sure not all abandoned traditional institutions, which remained sources for propelling and sustaining lived religion. But their monopoly was broken.

In the midst of this increasingly pluralistic and elusive spiritual environment, however, Americans by measurable standards remained extraordinarily religious. For roughly two-thirds of the century, pollsters had sampled the population to ascertain which religious beliefs Americans espoused, whether they belonged to religious institutions or attended religious services with any regularity, and whether they believed that religion was an important influence in common life. Consistently upwards of 95 percent of the population claimed belief in God, virtually the highest proportion of any nation. Although there was some variance, for most of the century nearly 60 percent claimed membership in a religious group; and around half the population reported attending religious services on a regular basis. Membership and statistics reported by organized religious groups, however, suggested that the actual figures were much lower. Even so, more Americans joined religious groups and attended religious services on a regular basis than in any other western nation. Statistics cannot of course adequately measure the religiosity, for example, of Jews for whom home- and family-centered religious observance has always been more vital than praying in a synagogue. Nor can percentages probe the spirituality entailed in crafting an eclectic, personal approach that does not associate itself with any one religious tradition.

When the twentieth century was born, religion was dominated by Protestant denominations and institutions. By the end of the century, religion was far more diffuse, harder to categorize, but thriving both in institutions that were changing to meet the times and in the very personal, eclectic lived religion of the people who made up the American nation.

REFERENCES AND FURTHER READING

Bellah, Robert N., Sullivan, William M., Swidler, Ann, and Tipton, Steven M. (1985) *Habits of the Heart: Individualism and Commitment in American Life.* Berkeley: University of California Press.

Carpenter, Joel A. (1997) *Revive Us Again: The Reawakening of American Fundamentalism.* New York: Oxford University Press.

Conser, Walter H., Jr. and Twiss, Sumner B. (eds.) (1997) *Religious Diversity and American Religious History: Studies in Traditions and Cultures.* Athens: University of Georgia Press.

Eck, Diana L. (2001) *A New Religious America: How a "Christian Country" Has Become the World's Most Religiously Diverse Nation.* San Francisco: HarperSanFrancisco.

Ellwood, Robert S. (1997) *The Fifties Spiritual Marketplace: American Religion in a Decade of Conflict.* New Brunswick, NJ: Rutgers University Press.

Ellwood, Robert S. and Partin, Harry B. (1988) *Religious and Spiritual Groups in Modern America,* 2nd edn. Englewood Cliffs, NJ: Prentice-Hall.

Gallup, George H., Jr. (1996) *Religion in America 1996*. Princeton, NJ: Princeton Religion Research Center.

Gallup, George H., Jr. and Castelli, Jim (1989) *The People's Religion: American Faith in the 90's*. New York: Macmillan.

Haddad, Yvonne Yazbeck and Smith, Jane Idleman (eds.) (1994) *Muslim Communities in North America*. Albany: State University of New York Press.

Herberg, Will (1960) *Protestant, Catholic, Jew: An Essay in American Religious Sociology*, rev. edn. Garden City, NY: Doubleday.

Hoge, Dean R., Johnson, Benton, and Luidens, Donald A. (1994) *Vanishing Boundaries: The Religion of Mainline Protestant Baby Boomers*. Louisville, Ky.: Westminster/John Knox Press.

Hudnut-Beumler, James (1994) *Looking for God in the Suburbs: The Religion of the American Dream and its Critics, 1945–1965*. New Brunswick, NJ: Rutgers University Press.

Krapohl, Robert H. and Lippy, Charles H. (1999) *The Evangelicals: A Historical, Thematic, and Biographical Guide*. Westport, Conn.: Greenwood Press.

Lippy, Charles H. (ed.) (1989) *Twentieth Century Shapers of American Popular Religion*. Westport, Conn.: Greenwood Press.

—— (2000) *Pluralism Comes of Age: American Religious Culture in the Twentieth Century*. Armonk, NY: M. E. Sharpe.

Marty, Martin. *Modern American Religion*. Vol. 1: *The Irony of It All, 1893–1919* (1986). Vol. 2: *The Noise of Conflict, 1919–1941* (1991). Vol. 3: *Under God, Indivisible, 1941–1960* (1996). Chicago: University of Chicago Press.

Massa, Mark (1999) *Catholics and American Culture: Fulton Sheen, Dorothy Day, and the Notre Dame Football Team*. New York: Crossroad.

Moore, R. Laurence (1994) *Selling God: American Religion in the Marketplace of Culture*. New York: Oxford University Press.

Neusner, Jacob (ed.) (1999) *World Religions in America: An Introduction*, 2nd edn. Louisville, Ky.: Westminster/John Knox.

Orsi, Robert A. (1985) *The Madonna of 115th Street: Faith and Community in Italian Harlem, 1880–1950*. New Haven, Conn.: Yale University Press.

—— (1996) *Thank You, St. Jude: Women's Devotion to the Patron Saint of Hopeless Causes*. New Haven, Conn.: Yale University Press.

Porterfield, Amanda (2001) *The Transformation of American Religion: The Story of a Late Twentieth Century Awakening*. New York: Oxford University Press.

Robbins, Thomas and Anthony, Dick (eds.) (1991) *In Gods We Trust: New Patterns of Religious Pluralism in America*. New Brunswick, NJ: Transaction.

Roof, Wade Clark (ed.) (1993) *Religion in the Nineties*. Annals of the American Academy of Political and Social Science, 527. Newbury Park, Calif.: Sage.

—— (1994) *A Generation of Seekers: The Spiritual Journeys of the Baby Boom Generation*. San Francisco: HarperSanFrancisco.

—— (1999) *Spiritual Marketplace: Baby Boomers and the Remaking of American Religion*. Princeton, NJ: Princeton University Press.

Roof, Wade Clark and McKinney, William (1987) *American Mainline Religion: Its Changing Shape and Future*. New Brunswick, NJ: Rutgers University Press.

Scanzoni, Letha Dawson and Hardesty, Nancy A. (1992) *All We're Meant to Be: Biblical Feminism for Today*, 3rd edn. Grand Rapids, Mich.: Eerdmans.

Scanzoni, Letha Dawson and Mollenkott, Virginia Ramey (1994) *Is the Homosexual My Neighbor? A Positive Christian Response*, rev. edn. San Francisco: HarperSanFrancisco.

Schneider, Herbert Wallace (1969) *Religion in 20th Century America*, rev. edn. New York: Atheneum.

Smith, Jane I. (1999) *Islam in America*. New York: Columbia University Press.

Tweed, Thomas A. (1997) *Our Lady of the Exile: Diasporic Religion at a Cuban Catholic Shrine in Miami.* New York: Oxford University Press.

Williams, Peter W. (ed.) (1999) *Perspectives on American Religion and Culture.* Oxford: Blackwell.

Williams, Raymond Brady (1988) *Religions of Immigrants from India and Pakistan: New Threads in the American Tapestry.* New York: Cambridge University Press.

Wuthnow, Robert (1988) *The Restructuring of American Religion: Society and Faith since World War II.* Princeton, NJ: Princeton University Press.

—— (1999) *After Heaven: Spirituality in America since the 1950s.* Berkeley: University of California Press.

CHAPTER TWENTY-FIVE

Ideas

WILFRED M. MCCLAY

Do Ideas Matter?

In his classic study, *Childhood and Society*, the psychologist Erik H. Erikson observed: "Whatever one may come to consider a truly American trait can be shown to have its equally characteristic opposite" (1950: 285). The observation has a certain plausibility, even though a similar ambivalence can be found in many national cultures, traceable to a variety of causes. Yet Erikson insisted that this bipolarity was especially pronounced in the modern American instance. In none of the other great nations of the world, he believed, were inhabitants subjected to more extreme contrasts than in the United States. The tensions between individualism and conformity, internationalism and isolationism, open-mindedness and closed-mindedness, cosmopolitanism and xenophobia, for example, have nowhere been as powerfully felt, he contended, as in America.

Such sweeping generalizations about "national character," American or otherwise, have come to be regarded as artifacts of the 1950s, and have long since passed out of favor, superseded by doctrines that emphasize pluralism and social heterogeneity, and stress the artificiality and "inventedness" of the modern nation-state. That trend is, in itself, representative of one of the central intellectual developments of the century. But there is plenty of evidence for the cogency of Erikson's dictum. Nowhere is it illustrated more vividly than in the paradoxical role of ideas in American culture. One can make an equally plausible case that ideas are both nowhere and everywhere; that they have played a uniquely insignificant role in American life, or a uniquely commanding one. Depending upon whom one asks, ideas are either among the least important, or among the most important, factors in the shaping of America. Which is why the status of ideas is one of the more intriguing puzzles of US history.

So which of the two assertions is the more accurate? At first blush, one would have to concede that the former proposition has had many more advocates. In that familiar view, Americans have generally been seen as a relentlessly action-oriented people, constituents of a thoroughgoing business civilization, a culture that respects knowledge only insofar as it can be shown to have immediately practical applications and commercial utility. This position can call upon a steady procession of distinguished witnesses to testify on its behalf. Alexis de Tocqueville gave voice to this theme early on in the nineteenth century. He remarked that, to the extent that Americans engaged in the cultivation of science, literature, and the arts, they invariably did so in the spirit of *usefulness*, not out of any high regard for the dignity of thought itself. Such an observation presaged what would become the consistent complaint of intellectuals from Walt Whitman to Matthew Arnold to Sinclair Lewis to George Steiner, modified now and then to fit then-current circumstances, but always adding up to the same general message: America was a hopelessly philistine society, interested only in the arts of self-aggrandizement and enhanced material well-being, reflexively anti-intellectual, utterly lacking in the resources needed to support the high and disinterested curiosity that is the stuff of genuine cultural achievement.

A variation on this theme, also staked out early on by Tocqueville, was that America had the historical distinction of embodying a fresh and distinctive theory of man and government, even though its citizenry couldn't even begin to articulate what that theory was. Tocqueville claimed that there was no country in the civilized world where less attention was paid to philosophy – and yet Americans seemed to be uniformly and enthusiastically committed to a particular, and very modern, philosophical method. Their country, he quipped, was the place where the precepts of Descartes are least studied and best applied. Yet the range of ideological possibilities in America was remarkably narrow, with comparatively little space between the supposed opposites of "left" and "right," and relatively little deviation from fundamental liberal principles. Therefore the very notion of lively intellectual debate, as a process of public wrangling over alternative ideas about the political and social order and the public good, tended to be tacitly regarded as anathema, even dangerous.

In 1953 the historian Daniel Boorstin even went so far as to argue that the absence of debates over American political theory was one of the nation's chief *virtues*. The unpremeditated "givenness" of American political institutions constituted for him "the genius of American politics," defining the difference between the placid stability of American politics and the ideology-ridden horrors that had so recently erupted in European politics. "Our national well-being," Boorstin contended, is "in inverse proportion to the sharpness and extent of [our] theoretical differences" (1953: 3). Such a breathtaking statement formulates on a national scale the powerful, if largely informal, American social taboo against discussing either religion or politics in public. One can even concede that such a taboo makes for a considerable measure of social peace. But it would be hard to imagine a deeper devaluation of the role of ideas.

Small wonder that Boorstin became one of the principal exponents of the "consensus" view of American history. They argued that there was a rough but stable ideological homogeneity encompassing nearly all the American people, built upon the cultural and economic premises of liberal capitalism. Contemporaries of Boorstin who were associated with the consensus view, such as Hofstadter and the political scientist Louis Hartz, took a far less positive view of this alleged homogeneity. Yes, they sighed, Americans all thought the same way, and more's the pity. But they did not challenge its basic outlines. Nor, for that matter, was there much fundamental disagreement to be found in the writings of the consensus theorists' immediate predecessors, such as Vernon Louis Parrington, Charles Beard, and Frederick Jackson Turner. Although all of these scholars saw conflict rather than consensus as the most salient characteristic of American history, they conceived the conflict as primarily one between rival material interests, a struggle in which ideas played, at best, a supporting or derivative role.

There is thus a well-established tradition that intellectuals and non-intellectuals shared, which holds that ideas have been largely irrelevant to the nation's practical concerns, and therefore tangential to the real business of American life. Such a belief has frequently been entwined in the perpetually tension-ridden relationship between America and Europe. After all, such tensions were integral to the way America defined itself from the very start. The contrast between America and Europe, it was thought, was the contrast between youth and age, novelty versus venerability, innocence versus experience, naturalness versus artificiality, purity versus corruption, guilelessness versus sophistication. "Nature" played an especially important part in equalizing the imbalance between the two, since whatever America lacked in illustrious precedents or historical weight and groundedness, it could more than make up with the claim to be more "natural."

However distinct it may have wanted to be, however, American intellectual culture was from the start an extension of Europe's, linked to European evaluative standards. Hence that culture should be understood, at least in its early history, as an "American province," to use historian David Hollinger's apt term, with all the ambivalence such a term implies about Americans' sense of connection with, separation from, and competition with, Europe. America was a province, in the sense that its best and brightest minds yearned to be found worthy by the metropolitan arbiters of taste and sensibility. Their ultimate validation came not from Boston or New York, but from London or Paris. Yet this also was a province that yearned to breathe freely and independently, and resented the cultural subordination in which it found itself becalmed, long after political independence had been achieved.

The Dawn of the Century

At the birth of the twentieth century, intellectuals complained that the emergence of an authentic, non-imported, indigenous American culture was being blocked by the smothering influence of staid, artificial, European-derived Anglo-Victorian notions of high culture. Such slavish imitation of the mother continent bespoke cultural immaturity, they thought, and a lack of intellectual self-confidence and vigor. One of the most influential statements of this theme came from the Spanish-born American philosopher George Santayana, whose 1911 lecture entitled "The genteel tradition in American philosophy" not only bequeathed to subsequent observers an indispensable term of analysis – "the genteel tradition" – to describe what was wrong with American art and expression, but also contributed a far-reaching diagnosis of the underlying fault line in American culture (1967). What Stanley Coben called "the rebellion against Victorianism" was one of the principal ways that American intellectuals responded to Santayana's critique (Coben 1991). That rebellion would turn out to be one of the enduring organizing principles of twentieth-century intellectual activity, particularly in the realms of arts and letters. It is an *idée fixe* so durable that it survives even when there would seem to be precious few remnants of Victorian gentility left to resist.

According to Santayana, intellectual life was split in two. "One-half of the American mind," he asserted, the part that was "not occupied intensely in practical affairs," has remained "becalmed," floating "gently in the backwater" of American life – prim, polite, refined, and irrelevant. Meanwhile, at the very same time, the other half of the mind, that part concerned with material innovation, "was leaping down a sort of Niagara Rapids," surging ahead of the entire world "in invention and industry and social organization." The division was between what was inherited and what was native-born, between the legacy of Europe and the immediacy of America, or, in Santayana's words, between "the beliefs and standards of the fathers" and "the instincts, practices, and discoveries of the younger generation" (Hollinger and Capper 2001: 94). That division could be neatly symbolized in architectural terms: the former was like a reproduction of a colonial mansion, while the latter was like a modern skyscraper. The former represented the artificial, derivative, moralistic, and feeble world of genteel Victorian "culture": what passed for intellectual and artistic achievement in the American province. The latter represented the authentic, if somewhat callow, vitality of a young, prosperous, and enterprising industrial America. "The American Will inhabits the sky-scraper," he continued, while "the American Intellect inhabits the colonial mansion . . . The one is all aggressive enterprise, the other is all genteel tradition" (p. 95). Each needed, but lacked, the corrective of the other, and so both were diminished as a consequence. No wonder the realm of ideas was so unsatisfactory in America, given its lack of nourishment from all the vital streams of the nation's life.

Santayana's brilliant analysis of the national antithesis was further elaborated and popularized in literary critic Van Wyck Brooks's influential manifesto, *America's Coming-of-Age* (1915). Brooks saw the American mind split across the brow, riven between Highbrows and Lowbrows, between transcendent theory and "catchpenny realities," between "academic pedantry and pavement slang," between the pipe-dream of professors and the banal rhetoric of a William Jennings Bryan (Sprague 1993: 82–3). The literary Highbrows issued forth works of fastidious refinement and aloofness, too prissy to have any salutary influence on the coarse and unkempt Lowbrows. Yet the Lowbrow culture, for all its vitality, was too vulgar and business-oriented to accommodate serious criticism or disinterested reflection. Between the two, Brooks lamented, "there is no community, no genial middle ground" (Sprague 1993: 83).

Like Santayana, Brooks blamed this state of affairs on the early influence of Puritanism, less because of its specific tenets than because it forced upon early America an elaborate imported theology that was too arcane to address the real problems of men and women struggling to build a civilization in the wilderness. As a consequence, a parallel track of Yankee practicality developed, one that had nothing to do with the theological track deriving from Calvinism, and that was largely unleavened by more advanced thinking. The two sets of issues thereby created became separated into two distinct currents in the American mind. The Highbrow current of high-minded piety ran from Jonathan Edwards through the classic American writers, and issued in the "final unreality" of most contemporary American high culture. The Lowbrow current of "catchpenny opportunism" found expression in the cracker-barrel maxims of Ben Franklin, the American humorists, and finally in the vulgar and jocular atmosphere of contemporary business life (Sprague 1993: 83–4).

Despite certain differences of emphasis, both Santayana and Brooks were driving at the same point: Americans had a disordered relationship to the realm of ideas, treating ideas as something one escaped into, something entirely abstract and ethereal, rather than something one could use to make sense of the flow of one's practical experience. Such an analysis struck a resonant note for intellectuals of the early twentieth century, who were consumed with the quest to connect ideas with lived reality, and thereby render them more useful. "A philosophy is not genuine," Santayana remarked near the beginning of his genteel tradition lecture, "unless it inspires and expresses the life of those who cherish it" – the very things that the "hereditary philosophy" of America had signally failed to do (Hollinger and Capper 2001: 94). With these words, Santayana captured the spirit of what was to come, as opposition to "the genteel tradition" in American art and expression swelled into a generational rallying cry, and set the oppositional tone for much of the century's art and thought.

The rise of pragmatism, so often touted as America's chief contribution to western philosophy, can be connected with the effort to address the same perceived inadequacy (what William James dubbed "intellectualism") and thereby with the same effort to make ideas useful once again. Pragmatism put forward the notion that ideas were most vital and valuable when they were understood as tools for adaptive living, or blueprints for action, and when their truth or falsehood was judged not by arid deductive reasoning but by the real-world consequences that ensued from them. "What difference would it practically make to any one," asked James, "if this notion rather than that notion were true? If no practical difference whatever can be traced, then . . . all dispute is idle" (Hollinger and Capper 2001: 113). In such blunt, businesslike tones, James sought to banish unprofitable metaphysical pursuits, and to bring the ordering principle of utility, as well as the empirical discipline of the natural sciences, to the notoriously misty and self-referential enterprise of philosophy. Such anti-abstractionism and anti-formalism became the defining mark of a whole generation's worth of fresh contributions to American thought, ranging from the sociologically informed jurisprudence of Oliver Wendell Holmes, Jr. to the economic contextualism of Charles Beard and Thorstein Veblen, and the pragmatic experimentalism of John Dewey.

The bald consequentialism implicit in James's question – and answer – showed the profound influence of Darwinian biological science upon the making of pragmatism and other expressions of anti-formalism. That influence showed not only in the notion that human cognition should be understood as an adaptive tool in the struggle for evolutionary survival, like the wings of a bird or the claws of a cat, but also in the tendency to think of ideas themselves as resembling species, whose viability can be evaluated only by testing their ability to survive in action. Intellectual life in this view was, like the Darwinian vision of organic life itself, a ceaseless flux of fresh challenges and fresh adaptations, without an inflexible absolute anywhere in sight. Equally notable, though, is the fact that James was willing to talk frankly in the language of Lowbrows, and evaluate ideas in terms of their "cash value," their ability to produce fruitful outcomes. In any event, the intellectual adaptation called pragmatism did nothing to alter the fundamental, and characteristically American, contention that ideas matter only insofar as they meet the bottom-line requirement: they must have a demonstrable practical use.

The progressive movement of the early twentieth century tried to institutionalize this emphasis upon the usefulness of ideas, and thereby preserve the workings of democracy against the corruptions, both actual and potential, threatened by the rise of industrial capitalism. In the progressive vision, an army of middle-class specialists could be trained in the "science" of governance by the burgeoning new universities and municipal research bureaus, and could run the apparatus of government, using their ideas as blueprints for social reform and the protection and cultivation of the public interest. Such experts would be disinterested arbiters, bound by the logic of science and the self-regulating rational autonomy of professional organizations, rather than the vagaries of economic self-interest or power politics. Staffed with such workers, government would in time come to play the same flexible and organic role in the life of the nation that the mind plays in the life of an individual person, constantly adapting and reformulating its policies and initiatives in response to shifting circumstances. In one sense, such a dispensation would seem to elevate ideas to a very high level indeed, by making them explicit partners in democratic governance. Yet the fact remains that ideas were handmaidens rather than equal partners in this arrangement, since their activity was still relentlessly bound to the practical logic of purposive activity, and dedicated to the triumph – in Walter Lippmann's formulation – of "mastery" over "drift." Far from asserting the independent importance of ideas, progressivism actually served to codify their subordination.

The Meaning of America

In the face of such evidence, and such testimony, can one still seriously entertain the opposite side of the Eriksonian paradox? Have ideas played a *commanding* role in American history? Indeed, one can affirm it. For the *idea* of America itself remained powerful and alluring and multifaceted. If we do not readily perceive the ubiquity of ideas in American history, it is for the same reason that deep-sea fish do not perceive the existence of water: because ideas provide the very medium itself within which American life is conducted. It is impossible to study the nation's history for long without being struck by the degree to which it is permeated with large anticipations and larger meanings. Such visions of the meta-historical meaning of American history are to be found, not on the fringes of the story, but at its very core. They intrude themselves constantly, affecting not only the accounts of historians but the self-understanding of historical actors. One simply cannot tell the story without them.

Such thinking is often dismissed as a species of "American exceptionalism." But the very concept of "America" has always been heavily freighted with large, exceptional meanings. It even had a place made ready for it in the European imagination long before Columbus. From as early as the works of Homer and Hesiod, which located a blessed land beyond the setting sun, to Thomas More's *Utopia*, to the fervent dreams of English Puritans seeking Zion in the Massachusetts Bay colony, to the Swedish prairie homesteaders and Scotch-Irish hard-scrabble farmers and frontiersmen, to the Polish and Italian peasants who made the transatlantic voyage west in search of freedom and material promise, to the Asian and Latin American immigrants who have thronged to these shores and borders in recent decades – the mythic sense of America as an asylum, a land of renewal, regeneration, and fresh possibility, has remained remarkably deep and persistent.

Instead, it is virtually impossible to talk about America for long without talking about the palpable effects of its mythic dimension. As the sociologists say, whatever is believed to be real, even if it be demonstrably false, is real in its social consequences; and a mythic impulse asserts itself everywhere. Nor was such thinking a peculiar preoccupation of conservative nationalists. It is a staple of public rhetoric. Consider these words of Senator Bill Bradley, upon withdrawing from the presidential campaign of 2000:

> Abraham Lincoln once wrote that "the cause of liberty must not be surrendered at the end of one or even one hundred defeats." We have been defeated. But the cause for which I ran has not been. The cause of trying to create a new politics in this country, the cause of trying to fulfill our special promise as a nation, that cannot be defeated, by one or 100 defeats. (*New York Times*, March 10, 2000, A18)

Senator Bradley was arguably the most liberal major candidate running in the 2000 election; yet he found it both comfortable and necessary to invoke, at this critical moment, the old mythic language of America's "special promise." It would be hard to ask for a more full-throated affirmation of American exceptionalism – of the *idea* of America.

Almost everyone seems convinced that America *means* something. To be sure they don't agree on what it means, and the disagreements can be quite basic. Is, for example, the United States to be understood as a nation built upon the extension of European and especially British laws, institutions, and religious beliefs? Or is it more properly understood as a modern, Enlightenment-based post-ethnic nation built on acceptance of abstract principles, such as universal individual rights, rather than bonds of shared tradition, race, history, conventions, and language? Or is it a transnational and multicultural "nation of nations," in which a diversity of sub- or supra-national sources of identity – race, class, gender, ethnicity, national origin, religion, sexual identity, etc. – are the main thing, and only a thin and minimal sense of national culture and obligation is required? Or is it something else again? And what are the implications of each of those propositions for the answers one gives to the question: "What does it mean for me to be an American?"

Clearly each understanding will cause one to answer that last question in a different way. But each suggests, in its own way, that American history has a distinctive meaning. Our fellow citizens seemed disinclined to stop searching for a broad, expansive, mythic way to define their national distinctiveness. They have been remarkably active in this work in the past. Consider just this short collection of monikers that the nation has attracted over the years: The City Upon a Hill, The Empire of Reason, Novus Ordo Seclorum, The New Eden, The Nation Dedicated to a Proposition, The Melting Pot, Land of Opportunity, Nation of Immigrants, Nation of Nations, The First New Nation, The Unfinished Nation and, most recently, The Indispensable Nation.

Nor should one neglect the religious dimension of Americans' self-understanding, which continues to be powerfully present, even in the minds of the non-religious. The notion that America is a nation chosen by God, a New Israel destined for a providential mission of world redemption, has been a near-constant element of the national experience. The Puritan settlers in Massachusetts Bay's "city upon a hill" had a strong sense of historical accountability, and saw themselves as collective bearers of a world-historical destiny. What is more surprising, however, was how persistent that self-understanding would prove to be. The same convictions can be found in the rhetoric of the American Revolution, in the vision of Manifest Destiny, in the crusading sentiments of Civil War intellectuals, in the benevolent imperialism of *fin-de-siècle* apostles of Christian civilization, and in the fervent speeches of President Woodrow Wilson during the First World War.

This impulse survived largely intact, even into an age in which its original religious basis is almost completely gone. Indeed the missionary past of Protestant Christianity came to be regarded with horror or discomfort. Few presidents since Wilson cared to make a direct appeal to Americans' sense of chosenness by God as a justification for foreign policy, and the disastrous intervention in Vietnam especially provided a severe chastening of such ambitions. But, as the above quotation from his fellow Princetonian Bill Bradley strongly suggests, Wilson's sense of America's larger moral responsibility – particularly its open-ended obligation to uphold human rights, defend democracy, and impart American-style institutions, technologies, and values to the rest of the world – had not vanished by the end of the twentieth century.

To be sure, other strains of American thought have operated, including a sober realist tradition grounded in John Quincy Adams's famous assertion that the United States does not go abroad in search of monsters to destroy. There has been a reflexive, if shallow, reluctance in many quarters to "impose our values" on the rest of the world, although with the implicit view that the temptation to do so is somehow uniquely American. There was even a direct counter-strain, represented by the radical political views of the linguist Noam Chomsky, that envisions the United States as a uniquely pernicious force in human history, uniquely guilty rather than uniquely virtuous. One could say that this was American exceptionalism with a vengeance. All of which only goes to show how difficult it was for Americans, and others, to think of the United States as "just another nation." The idea of an American national destiny clings, as tenaciously as ever, to the nation's history.

So, if only by virtue of the influence of this one large idea, the second half of the Eriksonian paradox would seem to hold. And the fact that the myths of national destiny were so varied does nothing to weaken that claim. None of these mythic constructs enjoyed anything like unquestioned predominance in American conscious- ness. But none died, and all complicated the sense of national identity. That Americans believed in, and sought the evidence of, their special national destiny is simply a fact of American history. In the twentieth century it had become a fact of world history.

Out of Many, One

The nation's growing social diversity also helped tilt the balance in the direction of America as an idea. For much of the nation's history, the primacy of English-speaking white Anglo-Saxon Protestants was an established fact, to which immigrants and other minorities were expected to accommodate themselves. But by the beginning of the twentieth century, such primacy was already weakening, and by the end of the century it was largely gone. When commonalities of race, religion, ethnicity, history, and even language were eroded, they ceased serving as a basis for the cohesiveness of the nation; and abstract ideas moved in to take their place. America was now more likely to be defined in terms of the large ideas for which it stands, such as liberty, equality, and economic opportunity, than the history or geography or religion or customs or culture that Americans shared.

Hence the rise of concepts such as "pluralism" and "multiculturalism," which played no part in the thinking of the nation's founders. "Pluralism" proposes that the national culture of the United States ought to be able to make room for, and leave as undisturbed as possible, robust and independent subcultures, usually those based on race, ethnicity, religion, or country of origin, and often all four at once. It became one of the central ideas of the twentieth century. The German-Jewish immigrant Horace Kallen, the chief proponent of cultural pluralism, compared American culture to a vast and various symphony orchestra, whose musical richness was enhanced precisely by the tonal distinctiveness of each of its members. The assimilationist ideal of a "melting pot" would destroy that symphonic richness, and substitute for it a bland and homogeneous unison. There was of course the need for some kind of national culture, just as there was a need for a national government. But Kallen and other pluralists assumed that such a national culture could be thin and limited in character, allowing the richness and depth of more particular affiliations to be preserved.

"Pluralism" proved surprisingly compatible with American institutions, perhaps because the tension between particularistic and national identities was so similar to the tension between state and national identities built into the federal system. But it had its limitations. It is a delicate concept, poised as it is between particularism and cosmopolitanism, partaking of both while wholly embracing neither. Some of the chief problems with it have manifested themselves in the even more elusive idea of "multiculturalism," which has meant almost anything one wants it to mean, from taking a generous view of ethnic foods and customs to believing in the absolute cognitive separateness of the "cultures" making up modern America. In that latter acceptation, multiculturalism was an important expression of the intellectual mood of postmodernism, with its fondness for the politics of identity (based on race, class, gender, sexuality, etc.) and its programmatic suspicion of all meta-narratives (except those of identity groups). It was also vulnerable to the factionalization that such politics of identity can induce in the political and social order, since it offered no principle of commonality in the name of which disparate groups can be enjoined to cooperate.

But even in its most exaggerated form, multiculturalism served to raise a very useful question, which pluralism largely evaded: How does one simultaneously protect both the *distinctiveness* of racial and ethnic groups and their full *membership*, both collectively and individually, in the polity? How much diversity can America stand? How much of a uniform national culture does American society really need? And where will that uniformity come from? Certainly the last two of these questions, which found their way into debates over immigration and education policy, suggest that the task of defining America is incomplete, and is far more than an academic quest.

The Ambiguity of Science

What, then, were some of the most characteristic and salient ideas and concerns that we find weaving in and out of the discourse of the twentieth century? What generalizations might one make about its intellectual texture? Would it be possible, for example, to point to a specific cluster of ideas that occupied an especially prominent position during all or part of those years? Perhaps nothing can capture the ambivalent and reflexive intellectual mood of the century better than those Eriksonian paradoxes of 1950. For every intellectual theme that seems to proclaim its "mainstream" dominance, it takes little effort to find its antagonist redoubling its resistance, digging in its heels, managing to survive and thrive in the interstices of a vast and various culture. It is as if every dominant idea has the effect of automatically precipitating the existence of its own opposite, so that no victory (or defeat) is ever complete. Hence we may find it more fruitful to look for points of contention, rather than points of consensus, in discerning the true organizing patterns of twentieth-century intellectual life. Even highly polarized debates, however, reveal areas of agreement. Several themes were crucial in establishing the horizons of American thought and propelling the debates.

Foremost were the issues precipitated by the ever-growing prestige of science, which served, as it had in the nineteenth century, as the model for any field of human endeavor that made a claim to thoroughness, accuracy, reliability, and disinterested truth. Sinclair Lewis's 1925 novel *Arrowsmith* offered the scientist as a secular priest, and a moral exemplar for modern society, very much in contrast to Lewis's mocking depiction of the businessman in *Babbitt* (1922) and the clergyman in *Elmer Gantry* (1927). There was a comparative purity about the scientific ideal, not to mention a more impressive record of achievement. Indeed, the steady advance of scientific knowledge and technological innovation through the twentieth century, in America and elsewhere, a pageant that stretched from the perfecting of air and space travel to the unlocking of the atom to the discovery of the DNA double helix, the mapping of the human genome, and countless other fabulous accomplishments, has to be accounted one of the great success stories of human history.

Such success has inevitably given rise to efforts to apply scientific methods to the solving of the full range of human problems. No thinker of the twentieth century epitomized that quest more consistently than John Dewey. His astonishingly wide-ranging oeuvre, embracing subjects from aesthetics to education to epistemology to politics to metaphysics, was thoroughly imbued with reverence for the tentative, provisional, experimental methods of science, which he regarded as both the highest expression of human intellectual striving and a model for democratic discourse. For Dewey, who described his own intellectual movement as one "from absolutism to experimentalism," most of the questions that had preoccupied western philosophers in the past were no longer worthy of our attention. Instead what was needed was a fresh approach, building not upon inherited moral formulations or other forms of idealism but upon careful attention to experience and to the supple, non-dualistic interplay of mind and world. Science was nothing more than the most refined elaboration of precisely that effort. And science, because it was inherently transparent and non-authoritarian, improved the prospects for participatory democracy (Hickman and Alexander 1998: 14–21).

In keeping with this spirit, most of what are called "the social sciences" came to be dominated by schools of thought that set out to be as rigorously "scientific" as possible, which often meant redefining the animating questions of the field, and even defining the old questions out of existence. One example was the rise of J. B. Watson's behaviorism in the field of experimental psychology, or of behaviorism in the field of political science, in which only observable and measurable external behaviors were studied, and the murky realms of "introspection" and "values" were eschewed entirely. Growing knowledge of the ways in which genetic information is linked to observable phenomena has fueled the growing influence of various forms of socio-biology, which sought to connect social thought with the physiological bases of human behavior. The rallying cry of all such disciplines, and the stuff of university presidents' speeches, was always the quest to "push back the frontiers of knowledge," by making "new discoveries." To do so credibly, one had to examine problems that were susceptible of being formulated in precise, and preferably quantitative, terms. Even the humanities, where the "frontiers of knowledge" metaphor has always been highly inappropriate, were affected by this development. In the spirit of Dewey, and in the wake of Ludwig Wittgenstein, Bertrand Russell, A. J. Ayer, and Rudolph Carnap, various forms of analytic philosophy, for example, sought to emulate the rigorous spirit of science, and often elected, in the process, to dispose of philosophers' perennial questions – the existence of God, for example, or the meaning of good and evil – by dismissing them as mere byproducts of linguistic confusion.

A culmination of sorts for this triumphalist strain of scientific thought came in the lavishly ambitious 1998 book *Consilience: The Unity of Knowledge*, by the distinguished entomologist Edward O. Wilson, a pioneer figure of the sociobiology movement. In *Consilience*, Wilson proposed that a common body of inherent principles underlies the entire human endeavor. In short, the Enlightenment thinkers of the seventeenth and eighteenth centuries had it generally right, he believed; we live in a lawful, perfectible material world in which knowledge is unified across all the great branches of learning. Once all fields of inquiry are brought under the cope of science, we will be able to explain everything in the world through an understanding and application of a finite number of natural laws. The book stands as a summa of naturalistic reductionism, a monument to the "Enlightenment project."

Needless to say, the reception of Wilson's universalizing book was not universally warm. The poet, novelist, and social critic Wendell Berry wrote a scathing rebuttal called *Life is a Miracle* (2000); and such influential figures as the philosopher Richard Rorty brushed it aside with faint contempt. Even many of Wilson's fellow scientists, being generally much more comfortable working in their disciplinary cubby-holes, found in it an element of overreaching. But however one accounts for it, the critical response to *Consilience* showed that even the prestige of science has its distinct limits in American intellectual life; powerful counter-currents were also at work. The hegemony of science polarized a formidable reaction against it.

There are at least three crucial reasons for this. First, there is growing anxiety about scientists' alarming, and increasingly conspicuous, lack of social and moral responsibility. When atomic physicist J. Robert Oppenheimer famously described the development of sophisticated nuclear weapons as a "technically sweet" pursuit (quoted in Curtis 1955: 155), in which one invents first and decides what to do with the invention second, he seemed to many Americans to describe the nub of the problem with science, whether the procedure at issue involved the splitting of atoms or the cloning of rats and genetic melding of species. Efforts to offset the dangers of nuclear weaponry, for example, with visions of the beneficent effects of the "peaceful atom" have been, at best, only partially successful. The increasingly corporate and publicly funded character of modern science has made it vulnerable to many of the same corruptions and inefficiencies as large business corporations or governmental bureaucracies. The days of *Arrowsmith*, in short, were long past. Americans became ambivalent about scientific progress – not opposed, but ambivalent.

Second, religious faith and practice continued to thrive. Of all the surprises the twentieth century had in store, surely none was greater than the amazing persistence of piety. That was not what the sociologists had expected. To be sure, the century saw a profound renegotiation of the terms of separation between religion and public life, mostly favoring the strict separation of the two. But the grand predictions of secularization theorists that, in becoming modern, America would also become secular have simply not been borne out by history. Nor is this simply a matter of the persistence of religious faith among poorly educated sub-elite groups, for which various forms of fundamentalism and superstition might be thought (rightly or wrongly) to have particular appeal. In fact, a few of the most influential thinkers of the twentieth century – such as Reinhold Niebuhr, Walter Rauschenbusch, John Courtney Murray, and Richard John Neuhaus – have written from a theological perspective. Moreover, the precise relationship between religion and science is not always easily defined, and it is not necessarily one of warfare. But at the very least, the persistence of religion showed that, even at its acme, science has its profound inadequacies. For instance, it tells us very little about how to live, about the ends towards which we should be directed. Indeed, in so far as science avoids judgments about questions of value, such silence is one of its chief characteristics.

The third reason stems, in part, from the first two, but relates more directly to the realm of ideas. There was a steadily mounting critique of the claims of science for its own epistemological superiority and purity, and a growing emphasis upon understanding science as something inherently social and political, the work of particular communities of inquiry (i.e., groups of accredited scientists), rather than a heroic endeavor to disclose the foundations of objective truth about nature. The critique emerged in earnest in 1962, when Thomas Kuhn argued that new theories become accepted by a community of scientists not because of objective criteria of truth, but because of the way those theories addressed the needs of that particular certifying community of discourse. Other thinkers took this position still further. In arguing that the "foundations" sought by "objective" science were illusory, Richard Rorty contended that the work of science was really no different from the work of any other intellectual community. Furthermore, if the activity of science were to be deemed exemplary, it could be so only out of recognition for the exceptional degree and kind of "solidarity" that the scientific communities evinced (1979). Thus there was nothing special about scientific knowledge. It stood in a continuum with all other forms of knowledge, in being made "true" not by objective verification, but by the assent of interested and certified parties. The correspondence theory of truth – that truth could be ascertained by the degree to which ideas corresponded to objective reality – was no longer believable. Instead, all truth was unavoidably instrumental, and reflected the interests of those who certify it. Indeed, as feminist critics such as Evelyn Fox Keller contended, the agenda of modern science had largely been dictated by the cultural assumptions of the men who ran it, and whose mechanical vision of nature determined in advance what truths they would find (Keller 1985). So much for the disinterested heroism of science.

The Power of Culture

Such assertions showed, at the very least, the power that the concept of "culture" enjoyed in the twentieth century, particularly as a counter to "nature." Indeed, "culture" was a keyword, and its transformations and peregrinations serve to map much of the intellectual ebb and flow of the century. If the great project of modern science was the conquest of nature, then the concept of "culture" could be thought of as the pursuit of that conquest by other means.

In the nineteenth century, of course, "culture" referred both to a process of intellectual and moral cultivation, and to a body of distinguished works of arts and letters produced by and for elite groups. Matthew Arnold considered "culture" as the counter to "commerce," and a morally formative substitute for the lost verities of religion. As such, "culture" had a highly prescriptive element; it was regarded as the tutor of the human soul. "Culture" made one better; it was more about what one *aspires* to be than it is about what one is. It is not hard to see how such a perspective might lend itself to the artificial separation of "culture" from actual life, the very condition to which Brooks, Santayana, and others objected so strongly. The meaning of "culture" shifted dramatically, however, with the emergence of cultural anthropology. "Culture" became life as it already was, not life as it should be, or might become. The father of cultural anthropology in America was Columbia University's Franz Boas, a German-Jewish immigrant. From him and his many talented students, including Ruth Benedict and Margaret Mead, emerged an approach involving the sympathetic, descriptive, non-judgmental study of comparative social structures, with a strong presumption that every functioning culture has its own validity. Whether such an approach can rightly be called "cultural relativism" is debatable, since Boas also had strong value commitments, including a passionate hostility to racism. But cultural anthropology did promote a sense of the plasticity of human nature, and of the extent to which norms thought to be grounded in nature were instead products of culture.

Indeed, the anthropological concept of "culture" tended to redefine humanity in its own image. "Man" was not defined by innate faculties, biological wiring, or instincts. (And "woman" was not defined by anatomical destiny.) It was not the given hardware of nature but the acquired software of culture – and the remarkable human capacity to acquire and adapt such software – that made human beings what they are. Much we had thought of as "natural" was actually "culturally conditioned" (or, in the more recent usage, "socially constructed"). Such an idea, in optimistic and reform-minded America, tended to be used for progressive purposes. Margaret Mead's study of Samoan youth sought, under the pretext of a disinterested study of adolescent sexual behavior, to expose the artificiality of American norms, and, presumably, open the possibility of their revision (1928). In other words, cultural anthropology served as yet another tool in the rebellion against Victorianism. The field perhaps had its most powerful effects in the study of gender and sexuality, serving to underwrite a wholesale re-conceptualization of those two subjects. The very use of the term "gender," which was introduced in the 1970s to distinguish the cultural and social characteristics ascribed to the sexes from those that are strictly biological, is an indication of the central role played by the concept of "culture."

Feminists had long seen biological determinism as their sworn enemy, and "culture" gave them a way of defeating it, by understanding human identity and relations in a more fluid, open, and malleable way than the concept of "nature" would permit.

The anthropological conception of culture enjoyed enormous influence, both scholarly and popular, and served to underwrite a certain vague but amiable cultural relativism that became an essential marker of good intellectual breeding in the West. But by the end of the twentieth century, however, the concept of "culture" was fraying from overuse, and was in danger of turning into an empty signifier. It was not clear in what sense one could speak of the culture of the United States, the culture of Microsoft, the culture of country music, the culture of Harvard, the culture of PS 148, and the culture of poverty, and have any confidence that one was speaking of the same thing. The "cultures" that make up American "multiculturalism" are clearly not all coherent or genuine cultures, and certainly not in the same sense as the cultures found in "native" countries. A taboo against judging other cultures had also begun to seem ridiculous in the context of grotesque violations of human rights in some parts of the non-western world. It seems absurd to condemn as a form of ethnocentrism western opposition to practices like clitoridectomy and suttee. Thus did liberal (and Judeo-Christian) universalist notions begin to seep back into western discourse. In addition, the newly vitalized biological disciplines mounted a fresh challenge to the predominance of "culture," in the form of sociobiology, evolutionary psychology, and other emerging fields brimming with energy and confidence. The battle between nature and nurture was being re-fought again, and by the end of the twentieth century, "culture" was steadily losing ground.

Ideas in Public Life

In political thought, liberalism itself changed its meaning early on in the century, from an ideology of laissez-faire economics, decentralization, and limited government to the promotion of economic regulation, nationalization, and activist government. Herbert Croly orchestrated the shift to this latter meaning (1909), which became politically embodied in the administration of Franklin D. Roosevelt and has characterized the political meaning of liberalism ever since.

Yet the liberalism regnant in the United States at the end of the twentieth century registered an additional shift of meaning. Although still committed to the state's role in the provision of social welfare, liberalism gravitated towards a more deeply rights-based political philosophy, which subordinates considerations of the common good to the sovereign liberty of rights-bearing individuals, and exalts the choice-making capacity of an autonomous and unencumbered self over all else, including the commitments of family, community, nation, and religion. Croly's progressive liberalism had a strong emphasis upon the cultivation of social solidarity and national consciousness; it saw the individualistic tendencies of liberalism as a grave potential threat to other valuable goals. Not so the newer liberalism, which proposed that individual rights trump all other considerations. Such a view is especially closely associated with philosopher John Rawls, whose formidable 1971 book, *A Theory of Justice*, quickly became the key text of the new liberalism.

Such a shift in liberal thought led to its own excesses, including a corrosive tendency to reduce all questions of law and social policy to simplistic "rights talk."

Thus, it gave new life and plausibility to conservative alternatives, which had quietly been gathering intellectual strength since 1945. The theoretical works of political philosophers Leo Strauss and Eric Voegelin, the historically informed criticism of Richard Weaver and Russell Kirk, the sociological works of Robert Nisbet – all helped provide a pivot for the analysis and criticism of regnant liberalism. In addition, the hyper-trophy of "rights talk" precipitated a counter-movement within liberalism (though incorporating conservative elements, and drawing the support of some conservatives) called "communitarianism," which had established itself as a fresh alternative by the end of the twentieth century.

Harvard political scientist Michael J. Sandel, one of the most forceful liberal-communitarian critics of Rawlsian rights-based liberalism, argued against the liberalism of what he called "the procedural republic." Such liberalism makes government the referee of fair procedure and guarantor of individual rights, but insists that government be scrupulously neutral when it comes to passing judgment upon the substantive ends that individuals elect to pursue. This liberal-neutralist philosophy, Sandel asserted, proved to be inadequate to the needs of a democratic republic, since it failed to inculcate the civic virtues and qualities of character necessary to sustain liberty and self-governance. Instead, Sandel invoked the "republican" tradition of early American politics, which did not exalt the ideal of the freely choosing, unconditioned, unencumbered, autonomous individual, but rather exalted participation in the civic life of the *res publica* (1996). Others, such as the historian Christopher Lasch, shared Sandel's emphasis on a more participatory regime, but gave equal emphasis to the role of religion in the formation of souls (1995).

Communitarians objected to the liberal tendency to reify the individual as a free-standing and unencumbered agent, a stance that gave insufficient attention, they argued, to the specific institutions and practices that were needed to create and sustain such individuals. Communitarianism thus addressed a central paradox of twentieth-century thought: its inability to give equal attention both to the liberal ideal of individual freedom and to the social, historical, cultural, linguistic, and other contexts in which the self is both formed and embedded. The historian Thomas Haskell brilliantly pointed to the paradox that, at century's end, academic thought seemed simultaneously and equally committed to the inviolability of individual liberty and "rights talk" on the one hand, and to the complete and utter cultural "situatedness" and historicity of the self on the other (1998). Their conflict represented the most recent installation of one of the truly perennial problems of philosophy, the conflict between freedom and determinism.

Of course, no generic discussion of ideas in the twentieth century would be complete without a consideration of the changing social location of ideas. A keen awareness, sometimes bordering on obsession, emerged with the social and psychological roots of knowledge. In other words, the history of ideas was no longer viewed as a stately procession of alternative concepts, but instead provoked the impertinent question: "Says *who?*" Or, to unpack the question a bit: Where did these ideas come from? Who propounded them, and in response to what circumstances? What sort of people, standing where in the social order, with what kinds of psychological concerns? What kinds of institutions served to define their activity, whether by supporting them, or inhibiting them? Through what means and in what venues did they distribute their ideas? And to whom were the ideas distributed?

Such thick description of intellectual context can turn out (if sufficiently opaque) to be just as mechanically reductive and anti-intellectual as the most Lowbrow philistinism. Yet to ignore the question of social location, and of the specific communities in which knowledge is generated and validated, is to miss a crucial element in the story. One would miss a decisive institutional fact in failing to point out that the great underlying trend of intellectual life in the last century was the ascendancy of academe. A great many of the concerns and pathologies of contemporary intellectual life are traceable to, and inseparable from, the particular institutional frameworks within which our era generates and transmits ideas. The modern research university absorbed into itself an astonishingly large part of the nation's intellectual life.

The academy provided a haven for free and disinterested intellectual inquiry in a commercial society, and has given those who work in ideas and symbols a place to make a decent living while plying their trade. The division of knowledge into academic disciplines and distinct "communities of interpretation" made for greater rigor and clarity in the production of studies in nearly all fields. Occasionally the academy even served as a promising model for alternative forms of community, though that promise has sometimes raised expectations it cannot meet. But even with its failings, the academy has provided a highly serviceable context for intellectual activity of a very high order. Yet the costs were high, and mostly stemmed not from failure but from success. The modern university still proceeded from Enlightenment assumptions about the nature of knowledge, which are that it can be objective, universal, progressive, and cumulative. Those assumptions worked fairly well for the natural sciences, moderately well for the "hard" social sciences, but not at all for the softer social sciences and the humanities, which found themselves in deepening crisis. The logic of specialization contributed to the problem, by dividing inquiry into smaller and smaller sub-units, each with its indigenous jargon and distinct community of interpretation, each with little to communicate to the world beyond itself. Such sterility negated the broader social meaning of humanistic knowledge in a democracy.

Small wonder that a vogue of the "public intellectual" cropped up as an antidote to this regnant academicism, in an effort to restore what looked like a golden era of freewheeling, freelance intellectual life in the first half of the century. Inspired by Russell Jacoby (1987), and by the continuing romance of bourgeois society with its bohemian rebels, this movement looked back longingly to Van Wyck Brooks, Lewis Mumford, Dwight Macdonald, Irving Howe, David Riesman, Lionel Trilling, and Mary McCarthy, and to the lively intellectual journals in which they published, such as *The Dial, The Masses, Seven Arts*, and *Partisan Review*. In these magazines important ideas were discussed in accessible ways. Such a nostalgia was understandable and healthy, even if it romanticized the sometimes less-than-stellar quality of those earlier journals, and underestimated what is still possible in the late twentieth century. (*Partisan Review*, which the actuarial tables of "little magazines" would have otherwise consigned to an early death, was sustained for thirty-four years by the direct support of Rutgers and Boston Universities.)

Nevertheless the loss of the "general educated reader" over the course of the century was an intellectual, cultural, and moral calamity, and a betrayal of the nation's democratic hopes. The situation bore an uncanny resemblance to what Santayana and Brooks had described nearly a century earlier. The split in the American mind was still there (as sharply etched as ever), and it was still a division in terms of Highbrows and

Lowbrows. But the Highbrows became ponderous and impenetrable and highly professionalized academics, whose air-castles of thought were surrounded by moats of professional jargon, designed to keep the dabblers and dilettantes at bay. Ironically, they were the true legatees and custodians of the genteel tradition, despite the disappearance of almost every trace of Victorian reticence and belletristic pretension. The Lowbrows, meanwhile, were the manufacturers and purveyors of commercial mass entertainment, whose low aesthetic standards and coarsening effects on the populace were arrestingly described by Neil Postman (1986). Political discourse, rather than being elevated by contributions from on High – which had far too little to contribute – was debased by the domination of the Low.

As a result the vital center of ideas stood largely unoccupied. The leavening effect that the two halves of the American cultural schism might have had upon one another – and occasionally did – was elusive. Those few hardy souls who were willing and able to "crossover" (a Leonard Bernstein in music, a Tom Wolfe in literature, a David McCullough in history, an Andrew Wyeth in painting) had to expect the scorn (often masking envy) of the specialized illuminati, and the dismissive label of "middlebrow," "popularizer," or even "sellout," as a reward for their effort. Yet the genius of American culture has arguably been found in precisely that vibrant democratic middle ground, where ideas drawn from elite and popular cultures mix and mingle. Such was the hope both of Emerson and of Lincoln, whose uncommon eloquence sprang from the commonest of roots. Such was the promise of jazz, whose tangled and improvised mongrel beauty became, in some sense, the very image of modern America. The deepening bifurcation of twentieth-century American culture, intensified by both the heavy hand of the academy and the numbing effects of mass culture, did not made it any easier for these kinds of American ideas – possessing both intellectual sophistication and wide democratic scope – to flourish and find a receptive audience. But it was not impossible, and no worthier goal for an American artist or thinker has emerged.

REFERENCES AND FURTHER READING

Akam, Everett Helmut (2002) *Transnational America: Cultural Pluralist Thought in the Twentieth Century.* Lanham, Md.: Rowman and Littlefield.

Bender, Thomas (1993) *Intellect and Public Life: Essays on the Social History of Academic Intellectuals in the United States.* Baltimore, Md.: Johns Hopkins University Press.

Bender, Thomas and Schorske, Carl (eds.) (1997) *American Academic Culture in Transformation.* Princeton, NJ: Princeton University Press.

Blake, Casey Nelson (1990) *Beloved Community: The Cultural Criticism of Randolph Bourne, Van Wyck Brooks, Waldo Frank, and Lewis Mumford.* Chapel Hill: University of North Carolina Press.

Boorstin, Daniel J. (1953) *The Genius of American Politics.* Chicago: University of Chicago Press.

Coben, Stanley (1991) *Rebellion Against Victorianism: The Impetus for Cultural Change in 1920s America.* New York: Oxford University Press.

Cotkin, George (1990) *William James, Public Philosopher.* Baltimore, Md.: Johns Hopkins University Press.

—— (1992) *Reluctant Modernism: American Thought and Culture, 1880–1900.* Boston: Twayne.

Croly, Herbert (1909) *The Promise of American Life.* New York: Capricorn Books.

Curtis, Charles P. (1955) *The Oppenheimer Case: The Trial of a Security System.* New York: Simon and Schuster.

Degler, Carl N. (1991) *In Search of Human Nature: The Decline and Revival of Darwinism in American Social Thought.* New York: Oxford University Press.

Erikson, Erik H. (1950) *Childhood and Society.* New York: W. W. Norton.

Galston, William A. (1991) *Liberal Purposes: Goods, Virtues, and Diversity in the Liberal State.* New York: Cambridge University Press.

—— (2002) *Liberal Pluralism: The Implications of Value Pluralism for Political Theory and Practice.* New York: Cambridge University Press.

Geertz, Clifford (1973) *The Interpretation of Cultures: Selected Essays.* New York: Basic Books.

Glendon, Mary Ann A. (1991) *Rights Talk: The Impoverishment of Political Discourse.* New York: Free Press.

Gurstein, Rochelle (1996) *The Repeal of Reticence: A History of America's Cultural and Legal Struggles Over Free Speech, Obscenity, Sexual Liberation, and Modern Art.* New York: Hill and Wang.

Harvey, David (1989) *The Condition of Postmodernity.* Cambridge, Mass.: Blackwell.

Haskell, Thomas L. (1998) *Objectivity Is Not Neutrality: Explanatory Schemes in History.* Baltimore, Md.: Johns Hopkins University Press.

Hickman, Larry A. and Alexander, Thomas M. (eds.) (1998) *The Essential Dewey,* 2 vols. Bloomington, Ind.: Indiana University Press.

Hollinger, David A. (1985) *In the American Province: Studies in the History and Historiography of Ideas.* Baltimore, Md.: Johns Hopkins University Press.

—— (1995) *Postethnic America: Beyond Multiculturalism.* New York: Basic Books.

—— (1996) *Science, Jews and Secular Culture: Studies in Mid-Twentieth Century American Intellectual History.* Princeton, NJ: Princeton University Press.

Hollinger, David A. and Capper, Charles (eds.) (2001) *The American Intellectual Tradition,* 3rd. edn., vol. 2. New York: Oxford University Press.

Jacoby, Russell (1987) *The Last Intellectuals: American Culture in the Age of Academe.* New York: Basic Books.

James, William (1907) *Pragmatism.* New York: Longman.

Kauffman, Linda S. (ed.) (1993) *American Feminist Thought at Century's End.* Cambridge, Mass.: Harvard University Press.

Keller, Evelyn Fox (1985) *Reflections on Gender and Science.* New Haven, Conn.: Yale University Press.

Kloppenberg, James T. (1986) *Uncertain Victory: Social Democracy and Progressivism in European and American Thought, 1870–1920.* New York: Oxford University Press.

—— (1998) *The Virtues of Liberalism.* New York: Oxford University Press.

Kuhn, Thomas (1962) *The Structure of Scientific Revolutions.* Chicago: University of Chicago Press.

Lasch, Christopher (1965) *The New Radicalism in America, 1889–1963: The Intellectual as a Social Type.* New York: Alfred A. Knopf.

—— (1995) *The Revolt of the Elites and the Betrayal of Democracy.* New York: W. W. Norton.

Levine, Lawrence (1988) *Highbrow/Lowbrow: The Emergence of Cultural Hierarchy.* Cambridge, Mass.: Harvard University Press.

Lewis, Sinclair (1925) *Arrowsmith.* New York: Grosset and Dunlap.

Lipset, Seymour Martin (1996) *American Exceptionalism: A Double-Edged Sword.* New York: W. W. Norton.

May, Henry F. (1959) *The End of American Innocence: A Study of the First Years of Our Time.* New York: Alfred A. Knopf.

McClay, Wilfred M. (1994) *The Masterless: Self and Society in Modern America*. Chapel Hill: University of North Carolina Press.

McDougall, Walter A. (1997) *Promised Land, Crusader State: The American Encounter with the World since 1776*. Boston: Little, Brown.

Mead, Margaret (1928) *Coming of Age in Samoa: A Psychological Study of Primitive Youth for Western Civilization*. New York: William Morrow.

Nash, George H. (1976) *The Conservative Intellectual Movement in America since 1945*. New York: Basic Books.

Novick, Peter (1988) *That Noble Dream: The "Objectivity Question" and the American Historical Profession*. New York: Cambridge University Press.

Perry, Lewis (1989) *Intellectual Life in America*. Chicago: University of Chicago Press.

Postman, Neil (1986) *Amusing Ourselves to Death: Public Discourse in the Age of Show Business*. New York: Viking.

Rawls, John (1971) *A Theory of Justice*. Cambridge, Mass.: Harvard University Press.

Rorty, Richard (1979) *Philosophy and the Mirror of Nature*. Princeton, NJ: Princeton University Press.

Ross, Dorothy (1991) *The Origins of American Social Science*. New York: Cambridge University Press.

Sandel, Michael J. (1996) *Democracy's Discontent: America in Search of a Public Philosophy*. Cambridge, Mass.: Harvard University Press.

Santayana, George (1967) *The Genteel Tradition: Nine Essays*. Cambridge, Mass.: Harvard University Press.

Selznick, Philip (2001) *The Communitarian Persuasion*. Washington, DC: Woodrow Wilson Press.

Singal, Daniel Joseph (1982) *The War Within: From Victorian to Modernist Thought in the South, 1919–1945*. Chapel Hill: University of North Carolina Press.

Sprague, Claire (ed.) (1993) *Van Wyck Brooks: The Early Years*. Boston: Northeastern University Press.

Tocqueville, Alexis de (1990) *Democracy in America*, 2 vols., ed. Phillips Bradley. New York: Vintage.

Trilling, Lionel (1950) *The Liberal Imagination: Essays on Literature and Society*. New York: Viking Press.

Tuveson, Ernest Lee (1968) *Redeemer Nation: The Idea of America's Millennial Role*. Chicago: University of Chicago Press.

Weaver, Richard (1948) *Ideas Have Consequences*. Chicago: University of Chicago Press.

Westbrook, Robert B. (1991) *John Dewey and American Democracy*. Ithaca, NY: Cornell University Press.

White, Morton (1949) *Social Thought in America: The Revolt Against Formalism*. Boston: Beacon Press.

Whitfield, Stephen J. (1991) *The Culture of the Cold War*. Baltimore, Md.: Johns Hopkins University Press.

CHAPTER TWENTY-SIX

Science and Technology

CARROLL PURSELL

Among the shards of American culture in the twentieth century, surely science and technology hold pride of place. Modern science is at least three centuries old, and technology is so ancient as to be a marker of the difference between human beings and other animals. Yet the past century is often thought of as uniquely characterized by these activities. If science and technology were not unique to the national experience in the twentieth century, they enjoyed a cultural authority which came to rival, if not surpass, that of the church or state. Science is widely seen as a privileged type of knowledge, transcending social relations and representing a "truth" superior to other forms of knowledge. For its part, technology has moved from the status of being a tool with which social goods can be produced to that of the most common measure of such goods.

It is important to note, however, that science is a house with many mansions. At any one time not all sciences are equally exciting, honored, and supported; indeed, throughout American history one branch of science has usually been privileged over the others. In the nineteenth century, for example, the massive task of exploring the North American continent, and of inventorying and exploiting its vast natural resources, made the natural sciences, and especially geology, of signal importance. In the early twentieth century, and especially after World War I, chemistry enjoyed the highest prestige. The US Department of Agriculture battled mightily to get farmers to abandon their hard-won traditional knowledge and to adopt "scientific" methods, which increasingly meant depending upon chemical fertilizers and pesticides. During World War I the dramatic use of poison gas was only the most obvious reason to think of the conflict as a "chemists' war." A campaign by American scientists after the Armistice to sell the importance of industrial research led hundreds of firms to set up laboratories.

The reign of the chemists did not outlast World War II. From the radar which helped turn the tide in the Battle of Britain to the atomic bombs which so dramatically ended the war in the Pacific five years later, the work of physicists took on new stature. Whether one looked at the arms race, at the space race, or at the cornucopia of consumer technologies such as television, what seemed at the very heart of national progress were physics and its practical applications. The decades-long (and so far unsuccessful) attempt to use lasers to produce useful amounts of energy by fusion was one such costly example of physics-based projects. So great was the prestige of physics, however, that "practical application" was not always necessary. Giant and very expensive projects like the super-collider could be undertaken with not even a pretense of any gain beyond the vague virtues of "advancing scientific knowledge." The names associated with this period still resonate in the public mind: J. Robert Oppenheimer, the scientific director of the Manhattan Project, for example, as well as his nemesis, Edward Teller, the "father" of the hydrogen bomb. And above them all, of course, was Albert Einstein, who spent the last two decades of his career in the US. As historian Daniel J. Kevles has pointed out, by 1950 the nation's physicists could brag that "the springtime of Big Physics has arrived" (quoted in Kevles 1978: 367).

By the end of the twentieth century, however, the long reign of physics as queen of the sciences appeared to be over. The super-collider, for example, was only partially built and then cancelled. Instead of physics, biology appeared to be the premier science. Gene-sequencing, bio-engineering, the patenting of genetically altered mice, DNA sampling of the criminal (perhaps eventually the entire) population, hormones to stimulate milk production – an entire menu of biological fields and techniques were being closely followed by applied technologies in medicine, agriculture, and social control. Alarms were sounded from those scientific specialties that were still not privileged. Yet the fields of geology, chemistry, physics, and a host of others remain exciting, useful, and (by the standards of the social sciences, the arts, and the humanities) lavishly funded by both government and corporate sources.

Estates of Science

Just as the predominant sciences change over time, so does the relative primacy of the several "estates of science." In the nineteenth century, higher education had stood out as perhaps the most important home and supporter of science. From the very beginning of the republic, however, the federal government had organized scientific bureaus and sponsored scientific expeditions. By the end of the nineteenth century state governments had also began to sponsor geological surveys, for example, and sometimes appointed agricultural scientists to the government. It was not until the demands of regulatory agencies, put into place or revitalized by the administrations of the Progressive Era, that science in the federal government began to grow significantly. With the massive scientific investments made during World War II, the government became a major player in the support and shaping of the nation's scientific activities. But the federal government was a key patron of science long before the war began (Dupree 1957).

Gradually, over the course of the nineteenth century, private philanthropy had grown in importance as well. Scientific schools at Harvard and Yale, for example, were funded and named for wealthy businessmen. By the end of the century Charles T. Yerkes in Illinois and James Lick in California had funded large telescopes which initiated American dominance in that field. After the turn of the twentieth century the great fortunes amassed by John D. Rockefeller, Andrew Carnegie, and others were partially diverted into philanthropic foundations, which undertook to seed new scientific fields and investigations through grants and fellowships. Such support remained important throughout the century, though overshadowed by federal funding. Colleges had been sites of scientific study since the colonial period, but organized research joined education only late in the nineteenth century. The land-grant colleges, established in the 1860s, envisioned scientific progress in both agriculture and mechanics as pivotal to their missions; and the great research universities, based on the German model, emerged by the turn of the twentieth century. The "multiversity," as exemplified by the University of California, were creatures of World War II grants and contracts from the federal government. Financed partly by states, significantly by the federal government, and to some extent by foundations (though surprisingly little by corporations), the nation's colleges and universities were major agents of both scientific and technological development.

These colleges and universities were not simply sites of research, of course. By the beginning of the twentieth century they had already become committed to the education, at both undergraduate and postgraduate levels, of scientists and engineers themselves. Even before there were careers in science to be made outside of teaching, medical students often chose science curricula. By the end of the nineteenth century, as research lives became possible, science offered a career path that was both genteel and modern. As late as the 1930s, however, postgraduate work in Europe (particularly Germany) was still a useful – if not quite necessary – part of preparation for a life in science. After World War II the flow was dramatically reversed, and the United States became the necessary destination of serious science students from all nations outside the Soviet bloc.

Although most universities, and especially the large land-grant state schools, had attached engineering colleges by 1900, the free-standing institute of technology was widely popular. As historian Monte A. Calvert pointed out, the demise of a "shop culture" and hegemonic rise of a "school culture" was well underway before the twentieth century (Calvert 1967). During the 1910s and 1920s graduate programs in engineering proliferated; and the idea of "engineering research" took its place alongside that of "scientific research." Importantly, however, engineering remains one of the few professions available to those with only a baccalaureate degree.

The great flowering of technology and science in the years before World War II meant that engineers and scientists enjoyed unprecedented prestige during this period. Sinclair Lewis's novel *Arrowsmith* (1925) romanticized the scientist as an incorruptible researcher who pursued Truth passionately. A 1908 novel by John Fox, Jr., *The Trail of the Lonesome Pine*, was turned into a successful motion picture in 1936. Its engineer-protagonist brought peace to feuding families, developed the mineral wealth of the region, and won the heart of a young woman. A virtual flood of juvenile novels were aimed at boys; from the Tom Swift series to "The Young Engineers" (a series beginning in 1912), they glamorized the exciting adventures of scientists, engineers, and inventors. The "machine world of the gear-and-girder technology had vast implications for all of American culture during the late nineteenth and earlier twentieth centuries," literary scholar Cecelia Tichi concluded (Tichi 1987: xiii). Popular culture usually gave these implications larger play than did the elite culture of the time. Only a few serious works of fiction, like Willa Cather's first novel (*Alexander's Bridge*, 1912), told a cautionary tale of engineering hubris and its dangers. This was a rare exception. In the last half of the century, the genre of science fiction, both in films and in literature, took the lead in exploring the utopian and dystopian issues of science and technology.

Yet in the universities as well as out, in science and particularly in engineering, women were hardly welcomed. In the late nineteenth century the convergence of the growth of scientific fields, and the increasing number of women who sought careers in them, led to a growing cadre of women scientists, as historian Margaret W. Rossiter claimed, but also to "a pattern of segregated employment and under-recognition, which, try as they might, women could not escape" (Rossiter 1982: xviii). She found that, despite the scientific expansions during World War II and the early Cold War, the very growth and affluence of science during the period "generally unleashed certain forces that hastened the women's exit and subsequent marginalization and under-utilization, which could then be cited to justify denying further training for their successors" (Rossiter 1995: xv). In engineering the circumstances were even worse. It was, as late as the 1970s, the single most sexually-segregated profession in the country, and by the end of the century stubbornly remained an almost exclusively male bastion.

The most recent source of support for science and technology has been corporations, whether through work in their own laboratories (industrial research), or through grants and contracts to colleges, or in various cooperative arrangements with the federal government. Throughout the twentieth century, corporations – usually, but not always, the largest and wealthiest – made crucial contributions to the rising tide of engineering and scientific research and development. This fourth "estate," like the others, tended to fill a special niche in the overall enterprise. But the tangle of interests, agencies, and sources of monies was so complex that they tended to act as a whole. A single project in agricultural science, for example, might involve the US Department of Agriculture, a large state university, and such large chemical firms as Dow and Monsanto. A rocket project might involve the California Institute of Technology, the National Aeronautics and Space Administration (NASA), the Department of Defense, General Dynamics, and Boeing. Nor might it be easily determined whose money was being spent and whose interests were served. Such ambiguities would eventually spark the critique of the military-industrial complex.

Over the last four decades of the century, significant shifts occurred in the mix of support for research and development. In 1960 a total of $13.6 billion was spent for this purpose, with the federal government providing $8.8 billion (about 65 percent), industry $4.5 billion, universities and colleges $66 million, and non-profits $122 million. Of this total 53 percent was defense-related. The preliminary figures for 1998 indicated dramatic shifts. Spending had risen to $220.6 billion, of which the federal government provided only $66.6 (about 30 percent), industry $143.7 (over twice as much as the government), colleges and universities $4.9 billion, and philanthropic agencies $3.4 billion. Of this vastly larger sum, defense took only 16 percent.

Industrial Research and Changing Technologies

The overwhelming importance of industrial research at the end of the century could hardly have been predicted at the beginning. Tied partly to resource exploitation, but more especially to industrial production generally, science began to appear important to manufacturing progress in the early years of the century. The new emphasis was signaled by the founding of the research laboratory at General Electric (GE) in 1900. Not the first but arguably the most famous, the GE laboratories embodied the notion that new and improved products and processes came not simply through genius, but through expertise. As the Du Pont Company famously phrased it, discoveries could provide "Better Things for Better Living Through Chemistry." In 1917, when the United States entered World War I, 375 industrial research laboratories were operating. That number increased to 1,600 by 1931. In addition, a number of independent research laboratories, such as Arthur D. Little, stood ready to contract with firms to develop, test, and improve commercial products for companies that chose not to invest in or expand their own research facilities.

The rise of industrial research was not inevitable, nor was the shape it took. The familiar term "research and development" makes the point well. The most obvious reading of the phrase is that research stands for science, and development for technology. Furthermore, the order of the two words makes it obvious that, at least in this formulation, research literally comes first and development follows. Taken as a whole, the meaning is that science is a necessary precursor of technology: that technology is, in effect, merely applied science. Thus the phrase "research and development" is a nice match for the phrase "science and technology"; they both slide over the tongue without friction. If the order of words in these phrases is reversed, however, another possibility emerges. If one wants to build a better mousetrap (development), perhaps one should begin the project and then resort to research only when some new and unexplained problem arises – perhaps the need for a new material with special characteristics. One can speak perhaps of "technology and science," although the tongue finds that a more awkward pronunciation. Implications in the real world are many; for instance, one might want to start by hiring engineers, and consult scientists only when necessary. By the 1930s industrial research was defined as a scientific enterprise, which was a tribute to the hard work and effective lobbying of the scientific community.

While much of industrial research was carried on at the level of analytical chemistry and handbook engineering design, high science was occasionally involved. In 1932 Irving Langmuir of General Electric Research Laboratories won the Nobel Prize for basic science he had done on surface chemistry. Certain industries besides electricity, such as chemicals and pharmaceuticals, seemed almost inevitably science-based. Certain other businesses, like automobiles and furniture, mostly got along with little or no scientific input. The huge annual investment of over $143.7 billion in research and development in 1998 was a dramatic measure, however, of just how ubiquitous this activity has become, and how much science-based industries have proliferated.

The convergence of science and technology in industry was not limited to research and development for new products. In an influential tract, *The Principles of Scientific Management* (1911), the mechanical engineer Frederick Winslow Taylor declared that, for every task to be done in industry, there was one best way to do it and one best tool to use. Which one, he insisted, could only be discovered through the strict and careful application of science. Once discovered, work would be reorganized and workers taught to work "scientifically" rather than traditionally. It was to be a perfect application of the future motto of the 1932 Chicago Century of Progress celebration: "Science Finds, Industry Applies, Man Conforms." Taylorism, as it was called, quickly became an effective tool for transferring power on the shop floor from workers to management.

In the four decades before the Second World War a cornucopia of new technologies, many of them consumer durables, poured from American industry, sometimes partly through the agency of research and development, but more often not. The automobile was a notable example. Invented in France late in the previous century, this vehicle became widely available and indispensable, owing largely to the design decisions and production innovations of Henry Ford. He designed a vehicle that was light and flexible, capable of navigating not only the poor roads of rural America but also the very farm fields themselves. His invention of mass production was then critical to making his Model T sufficiently inexpensive that it could truly become a people's car. For this achievement he drew upon techniques such as electric-resistance welding and sheet-metal stamping, which were borrowed from the manufacture of bicycles. His own central innovation was the moving assembly line, along which the vehicles passed as workers added parts delivered directly to them. Most earlier automobiles had been assembled out of components virtually hand-made by skilled craftspeople. Instead Ford used dedicated machine tools (a part of the nineteenth-century armory practice) to produce uniform and interchangeable parts. The result was hailed worldwide as revolutionary: the manufacture of large quantities of uniform products at ever-lower prices became known all over the world as Fordism.

It is important to resist the temptation, however, to see Ford's assembly line as the only "modern" way to produce goods, and to make it the measure of all other industries. During the nineteenth century, some goods were custom-made; others were produced in (mostly small) batches. Mass production augmented but did not displace these other methods. Some very high-tech products, like space laboratories, are essentially custom-made. Other products, like furniture or costume jewelry, are still made in batches because the multiple styles offered as well as rapid changes in fashion make the manufacture of large numbers of any single item uneconomical. Late in the twentieth century, ideas of "lean production" were borrowed from Japanese industry, particularly Toyota, and were introduced into American industrial settings. Lean production was strikingly similar to many of the "batch" processes long ignored or disparaged as less than modern. The nature and origins of mass production were studied by David A. Hounshell in his classic work *From the American System to Mass Production, 1800–1932* (1984). More recently Philip Scranton, in *Endless Novelty* (1997), has rescued the history of alternatives to mass production, notably custom and batch production, from the long shadow cast by Henry Ford's famous innovations.

Yet technologies always exist in systems; and the growing number of cars on the road triggered changes – some technological, some social – in other areas (Hughes 1983). The petroleum industry had long been dependent upon selling kerosene for illumination, and in the twentieth century found its *raison d'être* in the refining of gasoline to fuel the cars. A Good Roads Movement demanded better highways, leading to a vast public investment in road construction; over a billion dollars was spent in 1925 alone. In 1919 the General Motors Acceptance Corporation (GMAC) was formed to extend credit to consumers who wished to buy a GM car; this was the grandparent of subsequent consumer credit schemes. Consumer demand for cars invigorated the economic boom of the 1920s, and declining purchases helped contribute to the onset of the Great Depression. The value of cars produced in the country ballooned from just over $4 million in 1899 to $2.5 billion three decades later.

The automobile was wildly popular, but other consumer durable technologies also came into their own in the years before World War II. The radio, for example, had been invented by an Italian, Guglielmo Marconi, and joined motion pictures as popular forms of entertainment and culture. $14.3 million worth of radios were manufactured in 1919, $218 million worth in 1937. As with cars, radios could operate only as parts of a larger technical system; they were useless without available electricity and without broadcasting stations as well as receivers. A host of home appliances, from toasters and irons to refrigerators and vacuum cleaners, appeared and became necessities for the modern homes, which were wired as quickly as possible for electricity; and sufficient wall outlets were installed. Industries produced $1.9 million worth of electrical household appliances and supplies in 1899, but by 1937 that figure had grown to $332.6 million. This massive change has been characterized as an "Industrial Revolution" of the home (Cowan 1983).

Government Science and Technology Projects

Between the world wars the revolution in household technologies was largely confined to the urban and suburban homes of the middle and upper classes. Rural households found that electrical utility companies were reluctant to run long power lines to widely separated farms, of which only about 10 percent were served by central power stations by the mid-1930s. In 1936 President Franklin D. Roosevelt responded to this reluctance by establishing the Rural Electrification Administration (REA), which brought the benefits of electricity to farm operations in both the home and the barn through guaranteed loans to local cooperatives. The REA was only one of several large-scale technological interventions that the federal government made in the American economy. The REA did not itself produce electricity; but the same was not true for the Tennessee Valley Authority (TVA), authorized in 1933. This broad-scale, multipurpose project was designed not only to control flooding and produce electricity, but to accomplish nothing less than the economic and social rehabilitation of the entire Tennessee River valley. Earlier still, the Hoover Dam had been authorized in 1928 to impound part of the Colorado River for irrigation as well as hydroelectric power. Along with the Grand Coulee Dam and other massive constructions in the West, the REA, the TVA, and the Hoover Dam demonstrated both the resources and the authority of the federal government to undertake very large and complex technological projects for the national welfare.

There was a limit, however, to the political will to harness science and technology for common purposes. American culture in the 1920s was often characterized as a machine civilization, but the Depression that crashed down on the nation in 1929 made it clear that technical progress did not always and inevitably translate into sustained prosperity. There were calls for a "moratorium on research," as well as demands that science and technology be mobilized, under federal auspices, to return the nation to economic and social health. Neither course was taken until war in Europe made it apparent to the Roosevelt administration that national defense, as well as the common welfare, was at stake.

In the spring of 1940, with the Battle of Britain underway and the Nazi blitzkrieg sweeping across western Europe, a handful of US scientists and engineers formed, with Roosevelt's blessing, the National Defense Research Committee (NDRC). The next year the Office of Scientific Research and Development (OSRD) was established. For the duration of the war this group, headed by the electrical engineer Vannevar

Bush, directed that large part of the nation's scientific and technical war effort that was not under the direct control of the armed services themselves. Though not without precedent, the operations of the OSRD profoundly altered the shape of science and technology support and governance in the US, and therefore the character of science and technology.

First, the agency set goals and agendas, then contracted with scientists and engineers *in situ* to carry on the work. Before then government-sponsored research and development had largely been conducted in government laboratories organized as part of an operating agency. The postwar world of science and technology would be very much a contract state, in which the public's business was mostly carried on by private entities. A second characteristic of wartime science and technology was its heavy concentration in only a few universities and corporations. Among the former, the Massachusetts Institute of Technology (MIT), the California Institute of Technology, Harvard, Columbia, the University of California, and Johns Hopkins each received over $10 million in contracts. In 1964 three of those schools were still among the top ten recipients of funding for defense research and development. Among corporations, the top ten OSRD contractors included Western Electric (the manufacturing arm of AT&T), GE, the Radio Corporation of America (RCA), and E. I. Du Pont. In 1969 GE and AT&T were still among the top ten defense contractors in the country. The OSRD strategy had been clear: it went where the best scientists and engineers already were. Not only did the rich get richer, but the advantages of massive scientific and engineering resources during the Second World War also benefited these universities and corporations during the Cold War.

Thirdly, not all fields of science and technology were seen as equally relevant to the nation's war effort. Bush himself was an electrical engineer; and his chief lieutenants were drawn predominantly from the physical sciences, and especially physics. Weapons such as radar, proximity fuzzes, and the atomic bomb drew heavily upon such disciplines; and the men at the top of the OSRD could find little work for geologists, say, or ornithologists. OSRD was busily creating an electronic environment for war, partly because that seemed the most likely route to victory, and perhaps partly because it was the path the agency's key figures knew best. At any rate, physics emerged from the war as the most prestigious discipline within the sciences, and electrical engineering as the pre-eminent specialty within that field. And finally, growing out of the OSRD's experience, Bush proposed – most famously in his 1945 report, *Science: The Endless Frontier* – that Washington continue to play a leading role in stimulating and shaping American science and technology. He included in this call a commitment to the long-term support of what he called basic research, that is, fundamental research not closely related to predetermined outcomes.

The Military-Industrial Complex

In his farewell address to the American people on January 17, 1961, President Dwight D. Eisenhower issued a jeremiad against what he called a new "military-industrial complex": the "conjunction of an immense military establishment and a large arms industry." In a less well-known passage, however, he also warned against the possibility that "public policy could itself become the captive of a scientific-technological elite." This possibility loomed, he warned, because "research has become central; it also becomes more formalized, complex, and costly. A steadily increasing share," he noted, "is conducted for, by, or at the direction of the federal government" (quoted in Pursell 1972: 206–7). By 1961 the postwar configuration of science and technology was firmly in place. The US navy had provided for itself through a new Office of Naval Research, which generously funded university scientists for research often only vaguely related to naval warfare; and the newly independent air force created the RAND Corporation (for research and development). The Pentagon itself, of course, maintained a massive research and development program, largely administered through grants and contracts.

The imperative to address nuclear matters led in 1946 to the creation of the Atomic Energy Commission (AEC). A greatly expanded National Institutes of Health (NIH) supported not only medical research but quickly became a major source of support for the biological sciences generally. In 1950 the National Science Foundation (NSF) was created to fund basic research in colleges and universities and to support scientific education in schools at all levels. A year after the shock of *sputnik*, which the Soviet Union orbited in October of 1957, the National Advisory Committee on Aeronautics (which had existed since 1915) was folded into NASA. Whether caught up in the arms race, the space race, or just a "war against cancer," all of these agencies sought and usually received increased budgets, which were then channeled to scientists and engineers working in universities or in private industries. The national defense, public health, economic well-being, and the common welfare all seemed to demand the kind of progress that could only come through research and development. The science and technology that had contributed so much to the winning of the war against the Axis were fully enlisted to win the Cold War as well, whether fought on the battlefield, through a struggle for the world's resources and markets, or in the arena of international prestige. A plan to detonate a nuclear weapon on the moon, while never adopted, was typical, since the idea represented equal parts of science, technology, and theater.

Perhaps the Star Wars program of Ronald Reagan's presidency best demonstrated the convergence of interests that emerged during the Cold War. Designed as a Strategic Defense Initiative (SDI), the scheme was to create a system of anti-ballistic missiles that could shoot down all incoming nuclear warheads. Since the technology did not exist to create such a system – and indeed some scientists warned that it could never be developed – very large sums were appropriated and spent on research and development to push the technical envelope. Although the project was put on the back burner, it had already cost $30 billion by 1999. Since no system was ever developed, most of this funding went for research and development. Even some scientists who did not believe that SDI would ever be feasible accepted grants to do research which might serve some other useful purpose, or might prove to be interesting in its own right. Two administrations after Reagan proposed SDI, President Bill Clinton resurrected the scheme and called for a scaled-down version of it.

So great was the prestige of science, and of physics in particular, that some very large and expensive projects were undertaken even though they seemed far removed from immediate payoffs. In 1990 the space shuttle Discovery launched the Hubble telescope, a $1.5 billion project designed to provide the clearest pictures yet of the universe. Its 94.5-inch (2.4 m) polished mirror turned out to be faulty, but three years later astronauts added corrective optics while the telescope was still in orbit. It was a scientific instrument directly in line with the privately-funded telescopes of the late nineteenth century. By no means all defense-related research and development ended in wasteful extravagance; consider the dramatic example of the computer and its spin-off industries. The first successful computer, an electro-mechanical device, was built in 1937 by Howard Aiken. Delivered to Harvard by IBM in 1944, it was called the Mark I. The next important computer, the University of Pennsylvania's ENIAC, which began operations in 1946, was significant for at least two reasons: first, it was electronic rather than electro-mechanical, and second, it had been sponsored by the US army and was designed to do ballistic calculations.

The substitution of transistors for vacuum tubes and the development of printed circuit boards to substitute for wired circuits led to ever smaller and more powerful computers over the next generation. But the commitment to building large mainframes resulted directly from the continued focus on research and development. Large and powerful machines, capable of crunching almost unimaginable numbers, were particularly (one might almost say only) useful to scientists and engineers working on the federal government's defense projects. ARPANET, developed by the Pentagon's Advanced Research Projects Agency, grew out of the military's interest in C3 (command, control, and communication). Issues such as time sharing and interactive computing had their physical base in networks of individual computers connected to large mainframes. Having begun in 1966, the ARPANET project held its initial public demonstration at the first International Conference on Computer Communication, in Washington, DC, in 1972. Individual computers communicating with one another through telephone lines proved to be a powerfully attractive technology. ARPANET was designed to allow defense researchers, based mostly at universities, to share data. But within a year three-quarters of the activity on the network took the form of email messages. In 1983 the Pentagon spun off MILNET for its own military purposes, and five years later the NSF set up five supercomputer centers for researchers to use at universities. In the 1990s the creation of search engines (browsers) and the World Wide Web spurred the widespread use of the internet.

By this time, of course, the scientists and engineers who were working on defense projects, plus the military planners and the university computer researchers, had been joined by many millions of people around the world who used small personal computers for sending email to friends, for word processing, for web-surfing, and for e-commerce. The machines they used had evolved from the first personal computers, made by Stephen Wozniak and his friends in Silicon Valley. In 1976 Wozniak and Steve Jobs set up Apple Computers; and by 1984, when they introduced the first Macintosh, the company had sales of $1.5 billion. The computer had strayed far from its roots in the needs and dreams of the Pentagon.

The Book of Life

Even while old projects slumbered or were transformed, new enthusiasms continued to be advanced. By the end of the twentieth century, biology rather than physics had become the most glamorous of all scientific disciplines. As a result of the deciphering of the DNA structure by James Watson and Francis Crick at Cambridge University in

1953, the molecule became the preferred research subject in biology. By the mid-1980s, the notion of mapping the human genome began to take shape. In 1990 the Department of Energy (DOE) and the NIH launched a joint Human Genome Project (HGP) to spend $3 billion over fifteen years in an effort to find all the human genes (perhaps 100,000 in number) and sequence the three billion DNA basepairs. The head of the HGP was none other than James Watson, the co-discoverer of the structure of DNA. He asserted that "similar to the 1961 decision to send a man to the moon, the United States has committed itself to a highly visible and important goal" (Watson 1990: 44). Enthusiasts also compared the HGP to the wartime Manhattan Project that had developed the atomic bomb, a clear signal that it was the turn of biologists to receive headlines and big budgets.

What made this transformation to Big Science even more dramatic was that the NIH had operated as an increasingly old-fashioned cottage industry. Traditionally the main support for biologists, the NIH made individual grants to scientists who brought to the agency their research ideas for approval and funding. Now this " 'moon shot'-type macro project," as it was termed, was set to industrialize yet another branch of science. If experience was any guide, biology was about to experience a bureaucratic and hierarchical form of management, with work tightly coordinated by professional administrators rather than by bench scientists, and conducted in large, heavily-financed centers. To extend the industrial metaphor even further, it was assumed that the actual work of mapping the genome would be done by at least semi-automated machinery. Such work was exacting and excruciatingly boring.

If few wanted to do the dog-work of mapping, the glamour and possible profit of interpreting the data and patenting new processes and even life forms attracted many biologists, plus more than a few pharmaceutical companies. The fact that the HGP was to be an international effort, with major teams in the United Kingdom, Germany, France, Japan, and China, made the stakes much larger than simply scientific fame and glory. With biotech engineering projected to be the high-technology industry of the twenty-first century, industrial competition and national standing were of major consideration. The "post-genomic world" may find biologists "on the verge of new knowledge, vast in scale and thrilling in importance" (Wheeler 1999: A-17). But as the history of the intertwined technology and science of the twentieth century suggests, intellectual rewards promised to be only a part of the payoff.

Why America?

It is instructive to ask why, by the mid-twentieth century, the United States of America had become the world leader in things scientific and technological, especially in those technologies that were heavily dependent upon science. Part of the explanation, surely, is that the United States is a large and populous nation, lavishly endowed with natural and human resources. The sociologist Joseph Ben-David, however, has also emphasized the character of American universities. In the US could be found an "enterprising system of universities working within a pluralistic, education, and economic system [which] has created an unprecedentedly widespread demand for knowledge and research and has turned science into an important economic resource" (Ben-David 1984: 162). "Enterprising" and "pluralistic" are the key words here, and the harvest was not only in Nobel Prizes but also in the tens of thousands of students who flocked to American science and technology programs from around the world. Lavish funding was a necessary but hardly sufficient cause. The rich mix of scientific institutions ("estates"), and the freedom with which monies and ideas flowed back and forth between them, created a system within which feed-backs could occur and synergies develop.

One other reason for the power of science and technology in the United States was that, by the opening of the twentieth century, Americans were very familiar with applying to both, in pursuing social as well as personal goals. The national aspiration to life, liberty, and the pursuit of happiness was a political promise. But politics could be difficult and messy, with losers as well as winners. Over the nineteenth century Americans had gotten into the habit of using science and technology in an attempt to avoid compromise, frustration, and failure (often associated with politics). Goals could be achieved rather less painfully through research and development.

In the decade of the First World War, Frederick Winslow Taylor told a congressional committee that conflict over "dividing the pie" was leading to class warfare, and that both labor and capital should cooperate instead – so that the pie could be made larger. About the same time Henry Ford famously proposed to solve the urban problems by providing cars cheaply enough for people to leave the cities easily. Both men were advocating a technological fix for problems that were essentially political in nature, and their kind of argument struck a responsive chord in the public. From the belief that missiles in space are the best way to make us safe to the faith that a new car will make us popular and sexy, technology has become the preferred method of solving problems. And from putting off government regulations until "more re-search" is done to the appointment of panels of experts to find "scientific" (and therefore presumably disinterested) solutions to problems, science has become an equally attractive way to avoid (or at least camouflage) difficult political choices. Throughout the past century Americans favored technology and science because they could apparently deliver the good life, though the politics the citizenry hoped to avoid were exacerbated by being deflected and disguised.

By the close of the twentieth century, most historians and sociologists of science and technology had reached the conclusion that, at least to some degree, science and technology were socially constructed. Scientists and engineers have been alarmed at this notion, insisting that scientific laws are more than just agreed-upon stories. But those historians and sociologists insist that they *are* stories, and that they are agreed upon, at least until the community of practitioners agrees upon some different story. These stories can be analyzed not just for how much "truth" they contain, but also by their narrative strategies, their recourse to gendered assumptions, for example, and for their omissions: what they leave out of their frame. At the same time, scientific and technical activity and understandings occur within the society with which they interact. Politics, economics, and issues of cultural authority are never far away from what may look, at first, like purely "technical" decisions and choices.

REFERENCES AND FURTHER READING

Ben-David, Joseph (1984) *The Scientist's Role in Society: A Comparative Study.* Chicago: University of Chicago Press.

Calvert, Monte A. (1967) *The Mechanical Engineer in America, 1830–1910: Professional Cultures in Conflict*. Baltimore, Md.: Johns Hopkins University Press.

Collins, Harry and Pinch, Trevor (1998) *The Golem at Large: What You Should Know about Technology*. Cambridge: Cambridge University Press.

Cowan, Ruth Schwartz (1983) *More Work for Mother: The Ironies of Household Technology from the Open Hearth to the Microwave*. New York: Basic Books.

—— (1997) *A Social History of American Technology*. New York: Oxford University Press.

Dupree, A. Hunter (1957) *Science in the Federal Government: A History of Policies and Activities to 1940*. Cambridge, Mass.: Harvard University Press.

FitzGerald, Frances (2000) *Way Out There in the Blue: Reagan, Star Wars, and the End of the Cold War*. New York: Simon and Schuster.

Hounshell, David A. (1984) *From the American System to Mass Production, 1800–1932: The Development of Manufacturing Technology*. Baltimore, Md.: Johns Hopkins University Press.

Hughes, Thomas P. (1983) *Networks of Power: Electrification in Western Society, 1880–1930*. Baltimore, Md.: Johns Hopkins University Press.

—— (1989) *American Genesis: A Century of Invention and Technological Enthusiasm*. New York: Viking Press.

—— (1998) *Rescuing Prometheus*. New York: Pantheon.

Kevles, Daniel J. (1978) *The Physicists: The History of a Scientific Community in Modern America*. New York: Alfred A. Knopf.

Kevles, Daniel J. and Hood, Leroy (eds.) (1992) *The Code of Codes: Scientific and Social Issues in the Human Genome Project*. Cambridge, Mass.: Harvard University Press.

Kohlstedt, Sally Gregory and Rossiter, Margaret W. (eds.) (1985) "Historical writing on American science," *Osiris*, 2nd ser. 1, pp. 5–32.

Leslie, Stuart W. (1993) *The Cold War and American Science: The Military-Industrial-Academic Complex at MIT and Stanford*. New York: Columbia University Press.

Penick, Jr., James L. et al. (eds.) (1972) *The Politics of American Science: 1939 to the Present*, rev. edn. Cambridge, Mass.: MIT Press.

Pursell, Carroll (ed.) (1972) *The Military-Industrial Complex*. New York: Harper and Row.

—— (1995) *The Machine in America: A Social History of Technology*. Baltimore, Md.: Johns Hopkins University Press.

Reich, Leonard S. (1985) *The Making of American Industrial Research: Science and Business at GE and Bell, 1876–1926*. New York: Cambridge University Press.

Rossiter, Margaret W. (1982) *Women Scientists in America: Struggles and Strategies to 1940*. Baltimore, Md.: Johns Hopkins University Press.

—— (1995) *Women Scientists in America: Before Affirmative Action, 1940–1972*. Baltimore, Md.: Johns Hopkins University Press.

Scranton, Philip (1997) *Endless Novelty: Specialty Production and American Industrialization, 1865–1925*. Princeton, NJ: Princeton University Press.

Tichi, Cecelia (1987) *Shifting Gears: Technology, Literature, Culture in Modernist America*. Chapel Hill: University of North Carolina Press.

Watson, James (1990) "The human genome: past, present, and future," *Science* 248, pp. 44–9.

Wheeler, David L. (1999) "For biologists, the post-genomic world promises vast and thrilling knowledge," *Chronicle of Higher Education* 45, pp. A17–A18.

Womack, James P., Jones, Daniel T., and Roos, Daniel (1990) *The Machine that Changed the World*. New York: Rawson Associates.

CHAPTER TWENTY-SEVEN

Conservatism

EDWARD S. SHAPIRO

Although many of their fellow citizens have described themselves as "conservative," American intellectuals and historians have tended to view conservatism as an exotic European import. What relevance, after all, do the classic conservative values of status, stability, tradition, order, community, authority, and deference have for a nation born in revolution and permeated with capitalism, industrialism, individualism, mass democracy, social fluidity, and egalitarianism? Conservative thinkers have often been overwhelmed by a sense of their own irrelevance. The original title of Russell Kirk's *The Conservative Mind* was "The Conservatives' Rout"; Albert Jay Nock titled his autobiography *Memoirs of a Superfluous Man*; Robert Crunden named his anthology of writings of twentieth-century conservative critics of American culture *The Superfluous Men*; the subtitle of the second edition of Clinton Rossiter's history of conservatism is *The Thankless Persuasion*; and Samuel Francis called his morose collection of essays *Beautiful Losers: Essays on the Failure of American Conservatism*.

Little wonder, then, that the historian Alan Brinkley described conservatism as "an orphan in historical scholarship . . . While historians have displayed impressive powers of imagination in creating empathetic accounts of many once obscure areas of the past, they have seldom done so in considering the character of conservative lives and ideas." He suspected "a basic lack of sympathy for the right among many scholars. But it is a result, too, of the powerful, if not always fully recognized, progressive assumptions embedded in most of the leading paradigms with which historians approach their work" (Brinkley 1998: 277, 296). The task of most historians of twentieth-century American politics has been to explain why liberalism has not been more successful, the assumption being that under normal circumstances liberal reforms should have carried the day. Few historians have focused on the question why conservatism did not triumph, since the answer to that seemed so obvious.

Liberal intellectuals have argued that "American conservatism" is a contradiction in terms. For the historian Arthur M. Schlesinger, Jr., egalitarian liberalism has been "the" authentic political tradition of the republic. He has been fond of quoting Ralph Waldo Emerson's famous statement that the essence of politics is the conflict between "the party of Conservatism and that of Innovation." The conservative party, Emerson explained, "vindicates no right, it aspires to no real good, it brands no crime, it proposes no generous policy, it does not build, nor write, nor cherish the arts, nor foster religion, nor establish schools, nor encourage science, nor emancipate slaves, nor befriend the poor, or the Indian or the immigrant." For Emerson there was "always a certain meanness in the argument of Conservatism" (quoted in Schlesinger 1986: 23, 47). This charge was not true when Emerson made it, nor has it been true since. But it is symptomatic of the difficulty that conservatives have had in getting Americans to take their ideas seriously.

Schlesinger has believed in the cyclical nature of American politics: periods of public purpose have been followed by periods of private interest, stemming from the fatigue brought on by liberal activism rather than by the attractiveness of conservative ideas. "A nation's capacity for high-tension political commitment is limited," he noted. "Nature insists on a respite. People can no longer gird themselves for heroic effort. They yearn to immerse themselves in the privacies of life. Worn out by the constant summons to battle, weary of ceaseless national activity, disillusioned by the results, they seek a new dispensation, an interlude of rest and recuperation" (Schlesinger 1986: 28). And they find it in that privatization, materialism, and personal gratification, which Schlesinger has believed to be the essence of conservatism. In *The Vital Center* (1949), he conflated America's authentic politics with the social and economic liberalism of the New and Fair Deals.

A professor of government at Harvard provided the most influential case for the supposed irrelevance of conservatism. In *The Liberal Tradition in America: An Interpretation of American Political Thought since the Revolution*, Louis Hartz claimed that conservatism never took root in the United States because the nation lacked the feudal past that was the basis of all modern conservative movements. As a result, the debate over politics has always taken place within liberal parameters, with virtually everyone accepting the central tenets of nineteenth-century liberalism: private enterprise, individualism, the sanctity of property, and democracy. America "represents the liberal mechanism of Europe functioning without the European social antagonisms" (Hartz 1955: 16). Hartz believed this to have been unfortunate, since dissenting political views such as conservatism and Marxism could not seriously challenge this Lockean ideological straitjacket.

The most controversial attempt to marginalize conservatism was in the socio-psychological book *The Authoritarian Personality* (1950), by T. W. Adorno and others. Influenced by German neo-Marxism, *The Authoritarian Personality* posited a correlation between conservatism and authoritarianism, and described conservatives as anti-Semitic, ethnocentric, prone to violence, and uncomfortable with ambiguity. Conservative ideas need not be taken seriously since they are the products of a diseased personality, and conservatism is less an ideology deserving of refutation than a pathological condition requiring healing.

But what about citizens who still insist on describing themselves as conservatives? For Hartz, conservatism was merely a variant of liberalism, since conservatives sought to conserve a liberal society. How else could one explain the fact that President Herbert Hoover and Senator Robert A. Taft, Jr., the leading Republican opponents of the New Deal and the Fair Deal, as well as the free-market economists Friedrich von Hayek and Milton Friedman, all claimed that they were not conservatives but classical liberals? "American conservatism," the political scientist Sheldon Wolin argued, "was drawn to the defense of liberal principles and practices. While this confluence of liberals and conservatives produced a 'mainstream' of American politics, it left conservatism in something like a permanent identity crisis, without a distinctive idiom or vision." Although Wolin believed it feasible "to identify particular American writers as conservative in outlook, American society, Wolin concluded, "presents a formidable challenge to the conservative imagination" (quoted in Steinfels 1979: 17–18).

Rossiter also questioned whether American conservatism could truly be called Conservative, with a capital "C." "The reason the American Right is not Conservative today," he wrote, "is that it has not been Conservative for more than a hundred years." Not only had conservatives shared in the national celebration of the triumph of democracy, industrialism, capitalism, and individualism. The social and cultural conditions in America were also simply incompatible with traditional Conservatism. "When the one glorious thing to be conservative about was the Liberal tradition of the world's most liberal society," Rossiter asked, "how could a conservative be expected to be Conservative?" (Rossiter 1955: 219, 224). The republic had not produced a Burke or a Disraeli, nor was it ever likely to nurture anyone like them.

The Cornell political scientist was certainly correct in arguing that American conservatives bore little relationship to their European counterparts, and that the place of an American conservative movement in a liberal society has been perplexing. He suggested that the best conservatives could hope for was to modify, but not supplant, the reigning liberalism, to fuse "the rigorous teachings of the Conservative tradition and the happy promises of the American tradition." At its best, American conservatism "will be conservative without being Conservative" (Rossiter 1955: 299–300). This problematic status partially explains the fervent debate within the Right regarding the meaning of "conservatism," and why a host of incompatible groups have claimed title to the conservative legacy. With Burkeans, Spencerians, economic nationalists, free-marketers, individualists, and New Rightists all claiming to be conservatives, the label verges on incoherence.

It was not so long ago, conservative columnist George F. Will noted, that conservatism "was widely considered, at best, an eccentricity and 'conservative' was an epithet." In 1950 a citizen was arrested for creating a public disturbance. A witness to this wrongdoing stated: "He was using abusive language, calling people conservative and all that" (Will 1997: 79). That same year the literary critic Lionel Trilling stressed, in the introduction to his first collection of essays, *The Liberal Imagination*, the irrelevance of what then passed for conservatism. "In the United States at this time," he wrote, "liberalism is not only the dominant but even the sole intellectual tradition." Trilling did not mean, of course, "that there is no impulse to conservatism or to reaction. Such impulses are certainly very strong, perhaps even stronger than most of us know. But the conservative impulse and the reactionary impulse do not, with some isolated and some ecclesiastical exceptions, express themselves in ideas but only in action or in irritable mental gestures which seek to resemble ideas" (Trilling 1950: vii). He could not have foreseen the challenge that conservatism would make to the regnant climate of opinion. *The Liberal Imagination* appeared six years after the publication of Hayek's *The Road to Serfdom*, two years after Richard Weaver's *Ideas Have Consequences*, one year after Peter Viereck's *Conservatism Revisited*, one year before Francis G. Wilson's *The Case for Conservatism*, two years before Bernard Iddings Bell's *Crowd Culture*, three years before Daniel Boorstin's *The Genius of American Politics*, Leo Strauss's *Natural Right and History*, Robert A. Nisbet's *The*

Quest for Community, and Kirk's *The Conservative Mind*, four years before John Hallowell's *The Moral Foundation of Democracy*, and five years before Walter Lippmann's *Essays in the Public Philosophy*. Coming in the midst of this efflorescence of conservative thinking, Trilling's sentiments tell us more about postwar conventional wisdom than they do about the state of American conservative ideas.

There had certainly been conservative voices in America in the United States prior to World War II, including George Santayana, Ralph Adams Cram, Paul Elmer More, Irving Babbitt, the Southern Agrarians of *I'll Take My Stand* (1930), the contributors to the 1936 book edited by Herbert Agar and Allen Tate, *Who Owns America? A New Declaration of Independence*, and the Lippmann of *The Good Society* (1937). There was no conservative "movement," however, to speak of. Conservatism was the preserve of individuals, some of whom were eccentrics, if not outright cranks. They were united by a distaste for the post-Civil War transformation of America from an agrarian republic into a mass democracy of factories, large cities, and immigrant populations.

In the case of Henry and Brooks Adams, this change had been accompanied by a dramatic fall in their own social standing. These grandsons and great-grandsons of US presidents lacked the status, influence, and wealth of their ancestors, and believed that they were condemned to living on the margins of American society. This fall in status resulted in anti-Semitism. The immigrant Jew personified for the Adamses the loathsome finance capitalism that had transformed them into anachronisms. Even "a furtive Yacoob or Ysaac still reeking of the Ghetto, snarling a weird Yiddish," Henry Adams complained in his 1918 autobiography, "had a keener instinct, and intenser energy, and a freer hand than he – American of Americans" (Adams 1931: 238). He nevertheless beheld a greater threat to the nation, believing that the socialists were a more formidable danger to his America than capitalist Jews.

Both Adamses longed for a return to the values of the twelfth and thirteenth centuries. *The Law of Civilization and Decay* (Brooks Adams, 1898) and *Mont-Saint-Michel and Chartres* (Henry Adams, 1913) identified Jews with capitalism, emphasized the conflict in the Middle Ages between the church and the synagogue, and used the cathedrals as symbols for the anti-capitalist values of medieval society. Americans, the brothers believed, were at a crossroads. They had to decide between the values of the Virgin and those of the Dynamo, and the Adamses were not sure whether the degradation of the United States could be reversed. One aspect of this declension was the status of woman, who was "the cement of society, the head of the family, and the center of cohesion," Brooks Adams argued. She "has, for all intents and purposes, ceased to exist. She has become a wandering isolated unit, rather a dispersive than a collective force" (quoted in Kirk 1953: 323). As the diminished position of her gender demonstrated, the theory of progress was a delusion. "The progress of evolution, from President Washington to President Grant, was alone enough to upset Darwin," Henry Adams quipped (quoted in Kirk 1953: 316).

Russell Kirk called Henry Adams the most irritating of American writers. While only his brother came close to matching his pessimism, other conservative thinkers shared their fears for an America seemingly addicted to economic and political concentration, heedless social change, and intellectual novelty. But their warnings went unheeded in a nation that would soon deify Henry Ford and Charles Lindbergh. By the time of World War I, Kirk observed, conservatism existed "only in little circles of stubborn men who refused to be caught up in the expansive lust of their epoch, or in the vague resistance to change still prevalent among the rural population, or, in a muddled and half-hearted fashion, within certain churches and colleges. Everywhere else, change was preferred to continuity" (Kirk 1953: 325).

Of these "stubborn men," Henry Louis Mencken, the *enfant terrible* of American letters, was the most interesting and influential. Few conservatives have accorded him a place in the pantheon of conservative thinkers because of his disdain for fundamentalist religion and his support of socially conscious writers such as Theodore Dreiser. In fact Mencken had a fiercely conservative temperament, and disdained mass democracy, economic and social egalitarianism, and intrusive government. Never comfortable in New York City, he preferred the slower and more traditional pace of life in his beloved Baltimore. His view of culture, marriage, economics, and education was traditionalist; and he was contemptuous of do-gooding politicians like William Jennings Bryan: "an oily fellow, an adept opportunist. His specialty is capitalizing on grievances" (Moos 1960: 12). Bryan, Mencken maintained, was consumed by a dreadful fury against his social and intellectual betters. Woodrow Wilson was a "the perfect model of a Christian cad," "the self-bamboozled Presbyterian," and "a congenital liar" (quoted in Manchester 1962: 145, 172).

But Mencken's greatest scorn was reserved for Franklin D. Roosevelt, who was "the boldest and most preposterous practitioner" of political quackery in modern times. His New Deal saddled the country with a "camorra of quarreling crackpots, each bent upon only prospering his own brand of quackery and augmenting his own power." "The greatest President since Hoover," Roosevelt "carried on his job with an ingratiating grin upon his face, like that of a snake pill vender at a village carnival, and he has exhibited precisely the same sense of responsibility" (quoted in Manchester 1962: 311). More than anything, Mencken wished that such politicians would leave him alone. Unfortunately, they had fallen under the influence of intellectuals such as the Democratic administration's "Brain Trust," which wished to redeem the world from sloth and ignorance. Intellectuals were far worse than politicians, whom Mencken found much more amusing.

Nock's autobiography *Memoirs of a Superfluous Man* appeared in 1943 in the midst of a war that had made a mockery of his Jeffersonian and libertarian values. For Nock there seemed little hope for a conservatism that would extol small government, libertarianism, decentralized property holdings, and what Edmund Burke called "the unbought grace of life." Conservatives shared Nock's assumption that they were fated to be superfluous, to live in a state of permanent estrangement from their countrymen. Little in American culture seemed to give sustenance to a conservative sensibility. Instead, Henry Adams had looked to the Middle Ages, Ralph Adams Cram to English Gothic architecture, Paul Elmer More to classical Greece, the Southern Agrarians to the antebellum South, T. S. Eliot to England, and Nock to France and Belgium. When asked why, if he found America so distasteful, he remained in the United States, Mencken answered: "Why do some people go to zoos?"

Nock died in 1945, and one wonders whether he would have felt so superfluous in an era that saw conservatism come of age. Only after World War II was it possible to speak of such a movement, with its own magazines (including *National Review* and *Modern Age*), organizations, publishing houses, foundations, institutes, and academic redoubts. And it was only then that the literate public began taking conservative ideas seriously. Some citizens were pushed to the right in opposition to the economic and political collectivism accompanying the New Deal and American involvement in World War II, while others moved to the right out of fear of Communism. Whatever the reasons, it is clear that the watershed of modern American conservatism was the 1930s and 1940s.

Rossiter began his *Conservatism in America* by noting that "one of the wonders of the postwar decade has been the revival of conservatism." This rebirth was "hardly as startling in immediate impact as the onslaught of television, the development of the H-bomb, or the outlawing of segregation in education." Yet "the reappearance of conservatism may yet be judged an equally momentous event in the history of the Republic," he predicted. " 'Creeping conservatism' rather than 'creeping socialism' is the grand trend of our times, and there is every reason to believe that the trend will continue for some years to come." But whether conservatism would exhibit the grumpiness and eccentricity that had characterized it prior to World War II or strive for something more elevated was still to be determined. "A high-mined conservatism is America's most urgent need for the years ahead," and until it appears it will be unclear "whether our descendants will look upon the conservative revival of the mid-twentieth century as one of the most fortunate or tragic events in the history of the Republic" (Rossiter 1955: 2–4).

Rossiter was prescient. The postwar conservative movement gathered strength among intellectuals, whose influence spread to the general public. By the 1990s twice as many Americans identified themselves as conservatives as liberals. For the first time in generations, conservative ideas were in the ascendancy during the Reagan administration, and were even being translated into public policy. A decade later Irving Kristol, the "godfather of neo-conservatism," could describe the United States as the only western democracy experiencing a serious revival in conservative thinking. Such comments, however, failed to dissipate the despondency among intellectual conservatives, who suspected that Hartz and Trilling were correct in excluding conservatism from the mainstream. Many of the century's major American conservative books, particularly those written by traditionalists, reflected their authors' unhappiness with American society. This is surprising, coming from authors who stressed the need for community. But, as the conservative historian and poet Peter Viereck noted, conservatives have often exhibited a "rootless nostalgia for roots" (Viereck 1962: 124). Traditionalists like Kirk have had to look to Europe for the sources of an American conservatism. There was a world of difference between Kirk and his hero Edmund Burke, who, according to historian Ronald Lora, "defended the social order that existed; Kirk repudiated his world" (Lora 1971: 180).

This conservative pessimism even continued into the 1980s and 1990s. By then, by all rights, conservatives should have been trumpeting their accomplishments. The economy had emerged out of the doldrums of the 1970s, in part owing to a lowering of tax rates and to a lifting of regulations on business enterprise encouraged by the proudly conservative administration of Ronald Reagan. In addition, the dissolution of the Soviet empire in 1989 and the ending of Communist rule in Russia in 1991 should have been music to the ears of hard-line anti-Communists. And so should also have been the growing national consensus that liberalism lacked the answers to the problems troubling the polity and society. Perhaps at no time in the twentieth century did conservatives have greater reason to be optimistic. Instead, they preferred melancholy.

Conservatives were also depressed by the hold that liberalism continued to exert in the media and academia. With the failures of liberal social and economic planning so obvious, conservatives asked, why had conservatism not won the battle of ideas on the campus or in the studios? Even the most obtuse should presumably have realized that liberalism bore some responsibility for the dreadful conditions of the inner cities, the increasingly dysfunctional behavior of a large segment of the populace intoxicated by dreams of self-actualization and liberation, the cheapening of educational standards, and the decline of civility and manners. As William Bennett, Robert Bork, Gertrude Himmelfarb, and other conservative moralists emphasized, the ethical compass of the citizenry seems to be malfunctioning. They wondered whether there was something inherent in American culture that made it inhospitable to the conservative message.

Indeed, pessimism seems congenital to the temperament of conservatives, who tend to harbor a bleak view of human nature. Their gloom was also fostered by the continuing internecine struggle that has afflicted their movement for much of its duration. Ironically, conflicts within the Right intensified with the demise of Communism, the lessening credibility of liberalism, and the worldwide triumph of free-market economics. Their enemies defeated, conservatives had the luxury of quarreling among themselves; and quarrel they did.

Conservatives frequently used terms such as "unraveling" and "crack-up" to describe the condition of their movement. Historian Paul Gottfried ended *The Conservative Movement* with a chapter entitled "The unraveling of the conservative movement." This defender of the pre-World War II American Right wrote, "the conservative movement reached first maturity and then senescence, and hardly a month goes by without a new analysis of its decline" (Gottfried 1993: 142). The next year he published an article in *Society* entitled "Conservative crack-up continued." R. Emmett Tyrrell, Jr., the publisher of the conservative monthly *American Spectator*, was particularly fond of "crack-up." In 1987 he asked on the editorial page of *The Wall Street Journal* about "A coming conservative crack-up?". By 1992 his uncertainty had evidently disappeared; that year Tyrrell published *The Conservative Crack-Up*, without the question mark.

His book asked why, after so much huffing and puffing, an enduring conservative movement had not emerged. Did it not suffer from an excess of ideological posturing, intellectual dogmatism, and cultural parochialism, and from a failure to deal with political realities? "The Liberals have not had a new idea since the last Ice Age," Tyrrell wrote. Conservatives, by contrast, "have coherent ideas but they have very few gifted pols. The conservatives' relish for politics is only sporadic and almost wholly dependent on their perception that some zany reformer has become a threat to home sweet home" (Tyrrell 1992: 14). While liberals had a zest for practical politics, conservatives had an instinctive dislike for political activity and for creating a vibrant conservative counterculture. Instead, they preferred to contemplate the glories of Rome, of the Middle Ages, and of the antebellum South.

The problem of twentieth-century conservatives stemmed from more than simply a distaste for the practical world of politics. A more important issue was the relevance of conservative ideas to the most salient characteristics of the country. The United States was not only the world's pre-eminent industrial power, but also the world's most mobile society. Its citizens were accustomed to uprooting themselves and moving every decade or so. Their heroes embodied this national trait: Daniel Boone blazing a new trail in Kentucky, the Pony Express bringing mail to the new settlements of the West, the railroad pioneers building tracks that cross the continent, cowboys roaming around the West on their horses. The very language of Americans emphasizes their proclivity to migrate. "Stick-in-the-mud" and "stand-patter" are insults, while "go-getter" and "a mover and a shaker" are compliments. Politicians who stand for office in Britain run for office in America.

Added to this demographic mobility is social mobility, which Americans celebrate as one of the supreme virtues of their society. To have moved from rags to riches is admirable, while to be born with a silver spoon in your mouth is a prescription for a wasted life. The most popular novelist of the nineteenth century was Horatio Alger, whose tales advised boys on how to escape from poverty to middle-class respectability. The exemplar of social mobility was that most revered of Americans, Abraham Lincoln, born poor in Kentucky and educated by candle-light. What place was there in a society of movement, mobility, and migration, conservatives wondered, for ideals of stasis, harmony, and stability?

The warnings of conservative traditionalists who addressed technology, science, and economic progress also appeared incongruous in the most technologically-oriented of all nations. Paul Elmer More, Irving Babbitt, Albert Jay Nock, the Southern Agrarians, and the New Humanists were students of literature, and had shared its animosity toward science and technology. This hostility appeared particularly incongruous as the twentieth century came to a close in the computer age. Even the self-styled conservative politician Congressman Newt Gingrich admired the new electronic technology, proposed to cure educational ills by providing every child with a spanking new computer to surf the Net, and flaunted his friendship with the author of *Future Shock*.

The conservative distrust of change also struck a discordant note in a nation which, from its beginning, has prided itself on its novelty and openness to innovation. Edward Johnson, in his *Wonder-Working Providence of Zion's Savior* (1654), a history of Puritan settlement in the New World, emphasized how new this "New" England was. Because "every corner of England was filled with the fury of malignant adversaries," God had created "a new England to muster up the first of his forces in." This concept of novelty was secularized in the eighteenth century, when the Framers stressed not God's mercy but the uniqueness of America's republican political principles. Thomas Jefferson even suggested that a revolution every twenty years or so was necessary in order to wipe away the vestiges of the past. It is not surprising then that the motto *novus ordo seclorum* (a new order of the ages) was placed on the Great Seal, or that successful politicians of the twentieth century have highlighted the novelty of their programs, whether Wilson's New Freedom, Roosevelt's New Deal, John F. Kennedy's New Frontier, and Richard M. Nixon's New Federalism. In its infancy the postwar conservative intellectual movement was even given the seemingly oxymoronic title "The New Conservatism."

This stress on the new was accompanied by an impatience with history. What use was history to a nation that looked to the future and not to the past? Americans look, as one Hollywood film put it, *Back to the Future*. History is "bunk," declared Henry

Ford, that most revolutionary of all Americans, while lexicographer Ambrose Bierce defined history as "an account mostly false, of events unimportant, which are brought about by rulers mostly knaves, and soldiers mostly fools." This sense of freedom from the past strengthened the belief in American uniqueness. According to our national conceit, the United States did not suffer from the corruptions of Europe. (A 1996 poll reported that while 90 percent of Americans believed in heaven, only 65 percent believed in the devil.) The idea that we are "God's nation" fortifies an optimism that conservatives have believed runs contrary to the lessons of historic experience.

The past strengthened this national belief in the irrelevance of sin and limitations. America was a success story. The United States enjoyed the highest standard of living in the world, had absorbed tens of millions of immigrants, had subdued the West, and, until the Vietnam War, had not lost any of its wars. "We're number one," Americans understandably screamed in international athletic competitions. This confidence and optimism is the ultimate source for the reformist strain in American history, for the belief in the perfectibility of individuals and society. Poverty is seen as a problem rather than a condition, against which presidents have waged war.

In such a country, the warnings of conservatives would not be popular. "The American political mind has been a liberal mind," Rossiter said, "for change and progress have been the American way of life." Its articles of faith have been "perfectibility, progress, liberty, equality, democracy, and individualism" (Rossiter 1955: 66). Conservatives, by contrast, are suspicious of change, believe progress to be a mirage, reject egalitarianism, are skeptical about democratic impulses not grounded in religious teachings and historical precedents, and emphasize community over individualism. Conservative principles underscore limitations rather than liberation, and these are of limited appeal to a people who have been taught to believe that they can scale every mountain and cross every stream. Democracy is also problematic to conservatives, particularly when it has degenerated into a democracy of pandering politicians, cheap popular culture, tabloid journalism, and the pursuit of material pleasures. Paul Elmer More wondered whether his country, "newly shaking itself free from a disguised plutocratic regime," would accept the leadership "of a natural aristocracy which has none of the insignia of an old prescription to impose its authority" (quoted in Kirk 1953: 377).

Another factor in the conservatives' discontent has been their struggle over just precisely what their principles are. Conservatism, along with liberalism, is a notoriously slippery word; and the conservative movement has been racked by conflicts between opposing groups: libertarians and cultural traditionalists, free-market internationalists and economic nationalists, isolationists and militant anti-Communists eager to roll back their enemies. Each claimed to possess the true conservative patrimony and accused the others of heresy. Perhaps the bitter struggles between conservative factions were signs of health and not of sickness. Sociological studies of the American military during World War II revealed that the military units with the highest morale also were those which did the most complaining. Their complaints did not indicate opposition or indifference to the conduct of the war, but precisely the opposite. People gripe the most about that which is most important to them. The same principle holds true for social and intellectual movements. The heartiest of these movements are often those racked by dissent and schism, and this is because their members passionately care about what these movements champion. That the conservative movement had become variegated and able to spawn seeming heresies indicated vigor, not infirmity. These intra-conservative rumbles also obscured the consensus among conservatives regarding certain bedrock ideas.

There has been no shortage of attempts to delineate conservatives' most important beliefs. Kirk's *The Conservative Mind* listed the six canons of conservative thought, and in *The Politics of Prudence* he enumerated the ten most important conservative principles. In *The Conservative Tradition in America* (1996), Charles W. Dunn and J. David Woodard listed the ten most prominent beliefs of conservatism. Jerry Z. Muller's anthology (1997) of conservative writing contains the nine recurrent themes in conservative political and social thought. Rossiter's inventory of conservative concepts in his history of American conservatism comprises twenty-one items. These include the natural inequality of man and the folly of economic and social leveling; the potential tyranny of majority rule; the fallibility of human reason; the civilizing, as distinguished from the vocational, mission of education; the primacy of duty over rights and of the community over the individual; the decentralization of social, political, and economic power; and the widespread distribution of property.

An alternative way to understand the nature of conservatism is to examine its history. Conservatism as a movement, in contrast to conservatism as a disposition, arose in the late eighteenth century in reaction to the French Revolution. In his influential book *The Quest for Community*, Robert Nisbet emphasized that conservatism began in response to the revolution's destruction of what Edmund Burke called the "little platoons," the independent social institutions of the *ancien régime*. This social vacuum was then filled by the single most important political and social phenomenon of the past two centuries, the modern bureaucratic state. The state demanded "the supreme allegiance of men and, in most recent times, [provided] the greatest refuge from the insecurities and frustrations of other spheres of life" (Nisbet 1953: 99). Taken to the extreme, this led to totalitarianism. If freedom, social order, and personal adjustment were to be restored, the citizen would need to recover a sense of being part of significant local relationships, including kinship, religion, vocation, and neighborhood. Thus the essence of conservatism was "the protection of the social order – family, neighborhood, local community, and region foremost – from the ravishments of the centralized political state" (Nisbet 1982: 55).

Nisbet's emphasis on the "quest for community" was written against the backdrop of the rise of Communism and Nazism; and the relevance of his argument to America is not so clear-cut, since the United States never experienced anything remotely similar to European-style totalitarianism. The social, economic, ethnic, and religious diversity of America, as well as its numerous private associations, many religious groups, and independent judiciary emphasized by Alexis de Tocqueville, have been barriers to the powerful political state that Nisbet feared. Foreign and domestic observers have been impressed by the impotence, and not the power, of Washington. Americans have an almost hereditary distrust of politics and of its practitioners.

American conservatives have always been more concerned with repelling the encroachments of the state against individual rights and private enterprise than in defending the prerogatives of Burke's little platoons. They have never felt that visceral dislike of individualism and free-market economics characteristic of European conservatives, and in this respect have been more American than conservative. Individualism, as Tocqueville underscored, has been an important characteristic of American life. In what is arguably America's greatest novel (and certainly its most famous), Huck Finn rejects family, town, and conventional morality, and escapes to the unencumbered and unlimited possibilities of the future via the Mississippi River and the frontier. And if the frontier was as important in national development as the historian Frederick Jackson Turner claimed, then American history could be interpreted as a continual stripping away of social ties, with the individual constantly being forced back upon his own resources. It is not accidental that the great American folk hero is the unattached westerner who, as in the case of the marshal of the classic movie *High Noon* (1952), confronts the forces of evil alone, or that Lindbergh's nickname was "the lone eagle." In its sixtieth anniversary issue, the editors of *Time* summarized in one word the period since the magazine's founding in 1923: "freedom." The nation "was not merely free; it was freed, unshackled," they wrote. "To be free was to be modern; behind most of these events lay the assumption, almost a moral imperative, that what was not free ought to be free, that limits were intrinsically evil." What relevance does a conservatism of community have in the land of Natty Bumppo?

The great concern of twentieth-century American conservative thinkers has been the scope and salience of individualism, and the need to reconcile it, Kirk argued, with the defense of community. Thus the most important traditionalist American intellectual of the second half of the twentieth century recognized the importance of nineteenth-century liberalism and its institutions for America in general and for conservatism in particular. His call to make individualism and community compatible was complicated by the fact that the most prominent exponents on the right of liberty and individualism identified with the interests of industry and big business.

Traditionalist conservatives have distrusted industrialization and big business as revolutionary forces, which have obliterated traditional rural life, created hideous factories and slums, centralized the ownership of property and undermined proprietorship, transformed workers into propertyless proletarians, encouraged demographic mobility at the expense of communal stability, replaced relationships of kin, community, and religion with a cash nexus, disseminated a message of personal salvation through material gratification and hedonism, undermined traditional values of thrift and self-denial, and continually incited dissatisfaction through advertising and installment buying. Amenities, the Southern Agrarians declared in their 1930 manifesto, *I'll Take My Stand: The South and the Agrarian Tradition*, "suffer under the course of a strictly-business or industrial civilization. They consist in such practices as manners, conversation, hospitality, sympathy, family life, romantic love – in the social exchanges which reveal and develop sensibility in human affairs" (Ransom, Davidson et al. 1983: lxiii).

The historian Christopher Lasch argued in 1991 that traditional conservatism, with its respect for limits and localism and its skepticism toward economic growth, the consolidation of productive property accompanying unregulated economic enterprise, and the ideology of progress, was more compatible with the populist tradition than with the free-market tradition of mainstream conservatism. Having become increasingly sympathetic to traditional conservatism in his later years, Lasch was particularly disturbed by the deleterious impact of capitalism on the distribution of property. He believed that the great task of contemporary conservatism was to help restore the widespread distribution of property and revive the ideal of proprietorship

(Lasch 1991). The Jewish theologian Will Herberg joined Lasch in doubting the conservative credentials of the business class. "Is not the temper of dynamic American business too essentially liberal, too essentially radical?," he asked. "Who is more of a rationalistic innovator in his own field, who is less given to tradition, than the American business man, for whom 'revolutionary' is a term of the highest praise in matters of industrial engineering or marketing technique?" (Herberg 1955: 14–15).

But if conservatism implies the preservation of long-standing institutions and values, then advocates of capitalism are not totally mistaken in calling themselves conservatives. Capitalism has been the fundamental economic system of the United States, which has been the world's capitalist power *par excellence*. Of all the major industrial powers, the United States is unique in never having had a vibrant socialist movement, nor an influential critique of capitalism from the Right. Mencken, Nock, Babbitt, More, and Kirk criticized the capitalist mind. But they were isolated, particularly when compared with their counterparts in Europe.

The ambiguous relationship between individualism and conservatism is responsible for the conflict between the libertarian apostles of freedom and the traditionalist champions of virtue, the most important schism within twentieth-century conservatism. While libertarians and traditionalists both opposed the centralized and bureaucratized state, they disagreed regarding the primacy of individual liberty. The libertarian brand of conservatism had its roots in the nineteenth-century liberalism of John Stuart Mill, who claimed that the state should not restrict an individual's actions except when they threatened to harm another. Since a person's right over his body and mind was complete, the state should not interfere even if this would benefit him physically or morally. Taken to an extreme, libertarianism led to the objectivism of novelist Ayn Rand. To flaunt her support of egotism, Rand frequently wore a jewelry pin shaped in the form of the dollar sign.

Traditionalist conservatives favored liberty, but even more they valued tradition, virtue, and ancestral cultural standards. "If we achieve full employment and greater economic growth – if we have cities of gold and alabaster – but our children have not learned how to walk in goodness, justice and mercy," William Bennett asserted, "then the American experiment, no matter how gilded, will have failed" (quoted in Dunn and Woodard 1996: 145). For conservatives such as Bennett, society is more than a sum of discrete individuals. It is a community of shared values and inherited institutions, and the government should strive to inculcate in the people respect for these values and institutions. The family, educational institutions, and private organizations have the major responsibility for maintaining the barriers that separate the virtuous from the decadent. But government and law also have a role. This is particularly true in a republic, bereft of an established church or aristocracy that might maintain moral and cultural norms. In his book *Slouching Towards Gomorrah*, Judge Robert Bork pondered whether censorship of movies, television, records, and books might be necessary to reverse the degradation of popular culture.

This split between the libertarians and traditionalist conservatives prompted Frank Meyer to propose in his 1962 book *In Defense of Freedom* a "fusion" between the two groups. Other thinkers also believed that their shared opposition to statism was more important than their differences. By 1980 Nisbet was asserting that there was little to distinguish conservative from libertarian attitudes toward state power. The two groups agree on the necessity of freedom, particularly economic freedom, on the rejection of egalitarianism except for equality before the law, and on the danger of war and militarization. Finally and most importantly, both abhor contemporary American liberalism.

Nisbet nevertheless noted that there remained an unbridgeable gulf between the libertarianism of a Frank Chodorov, who founded the Intercollegiate Society of Individualists, and the conservatism of a Leo Strauss or a Russell Kirk. Libertarians believe the primary social unit to be the individual, while conservatives claim it is the group. Libertarians and conservatives also disagree about the nature of the authority exercised by private social groups, such as family and church. For conservatives this authority is natural, while for libertarians it may threaten the autonomy of the individual. Kirk was particularly distrustful of these "chirping sectaries" of libertarianism. Their political fanaticism was held to be alien to the conservative temperament. "The libertarian thinks that this world is chiefly a stage for the swaggering ego," he wrote, while "the conservative finds himself instead a pilgrim in a realm of mystery and wonder, where duty, discipline, and sacrifice are required – and where the reward is that love which passeth all understanding." Libertarianism, by contrast, seeks a world in which custom, prescription, and tradition are replaced by a lust for novelty, where people are "oblivious to the wisdom of their ancestors, and form every opinion merely under the pressure of the fad, the foible, the passion of the hour" (Kirk 1996: 275, 281).

Closely related to this conflict between traditionalists and libertarians has been the division between economic conservatives and cultural conservatives. The economic conservatives focus on encouraging economic growth through lower taxes, stable monetary policy, and reducing government's role in the economy. The cultural conservatives, by contrast, emphasize the realm of values. They seek to shore up the traditional family, bolster traditional gender roles, and inculcate an ethic of self-control, deferral of gratification, personal responsibility, and traditional morality. Beginning in the 1960s, cultural conservatives became increasingly pessimistic. The spread of pornography along with higher rates of family breakup, abortion, illegitimacy, sexual promiscuity, drug abuse, violent crime, and welfare dependency indicated a coarsening of American behavior. The diseases that faced the nation, the historian Gertrude Himmelfarb wrote, were moral and cultural rather than political or economic: "the collapse of ethical principles and habits, the loss of respect for authorities and institutions, the breakdown of the family, the decline of civility, the vulgarization of high culture, and the degradation of popular culture" (Himmelfarb 1999: 20). Only a return to traditional values could contain the rot spreading throughout the culture. The Institute for Cultural Conservatism's *Cultural Conservatism: Toward a New Cultural Agenda* (1987), the bible of the cultural conservatives, argued that this reversal could not occur without the active involvement of local, state, and federal governments.

The last of the major conflicts within conservatism was between devotees of the pre-World War II Right, or "paleo-conservatives," and the "neo-conservatives." This tension began in the 1970s and continued through the 1990s. Neo-conservatives were a group of former liberals, disenchanted with the Left because of its flirtation with isolationism, racial and gender favoritism, the counterculture, and bureaucratic social engineering. Paleo-conservatives were suspicious of the conservative credentials of such neo-cons as Irving Kristol, Nathan Glazer, and Norman Podhoretz. They were accused of being merely disaffected liberals and welfare state devotees. In this the "paleos" were not mistaken. Kristol noted that "neo-cons" saw their great task as reinvigorating the heritage of nineteenth-century liberal capitalism by returning "to the original sources of liberal vision and liberal energy so as to correct the warped vision of liberalism that is today's orthodoxy." A neo-conservative, in Kristol's definition, was "a liberal who has been mugged by reality" (1983: 75). But this mugging did not mean that the victim had dispensed with his liberal mind-set.

Clyde Wilson, a paleo historian of the American South, accused the neo-cons of being liberal wolves in conservative clothing. "These refugees now speak in our name, but the language they speak is the same one they have always spoken," he said. "We have grown familiar with it; we have learned to tolerate it, but it is tolerable only by contrast to the harsh syllables of the barbarians over the border. It contains no words for the things that we value. Our estate has been taken over by an imposter, just as we were about to inherit" (Wilson 1986: 6–7). The greatest of the neo-con sins was modernism, an indifference to the great philosophical and theological concerns that the "paleos" held dear. Thus George A. Panichas, the editor of *Modern Age*, criticized the neo-conservatism of *Commentary*, which "merely temporalizes and trivializes and dissimulates spiritual laws and truths. Such a conservatism belongs almost exclusively to the world and is impervious to the primacy of God as the measure of the soul." The theology of conservatism, Panichas said, was being "sacrificed to the new god and the new morality of modernity" (1986: 23).

While suspicious of neo-conservatism, Kirk warned his fellow traditionalists to refrain from heresy-hunting. "Various emphases upon this or that aspect of public policy will remain among the several conservative groupings," he noted, "but enough common ground can be cultivated to maintain a useful unity on certain large questions – supposing we abjure narrow ideology and condescend to think" (Kirk 1986: 27). But to what common ground did Kirk refer? Did social conservatives, libertarians, neo-conservatives, and the traditionalists have anything in common to justify the notion that there is, in fact, a conservative intellectual movement? When the first issue of William F. Buckley, Jr.'s *National Review* appeared in November, 1955, it was accompanied by a "Publisher's statement" providing the rationale for the new magazine. It "stands athwart history, yelling Stop, at a time when no one is inclined to do so, or to have much patience with those who do." Buckley captured the reactive character of conservatism. Its devotees have often been better at identifying what they oppose than what they favor. Twentieth-century conservatism would never have emerged without certain social, economic, and political trends, such as political centralization, egalitarianism, economic consolidation, militarism, and diplomatic interventionism. As a reactive movement, conservatism has changed in response to the latest threats to religion, local institutions, individual freedom, property rights, constitutionalism, and the traditional moral order. The conservative movement, Gottfried noted, had been held together by episodic crusades against Communism, the counterculture, and the welfare state. At certain times the Right has emphasized the marketplace and the teachings of Adam Smith. At other times it has defended tradition, morality, religion, and localism against the forces of modern capitalism and political centralization. The means differed, but the goal remained the same: the protection of what Lippmann called "the good society."

Conservatives have asked whether it is too late to reverse the retreat from bourgeois moral values and the spread of "expressivist" individualism and alternative life-styles. The source of this cultural decline, conservatives agreed, was liberalism. America, Kristol warns, had been corrupted by a liberal ethos of political and economic collectivism on the one hand, and of moral chaos on the other. At a time when the welfare state has extended to all sectors of the society and when a message of individual autonomy and material indulgence dominates the mass media, will the public be attracted to the conservative virtues of localism, decentralization, private property, family, neighborhood, and traditional morality? It is improbable that a conservatism of ideas will prevail in America at a time when the interests of a large percentage of the population are tied to the benefits provided by the federal and state governments. It is thus unlikely that conservative thinkers will cease thinking of themselves as a beleaguered minority. Their mission remains what it has been for the past century: to shout "stop" and hope that someone is listening.

REFERENCES AND FURTHER READING

Adams, Henry (1931) [1918] *The Education of Henry Adams.* New York: Modern Library.

Allitt, Patrick (1993) *Catholic Intellectuals and Conservative Politics in America, 1950–1985.* Ithaca, NY: Cornell University Press.

Brinkley, Alan (1998) *Liberalism and its Discontents.* Cambridge, Mass.: Harvard University Press.

Buckley, William F., Jr. and Kesler, Charles R. (eds.) (1988) *Keeping the Tablets: Modern American Conservative Thought.* New York: Harper and Row.

Carey, George W. (ed.) (1998) *Freedom and Virtue: The Conservative/Libertarian Debate.* Wilmington, Del.: Intercollegiate Studies Institute.

Crunden, Robert M. (ed.) (1977) *The Superfluous Men: Conservative Critics of American Culture, 1900–1945.* Austin: University of Texas Press.

Dorrien, Gary (1993) *The Neoconservative Mind: Politics, Culture, and the War of Ideology.* Philadelphia: Temple University Press.

Dunn, Charles W. and Woodard, J. David (1996) *The Conservative Tradition in America.* Lanham, Md.: Rowman and Littlefield.

Francis, Samuel (1993) *Beautiful Losers: Essays on the Failure of American Conservatism.* Columbia: University of Missouri Press.

Frum, David (1994) *Dead Right.* New York: Basic Books.

Genovese, Eugene D. (1994) *The Southern Tradition: The Achievement and Limitations of an American Conservatism.* Cambridge, Mass.: Harvard University Press.

Gerson, Mark (1996) *The Neoconservative Vision: From the Cold War to the Culture Wars.* Lanham, Md.: Madison.

Gottfried, Paul (1993) *The Conservative Movement,* rev. edn. New York: Twayne.

Hartz, Louis (1955) *The Liberal Tradition in America: An Interpretation of American Political Thought since the Revolution.* New York: Harcourt Brace.

Herberg, Will (1955) "Our conservative heritage recaptured," *New Leader* 38, pp. 14–15.

Himmelfarb, Gertrude (1999) *One Nation, Two Cultures.* New York: Alfred A. Knopf.

Institute for Cultural Conservatism (1987) *Cultural Conservatism: Toward A New Cultural Agenda.* Lanham, Md.: Free Congress Research and Education Foundation.

Kirk, Russell (1953) *The Conservative Mind: From Burke to Santayana.* Chicago: Henry Regnery.

—— (1986) "Enlivening the conservative mind," *Intercollegiate Review* 21, pp. 25–8.

—— (1996) *Redeeming the Time*. Wilmington, Del.: Intercollegiate Studies Institute.

Kristol, Irving (1983) *Reflections of a Neoconservative*. New York: Basic Books.

—— (1995) *Neoconservatism: The Autobiography of an Idea*. New York: Free Press.

Lasch, Christopher (1991) *The True and Only Heaven: Progress and its Critics*. New York: W. W. Norton.

Lora, Ronald (1971) *Conservative Minds in America*. Chicago: Rand McNally.

Manchester, William (1962) *H. L. Mencken: Disturber of the Peace*. New York: Collier.

Moos, Malcolm (ed.) (1960) *H. L. Mencken on Politics: A Carnival of Buncombe*. New York: Vintage.

Muller, Jerry Z. (ed.) (1997) *Conservatism: An Anthology of Social and Political Thought from David Hume to the Present*. Princeton, NJ: Princeton University Press.

Nash, George H. (1996) *The Conservative Intellectual Movement in America: Since 1945*. Wilmington, Del.: Intercollegiate Studies Institute.

Nisbet, Robert A. (1953) *The Quest for Community: A Study in the Ethics of Order and Freedom*. New York: Oxford University Press.

—— (1982) *Prejudices: A Philosophical Dictionary*. Cambridge, Mass.: Harvard University Press.

Nock, Albert Jay (1968) [1943] *Memoirs of a Superfluous Man*. Chicago: Henry Regnery.

Panichas, George A. (1986) "Conservatism and the life of the spirit," *Intercollegiate Review* 21, pp. 22–5.

Ransom, John Crowe, Davidson, Donald et al. (1983) *I'll Take My Stand: The South and the Agrarian Tradition*. Baton Rouge: Louisiana State University Press.

Rossiter, Clinton (1955) *Conservatism in America*. New York: Alfred A. Knopf. 2nd edn. (1962) New York: Viking.

Schlesinger, Arthur M., Jr. (1986) *The Cycles of American History*. Boston: Houghton Mifflin.

Steinfels, Peter (1979) *The Neoconservatives: The Men who are Changing America's Politics*. New York: Touchstone.

Trilling, Lionel (1950) *The Liberal Imagination: Essays on Literature and Society*. New York: Viking Press.

Tyrrell, R. Emmett, Jr. (1992) *The Conservative Crack-Up*. New York: Simon and Schuster.

Viereck, Peter (1962) *Conservatism Revisited*. New York: Collier.

Will, George F. (1997) *The Woven Figure: Conservatism and America's Fabric*. New York: Touchstone.

Wilson, Clyde (1986) "The conservative identity," *Intercollegiate Review* 21, pp. 5–8.

Chapter Twenty-eight

Liberalism

Hans Vorländer

America's liberal tradition has often been disputed but has not yet been disproved. Liberalism not only represents the most powerful strand of political thought in the United States, but is also the pre-eminent means of collective representation and self-interpretation.

The historian Louis Hartz once spoke of an American "mass Lockeanism" (1955: 12), indicating that Americans constituted something of a Lockean mass movement, unconscious subscribers to John Locke's theory of civic society. Hartz, too, conceded that the inhabitants of the United States, though no theorists, had developed a mind-set of "natural liberalism." Their social and political actions were in accordance with the principal Lockean values. Freedom, constitutionalism, limited government, and the protection of property constituted a classical liberal worldview that continued to dominate politics and values well beyond the nineteenth century.

Hartz's argument on the liberal legacy, which was preceded by Richard Hofstadter's work on the nation's political tradition (1948), has consistently been proven true by empirical research on political culture. According to such research, the pattern of opinions, values, and beliefs that can be called liberal remained stable in the twentieth century and is sustained by considerable popular approval and by officials and other politicians. Liberalism as the dominant political and cultural tradition therefore constitutes the specific way this society understands itself.

The hegemony of liberalism in the United States is due to a specific historical development. European liberalism had to prevail against feudalism and absolutism at the end of the eighteenth century and in the early nineteenth century, and then, when industrial capitalism emerged, tried to sustain itself against labor movements and against socialist parties or socialist political thought. But the United States lacked an aristocracy and also, to the amazement of many – especially European – analysts, an influential socialism (both in theory and in political practice). The Americans, as Alexis de Tocqueville noted in 1835, were "born equal" and thus had no need to become so.

Liberalism originated from the double heritage of religious Puritanism and classic republicanism. Its first modern expression is the constitutional theory – a new science of politics – found in the *Federalist Papers*, and its form is the Constitution of

1787–91. Thomas Jefferson's idea of society as well as the political agenda and practice of his presidency, plus that of Andrew Jackson, account for the second period in which American liberalism underwent its crucial social delineation. Jefferson's vision of a classless society of yeoman farmers, which linked political freedom, democratic participation, and economic independence to the prospect of prosperity, is the promise of the "American dream." This was to be an egalitarian, middle-class society of virtuous tillers of the soil and of self-made small businessmen. In this ideal of America, everyone can make a living; and no one enjoys special privileges. Never mind that Jefferson himself kept human beings in bondage; never mind that a republic in which blacks and whites would experience equal treatment was barely conceivable (nor did many whites desire it). Jefferson's vision of a society of free and equal men (if not women) had, at least briefly, an enormous appeal.

But already in the Jacksonian era, this tangible utopia came to an end. The economic and social development put this celebration of opportunity for the common man on the defensive and led to a populist radicalization – marked above all by President Jackson's battle against the second National Bank of the United States. The end of the age of Jackson was also the beginning of the cultural extrication of liberalism from its agrarian and early industrial roots. Even though the social expectations linked to the Jeffersonian ideal of democracy were not met, owing to the changing socioeconomic context, liberalism continued to be the ideological and cultural medium of American self-understanding, in which the hope for individual liberty and economic opportunity had formed a powerful alliance with specifically liberal ideas of order. The main demand of Jefferson's and Jackson's followers for a frugal government, for political minimalism, had been an expression of the belief – not unreasonable then – that society would generate a just and harmonious order by itself. By contrast state interventions in the name of industrial or market interests would inscribe a structure of privileges and thus disturb the natural balance of society. The no-holds-barred laissez-faire rambunctiousness of the Gilded Age, which symbolized the dominant position of liberalism most dramatically, was nothing but social Darwinism employed to rationalize and justify the rapid process of industrial development and concentration. *Laissez-faire* was hence no more than the economically reduced form of an originally much more comprehensive liberal model of society.

In the 1880s and 1890s the disparity between the concentration on industrial capitalism and the model of social expectations of the classic liberalism of an agrarian society led to protests from populists from the countryside and from the early labor movement of the cities. These challenges represented a defense of the former nexus between cultivation and ownership of land and between labor and just wages, which were pitted against the power of the great railway companies and the emergence of the trusts. At the same time, the protesters championed an agrarian and early small-scale industrial America against the tendency of their "incorporation" into a national, urbanized and highly organized society. But this was no fundamental revolt against liberalism. Protest was articulated in the name of classic individual capitalism against corporatism, its perverted form. The hegemonic position of liberalism – in admittedly a slightly social and modified form – prevailed as the system of reference, even after the turn of the century, when socialism was excluded as a political and intellectual option for the transformation of the polity in the United States.

The framework of liberalism can be understood as a continuous tradition of a specific culture of interpretation, in which the national self-understanding is discussed, modified, and confirmed. This culture of interpretation is the turf on which battles are fought over the conceptions of the political world and the "collective" theory of social and political development in the United States. The language of this confrontation, on the political as well as the intellectual level, is by and large (though not exclusively) the language of liberalism. The hegemony of a liberally defined cultural interpretation excludes other languages (though not all) from public discourse, especially those that question the central assumptions of liberalism. Those individuals or movements that propose reforms of or alternatives to dominant middle-class America are forced to legitimize themselves within the scope of liberalism, or to revitalize public forms of expression springing from Puritan or republican traditions that point to the beginning of settlement in North America or to periods of revolution or constitution. These belong to the civil religion of "Americanism" and draw their legitimacy from it.

The liberal tradition cannot be interpreted as a linear development, however. Republicanism and Puritanism have always existed in tension with the dominant liberal currents. This applies to twentieth-century thought as to the early liberalism of the Founders. Those protest and reform movements stemming from Puritan sources led, above all, to a change in liberalism itself. This is especially true for the beginning of the twentieth century: the Progressive Era, when the forces and ideas promoting reform reverted to the strongly republican-influenced philosophy of community, so that a new social philosophy of civic betterment might be formulated. This recourse to communitarian, ethical, and moral elements, which may well be attributed to the traditions of republicanism and religious Puritanism, led to the transformation of minimalism and laissez-faire economics into reformist social liberalism. This change was to become a characteristic of the twentieth century.

Politics within the Framework of the Liberal Tradition

The liberal tradition delineates the political and cultural framework for the political currents and social movements of influence in the nineteenth and twentieth centuries. Alternatives had always been excluded, among them, above all, socialist but also conservative political currents. Since neither an absolute monarchy nor feudalism had ever existed in North America, no European-style aristocratic, counter-Enlightenment conservatism could develop. Hence, there was also no conservative movement (except in the antebellum South) or monarchist party in the nineteenth century. Conversely, those currents that questioned the fundamental national values of liberty, equal opportunity, and a free economic system had particular difficulty surviving in a hegemonic liberal political culture. Models for reform which, at the end of the nineteenth century, strove to restructure the existing industrial society according to the European socialist model never had a real chance in the United States (Ross 1977/8, Vorländer 1997). Except for a few brief successes that Eugene V. Debs's Socialist Party enjoyed, and except for a few instances of syndicalism within the labor movement, socialism in the United States failed to erupt as a powerful political and social movement.

In 1906 the German social scientist Werner Sombart asked why there was no socialism in the United States, although the environment for it was much more favorable than in European industrial societies. Like his American contemporaries, Sombart could not help noting that hegemonic liberalism effected a cultural barrier in the United States. Sombart found that workers had a positive attitude towards capitalism, that the political system met with their approval, and that America – compared to Europe – was socially quite permeable. Thus workers had bigger chances for upward mobility than in the Old World. Apple pie and roast beef, so it seemed to Sombart, constituted the palliative that apparently prevented socialism from emerging in the United States. Since European-style conservatism was an alternative in American development that was excluded as fully as a powerful socialist organization of workers and labor unions, only those political currents that stayed within the given political and cultural framework of liberalism could count on support and success. A social and political reform movement had to prove that it could be reconciled with the frame of mind of liberalism. An authentic conservatism had to legitimize itself by referring to traditional American values and morality.

In the course of the twentieth century, "liberal" and "conservative" became terms of political direction and structured the spectrum of political parties. Republicans began to picture themselves as "conservative" in their opposition to Franklin D. Roosevelt's New Deal and later in their opposition to Lyndon B. Johnson's Great Society. Roosevelt called his attempts at political reform New Deal Liberalism, in imitation of the New Liberalism of the English Liberal Party at the turn of the century. In doing so, he picked up the thread of the progressive movement from his predecessors Theodore Roosevelt and Woodrow Wilson during the first two decades of the twentieth century. FDR introduced the term "liberalism" into everyday political language (Rotunda 1986) in order to define his agenda for a new national politics, which would lift the economy out of the Great Depression and reduce unemployment by means of industrial and social policy. This constituted the first era of conscious ideologizing of American politics, using a European term to denote a political persuasion. Yet the avoidance of such adjectives as "socialist" or "social democratic" was deliberate; Roosevelt knew that such labels would not conform with American tradition. However, by labeling the reform policy "New Deal," the economic aspirations of the country were specified and fused to a social-liberal identity, thus shaping the next three decades of domestic politics.

Designing the Twentieth Century: The Progressive Movement

Two decades earlier, during the Progressive Era, the approach to such a reform program had already been conceived and justified, and had been "fitted into" the American political culture. At the turn to the twentieth century, the economic, social, and cultural changes that had occurred since the end of the Civil War had created a critical awareness of a radical upheaval – both internal and external – that could no longer be defined in terms of the liberalism of Jefferson and Jackson. With the abandonment of geopolitical isolation, marked by the Spanish-American war in the Philippines, the United States had lost its "innocence" (May 1964) and was poised to become an economic world power. The individualistic and egalitarian "promise" of the "American dream" – equal rights for all, special privileges for none, as phrased during the Jacksonian era – seemed to have run dry at the beginning of the twentieth century (Croly 1965). Upon reaching the Pacific Ocean, continental expansion had come to an end; and the Census Bureau declared the frontier closed as of 1890. Fears of the closure of a safety valve, which had enabled the discontented to escape from the social conflicts of urbanized industrial centers and to settle in the rural West, seemed to be well-founded (Turner 1963). Bitter strikes shook the coal mines, the steel industry, and the railway companies, and demonstrated that the nation would not be spared from violent class conflicts. Blue-collar workers and the urban middle class of the industrial East and the Midwest were under the impression that opportunities for individual ascent and social solidarity were threatened. Large-scale corporate mergers, the awesome power of the trusts, the social power of the new capitalist elite ("plutocrats" or "robber barons"), and the political corruption of which the party machinery of large cities and their "bosses" were so often accused – these were fresh and formidable challenges to the liberal faith.

The United States, therefore, was decidedly no longer an agrarian capitalist state that depended on wealth originating in unlimited space and resources. What would happen to an ideal of success, historically due to a work ethic based on religion, equal opportunity, small-scale democratic organization, and geopolitical isolation? The Jeffersonian model of a self-sufficient republican society based on independent and free yeomen had been entirely superseded by the economic, social, and cultural developments of the Gilded Age. In attempting to draw conclusions from those developments, the progressives had to assume that socialist formulas – a fundamental transformation of the liberal capitalist system – would not fall on fertile ground in the United States. Equally unrealistic was a restoration of liberal and individualistic capitalism, which the Populists had propagated shortly before the turn of the century. The upheavals in the industrial order had been too radical and widespread to offer an expectation that such a nostalgic approach might work. The progressive movement was thus charged with the task of political and cultural adaptation, so that the United States, as an industrial nation bursting with ambitions for world power, might flourish under changed conditions.

During the administrations of Theodore Roosevelt, William Howard Taft, and Woodrow Wilson, progressivism was able to credit itself with the fulfillment of several attempts at economic and political reform. However, the progressive movement was too heterogeneous to accomplish a comprehensive and uni-directional political plan for reform. Wilson's New Freedom policies sought anti-trust legislation, plus at least a partial restoration of the economic *status quo ante*. Regulatory legislation dealt with international trade and the monopolies of the railroads. Other reforms aimed at democratizing the political system. To a large degree Wilson's program once more revived the classic liberalism of Jefferson. The winner of the presidential election in 1912 had the "common man" in mind – the man on the make – and made him the model for reform policies (Wilson 1913).

The other flank within progressivism, formed from 1912 onwards around former President Theodore Roosevelt and his Progressive (or Bull Moose) Party, was less concerned with the restoration of the old America and a revival of Jeffersonian democracy. In contrast to Wilson's New Freedom, the Bull Moosers backed a politics of "New Nationalism," the most striking characteristic of which was the acceptance of size as a political, economic, and national principle of organization. Accordingly, reorientation was urgently required in three areas. First, a centralization of the federal government was to meet effectively the challenge of the nationalization of the economy and the new social problems that ensued. A rejection of Jeffersonian minimalism and a reversion to Alexander Hamilton's plea for energetic national government was necessary to this process. Second, a new political, economic, and intellectual elite on a national level had to be formed so that, third, the United States could culturally renew itself under the auspices of this new national elite.

The individualistic Protestant community, whether the New England town or the southern farm and village, would no longer be the uncontested collective goal of the good life. Rather, it was imperative to assimilate *culturally* to the new large-scale economic and political structure. That, in turn, could only be accomplished by applying and adapting earlier American traditions. A fresh "public philosophy" was to provide the citizenry with an orientation toward the new realm of industry and world politics.

Beginning in 1914, a liberal journal of opinion, the *New Republic*, aspired to leadership in the formation of this public philosophy. The magazine's editors and contributors, especially the pragmatist philosopher John Dewey, were the "Young Intellectuals" – as Harold Stearns (1973) labelled them – of the Progressive Era and its aftermath. They believed that mastery rather than passivity, conscious direction rather than drift, needed to be adopted, to guarantee national integration and achieve cultural renewal. These Young Intellectuals were liberal pragmatists. Dewey as well as the editors of the *New Republic* (Herbert Croly, Walter Lippmann, and Walter Weyl), supported the US involvement in the First World War. Those most closely associated with the weekly also tended to exercise political influence by offering advice to officials and by helping to shape public policy (Forcey 1961; Steel 1980; Stettner 1993). The New Republic has continued to serve to the present as the voice of modern liberal reform, especially from its perch on the East Coast and among intellectuals (Seideman 1986). The editors of the magazine had learned from the experience of the First World War that governmental action could be decisive in shaping the forces of history. The war economy had demonstrated the necessity as well as the feasibility of a federal system devoted to administrative and regulatory authority. Even in times of peace, centralized activism could be expected to guarantee the efficient administration of an industrial order. Scientific knowledge findings and professional experience were exalted, as the best means of overcoming the nineteenth-century "natural order" and laissez-faire ideology that would have meant "social chaos" in the changed context of industrial development. Drift might finally be replaced by mastery (Lippmann 1985).

Just as regulated trusts could contribute to overcoming the anarchy that capitalist competitiveness risked, politics could be called upon to solve, with the help of "experts," the social problems resulting from industrialization and social incorporation. This would, according to the New Nationalists, achieve political adaptation to the changes in the industrialized economy. In this manner, a federal government that regulates capitalism and provides for social security could be imagined and worked for in the United States. In this respect the reformers acted as modernizers. But the program for cultural and moral renewal was clearly intended to constitute a limited modernization, and was not meant to be a radical rejection of sacrosanct traditions. The reformist program adhered to both liberal individualism and the residue of

Puritanism, and Dewey in particular sought to adapt the republican ideas of community to the industrial order. Venerable American traditions came with a new look; the acceptance of the modern industrial age coincided with the affirmation of long-standing cultural values. Croly's program of "cultural reconstruction" (1965: 417) championed individual regeneration and the revitalization of an ethos that not only allowed for material wealth but also made work itself – the striving for "excellency" – the purpose of life.

What remained of Croly's extravagant claim to redefine completely "the promise of American life" (1965) was, in the end, not much more than a proposal to empower a new intellectual elite, which would be entrusted with furthering the nation's development for the remainder of the twentieth century. The claim of embodying expert knowledge and enlightened leadership in this necessary national reconstruction reinforced the project of progressivism. Seven decades later, however, such a claim looked like a setback, discrediting liberal reform as out of touch with popular sentiment. The cultural and economic conservatism of the 1980s and 1990s was delighted to criticize the alleged arrogance of the intellectual "experts" and made liberalism itself sound like a term of reproach.

It should not be overlooked, however, that the progressives widened the spectrum of accepted political alternatives to include acceptance of at least the outlines of the welfare state. Although social policy as such remained vague, the progressives' reform model of the polity as well as admittedly brief "test run" during the First World War foreshadowed the essence of the New Deal and even of its internationalism. Progressivism thus anticipated the liberal ideology and practice of the New Deal, which exercised a certain hegemony until the 1980s and the "Reagan revolution." It follows that, after turning from the dominating figure of Theodore Roosevelt to President Wilson after 1916, the progressives increasingly regarded themselves as reformers and thus reshaped the meaning of liberalism (Forcey 1961). They contributed to the breakthrough of the idea of a positive attitude toward the (federal) government. That reorientation did not negate – but somewhat qualified – Jeffersonian anti-statism. The way was thus paved for a development of the rationale for much greater federal regulation of the economy and for intervention in social matters as well. The liberalism of the modern welfare state had become conceivable.

Testing the Limits of Liberalism: The New Deal and the Great Society

Franklin D. Roosevelt was able to build upon the foundations laid by the progressive movement, and his social and economic policy enabled him to advance the establishment of the regulatory state and the welfare state. In 1935 he introduced the federal system of Social Security, and the Wagner Labor Relations Act made labor unions into full partners in the process of collective bargaining with employers. Agricultural markets were controlled through the subsidizing of the prices of farm products. The National Industry Recovery Act permitted the planning and stimulation of the manufacturing economy, though this positive role for the federal government was soon declared unconstitutional by the Supreme Court. As public entrepreneur, the federal government also affected the infrastructure by providing a public utility, the Tennessee Valley Authority. In helping to plan and stimulate the economy, the New Deal adapted the European social liberalism of the dawn of the twentieth century

(Holl et al. 1986). Washington, DC, became a broker, adjudicating the interests of various players in the economy and society. Only with the Second World War and the boom thereafter was it evident that prosperity could be achieved without deploying the instruments of a planned economy. A Keynesian strategy could be accomplished – government spending (especially for war and defense) could substitute for insufficient consumer demand – without enlarging the welfare state to the degree that the European industrial democracies had to do.

The New Deal was certainly a deviation from the laissez-faire version of liberalism that had previously dominated discussions of the role of government in the economy. The federal guarantee of social security broke with the ethos of individual account-ability, by making the government responsible for protecting the citizenry from the uncertainties and ravages of capitalism. Roosevelt did not intend, however, to estab-lish an egalitarian socialism. He remained within the framework of the political ideas of liberalism, even as he altered the balance away from laissez-faire toward a more social emphasis. The concentration of capital, the rapid urbanization and industrial-ization of the United States had been noticeable as far back as the Gilded Age. But before Franklin D. Roosevelt, no politician had won such popular approval for a program of reforms that drew so systematic a conclusion from the drastic structural changes in industry and society.

Social liberalism, which dictated domestic politics from the New Deal into the 1960s, marked the limits of welfare state activity as determined and limited by the individualistic political culture of the United States. This was illustrated by the fate of Lyndon B. Johnson's Great Society, a program that attempted to enlarge social-liberal approaches to politics into social-democratic welfare programs. Whenever the federal government attempted to assume a more active role in welfare and economic planning, the popular appeal that such liberalism hoped for waned. Repub-licans and neo-conservatives attacked the spending policies and intervention of the Washington establishment, and Southern Democrats withdrew their support. The policies of the Great Society, which may be termed socially ambitious liberalism, did not fail in all respects. The "war on poverty" drastically reduced the poverty rate, particularly among the elderly. The civil rights policies of all branches of the federal government were quite successful in reducing racial discrimination. In addition, a series of transfer payments improved the chances for members of the lower classes. Yet the welfare programs of the Great Society were on the whole considered to be a failure. The Great Society provoked its conservative opponents into action; these critics of welfare-state activism also lamented the decline of cultural values. Political conservatism received such a boost in the 1970s that the "Reagan revolution" swept into office in the 1980 presidential elections.

The New Deal coalition of Democrats had consisted of southern whites, union members in the Northeast and Midwest in particular, Catholics of Irish, Italian, and Polish descent, blacks and Jews. This coalition had survived into the 1960s. In 1968 its majority status disappeared. The Democratic Party machinery of the industrial Midwest and East Coast lost its influence over its constituents; and union power stagnated, as the percentage of workers belonging to trade unions declined signifi-cantly. The social advance of the children and grandchildren of the immigrants from Ireland and from southern and eastern Europe altered voting patterns, which became more conservative. At the same time, new groups conspicuously emerged from the movements of the 1960s and joined the ranks of blacks, Jews, and urban intellectuals within the Democratic Party, such as feminists, Hispanics (other than Cuban Americans), and homosexuals. In some respects the Old Left of the 1930s had become the New Left of the 1960s and 1970s. Marked by the New Politics, the Democratic Party thus developed into a coalition of minority groups and ailing unions – and marginalized itself from masses of American voters. White southerners, members of an amorphous middle class, and yuppies in the cohort of baby-boomers became independent or unaffiliated voters, or joined the Republican Party.

The economic conservatism of these groups contributed considerably to the success of the Reagan coalitions that swept to victory in 1980 and 1984. The old idea of the reduction of government influence on the economy – the promised emancipation of private enterprise from governmental monitoring – made headway. Reaganomics was a mixture of fiscal conservatism, military Keynesianism, and a rigid monetarist policy. The social liberalism of the New Deal was deprived of its sanction in Washington, which promoted the shift of political and economic momentum from the Rustbelt to the Sunbelt. The decay of the coal and steel industries and of the manufacturing of many mass-produced goods (such as rubber tires) stood in contrast to emerging new industries, not only the long-powerful oil and chemical industries but especially high-tech electronic companies. Between 1970 and 1980, the creation of new jobs, particularly in the Southeast and Southwest, triggered the migration of 20 million Americans from the Northeast and the Midwest to the Sunbelt. There the American dream was revived, encompassing an entrepreneurial spirit and upward social mobility. Conservative voters seemed to make obsolete that type of moderate social-liberal government associated with the New Deal.

The "Reagan revolution" not only involved the return of economic and fiscal conservatism, but also – above all – spurred a renaissance of cultural conservatism, as though traditional American values were being juiced with new life. Two targets were identified: the Communist-socialist enemy in the geopolitical competition abroad, and liberal and permissive attitudes linked to the counterculture within the United States. Cultural conservatism was a position that united otherwise disparate conservative movements, whether the fundamentalist evangelical Moral Majority and the New Right, or the intellectuals who championed neo-conservatism.

Getting Nervous: Liberals Turning into Neo-conservatives

For a while, it appeared as if the neo-conservatives would finally be able to help establish an authentic American conservatism. They were often Jewish intellectuals who had emerged from the intensely political environment of New York's City College. These neo-conservatives were called – with good reason – "nervous liberals" (Walzer 1980). In the 1960s, most of them had conceived of themselves as liberals who supported Kennedy and Johnson, the politics of civil rights, and opportunities for social equality. That support evaporated, thanks to the student rebellion, the growth of an extensive and centralized welfare state, the formulation of affirmative action, and the clamor of ideological and sexual minorities for public recognition and representation. Some liberals were sufficiently irritated to become neo-conservatives (Steinfels 1979). *The Public Interest*, a quarterly founded in 1964 by Daniel Bell and Irving Kristol, gradually became more conservative, as did *Commentary*, edited by

Norman Podhoretz. Such neo-conservatives wanted to articulate a more modest scope for governmental action. In their view the proper functioning of democracy was threatened: interest groups had seized the political process of opinion-formation and decision-making, and threatened to carry interventionist activism in both the economy and society too far. Sociologist Nathan Glazer criticized the failures of the welfare system in lifting its beneficiaries from dependency, and doubted that the war on poverty could be won by means of government intervention.

In general, neo-conservative criticism was not deeply marked by anti-statist polemics. Having risen socially and professionally on their own from a minority position, without government support, neo-conservatives tended to disapprove of a paternalist state, which claimed to solve political problems but which may in fact have created new ones. Neo-conservatives invoked traditional virtues of individual initiative and favored a free-market economy, since both promised more efficient solutions to the problems posed by industrialization. Yet their own enthusiasm for free enterprise was tempered by a recognition that an unleashed capitalism was itself a major cause of instability and disruption that collided with traditional values. What Judeo-Christian tradition had bequeathed was also threatened by the counterculture, whose advocates and exemplars among students, blacks, homosexuals, and feminists risked turning the venerable Protestant ethic into a "psychedelic bazaar" (Bell 1978: 54).

The neo-conservatives were too intellectual and too academic to rally a broad political movement that could lay claim to the formation of a long-lost, genuine American conservatism. They were nevertheless able to record an enduring success in changing the parameters of public debate. Owing above all to Irving Kristol, who was very influential in business circles, they managed to pave the intellectual way for the Reagan revolution. However, their distance from day-to-day politics showed that not all neo-conservatives became enthusiastic Reagan supporters; and they maintained a distance from evangelical and fundamentalist conservatives, who became an integral part of the Reagan coalition.

The fundamentalist right of the Moral Majority were much less imposing intellectually, but enlisted considerable popular support in the Bible Belt of the South and in the Midwest. Not only did the fundamentalist movement help bring Reagan his impressive victory in the 1980 presidential elections; this New Right also revived the structural majority of the Republicans on the national level and thus left liberalism enfeebled. Such conservatives dreamed of restoring an "old" America, which included the "devolution" of the federal government, the reduction of federal intervention in the marketplace, and greater autonomy for state and local government. The conservative revolution regarded itself first and foremost as a cultural movement, since the "old" America was associated with a virtuous society in which the values of family, religion, and community were pronounced. The New Right and the self-proclaimed Moral Majority protested the influence of liberalism, by criticizing affirmative action, the legalization of abortion, the prohibition of mandatory school prayer, "value-relativizing" education, and pornography in print and the electronic media. The dream was to re-create a society that had allegedly flourished before the civil rights movement, before the emancipatory spirit of the 1960s, before the ambitious liberalism of the Great Society.

To the authoritarian moralism of the Christian Right, secular humanism, and liberal thought in general, could be defined as the arch-enemy. Thus was revitalized that religious fundamentalism in American politics that had marked periods of "creedal passions" in American history (Huntington 1981: 85). This Christian evangelism was able to become politically powerful and to organize national and local campaigns against the right to an abortion and the implementation of affirmative action, and for a return to the family values of white America. Such campaigns were activated through a sophisticated knowledge of the methods of modern political management, and through an ability to rally continued support from eloquent televangelists, especially Jerry Falwell, who played an important role in the development of the Moral Majority. The Christian Right rose to become a powerful pressure group and was decisive in giving the Republican Party a landslide victory in the 1994 congressional election.

However, success and failure were closely entwined in the "conservative revolution" of the 1980s and 1990s. The comet-like rise of Congressman Newt Gingrich, a Georgia Republican, as Speaker of the House of Representatives exemplified how quickly a self-proclaimed prophet could become the victim of the very radicalization that he himself had brought about. By going too far in his programmatic "roll-back" policy against liberalism, Gingrich scared off middle-of-the-road voters upon whom the Republican Party also depended; and his power had largely evaporated by the summer of 1996. Gingrich nevertheless managed to challenge President Bill Clinton with numerous legislative maneuvers, which resulted in fundamental changes in various fields of politics, especially in welfare reform. The social liberalism that had been born in the Progressive Era was barely breathing by the beginning of the twenty-first century.

Reconsidering Liberalism: The Critique from Outside

In the 1970s American liberalism was put under pressure from different angles. It was challenged not only by the political and cultural conservatism of the New Right and the Moral Majority, but also by multiculturalism, by the women's movement, and by communitarianism. All of these tendencies doubted the feasibility of core liberal political concepts. The radical challenge that liberalism faced from the left was far more than a simple political conflict. It threatened to undermine the genuinely liberal identity of American society.

By then the development of liberal theory had reached its peak and also its temporary culmination with John Rawls's *A Theory of Justice* (1971). Its author had intended to draft a general theory of justice for modern society. But Rawls, a philosopher at Harvard, also impressively managed to define the specifically American experience of a political order based on law. That order could lay claim to the principle of fairness. In this respect his interpretation of justice aimed at constituting a universal theory, which was Kantian in its rationalism and contractualism. Yet *A Theory of Justice* is distinctly American in its effort to capture the evolution of the nation's liberal political development. Rawls insisted that any satisfactory defense of the ideal of justice had to be founded upon a system of rights. Only in this way could equal liberties be guaranteed. In fact, American political development, particularly the reform liberalism of the era after the Second World War, was based on the enforcement of basic constitutional and civil rights. The contours of a rights-based liberalism became clear with the civil rights activism of the Supreme Court, highlighted in *Brown* v. *Board of Education* (1954) if not earlier, and gaining in momentum with the civil rights legislation of Johnson's Great Society. Rawls also gave warrant to the moderate social liberalism of redistribution with his "difference principle," according to which those persons benefiting the least from their status in society can at least demand the prospect of a better position. In this respect Rawls's *Theory of Justice* reconciled classic liberalism with its modern reform-oriented variant and successor, social liberalism.

However, this great philosophical achievement could not prevent the radical criticism that was to follow. On the whole the feminist movement could still be regarded as a political attempt to demand full equality based on a system of rights. By no means did this constitute a deviation from the liberal tradition of individual rights – no more than the civil rights movement had deviated from that faith in the 1960s. What called that faith into question was how affirmative action policies might be justified. Could the aim of equal rights for everyone under a color-blind Constitution be rendered compatible with the persistence of racial differences and discrimination? Could equality of opportunity be achieved by demanding equality of result? Could individual rights be made consistent with a recognition of group interests (Young 1996)? Even though the imperatives of pluralism appeared to be in accordance with a liberal, individualist interpretation of rights, the multiculturalist insistence upon the value of diversity and difference was very likely to extend beyond the boundaries of the liberal tradition.

Also aiming at a radical critique of liberalism was communitarianism, which argued that the modern liberal self can only develop in the nexus of society. Yet liberalism often seemed unaware of this underlying reality. Communitarianism insisted on the prevalence of the "good" over the "right" (Sandel 1982). This criticism was mainly directed at Rawls's *Theory of Justice*, but all variants of a rights-based liberalism were inevitably targeted. "Good" was defined as those ideas and values that provide the only basis to develop a meaningful life and that are shared by the members of society. According to this argument, any philosophy that defines the individual as a bearer of rights wrongly ignores the fact that rights are only anchored in social practice. Because liberalism is blind to the communal prerequisites of society, the view of the conditions for social integration is obstructed. Rawls, as did the representatives of political liberalism in general, took these arguments seriously, but continued to adhere to their own conception of rights on reasonable grounds. This stance, one could argue, had the advantage of allowing for various conceptions of the "good." The principle of an "overlapping consensus" renders social difference – and thus different life-styles and subcultures – possible (Rawls 1993).

At the same time, however, the cultural version of communitarianism drew attention to a potential threat to the cohesion of contemporary American society. According to this criticism, individual freedom had been socially rooted in family, community, and religious groups in the eighteenth and nineteenth centuries. The advance of liberal and industrial capitalism at the turn to the twentieth century shifted the social balance towards economic achievement and enrichment. Earlier religious and moral restrictions thus became obsolescent. Losers in this process were the small social units and communities of the past as well as the vigor of public life itself. Citizens were too easily tempted to withdraw into privacy and to forget their civic commitments and general obligations. With the increasing atomization of society, plus the intrusion of the various bureaucracies of the welfare state, the citizens' initiative and the self-healing capacities of society had become paralyzed.

Tocqueville in particular had already voiced this concern in his analysis of the mass democracy of the United States in the 1830s. He, too, pointed out that such a society – made up of newcomers – is dependent upon intermediate associations and civic spirit in order to provide society with stability. American communitarianism could hence be understood as a reflection of those forms of community, ranging from immigrant groups, religious sects, and other voluntary associations. From republican and Puritan origins came modern individualism and liberalism, as Max Weber had so impressively demonstrated. The communitarian critique was not necessarily a denial of the liberal tradition, but could be read as an effort to remind liberalism of the social, cultural, and moral prerequisites on which a worthy polity might be based. Communitarianism, as political theorist Michael Walzer (1990) understood it, could well be read as a self-criticism of liberalism, a way of strengthening it instead of displacing it.

What Remains of Liberalism?

The liberal tradition emerged at the end of the eighteenth century and flourished in the nineteenth century. This heritage was culturally thick and resonantly expressed the national self-image. The American liberal tradition could best be understood as a shared culture of political self-understanding and self-interpretation. At the turn to the twentieth century, however, the American liberal tradition underwent a double transformation. What had earlier been imagined as a single legacy split into a branch of classical liberalism and into another branch of social liberalism. The progressive movement can be understood as a social, moderate reform-liberalism, which had much in common with the English New Liberalism and its counterpart on the European continent. There was a transatlantic reform community stemming mainly from religious, ethical sources and from social thought. At the same time, however, classical economic liberalism mutated into a form of ideological conservatism. While progressivism, the New Deal, and the Great Society aimed to develop a welfare liberalism, conservatism sought to protect free enterprise from undue government intervention in the economy and from collective social security systems that seemed to deny the value of self-reliance.

The "conservative revolution" of the 1980s and 1990s forced reformist liberalism onto the defensive. In particular the Clinton administration had to yield to funda-mental changes, especially in welfare politics. Health-care reform, which Governor Clinton had as a presidential candidate in 1992 labeled his most important reform project, failed. Social Security reform also had to be postponed; and in the summer of 1996, the most drastic reduction of welfare programs occurred when Clinton signed a comprehensive welfare reform act into law. This astonishing reversal in social policy, the radical cut of aid programs, the transfer of federal programs to the states, and the switch from welfare rolls to payrolls meant nothing less than the termination of the welfare liberalism instituted during the New Deal. The defeat of the liberalism that had been inaugurated by Franklin D. Roosevelt was the greatest achievement of the conservative revolution of the end of the twentieth century. If there is to be a twenty-first-century American liberalism, it will have to be reinvented.

REFERENCES AND FURTHER READING

Appleby, Joyce (1992) *Liberalism and Republicanism in the Historical Imagination*. Cambridge, Mass.: Harvard University Press.

Bell, Daniel (1978) *The Cultural Contradictions of Capitalism*. New York: Basic Books.

Bellah, Robert N., Sullivan, William M., Swidler, Ann and Tipton, Steven M. (1985) *Habits of the Heart: Individualism and Commitment in American Life*. Berkeley: University of California Press.

Croly, Herbert (1965) [1909] *The Promise of American Life*, ed. Arthur M. Schlesinger, Jr. Cambridge, Mass.: Harvard University Press.

Diggins, John Patrick (1984) *The Lost Soul of American Politics: Virtue, Self-Interest, and the Foundations of Liberalism*. New York: Basic Books.

Forcey, Charles (1961) *The Crossroads of Liberalism: Croly, Weyl, Lippmann and the Progressive Era, 1900–1925*. New York: Oxford University Press.

Galston, William A. (1991) *Liberal Purposes: Goods, Virtues and Diversity in the Liberal State*. New York: Cambridge University Press.

Glendon, Mary Ann (1991) *Rights Talk: The Impoverishment of Political Discourse*. New York: Free Press.

Hartz, Louis (1955) *The Liberal Tradition in America: An Interpretation of American Political Thought since the Revolution*. New York: Harcourt, Brace.

Hofstadter, Richard (1948) *The American Political Tradition and the Men Who Made It*. New York: Alfred A. Knopf.

Holl, Karl, Trautmann, Günter, and Vorländer, Hans (eds.) (1986) *Sozialer Liberalismus* [*Social Liberalism*]. Göttingen: Vandenhoeck and Ruprecht.

Hollinger, David A. (1995) *Postethnic America: Beyond Multiculturalism*. New York: Basic Books.

Huntington, Samuel P. (1981) *American Politics: The Promise of Disharmony*. Cambridge, Mass.: Harvard University Press.

Kloppenberg, James T. (1986) *Uncertain Victory: Social Democracy and Progressivism in European and American Thought, 1870–1920*. New York: Oxford University Press.

—— (1989) *The Virtues of Liberalism*. New York: Oxford University Press.

Laslett, John H. M. and Lipset, Seymour Martin (eds.) (1974) *Failure of a Dream?: Essays in the History of American Socialism*. Garden City, NY: Anchor Books.

Lippmann, Walter (1985) [1914] *Drift and Mastery: An Attempt to Diagnose the Current Unrest*. Madison: University of Wisconsin Press.

Lipset, Seymour Martin (1996) *American Exceptionalism: A Double-Edged Sword*. New York: W. W. Norton.

May, Henry F. (1964) *The End of American Innocence: A Study of the First Years of Our Own Time, 1912–1917*. Chicago: Quadrangle Books.

McCloskey, Herbert and Zaller, John (1984) *The American Ethos: Public Attitude towards Capitalism and Democracy*. Cambridge, Mass.: Harvard University Press.

Pells, Richard H. (1973) *Radical Visions and American Dreams: Culture and Social Thought in the Depression Years*. New York: Harper and Row.

Rawls, John (1971) *A Theory of Justice*. Cambridge, Mass.: Harvard University Press.

—— (1993) *Political Liberalism*. New York: Columbia University Press.

Rodgers, Daniel T. (1987) *Contested Truths: Key Words in American Politics since Independence*. New York: Basic Books.

—— (1998) *Atlantic Crossings: Social Politics in a Progressive Age*. Cambridge, Mass.: Harvard University Press.

Rosenblum, Nancy (ed.) (1989) *Liberalism and the Moral Life*. Cambridge, Mass.: Harvard University Press.

Ross, Dorothy (1977–8) "Socialism and American liberalism: academic social thought in the 1880s," *Perspectives in American History* 11, pp. 7–79.

Rotunda, R. D. (1986) *The Politics of Language: Liberalism as Word and Symbol.* Iowa City: University of Iowa Press.

Sandel, Michael J. (1982) *Liberalism and the Limits of Justice.* Cambridge: Cambridge University Press.

—— (ed.) (1984) *Liberalism and its Critics.* Oxford: Blackwell.

Schlesinger, Arthur M., Jr. (1986) *The Cycles of American History.* Boston: Houghton Mifflin.

Seideman, David (1986) *The New Republic: A Voice of Modern Liberalism.* New York: Praeger.

Smith, Rogers M. (1993) "Beyond Tocqueville, Myrdal, and Hartz: the multiple traditions in America," *American Political Science Review* 87, pp. 549–66.

—— (1997) *Civic Ideas: Conflicting Visions of Citizenship in US History.* New Haven, Conn.: Yale University Press.

Sombart, Werner (1969) [1906] *Warum gibt es in den Vereinigten Staaten keinen Sozialismus?.* Darmstadt: Wissenschaftliche Buchgesellschaft, 1969. (1976) *Why is There No Socialism in the United States?,* trans. P. M. Hocking and C. T. Husbands. White Plains, NY: International Arts and Sciences Press.

Stearns, Harold (1973) [1921] *America and the Young Intellectual.* Westport, Conn.: Greenwood Press.

Steel, Ronald (1980) *Walter Lippmann and the American Century.* Boston: Little, Brown.

Steinfels, Peter (1979) *The Neoconservatives: The Men Who Are Changing America's Politics.* New York: Simon and Schuster.

Stettner, E. A. (1993) *Shaping Modern Liberalism: Herbert Croly and Progressive Thought.* Lawrence: University Press of Kansas.

Turner, Frederick Jackson (1963) [1894] *The Significance of the Frontier in American History.* New York: Ungar.

Vorländer, Hans (1988) "Transatlantische Reformgemeinschaft an der Wiege des 20. Jahrhundert," *Liberal* 30, pp. 87–91.

—— (1997) *Hegemonialer Liberalismus: Politisches Denken und politische Kultur in den USA 1776–1920* [*Hegemonic Liberalism: Political Thought and Political Culture in the USA 1776–1920*]. Frankfurt-am-Main: Campus.

Walzer, Michael (1980) *Radical Principles: Reflections of an Unreconstructed Democrat.* New York: Basic Books.

—— (1990) "The communitarian critique of liberalism," *Political Theory* 18, pp. 6–23.

Westbrook, Robert B. (1991) *John Dewey and American Democracy.* Ithaca, NY: Cornell University Press.

Wilson, Woodrow (1913) *The New Freedom: A Call for the Emancipation of the Generous Energies of a People.* Garden City, NY: Doubleday, Page.

Young, J. P. (1996) *American Liberalism: The Troubled Odyssey of the Liberal Idea.* Boulder, Colo.: Westview Press.

CHAPTER TWENTY-NINE

The Visual Arts

DOUGLAS TALLACK

An American Century

The Whitney's blockbuster exhibition of 1999, *The American Century: Art and Culture*, derived its title from Henry Luce's editorial in *Life* magazine for February, 1941. Luce believed that a United States, speaking with one voice, must have a world role. But if he correctly anticipated an American process of cultural globalization, he failed to recognize differences within the country and the buffeting that national identity would endure once a wartime unity had been dissipated. Luce's own media business did, however, symbolize the confluence of commerce and culture in an ambiguous logic of innovation and yet sameness, which has characterized the American century as one of reproducible images and populist sentiments, expressed through a battery of cultural forms from print to digitized media.

Within this socioeconomic and technological context and under the impact of modernism – overall, still the cultural movement of the American century – the visual arts have sought to identify what constitutes art and, concomitantly, to formulate relationships between art and life, beginning with what we still call "realism" and continuing through modernism to postmodernism. Indeed, the increasing interdependence of modes of production and dissemination within the culture industry has turned out to be a source of aesthetic innovation. Twentieth-century American artists, aided by Marcel Duchamp (who took US citizenship in 1954), have posed some of the most important questions about art precisely by focusing upon intersections between art forms and also between art and the consumer and industrial culture. In retrospect, we can recognize that this debate is at least as central as the one between stubborn adherents of realism and what was initially a European but, by mid-century, had become an American modernist attack on pictorial representation.

The global reach to which Henry Luce and other forces within the culture industry have aspired has, ironically, undermined not simply the supposed aura of the artwork but, equally, the very idea that there can be a national art. The culture industry needs a cosmopolitan world of rapid technical and industrial change and this formation has eroded the rural base from which nineteenth-century American art drew its strength. In historian Richard Hofstadter's words, "The United States was born in the country and has moved to the city" (Hofstadter 1962: 23); and, subsequently, to the suburb, we can add, thinking of the most important of Frank Lloyd Wright's houses in Chicago and Los Angeles or, in downbeat mood, thinking of what Edward Hopper calls "this sad desolation of our suburban landscape" (quoted in Hughes 1997: 427) and its makeover in the curiously depthless works painted by Eric Fischl in the 1980s. Nature has had its proponents, though: abstract artist Arthur Dove; Ansel Adams, notably in his photographs of Yosemite and Snake River, Wyoming; American Scene painters (Thomas Hart Benson, John Stuart Curry, and Grant Wood) and, also from the 1930s but in an anguished vein, the seascapes of Marsden Hartley; and, in a comprehensive combination of sculpture and architecture, the earthworks of the 1960s and 1970s by Michael Heizer (*Complex One* in Nevada, 1972), James Turrell (his excavation and transformation of the Roden Crater in Arizona), and Robert Smithson. A photograph of *Spiral Jetty* (1970) was chosen for the frontispiece to the catalogue for the second half of the Whitney's exhibition, while Robert Hughes punctuated his eight-part television series, *American Visions* (1997), with low-level aerial swoops over the American landscape and a concluding celebratory analysis of Smithson's astonishing project.

The larger patterns and debates within painting, photography, and architecture – the three visual forms which have been pre-eminent in twentieth-century America – have often been keyed quite directly to exhibitions. Thus the Armory Show of 1913 and the MoMA exhibition of 1932 brought, respectively, European art and architecture to the United States, while the 1999 Whitney show attempted to sum up a century that closed with America pre-eminent in visual culture. Of course, when one stands in front of Jackson Pollock's *Lavender Mist* (1950) or Wright's Robie House (1909) and then walks through its rooms, or goes, page by page, through Walker Evans's *American Photographs* (1938), the broad cultural patterns and theoretical debates hardly seem to matter. Even so, it can be helpful to have in mind the few claims outlined in this introductory section as a measure against which to put one's own "immediate experience," not least because critic Robert Warshow used this expression in the early 1950s when he felt most embattled against the onslaught of mid-century American mass culture (Warshow 1974: 26). It is one of the twentieth-century's legacies that we cannot now ignore the scare-quotes around any claim for direct access to "experience," "truth," and "reality." It does not necessarily follow, however, that we should accept the mediated society or its theoretical underpinning to the extent that we comfortably assume that no such access is possible through art or any other means.

Realism and Modernism, 1890s–1930s

In 1907 the National Academy of Design, an embodiment of the Victorian genteel tradition in America, rejected some works by John Sloan, George Luks, and William Glackens. Generally, these painters, along with Robert Henri, George Bellows, and Everett Shinn, were thought artistically crude and overly preoccupied with the underside of modernity. At the other end of the century, the European curators of the Whitney's immediate forerunner, *American Art in the Twentieth Century* (1993), effectively excluded the group now known as the Ashcan School by opening their survey with the Armory Show (Joachimides et al. 1993). Yet in spite of this reaction from the modernist end of the spectrum, the Ashcan artists can quite justifiably be regarded as among the first painters of modern American life (Weinberg et al. 1994 and Zurier et al. 1995).

George Bellows's *New York* (1911) at once sums up the Ashcan artists' preoccupation with urban modernity and highlights their regularly overlooked formal innovations. It is as full of painterly activity as a Jackson Pollock all-over work and if one stares long enough at the gridded windows of the skyscrapers in the background of this busy urban scene, the illusion of three-dimensionality begins to break down, rather as a familiar word takes on an arbitrary quality if repeated over and over. While Bellows is clearly in the tradition of realism, there is something of the modernist ambition to paint an abstract concept all at once; but instead of calling his painting "Energy," or "The City" Bellows opts for "New York." However, when *New York* was included in the 1995 exhibition, *Metropolitan Lives*, the wall-caption informed visitors that Bellows, in his effort to live up to his title and capture the totality of New York, surreptitiously brings together details of more than one location. Those buses and trolleys and the elevated railroad could only have met in the space of *New York*; never in the physical space of a specific New York location (Zurier et al. 1995). The heroism of Bellows and other Ashcan painters, who held on to the impulse to paint human figures in the face of a city that was growing so rapidly as to defeat standard forms of representation, is highlighted by Charles Sheeler's *View of New York* (1931), done in the hard-edged, designer-realism known as "Precisionism." The painting depicts Sheeler's own studio, his camera – which is shrouded as though to suggest that even the camera could not capture reality – and an open window. But through the window – ever since the Renaissance a motif for pictorial representation – we see only a few clouds in an otherwise empty sky. New York has not become an abstraction, as it would in certain modernist works; it has simply disappeared, along with the confidence that New York could be represented. The Ashcan legacy did survive the Armory Show, however, and can be picked up in the local scenes painted over a long career by Edward Hopper (who acknowledged the influence of John Sloan), in the busy realism of Reginald Marsh in the 1920s and 1930s, and – much more distantly – in the sculpture of Duane Hanson.

The early American modernists found in the example of European modernists different ways of painting the energy and power of modern life (Davidson 1994). Unlike such later American Modernists as Pollock, de Kooning, and Rothko, early American modernists like Max Weber, John Marin, Georgia O'Keeffe, Joseph Stella, and the Precisionists, Charles Demuth and (in most cases) Charles Sheeler, maintained more contact with their subject matter, particularly when they painted New York City. That is to say, they were modernists because they were both seeking ways to convey the pace and dynamism of modernity and were part of the revolution in perception that made the surface of the work of art the focus of attention, a tendency that we have already picked up in the one Ashcan painting ambitious enough to be entitled *New York*. There are elevated trains and skyscrapers in Weber's *New York* (1913) and Marin's *Lower Manhattan* (1920); *Brooklyn Bridge* is unmistakably the subject that Stella painted over and over again between 1917 and the 1940s; and we can recognize the Radiator Building in O'Keeffe's *The Radiator Building – Night, New York* (1927). Nevertheless, we cannot easily look through the overlapping shapes in Weber or the wash of water-colors in Marin or get away from the fact that O'Keeffe's is indisputably a painted building: partially gridded, be-hatted by its crown, and centered by the searchlights arrowing into it only to be dispersed by the distracting red neon letters "Stieglitz" (O'Keeffe's husband). Simi-larly, the painterly sheen that Stella imparts to his depiction of the steel cables of the Brooklyn Bridge arrests our efforts to attach signifier to signified. If we do persist, then we "see" the electricity (rather than the bridge's steel cables) that fascinated Stella, the Italian immigrant, as it did the Italian Futurists whose work he had seen at the Galerie Bernheim-Jeune in Paris in 1912.

Marsden Hartley was not an urban artist as such, though he was excited by Berlin's social and cultural life between 1913 and 1915. What has given him a special place in the first American avant-garde is the particular way he went about making the surface of the painting the place of meaning (rather than – to labor a point – the objective reality to which the painted signs refer). Hartley's method in *Portrait of a German Officer* (1914) and a number of other paintings that followed the death, in action, of his German lover is to paint the military insignia his lover would have worn, together with other somewhat enigmatic letters and numbers. This painted assemblage takes over the surface in almost Cubist fashion, but continues to signify emblematically while also resembling, in outline, a human body. Although the prevalence of objects and signs might suggest an early form of Pop Art, they give the impression of being crafted and full of, rather than bereft of, personal memories. Arthur Dove is the other early modernist whose reputation, along with Hartley's, had markedly risen by the end of the twentieth century. Dove's *Abstractions* of 1910–11 and *The Ten Com-mandments* of 1910–12 stand at the beginning of American non-objective art; and he went on, in *Plant Forms* (1915) and in a collage entitled *Grandmother* (1925), to work out an understanding of Cubist and Dada collage which, unusually among the largely New York-based modernists, allowed him to relate abstraction to symbolist, even Romantic, traditions of thought about nature. He also contributed presciently to the conundrum to which the Whitney's exhibition of 1999 was still seeking an answer:

> What do we call "America" outside of painting? Inventiveness, restlessness, speed, change. Well, a painter may put all of these qualities in a still-life or an abstraction, and be going more native than another who sits quietly copying a skyscraper. (quoted in Hughes, 1997: 344)

Although these early American modernists fail to fit European art-historical termin-ology, they share, to varying degrees, the Cubists' inclusion of multiple perspectives into one space; the Impressionists' efforts to paint the process of seeing (or of wondering what it was that one was seeing); the Fauves' deliberate mismatch between color and object; the Futurists' understanding of speed and energy and what tech-nology could do to, or for, representation; and, finally, Marcel Duchamp's insight that an art-object could exist by virtue of the artist's insistence that there was no reason why a coat-rack, a urinal, or an up-turned bicycle wheel could not be con-sidered works of art. When Duchamp even welcomed the cracks that appeared in his *The Bride Stripped Bare by her Bachelors Even (The Great Glass)* (1915–23), then a link between art and the accidental, as well as between art and commerce, was fairly instituted.

It was probably Man Ray who most capitalized upon the lessons taught by Marcel Duchamp. In his "aerographs" and "Rayographs," the latter abstract images created by exposing and developing light-sensitive paper onto which objects had been placed, Man Ray used photographic technology and techniques for quite different purposes from those intended by art- and amateur-photographers. His were, therefore, the most significant avant-gardist ventures made by a photographer between the 1890s and 1930s, though Edward Steichen's enigmatic *Time-Space Continuum* (1920) is perhaps the single most arresting modernist photograph. Paul Strand's *Akeley Motion Picture Camera* (1923) is certainly a startling abstraction, yet the object remains fully in place once we realize that it is a close-up of machinery. Even in Alvin Langdon Coburn's *The Octopus* (1912), the viewing position on top of a tall building looking down upon the garden design in Madison Square can be reconstructed.

In the period under discussion (and through to the 1970s), photographers, unlike painters responding to modernism, do not generally contest the fact that for the photograph to exist the object also needed to exist. They sought innovation elsewhere. The photographs by Strand and Coburn mentioned above, together with Stieglitz's *Sunlight and Shadows, Paula, Berlin* (1889), *The Hand of Man* (1902), and *The Steerage* (1907), display a modernist sensibility in their making of the subject matter and process of photography into the achieved form. Stieglitz's journal, *Camera Work* (1903–1917), and his 291 Gallery encouraged this phase of photographic modernism when he, Steichen, Gertrude Käsebier, and other Photo-Secessionists argued for photography as an art.

Nevertheless, however useful it is to distinguish between art photography and the documentary tradition of Jacob Riis, Lewis Hine, and, in the 1930s, Walker Evans, Dorothea Lange, and Berenice Abbott, such is the perplexity of this apparently straightforward visual medium that ambiguity is to be found on both sides of the line. Indeed, in a photograph by Jacob Riis, who regarded photography as a means to a reformist not aesthetic end, the ambiguities are, if anything, greater than in Stieglitz's work. The photograph carries the caption *Minding the Baby . . . A Whirlwind Scene, Gotham Court*, dates from around 1889, and depicts a small boy holding a smaller girl, probably his sister, in front of a wooden shed, while the blurred figure of a woman, probably their mother, reaches out for them. It is the issue of temporality that renders this photograph and, indeed, any photograph, unerringly uncanny. Is the woman reaching out for the children because the boy is about to drop his sister? Or because the little girl is calling for her mother? Or because the mother wants the children to be posed to their best advantage for the photographer? Or is she protecting them from the intrusive advances of the photographer/camera? If there is anything certain to be concluded from looking at this image, it is that it could not exist without the camera – not in the obvious sense but, in two other senses: first, that the camera can record a (blurred) reality invisible to the naked eye; and, second, that the photograph records the moment when photography constructed the object.

Even when the object presses its reality upon us through the great photographs of the twentieth century, from one captioned *An unnamed man faces death in the electric chair at Sing Sing, a New York State prison* (1900), through Strand's *Blind Woman* (1916) to the shocking image of a South Vietnamese officer shooting a Vietcong prisoner through the head, we cannot overlook the presence of the camera and the photographer. Nor can we be oblivious of the choices that the photographer had to make: To intervene? To photograph? To photograph a sightless person? This awareness does not diminish the impact of a photograph but adds a further dimension to it, namely the participation of photographer and now the viewer. Similarly, in James Van Der Zee's 1932 photograph, captioned *A couple wearing raccoon coats with a Cadillac, taken on West 127th Street*, we come to realize that the black man and woman in their expensive clothes, leaning nonchalantly against a luxury car, are looking at a photographer and, beyond Van Der Zee, at whoever looks at the photograph. It is this relay of looking that gives the image its ambiguous political resonance. And, when photography fully resumed its documentary vocation under the impact of the Great Depression, we cannot overlook the fact that the men and women photographed by Walker Evans are looking at him and his camera at that historical moment. This is why the series of re-photographs of the work of Evans and other classic photographers by Sherrie Levine in 1986 only tells us what we already knew: that we are intrigued and troubled by the moment of time photographed by Evans. In theory, we should have a similar reaction to the moment of re-photography by Levine but . . .

Once photography is put alongside painting in any survey of visual culture, it tends to assume its traditional role of reminding us of how unrealistic are marks on a canvas. Consequently, while noting a return to realism in American painting of the 1930s and, indeed, a hostility toward the foreignness of modernism, work by Evans, Lange, and Abbott introduces a heightened awareness of what the Social Realists, the American Scene artists and the unclassifiable Edward Hopper were doing. Hopper picks up the Ashcan artists' interest in everyday life but is drawn to the lonely, alienated side of modernity. He painted many scenes without people but even in populated scenes the people in the diner in *Nighthawks* (1942) or the couple in the truly despairing work, *Hotel by a Railroad* (1952), barely communicate. This lack of communication is, though, part of a more general editing out of other "in-betweens" which the realism of both photography and Ashcan painting include. Between the sketches and the finished paintings, *Dawn in Pennsylvania* (1942) and *Hotel Lobby* (1943), Hopper removed, respectively, the details of a station platform and additional figures in the lobby, together with most signs of interaction between those who remain. The modernist architect Mies van der Rohe famously coined the pronouncement "less is more"; and this could well be a reminder to notice the overlooked modernist elements in Hopper, that most realist of American artists. Instead of the detail that is the essence of realism, Hopper increasingly gives us large expanses of paint: from *Compartment C, Car 293* (1938) to *Sun in an Empty Room* (1963), the latter as abstract a realist work of art as one could imagine.

It is curious that while Hopper the realist edits out reality, the work of the leading American modernist of the prewar period, Stuart Davis, gets more and more full. But – and this is the nub of his difference from the Ashcan art which earlier had inspired him as well as Hopper – Davis's was not the non-objectivity practiced and theorized by Kandinsky but, rather, a painterly technique derived from collage. In line with his dictum "Copy the nature of the present – photography and advertisements" (quoted in Hughes 1997: 433), Davis includes in *Lucky Strike* (1921), *New York Mural* (1932), and so much of his work, not the signs of an urban society – as in collage – but painted signs. His is almost a still-life technique but adapted to a consumer-culture that has emptied out the content of objects while leaving their form intact. Within that painted culture, as Davis saw it, a pipe, a ticket machine, a brown derby, a gas pump, and images and words from packaging all match skyscrapers and sections of the elevated railroad for size and so inhabit each other's space. In the mural *Swing Landscape* (1938), Davis even succeeded in painting abstractly when employed by the Works Progress Administration's Federal Arts Project, with its orthodoxy of New Deal realism. As the claims that painting could convey three-dimensional space gave way under the combined impact of the various modernisms, not to mention the challenge of still and then moving photographs, so Davis opted for the alternative basis for modernist art, namely that it responds to its time using whatever techniques seem appropriate. What makes Davis unusual in the context of the 1930s in America is that, like a more numerous and better-known group of European artists and thinkers, which included Bertolt Brecht and the Frankfurt School, he saw modernist techniques as compatible with political radicalism.

It is stretching the term "modernism" but something similar can be said about Jacob Lawrence's *The Migration Series* (1940–1). This is a remarkable set of sixty paintings in which human figures are reduced to the essentials of representation – they are angular and simplified – but without any loss of emotion or historical significance. In *The Female Worker was also One of the Last to Leave the South*, the "background" of overlapping shapes comes "forward" to the surface to become one with the single human figure. Though socially and politically conscious, Lawrence manages to eschew all of the populist sentimentality which one finds in portrayals of "the people" (black and white) in American Scene and Social Realist art.

By the time of the 1932 MoMA exhibition, which was architecture's Armory Show, some important American sources of the modern were being sidelined. At the exhibition that inaugurated the phrase "the International Style," only Frank Lloyd Wright seriously competed with the European leaders of modernism: Richard Neutra, Le Corbusier, Mies van der Rohe, J. J. P. Oud, and Walter Gropius. Yet Gropius had found in common American grain elevators an example of what a new, rational architecture needed in its revolution against over-elaborated surfaces. Along with grain elevators, a second, more probable influence upon Gropius and other German modernists was their reading in 1910 of the Wasmuth edition of Frank Lloyd Wright's writings. And, finally, there is just too much of D. H. Burnham and Company's Reliance Building (Chicago, 1985) in Mies van der Rohe's project for a Glass Skyscraper (Berlin, 1922) to ignore the contribution of the Chicago School of architecture. Consequently, unlike the situation in painting, American architecture, in theory and practice, was part of a reaction against the past. And, to a degree, that past was European.

When leading European modernist architects de-camped to the US in a parallel expatriation to that of painters before and during World War II, the International Style seemed to take over. The result was what Tom Wolfe called the "Rue de Regret: The Avenue of the Americas in New York. Row after Mies van der row of glass boxes. Worker housing pitched up fifty stories high" (Wolfe 1983: 4). Yet Frank Lloyd Wright had already established an American modern tradition: the low-slung Prairie House, of which the Robie House in Hyde Park and the Elizabeth Gale House (1909) in Oak Park (both Chicago suburbs) are wonderful examples. A few years after the MoMA exhibition, Wright came up with an equivalent in the commercial sphere to the domestic modernism of the Prairie style house: the Johnson Wax Building (1936–9). But it was in the Midway Gardens (1914) that Wright comes closest to an American ideal: the marrying of the popular impulse and the modernist drive for planned results, a combination that largely disappears with the MoMA-endorsed arrival of the International Style three years after Midway Gardens was demolished. With its al fresco concert and dining area, interior dinner-dancing space, tavern, and sunken garden and with Wright's efforts to inscribe into the design future bookings that would span the supposed divide between imported European traditions of music and music with genuine popular appeal, Midway Gardens is one of those originals that twentieth-century American culture occasionally produces (but at least there are more occasions than in European culture).

In the inter-war years – again before the full impact of programmatic, functionalist, ex-Bauhaus modernism hit the US – there was a series of such occasions in American architecture. William van Alen's Chrysler Building (1930) – a defiant response to the Depression – brought together German Expressionism, Coney Island's Dreamland designs, and automobile motifs (the famous Chrysler hubcaps and eagle-design radiator caps). Shreve, Lamb, and Harmon's Empire State Building (1931) lacks the exuberance of the Chrysler Building, but the sheer vertical mass of what was then the tallest building in the world gives it an extraordinary authority; moreover, its observation decks offered the best view in town of the magical Chrysler Building, especially at night. Rockefeller Center (whose first phase, of 1929–39, is associated primarily with the architect Raymond Hood) is the third significant expression of the crossover between high and popular culture, which the Chrysler and Empire State Buildings inaugurated during the years that the Bauhaus was refining a more theoretically sophisticated version of the relationship between architecture and society. Even the high (European) modernist architectural critic Siegfried Giedion singled out Rockefeller Center as offering a time-space equation that he held to be central to modernist art and architecture alike (Giedion 1947: 574–8). Yet Rockefeller Center is important less because of its experiential collage of architectural shapes than for its endeavor to combine commercial, entertainment, and public spaces on its site between Fifth and Sixth Avenues and 48th and 51st Streets. If the full plan for Rockefeller Center had been realized then Radio City Music Hall would have been linked with the Museum of Modern Art on 53rd Street. And if Nelson Rockefeller had not been so vigilant, then Diego Rivera's revolutionary mural *Man at the Crossroads*, in the lobby, would not only have survived but would have retained its image of Lenin at the heart of urban capitalism. All of this can be found in a complex whose restrooms contain murals by Stuart Davis and Georgia O'Keeffe and whose Music Hall accommodated, on the opening night, both Martha Graham and the Roxyettes (later, Rockettes), the dancers whose syncopated movements are themselves a form of modernist abstraction of the body. With such opposites contained within the walls of the complex and such an uplifting vision of public space, it is sad that by the 1990s the rooftop gardens had been restricted to corporate use.

Late Modernism and Postmodernism, 1940s–1990s

Judging by reviews and overheard conversations, a fairly common response to the big 1999 Jackson Pollock retrospective at the Tate Gallery in London was an acknowledgment of the sheer beauty of *Number 1 (Lavender Mist)* (1950) and *Autumn Rhythm: Number 30* (1950), in particular. Even the selective use of soft colors (mixed in with harsh colors) in Willem de Kooning's mid-century work can strike us as beautiful and as part of a development toward *Pirate (Untitled II)* (1981) and other late works. Nevertheless, the overwhelming impression in *Woman I* (1950–2) and others in that series remains the Picasso-like violence, while the African-American artist, Robert Colescott, discerns another kind of insensitivity in *I Gets a Thrill Too When I Sees de Koo* (1978), with its Aunt Jemima head substituted for de Kooning's female faces. Yet there is enough mellowing of judgments, even of Pollock and de Kooning, for Abstract Expressionism to have assumed canonic status and to justify at least a brief reminder of how radical these modernists were.

Before returning to the Abstract Expressionists, it is important to acknowledge that the sculpture of mid-century America is now fully recognized in its own right, with David Smith pre-eminent. The brown-painted welded steel of his *Hudson River Landscape* (1951) incorporates both the Hudson River landscape that he had seen through a train window while at a station, the window, and – in the most geometrical part of the work – the steps to the station platform. The whole is a tree-shape and suggests that, even as nature was registering less in twentieth-century art, sculptural abstraction offered some options for maintaining a contact with earlier traditions. In such works as *Home of the Welder* (1945), *Steel Drawing* (1945), and *Agricola VIII* (1952), Smith unites a knowledge of the metal sculpture of Picasso and Julio González and a background as a welder and an inhabitant of an America of railroad and agricultural machinery.

MoMA's 1936 exhibitions, *Cubism and Abstract Art* and *Fantastic Art, Dada and Surrealism*, together with the physical re-location of, among others, Piet Mondrian, André Breton, André Masson, Max Ernst, and Salvador Dali to New York during World War II, gave an art-historical platform for the full emergence of Abstract Expressionism. However, these explanatory factors cannot diminish the impact of some of the very large and – in some cases – mural-like, paintings by Pollock, Clyfford Still, Mark Rothko, Robert Motherwell, Barnett Newman, Lee Krasner, and Franz Kline, or the radical techniques for applying paint to the canvas in these artists, as well as in de Kooning and Joan Mitchell. It is worth noting that as Pollock refined his drip-technique so Hans Namuth's film of Pollock rapidly moving around the edges of the canvas stretched on the floor has itself become part of the meaning of this aspect of Abstract Expressionism. Harold Rosenberg, writing from within the period, gets it just right:

> At a certain moment the canvas began to appear to one American painter after another as an arena in which to act – rather than as a space in which to reproduce, re-design, analyze or "express" an object, actual or imagined. What was to go on the canvas was not a picture but an event. (Rosenberg 1982: 25)

The Abstract Expressionists' paintings about the act of painting never became hermetic and, indeed, influenced the anti-formalist, open work with everyday materials of Richard Serra (*Scatter Piece*, 1967), Alan Sarat (*True Jungle*, 1968), and Eva Hesse (*Untitled (Rope Piece)*, 1970). It is hard not to look for meanings: for instance, Muybridge-like figures on the move across *Mural* (1943), the landmark and seemingly completely abstract work commissioned by Peggy Guggenheim. Arguably, the drive to interpret is stronger when faced with Clyfford Still's paintings, with their "rips" of unpainted canvas showing through their moody colors. Characteristic of Kline are vast daubs of black paint on an over-painted, off-white surface, which make us think of hieroglyphs. They remain indecipherable, however, because Kline gives us only a "close-up" fragment of a modernist script. For all this search for meaning there is no subject matter in the conventional sense in these late-modernists and – particularly in Jackson Pollock's work – certainly no top or bottom, beginning or end, or point of focus or entry to the painting.

In contrast to Harold Rosenberg, Clement Greenberg's influential explanatory defense of this new American art emphasizes the inescapable facts of the completed painting. His seminal statement comes in "Modernist painting":

> Each art had to determine, through the operations peculiar to itself, the effects peculiar and exclusive to itself . . . Realistic, illusionist art had dissembled the medium, using art to conceal art. Modernism used art to call attention to art . . . It was the stressing, however, of the ineluctable flatness of the support that remained most fundamental in the processes by which pictorial art criticized and defined itself under Modernism . . . Flatness, two-dimensionality, was the only condition painting shared with no other art, and so Modernist painting oriented itself to flatness as it did to nothing else. (Greenberg 1982b: 5 and 6)

It is, honestly, difficult to think of any informed understanding of modernist painting that can do without Greenberg's insights into flatness. That is why the best reactions against him still depend upon him. He tells us to look with due care at the surface of the great color field paintings of Barnett Newman, the evocative brushstrokes of Joan Mitchell's *Hemlock* of 1956, Mark Rothko's floating rectangles, the loss of figure-ground relations in Pollock's drip-paintings, and succeeding artists, such as Helen Frankenthaler, Richard Diebenkorn, Kevin Noland, Morris Louis, and the Minimalists, Ad Reinhardt, Agnes Martin, and Robert Ryman. Possibly, Greenberg's explanation works best with Frankenthaler and Reinhardt. For *Mountain and Sea* (1952), Frankenthaler thinned her oil paints almost to the point that they resembled water colors and then she poured the paint and stained the canvas. The chief consequence of this technique, this concentration upon the surface, is that the colors relate to each other within the space of the painting. Any suggestion that the colors merely decorate or represent something else, something outside of, or pre-existing, the painting, is countered by the staining technique.

Ad Reinhardt's large black paintings of 1960–1, all entitled *Abstract Painting*, recall an aspect of Greenberg's critical project that has been attacked by T. J. Clark and others, who argue for a social rather than an internalist history of art (Frascina 1985). By eliminating everything that, he believed, should not be in a painting Reinhardt marks out a sphere for art. With Reinhardt we are a very long way from the engagement with the materiality of modernity in the early American modernists. It is impossible to say exactly what happened in between Marin, Weber, Joseph Stella, and other early American modernists and Ad Reinhardt's preoccupation with paint. However, the increasing spread of mass culture and the multiplying interrelations between media within the logic of product differentiation both inside and outside what is thought to be the aesthetic sphere is probably as good an answer as we will get.

In "Avant-garde and kitsch" (1982a) Greenberg sets out to differentiate painting from other art forms. However, more tellingly – given his extreme formalism in "Modernist painting" and essays through into the 1960s – he sets out to differentiate art from mass cultural products. Looked at positively, a rigorously reductive art, such as Reinhardt's, cannot easily be co-opted for cultural consumption or political propaganda. Greenberg began his critical campaign in the 1930s when totalitarianisms of the Right and the Left were unavoidable facts of political life. It is ironic, then, that Greenberg's essays and their purist gospel paved the way for abstract art to become a valuable commodity.

Before touching upon reactions against Abstract Expressionism, further discussion of late-1950s and 1960s minimalist art permits an important cross-reference to a number of modernist architects and sculptors. In the work of Ad Reinhardt, Agnes Martin, Robert Ryman, Elsworth Kelly, Frank Stella, Donald Judd, Robert Morris, and Carl André, there is a reduction to the essentials of form and mass. Frank Stella's *Die Fahne Hoch* (1959) refers in its title to a Nazi marching song but Stella is perversely insistent that his painting only represents its structure: the painting is divided into four equal rectangles by the central lines (all the lines are in fact left unpainted on the black canvas) and this repeats the structure of the support on the back of the painting. As Stella remarks, "what you see is what you see" (quoted in Phillips 1999: 145); that is to say, paint on the canvas. The move from minimalist painting to sculpture is quite logical for Donald Judd who – while a purist – interjects into the theoretical project associated with Clement Greenberg the observation that even one painted mark implies the third dimension that accommodates his own large sculptured objects. For example, *Untitled* (1969) is a set of evenly spaced plexiglass units attached to steel wall brackets and rising towards the ceiling. Once Picasso's *Guitar* (1912–13) had signalled that sculpture could embrace the world of object-hood and not be confined to representations of the human body, the way was open to the directions taken by Judd's almost wholly abstract work, the organicist sculpture of David Smith in the 1950s, and the modernist architecture of the 1950s and 1960s. To walk around the steel pillars at the base of Gordon Bunshaft's glass-walled Lever House (1950–2) on Park Avenue, New York, or to walk around Isamu Noguchi's sculpture, *Cube*, on the travertine plaza of Bunshaft's Marine Midland Bank Building (now 140 Broadway, New York) is to recognize the intriguing overlap between the different aspects of abstract art that constituted the high point of a reductive but unified modernism.

Mies van der Rohe's pronouncement that "less is more" is exemplified in his adaptation of the modernist grid on the vertical plane in the Lake Shore Drive apartments in Chicago (1950) and the Seagram Building in New York City (1958). These buildings demonstrate a synergy between the thinking that informed both International Style modernism and the austere minimalism of Stella and Judd. Twenty years later, the exact repetition of aluminium-covered 18-inch (45 cm) columns across the twin towers of Minoru Yamasaki and Emory Roth and Sons' World Trade Center (1973 and 1974) proved to be about as minimalist as one can get in a skyscraper. Fortunately, architectural modernism went in other directions as well. Wright's Guggenheim Museum (1956–9), for instance, maintained his pre-eminence into the postwar period. Charles Eames's contribution to the Case Study House Program (1945–66) linked Mondrian-type motifs with a very different kind of architectural transparency from that pioneered by Mies. His Charles Eames House, Pacific Palisades, California of 1949 allows for transitions between the outside and inside which link the house to its surroundings rather than seal it off. And Frank Gehry's modest but welcoming museum in Santa Monica (Edgemar Development, 1984–8) demonstrates that this option is available for buildings in downtown areas as well.

Having said all this, modernist architecture did become more and more functional and less and less expressive of other human needs to the point that the demolition in 1972 of Minoru Yamasaki's high-rise Pruitt-Igoe public housing complex in St Louis (1952–5) was the inevitable outcome. Shortly afterwards, in 1977, in *The Language of Post-Modern Architecture*, Charles Jenks identified a reaction, though Robert Venturi's *Complexity and Contradiction in Architecture* (1966) was the really important manifesto, indicating how early postmodernism set in. When Venturi singles out Mies's "less is more" dictum for sharp criticism, he reminds us that that architectural modernism (at least in its International Style version) was the culmination of the eighteenth-century Enlightenment project of emerging rationality and transparency of purpose. Thus, whereas modernist art is mostly a rupture in pictorial perceptions dating back to the Renaissance, architectural Modernism is the apogee of the Enlightenment tradition.

Robert Venturi and Associates' Guild House (1960–3, Philadelphia), together with Michael Graves's Portland Public Services Building (1980–2), Charles Moore's Piazza d'Italia, New Orleans (1975–80), and Philip Johnson's AT&T (now Sony) skyscraper in New York (1978–84), have become canonic postmodern buildings, odd though it sounds to so categorize such eclectic architecture. Johnson's playfulness was the most calculated and, in an interview included in the British television series, *Architecture at the Crossroads*, he carefully marks his own departure from the modernist tenets of his mentor: "Mies is such a genius! But I grow old! And bored!" (quoted in Jenks 1985: 198). Yet it was modernism, with its exploitation of the steel frame in the direction of the curtain wall and – in its most typical manifestation – the glass wall, that made postmodernist playfulness possible. If Mies interpreted the steel frame as the opportunity to reduce the surface to a minimum level of expressiveness, postmodern architects realized that the move away from a load-bearing wall, dating back to the 1890s and the Chicago School of architecture, makes the surface an arena for historical allusion, decoration, sculpted cut-outs and outcrops, and references to popular culture. Postmodernist architects adopted an explicitly populist outlook, though this was not without its ambiguities: Frank Gehry's own house in a Santa Monica suburb, with its mock-up boat in the backyard and chain-linked fences flung up at angles like re-entry shields on a space capsule, irritated some people to the point that it was shot at on occasions. More typically, there is a tension between inclusiveness and exclusiveness based on ability to spend, and this characterizes the architectural environment of suburban and downtown malls.

If there are interesting confluences between modernist painting, sculpture, and architecture in the twenty years after World War II, the decisive move had been in the post-Armory Show years with Marcel Duchamp's ready-mades and *The Large Glass*. His lead was followed most fully in the 1960s with Pop Art's eclectic and street-wise reaction against Greenberg's tenets. In the context of pop music and the exporting of American consumerism to countries emerging from postwar austerity, the work of Roy Lichtenstein, Claes Oldenberg, Ed Ruscha, Tom Wesselmann, James Rosenquist, and especially Andy Warhol has none of the angst that we find in the Abstract Expressionists. If modernist qualities include seriousness and difficulty as well as emotion, at least in the more expressive versions, then Warhol stands for the reverse in each case, with the notion of the affectless image central to his work. There is, it is true, a degree of chance or risk in Warhol's silkscreen technique. His Coca-Cola bottles and Marilyns differ slightly from each other, but this is not comparable to the chances Pollock took while dancing around his canvas. The only chance Warhol took was that he might be sued for breach of copyright by Coca-Cola or another corporation. This was unlikely, however, since he was providing free advertising for their products, a telling riposte to those who see in the repetitiveness and seriality of Pop Art a subtle critique of consumer culture.

Yet distinctions can be made within Pop. When parodying the gestural brushwork of the Abstract Expressionists, Roy Lichtenstein is engaged in a serious critique of the objectification of art. And, aimed at the other end of the cultural spectrum, his *Blang* and *Blam* (both 1962) evince a meticulous reworking and magnifying of the cartoon image, even if the political insights that inform the selection and arrangement of icons in Stuart Davis's work are largely missing. Claes Oldenberg broke interestingly with the tradition of sculpture, whether figurative or abstract, when he used vinyl in *Soft Washstand* (1965) and *Soft Toilet* (1966). These are both intriguing anthropomorphic takes on the "matter-of-fact," while no one could feel other than defamiliarized in *Bedroom Ensemble* (1969), with its mismatch of materials with function and its decorative "Pollocks" on the wall.

A strict art-historical account has Robert Rauschenberg and Jasper Johns marking the break from Abstract Expressionism and thereby preparing the way for Pop Art. But there is a radical quality in works such as Rauschenberg's *Untitled (Red Painting)* (1953) and Johns's *Flag* series, begun in 1955; and it lies, in part, in the artists' close links with, but separation from, Abstract Expressionism. That it could well have taken longer for Rauschenberg to erase a drawing by De Kooning (to produce *Erased de Kooning Drawing*, 1953) than it took the latter to draw it suggests the nature of the separation. Rauschenberg gives a twist to the old question of the relationship between representation and life by accumulating society's junk (*Canyon*, 1955–9; *Monogram*, 1955–9; *Factum I*, 1957; and *Factum II*, 1957) and building up the work's surface, so that it very noticeably appears in the space of the viewer. In Rauschenberg's words: "I don't want a picture to look like something it isn't. I want it to look like something it is. And I think a picture is more like the real world when it's made out of the real world" (quoted in Phillips 1999: 83). There is nothing special about Rauschenberg's materials but they are marked by his own painterly performance in making what he called "combine paintings."

Jasper Johns builds up the surface of *Flag* (1954–5) by covering newspapers with wax encaustic paint and oil paint, lavishing extreme care upon this representation of an abstraction, the Stars and Stripes, to the point that the painting becomes an object; perhaps even a flag. After all, for the 1969 moon-landing a stiff, corrugated flag was needed to simulate what the real flag would look like in a wind. With so much happening in "the world," Johns opted, instead, subtly to ring the changes on a few themes. *Flag* became *White Flag* (1955) and *Three Flags* (1958); about the same time he began his series of targets (again, were these paintings of targets or targets?): *Target with Four Faces* (1955), *Green Target* (1955), *Target with Plaster Casts* (1955), and *Target* (1958). The work of Rauschenberg and Johns, with Pollock's action-painting in their artistic background, became a factor in the assemblage spaces of Oldenburg, Jim Dine, and Red Grooms, and even influenced performance art and the Happenings, led principally by Allan Kaprow. Hans Namuth's film of Pollock painting was interpreted as a "happening" and this further helped to break down the boundaries which, in his promotion of Pollock, Clement Greenberg had sought to patrol.

Sol LeWitt's *On black walls, all two-part combinations of white arcs from corners and sides, and white straight, not straight, and broken lines* (1975) can serve as an example of both conceptual and open, site-related art of the late 1960s and 1970s. It, too, shows the influence of Pollock and the breaking away from hermetic modernism. LeWitt's *On black walls* . . . has been exhibited many times, but in each location it has to be re-created using written instructions and adapted to the shape of the exhibition space. At MoMA's *Modern Starts* exhibition (1999–2000), for example, Anthony Sansotta and John Wagner re-created this intriguing white crayon work on a different configuration of black walls, which were marked out with a barely perceptible black grid. LeWitt's is therefore a piece of conceptual art – it exists fundamentally in the idea (which a museum purchases) – but it is then altered in its re-presentation, an acknowledgment by LeWitt that the concept is most interesting when it comes into physical contact with a site and when one knows that the resulting work will be emulsioned over as soon as the show closes.

There are two works that arise from this concern with site and materials but that – for rather old-fashioned reasons – seem different. There is no obvious -ism or phase of art into which *The Rose* (1958–66) by West Coast artist Jay DeFeo can be conveniently slotted. Though made primarily of oil paint, wood, and mica on canvas, its dimensions are approximately eleven by eight foot and eleven inches thick in the center (approximately 3.35 by 2.44 meters and 28 cm thick in the center), from which lines radiate out. It is faceted like a stone and seems almost to be a sculpture except that it is painted, using over 2,200 pounds (1,000 kilos) of paint and incorporating odds and ends that do not protrude but are subsumed in the overall shape. DeFeo worked on it alone between 1958 and 1966 and it took over her life as well as her San Francisco apartment. It was later removed (with difficulty) and stored for twenty years before eventually taking its place at the Whitney. It is quite compelling, even without the history that attended its making, and it shares with Robert Smithson's *Spiral Jetty* (1969–70), a heroic, sticking-in-there quality, the sense of a project, not a skirmish or a "theoretical intervention" or a "strategic engagement."

Robert Smithson – beginning with his essay-with-photographs, *The Monuments of Passaic* (1967) and his exhibition, *Earthworks*, of 1968 – moved on from the museum (to which materials were brought, as in *Non-Site* of 1968) to the American landscape itself. Earth-moving equipment shoved rock, earth, and salt crystals into a 1,500-foot (460-meter) spiral in a virtually inaccessible, yet polluted, part of the Great Salt Lake. As the water level changed over the years, so *Spiral Jetty* disappeared, reappeared, disappeared, and, apparently, has partly reappeared. Its construction was captured on video; and in *this* form Smithson is also able to claim that the journey to this desolate landscape in Utah was one that drew in mythological and evolutionary journeys. In this context, the earth-moving equipment looks and sounds like a dinosaur, while the jetty, seen from a helicopter, resembles a fossil. Smithson plays with perspective on a grand scale, journeying to the site via old maps, the actual roads, and mythological narratives and, once there, so immerses the viewer in the process of construction that there is, at first, little sense of the shape of the earthwork. When the spiral is complete (allowing, of course, for environmental action), the viewer sees it in its totality, only for the camera to zoom in for an almost microscopic view of a crystal, much as Robert Altman's camera closes in on Julie Christie's drugged eyeball at the end of *McCabe and Mrs. Miller*, another complex return to nature of the 1970s.

With the exception of the more pictorialist wing of the Photo-Secession and forays into abstraction by Paul Strand and Edward Steichen, for example, photography pursued the realist project throughout the century. In the Whitney's *The American Century* there seemed to be no easy way to keep the story of American photography going when painting took center-stage. Thus Harry Callaghan appears rather awkwardly in a room of mostly Abstract Expressionist works, and in the catalog Lisa Phillips hesitantly puts the New York School of photography alongside the New York School of painting (in effect Abstract Expressionism again). Arguably, only William Klein's photograph *Selwyn, New York* (1955) has much in common with the painters. The shiny curves of the automobile in the foreground give back a distorted mirroring image of the movie theater signs. On the whole, though, what links Klein and Weegee, Diane Arbus, Robert Frank (in *The Americans*, 1958–9) and Helen Levitt is that their street-style eschews the more composed images of both the WPA photographers in the 1930s and Lewis Hine in the earlier phase of documentary photography which he and Jacob Riis dominated.

The mid-century photographers do differ from each other as well as from their predecessors. Weegee's camera is unforgiving in its invasiveness, while Frank seemingly managed to go everywhere across the country with only the local police objecting when he explained his activities as "looking." A tendency towards an "on the run," at-an-angle, spontaneous style is more marked still in Garry Winogrand and is typified by *Untitled* from his *Women are Beautiful* series of 1961. A young woman lighting a cigarette is at the center of the photograph, but the downward angle is peculiar, putting the figures in the background on the slant, while most of the left half of the photograph is taken up by another woman who seems to have wandered into the frame. Her head is partly obscured by a sun-spot. Faced with an almost accidental image such as this, one can understand Winogrand's statement, "I photograph to see what the photograph will look like photographed" (quoted in Sandler 1989: 235).

It is apparent from overview accounts such as Hughes's *American Visions* and the Whitney's *American Century* that painting has occupied the center-ground (including the center-ground of the avant-garde) throughout the twentieth century. This was so even when Stieglitz was at his most influential and in spite of such landmark photographic texts as *Camera Work*, Walker Evans's *American Photographs* (1938), Robert Frank's *The Americans* (1953–7), Edward Steichen's *The Family of Man* (1955), and Richard Avedon's *In the American West* (1985). It is significant, therefore, that photography came closer to the forward edge of artistic change when it started to question its ability to capture reality (including off-center reality) and, instead, commented critically upon the image-filled world, a world to which it had made the crucial contribution when Kodak advertisements in the early twentieth century announced "You press the button, we do the rest." As the influential theorist Douglas Crimp remarks, "While it once seemed that pictures had the function of interpreting reality it now seems that they have usurped it" (quoted in Phillips 1999: 274). Hence the thrust of Sherrie Levine's re-photography, the hyperbolic gaze that Barbara Kruger directs at poster-ads, and Cindy Sherman's sustained play on the relationship between object and subject in her *Untitled Film Stills* (1978) or her series in 1984 for *Vogue* magazine in which she makes any viewer – but particularly a male viewer – uncomfortable with the act of looking at a photographed woman. That woman is herself but in the British television series based on Sandy Nairne's *State of the Art: Ideas and Images in the 1980s* (1987), the photographs she selects for exhibition are those in which she cannot easily recognize herself.

The ever-quickening pace of innovation in the visual arts pushed the Whitney's *American Century* exhibition (and virtually every other millennial publication or pronouncement) towards prediction. However, two works – or at least a fairly common response to them – warn us against missing the point of so much of twentieth-century art (and that which went before) by slipstreaming behind the onward push of innovation and its legitimating postmodern discourse. Part way through the second half of *The American Century* an alcove of works by Lichtenstein and Oldenberg drew viewers' attention. This was expertly harnessed by the docent conducting a tour until, one by one, almost every viewer realized that the old lady standing behind them, burdened with shopping bags, was not real. Duane Hanson's *The Shopper* is lifesize, has real human hair, and she (it is difficult not to refer to Hanson's artwork in any other way) has a sense of weariness beyond that of shopping fatigue. Even if one had been expecting to come across a Duane Hanson somewhere in the exhibition, the shock of the real was tangible. Quite a few people peered into her eyes. One visitor looked, sheepishly, into her shopping bags. Others checked whether the nearby museum attendant was real. Arguably, no other artwork in that exhibition, however disturbing, produced the same level of response as this now somewhat dated piece. A reasonable guess would be that it was a response to the disorientating ordinariness of the human condition focused on a representation of the human body.

Something of the extraordinariness of the human condition, seen through the body, can be glimpsed in Bill Viola's video/sound installation, *The Crossing* (1996). At the Stedelikj Museum in Amsterdam in 1998, for instance, the giant frameless image of a man was projected in the air at the top of the main staircase. The man is deluged by water, beginning with an isolated drop. Round the "back" of the invisible screen, viewers see the man being consumed by fire, beginning with a small flame breaking out on the ground beside him. People stood for lengthy periods at the foot of the stairs, walked up the stairs equally transfixed as the show was replayed, and watched it from "behind." Anyone who had seen *The Crossing* and who then queued up, a little apprehensively, near the end of the *American Century* exhibition to see another of Viola's "works," *Tree of Knowledge*, could be forgiven for thinking that the figure at the far end of the corridor silhouetted against the interactive tree was one of Viola's projected images. It turned out to be the person currently experiencing the show and soon to be replaced by oneself.

REFERENCES AND FURTHER READING

Clark, T. J. (1985) "Clement Greenberg's theory of art," in Francis Frascina (ed.) *Pollock and After: The Critical Debate*. London: Harper and Row.

Conrad, P. (1998) *Modern Times, Modern Places: Life and Art in the 20th Century.* London: Thames and Hudson.

Davidson, A. A. (1994) *Early American Modernist Painting, 1910–1935.* New York: Da Capo Press.

Elderfield, J., Reed, P., Chan, M., and Del Carmen González, M. (1999) *Modern Starts: People, Places, Things.* New York: Museum of Modern Art.

Frascina, Francis (ed.) (1985) *Pollock and After: The Critical Debate.* London: Harper and Row.

Giedion, Siegfried (1947) *Space, Time and Architecture: The Growth of a New Tradition.* London: Oxford University Press.

Greenberg, Clement (1982a) [1939] "Avant-garde and kitsch," in Francis Frascina and Charles Harrison (eds.) *Modern Art and Modernism: A Critical Anthology.* London: Harper and Row.

—— (1982b) [1965] "Modernist painting," in Francis Frascina and Charles Harrison (eds.) *Modern Art and Modernism: A Critical Anthology.* London: Harper and Row.

Haskell, Barbara (1999) *The American Century: Art and Culture, 1900–1950.* New York: Whitney Museum of American Art, in association with W. W. Norton.

Hofstadter, Richard (1962) *The Age of Reform: From Bryan to F.D.R.* London: Jonathan Cape.

Hughes, Robert (1997) *American Visions: The Epic History of Art in America.* New York: Alfred A. Knopf.

Jenks, Charles (1985) *Modern Movements in Architecture*, 2nd edn. Harmondsworth: Penguin.

Joachimides, Christos M. and Rosenthal, Norman (1993) *American Art in the 20th Century: Painting and Sculpture, 1913–1993.* London: Prestel.

Nairne, Sandy (1987) *State of the Art: Ideas and Images in the 1980s.* London: Chatto and Windus.

Phillips, Lisa (1999) *The American Century: Art and Culture, 1950–2000.* New York: Whitney Museum of American Art, in association with W. W. Norton.

Rosenberg, Harold (1982) *The Tradition of the New.* Chicago: University of Chicago Press.

Sandler, Martin W. (1989) *American Image: Photographing One Hundred Fifty Years in the Life of a Nation.* Chicago: Contemporary Books.

Warshow, Robert (1974) *The Immediate Experience: Movies, Comics, Theatre and Other Aspects of Popular Culture.* New York: Atheneum.

Weinberg, Barbara, Bolger, Doreen, and Curry, David Park (1994) *American Impressionism and Realism: The Painting of Modern Life, 1885–1915.* New York: The Metropolitan Museum of Art.

Wolfe, Tom (1983) *From Bauhaus to Our House.* London: Abacus.

Zurier, Rebecca, Snyder, Robert W., and Mecklenburg, Virginia M. (1995) *Metropolitan Lives: The Ashcan Artists and their New York.* Washington, DC: National Museum of American Art.

Bibliography

Abrahamson, David (1995) *Magazine-Made America: The Cultural Transformation of the Postwar Periodical.* Cresskill, NJ: Hampton Press.

Acuña, Rodolfo (2000) *Occupied America: A History of Chicanos,* 4th edn. New York: Harper and Row.

Adams, Henry (1931) *The Education of Henry Adams.* New York: Modern Library.

Adams, Michael C. C. (1994) *The Best War Ever: America and World War II.* Baltimore, Md.: Johns Hopkins University Press.

Addams, Jane (1961) [1910] *Twenty Years at Hull-House.* New York: New American Library.

Adler, Les K. and Paterson, Thomas G. (1970) "Red fascism: the merger of Nazi Germany and Soviet Russia in the American image of totalitarianism, 1930's–1950's," *American Historical Review* 75, pp. 1046–64.

Adler, Selig (1957) *The Isolationist Impulse: Its Twentieth Century Reaction.* New York: Abelard-Schuman.

Agnew, Jean-Christophe (1990) "Coming up for air: consumer culture in historical perspective," *Intellectual History Newsletter* 12, pp. 3–21.

Akam, Everett Helmut (2002) *Transnational America: Cultural Pluralist Thought in the Twentieth Century.* Lanham, Md.: Rowman and Littlefield.

Alba, Richard (1990) *Ethnic Identity: The Transformation of White America.* New Haven, Conn.: Yale University Press.

Allitt, Patrick (1993) *Catholic Intellectuals and Conservative Politics in America, 1950–1985.* Ithaca, NY: Cornell University Press.

Allport, Gordon W. (1958) *The Nature of Prejudice.* Garden City, NY: Doubleday.

Allyn, David (2000) *Make Love Not War: The Sexual Revolution, an Unfettered History.* Boston: Little, Brown.

Alvarez, Robert R. (1987) *Familia: Migration and Adaptation in Baja and Alta California, 1800–1975.* Berkeley: University of California Press.

Ambrose, Stephen E. (1984) *Eisenhower.* New York: Simon and Schuster.

Ambrosius, Lloyd E. (1987) *Woodrow Wilson and the American Diplomatic Tradition: The Treaty Fight in Perspective.* New York: Cambridge University Press.

—— (1991) *Wilsonian Statecraft: Theory and Practice of Liberal Internationalism during World War I.* Wilmington, Del.: SR Books.

Anderson, Karen (1981) *Wartime Women: Sex Roles, Family Relations, and the Status of Women during World War II.* Westport, Conn.: Greenwood Press.

Andrew, John A., III (1997) *The Other Side of the Sixties: Young Americans for Freedom and the Rise of Conservative Politics*. New Brunswick, NJ: Rutgers University Press.

Applebome, Peter (1996) *Dixie Rising: How the South is Shaping American Values, Politics, and Culture*. New York: Times Books.

Appleby, Joyce (1992) *Liberalism and Republicanism in the Historical Imagination*. Cambridge, Mass.: Harvard University Press.

Archdeacon, Thomas (1983) *Becoming American: An Ethnic History*. New York: Free Press.

Archibald, Robert (1978) *The Economic Aspects of the California Missions*. Washington, DC: Academy of American Franciscan History.

Armitage, Susan and Jameson, Elizabeth (1987) *The Women's West*. Norman: University of Oklahoma Press.

Arnold, Joseph L. (1971) *The New Deal in the Suburbs: A History of the Greenbelt Town Program, 1935–1954*. Columbus: Ohio State University Press.

Aron, Cindy S. (1999) *Working at Play: A History of Vacations in the United States*. New York: Oxford University Press.

Arsenault, Raymond (1984) "The end of the long hot summer: the air conditioner and southern culture," *Journal of Southern History* 50(4) (November), pp. 597–628.

—— (1984) *The Wild Ass of the Ozarks: Jeff Davis and the Social Bases of Southern Politics*. Philadelphia: Temple University Press.

—— (1996) "The folklore of southern demagoguery," in Charles Eagles (ed.) *Is There a Southern Political Tradition?* Jackson: University Press of Mississippi.

Asbell, Bernard (1961) *The Day FDR Died*. New York: Holt, Rinehart, and Winston.

Athearn, Robert (1978) *In Search of Canaan: Black Migration to Kansas, 1879–80*. Lawrence: Regents Press of Kansas.

Atherton, Lewis (1954) *Main Street on the Middle Border*. Bloomington: Indiana University Press.

Atkinson, Rich (1993) *Crusade: The Untold Story of the Persian Gulf War*. Boston: Houghton Mifflin.

Auerbach, Jerold (1969) "New Deal, old deal, or raw deal: some thoughts on New Left historiography," *Journal of Southern History* 35, pp. 18–30.

Ayers, Edward L. (1992) *The Promise of the New South: Life After Reconstruction*. New York: Oxford University Press.

Bacevich, A. J. (1986) *The Pentomic Era: The US Army between Korea and Vietnam*. Washington, DC: National Defense University Press.

Baer, George W. (1994) *One Hundred Years of Sea Power: The US Navy, 1890–1990*. Stanford, Calif.: Stanford University Press.

Bailey, Beth (1999) *Sex in the Heartland*. Cambridge, Mass.: Harvard University Press.

Baker, Ray Stannard (ed.) (1927–39) *Woodrow Wilson: Life and Letters*, 8 vols. Garden City, NY: Doubleday, Page.

Baker, Ray Stannard and Dodd, William E. (eds.) (1925) *The Public Papers of Woodrow Wilson*, vol. 2. New York: Harper.

Baldasty, Gerald (1992) *The Commercialization of News in the Nineteenth Century*. Madison: University of Wisconsin Press.

Balio, Tino (1976) *United Artists: The Company Built by the Stars*. Madison: University of Wisconsin Press.

—— (ed.) (1990) *Hollywood in the Age of Television*. Boston: Unwin Hyman.

Balogh, Brian (1991) *Chain Reaction: Expert Debate and Public Participation in American Commercial Nuclear Power, 1945–1975*. New York: Cambridge University Press.

Bao, Xiaolan (2001) *Holding Up More than Half the Sky: Chinese Women Garment Workers in New York City, 1948–1992*. Urbana: University of Illinois Press.

Barbeau, Arthur E. and Henri, Florette (1974) *The Unknown Soldiers: Black American Troops in World War I*. Philadelphia: Temple University Press.

Barber, William S. (1996) *Designs Within Disorder: Franklin D. Roosevelt, the Economists, and the Shaping of American Economic Policy, 1933–1945.* New York: Cambridge University Press.

Barkan, Elliott R. (1992) *Asian and Pacific Islander Migration to the United States: A Model of New Global Patterns.* Westport, Conn.: Greenwood.

Barnouw, Erik (1966) *A Tower in Babel: A History of Broadcasting in the United States, to 1933.* New York: Oxford University Press.

—— (1968) *The Golden Web: A History of Broadcasting in the United States, 1933–1953.* New York: Oxford University Press.

—— (1970) *The Image Empire: A History of Broadcasting in the United States, from 1953.* New York: Oxford University Press.

Barth, Gunther (1980) *City People: The Rise of Modern City Culture in Nineteenth-Century America.* New York: Oxford University Press.

Bartley, Numan V. (1969) *The Rise of Massive Resistance: Race and Politics in the South During the 1950s.* Baton Rouge: Louisiana State University Press.

—— (1995) *The New South, 1945–1980.* Baton Rouge: Louisiana State University Press.

Bartley, Numan V. and Graham, Hugh D. (1975) *Southern Politics and the Second Reconstruction.* Baltimore, Md.: Johns Hopkins University Press.

Barton, Bruce (1925) *The Man Nobody Knows: A Discovery of Jesus.* Indianapolis: Bobbs-Merrill.

Barton, Josef (1975) *Peasants and Strangers: Italians, Rumanians, and Slovaks in an American City, 1890–1950.* Cambridge, Mass.: Harvard University Press.

Bass, Jack and De Vries, Walter (1976) *The Transformation of Southern Politics: Social Change and Political Consequence since 1945.* New York: Basic Books.

Baughman, James L. (1997) *The Republic of Mass Culture: Journalism, Filmmaking, and Broadcasting in America since 1941,* 2nd edn. Baltimore, Md.: Johns Hopkins University Press.

—— (2001) *Henry R. Luce and the Rise of the American News Media,* rev. edn. Baltimore, Md.: Johns Hopkins University Press.

Beard, Charles A. and Beard, Mary R. (1930) [1927] *The Rise of American Civilization.* New York: Macmillan.

Beard, Mary (ed.) (1976) *America Through Women's Eyes.* New York: Greenwood Press.

Becker, Susan D. (1981) *The Origins of the Equal Rights Amendment: American Feminism between the Wars.* Westport, Conn.: Greenwood Press.

Becker, William H. (1999) *"Lean and Mean": Corporate Restructuring and the Resurgence of the American Economy in the 1990s.* Singapore: National University of Singapore.

Bell, Daniel (ed.) (1955) *The New American Right.* New York: Criterion Books.

—— (1978) *The Cultural Contradictions of Capitalism.* New York: Basic Books.

Bell, Derrick A., Jr. (1973) *Race, Racism and American Law.* Boston: Little, Brown.

Bellah, Robert N., Sullivan, William M., Swidler, Ann, and Tipton, Steven M. (1985) *Habits of the Heart: Individualism and Commitment in American Life.* Berkeley: University of California Press.

Belz, Herman (1990) *Equality Transformed: A Quarter-Century of Affirmative Action.* New Brunswick, NJ: Transaction.

Bemis, Samuel Flagg (1955) *A Diplomatic History of the United States,* 4th edn. New York: Holt, Rinehart, and Winston.

Ben-David, Joseph (1984) *The Scientist's Role in Society: A Comparative Study.* Chicago: University of Chicago Press.

Bender, Thomas (1993) *Intellect and Public Life: Essays on the Social History of Academic Intellectuals in the United States.* Baltimore, Md.: Johns Hopkins University Press.

Bender, Thomas and Schorske, Carl (eds.) (1997) *American Academic Culture in Transformation*. Princeton, NJ: Princeton University Press.

Bennett, Edward M. (1990) *Franklin D. Roosevelt and the Search for Victory: American–Soviet Relations, 1939–1945*. Wilmington, Del.: Scholarly Resources.

Benson, Susan Porter (1986) *Counter Cultures: Saleswomen, Managers, and Customers in American Department Stores, 1890–1940*. Urbana: University of Illinois Press.

Berger, Morroe (1950) *Equality by Statute: The Revolution in Civil Rights*. New York: Doubleday.

Berman, William C. (1998) *America's Right Turn: From Nixon to Clinton*. Baltimore, Md.: Johns Hopkins University Press.

Bernhard, Nancy E. (1999) *US Television News and Cold War Propaganda, 1947–1960*. New York: Cambridge University Press.

Bernstein, Barton J. (1968) "The New Deal: the conservative achievements of liberal reform," in B. Bernstein (ed.) *Towards a New Past: Dissenting Essays in American History*. New York: Random House.

—— (1970) "American foreign policy and the origins of the Cold War," in Barton J. Bernstein (ed.) *Politics and Policies of the Truman Administration*. Chicago: Quadrangle Books.

—— (1975) "Roosevelt, Truman, and the atomic bomb: 1941–1945: a reinterpretation," *Political Science Quarterly* 90 (Spring), pp. 23–69.

Bernstein, Irving (1966) *The Lean Years: A History of the American Worker, 1920–1933*. Baltimore, Md.: Johns Hopkins University Press.

Bernstein, Michael (1987) *The Great Depression: Delayed Recovery and Economic Change in America, 1929–1939*. New York: Cambridge University Press.

Beschloss, Michael and Talbott, Strobe (1993) *At the Highest Levels: The Inside Story of the End of the Cold War*. Boston: Little, Brown.

Best, Gary (1991) *Pride, Prejudice, and Politics: Roosevelt versus Recovery, 1933–1938*. New York: Praeger.

Billings, Dwight B., Jr. (1979) *Planters and the Making of a "New South": Class, Politics, and Development in North Carolina, 1865–1900*. Chapel Hill: University of North Carolina Press.

Bird, William L. (1999) *Better Living: Advertising, Media and the New Vocabulary of Business Leadership, 1935–1955*. Evanston, Ill.: Northwestern University Press.

Birdsall, Paul (1939) "Neutrality and economic pressures, 1914–1917," *Science and Society* 3, pp. 217–28.

Biven, W. Carl (2002) *Jimmy Carter's Economy: Policy in an Age of Limits*. Chapel Hill: Univerisity of North Carolina Press.

Black, Earl and Black, Merle (1987) *Politics and Society in the South*. Cambridge, Mass.: Harvard University Press.

Blackford, Mansel G. (1991) *A History of Small Business in America*. New York: Twayne.

Blake, Casey Nelson (1990) *Beloved Community: The Cultural Criticism of Randolph Bourne, Van Wyck Brooks, Waldo Frank, and Lewis Mumford*. Chapel Hill: University of North Carolina Press.

Blee, Kathleen M. (1991) *Women of the Klan: Racism and Gender in the 1920s*. Berkeley: University of California Press.

Bloom, Jack (1987) *Class, Race, and the Civil Rights Movement*. Bloomington: Indiana University Press.

Blum, John Morton (1965) *The Republican Roosevelt*. New York: Atheneum.

—— (1967) *From the Morgenthau Diaries: Years of War, 1941–1945*. Boston: Houghton Mifflin.

—— (1976) *V Was for Victory: Politics and American Culture During World War II*. New York: Harcourt Brace Jovanovich.

Blumenthal, Sidney (1990) *Pledging Allegiance: The Last Campaign of the Cold War*. New York: HarperCollins.

Blumenthal, Sidney and Edsall, Thomas Byrne (eds.) (1988) *The Reagan Legacy*. New York: Pantheon.

Boddy, William F. (1990) *Fifties Television: The Industry and its Critics*. Urbana: University of Illinois Press.

Bodnar, John (1985) *The Transplanted: A History of Immigrants in Urban America*. Bloomington: Indiana University Press.

Bogart, Leo (1982) "Newspapers in transition," *Wilson Quarterly* 6, pp. 58–70.

—— (1985) "How US newspaper content is changing," *Journal of Communication* 35, pp. 82–90.

Boles, John B. (ed.) (2002) *A Companion to the American South*. Oxford: Blackwell..

Boles, John B. and Nolen, Evelyn Thomas (eds.) (1987) *Interpreting Southern History: Historiographical Essays in Honor of Sanford W. Higginbotham*. Baton Rouge: Louisiana State University Press.

Bolton Valencius, Conevery (2002) *The Health of the Country: How American Settlers Understood Themselves and Their Land*. New York: Basic Books.

Boorstin, Daniel J. (1953) *The Genius of American Politics*. Chicago: University of Chicago Press.

Borstelmann, Thomas (2001) *The Cold War and the Color Line: American Race Relations in the Global Arena*. Cambridge, Mass.: Harvard University Press.

Bottles, Scott L. (1987) *Los Angeles and the Automobile: The Making of the Modern City*. Berkeley: University of California Press.

Bourdieu, Pierre (1990) *The Logic of Practice*. Palo Alto, Calif.: Stanford University Press.

Boyer, Paul (1978) *Urban Masses and Moral Order in America, 1820–1920*. Cambridge, Mass.: Harvard University Press.

Boylan, James (1986) "Declarations of independence," *Columbia Journalism Review* 25, pp. 30–45.

Branch, Taylor (1988) *Parting the Waters: America in the King Years, 1954–63*. New York: Simon and Schuster.

Brazil, John (1981) "Murder trials, murder, and twenties America," *American Quarterly* 33, pp. 163–84.

Breines, Winifred (1988) "Whose New Left?," *Journal of American History* 75, pp. 528–45.

Breitman, Richard and Kraut, Alan M. (1987) *American Refugee Policy and European Jewry*. Bloomington: Indiana University Press.

Brennan, Mary C. (1995) *Turning Right in the Sixties: The Conservative Capture of the GOP*. Chapel Hill: University of North Carolina Press.

Breslin, Jimmy (1975) *How the Good Guys Finally Won: Notes from an Impeachment Summer*. New York: Viking.

Brinkley, Alan (1982) *Voices of Protest: Huey Long, Father Coughlin, and the Great Depression*. New York: Alfred A. Knopf.

—— (1995) *The End of Reform: New Deal Liberalism in Recession and War*. New York: Alfred A. Knopf.

—— (1998) *Liberalism and its Discontents*. Cambridge, Mass.: Harvard University Press.

Brody, David (1960) *Steelworkers in America: The Nonunion Era*. Cambridge, Mass.: Harvard University Press.

—— (1993) *Workers in Industrial America: Essays on the Twentieth Century Struggle*, 2nd edn. New York: Oxford University Press.

Brokaw, Tom (1998) *The Greatest Generation*. New York: Random House.

Brown, Dorothy M. (1987) *Setting a Course: American Women in the 1920s*. Boston: Twayne.

Brown, Richard Maxwell (1975) *Strain of Violence: Historical Studies of American Violence and Vigilantism*. New York: Oxford University Press.

Brundage, W. Fitzhugh (1993) *Lynching in the New South: Georgia and Virginia, 1880–1930*. Urbana: University of Illinois Press.

Brune, Lester H. (1998) *The United States and Post-Cold War Interventions: Bush and Clinton in Somalia, Haiti, and Bosnia, 1992–1998*. Claremont, Calif.: Regina Books.

Buckley, William F., Jr., and Kesler, Charles R. (eds.) (1988) *Keeping the Tablets: Modern American Conservative Thought*. New York: Harper and Row.

Buckowczyk, John J. (1987) *And My Children Did not Know Me*. Bloomington: Indiana University Press.

Buenker, John D. (1973) *Urban Liberalism and Progressive Reform*. New York: Scribner.

—— (1976) "The New Era business philosophy of the 1920s," *Illinois Quarterly* 38, pp. 20–49.

Bullard, Robert D. (1990) *Dumping in Dixie: Race, Class, and Environmental Quality*. Boulder, Colo.: Westview Press.

Burk, Kathleen (1985) *Britain, America, and the Sinews of War, 1914–1918*. Boston: Allen and Unwin.

Burner, David M. (1968) *The Politics of Provincialism: The Democratic Party in Transition, 1918–1932*. New York: Alfred A. Knopf.

—— (1996) *Making Peace with the 60s*. Princeton, NJ: Princeton University Press.

Burns, James MacGregor (1956) *Roosevelt: The Lion and the Fox*. New York: Harcourt Brace.

Busterna, John C. (1988) "Trends in daily newspaper ownership," *Journalism Quarterly* 65, pp. 831–8.

Butler, Jon (2000) *Becoming America: The Revolution before 1776*. Cambridge, Mass.: Harvard University Press.

Byrnes, James F. (1947) *Speaking Frankly*. New York: Harper.

Cahn, Susan K. (1990) "Coming on strong: gender and sexuality in women's sport, 1900–1960." PhD dissertation, University of Minnesota.

Calvert, Monte A. (1967) *The Mechanical Engineer in America, 1830–1910: Professional Cultures in Conflict*. Baltimore, Md.: Johns Hopkins University Press.

Campos, Paul (1999) *Jurismania: The Madness of American Law*. New York: Oxford University Press.

Cannon, Lou (1991) *President Reagan: The Role of a Lifetime*. New York: Simon and Schuster.

Carey, George W. (ed.) (1998) *Freedom and Virtue: The Conservative/Libertarian Debate*. Wilmington, Del.: Intercollegiate Studies Institute.

Carpenter, Joel A. (1997) *Revive Us Again: The Reawakening of American Fundamentalism*. New York: Oxford University Press.

Carroll, Peter (1982) *It Seemed Like Nothing Happened: The Tragedy and Promise of America in the 1970s*. New York: Holt, Rinehart, and Winston.

Carson, Clayborne (1981) *In Struggle: SNCC and the Black Awakening of the 1960s*. Cambridge, Mass.: Harvard University Press.

Carter, Bill (1997) "The networks lose viewers to cable, again," New York *Times*, May 22, p. B3.

Carter, Dan T. (1969) *Scottsboro: A Tragedy of the American South*. Baton Rouge: Louisiana State University Press.

—— (1995) *The Politics of Rage: George Wallace, the Origins of the New Conservatism, and the Transformation of American Politics*. New York: Simon and Schuster.

—— (1996) *From George Wallace to Newt Gingrich: Race in the Conservative Counterrevolution, 1963–1994*. Baton Rouge: Louisiana State University Press.

Cash, W. J. (1941) *The Mind of the South*. New York: Alfred A. Knopf.

Cassidy, John (2002) *Dot.con: The Greatest Story Ever Sold*. New York: HarperCollins.

Caute, David (1978) *The Great Fear: The Anti-Communist Purge under Truman and Eisenhower*. New York: Simon and Schuster.

Ceruzzi, Paul E. (1998) *A History of Modern Computing*. Cambridge, Mass.: MIT Press.

Chafe, William H. (1972) *The American Woman: Her Changing Social, Economic, and Political Roles, 1920–1970*. New York: Oxford University Press.

—— (1980) *Civilities and Civil Rights: Greensboro, North Carolina, and the Black Struggle for Freedom*. New York: Oxford University Press.

Chamberlin, William Henry (1950) *America's Second Crusade*. Chicago: Henry Regnery.

Chan, Sucheng (1991) *Asian Americans: An Interpretive History*. Boston: Twayne.

Chandler, Alfred D., Jr. (1997) [1977] "The United States: engines of economic growth in the capital-intensive and knowledge-intensive industries," in Alfred D. Chandler, Jr., Franco Amatori, and Takashi Hikino (eds.) *Big Business and the Wealth of Nations*. Cambridge: Cambridge University Press.

—— (1977) *The Visible Hand: The Managerial Revolution in American Business*. Cambridge, Mass.: Harvard University Press.

Chomsky, Noam (1987) *On Power and Ideology: The Managua Lectures*. Boston: South End Press.

Churchill, Winston S. (1953) *The Second World War*, vol. 2. New York: Bantam.

Clark, Norman H. (1976) *Deliver Us From Evil: An Interpretation of American Prohibition*. New York: W. W. Norton.

Clark, T. J. (1985) "Clement Greenberg's theory of art," in Francis Frascina (ed.) *Pollock and After: The Critical Debate*. London: Harper and Row.

Cleaver, Eldridge (1968) *Soul on Ice*. New York: McGraw Hill.

Clecak, Peter (1983) *America's Quest for the Ideal Self: Dissent and Fulfillment in the '60s and '70s*. New York: Oxford University Press.

Clemens, Samuel Langhorne (1980) *Pudd'nhead Wilson and Those Extraordinary Twins*, ed. Sidney E. Berger. New York: W. W. Norton.

Clements, Kendrick (1987) *Woodrow Wilson: World Statesman*. Boston: Twayne.

—— (1992) *The Presidency of Woodrow Wilson*. Lawrence: University Press of Kansas.

Cobb, James C. (1982) *The Selling of the South: The Southern Crusade for Industrial Development, 1936–1980*. Baton Rouge: Louisiana State University Press.

—— (1992) *The Most Southern Place on Earth: The Mississippi Delta and the Roots of Regional Identity*. New York: Oxford University Press.

Coben, Stanley (1991) *Rebellion Against Victorianism: The Impetus for Cultural Change in 1920s America*. New York: Oxford University Press.

Cohen, Lizabeth (1990) *Making a New Deal: Industrial Workers in Chicago, 1919–1939*. New York: Cambridge University Press.

—— (2003) *A Consumer's Republic: The Politics of Mass Consumption in Postwar America*. New York: Alfred A. Knopf.

Cohen, Lucy (ed.) (1960) *The Legal Conscience: The Collected Papers of Felix S. Cohen*. New Haven, Conn.: Yale University Press.

Cohen, Warren I. (1967) *The American Revisionists: The Lessons of Intervention in World War I*. Chicago: University of Chicago Press.

—— (1987) *Empire Without Tears: America's Foreign Relations, 1921–1933*. Philadelphia: Temple University Press.

Collins, Harry and Pinch, Trevor (1998) *The Golem at Large: What You Should Know about Technology*. Cambridge: Cambridge University Press.

Commager, Henry Steele (ed.) (1948) *Documents of American History*. New York: Appleton-Century-Crofts.

Commons, John R. et al. (1921–35) *History of Labor in the United States*, 4 vols. New York: Macmillan.

Conkin, Paul (1967) *The New Deal*. Arlington Heights, Ill.: Harlan Davidson.

Connolly, James J. (1998) *The Triumph of Ethnic Progressivism: Urban Political Culture in Boston, 1900–1925*. Cambridge, Mass.: Harvard University Press.

Conrad, P. (1998) *Modern Times, Modern Places: Life and Art in the 20th Century*. London: Thames and Hudson.

Conser, Walter H., Jr. and Twiss, Sumner B. (eds.) (1997) *Religious Diversity and American Religious History: Studies in Traditions and Cultures*. Athens: University of Georgia Press.

Conzen, Kathleen N. (1976) *Immigrant Milwaukee, 1836–1860*. Cambridge, Mass.: Harvard University Press.

Coogan, John W. (1981) *The End of Neutrality: The United States, Britain, and Maritime Rights, 1899–1915*. Ithaca, NY: Cornell University Press.

—— (1994) "Wilsonian diplomacy in war and peace," in Gordon Martel (ed.) *American Foreign Relations Reconsidered, 1890–1993*. London: Routledge.

Cook, Blanche Wiesen (1992, 1999), *Eleanor Roosevelt*, 2 vols. New York: Viking Press.

Cooper, John Milton, Jr. (1980) "World War I: European origins and American intervention," *Virginia Quarterly Review* 56, pp. 1–18.

—— (2001) *Breaking the Heart of the World: Woodrow Wilson and the Fight for the League of Nations*. New York: Cambridge University Press.

Corwin, Edward (1941) *Constitutional Revolution, Ltd*. Claremont, Calif.: The Pomona Colleges.

Cotkin, George (1990) *William James, Public Philosopher*. Baltimore, Md.: Johns Hopkins University Press.

—— (1992) *Reluctant Modernism: American Thought and Culture, 1880–1900*. Boston: Twayne.

Cott, Nancy F. (1987) *The Grounding of Modern Feminism*. New Haven, Conn.: Yale University Press.

Cowan, Ruth Schwartz (1983) *More Work for Mother: The Ironies of Household Technology from the Open Hearth to the Microwave*. New York: Basic Books.

—— (1997) *A Social History of American Technology*. New York: Oxford University Press.

Cowdrey, Albert E. (1983) *This Land, This South: An Environmental History*. Lexington: University Press of Kentucky.

Craig, Douglas B. (1992) *After Wilson: The Struggle for the Democratic Party, 1920–1934*. Chapel Hill: University of North Carolina Press.

—— (2000) *Fireside Politics: Radio and Political Culture in the United States, 1920–1940*. Baltimore, Md.: Johns Hopkins University Press.

Crampton, Gregory C. (1977) *The Zunis of Cibola*. Salt Lake City: University of Utah Press.

Critoph, Gerald E. (1975) "The flapper and her critics," in Carol V. R. George (ed.) *"Remember the Ladies": New Perspectives on Women in American History*. Syracuse, NY: Syracuse University Press.

Crockett, Norman L. (1979) *The Black Towns*. Lawrence: Regents Press of Kansas.

Croly, Herbert (1964) [1909] *The Promise of American Life*. New York: Capricorn Books. Also (1965) ed. Arthur M. Schlesinger, Jr. Cambridge, Mass.: Harvard University Press.

Cronon, William (1991) *Nature's Metropolis: Chicago and the Great West*. New York: W. W. Norton.

—— (ed.) (1996) *Uncommon Ground: Rethinking the Human Place in Nature*. New York: W. W. Norton.

Crosby, Alfred W. (1989) *America's Forgotten Pandemic: The Influenza of 1918*. New York: Cambridge University Press.

Cross, Gary S. (1997) *Kids' Stuff: Toys and the Changing World of American Childhood*. Cambridge, Mass.: Harvard University Press.

—— (2000) *An All-Consuming Century: Why Commercialism Won in Modern America.* New York: Columbia University Press.

Crunden, Robert M. (ed.) (1977) *The Superfluous Men: Conservative Critics of American Culture, 1900–1945.* Austin: University of Texas Press.

Cuff, Robert D. (1973) *The War Industries Board: Business–Government Relations During World War I.* Baltimore, Md.: Johns Hopkins University Press.

Curtis, Charles P. (1955) *The Oppenheimer Case: The Trial of a Security System.* New York: Simon and Schuster.

Cushman, Barry (1998) *Rethinking the New Deal Court: The Structure of a Constitutional Revolution.* New York: Oxford University Press.

Dahl, Robert (1965) *Who Governs?: Democracy and Power in an American City.* New Haven, Conn.: Yale University Press.

Dalfiume, Richard M. (1968) "The forgotten years of the Negro revolution," *Journal of American History* 55 (June), pp. 90–106.

Dallek, Robert (1979) *Franklin D. Roosevelt and American Foreign Policy, 1932–1945.* New York: Oxford University Press.

Daniel, Pete (1972) *The Shadow of Slavery: Peonage in the South, 1901–1969.* New York: Oxford University Press.

—— (2000) *Lost Revolutions: The South in the 1950s.* Chapel Hill: University of North Carolina Press.

Daniels, Roger (1983) "American Refugee Policy in Historical Perspective," in Jarrell C. Jackman and Carla M. Borden (eds.) *The Muses Flee Hitler.* Washington, DC: Smithsonian Institution Press.

—— (1993) *Prisoners Without Trial: Japanese Americans in World War II.* New York: Hill and Wang.

—— (1997) *Not Like Us: Immigrants and Minorities in America, 1890–1924.* Chicago: Ivan R. Dee.

—— (2002) *Coming to America: A History of Immigration and Ethnicity in American Life,* 2nd edn. New York: HarperCollins.

—— (2003) *Guarding the Golden Door: American Immigration Policy and Immigrants since 1882.* New York: Hill and Wang.

Daniels, Roger and Otis, Graham (2001) *Debating American Immigration.* Lanham, Md.: Rowman and Littlefield.

Davidson, A. A. (1994) *Early American Modernist Painting, 1910–1935.* New York: Da Capo Press.

Davis, Allen F. (1967) *Spearheads for Reform: The Social Settlements and the Progressive Movement, 1890–1914.* New York: Oxford University Press.

Davis, Flora (1999) *Moving the Mountain: The Women's Movement in the United States Since 1960.* Urbana: University of Illinois Press.

Davis, Jack E. (2001) *Race against Time: Culture and Separation in Natchez since 1930.* Baton Rouge: Louisiana State University Press.

Davis, Mike (1998) *The Ecology of Fear: Los Angeles and the Imagination of Disaster.* New York: Metropolitan Books.

Davis, Susan (1997) *Spectacular Nature: Corporate Culture and the Sea World Experience.* Berkeley: University of California Press.

De León, Arnoldo (1983) *They Called Them Greasers: Anglo Attitudes Toward Mexicans in Texas, 1821–1900.* Austin: University of Texas Press.

De Witt, Benjamin Parke (1968) [1915] *The Progressive Movement.* Seattle: University of Washington Press.

Deedy, John (1987) *American Catholicism: And Now Where?* New York: Plenum Press.

Degler, Carl N. (1956) *Out of Our Past.* New York: Harper and Row.

—— (1980) *At Odds: Women and the Family in America from the Revolution to the Present.* New York: Oxford University Press.

—— (1991) *In Search of Human Nature: The Decline and Revival of Darwinism in American Social Thought.* New York: Oxford University Press.

Delgado, Richard and Stefancic, Jean (2001) *Critical Race Theory: An Introduction.* New York: New York University Press.

Deloria, Vine, Jr. (1969) *Custer Died for Your Sins: An Indian Manifesto.* New York: Macmillan.

D'Emilio, John and Freedman, Estelle B. (1988) *Intimate Matters: A History of Sexuality in America.* New York: Harper and Row.

Deutsch, Sarah (1987) *No Separate Refuge: Culture, Class, and Gender on an Anglo-Hispanic Frontier, 1880–1940.* New York: Oxford University Press.

Devlin, Patrick (1974) *Too Proud to Fight: Woodrow Wilson's Neutrality.* New York: Oxford University Press. Reprinted 1975.

Devroy, Ann and Smith, R. Jeffrey (1993) "Clinton re-examines a foreign policy under siege," *Washington Post*, October 17.

Diggins, John Patrick (1984) *The Lost Soul of American Politics: Virtue, Self-Interest, and the Foundations of Liberalism.* New York: Basic Books.

Diner, Hasia R. (1977) *In the Almost Promised Land: American Jews and Blacks, 1915–1935.* Westport, Conn.: Greenwood Press.

—— (1983) *Erin's Daughters in America: Irish Immigrant Women in the Nineteenth Century.* Baltimore, Md.: Johns Hopkins University Press.

Diner, Steven J. (1980) *A City and its Universities: Public Policy in Chicago, 1892–1919.* Chapel Hill: University of North Carolina Press.

—— (1998) *A Very Different Age: Americans of the Progressive Era.* New York: Hill and Wang.

Dinnerstein, Leonard (1982) *America and the Survivors of the Holocaust.* New York: Columbia University Press.

Dionne, E. J., Jr. (1988) "Dukakis and Bush trade fire in heavy barrages," *New York Times*, August 31.

Dittmer, John (1994) *Local People: The Struggle for Civil Rights in Mississippi.* Urbana: University of Illinois Press.

Doenecke, Justus D. and Wilz, John E. (2003) *From Isolation to War, 1931–1941*, 3rd edn. Wheeling, Ill.: Harlan Davidson.

Dolan, Jay P. (1975) *The Immigrant Church: New York's Irish and German Catholics, 1815–1865.* Baltimore, Md.: Johns Hopkins University Press.

Donner, Frank J. (1980) *The Age of Surveillance: The Aims and Methods of America's Political Intelligence System.* New York: Alfred A. Knopf.

Dorman, Robert L. (1993) *Revolt of the Provinces: The Regionalist Movement in America, 1920–1945.* Chapel Hill: University of North Carolina Press.

Dorrien, Gary (1993) *The Neoconservative Mind: Politics, Culture, and the War of Ideology.* Philadelphia: Temple University Press.

Douglas, Susan J. (1999) *Listening In: Radio and the American Imagination.* New York: Times Books.

Douglass, Harlan Paul (1925) *The Suburban Trend.* New York: Century.

Draper, Theodore (1991) *A Very Thin Line: The Iran-Contra Affairs.* New York: Hill and Wang.

Drew, Elizabeth (1995) *On the Edge: The Clinton Presidency.* New York: Touchstone Press.

Duany, Andres, Plater-Zyberk, Elizabeth, and Speck, Jeff (2000) *Suburban Nation: The Rise of Sprawl and the Decline of the American Dream.* New York: North Point Press.

Dubofsky, Melvyn (1988) *We Shall Be All: A History of the Industrial Workers of the World.* Urbana: University of Illinois Press.

—— (1994) *The State and Labor in Modern America.* Chapel Hill: University of North Carolina Press.

Dubofsky, Melvyn and Van Tine, Warren (1977) *John L. Lewis: A Biography*. New York: Quadrangle/New York Times.

Dudziak, Mary L. (2000) *Cold War Civil Rights: Race and the Image of American Democracy*. Princeton, NJ: Princeton University Press.

Dumenil, Lynn (1995) *The Modern Temper: American Culture and Society in the 1920s*. New York: Hill and Wang.

Dunlap, Thomas R. (1981) *DDT: Scientists, Citizens, and Public Policy*. Princeton, NJ: Princeton University Press.

—— (1988) *Saving America's Wildlife*. Princeton, NJ: Princeton University Press.

Dunn, Charles W. and Woodard, J. David (1996) *The Conservative Tradition in America*. Lanham, Md.: Rowman and Littlefield.

Dunn, Joe P. and Preston, Howard L. (eds.) (1991) *The Future South: A Historical Perspective for the Twenty-first Century*. Urbana: University of Illinois Press.

Dunnigan, James F. and Macedonia, Raymond M. (1995) *Getting It Right: American Military Reform after Vietnam to the Gulf War*. New York: William Morrow.

Dupree, A. Hunter (1957) *Science in the Federal Government: A History of Policies and Activities to 1940*. Cambridge, Mass.: Harvard University Press.

Duxbury, Neil (1995) *Patterns of American Jurisprudence*. New York: Oxford University Press.

Eagles, Charles W. (2000) "Towards new histories of the civil rights era," *Journal of Southern History* 66(4) (November), pp. 815–48.

Echols, Alice (1989) *Daring to Be Bad: Radical Feminism in America, 1967–1975*. Minneapolis: University of Minnesota Press.

Eck, Diana L. (2001) *A New Religious America: How a "Christian Country" Has Become the World's Most Religiously Diverse Nation*. San Francisco: HarperSanFrancisco.

Eden, Robert (ed.) (1989) *The New Deal and its Legacy: Critique and Appraisal*. Westport, Conn: Greenwood Press.

Edmunds, R. David (1978) *The Potowatomis: Keepers of the Fire*. Norman: University of Oklahoma Press.

—— (1983) *The Shawnee Prophet*. Lincoln: University of Nebraska Press.

—— (1984) *Tecumseh and the Quest for Indian Leadership*. Boston: Little, Brown.

Egerton, John (1974) *The Americanization of Dixie: The Southernization of America*. New York: Harper's Magazine Press.

—— (1994) *Speak Now Against the Day: The Generation before the Civil Rights Movement in the South*. New York: Alfred A. Knopf.

Ehrenhalt, Alan (1995) *The Lost City: The Forgotten Virtues of Community in America*. New York: Basic Books.

Ehrenreich, Barbara (1983) *The Hearts of Men: American Dreams and the Flight from Commitment*. Garden City, NY: Doubleday.

Eichengreen, Barry J. (1992) *Golden Fetters: The Gold Standard and the Great Depression, 1919–1939*. New York: Oxford University Press.

Elderfield, J., Reed, P., Chan, M., and Del Carmen González, M. (1999) *Modern Starts: People, Places, Things*. New York: Museum of Modern Art.

Ellwood, Robert S. (1997) *The Fifties Spiritual Marketplace: American Religion in a Decade of Conflict*. New Brunswick, NJ: Rutgers University Press.

Ellwood, Robert S. and Partin, Harry B. (1988) *Religious and Spiritual Groups in Modern America*, 2nd edn. Englewood Cliffs, NJ: Prentice-Hall.

Emmons, David M. (1989) *The Butte Irish: Class and Ethnicity in an American Mining Town, 1875–1925*. Urbana: University of Illinois Press.

Erikson, Erik H. (1950) *Childhood and Society*. New York: W. W. Norton.

Evans, Sara M. (1979) *Personal Politics: The Roots of Women's Liberation in the Civil Rights Movement and the New Left*. New York: Vintage.

—— (1989) *Born for Liberty: A History of Women in America*. New York: Free Press.

Ewen, Elizabeth (1985) *Immigrant Women in the Land of Dollars: Life and Culture on the Lower East Side, 1890–1925*. New York: Monthly Review Press.

Faragher, John Mack (1979) *Women and Men on the Overland Trail*. New Haven, Conn.: Yale University Press.

—— (1986) *Sugar Creek: Life on the Illinois Prairie*. New Haven, Conn.: Yale University Press.

Farley, Christopher John (1999) "Hip-hop special," *Guardian* (London), March 19.

Farrell, James J. (1997) *The Spirit of the Sixties: The Making of Postwar Radicalism*. New York: Routledge.

Faue, Lizabeth (1991) *Community of Suffering and Struggle: Women, Men, and the Labor Movement in Minneapolis, 1915–1945*. Chapel Hill: University of North Carolina Press.

Feldman, Stephen (2000) *American Legal Thought from Premodernism and Postmodernism: An Intellectual Voyage*. New York: Oxford University Press.

Ferguson, Thomas (1991) "Industrial structure and party competition in the New Deal," *Sociological Perspectives* 34, pp. 498–523.

Ferrell, Robert H. (1985) *Woodrow Wilson and World War I, 1917–1921*. New York: Harper and Row.

—— (1996) *The Strange Deaths of President Harding*. Columbia: University of Missouri Press.

—— (1998) *The Dying President: Franklin D. Roosevelt, 1944–1945*. Columbia: University of Missouri Press.

—— (1998) *The Presidency of Calvin Coolidge*. Lawrence: University Press of Kansas.

Fiege, Mark (1999) *Irrigated Eden: The Making of an Agricultural Landscape in the American West*. Seattle: University of Washington Press.

Filene, Peter G. (1970) "An obituary for 'the Progressive Movement,' " *American Quarterly* 22, pp. 20–34.

Fink, Gary M. and Graham, Hugh Davis (eds.) (1998) *The Carter Presidency: Policy Choices in the Post-New Deal Era*. Lawrence: University Press of Kansas

Fink, Gary M. and Reed, Merl E. (eds.) (1994) *Race, Class, and Community in Southern Labor History*. Tuscaloosa: University of Alabama Press.

Fink, Leon (1997) *Progressive Intellectuals and the Dilemmas of Democratic Commitment*. Cambridge, Mass.: Harvard University Press.

Fischer, David Hackett (1989) *Albion's Seed: Four British Folkways in America*. New York: Oxford University Press.

Fisher, William W., III, Horwitz, Morton J., and Reed, Thomas A. (eds.) (1993) *American Legal Realism*. New York: Oxford University Press.

Fishman, Robert (1977) *Urban Utopias in the Twentieth Century: Ebenezer Howard, Frank Lloyd Wright, and Le Corbusier*. New York: Basic Books.

—— (1987) *Bourgeois Utopias: The Rise and Fall of Suburbia*. New York: Basic Books.

Fiske, John (1994) *Media Matters: Race and Gender in US Politics*. Minneapolis: University of Minnesota Press.

Fitzgerald, Deborah (1990) *The Business of Breeding: Hybrid Corn in Illinois, 1890–1940*. Ithaca, NY: Cornell University Press.

FitzGerald, Frances (2000) *Way Out There in the Blue: Reagan, Star Wars, and the End of the Cold War*. New York: Simon and Schuster.

Fleming, Cynthia G. (1998) *Soon We Will Not Cry: The Liberation of Ruby Doris Smith Robinson*. Lanham, Md.: Rowman and Littlefield.

Fleming, Denna F. (1932) *The United States and the League of Nations, 1918–1920*. New York: G. P. Putnam's Sons.

Fleming, Thomas and Gottfried, Paul (1988) *The Conservative Movement*. Boston: Twayne.

Flexner, Eleanor (1959) *Century of Struggle: The Women's Rights Movement in the United States*. Cambridge, Mass.: Harvard University Press.

Flynn, John T. (1948) *The Roosevelt Myth*. New York: Devin-Adair.

Fogelson, Robert M. (2001) *Downtown: Its Rise and Fall, 1880–1950*. New Haven, Conn.: Yale University Press.

Foner, Nancy (ed.) (1987) *New Immigrants in New York*. New York: Columbia University Press.

Fones-Wolf, Elizabeth (1994) *Selling Free Enterprise: The Business Assault on Labor and Liberalism, 1945–1960*. Urbana: University of Illinois Press.

Forbath, William E. (1991) *Law and the Shaping of the American Labor Movement*. Cambridge, Mass.: Harvard University Press.

Forcey, Charles (1961) *The Crossroads of Liberalism: Croly, Weyl, Lippmann and the Progressive Era, 1900–1925*. New York: Oxford University Press.

Foreman, Grant (1932) *Indian Removal: The Emigration of the Five Civilized Tribes of Indians*. Norman: University of Oklahoma Press. Reprinted 1953.

Foreman, Joel (ed.) (1997) *The Other Fifties: Interrogating Midcentury American Icons*. Urbana: University of Illinois Press.

Foster, Gaines M. (1987) *Ghosts of the Confederacy: Defeat, the Lost Cause, and the Emergence of the New South, 1865–1913*. New York: Oxford University Press.

Foster, Mark S. (1981) *From Streetcar to Superhighway: American City Planners and Urban Transportation, 1900–1940*. Philadelphia: Temple University Press.

Fousek, John (2000) *To Lead the Free World: American Nationalism and the Cultural Roots of the Cold War*. Chapel Hill: University of North Carolina Press.

Francis, Samuel (1993) *Beautiful Losers: Essays on the Failure of American Conservatism*. Columbia: University of Missouri Press.

Frank, Jerome (1930) *Law and the Modern Mind*. New York: Brentano's.

Frank, Thomas (1997) *The Conquest of Cool: Business Culture, Counterculture, and the Rise of Hip Consumerism*. Chicago: University of Chicago Press.

Franklin, John Hope (1947) *From Slavery to Freedom*. New York: Macmillan.

Franklin, John Hope and Moss, Alfred A., Jr. (1994) *From Slavery to Freedom: A History of African Americans*, 7th edn. New York: Alfred A. Knopf.

Frascina, Francis (ed.) (1985) *Pollock and After: The Critical Debate*. London: Harper and Row.

Fraser, Steve (1991) *Labor Will Rule: Sidney Hillman and the Rise of American Labor*. New York: Free Press.

Fredrickson, George M. (1981) *White Supremacy: A Comparative Study in American and South African History*. New York: Oxford University Press.

Freeman, James M. (1990) *Hearts of Sorrow: Vietnamese-American Lives*. Stanford, Calif.: Stanford University Press.

Freidel, Frank (1952–78) *Franklin D. Roosevelt*, 4 vols. Boston: Little, Brown.

—— (1964) *The New Deal and the American People*. Englewood Cliffs, NJ: Prentice-Hall.

—— (1990) *Franklin D. Roosevelt: A Rendezvous with Destiny*. Boston: Little, Brown.

Fried, Richard M. (1990) *Nightmare in Red: The McCarthy Era in Perspective*. New York: Oxford University Press.

Friedan, Betty (1963) *The Feminine Mystique*. New York: W. W. Norton.

Friedman, Lawrence Meir (1999) *The Horizontal Society*. New Haven, Conn.: Yale University Press.

—— (2002) *American Law in the Twentieth Century*. New Haven, Conn.: Yale University Press.

Friedman, Richard (1994) "Switching time and other thought experiments: the Hughes Court and constitutional transformation," *University of Pennsylvania Law Review* 142, pp. 1891–943.

Friedman, Thomas L. (1999) *The Lexus and the Olive Tree*. New York: Farrar, Straus, Giroux.

Frum, David (1994) *Dead Right*. New York: Basic Books.

—— (2000) *How We Got Here: The '70s: The Decade that Brought You Modern Life (for Better or Worse)*. New York: Basic Books.

Fuchs, Lawrence H. (1990) *The American Kaleidoscope: Race, Ethnicity, and the Civic Culture.* Hanover, NH: Wesleyan University Press.

Fussell, Paul (1989) *Wartime: Understanding and Behavior in the Second World War.* New York: Oxford University Press.

Gabaccia, Donna (1995) *From the Other Side: Women, Gender, and Immigrant Life in the US, 1820–1990.* Bloomington: Indiana University Press.

Gabler, Neal (1995) "The culture wars," *Los Angeles Times,* September 17.

—— (1998) *Life the Movie: How Entertainment Conquered Reality.* New York: Alfred A. Knopf.

Gabriel, John (1998) *Whitewash: Racialized Politics and the Media.* New York: Routledge.

Gaddis, John Lewis (1982) *Strategies of Containment: A Critical Appraisal of Postwar American National Security Policy.* New York: Oxford University Press.

—— (1992) *The United States and the End of the Cold War: Implications, Reconsiderations, Provocations.* New York: Oxford University Press.

Galambos, Louis and Pratt, Joseph (1988) *The Rise of the Corporate Commonwealth: US Business and Public Policy in the Twentieth Century.* New York: Basic Books.

Galbraith, John Kenneth (1954) *The Great Crash: 1929.* Boston: Houghton Mifflin. 3rd edn. 1972

—— (1958) *The Affluent Society.* Boston: Houghton Mifflin.

Gallup, George H., Jr. (1996) *Religion in America 1996.* Princeton, NJ: Princeton Religion Research Center.

Gallup, George H., Jr. and Castelli, Jim (1989) *The People's Religion: American Faith in the 90's.* New York: Macmillan.

Galston, William A. (1991) *Liberal Purposes: Goods, Virtues, and Diversity in the Liberal State.* New York: Cambridge University Press.

—— (2002) *Liberal Pluralism: The Implications of Value Pluralism for Political Theory and Practice.* New York: Cambridge University Press.

Gamboa, Erasmo (1990) *Mexican Labor and World War II: Braceros in the Pacific Northwest, 1942–1947.* Austin: University of Texas Press.

Gamson, Joshua (1994) *Claims to Fame: Celebrity in Contemporary America.* Berkeley: University of California Press.

Gans, Herbert J. (1967) *The Levittowners: Ways of Life and Politics in a New Suburban Community.* New York: Pantheon.

—— (1979) *Deciding What's News: A Study of CBS Evening News, NBC Nightly News, Newsweek, and* Time. New York: Pantheon.

—— (1979) "Symbolic ethnicity in America," *Ethnic and Racial Studies* 2, pp. 1–20.

Garcia, Maria Christina (1996) *Havana USA: Cuban Exiles and Cuban Americans in South Florida, 1959–1994.* Berkeley: University of California Press.

Garcia, Richard A. (1989) *The Rise of the Mexican American Middle Class, San Antonio, 1929–1941.* College Station: Texas A&M University Press.

Gardner, Lloyd C. (1984) *Safe for Democracy: The Anglo-American Response to Revolution, 1913–1923.* New York: Oxford University Press.

—— (1995) *Pay Any Price: Lyndon Johnson and the Wars for Vietnam.* Chicago: Ivan R. Dee.

Garraty, John (1974) "The New Deal, National Socialism, and the Great Depression," *American Historical Review* 78, pp. 907–44.

—— (1986) *The Great Depression.* New York: Harcourt Brace.

Garreau, Joel (1991) *Edge City: Life on the New Frontier.* New York: Doubleday.

Garrow, David J. (1986) *Bearing the Cross: Martin Luther King, Jr. and the Southern Christian Leadership Conference.* New York: Morrow.

Garthoff, Raymond L. (1994) *Détente and Confrontation: American–Soviet Relations from Nixon to Reagan.* Washington, DC: Brookings.

—— (1994) *The Great Transition: American–Soviet Relations and the End of the Cold War.* Washington, DC: Brookings.

Garvey, Ellen Gruber (1996) *The Adman in the Parlor: Magazines and the Gendering of Consumer Culture, 1880s to 1920s.* New York: Oxford University Press.

Geertz, Clifford (1973) *The Interpretation of Cultures: Selected Essays.* New York: Basic Books.

Gelfand, Mark I. (1975) *A Nation of Cities: The Federal Government and Urban America, 1933–1965.* New York: Oxford University Press.

Genovese, Eugene D. (1994) *The Southern Tradition: The Achievement and Limitations of an American Conservatism.* Cambridge, Mass.: Harvard University Press.

Germond, Jack W. and Witcover, Jules (1989) *Whose Broad Stripes and Bright Stars: The Trivial Pursuit of the Presidency, 1988.* New York: Warner Books.

Gerson, Mark (1996) *The Neoconservative Vision: From the Cold War to the Culture Wars.* Lanham, Md.: Madison.

Gerstle, Gary (2001) *American Crucible: Race and Nation in the Twentieth Century.* Princeton, NJ: Princeton University Press.

Giedion, Siegfried (1947) *Space, Time and Architecture: The Growth of a New Tradition.* London: Oxford University Press.

Gillon, Steven M. (1992) *The Democrats' Dilemma: Walter F. Mondale and the Liberal Legacy.* New York: Columbia University Press.

Gilmore, Glenda E. (1996) *Gender and Jim Crow: Women and the Politics of White Supremacy in North Carolina, 1896–1920.* Chapel Hill: University of North Carolina Press.

Ginger, Ray (1958) *Six Days or Forever? Tennessee v. John Thomas Scopes.* Boston: Beacon.

Gitlin, Todd (1985) *Inside Prime Time.* New York: Pantheon.

—— (1987) *The Sixties: Years of Hope, Days of Rage.* New York: Bantam.

Gjerde, Jon (1997) *The Minds of the West: Ethnocultural Evolution in the Rural Middle West, 1830–1917.* Chapel Hill: University of North Carolina Press.

Glazer, Nathan (1975) *Affirmative Discrimination: Ethnic Inequality and Public Policy.* New York: Basic Books.

—— (1982) "The politics of a multiethnic society," in Lance Liebman (ed.) *Ethnic Relations in America.* Englewood Cliffs, NJ: Prentice-Hall.

Gleason, Philip (1992) *Speaking of Diversity: Language and Ethnicity in Twentieth-Century America.* Baltimore, Md.: Johns Hopkins University Press.

Glendon, Mary Ann (1991) *Rights Talk: The Impoverishment of Political Discourse.* New York: Free Press.

Glickman, Lawrence B. (1997) *A Living Wage: American Workers and the Making of Consumer Society.* Ithaca, NY: Cornell University Press.

—— (ed.) (1999) *Consumer Society in American History: A Reader.* Ithaca, NY: Cornell University Press.

Gluck, Sherna Berger (1987) *Rosie the Riveter Revisited: Women, The War, and Social Change.* Boston: Twayne Publishers.

Goldberg, David J. (1999) *Discontented America: The United States in the 1920s.* Baltimore, Md.: Johns Hopkins University Press.

Goldman, Eric F. (1961) *The Crucial Decade – and After: America, 1945–1960.* New York: Vintage.

Goldman, Nancy L. (ed.) (1982) *Female Soldiers: Combatants or Noncombatants.* Westport, Conn.: Greenwood Press.

Goldman, Peter and Mathews, Tom (1989) *The Quest for the Presidency: The 1988 Campaign.* New York: Touchstone.

Gonzalez, Gilbert G. (1990) *Chicano Education in the Era of Segregation.* Philadelphia: Balch Institute Press.

Gordon, Colin (1994) *New Deals: Business, Labor, and Politics in America, 1920–1935.* New York: Cambridge University Press.

Gordon, Linda (1976) *Woman's Body, Woman's Right: A Social History of Birth Control in America*. New York: Grossman.

Gorman, Paul R. (1996) *Left Intellectuals and Popular Culture in America*. Chapel Hill: University of North Carolina Press.

Gosse, Van (1993) *Where the Boys Are: Cuba, Cold War America, and the Making of a New Left*. New York: Verso.

Gossett, Thomas (1963) *Race: The History of an Idea in America*. Dallas: Southern Methodist University Press.

Gottfried, Paul (1993) *The Conservative Movement*, rev. edn. New York: Twayne.

Gottlieb, Robert (1993) *Forcing the Spring: The Transformation of the American Environmental Movement*. Washington, DC: Island Press.

Graebner, Norman (1984) *America as a World Power: A Realist Appraisal from Wilson to Reagan*. Wilmington, Del.: Scholarly Resources.

Graham, Hugh Davis (1990) *The Civil Rights Era: Origins and Development of National Policy, 1960–1972*. New York: Oxford University Press.

Grandstaff, Mark R. (1997) *Foundation of the Force: Air Force Enlisted Personnel Policy, 1907–1956*. Washington, DC: Air Force History and Museums Programs.

Grant, Joanne (1998) *Ella Baker: Freedom Bound*. New York: Wiley.

Grant, Madison (1916) *The Passing of the Great Race, Or The Racial Basis of European History*. New York: Scribner.

Grantham, Dewey W. (1958) *Hoke Smith and the Politics of the New South*. Baton Rouge: Louisiana State University Press.

—— (1983) *Southern Progressivism: The Reconciliation of Progress and Tradition*. Knoxville: University of Tennessee Press.

Graubard, Stephen R. (1992) *Mr. Bush's War: Adventures in the Politics of Illusion*. New York: Hill and Wang.

Grebler, Leo, Moore, Joan W., and Guzman, Ralph C. (1970) *The Mexican-American People: The Nation's Second Largest Minority*. New York: Free Press.

Green, Elna C. (1997) *Southern Strategies: Southern Women and the Woman Suffrage Question*. Chapel Hill: University of North Carolina Press.

Green, James R. (1978) *Grass-Roots Socialism: Radical Movements in the Southwest, 1895–1943*. Baton Rouge: Louisiana State University Press.

Greenberg, Clement (1982) [1939] "Avant-garde and kitsch," in Francis Frascina and Charles Harrison (eds.) *Modern Art and Modernism: A Critical Anthology*. London: Harper and Row.

—— (1982) [1965] "Modernist painting," in Francis Frascina and Charles Harrison (eds.) *Modern Art and Modernism: A Critical Anthology*. London: Harper and Row.

Greenberg, Jack (1959) *Race Relations and American Law*. New York: Columbia University Press.

Greene, Julie (1998) *Pure and Simple Politics: The American Federation of Labor and Political Activism, 1881–1917*. New York: Cambridge University Press.

Greene, John Robert (1995) *The Presidency of Gerald R. Ford*. Lawrence: University Press of Kansas.

—— (2000) *The Presidency of George Bush*. Lawrence: University Press of Kansas.

Greenstein, Fred I. (1982) *The Hidden-Hand Presidency: Eisenhower as Leader*. New York: Basic Books.

Gregory, Ross (1971) *The Origins of American Intervention in the First World War*. New York: W. W. Norton.

Griffith, Robert K., Jr. (1970) *The Politics of Fear: Joseph R. McCarthy and the Senate*. Lexington: University Press of Kentucky.

—— (1982) *Men Wanted for the United States Army: American Experience with an All Volunteer Army Between the Wars*. Westport, Conn.: Greenwood Press.

Griffith, Sally Foreman (1989) *Home Town News: William Allen White and the Emporia Gazette.* New York: Oxford University Press.

Guinsburg, Thomas N. (1982) *The Pursuit of Isolationism in the United States Senate from Versailles to Pearl Harbor.* New York: Garland.

Guralnick, Peter (1994) *Last Train to Memphis: The Rise of Elvis Presley.* Boston: Little, Brown.

Gurstein, Rochelle (1996) *The Repeal of Reticence: A History of America's Cultural and Legal Struggles Over Free Speech, Obscenity, Sexual Liberation, and Modern Art.* New York: Hill and Wang.

Habermas, Jürgen (1989) *The Structural Transformation of the Public Sphere: An Inquiry into a Category of Bourgeois Society,* trans. Thomas Burger. Cambridge, Mass.: MIT Press.

Hackney, Sheldon (1969) *Populism to Progressivism in Alabama.* Princeton, NJ: Princeton University Press.

—— (1972) "*Origins of the New South* in retrospect," *Journal of Southern History* 38(2) (May), pp. 191–216.

Haddad, Yvonne Yazbeck and Smith, Jane Idleman (eds.) (1994) *Muslim Communities in North America.* Albany: State University of New York Press.

Hagan, Kenneth J. and Roberts, William R. (eds.) (1986) *Against All Enemies: Interpretations of American Military History from Colonial Times to the Present.* Westport, Conn.: Greenwood Press.

Hagan, William T. (1976) *United States–Comanche Relations: The Reservation Years.* New Haven, Conn.: Yale University Press.

Haines, David W. (ed.) (1996) *Refugees in America in the 1990s: A Reference Handbook.* Westport, Conn.: Greenwood Press.

Hair, William Ivy (1991) *The Kingfish and his Realm: The Life and Times of Huey P. Long.* Baton Rouge: Louisiana State University Press.

Halberstam, David (1993) *The Fifties.* New York: Villard.

Hallin, Daniel C. (1986) *The "Uncensored War": The Media and Vietnam.* New York: Oxford University Press.

—— (1994) *We Keep America on Top of the World: Television Journalism and the Public Sphere.* London: Routledge.

Halter, Marilyn (1993) *Between Race and Ethnicity: Cape Verdean American Immigrants, 1860–1965.* Urbana: University of Illinois Press.

Hamby, Alonzo L. (1992) *Liberalism and its Challengers: From F.D.R. to Bush,* 2nd edn. New York: Oxford University Press.

—— (1995) *Man of the People: A Life of Harry S. Truman.* New York: Oxford University Press.

Handlin, Oscar (1941) *Boston's Immigrants, 1790–1865: A Study in Acculturation.* Cambridge, Mass.: Harvard University Press.

—— (1951) *The Uprooted: The Epic Story of the Great Migrations that Made the American People.* Boston: Little, Brown.

—— (1957) *Race and Nationality in American Life.* Boston: Little, Brown.

Hansen, Marcus Lee (1940) *The Immigrant in American History.* Cambridge, Mass.: Harvard University Press.

Hargrove, Erwin (1988) *Jimmy Carter as President: Leadership and the Politics of the Public Good.* Baton Rouge: Louisiana State University Press.

Harrison, Roderick J. and Bennett, Claudette E. (1995) "Racial and ethnic diversity," in Reynolds Farley (ed.) *State of the Union: America in the 1990s,* vol. 2: *Social Trends.* New York: Russell Sage.

Hartman, Susan M. (1982) *The Home Front and Beyond: American Women in the 1940s.* Boston: Twayne Publishers.

Hartz, Louis (1955) *The Liberal Tradition in America: An Interpretation of American Political Thought since the Revolution.* New York: Harcourt, Brace.

Harvey, David (1989) *The Condition of Postmodernity.* Cambridge, Mass.: Blackwell.

Harvey, Mark (1994) *A Symbol of Wilderness: Echo Park and the American Conservation Movement.* Albuquerque: University of New Mexico Press.

Haskell, Barbara (1999) *The American Century: Art and Culture, 1900–1950.* New York: Whitney Museum of American Art, in association with W. W. Norton.

Haskell, Molly (1974) *From Reverence to Rape: The Treatment of Women in the Movies.* New York: Penguin.

Haskell, Thomas L. (1998) *Objectivity Is Not Neutrality: Explanatory Schemes in History.* Baltimore, Md.: Johns Hopkins University Press.

Havard, William C. (ed.) (1972) *The Changing Politics of the South.* Baton Rouge: Louisiana State University Press.

Hawley, Ellis M. (1966) *The New Deal and the Problem of Monopoly: A Study in Economic Ambivalence.* Princeton, NJ: Princeton University Press.

—— (1992) *The Great War and the Search for a Modern Order: A History of the American People and their Institutions, 1917–1933,* 2nd edn. New York: St. Martin's Press.

Hays, Samuel P. (1957) *The Response to Industrialism, 1885–1914.* Chicago: University of Chicago Press.

—— (1959) *Conservation and the Gospel of Efficiency: The Progressive Conservation Movement, 1890–1920.* Cambridge, Mass.: Harvard University Press.

—— (1986) *Beauty, Health, and Permanence: Environmental Politics in the United States, 1955–1985.* New York: Cambridge University Press.

Heckscher, August (1991) *Woodrow Wilson: A Biography.* New York: Scribner's.

Hein, Jeffrey (1995) *From Vietnam, Laos, and Cambodia: A Refugee Experience in the United States.* New York: Twayne.

Heinze, Andrew R. (1990) *Adapting To Abundance: Jewish Immigrants, Mass Consumption and the Search for American Identity.* New York: Columbia University Press.

Henry, William A., III (1982) "The decline and fall of the New York *Daily News,*" *Washington Journalism Review* 4, pp. 18, 20, 22–3.

Herberg, Will (1955) "Our conservative heritage recaptured," *New Leader* 38, pp. 14–15.

—— (1960) *Protestant, Catholic, Jew: An Essay in American Religious Sociology,* rev. edn. Garden City, NY: Doubleday.

Hersey, John (1970) *Into the Valley: A Skirmish of the Marines.* New York: Alfred A. Knopf.

Hewes, James E. (1975) *From Root to McNamara: Army Organization and Administration, 1900–1963.* Washington, DC: US Army Center for Military History.

Hickman, Larry A. and Alexander, Thomas M. (eds.) (1998) *The Essential Dewey,* 2 vols. Bloomington, Ind.: Indiana University Press.

Hicks, John D. (1931) *The Populist Revolt: A History of the Farmers' Alliance and the People's Party.* Minneapolis: University of Minnesota Press.

—— (1960) *The Republican Ascendancy, 1921–1933.* New York: Harper and Row.

Higgs, Robert (1977) *Competition and Coercion: Blacks in the American Economy, 1865–1914.* Cambridge: Cambridge University Press.

Higham, John (1988) [1955] *Strangers in the Land: Patterns of American Nativism, 1860–1925.* New Brunswick, NJ: Rutgers University Press. Also reprinted 1963, New York: Atheneum.

—— (2001) *Hanging Together: Unity and Diversity in American Culture.* New Haven, Conn.: Yale University Press.

Hilmes, Michele (1990) *Hollywood and Broadcasting: From Radio to Cable.* Urbana: University of Illinois Press.

—— (1997) *Radio Voices: American Broadcasting, 1922–1952.* Minneapolis: University of Minnesota Press.

Himmelfarb, Gertrude (1999) *One Nation, Two Cultures.* New York: Alfred A. Knopf.

Hine, Darlene Clark and Thompson, Kathleen (1998) *A Shining Thread of Hope: The History of Black Women in America*. New York: Broadway.

Hine, Thomas (1986) *Populuxe*. New York: Alfred A. Knopf.

Hing, Bill Ong (1993) *Making and Remaking Asian America through Immigration Policy, 1850–1990*. Stanford, Calif.: Stanford University Press.

Hirt, Paul W. (1994) *A Conspiracy of Optimism: Management of the National Forests since World War Two*. Lincoln: University of Nebraska Press.

Hobson, Fred (1983) *Tell About the South: The Southern Rage to Explain*. Baton Rouge: Louisiana State University Press.

Hoerder, Dirk and Rossler, Horst (eds.) (1993) *Distant Magnets: Expectations and Realities in the Immigrant Experience, 1840–1930*. New York: Holmes and Meier.

Hofstadter, Richard (1948) *The American Political Tradition and the Men Who Made It*. New York: Alfred A. Knopf.

—— (1955) *The Age of Reform: From Bryan to FDR*. New York: Alfred A. Knopf, and London: Jonathan Cape. Reprinted 1962.

Hogan, Michael J. (1998) *A Cross of Iron: Harry S. Truman and the Origins of the National Security State, 1945–1954*. New York: Cambridge University Press.

Hoge, Dean R., Johnson, Benton, and Luidens, Donald A. (1994) *Vanishing Boundaries: The Religion of Mainline Protestant Baby Boomers*. Louisville, Ky.: Westminster/John Knox Press.

Holl, Karl, Trautmann, Günter, and Vorländer, Hans (eds.) (1986) *Sozialer Liberalismus* [*Social Liberalism*]. Göttingen: Vandenhoeck and Ruprecht.

Holland, Max (1989) *When the Machine Stopped: A Cautionary Tale from Industrial America*. Boston: Harvard Business School Press.

Hollinger, David A. (1985) *In the American Province: Studies in the History and Historiography of Ideas*. Baltimore, Md.: Johns Hopkins University Press.

—— (1995) *Postethnic America: Beyond Multiculturalism*. New York: Basic Books.

—— (1996) *Science, Jews and Secular Culture: Studies in Mid-Twentieth Century American Intellectual History*. Princeton, NJ: Princeton University Press.

Hollinger, David A. and Capper, Charles (eds.) (2001) *The American Intellectual Tradition*, 3rd. edn., vol. 2. New York: Oxford University Press.

Holmes, William F. (1970) *The White Chief: James Kimble Vardaman*. Baton Rouge: Louisiana State University Press.

Honey, Maureen (1984) *Creating Rosie the Riveter: Class, Gender, and Propaganda during World War II*. Amherst: University of Massachusetts Press.

Honey, Michael (1993) *Southern Labor and Black Civil Rights: Organizing Memphis Workers*. Urbana: University of Illinois Press.

Horowitz, Daniel (1985) *The Morality of Spending: Attitudes Toward the Consumer Society in America, 1875–1940*. Baltimore, Md.: Johns Hopkins University Press.

Horten, Gerd (2002) *Radio Goes to War: The Cultural Politics of Propaganda during World War II*. Berkeley: University of California Press.

Horwitz, Morton J. (1992) *The Transformation of American Law, 1870–1960: The Crisis of Legal Orthodoxy*. New York: Oxford University Press.

—— (1998) *The Warren Court and the Pursuit of Justice*. New York: Hill and Wang.

Hounshell, David A. (1984) *From the American System to Mass Production, 1800–1932: The Development of Manufacturing Technology*. Baltimore, Md.: Johns Hopkins University Press.

Howarth, Stephen (1991) *A History of the United States Navy, 1775–1991*. New York: Random House.

Howe, Irving (1985) *Socialism and America*. New York: Harcourt Brace Jovanovich.

Hoy, Suellen (1995) *Chasing Dirt: The American Pursuit of Cleanliness*. New York: Oxford University Press.

Hudnut-Beumler, James (1994) *Looking for God in the Suburbs: The Religion of the American Dream and its Critics, 1945–1965*. New Brunswick, NJ: Rutgers University Press.

Hughes, Robert (1997) *American Visions: The Epic History of Art in America*. New York: Alfred A. Knopf.

Hughes, Thomas P. (1983) *Networks of Power: Electrification in Western Society, 1880–1930*. Baltimore, Md.: Johns Hopkins University Press.

—— (1989) *American Genesis: A Century of Invention and Technological Enthusiasm*. New York: Viking.

—— (1998) *Rescuing Prometheus*. New York: Pantheon.

Hull, N. E. H. (1997) *Roscoe Pound and Karl Llewellyn: The Search for an American Jurisprudence*. Chicago: University of Chicago Press.

Hull, N. E. H. and Hoffer, Peter Charles (2001) *Roe v. Wade: The Abortion Rights Controversy in American History*. Lawrence: University Press of Kansas.

Huntington, Samuel P. (1981) *American Politics: The Promise of Disharmony*. Cambridge, Mass.: Harvard University Press.

Hurley, Andrew (1995) *Environmental Inequalities: Class, Race, and Industrial Pollution in Gary, Indiana, 1945–1980*. Chapel Hill: University of North Carolina Press.

Hurtado, Albert L. (1999) *Intimate Frontiers: Sex, Gender, and Culture in Old California*. Albuquerque: University of New Mexico Press.

Hutchinson, E. P. (1981) *Legislative History of American Immigration Policy, 1798–1965*. Philadelphia: University of Pennsylvania Press.

Huthmacher, J. Joseph (1962) "Urban liberalism and the age of reform," *Mississippi Valley Historical Review* 49, pp. 231–41.

Ickes, Harold L. (1954) *The Secret Diary of Harold L. Ickes*, vol. 2. New York: Simon and Schuster.

Igler, David (2001) *Industrial Cowboys: Miller and Lux and the Transformation of the Far West, 1850–1920*. Berkeley: University of California Press.

Institute for Cultural Conservatism (1987) *Cultural Conservatism: Toward A New Cultural Agenda*. Lanham, Md.: Free Congress Research and Education Foundation.

Irons, Peter (1982) *New Deal Lawyers*. Princeton, NJ: Princeton University Press.

Isaacson, Walter (1992) *Kissinger: A Biography*. New York: Simon and Schuster.

Isenberg, Andrew (2000) *The Destruction of the Bison: An Environmental History, 1750–1920*. New York: Cambridge University Press.

Isserman, Maurice (1987) *If I Had a Hammer . . .*: The Death of the Old Left and the Birth of the New Left. New York: Basic Books.

—— (1992) "You don't need a weatherman but a postman can be helpful: thoughts on the history of SDS and the antiwar movement," in Melvin Small and William D. Hoover (eds.) *Give Peace a Chance: Exploring the Vietnam Antiwar Movement*. Syracuse, NY: Syracuse University Press.

Isserman, Maurice and Kazin, Michael (1989) "The failure and success of the new radicalism," in Steve Fraser and Gary Gerstle (eds.) *The Rise and Fall of the New Deal Order, 1930–1980*. Princeton, NJ: Princeton University Press.

—— (2000) *America Divided: The Civil War of the Sixties*. New York: Oxford University Press.

Italian American Historical Society (1977) *The Urban Experience of Italian Americans*. Staten Island, NY: The Association.

Iverson, Peter (1998) "*We Are Still Here*": *American Indians in the Twentieth Century*. Wheeling, Ill.: Harlan Davidson.

Jackson, Charles O. (1970) *Food and Drug Legislation in the New Deal*. Princeton, NJ: Princeton University Press.

Jackson, Kenneth T. (1985) *Crabgrass Frontier: The Suburbanization of the United States*. New York: Oxford University Press.

Jackson, Walter A. (1990) *Gunnar Myrdal and America's Conscience: Social Engineering and Racial Liberalism, 1938–1987*. Chapel Hill: University of North Carolina Press.

Jacobs, Meg (1998) "How about some meat?: The Office of Price Administration, consumption politics, and state building from the bottom up, 1941–1946," *Journal of American History* 84, pp. 910–41.

Jacobsen, Hans-Adolf and Smith, Arthur L., Jr. (eds.) (1979) *World War II – Policy and Strategy: Selected Documents with Commentary*. Santa Barbara, Calif.: ABC-Clio.

Jacobson, Matthew Frye (1995) *Special Sorrows: The Diasporic Imagination of Irish, Polish and Jewish Immigrants in the United States*. Cambridge, Mass.: Harvard University Press.

—— (1998) *Whiteness of a Different Color: European Immigrants and the Alchemy of Race*. Cambridge, Mass.: Harvard University Press.

Jacoby, Karl (2001) *Crimes Against Nature: Squatters, Poachers, Thieves, and the Hidden History of American Conservation*. Berkeley: University of California Press.

Jacoby, Russell (1987) *The Last Intellectuals: American Culture in the Age of Academe*. New York: Basic Books.

Jacoby, Sanford (1997) *Modern Manors: Welfare Capitalism since the New Deal*. Princeton, NJ: Princeton University Press.

Jakle, John A. (2001) *City Lights: Illuminating the American Night*. Baltimore, Md.: Johns Hopkins University Press.

James, William (1907) *Pragmatism*. New York: Longman.

Jameson, Elizabeth (1998) *All that Glitters: Class, Conflict, and Community in Cripple Creek*. Urbana: University of Illinois Press.

Jameson, Fredric (1984) "Periodizing the 60s," in Sohnya Sayres et al. (eds.), *The 60s Without Apology*. Minneapolis: University of Minnesota Press.

Jeffries, John W. (1996) *Wartime America: The World War II Home Front*. Chicago: Ivan R. Dee.

Jenks, Charles (1985) *Modern Movements in Architecture*, 2nd edn. Harmondsworth: Penguin.

Jezer, Marty (1982) *The Dark Ages: Life in the United States, 1945–1960*. Boston: South End.

Joachimides, Christos M. and Rosenthal, Norman (1993) *American Art in the 20th Century: Painting and Sculpture, 1913–1993*. London: Prestel.

Johnson, Haynes (1991) *Sleepwalking Through History: America in the Reagan Years*. New York: Doubleday Anchor.

—— (1994) *Divided We Fall: Gambling with History in the Nineties*. New York: W. W. Norton.

—— (2001) *The Best of Times: America in the Age of Clinton*. New York: Harcourt.

Johnson, Lyndon B. (1967) *Public Papers, 1965*, vol. 2. Washington, DC: Government Printing Office.

Jones, James (1951) *From Here to Eternity*. New York: Scribner.

Jones, Landon Y. (1980) *Great Expectations: America and the Baby Boom Generation*. New York: Coward, McCann, and Geoghegan.

Jones, Maldwyn A. (1992) *American Immigration*, 2nd edn. Chicago: University of Chicago Press.

Jones, S. Shepard and Myers, Denys P. (eds.) (1940) *Documents on American Foreign Relations*, vol. 2. Boston: World Peace Foundation.

Jorstad, Erling (1990) *Holding Fast/Pressing On: Religion in America in the 1980s*. New York: Praeger.

Judd, Richard (1997) *Common Lands, Common People: The Origins of Conservation in Northern New England*. Cambridge, Mass.: Harvard University Press.

Kahn, Paul W. (1999) *The Cultural Study of Law: Reconstructing Legal Scholarship*. New Haven, Conn.: Yale University Press.

Kalman, Laura (1986) *Legal Realism at Yale, 1927–1960.* Chapel Hill: University of North Carolina Press.

—— (1996) *The Strange Career of Liberal Legalism.* New Haven, Conn.: Yale University Press.

Kammen, Michael (1999) *American Culture, American Tastes: Social Change and the Twentieth Century.* New York: Alfred A. Knopf.

Kantrowitz, Steve (2000) *Ben Tillman and the Reconstruction of White Supremacy.* Chapel Hill: University of North Carolina Press.

Karnow, Stanley (1991) *Vietnam: A History.* New York: Penguin.

Kasson, John F. (1978) *Amusing the Million: Coney Island at the Turn of the Century.* New York: Hill and Wang.

Katzman, David (1988) *Seven Days a Week: Women and Domestic Service in Industrializing America.* Champaign: University of Illinois Press.

Kauffman, Linda S. (ed.) (1993) *American Feminist Thought at Century's End.* Cambridge, Mass.: Harvard University Press.

Kaufman, Burton I. (1993) *The Presidency of James Earl Carter, Jr.* Lawrence: University Press of Kansas.

Kay, Jane Holtz (1997) *Asphalt Nation: How the Automobile Took Over America, and How We Can Take It Back.* New York: Crown.

Keats, John (1957) *The Crack in the Picture Window.* Boston: Houghton Mifflin.

—— (1958) *The Insolent Chariots.* Philadelphia: Lippincott.

Keller, Evelyn Fox (1985) *Reflections on Gender and Science.* New Haven, Conn.: Yale University Press.

Keller, Morton (1990) *Regulating a New Economy: Public Policy and Economic Change in America, 1900–1933.* Cambridge, Mass.: Harvard University Press.

—— (1994) *Regulating a New Society: Public Policy and Social Change in America, 1900–1933.* Cambridge, Mass.: Harvard University Press.

Kelley, Robin D. G. (1994) *Race Rebels: Culture, Politics, and the Black Working Class.* New York: Free Press.

Kennan, George F. (1947) X, "The sources of Soviet conduct," *Foreign Affairs* 25 (July), pp. 566–82.

—— (1951) *American Diplomacy, 1900–1950.* Chicago: University of Chicago Press.

Kennedy, David (1999) *Freedom from Fear: The American People in Depression and War, 1929–1945.* New York: Oxford University Press.

Kennedy, Duncan (1997) *A Critique of Adjudication (Fin de Siècle).* Cambridge, Mass.: Harvard University Press.

Kessler-Harris, Alice (1982) *Out to Work: A History of Wage-earning Women in the United States.* New York: Oxford University Press.

Kevles, Daniel J. (1978) *The Physicists: The History of a Scientific Community in Modern America.* New York: Alfred A. Knopf.

Kevles, Daniel J. and Hood, Leroy (eds.) (1992) *The Code of Codes: Scientific and Social Issues in the Human Genome Project.* Cambridge, Mass.: Harvard University Press.

Key, V. O. (1942) *Politics, Parties, and Pressure Groups.* New York: T. Y. Crowell.

—— (1949) *Southern Politics in State and Nation.* New York: Alfred A. Knopf.

Keyssar, Alexander (2000) *The Right to Vote: The Contested History of Democracy in the United States.* New York: Basic Books.

Kikumura, Akemi and Kitano, Harry H. (1973) "Interracial marriage: a picture of the Japanese Americans," *Journal of Social Issues* 29, pp. 67–82.

Kilian, Crawford (1978) *"Do Some Great Thing": The Black Pioneers of British Columbia.* Vancouver: Douglas and McIntyre.

Kimball, Warren F. (1969) *The Most Unsordid Act: Lend-Lease, 1939–1941.* Baltimore, Md.: Johns Hopkins University Press.

—— (1997) *Forged in War: Roosevelt, Churchill, and the Second World War.* New York: William Morrow.

Kimmel, Husband E. (1955) *Admiral Kimmel's Story.* Chicago: Henry Regnery.

King, Richard H. (1980) *A Southern Renaissance: The Cultural Awakening of the American South, 1930–1955.* New York: Oxford University Press.

Kirby, Jack Temple (1972) *Darkness at the Dawning: Race and Reform in the Progressive South.* Philadelphia: Lippincott.

Kirk, Russell (1953) *The Conservative Mind: From Burke to Santayana.* Chicago: Henry Regnery.

—— (1986) "Enlivening the conservative mind," *Intercollegiate Review* 21, pp. 25–8.

—— (1996) *Redeeming the Time.* Wilmington, Del.: Intercollegiate Studies Institute.

Kirwan, Albert W. (1951) *The Revolt of the Rednecks: Mississippi Politics, 1876–1925.* Lexington: University Press of Kentucky.

Kloppenberg, James T. (1986) *Uncertain Victory: Social Democracy and Progressivism in European and American Thought, 1870–1920.* New York: Oxford University Press.

—— (1998) *The Virtues of Liberalism.* New York: Oxford University Press.

Kluger, Richard (1976) *Simple Justice: The History of* Brown v. Board of Education *and Black America's Struggle for Equality.* New York: Alfred A. Knopf.

Kneebone, John T. (1985) *Southern Liberal Journalists and the Issue of Race, 1920–1944.* Chapel Hill: University of North Carolina Press.

Knock, Thomas J. (1992) *To End All Wars: Woodrow Wilson and the Quest for a New World Order.* Princeton, NJ: Princeton University Press.

Kohlstedt, Sally Gregory and Rossiter, Margaret W. (eds.) (1985) "Historical writing on American science," *Osiris*, 2nd ser. 1, pp. 5–32.

Kolb, Charles (1994) *White House Daze: The Unmaking of Domestic Policy in the Bush Years.* New York: Free Press.

Kolko, Gabriel (1963) *The Triumph of Conservatism: A Reinterpretation of American History, 1900–1916.* Chicago: Quadrangle Books.

Konvitz, Milton R. (1946) *The Alien and the Asiatic in American Law.* Ithaca, NY: Cornell University Press.

Kousser, J. Morgan (1974) *The Shaping of Southern Politics: Suffrage Restriction and the Establishment of the One-Party South, 1880–1910.* New Haven, Conn.: Yale University Press.

Kousser, J. Morgan and McPherson, James (eds.) (1982) *Region, Race, and Reconstruction: Essays in Honor of C. Vann Woodward.* New York: Oxford University Press.

Kramer, Larry D. (2001) "The Supreme Court 2000 term: Foreword: We the Court," *Harvard Law Review* 115, pp. 4–168.

Krapohl, Robert H. and Lippy, Charles H. (1999) *The Evangelicals: A Historical, Thematic, and Biographical Guide.* Westport, Conn.: Greenwood Press.

Kristol, Irving (1983) *Reflections of a Neoconservative.* New York: Basic Books.

—— (1995) *Neoconservatism: The Autobiography of an Idea.* New York: Free Press.

Kuhn, Thomas (1962) *The Structure of Scientific Revolutions.* Chicago: University of Chicago Press.

Kutler, Stanley I. (1984) *The American Inquisition: Justice and Injustice in the Cold War.* New York: Hill and Wang.

—— (1990) *The Wars of Watergate: The Last Crisis of Richard Nixon.* New York: Alfred A. Knopf.

Kwolek-Folland, Angel (1998) *Incorporating Women: A History of Women and Business in the United States.* New York: Twayne.

La Sorte, Michael (1985) *La Merica.* Philadelphia: Temple University Press.

LaFeber, Walter (1979) *The Panama Canal: The Crisis in Historical Perspective.* New York: Oxford University Press.

—— (1997) *America, Russia, and the Cold War, 1945–1996*, 8th edn. New York: McGraw Hill.

Laird, Pamela Walker (1998) *Advertising Progress: American Business and the Rise of Consumer Marketing*. Baltimore, Md.: Johns Hopkins University Press.

Langston, Nancy (1995) *Forest Dreams, Forest Nightmares: The Paradox of Old Growth in the Inland Northwest*. Seattle: University of Washington Press.

Lansing, Robert (1921) *The Peace Negotiations: A Personal Narrative*. Boston: Houghton Mifflin.

Lapp, Rudolph M. (1977) *Blacks in Gold Rush California*. New Haven, Conn.: Yale University Press.

Larson, Edward J. (1997) *Summer for the Gods: The Scopes Trial and America's Continuing Debate over Science and Religion*. New York: Basic Books.

Lasch, Christopher (1965) *The New Radicalism in America, 1889–1963: The Intellectual as a Social Type*. New York: Alfred A. Knopf.

—— (1979) *The Culture of Narcissism: American Life in an Age of Diminishing Expectations*. New York: W. W. Norton.

—— (1991) *The True and Only Heaven: Progress and its Critics*. New York: W. W. Norton.

—— (1995) *The Revolt of the Elites and the Betrayal of Democracy*. New York: W. W. Norton.

Laslett, John H. M. and Lipset, Seymour Martin (eds.) (1974) *Failure of a Dream?: Essays in the History of American Socialism*. Garden City, NY: Anchor Books.

Lay, Shawn (ed.) (1992) *The Invisible Empire in the West: Toward a New Historical Appraisal of the Ku Klux Klan of the 1920s*. Champaign: University of Illinois Press.

—— (1994) "Hooded populism: new assessments of the Ku Klux Klan of the 1920s," *Reviews in American History* 22, pp. 668–73.

Lazarsfeld, Paul F. and Field, Harry (1946) *The People Look at Radio*. Chapel Hill: University of North Carolina Press.

Leach, William (1993) *Land of Desire: Merchants, Power and the Rise of a New American Culture*. New York: Pantheon.

Lear, Linda (1997) *Rachel Carson: Witness for Nature*. New York: Henry Holt.

Lears, T. J. Jackson (1981) *No Place of Grace: Antimodernism and the Transformation of American Culture, 1880–1920*. New York: Pantheon.

—— (1994) *Fables of Abundance: A Cultural History of Advertising in America*. New York: Basic Books.

Lebergott, Stanley (1993) *Pursuing Happiness: American Consumers in the Twentieth Century*. Princeton, NJ: Princeton University Press.

Lee, Chana Kai (1999) *For Freedom's Sake: The Life of Fannie Lou Hamer*. Urbana: University of Illinois Press.

Leff, Mark H. (1984) *The Limits of Symbolic Reform: The New Deal and Taxation, 1933–1939*. New York: Cambridge University Press.

Leffler, Melvin P. (1992) *A Preponderance of Power: National Security, the Truman Administration, and the Cold War*. Stanford, Calif.: Stanford University Press.

Leonard, Thomas C. (1986) *The Power of the Press: The Birth of American Political Reporting*. New York: Oxford University Press.

—— (1995) *News for All: America's Coming-of-Age with the Press*. New York: Oxford University Press.

Lerner, Gerda (ed.) (1972) *Black Women in White America*. New York: Pantheon.

—— (1979) *The Majority Finds its Past: Placing Women in History*. New York: Oxford University Press.

Leslie, Stuart W. (1993) *The Cold War and American Science: The Military-Industrial-Academic Complex at MIT and Stanford*. New York: Columbia University Press.

Leuchtenburg, William E. (1963) *Franklin D. Roosevelt and the New Deal, 1932–1940*. New York: Harper and Row.

—— (1964) "The New Deal and the analogue of war," in John Braeman, Robert H. Bremner, and Everett Walters (eds.) *Change and Continuity in Twentieth Century America*. Columbus: Ohio State University Press.

—— (1993) *In the Shadow of FDR: From Harry Truman to Bill Clinton*. Ithaca, NY: Cornell University Press.

—— (1993) [1958] *The Perils of Prosperity, 1914–1932*, 2nd edn. Chicago: University of Chicago Press.

—— (1995) *The FDR Years: On Roosevelt and his Legacy*. New York: Columbia University Press.

—— (1995) *The Supreme Court Reborn: The Constitutional Revolution in the Age of Roosevelt*. New York: Oxford University Press.

Levin, N. Gordon (1968) *Woodrow Wilson and World Politics: America's Response to War and Revolution*. New York: Oxford University Press.

Levine, Lawrence (1988) *Highbrow/Lowbrow: The Emergence of Cultural Hierarchy*. Cambridge, Mass.: Harvard University Press.

—— (1993) *The Unpredictable Past: Explorations in American Cultural History*. New York: Oxford University Press.

Lewin, Kurt (1947) "Frontiers in group dynamics," *Human Relations* 1, pp. 5–41.

—— (1948) *Resolving Social Conflicts*. New York: Harper and Row.

Lewis, Sinclair (1925) *Arrowsmith*. New York: Grosset and Dunlap.

Lhamon, W. T., Jr. (1990) *Deliberate Speed: The Origins of a Cultural Style in the American 1950s*. Washington, DC: Smithsonian Institution.

Lichtenstein, Alex (1996) *Twice the Work of Free Labor: The Political Economy of Convict Labor in the South*. London: Verso.

Lichtenstein, Nelson (1982) *Labor's War at Home: The CIO in World War II*. New York: Cambridge University Press.

—— (1995) *The Most Dangerous Man in Detroit: Walter Reuther and the Fate of American Labor*. New York: Basic Books.

—— (2002) *State of the Union: A Century of American Labor*. Princeton, NJ: Princeton University Press.

Liddell Hart, B. H. (1970) *History of the Second World War*. New York: Putnam.

Lieberson, Stanley (1980) *A Piece of the Pie: Blacks and White Immigrants since 1880*. Berkeley: University of California Press.

Limerick, Patricia Nelson (1987) *The Legacy of Conquest: The Unbroken Past of the American West*. New York: W. W. Norton.

Link, Arthur S. (1954) *Woodrow Wilson and the Progressive Era, 1910–1917*. New York: Harper and Row.

—— (ed.) (1966–94) *The Papers of Woodrow Wilson*, 69 vols. Princeton, NJ: Princeton University Press.

—— (1979) *Woodrow Wilson: Revolution, War, and Peace*. Arlington Heights, Ill.: AHM Publishing.

Link, Arthur S. and McCormick, Richard L. (1983) *Progressivism*. Arlington Heights, Ill.: Harlan Davidson.

Link, Arthur S. and Patrick, Rembert W. (eds.) (1965) *Writing Southern History: Essays in Historiography in Honor of Fletcher M. Green*. Baton Rouge: Louisiana State University Press.

Linn, Brian (1997) *Guardians of Empire: The US Army and the Pacific, 1902–1940*. Chapel Hill: University of North Carolina Press.

Lippmann, Walter (1922) *Public Opinion*. New York: Macmillan.

—— (1985) [1914] *Drift and Mastery: An Attempt to Diagnose the Current Unrest*. Madison: University of Wisconsin Press.

Lippy, Charles H. (ed.) (1989) *Twentieth Century Shapers of American Popular Religion.* Westport, Conn.: Greenwood Press.

—— (2000) *Pluralism Comes of Age: American Religious Culture in the Twentieth Century.* Armonk, NY: M. E. Sharpe.

Lipset, Seymour Martin (1996) *American Exceptionalism: A Double-Edged Sword.* New York: W. W. Norton.

Lipsitz, George (1994) *A Rainbow at Midnight: Labor and Culture in the 1940s.* Champaign: University of Illinois Press.

—— (1998) *The Possessive Investment in Whiteness: How White People Profit from Identity Politics.* Philadelphia: Temple University Press.

Litwack, Leon F. (1998) *Trouble in Mind: Black Southerners in the Age of Jim Crow.* New York: Alfred A. Knopf.

Livingston, James (1994) *Pragmatism and the Political Economy of Cultural Revolution 1850–1940.* Chapel Hill: University of North Carolina Press.

—— (2001) *Pragmatism, Feminism, and Democracy: Rethinking the Politics of American History.* New York: Routledge.

Lora, Ronald (1971) *Conservative Minds in America.* Chicago: Rand McNally.

Lowenstein, Sharon R. (1986) *Token Refuge: The Story of the Jewish Refugee Shelter at Oswego, 1944–1946.* Bloomington: Indiana University Press.

Lowenthal, Leo (1979) [1944] "Biographies in popular magazines," in Paul F. Lazarsfeld and Frank N. Stanton (eds.) *Radio Research, 1942–1943.* New York: Arno Press.

Lunardini, Christine and Knock, Thomas J. (1981) "Woodrow Wilson and woman suffrage: a new look," *Political Science Quarterly* 95, pp. 655–71.

McCartin, Joseph A. (1997) *Labor's Great War: The Struggle for Industrial Democracy and the Origins of Modern American Labor Relations, 1912–1921.* Chapel Hill: University of North Carolina Press.

McChesney, Robert W. (1993) *Telecommunications, Mass Media, and Democracy: The Battle for the Control of US Broadcasting, 1928–1935.* New York: Oxford University Press.

McClay, Wilfred M. (1994) *The Masterless: Self and Society in Modern America.* Chapel Hill: University of North Carolina Press.

MacCleery, Douglas W. (1993) *American Forests: A History of Resiliency and Recovery.* Durham, NC: Forest History Society.

McCloskey, Herbert and Zaller, John (1984) *The American Ethos: Public Attitude towards Capitalism and Democracy.* Cambridge, Mass.: Harvard University Press.

McCormick, Richard L. (1986) *The Party Period and Public Policy: American Politics from the Age of Jackson to the Progressive Era.* New York: Oxford University Press.

McCormick, Thomas J. (1989) *America's Half-Century: United States Foreign Policy in the Cold War.* Baltimore, Md.: Johns Hopkins University Press.

McCraw, Thomas K. (1984) *Prophets of Regulation: Charles Francis Adams, Louis D. Brandeis, James M. Landis, Alfred E. Kahn.* Cambridge, Mass.: Harvard University Press.

McCullough, David (1992) *Truman.* New York: Simon and Schuster.

McDougall, Walter A. (1997) *Promised Land, Crusader State: The American Encounter with the World since 1776.* Boston: Little, Brown.

McEvoy, Arthur (1986) *The Fisherman's Problem: Ecology and Law in California Fisheries, 1850–1980.* New York: Cambridge University Press.

McFarland, Stephen L. (1995) *America's Pursuit of Precision Bombing, 1910–1945.* Washington, DC: Smithsonian Institution Press.

McGerr, Michael E. (1986) *The Decline of Popular Politics: The American North, 1865–1928.* New York: Oxford University Press.

McGovern, Charles F. (forthcoming) *Sold American: Inventing the Consumer, 1890–1945.* Chapel Hill: University of North Carolina Press.

McJimsey, George (2000) *The Presidency of Franklin Delano Roosevelt*. Lawrence: University Press of Kansas.

McKenna, Richard (1962) *The Sand Pebbles*. New York: Harper and Row.

McMillen, Neil R. (1989) *Dark Journey: Black Mississippians in the Age of Jim Crow*. Urbana: University of Illinois Press.

McNeill, J. R. (2000) *Something New under the Sun: An Environmental History of the Twentieth-Century World*. New York: W. W. Norton.

McQuaid, Kim (1994) *Uneasy Partners: Big Business and American Politics, 1945–1990*. Baltimore, Md.: Johns Hopkins University Press.

McWhorter, Diane (2001) *Carry Me Home: Birmingham, Alabama: The Climactic Battle of the Civil Rights Movement*. New York: Simon and Schuster.

Madigan, Tim (2001*) The Burning: Massacre, Destruction, and the Tulsa Race Riot of 1921*. New York: St. Martin's Press.

Mailer, Norman (1969) "Superman comes to the supermarket," in Harold Hayes (ed.) *Smiling Through the Apocalypse: Esquire's History of the Sixties*. New York: McCall.

Malin, James C. (1944) *Winter Wheat in the Golden Belt of Kansas: A Study in Adaptation to Subhumid Geographical Environment*. Lawrence: Regents Press of Kansas.

—— (1947) *The Grasslands of North America: Prolegomena to Its History, with Addenda and Postscript*. Lawrence, Kan.: James C. Malin.

Manchester, William (1962) *H. L. Mencken: Disturber of the Peace*. New York: Collier.

Mandle, Jay R. (1978) *The Roots of Black Poverty: The Southern Plantation Economy after the Civil War*. Durham, NC: Duke University Press.

Manis, Andrew M. (1999) *A Fire You Can't Put Out: The Civil Rights Life of Birmingham's Reverend Fred Shuttlesworth*. Tuscaloosa: University of Alabama Press.

Mann, Arthur (ed.) (1963) *Progressive Era: Liberal Renaissance or Liberal Failure?* New York: Holt, Rinehart, and Winston.

Marable, Manning (1984) *Race, Reform, and Rebellion: The Second Reconstruction in Black America, 1945–1982*. Jackson: University Press of Mississippi.

Maraniss, David (1996) *First in His Class: The Biography of Bill Clinton*. New York: Touchstone.

—— (1999) *When Pride Still Mattered: A Life of Vince Lombardi*. New York: Simon and Schuster.

Marchand, Roland (1985) *Advertising the American Dream: Making Way for Modernity, 1920–1940*. Berkeley: University of California Press.

—— (1998) *Creating the Corporate Soul: The Rise of Public Relations and Corporate Imagery in American Big Business*. Berkeley: University of California Press.

Marks, Frederick W., III (1988) *Wind Over Sand: The Diplomacy of Franklin Roosevelt*. Athens: University of Georgia Press.

Marling, Karal Ann (1994) *As Seen on TV: The Visual Culture of Everyday Life in the 1950s*. Cambridge, Mass.: Harvard University Press.

—— (2000) *Merry Christmas! Unwrapping America's Greatest Holiday*. Cambridge, Mass.: Harvard University Press.

Martin, William C. (1996) *With God on Our Side: The Rise of the Religious Right in America*. New York: Broadway Books.

Marty, Martin. *Modern American Religion*. Vol. 1: *The Irony of It All, 1893–1919* (1986). Vol. 2: *The Noise of Conflict, 1919–1941* (1991). Vol. 3: *Under God, Indivisible, 1941–1960* (1996). Chicago: University of Chicago Press.

Marvin, David (1996) *George Bush and the Guardianship Presidency*. New York: St. Martin's Press.

Marwick, Arthur (1998) *The Sixties: Cultural Revolution in Britain, France, Italy, and the United States, c.1958–c.1974*. New York: Oxford University Press.

Massa, Mark (1999) *Catholics and American Culture: Fulton Sheen, Dorothy Day, and the Notre Dame Football Team.* New York: Crossroad.

Matusow, Allen J. (1984) *The Unraveling of America: A History of Liberalism in the 1960s.* New York: Harper and Row.

May, Elaine Tyler (1988) *Homeward Bound: American Families in the Cold War Era.* New York: Basic Books.

May, Henry F. (1959) *The End of American Innocence: A Study of the First Years of Our Time.* New York: Alfred A. Knopf.

—— (1964) *The End of American Innocence: A Study of the First Years of Our Own Time, 1912–1917.* Chicago: Quadrangle Books.

May, Lary (1980) *Screening Out the Past: The Birth of Mass Culture and the Motion Picture Industry.* New York: Oxford University Press.

—— (2000) *The Big Tomorrow: Hollywood and the Politics of the American Way.* Chicago: University of Chicago Press.

Mayer, Arno (1959) *Political Origins of the New Diplomacy, 1917–1918.* New Haven, Conn.: Yale University Press.

Mayer, Jane and Abramson, Jill (1994) *Strange Justice: The Selling of Clarence Thomas.* Boston: Houghton Mifflin.

Mayer, Jane and McManus, Doyle (1988) *Landslide: The Unmaking of the President 1984–1988.* Boston: Houghton Mifflin.

Mayhew, Leon H. (1968) *Law and Equal Opportunity: A Study of the Massachusetts Commission against Discrimination.* Cambridge, Mass.: Harvard University Press.

Mead, Margaret. (1928) *Coming of Age in Samoa: A Psychological Study of Primitive Youth for Western Civilization.* New York: William Morrow.

Meier, August and Rudwick, Elliott (1973) *CORE: A Study in the Civil Rights Movement, 1942–1968.* New York: Oxford University Press.

Melosi, Martin (2000) *The Sanitary City: Urban Infrastructure from Colonial Times to the Present.* Baltimore, Md.: Johns Hopkins University Press.

Mershon, Sherie and Schlossman, Steven (1997) *Foxholes and Colorlines: Desegregating the US Armed Forces.* Baltimore, Md.: Johns Hopkins University Press.

Meyer, Roy W. (1977) *The Village Indians of the Upper Missouri: The Mandans, Hidatsas, and Arikaras.* Lincoln: University of Nebraska Press.

Meyerowitz, Joanne (ed.) (1994) *Not June Cleaver: Women and Gender in Postwar America, 1945–1960.* Philadelphia: Temple University Press.

Milazzo, Paul (2001) "Legislating the solution to pollution: Congress and the development of water pollution control policy, 1945–1972." PhD dissertation, University of Virginia.

Milkis, Sidney and Mileur, Jerome M. (eds.) (1999) *Progressivism and the New Democracy.* Amherst: University of Massachusetts Press.

Miller, Douglas T. and Nowak, Marion (1977) *The Fifties: The Way We Really Were.* Garden City, NY: Doubleday.

Miller, Herman (1971) *Rich Man, Poor Man.* New York: Thomas Y. Crowell.

Miller, James (1987) *"Democracy is in the Streets": From Port Huron to the Siege of Chicago.* New York: Simon and Schuster.

Miller, Randall M. and Pozzetta, George E. (eds.) (1988) *Shades of the Sunbelt: Essays on Ethnicity, Race, and the Urban South.* Westport, Conn.: Greenwood.

Millett, Allan R. (1991) *Semper Fidelis: The History of the United States Marine Corps*, rev., expanded edn. New York: Free Press.

Millett, Allan R. and Maslowski, Peter (1994) *For the Common Defense: A Military History of the United States of America*, rev., expanded edn. New York: Free Press.

Milner, Clyde A., II, O'Connor, Carol A., and Sandweiss, Martha A. (eds.) (1994) *The Oxford History of the American West.* New York: Oxford University Press.

Miner, H. Craig (1976) *The Corporation and the Indian: Tribal Sovereignty and Industrial Civilization in Indian Territory, 1865–1907*. Columbia: University of Missouri Press.

Mink, Gwendolyn (1986) *Old Labor and New Immigrants in American Political Development: Union, Party, and State*. Ithaca, NY: Cornell University Press.

Mitchell, Christopher (ed.) (1992) *Western Hemisphere Immigration and United States Foreign Policy*. University Park: Pennsylvania State University Press.

Moen, Matthew C. (1989) *The Christian Right and Congress*. Tuscaloosa: University of Alabama Press.

Mohl, Raymond A. (ed.) (1990) *Searching for the Sunbelt: Historical Perspectives on a Region*. Knoxville: University of Tennessee Press.

Montgomery, David (1987) *The Fall of the House of Labor: The Workplace, the State, and American Labor Activism, 1865–1925*. Cambridge and New York: Cambridge University Press.

—— (1987) "Thinking about American workers in the 1920s," *International Labor and Working-Class History* 32, pp. 4–38.

Moody, Kim (1988) *Injury to All: The Decline of American Unionism*. New York: Verso.

Moore, Leonard J. (1991) *Citizen Klansman: The Ku Klux Klan in Indiana, 1921–1928*. Chapel Hill: University of North Carolina Press.

Moore, R. Laurence (1994) *Selling God: American Religion in the Marketplace of Culture*. New York: Oxford University Press.

Moos, Malcolm (ed.) (1960) *H. L. Mencken on Politics: A Carnival of Buncombe*. New York: Vintage.

Morawska, Ewa (1985) *For Bread with Butter: The Life-Worlds of East Central Europeans in Johnstown, Pennsylvania, 1890–1940*. Cambridge: Cambridge University Press.

—— (1996) *Insecure Prosperity: Small-Town Jews in Industrial America, 1890–1940*. Princeton, NJ: Princeton University Press.

Morgan, Edward P. (1991) *The Sixties Experience: Hard Lessons about Modern America*. Philadelphia: Temple University Press.

Mormino, Gary R. and Pozzetta, George E. (1987) *The Immigrant World of Ybor City: Italians and their Latin Neighbors in Tampa, 1885–1985*. Urbana: University of Illinois Press.

Morris, Aldon (1984) *The Origins of the Civil Rights Movement: Black Communities Organizing for Change*. New York: Free Press.

Morris, Charles R. (1984) *A Time of Passion: America, 1960–1980*. New York: Penguin.

Morris, Dick (1997) *Behind the Oval Office: Winning the Presidency in the Nineties*. New York: Random House.

Morse, Arthur D. (1967) *While Six Million Died: A Chronicle of American Apathy*. New York: Random House.

Mosier, John (2001) *The Myth of the Great War: A New Military History of World War I*. New York: HarperCollins.

Mowry, George E. (1946) *Theodore Roosevelt and the Progressive Movement, 1900–1912*. New York: Hill and Wang.

Muller, Jerry Z. (ed.) (1997) *Conservatism: An Anthology of Social and Political Thought from David Hume to the Present*. Princeton, NJ: Princeton University Press.

Murphy, W. Tim (1997) *The Oldest Social Science?: Configurations of Law and Modernity*. New York: Oxford University Press.

Murray, Robert (1969) *The Harding Era: Warren G. Harding and his Administration*. Minneapolis: University of Minnesota Press.

—— (1973) *The Politics of Normalcy: Governmental Theory and Practice in the Harding–Coolidge Era*. New York: W. W. Norton.

Myrdal, Gunnar (1944) *An American Dilemma: The Negro Problem and Modern Democracy*. New York: Harper and Row.

Myres, Sandra L. (1982) *Westering Women and the Frontier Experience, 1815–1915*. Albuquerque: University of New Mexico Press.

Nairne, Sandy (1987) *State of the Art: Ideas and Images in the 1980s*. London: Chatto and Windus.

Nalty, Bernard C. (1986) *Strength for the Fight: A History of Black Americans in the Military*. New York: Free Press.

—— (ed.) (1997) *Winged Shield, Winged Sword: A History of the US Air Force*, 2 vols. Washington, DC: Air Force History and Museums Program.

Nasaw, David (1993) *Going Out: The Rise and Fall of Public Amusements*. New York: Basic Books.

Nash, George H. (1976) *The Conservative Intellectual Movement in America: Since 1945*. New York: Basic Books. Reprinted 1996, Wilmington, Del.: Intercollegiate Studies Institute.

Nash, Roderick (1982) *Wilderness and the American Mind*, 3rd edn. New Haven, Conn.: Yale University Press.

Neilson, Keith and Haycock, Ronald G. (eds.) (1990) *The Cold War and Defense*. New York: Praeger.

Nenninger, Timothy K. (1994) "Leavenworth and its critics: the US Army Command and General Staff School, 1920–1940," *Journal of Military History* 58, pp. 199–231.

Neusner, Jacob (ed.) (1999) *World Religions in America: An Introduction*, 2nd edn. Louisville, Ky.: Westminster/John Knox.

Newspaper Association of America (1998) "Facts about newspapers 1998" (www.naa.org/info/facts).

Nickles, Shelley (2002) "More is better: mass consumption, gender and class identity in postwar America," *American Quarterly* 54, pp. 581–622.

Nisbet, Robert A. (1953) *The Quest for Community: A Study in the Ethics of Order and Freedom*. New York: Oxford University Press.

—— (1982) *Prejudices: A Philosophical Dictionary*. Cambridge, Mass.: Harvard University Press.

Nock, Albert Jay (1968) [1943] *Memoirs of a Superfluous Man*. Chicago: Henry Regnery.

Nord, David Paul (1985) "The public community: the urbanization of journalism in Chicago," *Journal of Urban History* 11, pp. 411–41.

Norrell, Robert J. (1985) *Reaping the Whirlwind: The Civil Rights Movement in Tuskegee*. New York: Alfred A. Knopf.

Novak, William J. (1996) *The People's Welfare: Law and Regulation in Nineteenth-Century America*. Chapel Hill: University of North Carolina Press.

Novick, Peter (1988) *That Noble Dream: The "Objectivity Question" and the American Historical Profession*. New York: Cambridge University Press.

Nugent, Walter (1999) *Into the West: The Story of its People*. New York: Alfred A. Knopf.

Nye, David E. (1990) *Electrifying America: The Social Meanings of a New Technology, 1880–1940*. Cambridge, Mass.: MIT Press.

Oberdorfer, Don (1998) *From the Cold War to a New Era: The United States and the Soviet Union, 1983–1991*. Baltimore, Md.: Johns Hopkins University Press.

O'Brien, Michael (1979) *The Idea of the American South, 1920–1941*. Baltimore, Md.: Johns Hopkins University Press.

O'Brien, Tom (1990) *The Screening of America: Movies and Values from* Rocky *to* Rain Man. New York: Continuum.

O'Connor, Raymond G. (1971) *Diplomacy for Victory: FDR and Unconditional Surrender*. New York: W. W. Norton.

Ohmann, Richard M. (1996) *Selling Culture: Magazines, Markets, and Class at the Turn of the Century*. New York: Verso.

Olmsted, Kathryn S. (1996) *Challenging the Secret Government: The Post-Watergate Investi-gations of the CIA and the FBI*. Chapel Hill: University of North Carolina Press.

Olney, Martha L. (1991) *Buy Now, Pay Later: Advertising, Credit, and Consumer Durables in the 1920s*. Chapel Hill: University of North Carolina Press.

Olson, James S. and Wilson, Raymond (1984) *Native Americans in the Twentieth Century*. Urbana and Chicago: University of Illinois Press.

O'Neill, William L. (1986) *American High: The Years of Confidence, 1945–1960*. New York: Free Press.

Orsi, Robert A. (1985) *The Madonna of 115th Street: Faith and Community in Italian Harlem, 1880–1950*. New Haven, Conn.: Yale University Press.

—— (1996) *Thank You, St. Jude: Women's Devotion to the Patron Saint of Hopeless Causes*. New Haven, Conn.: Yale University Press.

Osgood, Robert E. (1953) *Ideals and Self-Interest in America's Foreign Relations: The Great Transformation of the Twentieth Century*. Chicago: University of Chicago Press.

Oshinsky, David M. (1983) *A Conspiracy So Immense: The World of Joe McCarthy*. New York: Free Press.

—— (1996) *"Worse Than Slavery": Parchman Farm and the Ordeal of Jim Crow Justice*. New York: Free Press.

Owen, Irma Watkins (1996) *Blood Relations: Caribbean Immigrants and the Harlem Commu-nity, 1900–1930*. Bloomington: Indiana University Press.

Ownby, Ted (1990) *Subduing Satan: Religion, Recreation, and Manhood in the Rural South, 1865–1920*. Chapel Hill: University of North Carolina Press.

—— (1999) *American Dream in Mississippi: Consumers, Poverty and Culture, 1830–1998*. Chapel Hill: University of North Carolina Press.

Page, Susan (2000) "President touts nation's prosperity, progress," *USA Today*, January 28.

Panichas, George A. (1986) "Conservatism and the life of the spirit," *Intercollegiate Review* 21, pp. 22–5.

Park, Robert E. (1925) "The natural history of the newspaper," in Robert E. Park, Ernest W. Burgess, and Roderick D. McKenzie, *The City*. Chicago: University of Chicago Press.

Parman, Donald (1976) *The Navajos and the New Deal*. New Haven, Conn.: Yale University Press.

Parrish, Michael E. (1992) *Anxious Decades: America in Prosperity and Depression, 1920–1941*. New York: W. W. Norton.

Pascoe, Peggy (1990) *Relations of Rescue: The Search for Female Moral Authority in the American West, 1874–1939*. New York: Oxford University Press.

Paterson, Thomas G. (1979) *On Every Front: The Making of the Cold War*. New York: W. W. Norton.

Patterson, James T. (1996) *Grand Expectations: The United States, 1945–1974*. New York: Oxford University Press.

Pauly, Philip (1996) "The beauty and menace of Japanese cherry trees: conflicting visions of American ecological independence," *Isis* 87, pp. 51–73.

Payne, Charles (1995) *I've Got the Light of Freedom: The Organizing Tradition and the Mississippi Freedom Struggle*. Berkeley: University of California Press.

Peele, Gillian (1984) *Revival and Reaction: The Right in Contemporary America*. New York: Oxford University Press.

Pegram, Thomas R. (1998) *Battling Demon Rum: The Struggle for a Dry America, 1800–1933*. Chicago: Ivan R. Dee.

Peiss, Kathy Lee (1986) *Cheap Amusements: Working Women and Leisure in New York City, 1880 to 1920*. Philadelphia: Temple University Press.

Pells, Richard H. (1973) *Radical Vision and American Dreams: Culture and Social Thought in the Depression Years*. New York: Harper and Row.

—— (1985) *The Liberal Mind in a Conservative Age: American Intellectuals in the 1940s and 1950s.* New York: Harper and Row.

Pemberton, William E. (1989) *Harry S. Truman: Fair Dealer and Cold Warrior.* Boston: Twayne.

—— (1998) *Exit with Honor: The Life and Presidency of Ronald Reagan.* Armonk, NY: M. E. Sharpe.

Penick, James L., Jr., et al. (eds.) (1972) *The Politics of American Science: 1939 to the Present,* rev. edn. Cambridge, Mass.: MIT Press.

Perkins, Dexter (1957) *The New Age of Franklin Roosevelt, 1932–1945.* Chicago: University of Chicago Press.

Perlmann, Joel and Waters, Mary C. (2002) *The New Race Question: How the Census Counts Multiracial Individuals.* New York: Russell Sage.

Perlstein, Rick (1996) "Who owns the sixties? The opening of a scholarly generation gap," *Linguafranca* 6, pp. 30–7.

Perman, Michael (2001) *Struggle for Mastery: Disfranchisement in the South, 1888–1908.* Chapel Hill: University of North Carolina Press.

Perrow, Charles (1972) *The Radical Attack on Business.* New York: Harcourt Brace Jovanovich.

Perry, Lewis (1989) *Intellectual Life in America.* Chicago: University of Chicago Press.

Petersen, William (1987) "Politics and the measurement of ethnicity," in William Alonzo and Paul Starr (eds.) *The Politics of Numbers.* New York: Russell Sage.

Phillips, Kevin P. (1969) *The Emerging Republican Majority.* New Rochelle, NY: Arlington House.

—— (1990) *The Politics of Rich and Poor: Wealth and the American Electorate in the Reagan Aftermath.* New York: Harper Perennial.

Phillips, Lisa (1999) *The American Century: Art and Culture, 1950–2000.* New York: Whitney Museum of American Art, in association with W. W. Norton.

Phillips, Ulrich Bonnell (1928) "The central theme of southern history," *American Historical Review* 34 (October), pp. 30–43.

Pisani, Donald (1992) *To Reclaim a Divided West: Water, Law, and Public Policy, 1848–1902.* Albuquerque: University of New Mexico Press.

Podhoretz, John (1993) *Hell of a Ride: Backstage at the White House Follies, 1989–1993.* New York: Simon and Schuster.

Pogue, Forrest C. (1963) *George C. Marshall: Education of a General, 1880–1939.* New York: Viking.

Polenberg, Richard (1992) "The good war? A reappraisal of how World War II affected American society," *The Virginia Magazine of History and Biography* 100 (July), pp. 295–322.

Pomper, Marlene Michels (ed.) (1981) *The Election of 1980: Reports and Interpretations.* Chatham, NJ: Chatham House.

—— (ed.) (1985) *The Election of 1984: Reports and Interpretations.* Chatham, NJ: Chatham House.

Porterfield, Amanda (2001) *The Transformation of American Religion: The Story of a Late Twentieth Century Awakening.* New York: Oxford University Press.

Posadas, Barbara M. (1999) *The Filipino Americans.* Westport, Conn.: Greenwood Press.

Posner, Richard A. (ed.) (1992) *The Essential Holmes: Selections from the Letters, Speeches, Judicial Opinions, and Other Writings of Oliver Wendell Holmes, Jr.* Chicago: University of Chicago Press.

—— (1999) *The Problematics of Moral and Legal Theory.* Cambridge, Mass.: Harvard University Press.

—— (2000) *An Affair of State: The Investigation, Impeachment, and Trial of President Clinton.* Cambridge, Mass.: Harvard University Press.

Post, Robert C. (ed.) (1998) *Censorship and Silencing: Practices of Cultural Regulation*. Los Angeles: Getty Research Institute.

Postman, Neil (1986) *Amusing Ourselves to Death: Public Discourse in the Age of Show Business*. New York: Viking.

Potter, David M. (1954) *People of Plenty: Economic Abundance and the American Character*. Chicago: University of Chicago Press.

Powe, Lucas A., Jr. (2000) *The Warren Court and American Politics*. Cambridge, Mass.: Harvard University Press.

Powers, Richard Gid (1987) *Secrecy and Power: The Life of J. Edgar Hoover*. New York: Free Press.

President's Commission on Immigration and Naturalization (1953) *Whom We Shall Welcome*. Washington, DC: Government Printing Office.

Price, Jennifer (1999) *Flight Maps: Adventures with Nature in Modern America*. New York: Basic Books.

Prince, Hugh (1997) *Wetlands of the American Midwest: A Historical Geography of Changing Attitudes*. Chicago: University of Chicago Press.

Purcell, Edward A., Jr. (1983) "Social thought," *American Quarterly* 35, pp. 80–100.

—— (2000) *Brandeis and the Progressive Constitution: Erie, the Judicial Power, and the Politics of the Federal Courts in Twentieth-Century America*. New Haven, Conn.: Yale University Press.

Pursell, Carroll (ed.) (1972) *The Military-Industrial Complex*. New York: Harper and Row.

—— (1995) *The Machine in America: A Social History of Technology*. Baltimore, Md.: Johns Hopkins University Press.

Pyne, Stephen (1982) *Fire in America: A Cultural History of Wildland and Rural Fire*. Princeton, NJ: Princeton University Press.

Quinn, D. Michael (1996) *Same Sex Dynamics among Nineteenth-century Americans: A Mormon Example*. Urbana: University of Illinois Press.

Rabinowitz, Howard N. (1978) *Race Relations in the Urban South, 1865–1890*. New York: Oxford University Press.

Ransom, John Crowe, Davidson, Donald et al. (1983) *I'll Take My Stand: The South and the Agrarian Tradition*. Baton Rouge: Louisiana State University Press.

Ransom, Roger L. and Sutch, Richard (1977) *One Kind of Freedom: The Economic Consequences of Emancipation*. Cambridge: Cambridge University Press.

Raper, Arthur F. (1933) *The Tragedy of Lynching*. Chapel Hill: University of North Carolina Press.

Rauch, Basil (1944) *The History of the New Deal*. New York: Creative Age Press.

Rawls, John (1971) *A Theory of Justice*. Cambridge, Mass.: Harvard University Press.

—— (1993) *Political Liberalism*. New York: Columbia University Press.

Reeves, Thomas C. (1982) *The Life and Times of Joe McCarthy: A Biography*. New York: Stein and Day.

Reich, Leonard S. (1985) *The Making of American Industrial Research: Science and Business at GE and Bell, 1876–1926*. New York: Cambridge University Press.

Reichley, A. James (1981) *Conservatives in an Age of Change: The Nixon and Ford Administrations*. Washington, DC: Brookings.

Reimers, David M. (1992) *Still the Golden Door: The Third World Comes to America*, 2nd edn. New York: Columbia University Press.

—— (1998) *Unwelcome Strangers: American Identity and the Turn Against Immigration*. New York: Columbia University Press.

Remnick, David (1998) *King of the World: Muhammad Ali and the Rise of an American Hero*. New York: Random House.

Restad, Penne L. (1995) *Christmas in America: A History*. New York: Oxford University Press.

Ribuffo, Leo P. (1981) "Jesus Christ as business statesman: Bruce Barton and the selling of corporate capitalism," *American Quarterly* 33, pp. 206–31.

—— (1997) "Malaise revisited: Jimmy Carter and the crisis of confidence," in John P. Diggins (ed.) *The Liberal Persuasion: Arthur Schlesinger, Jr. and the Challenge of the American Past.* Princeton, NJ: Princeton University Press.

Riess, Steven A. (ed.) (1984) *The American Sporting Experience.* West Point, NY: Leisure Press.

Riley, Glenda (1981) *Frontierswomen: The Iowa Experience.* Ames: Iowa State University Press.

—— (1984) *Women and Indians on the Frontier.* Albuquerque: University of New Mexico Press.

—— (1988) *The Female Frontier: A Comparative View of Women on the Prairie and the Plains.* Lawrence: University Press of Kansas.

—— (1992) *A Place to Grow: Women in the American West.* Arlington Heights, Ill.: Harlan Davidson.

—— (1996) *Building and Breaking Families in the American West.* Albuquerque: University of New Mexico Press.

—— (1999) *Women and Nature: Saving the Wild West.* Lincoln: University of Nebraska Press.

Robbins, Thomas and Anthony, Dick (eds.) (1991) *In Gods We Trust: New Patterns of Religious Pluralism in America.* New Brunswick, NJ: Transaction.

Roberts, Gene, Kunkel, Thomas, and Layton, Charles (eds.) (2001) *Leaving Readers Behind: The Age of Corporate Newspapering.* Fayetteville: University of Arkansas Press.

Robinson, Edgar (1955) *The Roosevelt Leadership, 1933–1945.* Philadelphia: Lippincott.

Rodgers, Daniel T. (1982) "In search of progressivism," *Reviews in American History* 10, pp. 113–32.

—— (1987) *Contested Truths: Key Words in American Politics since Independence.* New York: Basic Books.

—— (1998) *Atlantic Crossings: Social Politics in a Progressive Age.* Cambridge, Mass.: Harvard University Press.

Roeder, George H., Jr. (1993) *The Censored War: American Visual Experience During World War II.* New Haven, Conn.: Yale University Press.

Roediger, David (1991) *The Wages of Whiteness: Race and the Making of the American Working Class.* New York: Verso.

Rogin, Michael Paul (1967) *The Intellectuals and McCarthy: The Radical Specter.* Cambridge, Mass.: MIT Press.

Rohrbough, Malcolm J. (1997) *Days of Gold: The California Gold Rush and the American Nation.* Berkeley: University of California Press.

Roller, David C. and Twyman, Robert W. (1979) *The Encyclopedia of Southern History.* Baton Rouge: Louisiana State University Press.

Romasco, Albert (1965) *The Poverty of Abundance: Hoover, the Nation, the Depression.* New York: Oxford University Press.

Rome, Adam (2001) *The Bulldozer in the Countryside: Suburban Sprawl and the Rise of American Environmentalism.* New York: Cambridge University Press.

—— (2002) "What really matters in history?: environmental perspectives on modern America," *Environmental History* 7, pp. 303–18.

Roof, Wade Clark (ed.) (1993) *Religion in the Nineties.* Annals of the American Academy of Political and Social Science, 527. Newbury Park, Calif.: Sage.

—— (1994) *A Generation of Seekers: The Spiritual Journeys of the Baby Boom Generation.* San Francisco: HarperSanFrancisco.

—— (1999) *Spiritual Marketplace: Baby Boomers and the Remaking of American Religion.* Princeton, NJ: Princeton University Press.

Roof, Wade Clark and McKinney, William (1987) *American Mainline Religion: Its Changing Shape and Future.* New Brunswick, NJ: Rutgers University Press.

Rorty, Richard (1979) *Philosophy and the Mirror of Nature*. Princeton, NJ: Princeton University Press.

Rosen, Philip T. (1980) *The Modern Stentors: Radio Broadcasters and the Federal Government, 1920–1934*. Westport, Conn.: Greenwood Press.

Rosen, Ruth (2000) *The World Split Open: How the Modern Women's Movement Changed America*. New York: Penguin.

Rosenau, James N. (1963) *National Leadership and Foreign Policy: A Case Study in the Mobilization of Public Support*. Princeton, NJ: Princeton University Press.

Rosenberg, Bernard and White, David Manning (eds.) (1957) *Mass Culture: The Popular Arts in America*. Glencoe, Ill.: Free Press.

Rosenberg, Harold (1982) *The Tradition of the New*. Chicago: University of Chicago Press.

Rosenblum, Nancy (ed.) (1989) *Liberalism and the Moral Life*. Cambridge, Mass.: Harvard University Press.

Rosenzweig, Roy (1983) *Eight Hours For What We Will: Workers and Leisure in an Industrial City, 1870–1920*. Cambridge: Cambridge University Press.

Ross, Dorothy (1977–8) "Socialism and American liberalism: academic social thought in the 1880s," *Perspectives in American History*, 11, pp. 7–79.

—— (1991) *The Origins of American Social Science*. New York: Cambridge University Press.

Ross, Edward A. (1914) *The Old World in the New: The Significance of Past and Present Immigration to the American People*. New York: Century.

Rossinow, Doug (1998) *The Politics of Authenticity: Liberalism, Christianity, and the New Left in America*. New York: Columbia University Press.

Rossiter, Clinton (1955) *Conservatism in America*. New York: Alfred A. Knopf. 2nd edn. (1962) New York: Viking.

Rossiter, Margaret W. (1982) *Women Scientists in America: Struggles and Strategies to 1940*. Baltimore, Md.: Johns Hopkins University Press.

—— (1995) *Women Scientists in America: Before Affirmative Action, 1940–1972*. Baltimore, Md.: Johns Hopkins University Press.

Rotunda, R. D. (1986) *The Politics of Language: Liberalism as Word and Symbol*. Iowa City: University of Iowa Press.

Ruchames, Louis (1953) *Race, Jobs and Politics: The Story of FEPC*. New York: Columbia University Press.

Rupp, Leila and Taylor, Verta (1987) *Survival in the Doldrums: The American Woman's Rights Movement, 1945 to the 1960s*. New York: Oxford University Press.

Russell, Edmund (2000) *War and Nature: Fighting Humans and Insects with Chemicals from World War I to* Silent Spring. New York: Cambridge University Press.

Rutenberg, Jim (2000) "Number of debate viewers rises from the first but remains low," *New York Times*, October 19.

Rykken, Rolf (1989) "Readership decline brings newspapers to crossroads," *Presstime* 11, pp. 22–4.

Safire, William (1968) *The New Language of Politics*. New York: Random House.

Sale, Kirkpatrick (1990) *The Conquest of Paradise: Christopher Columbus and the Columbian Legacy*. New York: Alfred A. Knopf.

Salvatore, Nick (1982) *Eugene V. Debs: Citizen and Socialist*. Urbana: University of Illinois Press.

Samuel, Lawrence R. (2001) *Brought to You By: Postwar Television Advertising and the American Dream*. Austin: University of Texas Press.

Samuelson, Robert J. (1995) *The Good Life and its Discontents: The American Dream in the Age of Entitlement, 1945–1955*. New York: Times Books.

Sánchez, George J. (1993) *Becoming Mexican American: Ethnicity, Culture and Identity in Chicano Los Angeles, 1900–1945*. New York: Oxford University Press.

Sandel, Michael J. (1982) *Liberalism and the Limits of Justice.* Cambridge: Cambridge University Press.

—— (ed.) (1984) *Liberalism and its Critics.* Oxford: Blackwell.

—— (1996) *Democracy's Discontent: America in Search of a Public Philosophy.* Cambridge, Mass.: Harvard University Press.

Sanders, Elizabeth (1999) *Roots of Reform: Farmers, Workers, and the American State, 1877–1917.* Chicago: University of Chicago Press.

Sandler, Martin W. (1989) *American Image: Photographing One Hundred Fifty Years in the Life of a Nation.* Chicago: Contemporary Books.

Santayana, George (1967) *The Genteel Tradition: Nine Essays.* Cambridge, Mass.: Harvard University Press.

Sarat, Austin D. and Kearns, Thomas (eds.) (1996) *Legal Rights: Historical and Philosophical Perspectives.* Ann Arbor: University of Michigan Press.

—— and—— (eds.) (1998) *Law in the Domains of Culture.* Ann Arbor: University of Michigan Press.

Scanlon, Jennifer (1995) *Inarticulate Longings:* The Ladies' Home Journal, *Gender, and the Promises of Consumer Culture.* New York: Routledge.

Scanzoni, Letha Dawson and Hardesty, Nancy A. (1992) *All We're Meant to Be: Biblical Feminism for Today,* 3rd edn. Grand Rapids, Mich.: Eerdmans.

Scanzoni, Letha Dawson and Mollenkott, Virginia Ramey (1994) *Is the Homosexual My Neighbor? A Positive Christian Response,* rev. edn. San Francisco: HarperSanFrancisco.

Schaffer, Ronald (1991) *America in the Great War: The Rise of the War Welfare State.* New York: Oxford University Press.

Schlag, Pierre (1998) *The Enchantment of Reason.* Durham, NC: Duke University Press.

—— (2002) "The aesthetics of American law," *Harvard Law Review* 115, pp. 1047–118.

Schlesinger, Arthur M., Jr. (1957–60) *The Age of Roosevelt,* 3 vols. Boston: Houghton Mifflin.

—— (1967) "Origins of the Cold War," *Foreign Affairs* 46 (October), pp. 22–52.

—— (1986) *The Cycles of American History.* Boston: Houghton Mifflin.

—— (1991) *The Disuniting of America: Reflections on a Multicultural Society.* New York: W. W. Norton.

Schmitt, Peter (1969) *Back to Nature: The Arcadian Myth in Urban America.* New York: Oxford University Press.

Schneider, Herbert Wallace (1969) *Religion in 20th Century America,* rev. edn. New York: Atheneum.

Schneirov, Matthew (1994) *The Dream of a New Social Order: Popular Magazines in America, 1893–1914.* New York: Columbia University Press.

Schrag, Philip G. (2000) *A Well-Founded Fear: The Congressional Battle to Save Political Asylum in America.* New York: Routledge.

Schrecker, Ellen (1998) *Many Are the Crimes: McCarthyism in America.* Boston: Little, Brown.

Schudson, Michael (1978) *Discovering the News: A Social History of American Newspapers.* New York: Basic Books.

—— (1995) *The Power of News.* Cambridge, Mass.: Harvard University Press.

Schulman, Bruce J. (1991) *From Cotton Belt to Sunbelt: Federal Policy, Economic Development, and the Transformation of the South, 1938–1980.* New York: Oxford University Press.

—— (2001) *The Seventies: The Great Shift in American Culture, Society, and Politics.* New York: Free Press.

Schultz, George P. (1993) *Turmoil and Triumph: My Years as Secretary of State.* New York: Scribner.

Schulzinger, Robert D. (1997) *A Time for War: The United States and Vietnam, 1941–1975.* New York: Oxford University Press.

Schwartz, Herman (ed.) (1988) *The Burger Years: Rights and Wrongs in the Supreme Court.* New York: Penguin.

Scranton, Philip (1997) *Endless Novelty: Specialty Production and American Industrialization, 1865–1925.* Princeton, NJ: Princeton University Press.

Seideman, David (1986) *The New Republic: A Voice of Modern Liberalism.* New York: Praeger.

Seiter, Ellen (1993) *Sold Separately: Children and Parents in Consumer Culture.* New Brunswick, NJ: Rutgers University Press.

Sellars, Richard West (1997) *Preserving Nature in the National Parks: A History.* New Haven, Conn.: Yale University Press.

Sellers, Christopher (1997) *Hazards of the Job: From Industrial Disease to Environmental Health Science.* Chapel Hill: University of North Carolina Press.

Selznick, Philip (2001) *The Communitarian Persuasion.* Washington, DC: Woodrow Wilson Press.

Shaffer, Marguerite (2001) *See America First: Tourism and National Identity, 1880–1940.* Washington, DC: Smithsonian Institution.

Shamir, Ronen (1995) *Managing Uncertainty: Elite Lawyers in the New Deal.* Durham, NC: Duke University Press.

Shapiro, Herbert (1988) *White Violence and Black Response: From Reconstruction to Montgomery.* Amherst: University of Massachusetts Press.

Shawcross, William (1988) *The Shah's Last Ride: The Fate of an Ally.* New York: Simon and Schuster.

Sherrill, Robert (1983) *The Oil Follies of 1970–1980: How the Petroleum Industry Stole the Show (and Much More Besides).* Garden City, NY: Anchor.

Sherry, Michael S. (1995) *In the Shadow of War: The United States since the 1930s.* New Haven, Conn.: Yale University Press.

Sherwin, Martin J. (1975) *A World Destroyed: The Atomic Bomb and the Grand Alliance.* New York: Alfred A. Knopf.

Shilts, Randy (1993) *Conduct Unbecoming: Gays and Lesbians in the U.S. Military.* New York: St. Martin's Press.

Shogan, Robert (1995) *Hard Bargain: How FDR Twisted Churchill's Arm, Evaded the Law, and Changed the Role of the American Presidency.* New York: Scribner.

Sick, Gary (1986) *All Fall Down: America's Tragic Encounter with Iran.* New York: Penguin.

Silber, Norman Isaac (1983) *Test and Protest: The Influence of Consumers' Union.* New York: Holmes and Meier.

Simkins, Francis Butler (1944) *Pitchfork Ben Tillman, South Carolinian.* Baton Rouge: Louisiana State University Press.

Simon, Bryant (1998) *A Fabric of Defeat: The Politics of South Carolina Millhands, 1910–1948.* Chapel Hill: University of North Carolina Press.

Singal, Daniel Joseph (1982) *The War Within: From Victorian to Modernist Thought in the South, 1919–1945.* Chapel Hill: University of North Carolina Press.

Singh, Nikhil Pal (1998) "The Black Panthers and the 'undeveloped country of the left,' " in Charles E. Jones (ed.) *The Black Panther Party Reconsidered.* Baltimore, Md.: Black Classic Press.

Sitkoff, Harvard (1978) *A New Deal for Blacks: The Emergence of Civil Rights as a National Issue.* New York: Oxford University Press.

—— (1981) *The Struggle for Black Equality, 1954–1980.* New York: Hill and Wang.

Skerry, Peter (2000) *Counting on the Census? Race, Group Identity, and the Evasion of Politics.* Washington, DC: Brookings Institute Press.

Skidmore, David (1996) *Reversing Course: Carter's Foreign Policy, Domestic Politics, and the Failure of Reform.* Baton Rouge: Louisiana State University Press.

Sklar, Kathryn Kish (1995) *Florence Kelley and the Nation's Work.* New Haven, Conn.: Yale University Press.

Sklar, Martin J. (1988) *The Corporate Reconstruction of American Capitalism, 1890–1916: The Market, the Law, and Politics.* New York: Cambridge University Press.

Skocpol, Theda and Finegold, Kenneth (1982) "State capacity and economic intervention in the early New Deal," *Political Science Quarterly* 97, pp. 255–78.

Smith, Daniel M. (1965) *The Great Departure: The United States and World War I, 1914–1920.* New York: Wiley.

Smith, Gaddis (1985) *American Diplomacy during the Second World War, 1941–1945,* 2nd edn. New York: Alfred A. Knopf.

—— (1986) *Reality, Reason and Power: America Diplomacy in the Carter Years.* New York: Hill and Wang.

Smith, Jane I. (1999) *Islam in America.* New York: Columbia University Press.

Smith, Rogers M. (1993) "Beyond Tocqueville, Myrdal, and Hartz: the multiple traditions in America," *American Political Science Review* 87, pp. 549–66.

—— (1997) *Civic Ideals: Conflicting Visions of Citizenship in US History.* New Haven, Conn.: Yale University Press.

Smulyan, Susan (1994) *Selling Radio: The Commercialization of American Broadcasting, 1920–1934.* Washington, DC: Smithsonian Institution Press.

Sobel, Robert (1968) *The Great Bull Market: Wall Street in the 1920s.* New York: W. W. Norton.

Sochen, June (1973) *Movers and Shakers: Women Thinkers and Activists in America, 1900–1970.* New York: Quadrangle.

—— (1999) *From Mae to Madonna: Women Entertainers in Twentieth Century America.* Lexington: University Press of Kentucky.

Sollors, Werner (1986) *Beyond Ethnicity: Consent and Descent in American Culture.* New York: Oxford University Press.

Solomon, Barbara Miller (1956) *Ancestors and Immigrants: A Changing New England Tradition.* Cambridge, Mass.: Harvard University Press.

Sombart, Werner (1969) [1906] *Warum gibt es in den Vereinigten Staaten keinen Sozialismus?.* Darmstadt: Wissenschaftliche Buchgesellschaft, 1969. (1976) *Why is There No Socialism in the United States?,* trans. P. M. Hocking and C. T. Husbands. White Plains, NY: International Arts and Sciences Press.

Sosna, Morton (1977) *In Search of the Silent South: Southern Liberals and the Race Issue.* New York: Columbia University Press.

Sowell, Thomas (1981) *Ethnic America: A History.* New York: Basic Books.

Spence, Mark David (1999) *Dispossessing the Wilderness: Indian Removal and the Making of the National Parks.* New York: Oxford University Press.

Speranza, Gino (1925) *Race or Nation: A Conflict of Divided Loyalties.* Indianapolis, Ind.: Bobbs-Merrill. Reprinted 1975, New York: Arno Press.

Spigel, Lynn (1992) *Make Room for TV: Television and the Family Idea in Postwar America.* Chicago: University of Chicago Press.

Sprague, Claire (ed.) (1993) *Van Wyck Brooks: The Early Years.* Boston: Northeastern University Press.

Stage, Sarah J. (1983) "Women," *American Quarterly* 35, pp. 169–90.

Starr, Kenneth (1998) *The Starr Report: The Findings of Independent Counsel Kenneth W. Starr on President Clinton and the Lewinsky Affair.* Washington, DC: Public Affairs Press.

Stearns, Harold (1973) [1921] *America and the Young Intellectual.* Westport, Conn.: Greenwood Press.

Stedman, Lawrence C., Tinsley, Katherine, and Kaestle, Carl F. (1991) "Literacy as consumer activity," in Carl F. Kaestle et al., *Literacy in the United States: Readers and Reading since 1880.* New Haven, Conn.: Yale University Press.

Steel, Ronald (1980) *Walter Lippmann and the American Century.* Boston: Little, Brown.

Steele, Richard W. (1999) *Free Speech in the Good War.* New York: St. Martin's Press.

Stein, Herbert (1985) *Presidential Economics: The Making of Economic Policy from Roosevelt to Reagan and Beyond.* New York: Simon and Schuster.

Stein, Judith (1998) *Running Steel, Running America: Race, Economic Policy, and the Decline of Liberalism.* Chapel Hill: University of North Carolina Press.

Steinberg, Ted (2000) *Acts of God: The Unnatural History of Natural Disaster in America.* New York: Oxford University Press.

Steinfels, Peter (1979) *The Neoconservatives: The Men who are Changing America's Politics.* New York: Simon and Schuster.

Stern, Kenneth S. (1997) *A Force Upon the Plain: The American Militia Movement and the Politics of Hate.* Norman: University of Oklahoma Press.

Stettner, E. A. (1993) *Shaping Modern Liberalism: Herbert Croly and Progressive Thought.* Lawrence: University Press of Kansas.

Stewart, Barbara McDonald (1982) *United States Government Policy on Refugees from Nazism, 1933–1940.* New York: Garland.

Stewart, James (1997) *Blood Sport: The President and his Adversaries.* New York: Touchstone.

Stinnett, Robert B. (2000) *Day of Deceit: The Truth about FDR and Pearl Harbor.* New York: Touchstone.

Stoddard, Lothrop (1920) *The Rising Tide of Color against White World-Supremacy.* New York: Scribner.

—— (1922) *The Revolt against Civilization: The Menace of the Under Man.* New York: Scribner.

Storrs, Landon R. Y. (2000) *Civilizing Capitalism: The National Consumers' League, Women's Activism, and Labor Standards in the New Deal Era.* Chapel Hill: University of North Carolina Press.

Stott, William (1973) *Documentary Expression and Thirties America.* New York: Oxford University Press.

Strasser, Susan (1982) *Never Done: A History of American Housework.* New York: Pantheon.

—— (1989) *Satisfaction Guaranteed: The Making of the American Mass Market.* New York: Pantheon.

—— (1999) *Waste and Want: A Social History of Trash.* New York: Henry Holt.

Strickland, Rennard (1975) *Fire and Spirits: Cherokee Law from Clan to Court.* Norman: University of Oklahoma Press.

Strong, Robert A. (2000) *Working in the World: Jimmy Carter and the Making of American Foreign Policy.* Baton Rouge: Louisiana State University Press.

Sugrue, Thomas J. (1996) *The Origins of the Urban Crisis: Race and Inequality in Postwar Detroit.* Princeton, NJ: Princeton University Press.

Sullivan, Patricia (1996) *Days of Hope: Race and Democracy in the New Deal Era.* Chapel Hill: University of North Carolina Press.

Sunstein, Cass R. (1999) *One Case at a Time: Judicial Minimalism on the Supreme Court.* Cambridge, Mass.: Harvard University Press.

Sunstein, Cass R. and Epstein, Richard A. (eds.) (2001) *The Vote: Bush, Gore, and the Supreme Court.* Chicago: University of Chicago Press.

Susman, Warren I. (1984) *Culture as History: The Transformation of American Society in the Twentieth Century.* New York: Pantheon.

Sutter, Paul (2002) *Driven Wild: How the Fight against Automobiles Launched the Modern Wilderness Movement.* Seattle: University of Washington Press.

Swierenga, Robert P. (1994) *Dutch Jewry in the North American Diaspora.* Detroit: Wayne State University Press.

—— (2000) *Faith and Family: Dutch Immigration and Settlement in the United States.* New York: Holmes and Meier.

Tansill, Charles C. (1938) *America Goes to War.* Boston: Little, Brown.

Tarr, Joel (1996) *The Search for the Ultimate Sink: Urban Pollution in Historical Perspective.* Akron, Oh.: University of Akron Press.

Tatalovich, Raymond (1995) *Nativism Reborn: The Official English Language Movement and the American States.* Lexington: University Press of Kentucky.

Taylor, Joseph (1999) *Making Salmon: An Environmental History of the Northwest Fisheries Crisis.* Seattle: University of Washington Press.

Teaford, Jon C. (1979) *City and Suburb: The Political Fragmentation of Metropolitan America, 1850–1970.* Baltimore, Md.: Johns Hopkins University Press.

—— (1990) *The Rough Road to Renaissance: Urban Revitalization in America, 1940–1985.* Baltimore, Md.: Johns Hopkins University Press.

—— (1997) *Post-Suburbia: Government and Politics in the Edge Cities.* Baltimore, Md.: Johns Hopkins University Press.

Tedlow, Richard S. (1990) *New and Improved: The Story of Mass Marketing in America.* New York: Basic Books.

Terkel, Studs (1984) *"The Good War": An Oral History of World War Two.* New York: Pantheon Books.

Theobald, Robert A. (1954) *The Final Secret of Pearl Harbor: The Washington Contribution to the Japanese Attack.* New York: Devin-Adair.

Theoharis, Athan (1971) *Seeds of Repression: Harry S. Truman and the Origins of McCarthyism.* Chicago: Quadrangle.

Thernstrom, Abigail (1987) *Whose Votes Count? Affirmative Action and Minority Voting Rights.* Cambridge, Mass.: Harvard University Press.

Thernstrom, Stephan (1973) *The Other Bostonians: Poverty and Progress in the American Metropolis, 1880–1970.* Cambridge, Mass.: Harvard University Press.

—— (ed.) (1980) *The Harvard Encyclopedia of American Ethnic Groups.* Cambridge, Mass.: Harvard University Press.

—— (1992) "American ethnic statistics," in Donald L. Horowitz and Gerard Noiriel (eds.) *Immigrants in Two Democracies: French and American Experience.* New York: New York University Press.

—— (1992) "The Columbus Controversy," *American Educator* 16, pp. 24–32.

Thernstrom, Stephan and Thernstrom, Abigail (1997) *America in Black and White: One Nation, Indivisible.* New York: Simon and Schuster.

Thomas, Mary Martha (1992) *The New Woman in Alabama: Social Reforms and Suffrage, 1890–1920.* Tuscaloosa: University of Alabama Press.

Thomas, W. I. (1921) *Old World Traits Transplanted.* New York: Harper and Brothers.

Thompson, Gerald (1976) *The Army and the Navajo.* Tucson: University of Arizona Press.

Thornton, J. Mills, III (2002) *Dividing Lines: Municipal Politics and the Struggle for Civil Rights in Montgomery, Birmingham, and Selma.* Tuscaloosa: University of Alabama Press.

Thurow, Lester C. (1980) *The Zero-Sum Society: Distribution and the Possibilities for Economic Change.* New York: Penguin.

Tichi, Cecelia M. (1987) *Shifting Gears: Technology, Literature, Culture in Modernist America.* Chapel Hill: University of North Carolina Press.

—— (1991) *Electronic Hearth: Creating an American Television Culture.* New York: Oxford University Press.

Tiffany, Paul A. (1988) *The Decline of American Steel: How Management, Labor, and Government Went Wrong.* New York: Oxford University Press.

Tindall, George Brown (1967) *The Emergence of the New South, 1913–1945.* Baton Rouge: Louisiana State University Press.

—— (1995) *Natives and Newcomers: Ethnic Southerners and Southern Ethnics*. Athens: University of Georgia Press.

Tocqueville, Alexis de (1990) *Democracy in America*, 2 vols., ed. Phillips Bradley. New York: Vintage.

Toland, John (1982) *Infamy: Pearl Harbor and its Aftermath*. Garden City, NY: Doubleday.

Tomes, Nancy (1998) *The Gospel of Germs: Men, Women, and the Microbe in American Life*. Cambridge, Mass.: Harvard University Press.

Tomlins, Christopher (1985) *The State and the Unions: Labor Relations, Law, and the Organized Labor Movement in America, 1880–1960*. New York: Cambridge University Press.

Tong, Benson (1994) *Unsubmissive Women: Chinese Prostitutes in Nineteenth-century San Francisco*. Norman: University of Oklahoma Press.

Trani, Eugene P. and Wilson, David L. (1977) *The Presidency of Warren G. Harding*. Lawrence: Regents Press of Kansas.

Trask, David F. (1993) *The AEF and Coalition Warmaking, 1917–1918*. Lawrence: University Press of Kansas.

Trilling, Lionel (1950) *The Liberal Imagination: Essays on Literature and Society*. New York: Viking Press.

Truman, Harry S. (1955) *Memoirs: Year of Decisions*. Garden City, NY: Doubleday.

Tuchman, Barbara (1958) *The Zimmermann Telegram*. New York: Viking.

Tucker, Richard (2000) *Insatiable Appetite: The United States and the Ecological Degradation of the Tropical World*. Berkeley: University of California Press.

Turner, Frederick Jackson (1920) *The Frontier in American History*. New York: Henry Holt.

—— (1963) [1894] *The Significance of the Frontier in American History*. New York: Ungar.

Turow, Joseph (1997) *Breaking Up America: Advertisers and the New Media World*. Chicago: University of Chicago Press.

Tushnet, Mark V. (1997) *Making Constitutional Law: Thurgood Marshall and the Supreme Court*. New York: Oxford University Press.

Tuttle, William M., Jr. (1970) *Race Riot: Chicago in the Red Summer of 1919*. New York: Atheneum.

Tuveson, Ernest Lee (1968) *Redeemer Nation: The Idea of America's Millennial Role*. Chicago: University of Chicago Press.

Tweed, Thomas A. (1997) *Our Lady of the Exile: Diasporic Religion at a Cuban Catholic Shrine in Miami*. New York: Oxford University Press.

Tygiel, Jules (1983) *Baseball's Great Experiment: Jackie Robinson and his Legacy*. New York: Oxford University Press.

Tyrrell, Ian (1999) *True Gardens of the Gods: California–Australian Environmental Reform, 1860–1930*. Berkeley: University of California Press.

Tyrrell, R. Emmett, Jr. (1992) *The Conservative Crack-Up*. New York: Simon and Schuster.

Ueda, Reed (1980) "Citizenship and naturalization," in Stephan Thernstrom (ed.) *Harvard Encyclopedia of American Ethnic Groups*. Cambridge, Mass.: Harvard University Press.

Underwood, Kathleen (1987) *Town Building on the Colorado Frontier*. Albuquerque: University of New Mexico Press.

United States Bureau of the Census (1982) *Current Population Reports*, Series P-23, no. 116, *Ancestry and Language in the United States: November 1979*. Washington, DC: Government Printing Office.

—— (1993) *1990 Summary Population and Housing Reports*. Washington, DC: Government Printing Office.

United States Immigration Commission (1911) *Reports of the Immigration Commission*, 41 vols. Washington, DC: Government Printing Office. University of Tennessee Press.

Utley, Jonathan G. (1985) *Going to War with Japan, 1937–1941*. Knoxville: University of Tennessee Press.

Van Burkleo, Sandra, Kaczorowski, Robert J., and Hall, Kermit (eds.) (2002) *Constitutionalism and American Culture: Writing the New Constitutional History.* Lawrence: University Press of Kansas.

Vankin, Jonathan (1992) *Conspiracies, Cover-ups, and Crimes: Political Manipulation and Mind Control in America.* New York: Paragon House.

Vatter, Harold G. (1963) *The US Economy in the 1950s: An Economic History.* New York: W. W. Norton.

Vecoli, Rudolph J. and Sinke, Suzanne (eds.) (1992) *A Century of European Migrations, 1830–1930.* Urbana: University of Illinois Press.

Vickerman, Milton (1999) *Crosscurrents: West Indian Immigrants and Race.* New York: Oxford University Press.

Viereck, Peter (1962) *Conservatism Revisited.* New York: Collier.

Vietor, Richard H. K. (1994) *Contrived Competition: Regulation and Deregulation in America.* Cambridge, Mass.: Harvard University Press.

Vileisis, Ann (1997) *Discovering the Unknown Landscape: A History of America's Wetlands.* Washington, DC: Island Press.

Vincent, C. Paul (1985) *The Politics of Hunger: The Allied Blockade of Germany, 1915–1919.* Athens: Ohio University Press.

Vlahos, Michael (1980) *The Blue Sword: The Naval War College and the American Mission, 1919–1941.* Newport, RI: Naval War College Press.

Vogel, David (1989) *Fluctuating Fortunes: The Political Power of Business in America.* New York: Basic Books.

Vorländer, Hans (1988) "Transatlantische Reformgemeinschaft an der Wiege des 20. Jahrhundert," *Liberal* 30, pp. 87–91.

—— (1997) *Hegemonialer Liberalismus: Politisches Denken und politische Kultur in den USA 1776–1920* [*Hegemonic Liberalism: Political Thought and Political Culture in the USA 1776–1920*]. Frankfurt-am-Main: Campus.

Waits, William B. (1994) *The Modern Christmas in America: A Cultural History of Gift Giving.* New York: New York University Press

Walker, J. Samuel (1997) *Prompt and Utter Destruction: Truman and the Use of Atomic Bombs against Japan.* Chapel Hill: University of North Carolina Press.

Walker, Juliet E. K. (1998) *The History of Black Business in America: Capitalism, Race, Entrepreneurship.* New York: Macmillan Library Reference USA.

Walzer, Michael (1980) *Radical Principles: Reflections of an Unreconstructed Democrat.* New York: Basic Books.

—— (1990) "The communitarian critique of liberalism," *Political Theory* 18, pp. 6–23.

Warner, W. Lloyd and Lunt, Paul S. (1941) *The Social Life of a Modern Community.* New Haven, Conn.: Yale University Press.

Warren, Harris Gaylord (1959) *Herbert Hoover and the Great Depression.* New York: Oxford University Press.

Warren, Louis (1997) *The Hunter's Game: Poachers and Conservationists in Twentieth-Century America.* New Haven, Conn.: Yale University Press.

Warshow, Robert (1974) *The Immediate Experience: Movies, Comics, Theatre and Other Aspects of Popular Culture.* New York: Atheneum.

Waters, Mary (1990) *Ethnic Options: Choosing Identities in America.* Berkeley: University of California Press.

Watson, James (1990) "The human genome: past, present, and future," *Science* 248, pp. 44–9.

Wattenberg, Ben B. (1991) *The First Universal Nation: Leading Indicators and Ideas about the Surge in America in the 1990s.* New York: Free Press.

Weaver, Richard (1948) *Ideas Have Consequences.* Chicago: University of Chicago Press.

Webb, Walter Prescott (1931) *The Great Plains.* Boston: Ginn.

Weber, Adna Ferrin (1899) *The Growth of Cities in the Nineteenth Century.* New York: Macmillan.

Weber, David J. (1992) *The Spanish Frontier in North America.* New Haven, Conn.: Yale University Press.

Weems, Robert E. (1996) *Black Business in the Black Metropolis: The Chicago Metropolitan Assurance Company, 1925–1985.* Bloomington: Indiana University Press.

—— (1998) *Desegregating the Dollar: African American Consumerism in the Twentieth Century.* New York: New York University Press.

Weigley, Russell F. (1972) *The American Way of War: A History of United States Military Strategy and Policy.* New York: Macmillan.

—— (1984) *History of the United States Army,* enlarged edn. Bloomington: Indiana University Press.

Weinberg, Barbara, Bolger, Doreen, and Curry, David Park (1994) *American Impressionism and Realism: The Painting of Modern Life, 1885–1915.* New York: The Metropolitan Museum of Art.

Weinberg, Gerhard L. (1994) *A World at Arms: A Global History of World War II.* New York: Cambridge University Press.

Weinstein, James (1968) *The Corporate Ideal in the Liberal State, 1900–1918.* Boston: Beacon Press.

West, Elliott (1998) *Contested Plains: Indians, Goldseekers, and the Rush to Colorado.* Lawrence: University Press of Kansas.

Westbrook, Robert B. (1991) *John Dewey and American Democracy.* Ithaca, NY: Cornell University Press.

Wheeler, David L. (1999) "For biologists, the post-genomic world promises vast and thrilling knowledge," *Chronicle of Higher Education* 45, pp. A17–A18.

Wheeler, Marjorie Spruill (1993) *New Women of the New South: The Leaders of the Woman Suffrage Movement in the Southern States.* New York: Oxford University Press.

White, G. Edward (1993) *Justice Oliver Wendell Holmes, Jr.: Law and the Inner Self.* New York: Oxford University Press.

—— (2000) *The Constitution and the New Deal.* Cambridge, Mass.: Harvard University Press.

White, Morton (1949) *Social Thought in America: The Revolt Against Formalism.* Boston: Beacon Press.

White, Richard (1983) *The Roots of Dependency: Subsistence, Environment, and Social Change among the Choctaws, Pawnees, and Navajos.* Lincoln: University of Nebraska Press.

—— (1991) *"It's Your Misfortune and None of My Own": A History of the American West.* Norman: University of Oklahoma Press.

—— (1991) *The Middle Ground: Indians, Empires, and Republics in the Great Lakes Region, 1650–1815.* Cambridge: Cambridge University Press.

—— (1995) *The Organic Machine: The Remaking of the Columbia River.* New York: Hill and Wang.

White, Theodore H. (1961) *The Making of the President 1960.* New York: Atheneum.

Whitfield, Stephen J. (1988) *A Death in the Delta: The Story of Emmett Till.* New York: Free Press.

—— (1991) *The Culture of the Cold War.* Baltimore, Md.: Johns Hopkins University Press. 2nd edn. 1996.

Whyte, William H., Jr. (ed.) (1958) *The Exploding Metropolis.* Garden City, NY: Doubleday.

Wiebe, Robert H. (1967) *The Search for Order, 1877–1920.* New York: Hill and Wang.

Wiener, Jonathan M. (1978) *Social Origins of the New South: Alabama, 1860–1885.* Baton Rouge: Louisiana State University Press.

Will, George F. (1997) *The Woven Figure: Conservatism and America's Fabric.* New York: Touchstone.

Williams, Peter W. (ed.) (1999) *Perspectives on American Religion and Culture*. Oxford: Blackwell.

Williams, Raymond Brady (1988) *Religions of Immigrants from India and Pakistan: New Threads in the American Tapestry*. New York: Cambridge University Press.

Williams, T. Harry (1969) *Huey Long*. New York: Alfred A. Knopf.

Williams, William Appleman (1972) [1959] *The Tragedy of American Diplomacy*, rev. edn. New York: Dell.

Williamson, Joel (ed.) (1968) *The Origins of Segregation*. Boston: D. C. Heath.

—— (1984) *The Crucible of Race: Black–White Relations in the American South since Reconstruction*. New York: Oxford University Press.

—— (1997) "Wounds not scars: lynching, the national conscience, and the American historian," *Journal of American History* 83(4) (March), pp. 1221–53.

Wilson, Charles Reagan and Ferris, William (eds.) (1989) *Encyclopedia of Southern Culture*. Chapel Hill: University of North Carolina Press.

Wilson, Clyde (1986) "The conservative identity," *Intercollegiate Review* 21, pp. 5–8.

Wilson, Harold (1970) McClure's Magazine *and the Muckrakers*. Princeton, NJ: Princeton University Press.

Wilson, Joan Hoff (1975) *Herbert Hoover: Forgotten Progressive*. Boston: Little, Brown.

Wilson, Woodrow (1913) *The New Freedom: A Call for the Emancipation of the Generous Energies of a People*. Garden City, NY: Doubleday, Page.

Winkler, Allan M. (1978) *The Politics of Propaganda: The Office of War Information, 1942–1945*. New Haven, Conn.: Yale University Press.

—— (1993) *Life Under a Cloud: American Anxiety about the Atom*. New York: Oxford University Press.

—— (2000) *Home Front, U.S.A.: America during World War II*, 2nd edn. Arlington Heights, Ill.: Harlan Davidson.

—— (2000) *The Cold War: A History in Documents*. New York: Oxford University Press.

Wirth, Louis (1928) *The Ghetto*. Chicago: University of Chicago Press.

Witcover, Jules (1977) *Marathon: The Pursuit of the Presidency 1972–1976*. New York: Viking.

Wohlstetter, Roberta (1962) *Pearl Harbor: Warning and Decision*. Stanford, Calif.: Stanford University Press.

Wokeck, Marianne S. (1999) *A Trade in Strangers: The Beginnings of Mass Migration to North America*. University Park: Pennsylvania State University Press.

Wolfe, Margaret Ripley (1995) *Daughters of Canaan: A Saga of Southern Women*. Lexington: University Press of Kentucky.

Wolfe, Tom (1983) *From Bauhaus to Our House*. London: Abacus.

Wollenberg, Charles M. (1976) *All Deliberate Speed: Segregation and Exclusion in California Schools, 1855–1975*. Berkeley: University of California Press.

Womack, James P., Jones, Daniel T., and Roos, Daniel (1990) *The Machine that Changed the World*. New York: Rawson Associates.

Woodward, Bob (1994) *The Agenda: Inside the Clinton White House*. New York: Simon and Schuster.

Woodward, C. Vann (1938) *Tom Watson: Agrarian Rebel*. New York: Macmillan.

—— (1951) *Origins of the New South, 1877–1913*. Baton Rouge: Louisiana State University Press.

—— (1955) *The Strange Career of Jim Crow*. New York: Oxford University Press. Revised editions: 1966, 1974, 1990, 2002.

—— (1960) *The Burden of Southern History*. Baton Rouge: Louisiana State University Press. Revised editions: 1968, 1993.

—— (1971) *American Counterpoint: Slavery and Racism in the North–South Dialogue.* Boston: Little, Brown.

—— (1986) *Thinking Back: The Perils of Writing History.* Baton Rouge: Louisiana State University Press.

Woodward, David R. (1993) *Trial by Friendship: Anglo-American Relations, 1917–1918.* Lexington: University Press of Kentucky.

Worley, William S. (1990) *J. C. Nichols and the Shaping of Kansas City.* Columbia: University of Missouri Press.

Worster, Donald (1979) *Dust Bowl: The Southern Plains during the 1930s.* New York: Oxford University Press.

—— (1985) *Rivers of Empire: Water, Aridity, and the Growth of the American West.* New York: Pantheon.

—— (1994) *Nature's Economy: A History of Ecological Ideas,* 2nd edn. New York: Cambridge University Press.

—— (2001) *A River Running West: The Life of John Wesley Powell.* New York: Oxford University Press.

Wright, Frank Lloyd (1932) *The Disappearing City.* New York: William Farquhar Payson.

Wright, Gavin (1986) *Old South, New South: Revolutions in the Southern Economy since the Civil War.* New York: Basic Books.

Wuthnow, Robert (1988) *The Restructuring of American Religion: Society and Faith since World War II.* Princeton, NJ: Princeton University Press.

—— (1999) *After Heaven: Spirituality in America since the 1950s.* Berkeley: University of California Press.

Wyman, Mark (1993) *Round-Trip to America: The Immigrants Return to Europe, 1880–1930.* Ithaca, NY: Cornell University Press.

Wynn, Neil A. (1976) *The Afro-American and the Second World War.* New York: Holmes and Meier.

Yans-McLaughlin, Virginia (1977) *Family and Community: Italian Immigrants in Buffalo, 1880–1930.* Ithaca, NY: Cornell University Press.

—— (ed.) (1990) *Immigration Reconsidered: History, Sociology, and Politics.* New York: Oxford University Press.

Young, J. P. (1996) *American Liberalism: The Troubled Odyssey of the Liberal Idea.* Boulder, Colo.: Westview Press.

Yung, Judy (1995) *Unbound Feet: A Social History of Chinese Women in San Francisco.* Berkeley: University of California Press.

Zamora, Emilio (1993) *The World of the Mexican Worker in Texas.* College Station, Tex.: Texas A&M University Press.

Zangrando, Robert L. (1980) *The NAACP Crusade Against Lynching, 1909–1950.* Philadelphia: Temple University Press.

Zieger, Robert H. (ed.) (1991) *Organized Labor in the Twentieth-Century South.* Knoxville: University of Tennessee Press.

—— (1995) *The CIO, 1935–1955.* Chapel Hill: University of North Carolina Press.

—— (ed.) (1997) *Southern Labor in Transition, 1940–1995.* Knoxville: University of Tennessee Press.

—— (2000) *America's Great War: World War I and the American Experience.* Lanham, Md.: Rowman and Littlefield.

Zinn, Howard (ed.) (1966) *New Deal Thought.* Indianapolis: Bobbs-Merrill.

Zucker, Norman L. and Zucker, Naomi F. (1987) *The Guarded Gate: The Reality of American Refugee Policy.* San Diego, Calif.: Harcourt Brace Jovanovich.

Zunz, Olivier (1990) *Making America Corporate, 1870–1920.* Chicago: University of Chicago Press.

Zurier, Rebecca, Snyder, Robert W., and Mecklenburg, Virginia M. (1995) *Metropolitan Lives: The Ashcan Artists and their New York.* Washington, DC: National Museum of American Art.

Index

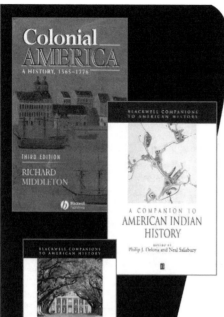